International Investment Law and Arbitration
SECOND EDITION

International investment law and arbitration form a rapidly evolving field, and can be difficult for students to acquire a firm understanding of, given the considerable number of published awards and legal writings. The first edition of this text, cited by courts in Singapore and Colombia, overcame this challenge by interweaving extracts from these arbitral decisions, treaties and scholarly works with concise, up-to-date and reliable commentary. Now fully updated and with a new chapter on arbitrators, the second edition retains this practical structure, along with carefully curated end-of-chapter questions and readings. The authors consider the new chapter an essential revision to the text, and a discussion that is indispensable to understanding present calls for reform of investment arbitration. The coverage of the book has also been expanded, with the inclusion of over sixty new awards and judicial decisions, comprising both recent and well-established jurisprudence. This textbook will appeal to graduates studying international investment law and international arbitration, as well as being of interest to practitioners in this area.

CHIN LENG LIM is the Choh-Ming Li Professor of Law at The Chinese University of Hong Kong, a Visiting Professor at King's College London and Honorary Senior Fellow of the British Institute of International & Comparative Law. He practises as a barrister with Keating Chambers, London. Lim worked previously as international law counsel for a government as well as at the United Nations Compensation Commission in Geneva, and he served three terms on a committee advising Hong Kong's Commerce Secretary. He is currently participating in the UNCITRAL WG III deliberations in which he represents an observer entity.

JEAN HO is Associate Professor of Law at the National University of Singapore. She previously practised international investment law and arbitration at Shearman & Sterling LLP and now acts as counsel in investor–State disputes. She is an elected Member of the Executive Council of the Asian Society of International Law, an elected Member of the Steering Committee of the Academic Forum on Investor–State Dispute Settlement, and a US-nominated Expert on the UNIDROIT Working Group on Agricultural Land Investment Contracts.

MARTINS PAPARINSKIS is Reader in Public International Law at University College London, Faculty of Laws. He is the Book Review Editor of the *Journal of World Investment and Trade*, a Member of the Permanent Court of Arbitration, and a Member of the Panels of Arbitrators and of Conciliators of the International Centre for Settlement of Investment Disputes.

International Investment Law and Arbitration

COMMENTARY, AWARDS AND OTHER MATERIALS

Second Edition

Chin Leng Lim
The Chinese University of Hong Kong

Jean Ho
National University of Singapore

Martins Paparinskis
University College London

CAMBRIDGE
UNIVERSITY PRESS

CAMBRIDGE
UNIVERSITY PRESS

University Printing House, Cambridge CB2 8BS, United Kingdom

One Liberty Plaza, 20th Floor, New York, NY 10006, USA

477 Williamstown Road, Port Melbourne, VIC 3207, Australia

314–321, 3rd Floor, Plot 3, Splendor Forum, Jasola District Centre, New Delhi – 110025, India

79 Anson Road, #06–04/06, Singapore 079906

Cambridge University Press is part of the University of Cambridge.

It furthers the University's mission by disseminating knowledge in the pursuit of
education, learning, and research at the highest international levels of excellence.

www.cambridge.org
Information on this title: www.cambridge.org/9781108842990
DOI: 10.1017/9781108913652

First published 2018
3rd printing 2019
Second edition 2021

Printed in the United Kingdom by TJ Books Limited, Padstow Cornwall, 2021

A catalogue record for this publication is available from the British Library.

Library of Congress Cataloging-in-Publication Data
Names: Lim, C. L. (Chin L.), author. | Ho, Jean, author. | Paparinskis, Mārtiņš, author.
Title: International investment law and arbitration : commentary, awards,
and other materials / Chin Leng Lim, The Chinese University of Hong
Kong; Jean Ho, National University of Singapore; Martins Paparinskis, University College London.
Description: Second edition. | Cambridge, United Kingdom ; New York, NY :
Cambridge University Press, [2021?] | Includes bibliographical
references and index. | Contents: The origins of investment protection
and international investment law – Investment contracts and internationalisation –
The metamorphosis of investment treaties – Investment dispute settlement –
Jurisdiction, admissibility, and parallel proceedings – Applicable laws - Arbitrators – Evidence –
Provisional measures – Protected investments – Prß otected investors –
Fair and equitable treatment, and full protection and security –
Contingent standards : national treatment and most-favoured nation treatment –
Expropriation – Umbrella clauses – Defences – Remedies – Costs and legal fees -
Challenging and enforcing awards, and the question of foreign state immunities –
New directions in international investment law and arbitration.
Identifiers: LCCN 2020042862 (print) | LCCN 2020042863 (ebook) |
ISBN 9781108842990 (hardback) | ISBN 9781108913652 (ebook)
Subjects: LCSH: Investments, Foreign (International law) | International
commercial arbitration. | Investments, Foreign–Law and legislation.
Classification: LCC K3830 .L5826 2021 (print) | LCC K3830 (ebook) | ¡DDC 346/.092–dc23
LC record available at https://lccn.loc.gov/2020042862
LC ebook record available at https://lccn.loc.gov/2020042863

ISBN 978-1-108-84299-0 Hardback
ISBN 978-1-108-82320-3 Paperback

Contents

Foreword to the Second Edition

International investment law and arbitration commands global interest. It is the arena in which investor–State dispute settlement unfolds, a taught subject at the undergraduate and postgraduate levels, a field of practice, an academic pursuit and even a political campaign. Shaped by general international law, investment treaties, arbitral jurisprudence and academic writings, international investment law and arbitration is as dynamic as its constituent variables. The variety of viewpoints on virtually every legal issue sustains an intense, ongoing international dialogue. Yet this variety also poses a serious challenge to the systematic study of international investment law and arbitration.

This book is the first to synthesise the moving parts of international investment law and arbitration into a comprehensive narrative with a hybrid casebook–textbook format. By pairing carefully curated extracts from voluminous Awards and other documents with original commentary and analysis, Lim, Ho and Paparinskis deftly enhance the informative value of a traditional casebook with the explanatory value of a traditional textbook. And in doing so, they have written a book that gives their readers the best of both worlds.

Relying on their significant combined teaching, publishing and practical experience, Lim, Ho and Paparinskis deconstruct the many legal complexities and controversies of international investment law and arbitration in 20 meticulous and engaging chapters. *International Investment Law and Arbitration: Commentary, Awards and Other Materials* fills the niche in the market for a compact general treatise which strikes a fine balance between doctrinal rigour and practical relevance. It is a book that both students and specialists will find accessible and instructive.

Since the publication of the remarkable first edition in April 2018, this book has already been cited with approval by the Constitutional Court of Colombia and by the Court of Appeal of Singapore. The second edition, which promises to be as impactful as the first, will continue to be an indispensable resource and an important contribution to the mastery of a prominent discipline.

Emmanuel Gaillard
Global Head of International Arbitration, Shearman & Sterling LLP
Visiting Professor of Law, Yale Law School and Harvard Law School

Preface to the First Edition

The past two decades epitomised the emergence of international investment arbitration as one of the most dynamic areas of legal practice. Given the considerable number of published arbitral awards and legal writings, and the underlying public international law principles, acquiring a firm understanding of international investment law and arbitration has become harder for students, practitioners and others. There is a place for a book which reproduces within a single, portable volume selected extracts from arbitral decisions, other documents and legal writings, accompanied by concise, up-to-date and reliable commentary on both the law and procedure of international investment arbitration. Questions of procedure and practice have become bound up with the application of substantive international law protections, raising important questions of technical international law. There is also the need for the subject to be explained in academic institutions in a way which reflects its historical development, conceptual basis and intellectual contribution to the peaceful settlement of disputes. It is this combination of aims which this book seeks to advance.

A further justification is that the field is in a renewed state of flux. It appeared to us that there is scope for a book which aims to convey the effect of these broader developments, not least on the latest innovations in treaty design and language. However, we have also been wary of exaggerating the current backlash against investment treaties and arbitration. While this book is alive to the gathering forces of change, for now one need look no further than the facts of daily legal practice and the largely unaltered aims of the subject.

The present book draws upon the experience derived from teaching the subject in three different jurisdictions. No work can be faultless. It is especially true of a first edition and we hope to benefit from the comments of our peers about the ways in which this first attempt might be improved. In terms of the allocation of writing responsibility, Lim was tasked with Chapters 1, 4, 8, 11, 14, 17, 18 and 19; Ho with Chapters 2, 3, 6, 7, 9, 10, 13 and 16; and Paparinskis with Chapters 5, 12 and 15. We have tried to state the law and its surrounding developments as they appeared to us in May 2017.

Preface to the Second Edition

The aim of the second edition remains that of the first. We are grateful to our colleagues in the law school teaching profession for adopting the first edition, which appeared just less than three years ago. When Cambridge University Press requested a new edition so swiftly, we did not hesitate due to the rapid, even clamorous, movements in the field.

The second edition is expanded slightly with a new chapter, Chapter 7, by Lim and Paparinskis on arbitrators, not least as the authors feel that this discussion is indispensable to an understanding of present calls for reform of investment arbitration. The concerns with a small club, double-hatting and repeat appointments go to the heart of the reform debate. Accordingly, the numbering of previous chapters has shifted, the old Chapter 7 having become Chapter 8 and so on, and there are now twenty rather than nineteen chapters. That apart, and as before, Lim was tasked with what now are Chapters 1, 4, 9, 12, 15, 18, 19 and 20, Ho with Chapters 2, 3, 6, 8, 10, 11, 14 and 17, and Paparinskis with what now are Chapters 5, 13 and 16. Altogether, over sixty new awards and judicial decisions have been added in this second edition. They consist not simply of those that have appeared since the publication of the first edition, but at times as an attempt to expand upon the coverage of the book, and consequently the stock of awards and judgments.

Chapter 1 remains largely unchanged. Chapter 2 contains new text on the involvement of indigenous communities as stakeholders in investment contracts, while Chapter 3 tracks new developments in treaty redesign and the further inroads made into the establishment of a multilateral investment court, the possible replacement of treaty protection with domestic legislation in the form of South Africa's Protection of Investment Act (Act No. 22 of 2015, Official Gazette, Vol. 606, No. 39514), the impact of COVID-19 on increasingly prominent issues such as investor responsibility and questions about whether investment treaties remain an appropriate tool for investment protection. Chapter 3 also touches now on the mass termination of intra-EU bilateral investment treaties. Chapter 4 now includes discussion of the US–Mexico–Canada Agreement and *Swissbourgh Diamond Mines (Pty) Ltd.* v. *Kingdom of Lesotho* [2018] SGCA 81.

The discussion of jurisdiction and admissibility in Chapter 5 was cited by the Singapore Court of Appeal in *Swissbourgh Diamond Mines (Pty) Limited and Others* v. *Kingdom* of Lesotho [2018] SGCA 81 and in *BBA & Others* v. *BAZ* [2020] SGCA 53. Both cases are discussed in this second edition. Other cases newly excerpted include the curious *Oded Besserglik* v. *Mozambique*, ICSID Case No. ARB(AF)/14/2, Award, 28 October 2019, where the non-existence of the treaty instrument providing consent was only discovered at a very late stage, and *Orascom TMT Investments S.à r.l.* v. *Algeria*, ICSID Case No. ARB/12/35, Award, 31 May 2017. This last provides an important gloss to *Ampal-American Israel Corp. and Others* v. *Egypt*, ICSID Case No. ARB/12/11, Decision on Jurisdiction, 1 February 2016, which had dominated discussion of the parallel proceedings jurisprudence in the previous edition. Chapter 6 retains the form and substance of the first edition.

Chapter 8 now includes *Tethyan Copper Company Pty Limited* v. *Islamic Republic of Pakistan*, ICSID Case No. ARB/12/1, Decision on Respondent's Application to Dismiss the Claims (With Reasons), 10 November 2017 as authority against a 'shifting' burden of proof, and fleshes out the operation and drawbacks of a malleable standard of proof which tribunals appear to apply when confronted with allegations of fraud and corruption on the part of both investors and States with reference to *Bernhard Friedrich Arnd Rüdiger von Pezold and Others* v. *Zimbabwe,* ICSID Case No. ARB/10/15, Award, 28 July 2015, *EDF (Services) Limited* v. *Romania*, ICSID Case No. ARB/05/13, Award, 8 October 2009, *Chevron Corporation and Texaco Petroleum Corporation* v. *The Republic of Ecuador*, UNCITRAL, PCA Case No. 2009–23, Second Partial Award on Track II, 30 August 2018, and *Spentex Netherlands, B.V.* v. *Republic of Uzbekistan*, ICSID Case No. ARB/13/26, Award, 27 December 2016. Chapter 9 remains essentially unchanged.

Chapter 10 delves now into the increasingly controversial objective criterion of capital contribution for the establishment of a protected investment. This has been held by some tribunals to require an active investment by the claimant. The debate over the eligibility of passive investments for treaty protection is borne out in a discussion of *Alapli Elektrik B.V.* v. *Republic of Turkey*, ICSID Case No. ARB/08/13, Award, 16 July 2012, *Anglo-Adriatic Group Limited* v. *Republic of Albania*, ICSID Case No. ARB/17/6, Award, 7 February 2019, *Quiborax S.A., Non Metallic Minerals S.A. and Allan Fosk Kaplún* v. *Plurinational State of Bolivia*, ICSID Case No. ARB/06/2, Decision on Jurisdiction, 27 September 2012, *Standard Chartered Bank* v. *The United Republic of Tanzania*, ICSID Case No. ARB/10/12, Award, 2 November 2012 and *Clorox Spain S.L.* v. *Bolivarian Republic of Venezuela*, PCA Case No. 2015–30, Award, 20 March 2019.

Chapter 11 now includes an extended discussion of the eligibility of dual nationals for treaty protection. It places the spotlight on the recent award in *Michael Ballantine and Lisa Ballantine* v. *The Dominican Republic*, PCA Case No. 2016–17 (UNCITRAL), Final Award, 3 September 2019. The chapter now follows up on the previous discussion of 'divisible investors' with the recent publication of *Lao Holdings* v. *Laos,* ICSID Case No. ARB(AF)/12/6, Award, 6 August 2019 and *Sanum Investments Ltd* v. *Government of Laos,* UNCITRAL, PCA Case No. 2013–13, Award, 6 August 2019. It explains how these awards enhance the risk of double recovery when claims by 'divisible investors' are entertained.

The discussions of fair and equitable treatment in Chapter 12, as with those on national treatment and most-favoured-nation treatment in Chapter 13, were cited in 2019 by the Colombian Constitutional Court in Judgment C-252/19. Additions now made to Chapter

12 include *Eiser Infrastructure Limited and Energía Solar Luxembourg S.à.r.l.* v. *Kingdom of Spain*, ICSID Case No. ARB/13/36, Award, 4 May 2017, where the tribunal links the stability and transparency requirements in the Energy Charter Treaty, and also the stability requirement with the investor's legitimate expectations. The tribunal in *Anglo American plc* v. *Bolivarian Republic of Venezuela*, ICSID Case No. ARB(AF)/14/1, Award, 18 January 2019 has since referred to the question of linking the fair and equitable treatment standard to a minimum customary standard as 'sterile', while at the same time supporting the view that the minimum standard of treatment under international custom has evolved. The tribunal also lent support to the view, discussed in the earlier edition, that the full protection and security standard extends beyond the assurance merely of physical security, and that it includes an assurance of legal stability.

Chapter 14 as it is now elaborates on the concept of expropriation with reference to *Waste Management Inc.* v. *Mexico ('No. 2')*, ICSID Case No. ARB(AF)00/3, Award, 30 April 2004, and on the exercise of a State's police powers with reference to *Emanuel Too* v. *Greater Modesto Insurance Associates*, Award, 29 December 1989, 23 Iran–United States Cl. Trib. Rep. 378. Chapter 14 also contains a new section on judicial expropriation which reproduces and critiques excerpts from a series of awards, namely *Saipem* v. *Bangladesh*, ICSID Case No. ARB/05/07, Award, 30 June 2009, *Swisslion DOO Skopje* v. *The Former Yugoslav Republic of Macedonia*, ICSID Case No. ARB/09/16, Award, 6 July 2012, *Garanti Koza LLP* v. *Turkmenistan*, ICSID Case No. ARB/11/20, Award, 19 December 2016 and *Krederi Ltd.* v. *Ukraine*, ICSID Case No. ARB/14/17, Award, 3 July 2018.

Chapter 15 on umbrella clauses has sought to include *WNC Factoring Ltd* v. *The Czech Republic,* PCA Case No. 2014–34, Award, 22 February 2017 in respect of a requirement of privity between Claimant and Respondent.

The law of defences, now in Chapter 16, will also be tested in the coming years by COVID-19-related claims. In this edition, the most significant addition is the duo of Indian telecommunication cases, discussing similar facts and prima facie similar rules but reaching very different conclusions on the point concerning the applicability of treaty exceptions: *CC/Devas (Mauritius) Ltd., Devas Employees Mauritius Private Limited and Telecom Devas Mauritius Limited* v. *India*, PCA Case No. 2013–09, Award on Jurisdiction and Merits, 25 July 2016 and *Deutsche Telekom AG* v. *India*, PCA Case No. 2014–10, Interim Award, 13 December 2017. A reminder, if one was needed, that the law of crises has moved on since the Argentinian decisions. Chapter 17 retains the form and substance of the first edition.

In the costs chapter (now Chapter 18) the available figures have been updated, and we have included *EuroGas Inc. and Belmont Resources Inc.* v. *Slovak Republic*, ICSID Case No. ARB/14/14, Award, 18 August 2017, where the tribunal considered the complexity of the legal issues, a factor which should be taken into account in cost allocation. This complements the broader view that a party should not be penalised on costs when the claim raises a novel legal issue. In the very recent decision in *Dirk Herzig as Insolvency Administrator over the Assets of Unionmatex Industrieanlagen GmbH* v. *Turkmenistan*, ICSID Case No. ARB/18/35, Decision on the Respondent's Request for Security for Costs and the Claimant's Request for Security for Claim, 27 January 2020, the tribunal rescinded its own previous order for security notwithstanding the existence of third-party funding. A comparison is to be drawn with the order in *RSM Production Corp.* v. *St Lucia*, ICSID Case No. ARB/12/10, Decision on St Lucia's Request for Security for Costs, 13 August 2014, which, as a landmark ruling, had been dominant in the previous edition's discussion of the subject.

Chapter 19 (Challenging and Enforcing Awards) now includes *Capital Financial Holdings Luxembourg SA* v. *République du Cameroun*, ICSID Case No. ARB/15/18, Award, 22 June 2017, which contains some attempt to clarify the 'Salini' criteria. Two new English judgments have been added. The first is *GPF GP S.à.r.l.* v. *The Republic of Poland* [2018] EWHC 409, which gives an example of an application under s. 67 of the Arbitration Act of 1996 in respect of an investment tribunal's award on jurisdiction. The second is the Supreme Court decision in *Micula and others* v. *Romania* [2020] UKSC 5. We have also been able to include *Eiser Infrastructure Limited and Energía Solar Luxembourg S.à r.l.* v. *Spain*, ICSID Case No. ARB/13/36, Decision on Annulment, 11 June 2020. It opens up two fronts, simultaneously, in respect of challenges against arbitrators and annulment on the ground of improper constitution of the tribunal.

Finally, in Chapter 20 (New Directions), quite apart from the discussions on creation of a multilateral investment court (MIC) in UNCITRAL Working Group III, the provisions in the EU–Canada Comprehensive Economic and Trade Agreement, the EU–Vietnam Investment Protection Agreement and the EU–Singapore Investment Protection Agreement that are relevant to that discussion have been included. Be that so, it remains the EU proposed text in connection with the moribund Trans-Atlantic Trade and Investment Partnership which is excerpted. Analogous provisions in CETA, as well as in the EU–Vietnam and EU–Singapore IPAs are referred to and discussed. Something needed to be, and is, said about the new US–Mexico–Canada Agreement.

Aside from that, there are other developments which have also been reflected throughout the new edition. For example, the previous edition contained several references to – and excerpts from – the Trans-Pacific Partnership. Some of these have been retained. However, references have now been added to the Comprehensive and Progressive Agreement for Trans-Pacific Partnership, which came into force on 30 December 2018. Perhaps the most important thing to note in terms of key differences in the substantive application of the CPTPP as compared with the TPP is that the TPP's clauses on investment agreements have been suspended under the CPTPP. Because, by and large, common provisions remain between the two treaty texts due to the wide harvesting in the CPTPP and transplantation of the TPP's parts as an organ donor, in such excerpts that refer both to the TPP and CPTPP a slash (/) symbol is used, as in 'Trans Pacific Partnership Agreement/Comprehensive Agreement for Trans-Pacific Partnership'. Elsewhere, reference is made simply to CPTPP.

We hope this new and expanded edition will prove as useful as the first, and we have endeavoured to take account of developments, and to state the law, as they appeared to us on 30 June 2020.

Acknowledgments

FIRST EDITION

With the usual caveat, we would like to express our immense gratitude to Finola O'Sullivan, Marta Walkowiak, Caitlin Lisle and Valerie Appleby at Cambridge University Press, without whose initial encouragement and enthusiasm, subsequent patience, forbearance, experience and expert guidance this book would not have been possible. We are likewise grateful to Sophie Rosinke and Amy Mower of Cambridge for their consummate professionalism during the copyediting and proofing stages. We would like to thank Chao Junqing at the University of Hong Kong and Alastair Simon Chetty at the National University of Singapore for their research and editorial assistance, and also Cheng Chi, now in practice, who provided much-needed assistance during the early stages of the book. Finally, we thank our students in Hong Kong, Singapore and London. Hopefully they will discover both things that are familiar as well as some improvements in this book. C. L. Lim acknowledges with gratitude Hong Kong University's grant of leave, the Class of '61's generosity which made a Lionel Astor Sheridan Visiting Professorship possible at the National University of Singapore and the support of King's College, London, the Shanghai 1000 Plan, Professor Zhang Lei and SUIBE, Shanghai. Jean Ho would like to acknowledge partial funding support from the Singapore Ministry of Education Academic Research Fund Tier 1 (WBS No. R-241-000-156-115).

SECOND EDITION

In respect of the preparation of this second edition, the authors are grateful to Yuanyuan Zhang and Xueji Su in Hong Kong, and also to Zhao Jingtong in Singapore. They have provided valuable assistance in one way or another.

Treaties and Other International Instruments, National Legislation, Cases and Awards

BILATERAL INVESTMENT TREATIES

ARBITRATION RULES

OTHER TREATIES

UN GENERAL ASSEMBLY AND SECURITY COUNCIL RESOLUTIONS

NATIONAL LEGISLATION BY COUNTRY

Australia

Canada

State Immunity Act 1980
Section 12(1)(a) 563

Egypt

Egyptian Law No. 43 of 1974 63

Hong Kong

International Organizations (Privileges and Immunities) (Permanent Court of
Arbitration) Order, LN 26 of 2016 260

Pakistan

State Immunity Ordinance 1981
Section 10 563

Singapore

Arbitration (International Investment Disputes Act) 1968 557
State Immunity Act 1979
Section 11 563

South Africa

Foreign States Immunities Act 1981
Section 10 563
Protection of Investment Act, Act No. 22 of 2015, Official Gazette, Vol. 606, No. 39514 75

United Kingdom

Arbitration (International Investment Disputes) Act 1966 549
Section 3(2) 568
Arbitration Act 1996 541, 556, 565, 568
Section 67 541, 564–565
Section 68 541, 564
Section 69 541
Civil Jurisdiction and Judgments Act 1992 255
Civil Jurisdiction and Judgments (Hague Convention on Choice of Court Agreements
2005) Regulations (SI 2015/1644) 608
State Immunity Act 1978 559
Section 9 563, 573

United States

International Cases

NATIONAL CASES BY COUNTRY

United States

Abbreviations

TREATIES AND OTHER INSTRUMENTS

ACIA	ASEAN Comprehensive Investment Agreement 2009
C–J–K TIT	China–Japan–Korea Trilateral Investment Treaty 2012
CETA	EU–Canada Comprehensive Economic and Trade Agreement 2016
CPTPP	Comprehensive and Progressive Agreement for Trans-Pacific Partnership 2018
DR–CAFTA	Dominican Republic–Central America Free Trade Agreement 2004
ECT	Energy Charter Treaty 1994
GATS	General Agreement on Trade in Services 1994
GATT	General Agreement on Tariffs and Trade 1947 and 1994
ICSID Convention	Convention on the Settlement of Investment Disputes between States and Nationals of Other States 1965
ICSID Arbitration Rules	Rules of Procedure for Arbitration Proceedings 2006
NAFTA	North American Free Trade Agreement 1992
New York Convention	Convention on the Recognition and Enforcement of Foreign Arbitral Awards 1958
TFEU	Treaty on the Functioning of the European Union 1958
TPP	Trans-Pacific Partnership 2016
TRIMS	Agreement on Trade-Related Investment Measures 1994
TTIP	Transatlantic Trade and Investment Partnership

UNCITRAL Model Law	UNCITRAL Model Law on International Commercial Arbitration, 1985, with Amendments as Adopted in 2006
UNCITRAL Rules	UNCITRAL Arbitration Rules 2010
USMCA	US–Mexico–Canada Agreement 2018
VCLT	Vienna Convention on the Law of Treaties 1969

Bodies

AALCO	Asian–African Legal Consultative Organisation
ACICA	Australian Centre for International Commercial Arbitration
AF	Additional Facility
ASEAN	Association of Southeast Asian Nations
BIICL	British Institute of International and Comparative Law
CAS	Court of Arbitration for Sports
EC	European Commission
EU	European Union
GCEU	General Court of the European Union
HKIAC	Hong Kong International Arbitration Centre
ICC	International Chamber of Commerce
ICJ	International Court of Justice
ICSID	International Centre for Settlement of Investment Disputes
ILC	International Law Commission
IUSCT	Iran–United States Claims Tribunal
LCIA	London Court of International Arbitration
NAFTA FTC	NAFTA Free Trade Commission
OECD	Organisation for Economic Co-operation and Development
PCA	Permanent Court of Arbitration
PCIJ	Permanent Court of International Justice
SCC	Stockholm Chamber of Commerce
SIAC	Singapore International Arbitration Centre
UN	United Nations
UNCC	UN Compensation Commission
UNCITRAL	UN Commission on International Trade Law
UNCTAD	UN Conference on Trade and Development
UNGA	UN General Assembly
WTO	World Trade Organization

Common Terms

ASR	Articles on State Responsibility
BIT	bilateral investment treaty
BOT	build-operate-and-transfer
CFtE	costs follow the event
CPG	Central People's Government of the People's Republic of China
CPR	Civil Procedure Rules
DCF	discounted cash flow
DELC	*damnum emergens* plus *lucrum cessans*
EPA	Economic Partnership Agreement
FCN	friendship, commerce and navigation
FET	fair and equitable treatment
FMV	fair market value
FPS	full protection and security
FTA	free trade agreement
GSP	Generalized System of Preferences
IIA	international investment agreement
IPA	investment protection agreement
ISDS	investor–State dispute settlement
MFN	most-favoured nation
MIT	multilateral investment treaty
MST	minimum standard of treatment
MTBE	methyl tertiary-butyl ether
NIEO	New International Economic Order
NT	national treatment
PPA	power purchase agreement
PPP	public–private partnership
PRC	People's Republic of China
US	United States
USSR	Union of Soviet Socialist Republics

The Origins of Investment Protection and International Investment Law

CHAPTER OUTLINE

Investment treaty arbitration derives from the consent of the host State, given under a treaty, to submit itself to arbitration in the event of a dispute with a foreign investor. Today, such treaty-based arbitration is the most prominent aspect of international investment arbitration, but it is only one aspect or form of it. Arbitration itself is only one of several means of settling investment disputes between foreign investors and host States. In the past, international investment disputes were resolved diplomatically by the 'home' State of the investor taking up its grievance against a foreign 'host' State, thereby making that grievance the home State's own. Such a claim might be pursued purely through diplomatic means, but throughout the nineteenth century and persisting well into the twentieth century there were several examples of the settlement of investment disputes through 'mixed' claims commissions. These were commissions of an international character which in time were supplemented by national claims commissions. Diplomatic espousal and mixed commissions operated in tandem. Where the commission failed, as it sometimes did, there were diplomatic negotiations leading to 'lump sum' settlements. Section 1 discusses these earlier forms of international investment dispute settlement. Section 2 goes on to discuss the unsettled period following the Second World War from 1945 to the 1970s, during which the standards of protection, particularly the standard of compensation, as well as the means of settlement – whether that ought to be in domestic courts or by way of international arbitration – were controversial. In response to controversy and uncertainty, there was an effort to transform the standards of protection into contractual terms, and to introduce contractual agreements to arbitrate any disputes. The attempt to 'contractualise' international investment protection became an attempt to elevate the contracts themselves onto the international plane, such that the contractual commitments to standards of protection and arbitration would themselves have the force of international law. That is the subject of Section 3. Section 4 deals with the rise, subsequently, of treaty-based protection and treaty-based arbitration in place of the role which contract had played. From this emerged today's ubiquitous bilateral investment treaties (BITs) and the sort of investment treaty arbitration for which they provide. Section 5 discusses related modern institutions: the International Centre for the Settlement of Investment Disputes (ICSID), as well as the inter-State adjudication of investment disputes before the International Court of Justice (ICJ). Section 6 rounds off this opening chapter with a brief introduction to the modern sources of international law usually relied upon by international investment tribunals.

INTRODUCTION

Many who know nothing of international law are likely to have heard of 'investor–State dispute settlement' (ISDS for short). Some of what has been heard may be discouraging.[1] What is meant by ISDS today is, often, a form of treaty-based arbitration – a late-twentieth-century development. Investment treaty arbitration is the principal focus of this book, although it is not its sole focus. In comparison, contractually based arbitration has had a longer and sturdier history. There are also forms of investment arbitration which are based neither on treaty nor contract, such as arbitrations brought by private claimants on the basis of a host State's consent to arbitration embodied in a national law, say a national petroleum law, or even in a host State's investment authorisation, or in some other document.[2]

Still, it is important to be reminded of history. The American Supreme Court Justice Oliver Wendell Holmes once wrote that 'time has upset many fighting faiths'.[3] The converse is true too. Old ideas return. They recur. Seemingly fresh ideas that are emerging, such as the European Union's current proposal that 'private' investment treaty arbitration should be replaced with a multilateral international investment court, cannot be appreciated fully without some acknowledgment of the history of the subject. History may also prove to be the best guide to the future where overbroad international protection for foreign investors is again being challenged, as it once was by the newly decolonised nations of Africa and Asia.

1. DIPLOMATIC ESPOUSAL AND MIXED OR SIMILAR COMMISSIONS

1.1 Diplomatic Espousal

We should begin, first, with diplomatic protection. Injury to an alien, including injury to a foreign investor, can trigger diplomatic protection by the investor's home State. The Permanent Court of International Justice, the predecessor to the present-day International Court of Justice, had put it this way:

---

[1] For which, see, e.g., P. Eberhardt and C. Olivet (with contributions from T. Amos and N. Buxton), *Profiting from Injustice: How Law Firms, Arbitrators and Financiers Are Fuelling an Investment Arbitration Boom* (Brussels/Amsterdam: Corporate Europe Observatory and the Transnational Institute, 2012).
[2] All of this we will come to in Chapter 4 of this book.
[3] *Abrams* v. *USA*, 250 US 616 (1919) (Holmes J).

> it is an elementary principle of international law that a state is entitled
> to protect its subjects, when injured by acts contrary to international law
> committed by another state, from whom they have been unable to obtain
> satisfaction through the ordinary channels.[4]

In the *Don Pacifico* affair, discussed in Section 1.2, to the question why the British government would be entitled to compensation had the Greek authorities taken no steps to protect Mr Pacifico and his property, Sir John Dodson answered:

> Simply, it is to be presumed, because it is the duty of every civilized Government to
> protect Persons and Property within its Jurisdiction, and, if, having the means at its
> disposal, it neglects to do so, it must be answerable for the consequences.[5]

The term 'diplomatic protection', however, is wide. In the view of the International Law Commission (ILC) – the body entrusted with the codification and progressive development of international law – the 'other means of peaceful settlement' include 'negotiation, mediation and conciliation' in addition to 'arbitral and judicial dispute settlement'. In its Draft Articles on Diplomatic Protection, the ILC defines diplomatic protection as:

> the invocation by a State, through diplomatic action or other means of peaceful
> settlement, of the responsibility of another State for an injury caused by an
> internationally wrongful act of that State to a natural or legal person that is a
> national of the former State with a view to the implementation of such responsibility.[6]

The aim is to ensure both protection and reparation for a national wronged by a foreign State.[7] It should be added, for the sake only of completeness, that this definition in the Draft Articles on Diplomatic Protection keeps to the formulation in the ILC's Draft Articles on Responsibility of States for Internationally Wrongful Acts.[8]

The legal fiction, said to originate with Vattel's dictum that whosoever injures a national injures the State itself,[9] is this: the claim becomes that of the home State itself, not that of the injured national.[10] It is a fiction which now more than ever is confronted with the reality of investors bringing claims directly before an investment arbitration tribunal. This book is about the new reality, particularly since the late 1990s, of investor–State arbitration. Although not unimaginable, this reality today was once thought to have been unlikely. In the beginning, diplomatic protection meant the espousal of an investor's claim by its own State.

---

[4] *Mavrommatis Palestine Concessions (Greece v. UK)* (1924) PCIJ Rep. Series A No. 2, 12.
[5] Sir John Dodson to Lord Palmerston, 13 July 1847: see note 12 below.
[6] Art. 1, Draft Articles on Diplomatic Protection, text adopted by the ILC at its 58th session, 2006, UN Doc. A/61/10; YrBk of the ILC, 2006, vol. II, Part Two, 24, 27. The page numbers refer to UN Doc. A/61/10.
[7] *Ibid.*, 24.
[8] For '[a]ny system of law must address the responsibility of its subjects for breaches of their obligations'; J. Crawford, *State Responsibility: The General Part* (Cambridge University Press, 2014), 3.
[9] E. de Vattel, *The Law of Nations or the Principles of Natural Law Applied to the Conduct and to the Affairs of Nations and Sovereigns* (Washington, DC: 1758, English translation by C. G. Fenwick, Carnegie Institution, 1916), vol. III, 136.
[10] See further A. Vermeer-Künzli, 'As If: The Legal Fiction in Diplomatic Protection' (2007) 18(1) *EJIL* 37.

Maximilian Koessler, 'Government Espousal of Private Claims before International Tribunals' (1946) 13 *Chicago L Rev* 180, 180–181

International law has not so far developed a generally accepted theory to explain the nature of 'diplomatic protection'. Yet in the postwar era this phrase will be employed to an extent unknown before the war to define the action taken by state against state to secure redress of alleged wrongs done to individuals or corporations. Although many of these claims will be settled by mutual agreement of the respective foreign offices, in many cases the issues will be submitted to an international body of arbitration or adjudication. Such litigation may become the most important aspect of postwar 'diplomatic protection'. The term itself is not very felicitous since it does not describe an essential or characteristic feature of the institution. The unique character of this international litigation does not lie in the employment of diplomatic measures. Its peculiarity is based on the fact that the claim of a private person, normally without judicial standing as against a foreign state, is espoused by a state and thus converted into a government claim which will be heard by the appropriate international tribunal. An historical analogy may be suggested. It appears that 'interposition', in the sense just referred to, is similar to the representation of the serf by his lord under feudal law. This feudal representation grew out of the fact that the serf, devoid of a standing in the barons' courts, would have been a defenseless victim of aggression by any other lord but for the championship of his own lord. Similarly, the private person today, unrecognized by international courts or arbitration bodies, would be without legal protection against an offending foreign state were not that private person's claim espoused by his government.

...

A streamlined law of nations, granting to private persons a standing before international courts and arbitration commissions, could do away with the roundabout relief through diplomatic protection, just as the emancipation of the serfs eliminated the need for feudal representation.

1.2 Diplomatic Espousal and Diplomatic Settlement

We have travelled far since. Diplomatic espousal was viewed as a thing fraught with risk. To paraphrase McNair, it arises at the behest of troublesome individuals who are prone to invent claims and were therefore a bit of a nuisance. It was also hardly irrelevant that claimants often asked for the right to wage private war through the grant of special reprisals.[11] McNair observed that the famous *Don Pacifico* incident was notable in that regard. A British subject, who suffered loss and injury when his house was broken into and plundered by a riotous mob, had sought and obtained British espousal of his claim for the loss and injury sustained to him and his family. Lord Palmerston was in that case

---

[11] Lord McNair, *International Law Opinions: Selected and Annotated* (Cambridge University Press, 1956), vol. 11, 197, 198.

advised by Sir John Dodson that the Greek authorities had breached 'the duty of every civilized Government to protect Persons and Property within its Jurisdiction'.[12] This led to a claim by the British government for losses sustained. The same principle had been expressed, as Professors Rudolf Dolzer and Christoph Schreuer have pointed out, by John Adams during the year before he became the president of the United States following the conclusion of a friendship, commerce and navigation (FCN) treaty with France[13] – a precursor to today's bilateral investment treaties.[14]

For our purposes, it would be excessive to explore the various criteria which have been applied by individual governments in deciding upon the exercise of their discretionary power. Suffice to say that the exhaustion of local remedies is typically a requirement,[15] so too the requirement that the injured party should have the protecting State's nationality, which in turn might involve further questions about the continuity of that nationality and its duration. The chief shortcoming of diplomatic espousal from the viewpoint of the private party who alleges injury is the discretionary nature of that remedy.[16] There is no assurance that protection will be forthcoming. In comparison, the investor may elect, on its own, whether or not to pursue that right directly and when to do so. This may be advantageous not just to the claimant, but also to the State, which is thereby spared the role of serving as a debt collector for its merchantmen.

The story of how diplomatic espousal, which although it remains, gave way to investor–State claims and arbitration, is a story of adaptation, experimentation and human ingenuity. The roots lie in the mixed international commissions of old.

1.3 Mixed International Commissions, National Commissions and Modern Claims Settlement

The idea of a 'mixed' dispute settlement mechanism, where commissioners of mixed nationalities are chosen by the States, has a long history. Such international claims commissions have existed since the earliest 'investment' disputes. International mixed claims commissions should also be distinguished from 'national' claims commissions, which represent a related, but distinct, device, as the extract by Professor Lillich, cited below, explains.

So far as mixed claims commissions were concerned, these were an inherently flexible device which had been designed to settle claims between the citizens of different States, between the citizens of one State against another State and also between the States

---

[12] Sir John Dodson to Lord Palmerston, 13 July 1847; reproduced in McNair, *International Law Opinions*, 239.
[13] Cited and quoted in R. Dolzer and C. Schreuer, *Principles of International Investment Law*, 2nd edn (Oxford University Press, 2012), 1.
[14] For the influence of FCN treaties today, see K. J. Vandevelde, *Bilateral Investment Treaties: History, Policy and Interpretation* (Oxford University Press, 2010).
[15] Flexibly interpreted, see, e.g., 'Letter of US Secretary of State to Minister to Turkey, 5 February 1853' (1906) 6 *Moore's Digest of International Law* 264, also reproduced in C. F. Dugan, D. Wallace, Jr, N. D. Rubins and B. Sabahi, *Investor-State Arbitration* (Oxford University Press, 2008), 28. Dugan *et al.* cite the Canadian Foreign Ministry's position, requiring nationality at the time of loss and presentation of claim and in the case of a company its formation under Canadian law prior to the time of the presentation of the claim, as well as the exhaustion of local remedies again flexibly interpreted (*ibid.*, 29–30).
[16] See the well-known passage in *Case Concerning Barcelona Traction, Light and Power Co., Ltd (Belgium v. Spain)* [1970] ICJ Rep. 3, p. 44.

themselves.[17] One should be careful to observe that this did not mean that individuals could simply appear to press their own claims as they can today in investment arbitration.[18] Typically, such commissions were established under treaty by States – i.e. by more than one State, unlike in the case of national commissions – and it is the States which played a key role in choosing the commissioners, who would thereby comprise a majority of their own nationals. Mixed commissions were most prominent during the nineteenth century, when some eighty or so of them replaced the single arbitrator tribunals of an earlier era. They presaged today's 'mixed' arbitral tribunals. Unlike diplomatic espousal, such commissions would not normally require the exhaustion of local remedies. The mixed claims commissions lasted well into the late 1930s,[19] one of the more prominent being perhaps the commission established by the United States and Mexico just before the Second World War in order to settle the Mexican agrarian expropriations.[20]

As for national commissions, these are explained in the extract by Professor Lillich below. The extract also refers to the three Jay Treaty commissions. That treaty of 1794, which was also the first commercial treaty between Great Britain and the United States, marked the passage from an older law of nations to the present international justice system in which international adjudication, in the form of arbitration, had re-emerged in modern times as an instrument of peace. Put differently, the Jay Treaty saw the introduction, or reintroduction, of international arbitration between States in modern times. Three commissions dealing with separate matters were introduced, two comprising panels of five commissioners of 'mixed' nationality and a third being a panel of three such commissioners. As Lillich notes, the commission dealing with pre-1783 Paris Peace Treaty debt claims of British subjects was to collapse into acrimony.[21]

Richard B. Lillich, *International Claims: Their Adjudication by National Commissions* (New York: Syracuse University Press, 1962), 6–11 (footnotes omitted)

Many proposals have been made through the years for the establishment of international judicial bodies to facilitate the settlement of claims. All would modify or eliminate the espousal concept and give the individuals more or less direct access to some form of permanent international tribunal. All, unfortunately, have come to naught. Nor have the increasing availability of municipal fora to aliens for the prosecution of direct claims

---

[17] See R. Dolzer, 'Mixed Claims Commissions' in *Max Planck Encyclopedia of Public International Law*, available at https://opil.ouplaw.com/view/10.1093/law:epil/9780199231690/law-9780199231690-e64 (accessed 29 September 2020). As ideas in the field tend to, this very flexibility now returns in modern form in the Iran–US Claims Tribunal and the UN Compensation Commission, discussed further below.

[18] This only appeared after the First World War (Dolzer, 'Mixed Claims Commissions').

[19] *Ibid.*

[20] Or at least those occurring after 1927. For the Mexican agrarian expropriations, see Section 2, below, which reproduces the US–Mexican correspondence of 1938. A further round of expropriations of British and American property in 1938 were settled by means of expert determination instead, in which both sides appointed expert assessors. See further A. Lowenfeld, *International Economic Law*, 2nd edn (Oxford University Press, 2008), 479–480.

[21] See G. Schwarzenberger, 'Present-Day Relevance of the Jay Treaty Arbitrations' (1978) 53 *Notre Dame LR* 715.

against the sovereign and the concurrent trend toward the restrictive theory of sovereign immunity alleviated the situation for the vast majority of aggrieved individuals, whose only recourse against a foreign state remains via the method of espousal.

The United States at an early date sought to avoid the unwieldy espousal concept whenever a large number of claims arose against a single state by resort to international claims commissions. Beginning with the Jay Treaty of 1794, regarded as the commencement of modern international arbitration, this country [i.e. the United States] pursued a policy of advocating the use of mixed claims commissions. These commissions, composed of nationals of the United States, the foreign country, and a third state, would receive and adjudicate claims brought by the United States on behalf of its nationals against the foreign country. Other states followed suit and 'gradually this jurisprudence attained an increasing influence on the development of international law' [quoting Professor Stuyt].

While the mixed claims commission promoted the rule of law in that it substituted a legal for a political determination, and while in a sense it relieved the Department of State of the burden of severally presenting many essentially nongovernmental claims, it soon became apparent that the success of a mixed commission depended to a disproportionate degree upon the ability of its commissioners. Indeed, the very nature of the device was such as to produce commissioners of nonjudicious, adversary temperament. If commissioners performed their duties with speed and impartiality the mixed commission was a useful device for the settlement of international claims and the development of customary international law. But too often this was not the case.

One of the Jay Treaty commissions, for instance, was rendered so ineffective by the conduct of the commissioners that it was eventually abandoned, the United States paying a lump sum to Great Britain and the latter establishing a national commission to distribute the money. The failure of this mixed commission was undoubtedly one reason why a year later, in 1803, the United States accepted a lump sum from France in settlement of certain American claims which it distributed by means of the first United States national claims commission. Thus it can be seen that 'the domestic claims commission is not an innovation' [Quoting Coerper] of recent years but a device dating back to the earliest days of modern international arbitration.

National commissions have been utilized frequently by the United States during the past 150 years. Such commissions have distributed funds under treaties, conventions, or agreements with Spain in 1819, Great Britain in 1826, Denmark in 1830, France in 1831, the Two Sicilies in 1832, Spain in 1834, Peru in 1841, Mexico in 1848, Brazil in 1849, China in 1858, Rumania, Italy, the U.S.S.R. and Czechoslovakia. Lump sum settlements with Rumania and Poland were concluded in 1960, and the Department of State currently is conducting negotiations with several Eastern European countries in an effort to achieve a settlement of outstanding claims. Future lump sum settlements with these countries will be handled by the Foreign Claims Settlement Commission, which is now processing Czech and Polish claims.

The wholehearted adoption by the United States of the lump sum method of handling large groups of international claims, indicated by the various settlements mentioned above and commented upon by many writers, was due less to the superior features of this method of adjudicating claims than to the inherent defects and repeated failures of mixed claims commissions. The ineffectiveness of one Jay Treaty commission leading to the utilization of the first United States national commission established a pattern which has been followed many times over. Indeed, in the case of the 1826 Convention with Great Britain, the 1848 Treaty with Mexico, and the 1934 and 1941 Conventions with Mexico, there had been prior attempts to settle these claims by means of mixed commissions which each time had failed. The failure of these mixed commissions led not only to an assumption of their work by national commissions, but also caused the Department of State to place increased reliance on the national commission technique of settling international claims. Following the 1826 Convention with Great Britain, for example, the United States negotiated lump sum settlements in 1830 with Denmark, in 1831 with France, in 1832 with the Two Sicilies, in 1834 with Spain, and in 1841 with Peru. After the 1848 Treaty with Mexico, lump sum settlements were concluded in 1849 with Brazil and in 1858 with China. The breakdown of the prewar mixed commissions with Mexico, followed by the 1934 and 1941 Conventions with that country, resulted in the national claims commission device being used by the United States almost to the exclusion of any other type.

Even if commissioners on a mixed commission could function smoothly, there is doubt whether the mixed commission would be adequate to handle the wholesale claims of the postwar period. As far back as 1938, McKernan noted that 'a large number of claims demands a certain speed of adjudication which is impossible if the claims are to be decided by commissioners of different nationalities, and language, and who are educated in different legal systems'. Six years later Hudson pointed out that extraordinary delays were a common characteristic of mixed commissions and had tended to jeopardize confidence in them.

The best-known modern successors of the mixed claims commissions of old are the Iran–US Claims Tribunal and, though fundamentally different for being strictly a claims-processing facility, the UN Compensation Commission.[22] The Iran–US Claims Tribunal in particular has contributed significantly to the jurisprudence on investment claims. Professor Lillich's account of mixed international claims commissions and national claims commissions provides a helpful introduction to a part of the controversy over the nature of the Iran–US Claims Tribunal.

The tribunal had been established under the 1981 Second Algiers Declaration ('the Claims Settlement Declaration'). One question had concerned the status of the tribunal since it was at least unclear whether the Claims Settlement Declaration was a treaty. It was argued that it was a treaty albeit concluded through an intermediary, and the tribunal itself considered it a treaty. Still it was not clear even then that what resulted was

[22] The UNCC, whose tasks are now practically completed, was not entrusted with the responsibility of deciding the question of liability itself, but merely questions of causation and quantum. There are other modern examples, such as the commissions for German forced labour during the Second World War, and the claims of Austrian Holocaust survivors and their heirs. See Dolzer, 'Mixed Claims Commissions'.

necessarily an international tribunal, even though Article II(1) of the Claims Settlement Declaration called it such.[23] This is Professor Lillich's point in the extract above – namely, that a treaty could be used to establish an agreement between two States, but, although still obligated under treaty, a State might establish a national, rather than an international, commission for the settlement of the relevant claims.

The Iran–US Claims Tribunal was established, as was typically the case, as a response to traumatic events, in this case flowing from the Iranian Revolution of 1979 and the Iran hostage crisis. The 1981 First Algiers Declaration broadly speaking dealt with, among other things, the hostage crisis, the return of Iranian assets, the settlement of Iranian bank loans and Iran's commitment to pay into a fund from which awards in successful claims against it might be paid. The second declaration, the Claims Settlement Declaration, with which we are primarily concerned, established a nine-member tribunal, three appointed by each side and three more by mutual agreement.[24] The UN Commission on International Trade Law (UNCITRAL) Arbitration Rules applied. Importantly, the tribunal was entrusted with, among other things, claims by the nationals of each State against the other (i.e. the United States and Iran) in respect of the assertion of private law rights.[25] Therein lies the resemblance with the mixed international commissions of old. In this case, it was a mixed international tribunal.

A further, contemporary, example of a bespoke arrangement is the UN Compensation Commission (UNCC),[26] which was established by the UN Security Council in Resolution 692 after the Gulf War.[27] The UNCC was established to effect war reparations, excluding such costs and losses and damage or injury borne by the Allied Coalition Forces during the Gulf War following Iraq's invasion and occupation of Kuwait. An important difference between the UNCC and the Iran–US Claims Tribunal is that Iraq's liability for injury, death, loss and damage to individuals, corporations and countries had already been determined by the UN Security Council.[28] All that remained were issues of claims

---

[23] See S. J. Toope, *Mixed International Arbitration: Studies in Arbitration between States and Private Persons* (Cambridge: Grotius, 1990), 266–268; citing, inter alia, *Case A-I* (1982), I Iran–USCTR 144 (First Phase).

[24] G. H. Aldrich, *The Jurisprudence of the Iran–US Claims Tribunal* (Oxford University Press, 1996), 2–6.

[25] Article II(1) of the Claims Settlement Declaration; see Toope, *Mixed International Arbitration*, 268; Aldrich, *The Jurisprudence of the Iran–US Claims Tribunal*, 6. Part of the complexity over determining the true nature, or status, of the tribunal concerns its varied mandate, since the tribunal was also charged with contractual claims between the United States and Iran themselves, as well as with the interpretation and application of the two Algiers Declarations (Aldrich, *The Jurisprudence of the Iran–US Claims Tribunal*, 6). The other part concerns whether claimants have direct rights, or whether the right of espousal by the State of nationality is retained (Toope, *Mixed International Arbitration*, 268). Yet this is not unique to the tribunal, and is a question which arises even with investment treaty arbitration, as this chapter goes on to discuss, immediately below.

[26] The UNCC's official internal designation within the United Nations was Ad Hoc Committee 26 of the UN Security Council. See further R. B. Lillich (ed.), *The United Nations Compensation Commission: Thirteenth Sokol Colloquium* (Irvington, NY: Transnational, 1995); M. Frigessi di Rattalma and T. Treves (eds), *The United Nations Compensation Commission: A Handbook* (The Hague: Martinus Nijhoff, 1999); C. S. Gibson, T. M. Rajah and T. J. Feighery (eds), *War Reparations and the UN Compensation Commission: Designing Compensation after Conflict* (Oxford University Press, 2015); C. L. Lim, 'On the Law, Procedures and Politics of United Nations Gulf War Reparations' (2000) 4 *SJICL* 435.

[27] Resolution 692 (UN Doc. S/RES/692 (1991), 20 May 1991) established the UNCC and the Compensation Fund.

[28] UN Security Council Resolution 687 (UN Doc. S/RES/687 (1991), 8 April 1991), para. 16: 'Reaffirms that Iraq, without prejudice to the debts and obligations of Iraq arising prior to 2 August 1990, which will be addressed through the normal mechanisms, is liable under international law for any direct loss, damage, including environmental damage and the depletion of natural resources, or injury to foreign Governments, nationals and corporations, as a result of Iraq's unlawful invasion and occupation of Kuwait.'

management, and the determination by three-person panels of UNCC Commissioners of issues of causation and the assessment of damages for a total of some 2.6 million claims subsequently filed against Iraq. Because liability had been determined beforehand and was not an issue before the panels of Commissioners, the UNCC is most aptly described as a claims-processing facility dealing only with the screening of claims and the actual disbursement of funds. Be that as it may, the panels applied international law principles as well as internal UNCC law,[29] and there was an acute sense of the requirements of due process as with any tribunal proceedings. Moreover, as with other dispute resolution methods, such as in the World Trade Organization (the WTO), the Commissioners did not hand down awards, but only made 'recommendations' for approval by a higher political body. That body was the UNCC Governing Council comprising all Members of the Security Council, sitting in committee in Geneva.

Section 2 describes the emergence of modern international investment arbitration, following an initial attempt to turn, first, to contract law both in respect of the provision of substantive legal standards of protection and as the basis of the agreement to arbitrate. Eventually, however, those who sought a more effective system of investment protection reached for another, wholly innovative device – namely, treaty-based investor–State arbitration, in which the promise to arbitrate was made by the host State to the claimant's home State. What follows is therefore a tale about the shift from what initially was a substantial reliance upon general, customary international law principles to a contractual, and thereafter to a treaty-based, system of law and dispute settlement which we now tend to think of when we refer to 'investment treaty arbitration'. Such investment treaty arbitration should be distinguished from the examples of investment claims settlement, inter-State forms of investment arbitration in which the claim is brought by the home State against the host State,[30] and international adjudication discussed earlier.

2. LEGAL UNCERTAINTY AND THE CONFLICTING ATTEMPTS TO RESTATE THE LAW IN THE UNITED NATIONS (1945–1970s)

In both contractual and treaty-based investment arbitration, a procedural innovation of great importance is that, unlike diplomatic espousals of the past, the claim is the investor's own, and in the case of a treaty between the investor's home State and the host State conferring the right to bring a claim, the home State has no business in respect of the claim, meaning it has no legal interest and no control over the commencement, advancement and management of the claim.[31] This idea may be traced to the manner in which

---

[29] This included the Decisions of the UNCC Governing Council, such as that adopting the UNCC's rules of procedure (officially, 'Provisional Rules for Claims Procedure') (UN Doc. S/AC.26/1992/INF.1).

[30] Although investment treaties can and do provide for both investor–State and inter-State claims, and thus there is a certain looseness even to the term 'investment treaty arbitration'.

[31] This view is at least forcefully argued in Z. Douglas, *The International Law of Investment Claims* (Cambridge University Press, 2009), 10 and esp. 19. Regarding this section of this chapter generally, see further, e.g., Lowenfeld, *International Economic Law*, 483–485.

diplomatic espousal had evolved into mixed claims commissions, in which agreements between disputing States had allowed commissions before which claimants might pursue their claims 'directly' against the host State.[32]

Yet, in order to understand how contractually based and treaty-based investment arbitration emerged, we should begin with the fluid state of customary international law principles during the 1960s, which persisted well into the 1980s. This had prompted multilateral diplomatic attempts to clarify such principles of customary law at the UN General Assembly (UNGA). The initial efforts at the United Nations, as we shall see, ultimately led to: (1) the articulation of principles (under UNGA Resolution 1803, for example) which sought to ensure that investors' *contracts* with host States had themselves some international law basis;[33] (2) investor rights eventually being placed upon a firm treaty footing instead;[34] and (3) the procedural innovation of allowing claimants to 'own' their claims without requiring the adoption of such claims by their home States.

2.1 Legal Chaos

In the *Don Pacifico* incident referred to earlier, there had been discussion of compensation, but no principles apart from the sanctity of foreign-owned property had apparently been relied on. The classical view on the appropriate standard of compensation for the expropriation of foreign-owned property is that expressed in the *Chorzów Factory* case, a case decided in 1927 by the Permanent Court of International Justice, the predecessor to the International Court of Justice. The case had involved the Polish forfeiture of two German companies in violation of a German–Polish treaty commitment.

Case Concerning the Factory at Chorzów (Claim for Indemnity) (Germany v. Poland),
Claim No. 13 (PCA), Merits (1928) PCIJ Series A No. 17, 47

The essential principle contained in the actual notion of an illegal act – a principle which seems to be established by international practice and in particular by the decisions of arbitral tribunals – is that reparation must, as far as possible, wipe out all the consequences of the illegal act and re-establish the situation which would, in all probability, have existed if that act had not been committed. Restitution in kind, or, if this is not possible, payment of a sum corresponding to the value which a restitution in kind would bear; the award, if need be, of damages for loss sustained which would not be covered by restitution in kind or payment in place of it – such are the principles which should serve to determine the amount of compensation due for an act contrary to international law.

---

[32] Douglas, *The International Law of Investment Claims*, 11.
[33] Section 3, this chapter. See also the theory of the internationalisation of State contracts in Chapter 2 of this book.
[34] Section 4, this chapter.

It was precisely the erosion of that view, prior to the widespread Arab oil nationalisations following the Second World War, which led to the sort of grave legal uncertainty about the appropriate customary international law standards and which,[35] in turn, triggered efforts at the UN General Assembly to restate the law.

The story of doubt over the legal principles governing compensation during the twentieth century is, typically, told by referring to a 1938 exchange of letters between the US Secretary of State Cordell Hull and his Mexican counterpart. In truth, it was not only the Mexican Revolution, but also the Russian Revolution, which had cast the key principles governing takings of alien property into doubt. The ideas which were subsequently to receive expression in the Mexican minister's correspondence trace their roots to the doctrine espoused by the Argentinian jurist Carlos Calvo in the previous century. This nineteenth-century doctrine stood, first, for the view that the foreign investor shall be accorded no better treatment than that accorded to the host State's own nationals. It stood, second, for insistence upon settlement by the domestic courts of the host State alone. Third, it stood for rejection of the home State's right to diplomatic espousal.[36] That idea was expressed most clearly in pre-Second World War diplomatic practice in the 1938 US–Mexican correspondence following the earlier Mexican policy of agrarian expropriations, which had, in turn, culminated in the then new 1917 Mexican Constitution. Parts of that correspondence are reproduced below. In the end, there was no agreement on the law, although Secretary Hull's position was taken to have stood for the view of 'Western' governments generally. In any event, it may be said that tribunals generally carried on applying the classical principles of protection of foreign-owned property, which is what makes the *Sabbatino* case, also reproduced below, so spectacular in its admission that customary international law had, by 1964, fallen into a state of considerable legal uncertainty.

Below are some excerpts from the US–Mexican correspondence of 1938.[37]

US Secretary of State to Mexican Ambassador to the United States, 21 July 1938

The taking of property without compensation is not expropriation. It is confiscation. It is no less confiscation because there may be an expressed intent to pay at some time in the future.

If it were permissible for a government to take the private property of the citizens of other countries and pay for it as and when, in the judgment of the government, its economic circumstances and its local legislation may perhaps permit, the safeguards which the constitutions of most countries and established international law have sought to provide would be illusory.

---

[35] For an overview, see the debate between Professors Schachter and Mendelson: O. Schachter, 'Compensation for Expropriation' (1984) 78 *AJIL* 121; M. H. Mendelson, 'Compensation for Expropriation: The Case-Law' (1985) 79 *AJIL* 414.

[36] See, e.g., Dolzer and Schreuer, *Principles of International Investment Law*, 1–2.

[37] See further G. H. Hackworth, *Digest of International Law* (Washington, DC: US Department of State, 1942), vol. III, 655–661; Lowenfeld, *International Economic Law*, 475–481, from which these excerpts are derived.

Mexican Minister of Foreign Affairs to US Ambassador, 3 August 1938

My Government maintains ... that there is in international law no rule universally accepted in theory nor carried out in practice, which makes obligatory the payment of immediate compensation nor even of deferred compensation, for expropriations of a general and impersonal character like those which Mexico has carried out for the purpose of redistribution of the land.

...

Nevertheless, Mexico admits, in obedience to her own laws, that she is indeed under obligation to indemnify in an adequate manner; but the doctrine which she maintains on the subject, which is based on the most authoritative opinions of writers of treaties on international law, is that the time and manner of such payment must be determined by her own laws.

Notice Mexico's proposition here: namely, that compensation is not payable under *international* law for *non-discriminatory* expropriation – expropriations of a 'general and impersonal character'.

US Secretary of State to Mexican Ambassador, 22 August 1938

The Government of the United States merely adverts to a self-evident fact when it notes that the applicable precedents and recognized authorities on international law support its declaration that, under every rule of law and equity, no government is entitled to expropriate [foreign-owned[38]] private property, for whatever purpose, without provision for prompt, adequate and effective payment therefor.

The Mexican Government refers to the fact that when it undertook suspension of the payment of its agrarian debt, the measure affected equally Mexicans and foreigners. It suggests that if Mexico had paid only the latter to the exclusion of its nationals, she would have violated a rule of equity.

...

Your Excellency's Government intimates that a demand for unequal treatment is implicit in the note of the United States ...

I must definitely dissent ...

...

There is now announced by your Government the astonishing theory that this treasured and cherished principle of equality, designed to protect both human and property rights, is to be invoked, not in the protection of personal rights and liberties, but as a chief ground of depriving and stripping individuals of their conceded rights. It is contended, in a word, that it is wholly justifiable to deprive an individual of his rights if all other persons are equally deprived, and if no victim is allowed to escape ... The proposition scarcely requires an answer.

---

[38] Secretary Hull had conceded in the 21 July note, cited above, that: 'We cannot question the right of a foreign government to treat its own nationals in this fashion if it so desires. This is a matter of domestic concern.'

By 1964, the world was at the height of the Cold War. Suddenly, there was a surprising and controversial concession by no less a body than the US Supreme Court. The case concerned the Cuban expropriation of American-owned properties, including a sugar company belonging to an American investor which had gone into receivership pending a determination of ownership by the courts, but whose temporary receiver – a certain Mr Sabbatino – had successfully persuaded the purchaser of a shipment of sugar not to pay the Cuban government itself, but rather the 'rightful' American owner of the expropriated sugar shipment. The claim in *Sabbatino* was, quite extraordinarily, a claim by the Banco Nacional de Cuba itself brought in the US courts for conversion and damages. In the court of appeals, Judge Waterman uttered a ringing endorsement of the role of the US courts in upholding international law, declaring in favour of the defendant that 'until the day of capable international adjudication among countries, the municipal courts must be the custodians of the concepts of international law, and they must expound, apply and develop that law whenever they are called upon to do so'.[39] International lawyers would have seen this as a classic call for 'piggy-backing' – i.e. using the various domestic courts of the world to uphold international law.

However, on appeal to the US Supreme Court, an eight-to-one majority judgment held against Sabbatino in favour of the Banco Nacional de Cuba on account of the fact that the Act of State doctrine prevented the court from inquiring into the validity of the actions of a foreign government on its own soil.[40] The reasoning, reproduced in part below, caused a scandal which prompted the US Congress to reverse that decision with its 'Sabbatino Amendment', also known as the 'Second Hickenlooper Amendment', which precluded the Act of State doctrine from being invoked in cases involving an unlawful – i.e. uncompensated, retaliatory and discriminatory – taking of foreign-owned property.[41] The judgment was delivered two years after the Cuban missile crisis, which was when the Cold War was at its most intense. The taking was evidently discriminatory, directed as it was as an act of retaliation against the United States. In the following extract, Justice Harlan addresses the well-couched argument by counsel that what was at stake was international law itself.

> **Banco Nacional de Cuba v. Sabbatino, 376 US 398, 428 (1964) (Justice Harlan)**
>
> [Sabbatino's] basic contention ... [is] ... that the United States' courts could make a significant contribution to the growth of international law, a contribution whose importance it is said, would be magnified by the relative paucity of decisional law by international bodies. But given the fluidity of present world conditions, the effectiveness of such a patchwork approach toward the formulation of an acceptable body of law concerning state responsibility for expropriations is, to say the least, highly conjectural.

[39] *Banco Nacional de Cuba* v. *Sabbatino*, 307 F2d 845 (2nd Cir. 1962).
[40] For the Act of State doctrine, see Chapter 19 of this book.
[41] See V. C. Folsom, 'The Sabbatino Case: Rule of Law or Rule of "No Law"?' (1965) 51 *ABA Journal* 725. The Amendment was swiftly applied on remand to the US Court of Appeals, from which the Supreme Court decision had originated, despite the fact that the statute was passed afterwards.

> Moreover, it rests upon the sanguine proposition that the decisions of the courts of the world's major capital exporting country and principal exponent of the free enterprise system would be accepted as disinterested expressions of sound legal principle by those adhering to widely different ideologies.

Perhaps there were more than a few persons who would have wondered if eight communists had somehow infiltrated the US Supreme Court. In any event, as one observer put it in a trenchantly worded piece in the *American Bar Association Journal*, it was a 'mistake' if the intent had been to 'balance the international "law" followed by the Communist countries against that followed by the free countries'.[42]

What was incontrovertible was the observation by Justice Harlan, writing for the majority, that the search for an appropriate, applicable, legal standard had become chaotic. In any case, the use of international legal principles in the settlement of foreign investment disputes had declined in favour of the kinds of lump-sum negotiated settlements referred to by Professor Lillich (see Section 1.3), without – as the late Andreas Lowenfeld put it – 'an attempt to fit them into international legal doctrine'.[43]

2.2 Efforts at the United Nations

By this time, there were concurrent efforts by the industrialised, developed countries to restate the principles governing the protection of foreign investments, most famously in the form of UN General Assembly Resolution 1803.

Observe paragraphs 4 and 8 of Resolution 1803, reproduced below. Notice the idea, introduced in paragraph 4, that by the agreement of 'sovereign States and other parties concerned' – i.e. investor–host State contracts – the parties can choose arbitration or international adjudication. The significance of this is that it responded to any contrary suggestion that it may be inimical to the sovereignty of a host State to agree to have investment disputes settled by an international arbitral tribunal. Contract became the device by which such a choice might be effected, an idea which in turn responded to the notion that a sovereign nation cannot be bound by contract under international law, as opposed to a contract under the host State's own law or the domestic contract law of some other municipal legal system.[44] For what did this resolution seek to do if not to declare the general or customary international law position during a time of grave uncertainty? This was, therefore, in many ways a critical moment in the history of investment arbitration. It brings us to the next noteworthy paragraph in Resolution

---

[42] *Ibid.*, 726.

[43] Lowenfeld, *International Economic Law*, 484–485. See further R. B. Lillich and B. H. Weston, *International Claims: Their Settlement by Lump Sum Agreements, Part I: The Commentary* (Charlottesville, VA: University Press of Virginia, 1975).

[44] See further C. L. Lim, 'The Worm's View of History and the Twailing Machine' in C. L. Lim (ed.), *Alternative Visions of the International Law on Foreign Investment: Essays in Honour of Muthucumaraswamy Sornarajah* (Cambridge University Press, 2016), 3, 4–5, 16–18.

1803, paragraph 8 (reproduced below), which speaks directly to the idea that a sovereign State can bind itself under international law by way of contract. As the first line of paragraph 8 puts it: 'Foreign investment agreements entered into by or between sovereign States shall be observed in good faith.' Notice too that paragraph 8 refers to foreign investment agreements 'entered into by or between sovereign States'. It thereby includes agreements between a host State and a private investor. The stipulation that such agreements shall be observed in good faith was intended to state that such agreements are binding under international law asopposed to the domestic contract law of some municipal legal system.

By the time another resolution, Resolution 3281, was passed, there had been significant changes in world events – not least in the proliferation of newly decolonised developing nations which had become members of the United Nations. The new member nations of Asia and Africa sought to restate international economic law in this field by using their greater numbers in an endeavour to outvote the power of the Western industrialised nations.[45] One outcome of all of this was the *Texaco* v. *Libya* Award, which is also reproduced below. Among the many awards flowing from the post-war oil nationalisations, *Texaco* was perhaps the most controversial of all, at least in the eyes of the developing countries and their lawyers.

UN General Assembly Resolution 1803 (XVII), 1194th plenary meeting, 14 December 1962, paras 4, 8

4. Nationalization, expropriation or requisitioning shall be based on grounds or reasons of public utility, security or the national interest which are recognized as overriding purely individual or private interests, both domestic and foreign. In such cases the owner shall be paid appropriate compensation, in accordance with the rules in force in the State taking such measures in the exercise of its sovereignty and in accordance with international law. In any case where the question of compensation gives rise to a controversy, the national jurisdiction of the State taking such measures shall be exhausted. However, upon agreement by sovereign States and other parties concerned, settlement of the dispute should be made through arbitration or international adjudication.

...

8. Foreign investment agreements freely entered into by or between sovereign States shall be observed in good faith; States and international organizations shall strictly and conscientiously respect the sovereignty of peoples and nations over their natural wealth and resources in accordance with the Charter and the principles set forth in the present resolution.

Notice that while paragraph 4 sought to uphold international arbitration or adjudication in preference to resolution by the host State's domestic courts and tribunals, in other

[45] See, e.g., C. L. Lim, 'Neither Sheep Nor Peacocks: T. O. Elias and Postcolonial International Law' (2008) 21 *Leiden J Int'l L* 295, 302–310.

words by introducing what was perceived to be a more neutral and effective device of delocalised third-party settlement, paragraph 8 sought to place the substantive rules of foreign investment protection upon a contractual footing. Contract and arbitration, as we go on to see below, became the devices of choice in the face of the turmoil in customary international law, although it was not the case that this effort went unchallenged, as Resolution 3281 shows.

> **UN General Assembly Resolution 3281(XXIX), Charter of Economic Rights and Duties of States, 2315th plenary meeting, 12 December 1974, Art. 2**
>
> 2. Each State has the right:
>
> ...
>
> (c) To nationalize, expropriate or transfer ownership of foreign property, in which case appropriate compensation should be paid by the State adopting such measures, taking into account its relevant laws and regulations and all circumstances that the State considers pertinent. In any case where the question of compensation gives rise to a controversy, it shall be settled under the domestic law of the nationalizing State and by its tribunals, unless it is freely and mutually agreed by all States concerned that other peaceful means be sought on the basis of the sovereign equality of States and in accordance with the principle of free choice of means

Resolution 3281 was part of a broader effort by the newly decolonised developing nations to construct a New International Economic Order (NIEO).[46] It was in that context that *Texaco* v. *Libya* became notable. Libya had raised the argument that Resolution 3281, in particular Article 2(2)(c), states the position under general customary international law. In the following extract, the arbitrator, René Jean Dupuy, rejects Libya's argument, stating that Resolution 1803 declares the position under customary international law.[47]

---

[46] It was a part of a broader effort to remake international law. A chief method involved an attempt to use the UN General Assembly as a permanent diplomatic law-making conference in order to restate or even remake international law, as exemplified by Resolution 3281. For the reader who is interested, the literature is voluminous, but see, e.g., Lim, 'Neither Sheep Nor Peacocks', 302–310; C. L. Lim, 'The Many-Headed Hydra' in Lim, *Alternative Visions*, 433–434; the first edition of Antonio Cassese's *International Law in a Divided World* (Oxford University Press, 1986), 364–375; R. P. Anand, *Studies in International Law and History* (Leiden: Brill, 2004), 252–256; and M. Sornarajah, *The Pursuit of Nationalized Property* (Dordrecht: Nijhoff, 1986), 14–21. For the effect of this period on (and on perceptions of) the sensibility of lawyers, including international investment lawyers, in the developing world, see A. Shalakany, 'Arbitration in the Third World: A Plea for Reassessing Bias under the Spectre of Neoliberalism' (2000) *Harvard ILJ* 419. On the more technical issue of the legal status of General Assembly resolutions, see F. Blaine Sloan, 'The Binding Force of a "Recommendation" of the General Assembly of the United Nations' (1948) XXV *BYbIL* 1; D. H. N. Johnson, 'The Effect of Resolutions of the General Assembly of the United Nations' (1956–7) XXXII *BYbIL* 97; O. Asamoah, 'The Legal Effect of Resolutions of the General Assembly' (1964) 3 *Columbia J Trans'l L* 210.

[47] See further J. Cantegreil, 'The Audacity of the *Texaco/Calasiatic* Award: René-Jean Dupuy and the Internationalization of Foreign Investment Law' (2011) 22 *EJIL* 441.

Texaco Overseas Petroleum Co./California Asiatic Oil Co. v. Government of Libya, Award on the Merits, 19 January 1977, 17 ILM 1, paras 84–90 (Dupuy) (footnotes omitted)

84. (1) With respect to the first point, Resolution 1803 (XVII) of 14 December 1962 was passed by the General Assembly by 87 votes to 2, with 12 abstentions. It is particularly important to note that the majority voted for this text, including many States of the Third World, but also several Western developed countries with market economies, including the most important one, the United States. The principles stated in this Resolution were therefore assented to by a great many States representing not only all geographical areas but also all economic systems. From this point of view, this Tribunal notes that the affirmative vote of several developed countries with a market economy was made possible in particular by the inclusion in the Resolution of two references to international law, and one passage relating to the importance of international cooperation for economic development. According to the representative of Tunisia:

> ... the result of the debate on this question was that the balance of the original draft resolution was improved – a balance between, on the one hand, the unequivocal affirmation of the inalienable right of States to exercise sovereignty over their natural resources and, on the other hand, the reconciliation or adaptation of this sovereignty to international law, equity and the principles of international cooperation (17 UN GAOR 1122, UN Doc. A/PV.1193 (1962)).

The reference to international law, in particular in the field of nationalization, was therefore an essential factor in the support given by several Western countries to Resolution 1803 (XVII).

85. On the contrary, it appears to this Tribunal that the conditions under which Resolutions 3171 (XXVII), 3201 (S-VI) and 3281 (XXIX) (Charter of the Economic Rights and Duties of States) were notably different:

> – Resolution 3171 (XXVII) was adopted by a recorded vote of 108 votes to 1, with 16 abstentions, but this Tribunal notes that a separate vote was requested with respect to the paragraph in the operative part mentioned in the Libyan Government's Memorandum whereby the General Assembly stated that the application of the principle according to which nationalizations effected by States as the expression of their sovereignty implied that it is within the right of each State to determine the amount of possible compensation and the means of their payment, and that any dispute which might arise should be settled in conformity with the national law of each State instituting measures of this kind. As a consequence of a roll-call, this paragraph was adopted by 86 votes to 11 (Federal Republic of Germany, Belgium, Spain, United States, France, Israel, Italy, Japan, The Netherlands, Portugal, United Kingdom), with 28 abstentions (South Africa, Australia, Austria, Barbados, Canada, Ivory Coast, Denmark, Finland, Ghana, Greece, Haiti, India, Indonesia, Ireland, Luxembourg, Malawi, Malaysia, Nepal, Nicaragua, Norway, New Zealand, Philippines, Rwanda, Singapore, Sri Lanka, Sweden, Thailand, Turkey).

This specific paragraph concerning nationalizations, disregarding the role of international law, not only was not consented to by the most important Western countries, but caused a number of the developing countries to abstain.

– Resolution 3201 (S-VI) was adopted without a vote by the General Assembly, but the statements made by 38 delegates showed clearly and explicitly what was the position of each main group of countries. The Tribunal should therefore note that the most important Western countries were opposed to abandoning the compromise solution contained in Resolution 1803 (XVII).

– The conditions under which, Resolution 3281 (XXIX), proclaiming the Charter of Economic Rights and Duties of States, was adopted also show unambiguously that there was no general consensus of the States with respect to the most important provisions and, in particular those concerning nationalization. Having been the subject matter of a roll-call vote, the Charter was adopted by 118 votes to 6, with 10 abstentions. The analysis of votes on specific sections of the Charter is most significant insofar as the present case is concerned. From this point of view, paragraph 2(c) of Article 2 of the Charter, which limits consideration of the characteristics of compensation to the State and does not refer to international law, was voted by 104 to 16, with 6 abstentions, all of the industrialized countries with market economies having abstained or having voted against it.

86. Taking into account the various circumstances of the votes with respect to these Resolutions, this Tribunal must specify the legal scope of the provisions of each of these Resolutions for the instant case. A first general indication of the intent of the drafters of the Charter of Economic Rights and Duties of States is afforded by the discussions which took place within the Working Group concerning the mandatory force of the future text. As early as the first session of the Working Group, differences of opinion as to the nature of the Charter envisaged gave rise to a very clear division between developed and developing countries. Thus, representatives of Iraq, Sri Lanka, Egypt, Kenya, Morocco, Nigeria, Zaire, Brazil, Chile, Guatemala, Jamaica, Mexico, Peru and Rumania held the view that the draft Charter should be a legal instrument of a binding nature and not merely a declaration of intention.

On the contrary, representatives of developed countries, such as Australia, France, Federal Republic of Germany, Italy, Japan, United Kingdom and United States expressed doubt that it was advisable, possible or even realistic to make the rights and duties set forth in a draft Charter binding upon States (Report of the Working Party on its 1st Session, U.N. Doc. TD/B/AC.12/ 1 (1973), at 6). The form of resolution adopted did not provide for the binding application of the text to those to which it applied, but the problem of the legal validity to be attached to the Charter is not thereby solved. In fact, while it is now possible to recognize that resolutions of the United Nations have a certain legal value, this legal value differs considerably, depending on the type of resolution and the conditions attached to its adoption and its provisions. Even under the assumption that they are resolutions of a declaratory nature, which is the case of the Charter of Economic Rights and Duties of States, the legal value is variable. Ambassador Castaneda, who was Chairman of the Working Group entrusted with the task of preparing this Charter, admitted that 'it is extremely difficult to determine with certainty the legal force of declaratory resolutions', that it is 'impossible to lay down a general rule in this respect', and that the legal value of the declaratory resolutions therefore includes 'an immense gamut of nuances' (La Valeur Juridique des Resolutions des Nations Unies, 129 R.C.A.D.I. 204 (1970), at 319–320).

As this Tribunal has already indicated, the legal value of the resolutions which are relevant to the present case can be determined on the basis of circumstances under which they were adopted and by analysis of the principles which they state:

   – With respect to the first point, the absence of any binding force of the resolutions of the General Assembly of the United Nations implies that such resolutions must be accepted by the Members of the United Nations in order to be legally binding. In this respect, the Tribunal notes that only Resolution 1803 (XVII) of 14 December 1962 was supported by a majority of Member States representing all of the various groups. By contrast, the other Resolutions mentioned above, and in particular those referred to in the Libyan Memorandum, were supported by a majority of States but not by any of the developed countries with market economies which carry on the largest part of international trade.

87. (2) With respect to the second point, to wit the appraisal of the legal value on the basis of the principles stated, it appears essential to this Tribunal to distinguish between those provisions stating the existence of a right on which the generality of the States has expressed agreement, and those provisions introducing new principles which were rejected by certain representative groups of States and having nothing more than a *de lege ferenda* value only in the eyes of the States which have adopted them; as far as the others are concerned, the rejection of these same principles implies that they consider them as being *contra legem*. With respect to the former, which proclaim rules recognized by the community of nations, they do not create a custom but confirm one by formulating it and specifying its scope, thereby making it possible to determine whether or not one is confronted with a legal rule. As has been noted by Ambassador Castaneda, '[such resolutions] do not create the law; they have a declaratory nature of noting what does exist' (129 R.O.A.D.I. 204 (1970), at 315). On the basis of the circumstances of adoption mentioned above and by expressing an *opinio juris communis*, Resolution 1803 (XVII) seems to this Tribunal to reflect the state of customary law existing in this field. Indeed, on the occasion of the vote on a resolution finding the existence of a customary rule, the States concerned clearly express their views. The consensus by a majority of States belonging to the various representative groups indicates without the slightest doubt universal recognition of the rules therein incorporated, i.e., with respect to nationalization and compensation the use of the rules in force in the nationalizing State, but all this in conformity with international law.

88. While Resolution 1803 (XVII) appears to a large extent as the expression of a real general will, this is not at all the case with respect to the other Resolutions mentioned above, which has been demonstrated previously by analysis of the circumstances of adoption. In particular, as regards the Charter of Economic Rights and Duties of States, several factors contribute to denying legal value to those provisions of the document which are of interest in the instant case.

    – In the first place, Article 2 of this Charter must be analyzed as a political rather than as a legal declaration concerned with the ideological strategy of development and, as such, supported only by non-industrialized States.

    – In the second place, this Tribunal notes that in the draft submitted by the Group of 77 to the Second Commission (U.N. Doc A/C.2/L. 1386 (1974), at 2), the General Assembly was invited to adopt the Charter 'as a first measure of codification and progressive development' within the field of the international law of development. However, because of the opposition of several States, this description was deleted from the text submitted to the vote of the Assembly. This important modification led Professor Virally to declare: 'It is therefore clear that the Charter is not a first step to codification and progressive development of international law, within the meaning of Article 13, para. 1(a) of the Charter of the United Nations, that is to say an instrument purporting to formulate in writing the rules of customary law and intended to better adjust its content to the requirements of international relations. The persisting difference of opinions in respect to some of its articles prevented reaching this goal and it is healthy that people have become aware of this' ('La Charte des Droits et Devoirs Economique des Etats. Notes de Lecture', 20 A.F.D.I. 57 (1974), at 59).

The absence of any connection between the procedure of compensation and international law and the subjection of this procedure solely to municipal law cannot be regarded by this Tribunal except as a *de lege ferenda* formulation, which even appears *contra legem* in the eyes of many developed countries. Similarly, several developing countries, although having voted favorably on the Charter of Economic Rights and Duties of States as a whole, in explaining their votes regretted the absence of any reference to international law.

    89. Such an attitude is further reinforced by an examination of the general practice of relations between States with respect to investments. This practice is in conformity, not with the provisions of Article 2(c) of the above-mentioned Charter conferring exclusive jurisdiction on domestic legislation and courts, but with the exception stated at the end of this paragraph. Thus a great many investment agreements entered into between industrial States or their nationals, on the one hand, and developing countries, on the other, state, in an objective way, the standards of compensation and further provide, in case of dispute regarding the level of such compensation, the possibility of resorting to an international tribunal. In this respect, it is particularly significant in the eyes of this Tribunal that no fewer than 65 States, as of 31 October 1974, had ratified the Convention on the Settlement of Investment Disputes between States and Nationals of other States, dated March 18, 1965.

    90. The argument of the Libyan Government, based on the relevant resolutions enacted by the General Assembly of the United Nations, that any dispute relating to nationalization or its consequences should be decided in conformity with the provisions of the municipal law of the nationalizing State and only in its courts, is also negated by a complete analysis of the whole text of the Charter of Economic Rights and Duties of States.

    From this point of view, even though Article 2 of the Charter does not explicitly refer to international law, this Tribunal concludes that the provisions referred to in this Article do not escape all norms of international law. Article 33, paragraph 2, of this Resolution states as follows: '2. In their interpretation and application, the provisions of the present Charter are interrelated and each provision should be construed in the context of the other provisions'. Now, among the fundamental elements of international economic relations quoted in the Charter, principle (j) is headed as follows: 'Fulfillment in good faith of International obligations'.

Analyzing the scope of these various provisions, Ambassador Castaneda, who chaired the Working Group charged with drawing up the Charter of Economic Rights and Duties of States, formally stated that the principle of performance in good faith of international obligations laid down in Chapter I(j) of the Charter applies to all matters governed by it, including, in particular, matters referred to in Article 2. Following his analysis, this particularly competent and eminent scholar concluded as follows: 'The Charter accepts that international law may operate as a factor limiting the freedom of the State should foreign interests be affected, even though Article 2 does not state this explicitly. This stems legally from the provisions included in other Articles of the Charter which should be interpreted and applied jointly with those of Article 2' ('La Charte des Droits et Devoirs Economiques dos Etats. Note sur son Processus d'Elaboration', 20 A.F.D.I. 31 (1974), at 54).

What these passages show is the treatment of UN General Assembly Resolution 1803 as a statement of the law. *Texaco* was a forceful and subsequently influential attempt to treat Resolution 1803 itself as a species of State practice and *opinio juris communis*.

3. THE CREATURE OF THE 'INTERNATIONALISED' CONTRACT

Resolution 1803 also stood for the proposition that investor–State contracts will not be governed by the law of the host State with which the contract might be presumed to have its closest connection, but rather by international law itself. The following passage from the *Texaco* Award, which is also discussed in greater detail in Chapter 2 of this book, purports to state the precise legal process and conditions under which a contract between the investor and the host State becomes 'automatically' internationalised.

Texaco Overseas Petroleum Co./California Asiatic Oil Co. v. Government of Libya, Award on the Merits, 19 January 1977, 17 ILM 1, paras 40–45 (Dupuy) (footnotes omitted)

40. As the Tribunal has already observed ... the internationalization of contracts entered into between States and foreign private persons can result in various ways ...

41 (a.a). At the outset, it is accepted that the reference made by the contract, in the clause concerning the governing law, to the general principles of law leads to this result.

These general principles, being those which are mentioned in Article 38 of the Statute of the International Court of Justice, are one of the sources of international law: they may appear alone in the clause or jointly with a national law, particularly with the law of the contracting State.

...

43. This evolution toward the internationalization of contracts was foreseeable: indeed, in its judgments in the cases relating to the *Serbian and Brazilian Loans* and on the occasion of the examination of the criteria which could be adopted for the determination of the applicable law, the Permanent Court of International Justice laid down a rule of great flexibility:

> 'The Court which has before it a dispute involving the question as to the law which governs the contractual obligations at issue, can determine what this law is only by reference to the actual nature of these obligations and to the circumstances attendant upon their creation, though it may also take into account the expressed or presumed intention of the Parties' ([1929] P.C.I.J., Ser. A, No. 20, at 41).

> The three criteria laid down by the Permanent Court of International Justice and derived from the nature of the obligations, the circumstances of their creation and the will of the parties, converge, in the instant case, to reverse the presumption which was established, in another connection, by the judgments of 1929, a presumption to which reference was made already (see para. 27 *supra, in fine*), and according to which a State cannot, from the outset, be presumed 'to have made the substance of its debt and the validity of the obligations accepted by it in respect thereof, subject to any law other than its own'.

44 (b.b.). Another process for the internationalization of a contract consists in inserting a clause providing that possible differences which may arise in respect of the interpretation and the performance of the contract shall be submitted to arbitration.

Such a clause has a twofold consequence:

> – on the one hand, as this Tribunal has already noted (see para. 16 *supra*), the institution of arbitration shall be that established by international law.
> – on the other hand, as regards the law applicable to the merits of the dispute itself, the inclusion of an arbitration clause leads to a reference to the rules of international law.

Even if one considers that the choice of international arbitration proceedings cannot by itself lead to the exclusive application of international law, it is one of the elements which makes it possible to detect a certain internationalization of the contract. The *Sapphire International Petroleum Ltd.* award is quite explicit: 'If no positive implication can be made from the arbitral clause, it is possible to find there a negative intention, namely to reject the exclusive application of Iranian law' (35 Int'l L.R. 136 (1963), at 172); this is what led the arbitrator in that case, in the absence of any explicit reference to the law applicable, not to apply automatically Iranian law, thus dismissing any presumption in its favor. It is therefore unquestionable that the reference to international arbitration is sufficient to internationalize a contract, in other words, to situate it within a specific legal order – the order of the international law of contracts.

45 (c). A third element of the internationalization of the contracts in dispute results from the fact that it takes on a dimension of a new category of agreements between States and private persons: economic development agreements ...

Several elements characterize these agreements: in the first place, their subject matter is particularly broad: they are not concerned only with an isolated purchase or performance, but tend to bring to developing countries investments and technical assistance, particularly in the field of research and exploitation of mineral resources, or in the construction of factories on a turnkey basis. Thus, they assume a real importance in the development of the country where they are performed: it will suffice to mention here the importance of the obligations assumed in the case under consideration by the concession holders in the field of road and port infrastructures and the training on the spot of qualified personnel. The party contracting with the State was thus associated with the realization of the economic and social progress of the host country.

In the second place, the long duration of these contracts implies close cooperation between the State and the contracting party and requires permanent installations as well as the acceptance of extensive responsibilities by the investor.

Finally, because of the purpose of the cooperation in which the contracting party must participate with the State and the magnitude of the investments to which it agreed, the contractual nature of this type of agreement is reinforced: the emphasis on the contractual nature of the legal relation between the host State and the investor is intended to bring about an equilibrium between the goal of the general interest sought by such relation and the profitability which is necessary for the pursuit of the task entrusted to the private enterprise. The effect is also to ensure to the private contracting party a certain stability which is justified by the considerable investments which it makes in the country concerned. The investor must in particular be protected against legislative uncertainties, that is to say the risks of the municipal law of the host country being modified, or against any government measures which would lead to an abrogation or rescission of the contract. Hence, the insertion, as in the present case, of so-called stabilization clauses: these clauses tend to remove all or part of the agreement from the internal law and to provide for its correlative submission to *sui generis* rules as stated in the *Aramco* award, or to a system which is properly an international law system. From this latter point of view, the following considerations should be noted, which were mentioned in the *Sapphire* award, and which stress the interest of the internationalization of the contract:

> 'Such a solution seems particularly suitable for giving the guarantees of protection which are indispensable for foreign companies, since these companies undergo very considerable risks in bringing financial and technical aid to countries in the process of development. It is in the interest of both parties to such agreements that any disputes between them should be settled according to the general principles universally recognized and should not be subject to the particular rules of national laws ...' (35 Int'l L.R. 136 (1963), at 175–176).

The upshot is that contract, specifically the creature of an 'internationalised contract', became one answer to the uncertainties of customary international law which had made resort to customary principles unreliable in practice. Insofar as custom might still be useful, it would simply lend the force of law to investor–host State contracts whose terms were to be negotiated with the foreign investor.

4. REACHING FOR TREATY-BASED INVESTOR–STATE ARBITRATION

Contracts, together with the endorsement of contractually based international arbitration, were viewed as promising solutions to the decline of international law principles in the settlement of foreign investment disputes. Yet the effort to steer clear of the muddy controversy over substantive customary international law principles on the protection of foreign investments did not result merely in the attempt to replace substantive customary principles with freely negotiated contractual principles. This would ultimately have such contractual principles placed upon a customary international law footing for their validity and application, or worse upon some lesser international law footing such as the writings of publicists as evidence of a *lex mercatoria*.[48] Such contractual commitments were eventually also sought to be placed upon a treaty footing in the famous Abs–Shawcross Draft.[49] Indeed, the entire body of preferred principles of customary international law on foreign investment protection was sought to be placed upon a treaty footing,[50] and so too with investor–host State arbitration.[51] Here lies the turn, finally, to treaty law as the foundation of international investment law and arbitration today.

Much has been written about the process triggered by the extraordinary attempt by Hermann Abs and Sir Hartley Shawcross to introduce a *magna carta* for foreign investors internationally, under which investment protection and third-party settlement would be placed instead upon a firm treaty footing. Suffice to say here that the idea of a multilateral investment treaty also led to an Organisation for Economic Co-operation and Development (OECD) Draft Convention, which was soon abandoned. In turn, there emerged bilateral investment treaties, so-called 'BITs', beginning with the 1959 Germany–Pakistan BIT, which was the first modern example of its kind.[52] Subsequently, there was

---

[48] Such as the general principles of law recognised by civilised nations, or what Sornarajah has called 'the low order sources' of international law (M. Sornarajah, 'The Myth of International Contract Law' (1981) 15 *J World Trade Law* 187, 199, 201, 202), also discussed in Lim, 'The Many-Headed Hydra', 434–435.

[49] See, e.g., G. Schwarzenberger, 'The Abs–Shawcross Draft on Investments Abroad: A Critical Commentary' (1960) 9 *J Pub L* 147, 154–155; I. Seidl-Hohenveldern, 'The Abs–Shawcross Draft Convention to Protect Private Foreign Investment: Comments on the Round Table' (1961) 10 *J Pub L* 100, 103 et seq. and the reply by Professor Stanley Metzger, *ibid.*, 110, at 111. Art. 2, Draft Convention on Investments Abroad, 1959, Article II; reproduced in A. Newcombe and L. Paradell, *Law and Practice of Investment Treaties* (The Hague: Kluwer Law International, 2009), 441; also in M. Paparinskis, *Basic Documents in International Investment Protection* (Oxford and Portland, OR: Hart, 2012), 6. Umbrella clauses are addressed in Chapter 15 of this book. See further, e.g., C. L. Lim, 'Is the Umbrella Clause Not Just Another Treaty Clause?' in Lim, *Alternative Visions*, 349, 351 and the references cited therein.

[50] Schwarzenberger, 'The Abs–Shawcross Draft on Investments Abroad', generally.

[51] *Ibid.*, 162–164.

[52] See, e.g., Dolzer and Schreuer, *Principles of International Investment Law*, 8; Newcombe and Paradell, *Law and Practice of Investment Treaties*, 21 et seq.

widespread adoption of such BITs by European States, and this was followed in the adaptation of the United States' earlier FCN treaties to the modern European form before such BITs spread worldwide.[53]

The BITs played a key role in forging the investment arbitration practice of today, which has grown from treaty claims brought from the 1990s onwards, almost three decades from the time of the first modern BIT mentioned above.[54] The key treaties had been Chapter 11 of a trilateral investment treaty, the North American Free Trade Agreement (NAFTA) and the Energy Charter Treaty (ECT).[55] In short, without the intervention of the treaty device in this sphere, there would be no law and practice of investment arbitration, which is another way of saying that investment arbitration as we know it today is largely investment treaty arbitration. The idea that contractually based investment arbitration would have taken pride of place has not been borne out. Rather, contractually based investment arbitration exists alongside treaty arbitration.

Investor–State arbitration is discussed in Chapter 4 of this book, in particular the idea that an 'offer' of the host State in an investment treaty is 'accepted', thereby perfecting consent to arbitration, when the investor initiates arbitration by way of its written notice of arbitration or other similar instrument.

5. ICSID, INTERNATIONAL COURTS AND OTHER MODERN INSTITUTIONS

The idea of a worldwide investment treaty which would offer substantive treaty protection against unlawful expropriation was not favoured by the World Bank, whose Office of General Counsel had long played an informal role in assisting with the settlement of investment disputes.[56] This was for the same reason as that expressed by detractors from the Abs–Shawcross Draft Convention – namely, that the developing, capital-importing countries would not come to agreement about the contents of such a treaty.[57] Indeed, the OECD's efforts in producing such a multilateral treaty had failed.[58] Scepticism about the prospects of a multilateral investment treaty which would provide substantive treaty protection had

---

[53] See K. J. Vandevelde, 'The Liberal Vision of the International Law on Foreign Investment' in Lim, *Alternative Visions*, 43.

[54] See also K. J. Vandevelde, 'A Brief History of International Investment Agreements' (2005) 12 *UC Davis J Int'l L & Pol* 157, 174, attributing the sudden emergence of BIT-based investment treaty arbitration to the conclusion of the 1965 ICSID Convention.

[55] NAFTA 1992 is a free trade agreement which contains an investment chapter in Chapter 11 which provides for investment arbitration; see, e.g., R. Folsom *et al.*, *Handbook of NAFTA Dispute Settlement* (Ardsley, NY: Transnational, 1998). The ECT 1994 is a multilateral treaty which governs energy cooperation, containing among others trade and investment disciplines, and providing for investment arbitration under Art. 29; see G. Coop and C. Ribeiro (eds), *Investment Protection and the Energy Charter Treaty* (New York: Juris, 2008). By 2012, there were 514 known cases against some ninety-five Respondent States. For the growth in cases between 1992 and 2012, see 'Recent Developments in Investor State Dispute Settlement', UNCTAD, IIA Issue Note No. 1, May 2013. On the effect of this explosion of arbitral jurisprudence on the subject, see S. W. Schill, 'W(h)ither Fragmentation? On the Literature and Sociology of International Investment Law' (2011) 22 *EJIL* 875.

[56] See, e.g., R. W. Edwards, Jr, 'The Role of a General Counsel of an International Financial Institution' (2008) 17 *Kansas JL Pub Pol'cy* 254, 258.

[57] Discussed in Seidl-Hohenveldern, 'The Abs–Shawcross Draft Convention', and also in the reply by Metzger in that article.

[58] Dolzer and Schreuer, *Principles of International Investment Law*, 8.

been confirmed by the World Bank's General Counsel at the time, Aron Broches. So, instead, Broches played a pivotal role in forging ahead with the Bank's idea of the establishment of a standing, multilateral foreign investment dispute settlement mechanism.[59]

Aron Broches, *Selected Essays: World Bank, ICSID, and Other Subjects of Public and Private International Law* (Dordrecht: Nijhoff, 1995), 264–266, 275–276, 278 (footnotes omitted)

In the early 1960s the World Bank found itself being urged from various sides to take some action to help overcome the political risk obstacle which was inhibiting the flow of private investment from the rich to the poor countries. Two approaches were being considered at the time. The direct approach was represented by the OECD's work on a multilateral convention for the protection of foreign property, often referred to at the time as a 'code of good behaviour'. Viewing the problem from an entirely different angle were the various proposals for multilateral insurance of investments against expropriation and other political risks. We in the World Bank did not consider that either of these approaches was a promising vehicle for Bank activity. The OECD Convention set forth rules of law which the developing countries were not prepared to accept in a multilateral context. A multilateral insurance scheme bristled with technical and policy problems, including issues of risk sharing, financing, subrogation of the insurance agency in the claim of a compensated investor and compulsory arbitration of disputes between the subrogated agency and the state which caused the event giving rise to the claim. Our assessment proved to be right. In 1967 the OECD abandoned its efforts to arrive at a multilaterally agreed Code of Good Behavior and notwithstanding some 25 years of discussion in various organizations, including the OECD, the Inter-American Development Bank and the World Bank, multilateral investment insurance has not yet become a reality.

   The management of the World Bank, and in particular Presidents Black (1949–1962) and Woods (1963–1968), opted for a more limited and more realistic approach, thinking that the Bank might make a modest contribution to an improvement of the investment climate by creating facilities for the Settlement of investment disputes through conciliation and/or arbitration proceedings to which the host country and the foreign investor would be parties on an equal procedural footing, and without either requiring or permitting the intervention of the Investor's national state, thereby contributing to a depoliticization of investment disputes. First discussed in 1962, the ICSID Convention was approved by the Executive Directors on March 18, 1965 for submission to governments and entered into force on October 14, 1966, after 20 governments had ratified it ... it will be sufficient to recall here only a few of its principal distinctive features:
(a) While recourse to the facilities of the Centre is voluntary, once such recourse has been
   agreed upon that agreement is irrevocable (Art. 5).

---

[59] *Ibid.*, 9; A. Broches, *Selected Essays: World Bank, ICSID, and Other Subjects of Public and Private International Law* (Dordrecht: Nijhoff, 1995).

(b) The Convention contains no rules of substantive law, no rules of conduct, but grants the parties unlimited freedom to agree on the rules of law to be applied by the tribunal in deciding the dispute. Absent such agreement the tribunal is to apply the law of the state party to the dispute 'and such rules of international law as may be applicable' (Art. 42).
(c) Awards are binding and not subject to appeal or to any other remedy except those provided for in the Convention (Art. 53).
(d) All Contracting States are obliged to recognize and enforce ICSID awards as if they were final judgments of domestic courts (Art. 54).
(e) The State party to an arbitration proceeding is under an obligation to 'abide by and comply with' the award rendered therein, but forcible execution of the award may founder on the gradually eroding rocks of sovereign immunity, if and to the extent such immunity is recognized by the forum state (Art. 55).[60]

The Convention has sometimes been regarded as an instrument for the protection of foreign private investment. This characterization is one-sided and too narrow. The purpose of the Convention is to promote private foreign investment by improving the investment climate for investors and host states alike, and the drafters took great care to make it a balanced instrument. The Convention permits proceedings at the initiative of an investor as well as at that of the host state.

...

ICSID arbitration is institutional arbitration. The proceedings are governed by the Convention and the Regulations and Rules adopted by the Administrative Council. These are highly technical and complex instruments whose application may pose problems not only for counsel but also for arbitrators. This is especially true of those whose experience is limited to arbitrations which while 'international' judged by subject-matter, nationality or residence of the parties or similar criteria, are nevertheless part of the national legal order.

They are governed by national laws, subject as to certain matters to applicable international agreements such as the 1958 New York Convention on the Recognition and Enforcement of Foreign Arbitral Awards or the 1961 European Convention on International Commercial Arbitration. In contrast, ICSID arbitration proceedings are governed entirely by public international procedural law. The Convention and the Arbitral Rules constitute the *lex arbitri*, the *loi de l'arbitrage*. The contrast is thus between restraints imposed by international law on national procedures, on the one hand, and a procedural system governed entirely by public international law, on the other.

---

[60] [Eds: Here, Broches refers to the fact that while immunity from award enforcement is waived by the State party to the ICSID Convention (Art. 54), 'execution' and 'attachment', unlike 'enforcement' of the Award, will still be subject to the laws of the State in which such execution and attachment is sought. In that regard, immunity from execution and attachment is the State's last refuge. Why is that so? The simple answer is that States are wary of interfering with each other's property. The issue of the immunity of a foreign State, which is always implicated in the enforcement of an arbitral award, is discussed further in Chapter 19 of this book.]

Because of these special characteristics and the fact that each proceeding includes a governmental party, the Arbitration Rules of the Centre envisage an important administrative role for the Secretary-General and, under his responsibility, for the secretaries of tribunals whom he is to appoint for each proceeding. This offers an opportunity to create an independent secretariat which through its familiarity with the institution can assist arbitrators in matters of procedure and 'manage' the proceedings.

...

Ad hoc arbitration need not be synonymous with unadministered arbitration. The *compromis* may provide for a secretariat to assist the tribunal. On the other hand, private law institutional arbitration of which ICC arbitration is the best known example in the international commercial field does not guarantee the degree of administration provided by the ICSID system. This degree of administration is available not only to assist proceedings governed by the Convention, but also those conducted under the Additional Facility which authorizes the ICSID secretariat to administer certain proceedings outside the scope of the Convention, for example a proceeding in which either the state party or the national state of the foreign investor is not a party to the Convention.

...

The ICSID Convention ... provides for a Panel of Conciliators and a Panel of Arbitrators to each of which Contracting States may designate up to four persons. However, drawing on the lessons of experience the Convention provides that the parties may, but need not, choose from the Panels. To that extent, the Panels serve as an aid to litigants, providing them with a list of arbitrators whose respective governments have deemed them worthy of inclusion. This freedom is not enjoyed by the Chairman of the centre's Administrative Council when he is called upon to designate arbitrators: he must choose from the Panel.

The advantages and disadvantages of International Centre for Settlement of Investment Disputes (ICSID) arbitration as compared to other forms of investment arbitration are discussed briefly in Chapter 4 of this book. In any event, starting in the 1970s and 1980s,[61] the ICSID's caseload picked up before the explosion of ICSID arbitrations, and indeed of foreign direct investment flows and BITs, during the 1990s. The increase in disputes submitted to ICSID arbitration was fuelled by NAFTA disputes and disputes involving the European Energy Charter treaty.[62]

It should not be forgotten, however, that investment disputes have for a long time also made their way to international State-to-State adjudication. Some of the most important, indeed seminal precedents on the protection which customary international law affords to

---

[61] C. F. Amerasinghe, 'Judging with and Legal Advising in International Organizations' (2001) 2 *Chicago J Int'l L* 283, 286.

[62] See A. Parra, 'Applicable Law in Investor-State Arbitration' in M. Rovine (ed.), *Contemporary Issues in International Arbitration and Mediation: The Fordham Papers* (The Hague: Martinus Nijhoff, 2008), 3, generally, for a survey of some of the more interesting figures.

foreign investments have derived from international adjudication. The *Chorzów Factory* case has already been mentioned. That important pronouncements have come from the International Court of Justice is wholly unsurprising when it is considered that international adjudication played – or was made to play – a crucial role in the twentieth-century development of the subject of the protection of foreign investments under international law. International adjudication was, after all, a great invention, some might say the greatest invention, of twentieth-century international law. Mention should be made here of at least three cases which went before the International Court of Justice – *Barcelona Traction*, *ELSI* and *Diallo*.

These three cases govern a question which, although of decreasing practical importance because of the advent of treaties, is nonetheless foundational – does customary international law (i.e. absent a treaty rule) allow derivative shareholders to claim against the host State? The Court in the *Barcelona Traction* case held against it,[63] but admitted that a treaty rule could provide otherwise,[64] as today's BITs have indeed shown. The Court also conceded that derivative shareholders may bring a claim where their own 'direct rights' as opposed to those of the company have been violated,[65] and that – perhaps – an exception might also be made where the home State and host State are one and the same.[66] An attempt was made to revisit the ruling in *Barcelona Traction* subsequently in the *ELSI* case – a case where the host State and home State of the company were one and the same. But although the Court did admit at one point that the US–Italian FCN Treaty would allow claims by the American derivative shareholders,[67] that decision was concerned largely with the construction of the terms of the relevant treaty. It was not until the *Diallo* case that consideration was again given to the situation where the host and home States were one and the same. The *Diallo* judgment applied the International Law Commission's view that, for an exception to be made to the '*Barcelona Traction* rule' in a case where the host and home States are the same, the investor must have been required or compelled to invest through local incorporation.[68] In *Diallo*, however, the Court observed that the investor had not been required to form a local subsidiary.

Lest it be forgotten, international arbitration historically had preceded international adjudication. This is no less true in the field of disputes over foreign-owned property. There are various examples of famous awards. The *Lena Goldfields* Award was one, involving an award against the USSR for the violation of a Tsarist-era exploration, mining and transportation concession. That Award was published in *The Times* of London

---

[63] *Case Concerning Barcelona Traction, Light & Power Co. (Belgium v. Spain)* [1970] ICJ Rep. 3, p. 36.
[64] *Ibid.*, p. 46.
[65] *Ibid.*, p. 36.
[66] *Ibid.*, p. 48, stating, however, that this was not the case at hand.
[67] *Case Concerning Elettronica Sicula SpA (ELSI) (USA v. Italy)* [1989] ICJ Rep. 15, 79–80. See further S. Kubiatowski, 'The Case of Elettronica Sicula S.p.A.: Toward Greater Protection of Shareholders' Rights in Foreign Investments' (1991) *Columbia J Trans'l L* 215, 237–238.
[68] *Case Concerning Ahmadou Sadio Diallo (Guinea v. Congo)* (Preliminary Objections) [2007] ICJ Rep. 579, 91–93. See ILC Draft Articles on Diplomatic Protection, Art. 11(b). See further, e.g., A. Alvarez-Jimènez, 'Foreign Investors, Diplomatic Protection and the International Court of Justice's Decision on Preliminary Objections in the Diallo Case' (2008) 33(3) *North Carolina J Int'l L & Comp Reg* 437, 450–453.

on 3 September 1930.[69] There were also the Libyan oil nationalisation cases, of which mention has already been made. These were unusual, as was observed at the time. They were three essentially 'private' arbitrations appearing before three eminent jurists, arising from similar facts and the same political context – namely, the 1970s oil crisis and the concurrent attempt by developing countries to rewrite the rules of the international economic order. These arbitrations subsequently came to light prominently in the public domain.[70] They were also part of a host of broader Arab oil nationalisation cases – the *Abu Dhabi* arbitration, which saw Lord Asquith as Umpire,[71] the *Qatar* arbitration[72] and the *Saudi Aramco* arbitration.[73] These marked the beginning of the internationalisation of State contracts through the insistence of the arbitrators that the Islamic laws of the host States were inadequate for the task of deciding petroleum disputes.[74] The Libyan disputes had, on the other hand, emerged from the Libyan oil nationalisations which occurred between 1971 and 1974,[75] and they were the famous *BP*,[76] *Texaco*[77] and *LIAMCO*[78] arbitrations brought against Libya.

Other institutional tribunals and similar bodies, particularly more recent ones which emerged in the twentieth and twenty-first centuries, such as the Iran–US Claims Tribunal and the UN Compensation Commission – a body established by the UN Security Council to administer Gulf War reparations against Iraq – have already been mentioned.

6. THE NATURE OF INVESTMENT TREATY ARBITRATION AND THE SOURCES OF THE INTERNATIONAL LAW ON FOREIGN INVESTMENT

The nature of investment treaty arbitration, being the most prominent form today of international investment arbitration, is no easy matter. But for the replacement of the reference to treaties, the description of investment treaty arbitration in the extract below refers just as adequately to investment contract arbitration. In place of the reference to investment treaty arbitration, should it be accepted that investment contracts may be and often are 'internationalised', one should simply insert a reference to investment contract arbitration? There is no doubt, however, of the 'hybrid', complex nature of international investment arbitration, and more specifically investment treaty arbitration today. Zachary Douglas has the following comments to make.

---

[69] A. Nussbaum, 'The Arbitration between the Lena Goldfields, Ltd. and the Soviet Government' (1950) 36(1) *Cornell L Rev* 31.

[70] Shalakany, 'Arbitration in the Third World', 426, quoting R. B. von Mehren and P. N. Kourides, 'International Arbitrations between States and Foreign Private Parties: The Libyan Nationalization Cases' (1981) 75 *AJIL* 476, 490.

[71] *Petroleum Development Ltd* v. *The Sheikh of Abu Dhabi* (1951) 18 ILR 144.

[72] (1953) 20 ILR 534.

[73] (1958) 27 ILR 117.

[74] See Sornarajah, *The Pursuit of Nationalized Property*, 113–115; M. Sornarajah, *The International Law on Foreign Investment*, 3rd edn (Cambridge University Press, 2010), 289–294.

[75] Shalakany, 'Arbitration in the Third World', 448.

[76] *BP Exploration Co. (Libya) Ltd* v. *Government of Libya* (1979) 53 ILR 297.

[77] *Texaco Overseas Petroleum Co./California Asiatic Oil Co.* v. *Government of Libya*, Award on the Merits, 19 January 1977, (1979) 53 ILR 389; (1978) 17 ILM 1.

[78] *Libyan American Oil Co.* v. *Government of Libya* (1977) 17 ILM 3.

Zachary Douglas, 'The Hybrid Foundations of Investment Treaty Arbitration' (2003) 74 *BYbIL* 151, 152–155

The analytical challenge presented by the investment treaty regime for the arbitration of investment disputes is that it cannot be adequately rationalised either as a form of public international or private transnational dispute resolution. Investment treaties are international instruments between states governed by the public international law of treaties. The principal beneficiary of the investment treaty regime is most often a corporate entity established under a municipal law, while the legal interests protected by the regime are a bundle of rights in an investment arising under a different municipal law. The standards of protection are fixed by an international treaty, but liability for their breach is said to give rise to a 'civil or commercial' award for enforcement purposes.

Even this superficial appraisal of the different legal relationships and categories arising out of the investment treaty regime is sufficient to disclose its hybrid or *sui generis* character. Nonetheless, the present tendency is for states to see elements of the international law of diplomatic protection lurking in the shadows cast by investment treaties, whereas investors are often convinced of a striking resemblance to international commercial arbitration. The *lex arbitri* created by the investment treaty regime, as this study will demonstrate, is a long way from both these legal institutions for the resolution of disputes.

There is nothing new in abandoning the simple dichotomy between public and private international law conceptions of dispute resolution. Modern international society and commerce are characterised by a complex and sometimes disordered web of interrelationships between sovereign states, individuals, international organisations, and multinational corporations. As this web grows in density and coverage, traversing territorial and jurisdictional frontiers, the challenges for the international or transnational legal order become more and more critical. The response to these challenges has often been in the form of innovative international treaties that introduce a bundle of substantive norms and a distinct dispute resolution mechanism. In the sphere of legal relationships between private entities and sovereign states, there are many parallels between the legal regime created by investment treaties on the one hand and those regimes established by the European Convention of Human Rights and the Algiers Accords (creating the Iran/US Claims Tribunal) on the other. Citizens of many European countries have the right to pursue remedies directly against a state for violations of international minimum standards of treatment, formulated as universal and inalienable human rights, before an international tribunal. Citizens of Iran and the United States have the right to pursue remedies directly against the other state for violations of international minimum standards of treatment, such as the prohibition against uncompensated expropriation, before an international tribunal. Recourse to the European Court of Human Rights, the Iran/US Claims Tribunal, and the international arbitral tribunals established pursuant to investment treaties has catapulted individuals and corporate entities into an international system of adjudication along-side states. In this respect also the traditional view of the international legal order that relegated individuals and corporate entities to the status of mere 'objects' of international law is no longer credible.

An analysis of these different treaty regimes can be distorted if one adheres to a strict distinction between public and private international law conceptions of dispute resolution.

Many of the awards of investment treaty tribunals – and the pleadings of parties to these disputes – proceed on the basis of a dogmatic distinction between 'international' or 'treaty' versus 'municipal' or 'contractual' spheres, as if the two can be strictly dissociated one from the other. Thus, by characterising the status of an investment treaty tribunal as 'international', arbitrators have professed to occupy a position of supremacy in a 'hierarchy' of legal orders, and thereby have dismissed the relevance of any competing law or jurisdiction. The principle of international law that is used to buttress this approach, whether expressly or implicitly, is the rule of state responsibility that a state cannot invoke provisions of its own law to justify a derogation from an international obligation. Article 3 of the ILC's Articles on the Responsibility of States for International Wrongs, titled 'Characterization of the act of a State as internationally wrongful', is a codification of this rule, which provides: 'The characterization of an act of a State as internationally wrongful is governed by international law. Such characterization is not affected by the characterization of the same act as lawful by internal law.' But investment disputes are only partly concerned with the compliance of acts attributable to a state with its treaty obligations; and the principle stated in Article 3 of the ILC Articles only comes into play when there is actual conflict between the two legal orders – orders which nonetheless coexist in principle (and in fact), in relation to any investment situation. In other words, investment disputes are significantly concerned with issues pertaining to the existence, nature, and scope of the private interests comprising the investment. These issues go beyond the purview of international law and the rule of state responsibility just recalled. To treat international law as a self-sufficient legal order in the sphere of foreign investment is plainly untenable.

Within this domain of private or commercial interests, problems relating to overlapping adjudicative competence and the application of municipal law cannot be resolved by playing the simple 'international trump card' of Article 3.

Insofar as the argument is that domestic law concepts and domestic law can come into play, there can be no controversy. Two quick examples can be provided here. International law, for example, turns to the nationality law of the home State in determining whether the investor in the host State qualifies as an 'investor' for the purposes of the definition of an 'investor' in a BIT,[79] which in turn would typically specify – among other things – that an 'investor' has to possess the nationality of the home State which is party to the BIT.

[79] And there it should end, but sometimes it does not. There could arise the argument that the same internal law of the State disapplies treaty protection to a particular area or class of persons, but in circumstances wherein it may be countered that this is irrelevant to international law. International law presumes that the treaties of a new metropolitan territory apply to a newly absorbed territorial unit, and that a treaty applies to the whole of a State's territory. Things may become more complicated when the metropolitan territory denies that there ever was a succession since sovereignty was never lost. For a vivid example, see the cases of Hong Kong and Macao in connection with the application of PRC investment treaties: C. L. Lim, 'Fragrant Harbour and Oyster Mirror' in L. E. Sachs and L. J. Johnson (eds), *Yearbook on International Investment Law & Policy 2015–2016* (Oxford University Press, 2018), 375.

Another example is where a treaty 'umbrella clause' states that a contractual breach (at least of a sufficiently serious nature) also amounts to a treaty breach. Whether or not there has been a breach of contract is determined by the (domestic) law governing the contract.

Whether such domestic law concepts can exist alongside international law rights should be taken as being uncontroversial. What is likely to provoke greater controversy is the notion that the usual principles of international law do not also apply, and insofar as these are the usual principles of international law concerning, for example, the principle that breach of an international legal obligation attracts responsibility, or that treaties are binding, we are speaking of the usual sources of international law – treaties, customary international law as evidence of a general practice accepted as law, the general principles of law recognised by civilised nations, as well as judicial decisions and the teachings of the most highly qualified publicists of the various nations.

Treaties are binding compacts between nations, and the law of treaties as it exists under customary international law is codified in the Vienna Convention on the Law of Treaties (VCLT). Custom is formed through the general practice of States (*usus*) coupled with the sense that such practice is required or permitted by international law (*opinio juris*). The form which State practice takes may include conduct, the absence of conduct where it might be expected, statements and even the act of forming treaty rules, such that one of the great controversies has concerned whether more than 3,000 BITs have themselves not formed new rules of customary international law.[80] The general principles of law recognised by civilised nations are derived from general, common principles which are to be found, for example, in the various national legal orders. Such principles, together with treaty and custom, have been termed the 'formal sources' of international law, unlike judicial decisions and the writings of publicists, which are only evidence of international law, do not themselves 'make' international law and are only 'material sources' of the law. In this respect, general principles are grouped together with the treaty and customary international law-making processes.[81] The distinction may not be of any great practical importance.[82] It is unsurprising, therefore, to find that, at least statistically,

---

[80] The point had been raised early on by the late F. A. Mann: see, e.g., F. A. Mann, 'British Treaties for the Promotion and Protection of Investments' (1981) 52 *BYbIL* 241, 249; also P. Dumberry, 'Are BITs Representing the "New" Customary International Law in International Investment Law?' (2010) 29 *Penn St Int'l L Rev* 675.

[81] G. Schwarzenberger, *International Law*, 3rd edn (London: Stevens, 1957), vol. I, 26–27. For the view that, as with custom and treaty, general principles are, in principle at least, derived from State 'consent' or 'assent', see O. A. Elias and C. L. Lim, 'General Principles of Law, "Soft Law" and the Identification of International Law' (1997) 28 *Netherlands YbIL* 3.

[82] This is not to say that various theoretical issues, if unresolved, will not affect the practical credibility of a particular source of law. See C. A. Bradley, 'Introduction: Custom's Future' in C. A. Bradley (ed.), *Custom's Future: International Law in a Changing World* (Cambridge University Press, 2016), 1–2. The more conceptually puzzling a supposed 'source' is, the less credible and therefore useful it may be. Questions abound, in particular, about custom, such as how new custom may be made if, as is commonly accepted, it is said to comprise both a component of state practice and *opinio juris*. There surely cannot be a sense of legal obligation about a rule which does not yet exist. Saying that custom is therefore made by a 'mistaken' view of the law may be true, but appears unattractive. Saying that States take a chance in advancing a new view in the hope that it may be accepted, albeit by insisting that such a view is already the law, is only marginally more attractive. See A. D'Amato, *The Concept of Custom in International Law* (Ithaca, NY: Cornell University Press, 1971). For these reasons, the ILC has seen urgency in providing closer guidance on custom and the customary law process. The reader may therefore wish, as a practical matter, to consult the ILC's 'Third Report on Identification of Customary International Law', by Sir Michael Wood of the United Kingdom (Special Rapporteur), 67th Session, 27 March 2015, UN Doc. A/CN.4/682. See also P. Dumberry, *The Formation and Identification of Rules of Customary International Law in International Investment Law* (Cambridge University Press, 2016).

custom is often said to have become formed in judicial statements which simply cite treaties as proof of the existence of custom.[83]

All this is mentioned only to show that the law which is applied in international investment arbitration often gives rise to complexity, and it is best to beware of this at the outset. In the course of this book, the reader will encounter questions about whether a particular customary standard has been shaped and the standard therein elevated by years of intervening, widespread treaty practice; but there is no sense in rushing the discussion.

CONCLUSION

In the past, investment disputes were typically resolved by the home State's diplomatic espousal of the investor's claim, putting settlement by means of gunboat diplomacy aside – Palmerston had defended the use of the threat of armed force during the *Don Pacifico* affair.[84] Fortunately, this approach has faded into the past, at least for now. There were other methods which existed alongside diplomatic settlement. Where the popularity of some methods waned, others would come to replace them. Development and refinement of the means for settling investment disputes did not proceed in a linear fashion. Certain ideas were carried into the future, waned and returned again as new forms and devices were developed which required them. It has been a process of adaptation, guided by the need to meet a constant practical objective whose controversies have never truly been resolved, for an irresolvable tension between investors' rights and host States' rights has continued throughout.

During the nineteenth century, mixed commissions replaced single umpires and existed alongside diplomatic negotiations. Such commissions persisted until the Second World War, and extended beyond it, before yielding to lump-sum negotiated settlements, while national commissions – as opposed to mixed international commissions – also came to feature. The debate over standards of protection, particularly over compensation, led to such conceptual and practical uncertainty that the attempt to set standards of protection of a contractual nature led also to attempts to have such contractual disputes referred to arbitration, typically in the single arbitrator or umpire scenarios of the early Middle Eastern petroleum arbitrations, which began in the 1950s. By the late 1950s, States were beginning to grant investors the right to bring treaty-based arbitration claims, although this form of arbitration was not to become a dominant feature until the 1990s. Thus was investment treaty arbitration born, existing alongside contractually based arbitration and the other forms of investment arbitration which we have today, not least the lurking, academic presence of inter-State arbitration. The law which is to be applied – international investment law – and which had developed out of customary international law, became based upon some 3,000 bilateral and other investment treaties which have emerged since 1959, their content and form changing over time. Much of this book will

[83] S. J. Choi and M. Gulati, 'Customary International Law: How Do Courts Do It?' in Bradley, *Custom's Future*, 117.

[84] O. T. Johnson, Jr and J. Gimblett, 'From Gunboats to BITs: The Evolution of Modern International Investment Law' in K. Sauvant (ed.), *Yearbook of International Investment Law and Policy 2010–2011* (Oxford University Press, 2012), 649, 652.

be spent discussing such treaty clauses which afford protection and stipulate the arbitration procedures to be followed, but new institutions have also emerged. By the 1960s, for our purposes the most important institution to have been created was the ICSID, in the expectation that investment arbitration should in future be preferred. Today, ICSID arbitration is well known and it coexists with ad hoc arbitration and other kinds of institutionally based investment arbitration, as well as inter-State adjudication before the ICJ.

By the time the reader reaches the final chapter of this book, he or she will be entitled to ask whether this picture will now change again, and if investment arbitration itself will not now yield to private claims brought against host States in a new form of international adjudication presided over by permanent, transnational judges. For now, the focus of anyone who is interested in investment disputes practice will still be on investment treaty arbitration and contractually based investor–State arbitration. This book is intended to assist those who wish to understand the law and procedure of this field of practice in the full light of its historical development, modern day context and current perplexities.

QUESTIONS

1. What were the disadvantages, if any, of diplomatic espousal and mixed commissions?
2. What are the differences between inter-State adjudication and investor–State arbitration?
3. How did uncertainty over the legal protection afforded to foreign investments shape the development of investment arbitration? How did such legal uncertainty arise?
4. How does international investment arbitration rest upon contractual agreements and treaty promises to arbitrate?
5. What role does the ICSID play in furthering the cause of investment arbitration?
6. What are the principal sources today of international investment law?

SUGGESTIONS FOR FURTHER READING

1. R. Dolzer, 'Mixed Claims Commissions' in *Max Planck Encyclopedia of Public International Law*, available at https://opil.ouplaw.com/view/10.1093/law:epil/9780199231690/law-9780199231690-e64 (accessed 29 September 2020).
2. A. Shalakany, 'Arbitration in the Third World: A Plea for Reassessing Bias under the Spectre of Neoliberalism' (2000) *Harvard ILJ* 419.
3. J. Paulsson, 'Arbitration without Privity' (1995) 10 *ICSID Review – FILJ* 232.
4. Z. Douglas, 'The Hybrid Foundations of Investment Treaty Arbitration' (2003) 74 *BYbIL* 151.
5. S. W. Schill, 'W(h)ither Fragmentation? On the Literature and Sociology of International Investment Law' (2011) 22 *EJIL* 875.
6. C. L. Lim and J. Ho, 'International Investment Arbitration' in *Oxford Bibliography of International Law*, available at www.oxfordbibliographies.com/view/document/obo-9780199796953/obo-9780199796953-0135.xml (accessed 29 September 2020).

2

Investment Contracts and Internationalisation

CHAPTER OUTLINE

This chapter deals with investment contracts and their protection through internationalisation. Internationalisation refers to the conversion of contractual obligations to international obligations, so that every breach of an investment contract amounts to a violation of international law. Section 1 excerpts the main arbitral awards on investment contract internationalisation, while Section 2 outlines the main objections to investment contract internationalisation. Section 3 addresses a subsidiary concern – different types of investment contracts and their respective characteristics.

INTRODUCTION

Most foreign investments begin life with investment contracts concluded between foreign investors and host States or State entities. Investment contracts are also a source of investor–State disputes. This is because investors crave stability in investment contracts, while States cherish the freedom to modify or even terminate investment contracts in accordance with their prevailing economic policy. As States tend to initiate contractual modification or termination, often to the detriment of investors, the quest for investment protection necessarily included attempts at shielding investment contracts from State interference. The most remarkable of these attempts, and the focus of this chapter, is the internationalisation of investment contracts. Internationalisation is the equation of contractual obligations to international obligations, so that every breach of an internationalised investment contract by a State constitutes a violation of international law.

International law sanctions State breaches of international obligations only, and not breaches of contractual obligations. Internationalisation is thus highly controversial because it erases the deeply entrenched distinction between obligations governed by international law and obligations – such as contractual obligations – which are traditionally governed by domestic law. Whether a State breaches international law by breaching an investment contract is a recurrent yet unresolved issue in international investment law.[1]

The idea of internationalisation surfaced in the 1930 arbitration between English company Lena Goldfields and the USSR. Although the term 'internationalisation' gained prominence with the writings of Frederick Mann and Wolfgang Friedmann in the 1960s,[2] the allusion to internationalisation was sufficiently strong in *Lena Goldfields* v. *USSR* for it to be credited as the award from which the notion of internationalisation grew.[3]

Lena Goldfields v. *USSR*, The Times, 3 September 1930, para. 22

It was admitted by Dr. Idelson, counsel for Lena, that on all domestic matters in the U.S.S.R. the laws of Soviet Russia applied except in so far as they were excluded by the contract, and accordingly that in regard to performances of the contract by both parties inside the U.S.S.R. Russian law was 'the proper law of the contract', i.e., the law by reference to which the contract should be interpreted.

But it was submitted by him that for other purposes the general principles of law such as those recognized by Article 38 of the Statute of the Permanent Court of International Justice at The Hague should be regarded as 'the proper law of the contract' and in support of this submission counsel for Lena pointed out that both the Concession Agreement itself and also the agreement of June, 1927, whereby the coal mines were handed over, were signed not only on behalf of the Executive Government of Russia generally but by the Acting Commissary for Foreign Affairs, and that many of the terms of the contract contemplated the application of international rather than merely national principles of law. In so far as any difference of interpretation might result the Court holds that this contention is correct.

The difficulty which Lena Goldfields faced, and which present-day foreign investors continue to face when seeking redress for a breach of contract, is the ability of a host State to change its own laws. The proper law of an investment contract is by default host State

---

[1] The topic is addressed in detail in J. Ho, *State Responsibility for Breaches of Investment Contracts* (Cambridge University Press, 2018). Earlier works include A. McNair, 'The General Principles of Law Recognized by Civilized Nations' (1957) 33 *BYbIL* 1; H. Wehberg, 'Pacta Sunt Servanda' (1959) 53 *AJIL* 775; R. Y. Jennings, 'State Contracts in International Law' (1961) 37 *BYIL* 156; A. Verdross, 'Quasi-International Agreements and International Economic Transactions' (1964) *Yearbook of World Affairs* 230; C. F. Amerasinghe, 'State Breaches of Contracts with Aliens and International Law' (1964) 58 *AJIL* 881; P. Weil, 'Problèmes Relatifs aux Contrats Passées entre un Etat et un Particulier' (1969) 128(III) *RDC* 95; A. A. Fatouros, 'International Law and the Internationalized Contract' (1980) 74 *AJIL* 134; S. M. Schwebel, 'On Whether the Breach by a State of a Contract with an Alien Is a Breach of International Law' in S. M. Schwebel (ed.), *Justice in International Law: Selected Writings of Stephen M. Schwebel* (Cambridge University Press, 1994), 425; C. Leben, *The Advancement of International Law* (Oxford University Press, 2010), 153; J. Cantergreil, 'The Audacity of the Texaco/Calasiatic Award: René-Jean Dupuy and the Internationalization of Foreign Investment Law' (2011) 22(2) *EJIL* 441; I. Alvik, *Contracting with Sovereignty* (Oxford University Press, 2011), 47–58; J. Ho, 'Internationalisation and State Contracts: Are State Contracts the Future or the Past?' in C. L. Lim (ed.), *Alternative Visions in the International Law on Foreign Investment* (Cambridge University Press, 2016), 377.

[2] F. A. Mann, 'State Contracts and State Responsibility' (1960) 54 *AJIL* 572; W. Friedmann, 'Half a Century of International Law' (1964) 50(8) *Virginia L Rev* 1333.

[3] V. V. Veeder considered this allusion of equal importance to 'the caveman's discovery of fire': 'The Lena Goldfields Arbitration: The Historical Roots of Three Ideas' (1998) 47 *ICLQ* 747, 772.

law, not international law. Legislation can end a contract, as well as disable its protective mechanisms, leaving an investor with no contract and no recourse. So long as the legality of a State's interference with an investment contract is determined solely by reference to that State's own law, the risk that States can and will interfere with investment contracts with apparent impunity exists.[4] This risk materialised in *Lena Goldfields* v. *USSR*.

The specific mischief that internationalisation tries to contain, therefore, is the avoidance of liability for contractual breaches engineered by changes to host State law. Whether internationalisation succeeds in what it sets out to do is debatable. Internationalisation rests on a series of six propositions which its advocates consider self-evident, but which its opponents do not:

(1) International law recognises the absolute sanctity of contract.
(2) Because international law recognises the absolute sanctity of contract, every breach of contract by a State is open to sanction by international law.
(3) An investment contract is better protected under international law than under domestic law.
(4) Regardless of what the original proper law of the investment contract is, it can be replaced with international law by using the tools of internationalisation.
(5) So long as the proper law of an investment contract is international law, contractual obligations are automatically transformed into international obligations.
(6) When contractual obligations are international obligations, every breach of contract by a State is a violation of international law.

Together, the foregoing propositions frame the ongoing debate over the legitimacy of internationalisation in the name of investment contract protection. Internationalisation was, however, destined to be controversial. As the product of arbitral rulings and academic writings, internationalisation was both radical and extreme in aim – the total constraint of sovereign power by private actors.

1. KEY AWARDS ON INTERNATIONALISATION

After *Lena Goldfields* v. *USSR*, the contours of internationalisation continued to be explored and refined by arbitral tribunals. There are five key awards on internationalisation, rendered between 1951 and 1979. They are, in chronological order, *Petroleum Development Ltd* v. *The Sheikh of Abu Dhabi*, *Ruler of Qatar* v. *International Marine Oil Co.*, *Saudi Arabia* v. *Arabian American Oil Co. (Aramco)*, *Sapphire International Petroleums Ltd* v. *National Iranian Oil Co.* and *Texaco* v. *Libya*. These awards serve as authoritative precedents for writers in favour of the internationalisation of investment contracts. The most important of these key awards, for its breadth and depth of reasoning, as well as the frequency with which it is discussed in academic writings, is arguably *Texaco* v. *Libya*.

---

[4] G. Delaume, 'State Contracts and Transnational Arbitration' (1981) 75 *AJIL* 784, 806; R. Kreindler, 'The Law Applicable to International Investment Disputes' in N. Horn and S. M. Kröll (eds), *Arbitrating Foreign Investment Disputes: Procedural and Substantive Legal Aspects* (The Hague: Kluwer Law International, 2004), 401, 417; Leben, *The Advancement of International Law*, 153.

The key awards on internationalisation share similar core factual attributes (disputes arising from the breach or termination of oil concessions by the host State), but differ in three important respects. First, the justification for internationalisation changed over time. While the inadequacy of primitive host State laws prompted the tribunals in the earlier *Abu Dhabi*, *Qatar* and *Aramco* arbitrations to favour internationalisation,[5] the tribunals in the later *Sapphire* and *Texaco* arbitrations were driven by the overhanging threat of the host State changing its own laws to the detriment of the foreign investor. Second, the tribunals' findings on internationalisation became more detailed and discursive over time. The *Texaco* award, which contains the most meticulous exposition of internationalisation, was rendered at the height of opposition to over-reliance on international law to govern foreign investment by developing States pursuing a New International Economic Order.[6] Third, the three earlier *Abu Dhabi*, *Qatar* and *Aramco* awards held that the tribunal could uphold internationalisation as a matter of common or commercial sense; but the later *Sapphire* and *Texaco* awards pointed to a contractual basis for internationalisation and, in doing so, tried to legitimise internationalisation through the will of the contracting parties. The excerpts from each award below have been chosen to demonstrate how the understanding of internationalisation evolved and became more refined with each new award that was rendered. Therefore, we recommend reading the excerpts in the order that they are presented.

Petroleum Development Ltd v. *The Sheikh of Abu Dhabi*, **Award, September 1951, 18 ILR 144, 149 (Lord Asquith of Bishopstone)**

What is the 'Proper Law' applicable in construing this contract? This is a contract made in Abu Dhabi and wholly to be performed in that country. If any municipal system of law were applicable, it would prima facie be that of Abu Dhabi. But no such law can reasonably be said to exist. The Sheikh administers a purely discretionary justice with the assistance of the Koran; and it would be fanciful to suggest that in this very primitive region there is any settled body of legal principles applicable to the construction of modern commercial instruments. Nor can I see any basis on which the municipal Law of England could apply. On the contrary, Clause 17 of the Agreement, cited above, repels the notion that the municipal Law of any country, as such, could be appropriate. The terms of that Clause invite, indeed prescribe, the application of principles rooted in the good sense and common practice of the generality of civilised nations – a sort of 'modern law of nature'. I do not think that on this point there is any conflict between the parties.

---

[5] Inadequate host State laws were regarded by McNair as a sound justification for internationalisation: 'The General Principles of Law', 4. Cf. A. S. El-Kosheri and T.F. Riad, 'The Law Governing a New Generation of Petroleum Agreements: Changes in the Arbitral Process' (1986) 1 *ICSID Review – FILJ* 257, 259; D. W. Bowett, 'State Contracts with Aliens: Contemporary Developments on Compensation for Termination or Breach' (1988) 58 *BYbIL* 49, 51.

[6] Declaration on the Establishment of a New International Economic Order (UNGA Res A/Res/3201 (S-VI) (9 May 1974); Programme of Action on the Establishment of a New International Economic Order (UNGA Res A/Res/3202 (S-VI) (15 May 1974); Charter of Economic Rights and Duties of States (UNGA Res A/Res/3281 (XXIX) (12 December 1974), Art. 2.

Ruler of Qatar v. *International Marine Oil Co.*, Award, June 1953, 20 ILR 534, 544–545 (Sir Alfred Bucknill) (footnote omitted)

The first question was whether the proper law to be applied in the construction of the Principal Agreement is Islamic law or the principles of natural justice and equity ...

...

There is nothing in the Principal or Supplemental Agreements which throws a clear light upon the intention of the parties on this point. If one considers the subject matter of the contract, it is oil to be taken out of ground within the jurisdiction of the Ruler. That fact, together with the fact that the Ruler is a party to the contract and had, in effect, the right to nominate Qatar as the place where any arbitration arising out of the contract should sit, and the fact that the agreement was written in Arabic as well as English, points to Islamic law, that being the law administered at Qatar, as the appropriate law.

On the other hand, there are at least two weighty considerations against that view.

One is that in my opinion, after hearing the evidence of the two experts in Islamic law, Mr. Anderson and Professor Milliot, 'there is no settled body of legal principles in Qatar applicable to the construction of modern commercial instruments' to quote and adapt the words of Lord Asquith of Bishopstone, in his Award as Referee in an Arbitration in 1951 in which the Shaikh of Abu Dhabi, a territory immediately adjacent to Qatar and in fact much larger than Qatar, was a party, and the Arbitration concerned the interpretation of words in an oil concession contract. I need not set out the evidence before me about the origin, history and development of Islamic law as applied in Qatar or as to the legal procedure in that country. I have no reason to suppose that Islamic law is not administered there strictly, but I am satisfied that the law does not contain any principles which would be sufficient to interpret this particular contract.

Arising out of that reason is the second reason, which is that both experts agreed that certain parts of the contract, if Islamic law was applicable, would be open to the grave criticism of being invalid. According to Professor Milliot, the Principal Agreement was full of irregularities from end to end according to Islamic law, as applied in Qatar.

This is a cogent reason for saying that such law does not contain a body of legal principles applicable to a modern commercial contract of this kind. I cannot think that the Ruler intended Islamic law to apply to a contract upon which he intended to enter, under which he was to receive considerable sums of money, although Islamic law would declare that the transaction was wholly or partially void. Still less would the Ruler so intend, and at the same time stipulate that these sums when paid were not to be repaid under any circumstances whatever. I am sure that Sir Hugh Weightman and Mr. Allan did not intend Islamic law to apply. In my opinion neither party intended Islamic law to apply, and intended that the agreement was to be governed by 'the principles of justice, equity and good conscience' as indeed each party pleads in Claim and Answer, alternatively to Islamic law, in the case of the Claimant.

Saudi Arabia v. *Arabian American Oil Co. (Aramco)*, Award, 23 August 1958, 27 ILR 117, 168 (Sauser-Hall, Referee; Badawi/Hassan; Habachy) (footnotes omitted)

Inasmuch as the law in force in Saudi Arabia did not contain any definite rule relating to the exploitation of oil deposits, because no such exploitation existed in that State before 1933, this lacuna was filled by the 1933 Concession Agreement, whose validity and legality under Saudi Arabian law are not disputed by either side. The present dispute only concerns the effects of the provisions contained in the Agreement.

The Concession Agreement is thus the fundamental law of the Parties, and the Arbitration Tribunal is bound to recognize its particular importance owing to the fact that it fills a gap in the legal system of Saudi Arabia with regard to the oil industry. The Tribunal holds that the Concession has the nature of a constitution which has the effect of conferring acquired rights on the contracting Parties. By reason of its very sovereignty within its territorial domain, the State possesses the legal power to grant rights which it forbids itself to withdraw before the end of the Concession, with the reservation of the Clauses of the Concession Agreement relating to its revocation. Nothing can prevent a State, in the exercise of its sovereignty, from binding itself irrevocably by the provisions of a concession and from granting to the concessionaire irretractable rights. Such rights have the character of acquired rights. Should a new concession contract incompatible with the first, or a subsequent statute, abolish totally or partially that which has been granted by a previous law or concession, this could constitute a clear infringement, by the second contract, of acquired rights or a violation, by the subsequent statute, of the principle of non-retroactivity of laws, with the only exception of rules of public policy. This is because a legal situation acquired by virtue of a previous special statute cannot be abrogated by a subsequent statute – *generalia specialibus non derogant* – unless the legislator has expressly given retroactive effect to such statute, which the State cannot do in respect of concessions, without engaging its responsibility.

In so far as doubts may remain on the content or on the meaning of the agreements of the Parties, it is necessary to resort to the general principles of law and to apply them in order to interpret, and even to supplement, the respective rights and obligations of the Parties.

The Arbitration Tribunal relies, by analogy, on the precedent of the *Lena Goldfields Arbitration* between the U.S.S.R. and a British corporation, with respect to mining concessions, and on the award given in that case on 3 September 1930. According to Article 75 of the concession contract, the concessionary company was subject to the whole present and future legislation of the U.S.S.R., but with the following important reservation: 'in so far as special provisions are not contained in the present agreement'. Further, under Article 76, the Government had undertaken not to modify the contract in any way, by order, by decree or by any other unilateral act, without the approval of the [*sic*] Lena Goldfields Ltd. The arbitrators (in the absence of the Government's arbitrator who refused to take part in the proceedings) adopted the following standpoint, in conformity with the submissions of the plaintiff:

'... On all domestic matters in the U.S.S.R., the laws of Soviet Russia applied except in so far as they were excluded by the contract, and accordingly that in regard to performance of the contract by both parties inside the U.S.S.R. Russian law was the "proper law of the contract".

'But ... for other purposes the general principles of law such as those recognised by Article 38 of the Statute of the Permanent Court of International Justice at The Hague should be regarded as the "proper law of the contract".

The latter solution seemed justified to the arbitrators because several provisions in the Concession called for the application of international law rather than that of municipal law (Cornell Law Quarterly, vol. 36, 1930, p. 50).

A similar decision is found in the Arbitral Award given by Lord Asquith of Bishopstone, in August 1951, in the case of *Abu Dhabi*. Looking for the law to be applied, the Arbitrator noted that the law of Abu Dhabi was applicable prima facie, as an oil concession was involved, but that this law did not contain any rules on the subject. Having, on the other hand, excluded the application of English law, as unwarranted, the Arbitrator held, therefore, that he had to resort to the general principles of law, as a kind of 'modern law of nature' (*Petroleum Development [Trucial Coast] Ltd.* v. *The Shaikh of Abu Dhabi: International and Comparative Law Quarterly*, vol. 1 [4th series] 1952, p. 247).

Sapphire International Petroleums Ltd v. National Iranian Oil Co., Award, 15 March 1963, 35 ILR 136, 172–176 (Cavin) (footnotes omitted)

2(i) The agreement contains an arbitration clause entrusting the task of arbitrating any possible dispute to an arbitrator chosen by the President of the Supreme Court of Switzerland, Denmark, Sweden, or Brazil.

Now in doctrine and in case law, an arbitral clause is generally regarded as 'one of the most frequent and most significant indications of what the parties considered to be the nature of their operation, by which the contract is connected to the legal system of the country thus chosen' (Batiffol, *Traité élémentaire de droit international privé*, 3rd ed. (Paris, 1959), No. 595, p. 648, as well as the different French and foreign cases cited in the note; Dicey, *Conflict of Laws*, 7th ed. (London, 1958), p. 731; Lord McNair, 'The General Principles of Law Recognized by Civilized Nations', in *B.Y.*, 33 (1957), p. 1, at p. 6).

Undoubtedly the localizing value of this connecting factor should not be overestimated (Cheshire, *Private International Law*, 6th ed. (Oxford, 1961), p. 226), particularly, as in this case, when the country where the arbitration takes place has no connection with the other elements of the agreement (Batiffol, op. cit. p. 649).

It is not feasible in the present case to imply an intention by the parties to submit to the substantive law of the forum of the arbitration, a forum which they did not know of at the time they concluded the agreement. However, if no positive implication can be made from the arbitral clause, it is possible to find there a negative intention, namely to reject the exclusive application of Iranian law. If in fact the parties had intended to submit their agreement to Iranian law and if the only significance of the arbitral clause was to deprive the Iranian authorities of jurisdiction in case of any dispute, the authors of the agreement – whom one must suppose were competent lawyers – would almost certainly not have failed to negative, by an express provision, any significance which such an arbitral clause normally carried as a connecting factor according to general doctrine.

(ii) Article 38 of the agreement, which confirms an intention already expressed in the preamble, provides that the parties undertake to carry out its provisions according to the principles of good faith and good will, and to respect the spirit as well as the letter of the agreement.

It has been held in several arbitral awards concerning similar legal relations to those binding the parties in the present case (*Lena Goldfields Arbitration: Cornell Law Quarterly*, 1950, p. 42; *Petroleum Developments Limited* v. *Ruler of Abu Dhabi: I.C.L.Q.*, 1952, p. 247; *Ruler of Qatar* v. *International Marine Oil Company Limited*), that such a clause is scarcely compatible with the strict application of the internal law of a particular country. It much more often calls for the application of general principles of law, based upon reason and upon the common practice of civilized countries, as was expressly recognized by the above-cited authorities. These authorities are approved of by Lord McNair, former President of the International Court of Justice (*loc. cit.*). In fact, in ordinary law, the judge who decides a dispute concerning the interpretation or performance of a contract normally refers to the complementary rules contained in the positive law applicable to the contract. On the other hand, a reference to rules of good faith, together with the absence of any reference to a national system of law, leads the judge to determine, according to the spirit of the agreement, what meaning he can reasonably give to a provision of the agreement which is in dispute. It is therefore perfectly legitimate to find in such a clause evidence of the intention of the parties not to apply the strict rules of a particular system but, rather, to rely upon the rules of law, based upon reason, which are common to civilized nations. These rules are enshrined in Article 38 of the Statute of the International Court of Justice as a source of law, and numerous decisions of international tribunals have made use of them and clarified them. Their application is particularly justified in the present contract, which was concluded between a State organ and a foreign company, and depends upon public law in certain of its aspects. This contract has therefore a quasi-international character which releases it from the sovereignty of a particular legal system, and it differs fundamentally from an ordinary commercial contract. It should be mentioned that the question of the law applicable did not altogether escape the draughtsman of the agreement – see paragraph (iv) below; and the absence of any reference to a national system of law can only confirm this conclusion.

Furthermore, according to the precedents cited above and to the conclusions reached by McNair, to which he refers, the arbitrator finds important evidence in Article 38, para. 1, of the agreement of the parties' intention to exclude the application of Iranian law and a fortiori any other national law, and to submit, so far as concerns the interpretation and performance of their agreement, to the general principles of law based upon the practice common to civilized countries.

...

(iv) Finally, the present contract is the last of several agreements made by NIOC which have the same object. First of all there is the agreement of October 1954, made with the International Oil Consortium. Article 41 of this agreement is identical with Article 38 of the present contract. In its Article 44 it contains clauses relating to arbitration which are in substance identical with those in the Sapphire contract. The difference between this contract and the other agreement is that the agreement made with the Consortium expressly lays down, in its Article 46, the law applicable as follows:

> 'In view of the diverse nationalities of the parties to this Agreement, it shall be governed by and interpreted and applied in accordance with the principles of law common to Iran and the several nations in which the other parties to this Agreement are incorporated, and in the absence of such common principles then by and in accordance with principles of law recognized by civilized nations in general, including such of those principles as may have been applied by international tribunals.'

A similar clause appears in the agreement made between NIOC and the company Agip Mineraria in July 1957. Undoubtedly, as Carabiber (*op. cit.* p. 49) points out, the wording of this provision was discussed at length at the time of the conclusion of the contract in 1954. The difficulties which the Iranian Treasury were undergoing and the necessity to put an end to a situation which was likely to become rapidly worse may have influenced the Iranian Government in adopting this clause. But it does not alter the fact that the parties to this agreement recognized that this was a legitimate means of guaranteeing the foreign companies against the unilateral decisions of Iran, which would automatically be applied if Iranian law had been declared applicable.

Furthermore the particular circumstances existing at the time of the 1954 agreement were no longer applicable for the agreement made with Agip in 1957, and yet this agreement, as has been seen, retained this clause.

It is true that there is no such provision in the present agreement, nor in the one made in 1958 with the Pan-American Petroleum Corporation. But the essential character of all these contracts is the same; they all have the same object and the same character, as is evidenced by the complete similarity of several of their clauses, particularly those dealing with performance and arbitration. By virtue of the principle of good faith, NIOC cannot claim that the absence of an express provision regarding the law applicable should be interpreted as a denial of a principle contained in previous agreements which had the same object. The requirements of a guarantee by the foreign company are the same; therefore, according to reason and good faith, the same solution should be adopted as NIOC formally agreed to with more powerful partners. If then, in the present contract, NIOC had intended to cast aside a principle which is recognized in the previous agreements and to refuse Sapphire a guarantee which they had previously conceded as legitimate, it must be presumed that the draughtsman of the contract would have expressly shown this intention.

3. It is quite clear from the above that the parties intended to exclude the application of Iranian law. But they have not chosen another positive legal system, and this omission is on all the evidence deliberate. All the connecting factors cited above point to the fact that the parties therefore intended to submit the interpretation and performance of their contract to the principles of law generally recognized by civilized nations, to which Article 37 of the agreement refers, this being the only clause which contains an express reference to an applicable law.

The arbitrator will therefore apply these principles, by following, when necessary, the decisions taken by international tribunals. He points out that, this being so, he has no intention of deciding the case according to 'equity', like an 'amiable compositeur'. On the contrary, he will try to disentangle the rules of positive law, common to civilized nations, such as are formulated in their statutes or are generally recognized in practice. With regard to each rule of law to be applied, he will show first its character as a rule of positive law, and then its generality. This solution, moreover, is the one advocated for such contracts by the following recognized authorities: McNair, *loc. cit.*, and Jessup, *Transnational Law* (Yale, 1956).

Such a solution seems particularly suitable for giving the guarantees of protection which are indispensable for foreign companies, since these companies undergo very considerable risks in bringing financial and technical aid to countries in the process of development. It is in the interest of both parties to such agreements that any disputes between them should be settled according to the general principles universally recognized and should not be subject to the particular rules of national laws, which are very often unsuitable for solving problems concerning the rights of the State where the contract is being carried out, and which are always subject to changes by this State and are often unknown or not fully known to one of the contracting parties.

Texaco Overseas Petroleum Co./California Asiatic Oil Co. v. *Government of Libya*, Award on the Merits, 19 January 1977, 17 ILM 1, paras 36, 40–45 (Dupuy) (footnotes omitted)

36. Under what circumstances was the choice of applicable law made and what consequences should be derived therefrom as to the internationalization of the Deeds of Concession in dispute?

   (a) In its final version, the clause designating the applicable law or the choice of law established by Clause 28 of the Deeds of Concession reads as follows:

   'This concession shall be governed by and interpreted in accordance with the principles of the law of Libya common to the principles of international law and, in the absence of such common principles, then by and in accordance with the general principles of law, including such of those principles as may have been applied by international tribunals.'

...

(b) The clause relating to the choice of law and the internationalization of the contract:

40. As the Tribunal has already observed (see *supra*, para. 31, *in fine*), the internationalization of contracts entered into between States and foreign private persons can result in various ways which it is now time to examine.

41 (a.a). At the outset, it is accepted that the reference made by the contract, in the clause concerning the governing law, to the general principles of law leads to this result. These general principles, being those which are mentioned in Article 38 of the Statute of the International Court of Justice, are one of the sources of international law: they may appear alone in the clause or jointly with a national law, particularly with the law of the contracting State.

In the present dispute, general principles of law have a subsidiary role in the governing law clause and apply in the case of lack of conformity between the principles of Libyan law and the principles of international law: but precisely the expression 'principles of international law' is of much wider scope than 'general principles of law', because the latter contribute with other elements (international custom and practice which is accepted by the law of nations) to constitute what is called the 'principles of international law'. To take the terms used by the Permanent Court of International Justice in its judgment in the '*Lotus*' case ([1927] P.C.I.J., No. 10, Ser. A, at 16): the meaning of the 'words "principles of international law", as ordinarily used, can only mean international law as it is applied between all nations belonging to the community of States'. Now, these principles of international law must, in the present case, be the standard for the application of Libyan law since it is only if Libyan law is in conformity with international law that it should be applied. Therefore, the reference which is made mainly to the principles of international law and, secondarily, to the general principles of law must have as a consequence the application of international law to the legal relations between the parties.

There are many international contracts comparable to the contracts in dispute which refer to the general principles of law. It will suffice to cite here: the contract between Iran and Agip Mineraria of 24 August 1954 (Art. 40), the contract between Iran and the Consortium of 19 September 1954 (Art. 46), the contract between Kuwait and Kuwait Shell Petroleum Company of 15 January 1961 (Art. 35), and the contract between the United Arab Republic and Pan America U.A.R. Oil Company, of 23 October 1963 (Art. 42).

42. International arbitration case law confirms that the reference to the general principles of law is always regarded to be a sufficient criterion for the internationalization of a contract. One should remember, in this respect, the awards delivered in *Lena Goldfields* v. *U.S.S.R.* in 1930, *Petroleum Development Ltd.* v. *Sovereign of Abu Dhabi* in 1951, and *International Marine Oil Company* v. *Sovereign of Qatar* in 1953, and in *Sapphire International Petroleum Ltd.* v. *N.I.O.C.*, all cases in which the arbitrators noted a reference to the general principles of law in order to reach their conclusions as to the internationalization of the contract.

It should be noted that the invocation of the general principles of law does not occur only when the municipal law of the contracting State is not suited to petroleum problems. Thus, for example, the Iranian law is without doubt particularly well suited for oil concessions but this does not prevent the contracts executed by Iran from referring very often to these general principles. The recourse to general principles is to be explained not only by the lack of adequate legislation in the State considered (which might have been the case, at one time, in certain oil Emirates). It is also justified by the need for the private contracting party to be protected against unilateral and abrupt modifications of the legislation in the contracting State: it plays, therefore, an important role in the contractual equilibrium intended by the parties.

43. This evolution toward the internationalization of contracts was foreseeable: indeed, in its judgments in the cases relating to the *Serbian and Brazilian Loans* and on the occasion of the examination of the criteria which could be adopted for the determination of the applicable law, the Permanent Court of International Justice laid down a rule of great flexibility:

> 'The Court which has before it a dispute involving the question as to the law which governs the contractual obligations at issue, can determine what this law is only by reference to the actual nature of these obligations and to the circumstances attendant upon their creation, though it may also take into account the expressed or presumed intention of the Parties.' ([1929] P.C.I.J., Ser. A, No. 20, at 41.)

The three criteria laid down by the Permanent Court of International Justice and derived from the nature of the obligations, the circumstances of their creation and the will of the parties, converge, in the instant case, to reverse the presumption which was established, in another connection, by the judgments of 1929, a presumption to which reference was made already (see para. 27 *supra, in fine*), and according to which a State cannot, from the outset, be presumed 'to have made the substance of its debt and the validity of the obligations accepted by it in respect thereof, subject to any law other than its own'.

44 (b.b.). Another process for the internationalization of a contract consists in inserting a clause providing that possible differences which may arise in respect of the interpretation and the performance of the contract shall be submitted to arbitration.

Such a clause has a twofold consequence:

- on the one hand, as this Tribunal has already noted (see para. 16 *supra*), the institution of arbitration shall be that established by international law.
- on the other hand, as regards the law applicable to the merits of the dispute itself, the inclusion of an arbitration clause leads to a reference to the rules of international law.

Even if one considers that the choice of international arbitration proceedings cannot by itself lead to the exclusive application of international law, it is one of the elements which makes it possible to detect a certain internationalization of the contract. The *Sapphire International Petroleum Ltd.* award is quite explicit: 'If no positive implication can be made from the arbitral clause, it is possible to find there a negative intention, namely to reject the exclusive application of Iranian law' (35 Int'l L.R. 136 (1963), at 172); this is what led the arbitrator in that case, in the absence of any explicit reference to the law applicable, not to apply automatically Iranian law, thus dismissing any presumption in its favor. It is therefore unquestionable that the reference to international arbitration is sufficient to internationalize a contract, in other words, to situate it within a specific legal order – the order of the international law of contracts.

45 (c). A third element of the internationalization of the contracts in dispute results from the fact that it takes on a dimension of a new category of agreements between States and private persons: economic development agreements (see Bourquin, 'Arbitration and Economic Development Agreements', 15 Bus. Law. 860 (1960); A. A. Fatouros, Government Guarantees to Foreign Investors (1962); Hyde, 'Economic Development Agreements', 105 Recueil des Cours de l'Académie de Droit International de la Haye ('R.C.A.D.I.') 267 (1962), and Verdross, 'The Status of Foreign Private Interests Stemming from Economic Development Agreements with Arbitration Clauses', in Selected Readings on Protection by Law of Private Foreign Investments 117 (1964)).

Several elements characterize these agreements: in the first place, their subject matter is particularly broad: they are not concerned only with an isolated purchase or performance, but tend to bring to developing countries investments and technical assistance, particularly in the field of research and exploitation of mineral resources, or in the construction of factories on a turnkey basis. Thus, they assume a real importance in the development of the country where they are performed: it will suffice to mention here the importance of the obligations assumed in the case under consideration by the concession holders in the field of road and port infrastructures and the training on the spot of qualified personnel. The party contracting with the State was thus associated with the realization of the economic and social progress of the host country.

In the second place, the long duration of these contracts implies close cooperation between the State and the contracting party and requires permanent installations as well as the acceptance of extensive responsibilities by the investor.

Finally, because of the purpose of the cooperation in which the contracting party must participate with the State and the magnitude of the investments to which it agreed, the contractual nature of this type of agreement is reinforced: the emphasis on the contractual nature of the legal relation between the host State and the investor is intended to bring about an equilibrium between the goal of the general interest sought by such relation and the profitability which is necessary for the pursuit of the task entrusted to the private enterprise. The effect is also to ensure to the private contracting party a certain stability which is justified by the considerable investments which it makes in the country concerned. The investor must in particular be protected against legislative uncertainties, that is to say the risks of the municipal law of the host country being modified, or against any government measures which would lead to an abrogation or rescission of the contract. Hence, the insertion, as in the present case, of so-called stabilization clauses: these clauses tend to remove all or part of the agreement from the internal law and to provide for its correlative submission to *sui generis* rules as stated in the *Aramco* award, or to a system which is properly an international law system.

From this latter point of view, the following considerations should be noted, which were mentioned in the *Sapphire* award, and which stress the interest of the internationalization of the contract:

'Such a solution seems particularly suitable for giving the guarantees of protection which are indispensable for foreign companies, since these companies undergo very considerable risks in bringing financial and technical aid to countries in the process of development. It is in the interest of both parties to such agreements that any disputes between them should be settled according to the general principles universally recognized and should not be subject to the particular rules of national laws ... ' (35 Int'l L.R. 136 (1963), at 175–176.)

It is apparent that none of the key awards contemplate the possibility that internationalisation may not be defensible on legal grounds. As a result, no attempt is made to counter objections to investment contract internationalisation. Sceptics soon latched onto this omission, and their reasoned objections to investment contract internationalisation gave rise to a backlash against internationalisation.

2. THE BACKLASH AGAINST INTERNATIONALISATION

Although arbitral tribunals often cite academic writings in support of internationalisation, there is also stiff opposition to internationalisation from academic writers.[7] Scepticism towards internationalisation intensified after it became clear that developing States considered internationalisation, which displaced national law in favour of international law as the governing law of an investment contract, an affront to their right to self-determination and their sovereignty. Developing States fought back against internationalisation, using their numerical edge in the United Nations General Assembly to press for a series of Resolutions that reaffirmed the centrality of host State law in the regulation of foreign investment.[8] Thereafter, the critics of internationalisation began dismantling its juridical foundations at a rate and frequency with which the advocates of internationalisation struggled to keep pace. Internationalisation was attacked on three main fronts.

First, critics rightly questioned if international law recognises the absolute sanctity of contract.[9] If it does not, the identification of international law as the proper law of the contract, and of tools to convert contractual obligations to international obligations, cannot beget a finding that a State violates international law simply by committing a breach of contract. Advocates of internationalisation liken contractual rights to property rights

[7] Jennings, 'State Contracts in International Law', 165–168; Amerasinghe, 'State Breaches of Contracts', 897; Fatouros, 'International Law and the Internationalized Contract', 136; El-Kosheri and Riad, 'The Law Governing a New Generation of Petroleum Agreements', 259; Bowett, 'State Contracts with Aliens', 51.

[8] Permanent Sovereignty Over Natural Resources, UNGA Res. 1803 (XVIII) (14 December 1962), GAOR Supp 17, 15; Declaration on the Establishment of a New International Economic Order; Programme of Action on the Establishment of a New International Economic Order; Charter of Economic Rights and Duties of States.

[9] M. Sornarajah, 'The Myth of International Contract Law' (1981) 15 *J World Trade Law* 187, 205–206.

and acquired rights,[10] but it is also well established under international law that there is no blanket prohibition from State interference with these rights. The clash between those for and against internationalisation revealed that while international law protects investment contracts, that protection is not absolute.

Second, as Asante points out in the extract below, the applicability of *pacta sunt servanda* (agreements must be kept), a fundamental principle of the law of treaties, to investment contracts[11] does not automatically turn breaches of contractual obligations into breaches of treaty or international obligations.[12]

S. Asante, 'International Law and Foreign Investment: A Reappraisal' (1988) 37 *ICLQ* 588, 612

However, assuming that such an agreement were subject to public international law, the doctrine of *pacta sunt servanda* would be effectively qualified by the equally well-established international legal principle, *clausula rebus sic stantibus*, which sanctions the revision of international agreements on the basis of a fundamental change of circumstances.

Third, critics doubted if choice-of-law clauses containing a reference to international law, arbitration clauses and stabilisation clauses are tools of internationalisation.[13] First, while there is contemporary support for choice-of-law clauses as tools of internationalisation,[14] the better view states that international law applies only to issues in a claim that fall to be determined by international law.[15] As a breach of contract is a matter for the proper law of the contract, in most cases national law, reference to international law in the choice-of-law clause need not remove the question of breach from the purview of national law. Second, there is also resistance to arbitration clause internationalisation because it turns a clause recording an agreed form of dispute settlement into a penalty clause for the State. Internationalisation alters the character of a State's contractual obligations, leaving the character of the investor's contractual obligations unchanged. Only a State can violate international law for breaching an internationalised investment contract, but not an investor whom internationalisation was conceived to benefit. Finally,

---

[10] *Aramco*, 168. See also *The Sopron-Köszeg Local Co*, Award, 18 June 1929, (1930) 24 AJIL 164, 167.

[11] Reliance on *pacta sunt servanda* to internationalise is often credited to the Vienna School, which extrapolated their theory of internationalisation from the writings of Hans Kelsen. It was the primary contention of the Vienna School that, since the conduct of States was in reality driven by individuals, individuals were the ultimate objects of regulation by international law. *Pacta sunt servanda* thus applied to contracts in the same way that it applied to treaties, and allowed contracts to be assimilated to treaties. The most notable followers of the Vienna School are Verdross and Wehberg.

[12] See also Mann, 'State Contracts and State Responsibility', 581.

[13] Fatouros, 'International Law and the Internationalized Contract', 136.

[14] H. E. Kjos, *Applicable Law in Investor-State Arbitration: The Interplay between National and International Law* (Oxford University Press, 2013), 213, 222.

[15] Z. Douglas, *The International Law of Investment Claims* (Cambridge University Press, 2012), 81–94 (Rules 10 and 11).

there is an objection to stabilisation clauses as tools of internationalisation which lies in their enforceability.[16]

The backlash against internationalisation greatly diminished, but did not wholly eradicate, support for internationalisation. Contemporary supporters reiterate the risk of sudden and adverse legislative changes which only internationalisation is able to counter. This gives internationalisation currency in the enduring search for balance between sovereign choices and sovereign constraints.

The pithy arguments made by opponents of investment contract internationalisation undermined the credibility of internationalisation and modern-day internationalists. But opponents did not provide an alternative solution to internationalisation when States unilaterally amend their own laws to evade contractual obligations. Opponents seemed content to accept that legislative activity was simply a risk that investors had to bear. Far from putting an end to the internationalisation debate, opponents of internationalisation appear to have inadvertently prolonged it by giving host States carte blanche to interfere with investment contracts through legislation.

3. TYPES OF INVESTMENT CONTRACT

Investment contracts, which can be in the form of a single document or a series of documents, manifest one or more of the following characteristics: a large capital outlay, long duration, risk, the importance of profitability and the presence of a contribution to the economic development of the host State.[17] They can be bilateral agreements between investors on the one hand and States or State entities on the other. They can also involve, in varying degrees and forms, multiple stakeholders such as indigenous communities, local goods and service providers, and other entities situated along the extractive, production, distribution, construction or management line. The most frequently concluded investment contracts take the form of natural resource concessions (Section 3.1), public service concessions (Section 3.2), build-operate-and-transfer (including engineering, construction and procurement) contracts (Section 3.3) and public–private partnerships (Section 3.4).

3.1 Natural Resource Concessions

Oil exploration, mineral mining, timber extraction and other forms of natural resource harvesting by foreign investors take place pursuant to the grant of a concession by the host State. The foreign investor is usually given exclusive access, for a specified period of time, to an area where the exploration or extraction takes place. Depending on the terms of the concession, the investor may pay the State a fixed sum for the resources extracted,

---

[16] R. Geiger, 'The Unilateral Change of Economic Development Agreements' (1974) 23 *ICLQ* 73, 101–102; P. Kahn, 'Contrats d'Etat et Nationalisation: Les Apports de la Sentence Arbitrale du 24 mars 1982' (1982) 109 *JDI* 844, 858. Cf. *AGIP SpA v. Government of Congo*, ICSID Case No. ARB/77/1, 67 ILR 318, Award, 30 November 1979, 85–87.

[17] For a critique of these indicia, see J. Ho, 'The Meaning of Investment in ICSID Arbitrations' (2010) 26(4) *Arb Int'l* 633.

or share in the proceeds of sale with the State. There are many detailed variations on these simple themes. Natural resource concessions tend to require considerable capital outlay from the foreign investor who supplies the expertise and equipment for exploration and extraction. They also carry considerable risk if the region earmarked for the concession yields fewer natural resources, and consequently less profit for the investor, than predicted. Historically, the most well-known disputes over natural resource concessions emerged from oil concessions.[18] When global oil prices began to rise in the 1950s, it became apparent to oil-rich States like Iran, Qatar, Saudi Arabia, Libya and Kuwait that they were not profiting from the price increase under the terms of existing oil concessions concluded with Anglo-American oil companies. These older concessions provided that the foreign investor would pay the State a nominal royalty in exchange for full retention of the sale proceeds. The interference by the State with these lucrative oil concessions led to a spate of disputes, most of which were submitted to international arbitration. These make up the key awards on internationalisation.

3.2 Public Service Concessions

Public service concessions are another common type of investment contract. Public service concessionaires differ from natural resource concessionaires in that they provide essential services to the general public of the host State. Investors holding public service concessions are usually remunerated through fees paid by the public or by a town or municipality as users of the service. Contracts for the provision of water and sewage facilities,[19] gas and electricity,[20] waste management[21] and even a national car registry are all examples of public service concessions.[22]

Many concluded and pending investor claims against Argentina before ICSID tribunals involve public service concessions. Argentina had embarked on a campaign of privatising its public utilities sector through the granting of concessions to private concessionaires during the 1990s. But these concessions were either revoked or renegotiated in light of the 2001 economic crisis. For many public services, responsibility for their provision reverted to the government. A number of investors prevailed in their claim that Argentina's economic recovery measures amounted to an unlawful expropriation of their public service concessions.[23]

---

[18] C. Greenwood, 'State Contracts in International Law – the Libyan Oil Arbitrations' (1982) 53 *BYbIL* 27.

[19] *Azurix Corp.* v. *Argentina*, ICSID Case No. ARB/01/12; *Aguas Provinciales de Santa Fe SA and Others* v. *Argentina*, ICSID Case No. ARB/03/17; *Aguas Cordobesesas SA and Another* v. *Argentina*, ICSID Case No. ARB/03/18; *Aguas Argentinas SA and Others* v. *Argentina*, ICSID Case No. ARB/03/19; *Impregilo SpA* v. *Argentina*, ICSID Case No. ARB/07/17.

[20] *LG&E Energy Corp. and Others* v. *Argentina*, ICSID Case No. ARB/02/1; *Sempra Energy International* v. *Argentina*, ICSID Case No. ARB/02/16; *El Paso Energy International Co.* v. *Argentina*, ICSID Case No. ARB/03/15; *EDF International SA and Others* v. *Argentina*, ICSID Case No. ARB/03/23; *Iberdrola Energía SA* v. *Guatemala*, ICSID Case No. ARB/09/5.

[21] *Metalclad Corp.* v. *Mexico*, ICSID Case No. ARB(AF)/97/1; *Waste Management Inc.* v. *Mexico*, ICSID Case No. ARB(AF)/00/3.

[22] *Gemplus SA and Another* v. *Mexico*, ICSID Case No. ARB(AF)/04/3; *Talsud SA* v. *Mexico*, ICSID Case No. ARB(AF)/04/4.

[23] See, for instance, *Metalclad Corp.* v. *Mexico*, ICSID Case No. ARB(AF)/97/1, Award, 30 August 2000, 99; *Gemplus SA and Another* v. *Mexico*, ICSID Case No. ARB(AF)/04/3, Award, 16 June 2010, 8–25.

3.3 Build-Operate-and-Transfer (BOT) Contracts

Contracts where investors build an infrastructure for the State, operate it for a period of time and then transfer operation to the State, are BOT contracts. The construction of highways and airports is often accomplished through BOT contracts. The investor normally aims to recoup its investment from the collection of tolls or fees when operating the infrastructure.[24] Due to the public benefit that some forms of infrastructure – highways, for example – bring, BOT contracts may resemble public service concessions. The difference between BOT contracts and public service concessions lies in the eventual handing over of operations to the State in BOT contracts. The investor in a BOT contract, unlike a public service concessionaire, does not perform a public service for the entire duration of the contract. Due to the scale and cost of the planned infrastructure, BOT contracts can be highly complex instruments that call for the close cooperation of main contractors, sub-contractors and State institutions.

3.4 Public–Private Partnerships (PPPs)

A public–private partnership, or PPP, is defined by the World Bank as '[a] long-term contract between a private party and a government entity, for providing a public asset or service, in which the private party bears significant risk and management responsibility, and remuneration is linked to performance'.[25] This broad definition encompasses natural resource concessions, public service concessions and even BOT contracts. With the exception of turnkey, management and financial lease contracts, which tend to be of a shorter duration and transfer fewer risks to the foreign investor, many investment contracts potentially qualify as PPPs. As PPP is an inclusive label, we use it to denote investment contracts that do not fall within the more established natural resource concession, public service concession and BOT contract categories, but which are nonetheless gaining visibility due to their scale and importance. Notable PPPs include the development of tourism sites,[26] housing projects[27] and the licensing of the telecommunications sector.[28]

---

[24] *Autopista Concesionada de Venezuela CA (Aucoven)* v. *Venezuela*, ICSID Case No. ARB/00/5 (highway construction); *Walter Bau AG (In Liquidation)* v. *Thailand*, UNCITRAL (highway construction); *Fraport AG Frankfurt Airport Services Worldwide* v. *Philippines*, ICSID Case No. ARB/03/25 (airport terminal construction); *Malicorp Ltd* v. *Egypt*, ICSID Case No. ARB/08/18 (airport construction).

[25] The World Bank, Asian Development Bank and the Inter-American Development Bank, 'Public–Private Partnership Reference Guide Version 2.0' (2014), https://ppp.worldbank.org/public-private-partnership/library/public-private-partnerships-reference-guide-version-20 (accessed 31 July 2020), 14.

[26] *Southern Pacific Properties and Another* v. *Egypt and Another*, ICC Case No. 3493, ICSID Case No. ARB/84/3; *Marion Unglaube* v. *Costa Rica*, ICSID Case No. ARB/08/1; *Mohamed Abdulmohsen Al-Kharafi & Sons Co.* v. *Libya and Others* (www.italaw.com, accessed 31 July 2020); *Vigotop Ltd* v. *Hungary*, ICSID Case No. ARB/11/22.

[27] *Dallah Real Estate and Tourism Holding Co.* v. *The Ministry of Religious Affairs, Government of Pakistan*, Final Award, 23 June 2006, unpublished, excerpted in [2010] UKSC 46.

[28] *Rumeli Telekom AS and Another* v. *Kazakhstan*, ICSID Case No. ARB/05/16; *Saba Fakes* v. *Turkey*, ICSID Case No. ARB/07/20; *Brandes Investment Partners LP* v. *Venezuela*, ICSID Case No. ARB/08/3.

CONCLUSION

By advocating the total constraint of sovereign powers by private actors, proponents of internationalisation thought they had found a straightforward solution to the problem of a host State changing its laws to evade its contractual obligations. However, the conversion of contractual obligations to international obligations does not occur on the say-so of any group of individuals. Resistance to investment contract internationalisation, canvassed in detail in Section 2, stemmed from the glaring absence of a cogent juridical basis for the conversion of contractual obligations to international obligations, canvassed in detail in Section 1. Over time, the series of six propositions laid out in the Introduction developed into a series of six counter-propositions:

(1) International law *does not* recognise the absolute sanctity of contract.
(2) Because international law *does not* recognise the absolute sanctity of contract, *not* every breach of contract by a State is open to sanction by international law.
(3) An investment contract is *not necessarily* better protected under international law than under domestic law.
(4) The original proper law of the investment contract *cannot* be *casually* replaced with international law.
(5) *Even if* the proper law of an investment contract is international law, contractual obligations are *not* automatically transformed into international obligations.
(6) *Since* contractual obligations are *not* international obligations, *not* every breach of contract by a State is a violation of international law.

Despite the apparent stalemate between proponents and opponents of internationalisation, investment contract internationalisation continues to feature in contemporary discourse because it represents the once-attainable ideal where investors were able to shield their contracts completely and successfully from State interference.

QUESTIONS

1. How exactly does international law preclude States from modifying or terminating investment contracts?
2. What tangible benefits, if any, do investors derive from enforcing their contractual rights through international law?
3. The current backlash against internationalisation has not led to its eradication. Internationalisation appears to live on in broadly worded umbrella clauses in investment treaties (see Chapter 15). Why does internationalisation continue to gain adherents?
4. Internationalisation has been justified on the basis that some investment contracts are of such great economic significance to the host State that they are akin to treaties. Is the assimilation of certain investment contracts to treaties defensible? Does this create

a sliding scale of importance for investment contracts, rendering some contracts more appropriate candidates for internationalisation than others? Is this desirable?

5. Are immutable investment contracts the surest form of protection for investors? If so why, and if not, why not? What are the alternatives?

SUGGESTIONS FOR FURTHER READING

1. J. Ho, *State Responsibility for Breaches of Investment Contracts* (Cambridge University Press, 2018), especially Chapter 5.
2. F. A. Mann, 'State Contracts and State Responsibility' (1960) 54 *AJIL* 572.
3. M. Sornarajah, 'The Myth of International Contract Law' (1981) 15 *J World Trade Law* 187.
4. S. M. Schwebel, 'On Whether the Breach by a State of a Contract with an Alien Is a Breach of International Law' in S. M. Schwebel (ed.), *Justice in International Law: Selected Writings of Stephen M Schwebel* (Cambridge: Grotius, 1994), 425.
5. J. Cantergreil, 'The Audacity of the Texaco/Calasiatic Award: René-Jean Dupuy and the Internationalization of Foreign Investment Law' (2011) 22(2) *EJIL* 441.

3

The Metamorphosis of Investment Treaties

CHAPTER OUTLINE

This chapter charts the rise of treaties as key instruments of foreign investment protection. In this chapter, the term investment treaties refers to bilateral or multilateral treaties that address investment protection exclusively, as well as chapters in free trade agreements that highlight investment protection as one of several trade-related concerns. There are currently more than 3,000 investment treaties in existence, weaving almost every country in the world into a vast, complex web of overlapping treaties. Today, foreign investment that is not subject to investment treaty protection is the exception to the norm. Section 1 situates the emergence of investment treaties in their proper historical, political and economic context. Section 2 discusses the period of rapid growth in the number of investment treaties, the ensuing surge in the invocation of investment treaties by foreign investors against host States and the consequences of the turn to investment treaty protection. Section 3 demonstrates how investment treaties, as well as the regime they fostered, are currently undergoing a period of resistance and change. Measures that purportedly achieve a better balance between the right of investors to protection and the right of States to regulate are being taken to address the deficiencies in the status quo.

INTRODUCTION

The rise of investment treaties as important instruments of foreign investment protection is a recent phenomenon. Although foreign investment has existed since the days of exploration and empire when foreign trade and settlement flourished, the traditional mode of recourse in the event of a dispute between the investor and the host State was diplomatic protection.[1] This involved the investor writing to their home State with a claim against the host State,

---

[1] The 2006 International Law Commission (ILC) Draft Articles on Diplomatic Protection define diplomatic protection in Art. 1 as 'the invocation by a State, through diplomatic action or other means of peaceful settlement, of the responsibility of another State for an injury caused by an internationally wrongful act of that State to a natural or legal person that is a national of the former State with a view to the implementation of such responsibility'. However, the exercise of diplomatic protection did not always bear such precise legal connotations: see F. A. Mann, 'The Law Governing State Contracts' (1944) 21 *BYbIL* 11, 14. In earlier

and the home State deciding whether to take up the matter with its foreign counterpart. However, the discretionary nature of diplomatic protection offered neither clarity nor certainty to investors seeking recompense for host State interference with their investments. The appeal of diplomatic protection waned in the aftermath of the two World Wars, which devastated national economies and ushered in a period of urgent economic rebuilding. States actively sought a way to stimulate the inward flow of foreign capital while simultaneously safeguarding that capital, thereby ensuring sustainable economic rejuvenation and development.[2] Investment treaties, which offer holders of foreign capital assurances that diplomatic protection does not, seemed to be a promising means to those ends.

Investment treaties, both bilateral (BITs) and multilateral (MITs), are concluded for the reciprocal promotion and protection of investment in the territory of the Contracting States.[3] This means that a Contracting State pledges to protect qualifying investments belonging to nationals of the other Contracting State(s) to the extent agreed upon in the treaty, and vice versa. Common assurances found in investment treaties include the obligation of Contracting States to treat protected investors and investments fairly and equitably (FET),[4] to guarantee their full protection and security (FPS),[5] not to expropriate without compensation,[6] to ensure no less favourable treatment than that given to local investors,[7] as well as no less favourable treatment than that given to investors from third States (also known as most-favoured-nation, or MFN, treatment).[8] Additionally, most investment treaties empower investors to bring claims against host States for treaty breaches before arbitral tribunals, granting them privileged status as third-party beneficiaries of treaty obligations.[9] Over time, the character and extent of pledged protection were articulated by arbitral tribunals interpreting the various treaty obligations. These findings, which are recorded in a growing body of often publicly available arbitral awards, have been criticised for overstating the extent of pledged protection, and for overstepping the inherent sovereign right to regulate.[10] Challenges have also been mounted to the propriety of allowing disgruntled investors to sue, and party-appointed arbitrators to rule, on commercially injurious State measures taken in an exercise of governance. The critics

---

times, diplomatic protection was a generic label for communications at the inter-State level, and which may today be subdivided into diplomatic protection, diplomatic representations or use of good offices, the latter two not amounting to diplomatic protection. As this chapter considers diplomatic protection in earlier times, it adopts a looser definition of diplomatic protection than that proposed by the ILC.

[2] For an account of the historical backdrop to the proliferation of investment treaties, see K. Miles, *The Origins of International Investment Law: Empire, Environment, and the Safeguarding of Capital* (Cambridge University Press, 2013), ch. 1.

[3] The text of the 3,000-plus investment treaties currently in existence can be perused online in a free and searchable database: http://investmentpolicyhub.unctad.org/IIA (accessed 31 July 2020).

[4] See discussion at Chapter 12.

[5] *Ibid.*

[6] See discussion at Chapter 14.

[7] See discussion at Chapter 13.

[8] *Ibid.*

[9] Investors, who are either natural or legal persons, cannot, by definition, be signatories to a treaty.

[10] A leading critic is M. Sornarajah. Of his numerous works, 'Evolution or Revolution in International Investment Arbitration? The Descent into Normlessness' in C. Brown and K. Miles (eds), *Evolution in Investment Treaty Law and Arbitration* (Cambridge University Press, 2011), 631, offers the most compact yet compelling account of his objections.

and the challengers stoked sufficient controversy,[11] impelling States to reconsider, and in some cases revise, the traditional laconicism of treaty language and the optimal mode for investor–State dispute settlement.

This chapter discusses the creation, implementation and reorientation of investment treaties, which are akin to sequential phases of a life cycle. Section 1 covers the period from 1959 to 1990, which witnessed the appearance of investment treaties and the absence of treaty-based investment arbitrations. Section 2 covers the period from the 1990s to 2007, which, in comparison with the preceding decades, marked an exponential increase in the number of investment treaties concluded, as well as a sudden spike in treaty claims brought by investors against States. Section 3 covers the period from 2007, the year when cracks in the investment treaty regime started to appear with the denunciation by Bolivia of the Convention on the Settlement of Investment Disputes between States and Nationals of Other States (ICSID Convention)[12] and threats by some States to terminate their investment treaties, to the present. Ways of repairing the cracks have abounded. Newer investment treaties proffer details on the scope and extent of pledged protection which older investment treaties lacked. Proposals for an appellate mechanism,[13] or for a standing tribunal with State-appointed members,[14] strive to address the legitimacy deficit that private adjudicators pronouncing on issues with a strong public dimension are said to face. Investment treaties, new and old, will remain a source of great dissatisfaction for some. But because more States appear to be choosing reform over rejection, '[i]nvestment treaties are here to stay'.[15]

1. CREATION: 1959–1990

The year 1959 is symbolic for investment treaties. In the autumn of 1959, Germany and Pakistan signed the very first BIT.[16] However, this BIT, which comprises fourteen tersely worded Articles, repeats the customary position on non-discrimination,[17]

---

[11] The bringing of a treaty claim by Swedish energy supplier Vattenfall against Germany over the latter's phasing out of nuclear power plants in 2009, and by tobacco giant Philip Morris against Australia over the latter's plain packaging regulations in 2011, catapulted investment treaties from a specialised vocation into popular consciousness. Partisan headlines in mainstream media, such as 'Investor-State Dispute Settlement – the Arbitration Game: Governments Are Souring on Treaties to Protect Foreign Investors', *The Economist*, 11 October 2014, keep the controversy alive.

[12] 18 March 1965. List of Contracting States and Other Signatories of the Convention, https://icsid.worldbank.org/about/member-states/database-of-member-stateshttps://icsid.worldbank.org/en/Documents/icsiddocs/List%20of%20Contracting%20States%20and%20Other%20Signatories%20of%20 the%20Convention%20-%20Latest.pdf (accessed 31 August 2020), 4–5.

[13] C. Tams, 'An Appealing Option? The Debate about an ICSID Appellate Structure' (2007) 4(5) *TDM* 1, 21–40.

[14] European Union (EU)–Canada Comprehensive Economic and Trade Agreement (CETA) (signed 30 October 2016, entered into force 15 February 2017), Art. 8.27. A standing tribunal, instead of institutional or ad hoc arbitration, to hear treaty claims is also on the negotiating table for the Transatlantic Trade and Investment Partnership (TTIP) between the European Union and the United States.

[15] J. Bonnitcha, L. N. Skovgaard Poulsen and M. Waibel, *The Political Economy of the Investment Treaty Regime* (Oxford University Press, 2017), 3.

[16] Treaty between the Federal Republic of Germany and Pakistan for the Promotion and Protection of Investments (signed 25 November 1959, entered into force 28 April 1962) (Germany–Pakistan BIT 1959), replaced by the Agreement on the Encouragement and Reciprocal Protection of Investments between the Federal Republic of Germany and Pakistan (signed 1 December 2009, not yet in force).

[17] Germany–Pakistan BIT 1959, Art. 2.

FPS,[18] compensable expropriation[19] and *pacta sunt servanda*[20] in the treatment of aliens and alien assets. It does not provide for FET of protected investors and investments, MFN treatment of protected investors and investments, or investor–State dispute settlement. In short, the most innovative, distinctive and controversial features of the modern-day investment treaty regime were not introduced by the 1959 Germany–Pakistan BIT.

While not a document of immense historic significance, the 1959 Germany–Pakistan BIT is notable for making investment protection the sole focus of a bilateral accord. It marked a lasting shift away from the conclusion of multi-focal friendship, commerce and navigation (FCN) treaties, a hallmark of US foreign policy in the nineteenth and early twentieth centuries. Some provisions in FCN treaties are relevant to investment protection. These include the guarantee that nationals of the other Contracting State will be accorded the same rights and privileges as 'native citizens',[21] and the guarantee that nationals and property belonging to nationals of the other Contracting State will enjoy the 'full protection' of the host State.[22] These provisions live on in BITs and MITs as national treatment clauses[23] and FPS clauses.[24] Therefore, FCN treaties are regarded as forerunners of investment treaties.[25]

Over the next four decades, States concluded more than 400 BITs, negotiated, signed and ratified the ICSID Convention, but showed little interest in attempts to draw up a multilateral investment convention. This Section examines key features of the earliest investment treaties (Section 1.1), the widespread support for the ICSID Convention (Section 1.2) and the failure to multilateralise (Section 1.3).

---

[18] *Ibid.*, Art. 3(1).

[19] *Ibid.*, Art. 3(2).

[20] *Ibid.*, Art. 7.

[21] See, e.g., Treaty of Friendship, Commerce and Navigation between Argentina and the United States (signed 27 July 1853, entered into force 20 December 1854) (Argentina–US FCN treaty), Art. VIII (excerpted): 'The citizens of the two contracting parties … shall have free and open access to the courts of justice in the said countries respectively, for the prosecution and defense of their just rights, and they shall be at liberty to employ in all cases such advocates, attorneys or agents as they may think proper; and they shall enjoy, in this respect, the same rights and privileges therein as native citizens.'

[22] See, e.g., Argentina–US FCN treaty, Art. XIII (excerpted): 'The citizens of the United States, and the citizens of the Argentine Confederation, respectively, residing in any of the territories of the other party, shall enjoy, in their houses, persons and properties, the full protection of the Government.'

[23] See discussion at Chapter 13. An example of a national treatment clause is Treaty between United States of America and the Argentine Republic Concerning the Reciprocal Encouragement and Protection of Investment (signed 14 November 1991, entered into force 20 October 1994) (US–Argentina BIT), Art. II(1): 'Each Party shall permit and treat investment, and activities associated therewith, on a basis no less favorable than that accorded in like situations to investment or associated activities of its own nationals or companies … subject to the right of each Party to make or maintain exceptions falling within one of the sectors or matters listed in the Protocol to this Treaty.'

[24] See discussion at Chapter 12. An example of a full protection and security clause is US–Argentina BIT, Art. II(2)(a): 'Investment shall at all times … enjoy full protection and security and shall in no case be accorded treatment less than that required by international law.'

[25] K. Vandevelde, 'The Bilateral Investment Treaty Program of the United States' (1988) 21 *Cornell ILJ* 203, 204.

1.1 The Earliest Investment Treaties

Germany took the lead in the 1960s, concluding close to half of the seventy-four BITs created during that time, mostly with developing African and Asian nations.[26] A total of 101 new BITs were concluded by 1980, and an additional 286 by 1990.[27] A total of twenty-four treaties containing investment provisions were concluded from 1960 to 1990.[28] The earliest investment treaties permit three observations.

First, virtually all the investment treaties of this period, predominantly BITs, were concluded between developed and developing States (the North–South model), with only a handful concluded between developing States (the South–South model). There appears to be no investment treaty between developed States (the North–North model).

Second, North–South treaties and South–South treaties vary considerably in content. Two BITs which showcase the contrast are the Convention between the Government of the French Republic and of the Democratic Republic of Sudan on the Encouragement and the Reciprocal Protection of Investments (France–Sudan BIT)[29] and the Agreement between the Government of the Socialist Republic of Romania and the Government of the Democratic Republic of the Sudan on the Mutual Promotion and Guarantee of Capital Investments (Romania–Sudan BIT),[30] both of which were signed in 1978. The France– Sudan BIT entitles protected investors and investment to FET,[31] national treatment,[32] MFN treatment[33] and compensable expropriation,[34] and empowers protected investors to bring claims for treaty breaches directly against the host State.[35] In contrast, the Romania–Sudan BIT guarantees only MFN treatment[36] and compensable expropriation.[37] There is no provision for investor–State dispute settlement. The types, wording and arrangement of substantive protection provisions in the France–Sudan BIT are virtually identical to other French BITs concluded in the period under study, strongly suggesting the existence of a French treaty template which its developing counterparts could simply endorse. Investment protection rules in the earliest North–South investment treaties were almost certainly determined and drafted by the developed Contracting State.

Third, although the first investment treaty appeared in 1959, it was not until 1975 that Contracting States started making provision for investor–State dispute settlement, under

---

[26] Figures obtained from the free, searchable database: http://investmentpolicyhub.unctad.org/IIA (accessed 31 July 2020).
[27] *Ibid.*
[28] *Ibid.*
[29] Signed 31 July 1978, entered into force 5 July 1980.
[30] Signed 8 December 1978, not yet in force.
[31] France–Sudan BIT, Art. 3.
[32] *Ibid.*
[33] *Ibid.*
[34] *Ibid.*, Art. 5.
[35] *Ibid.*, Art. 8.
[36] Romania–Sudan BIT, Art. 3(1) and (2).
[37] *Ibid.*, Art. 4.

the auspices of the ICSID and in accordance with the ICSID Convention. This provision contains the unilateral, irrevocable consent of the Contracting States to submit future disputes with protected investors to arbitration. Consent to arbitrate is perfected when the investor submits a request for arbitration to the ICSID. As arbitration is a form of private adjudication, disputing parties must consent to have their dispute settled by arbitration. Absent mutual consent to arbitrate, the arbitral tribunal has no jurisdiction over the dispute. The availability of arbitration precludes the investor from seeking diplomatic protection for its claim. An early example of an investor–State dispute settlement provision is Article 8 of the Agreement between the Government of the United Kingdom of Great Britain and Northern Ireland and the Government of the Arab Republic of Egypt (UK–Egypt BIT).[38]

UK–Egypt BIT, Art. 8 (footnote omitted)

(1) Each Contracting Party hereby consents to submit to the International Centre for the Settlement of Investment Disputes (hereinafter referred to as 'the Centre') for settlement by conciliation or arbitration under the Convention on the Settlement of Investment Disputes between States and of Other States opened for signature at Washington on 18 March 1965 any legal dispute arising between that Contracting Party and a national or company of the other Contracting Party concerning an investment of the territory of the former. Such a company of one Contracting Party of which before such a dispute arises the majority of shares are owned by nationals or companies of the other Contracting Party shall in accordance with Article 25(2)(b) of the Convention be treated for the purposes of the Convention as a company of the other Contracting Party. If any such dispute should arise and agreement cannot be reached within three months between the parties to this dispute through pursuit of local remedies, through conciliation or otherwise, then, if the national or company affected also consents in writing to submit the dispute to the Centre for settlement by conciliation or arbitration under the Convention, either party may institute proceedings by addressing a request to that effect to the Secretary-General of the Centre as provided in Articles 28 and 36 of the Convention. In the event of disagreement as to whether conciliation or arbitration is the more appropriate procedure the national or company affected shall have the right to choose.

(2) Neither Contracting Party shall pursue through diplomatic channels any dispute referred to the Centre unless
  (a) the Secretary-General of the Centre, or a conciliation commission or an arbitral tribunal constituted by it, decides that the dispute is not within the jurisdiction of the Centre, or
  (b) the other Contracting Party should fail to abide by or to comply with any award rendered by an arbitral tribunal.

[38] Signed 11 June 1975, entered into force 24 February 1976.

1.2 The ICSID Convention

The ICSID Convention was negotiated from 1962 to 1965 under the auspices of the World Bank. Given the Bank's mission to boost shared prosperity among nations, it 'had long taken an interest in the settlement of disputes between its member countries and foreign investors'.[39] The negotiations for a multilateral convention that established the procedures for the arbitration and conciliation of investment disputes between States and nationals of other States were facilitated by a draft convention prepared by the then General Counsel for the World Bank, Aron Broches.[40] The ICSID Convention was signed on 18 March 1965, and entered into force on 14 October 1966. As of 31 July 2020, the ICSID Convention has 163 signatories, of whom 155 have deposited instruments of ratification.[41]

The ICSID Convention secured widespread support among States because its text was deliberately formulated in a way 'which could be accepted by the largest possible number of governments'.[42] In the first place, the Convention's scope was limited to procedural matters, which are considerably less contentious than the nature and extent of substantive protection accorded to investments. Moreover, when a point of contention arose during the negotiations and for which no consensus was achievable, such as the definition of an 'investment' in Article 25 which delimits the jurisdiction of tribunals constituted pursuant to the ICSID Convention, the final text was silent on the matter. States could therefore sign the ICSID Convention and yet remain free to define 'investment' in whichever way they saw fit in BITs and MITs.[43]

Accession to the ICSID Convention is a firm commitment by a State to investor–State dispute settlement. An investor whose home State is a Contracting State to the ICSID Convention can bring a claim directly against a host State who is also a Contracting State, even in the absence of an applicable investment treaty. In the 'first World Bank arbitration',[44] *Holiday Inns SA and Others* v. *Morocco*, the US and Swiss investors invoked the arbitration clause in a hotel development contract with a Moroccan State entity, which referred the disputing parties to ICSID arbitration.[45] The ICSID Convention was, at the date of the Request for Arbitration, in force in Switzerland, the United States and Morocco. More than a decade later, in *Southern Pacific Properties (Middle East) Ltd* v. *Egypt*, the Hong Kong claimants invoked Egyptian Law No. 43 of 1974, which allowed foreign investors to submit investment disputes with the Egyptian Government

---

[39] Antonio Parra, *The History of ICSID*, 2nd edn (Oxford University Press, 2017), 20.

[40] *Ibid.*, 23–24.

[41] List of Contracting States (above n. 12), p. 1.

[42] ICSID, 'Report of the Executive Directors on the Convention on the Settlement of Investment Disputes between States and Nationals of Other States', 18 March 1965, p. 38.

[43] A. Broches, *Selected Essays: World Bank, ICSID, and Other Subjects of Public and Private International Law* (The Netherlands: Martinus Nijhoff, 1995), 168; A. Broches, 'Legal Committee on Settlement of Investment Disputes: Definition of "Investment", November 27, 1964' in *History of the ICSID Convention* (Washington, DC: ICSID, 1968), 843–844; ICSID, 'Memorandum of the Meeting of the Committee of the Whole, February 16, 1965' in *History of the ICSID Convention*, para. 65.

[44] P. Lalive, 'The First "World Bank" Arbitration (*Holiday Inns v. Morocco*) – Some Legal Problems' (1980) 51(1) BYbIL 123, 123. Lalive was counsel for claimants in this inaugural World Bank arbitration.

[45] ICSID Case No. ARB/72/1, Decision on Jurisdiction, 12 May 1974 (Legergren, Reuter, Schultz).

to ICSID arbitration.[46] Both the United Kingdom (of which Hong Kong was then a Crown colony) and Egypt had ratified the ICSID Convention by the time of promulgation of Law No. 43.

1.3 Draft Multilateral Investment Treaties

The readiness of States to accede to a multilateral investment dispute settlement treaty did not extend to draft multilateral treaties setting out common standards of protection for foreign investment. Three of the most prominent draft treaties proposed by private organisations or think-tanks were the 1959 Abs–Shawcross Draft Convention on Investments Abroad,[47] the 1961 Harvard Draft Convention on the Responsibility of States for Injuries to the Economic Interests of Aliens[48] and the 1967 OECD Draft Convention on the Protection of Private Foreign Investment.[49] None of these drafts benefited from State participation, and none garnered enough support from States to leave the drawing board and be put up for signature and ratification.

Diffidence towards multilateral investment treaties was an early sign of the inherent tension between the desire of States to attract foreign investment by guaranteeing protection from State interference, and the conviction that sovereign powers must not be unwittingly subordinated to the safeguarding of foreign capital. Developing States, who formed the overwhelming numerical majority of the family of nations from 1959 to 1990, were determined not to sacrifice sovereignty for investment protection. This ethos was expressed in their accession to the Final Act of the UN Conference on Trade and Employment 1948 (the Havana Charter),[50] and in their yes votes for the 1962 General Assembly Resolution on Permanent Sovereignty Over Natural Resources[51] and the 1974 General Assembly Resolution on a Charter of Economic Rights and Duties of States.[52] Article 12 of the Havana Charter captures this ethos and offers broad guidelines on the extent of investment protection that States should confer.

---

[46] ICSID Case No. ARB/84/3, Decision on Jurisdiction, 14 April 1988 (Jiménez de Arechaga, El Mahdi, Pietrowski). The UK–Egypt BIT, which entered into force in 1976, was not applicable because the extension of treaty protection to Hong Kong investors was conditional upon an Exchange of Notes between the United Kingdom and Egypt, which never took place. According to Art. 11: 'At the time of definitive entry into force of this Agreement or at any time thereafter, the provisions of this Agreement may be extended to such territories for whose international relations the Government of the United Kingdom are responsible as may be agreed between the Contracting Parties in an Exchange of Notes.'

[47] UNCTAD, *International Investment Instruments: A Compendium*, vol. 3, No. 159, www.unctad.org (accessed 31 July 2020).

[48] (1961) 55 AJIL 545.

[49] (12 October 1967) C(67)102, 14. For a list of other private efforts to multilateralise investment protection, see R. Ago, 'First Report on State Responsibility' (7 May 1969–20 January 1970) UN Doc. A/CN.4/217, 101, pp. 141–154.

[50] Signed 24 March 1948, not yet in force.

[51] UNGA Res. 1803 (XVIII) (14 December 1962), GAOR Supp. 17, 15.

[52] UNGA Res. A/Res/3281(XXIX) (12 December 1974). See especially Report of the Working Group of the Trade and Development Board (1 August 1974), TD/B/AC.12/4, partially reproduced in J. Kuusi, *The Host State and the Transnational Corporation* (Farnborough: Saxon House, 1979) 71, 131–135.

Havana Charter, Art. 12

1. The Members recognize that:
   (a) international investment, both public and private, can be of great value in promoting economic development and reconstruction, and consequent social progress;
   (b) the international flow of capital will be stimulated to the extent that Members afford nationals of other countries opportunities for investment and security for existing and future investments;
   (c) without prejudice to existing international agreements to which Members are parties, a Member has the right:
      (i) to take any appropriate safeguards necessary to ensure that foreign investment is not used as a basis for interference in its internal affairs or national policies;
      (ii) to determine whether and, to what extent and upon what terms it will allow future foreign investment;
      (iii) to prescribe and give effect on just terms to requirements as to the ownership of existing and future investments;
      (iv) to prescribe and give effect to other reasonable requirements with respect to existing and future investments;
   (d) the interests of Members whose nationals are in a position to provide capital for international investment and of Members who desire to obtain the use of such capital to promote their economic development or reconstruction may be promoted if such Members enter into bilateral or multilateral agreements relating to the opportunities and security for investment which the Members are prepared to offer and any limitations which they are prepared to accept of the rights referred to in sub-paragraph (c).
2. Members therefore undertake:
   (a) subject to the provisions of paragraph 1(c) and to any agreements entered into under paragraph 1(d),
      (i) to provide reasonable opportunities for investments acceptable to them and adequate security for existing and future investments, and
      (ii) to give due regard to the desirability of avoiding discrimination as between foreign investments;
   (b) upon the request of any Member and without prejudice to existing international agreements to which Members are parties, to enter into consultation or to participate in negotiations directed to the conclusion, if mutually acceptable, of an agreement of the kind referred to in paragraph 1(d).
3. Members shall promote co-operation between national and foreign enterprises or investors for the purpose of fostering economic development or reconstruction in cases where such co-operation appears to the Members concerned to be appropriate.

However, any perceived tension did not entirely dissuade States, especially developing States, from concluding investment treaties. Standards of investment protection that failed to secure consensus on a multilateral level[53] lent themselves to agreement on a bilateral basis. This trend continued from the 1990s to 2007.

The period of creation is marked by a successful foray into bilateralism in investment protection, the historic entry into force of the ICSID Convention and the repeated failure of multilateralism. BITs of this period were by no means homogenous in content. The option of investor–State dispute settlement only started appearing from 1975, and North–South investment treaties offered a spectrum of investment protection standards and the option of investor–State dispute settlement which South–South investment treaties did not. The period of creation is also marked by the absence of North–North investment treaties and of treaty-based investor–State disputes. This changed in the following period of accelerated growth.

2. ACCELERATED GROWTH: 1990s–2007

The 1990s to 2007 was a period of intense activity on two fronts. First, States concluded more than 2,500 investment treaties, more than a five-fold increase from the preceding decades. Some of the most frequently invoked investment treaties, such as the US–Argentina BIT and Chapter 11 of the North American Free Trade Agreement (NAFTA),[54] as well as a multilateral treaty specific to the energy sector, the Energy Charter Treaty (ECT),[55] were concluded during this period. North–North treaties, such as Chapter 11 of the US–Australia Free Trade Agreement (FTA),[56] were also inked. Notwithstanding the reluctance of States to commit to common standards of investment protection in a multi-lateral treaty, the content of the vast repository of bilateral treaties suggests convergence on some protective standards (Section 2.1).

Second, investors started bringing claims against States, invoking treaty protection from interference with their investments. Arbitral tribunals were constituted to hear these claims and to interpret the various open-textured substantive protection provisions in the applicable investment treaty/treaties. Numerous arbitral awards were rendered during this period and many have been made public with the consent of the disputing parties. As there is no system of binding precedent in international arbitration, positions taken by tribunals on the same legal issue in arbitral awards can vary. There may be several lines of authority on a given issue, but no *jurisprudence constante*. Any resulting inconsistency is a by-product of popularising dispute settlement by arbitration, but is more often cited to link investor–State dispute settlement to ad hoc justice (Section 2.2).

---

[53] The next attempt at multilateralism, this time with the participation of States, lasted from 1995 to 1998, and would have culminated in a Multilateral Agreement on Investment, but also ended in failure. For an overview, see P. Muchlinski, 'The Rise and Fall of the Multilateral Agreement on Investment: Where Now?' (2000) 34 *International Lawyer* 1033.

[54] Signed 17 December 1992, entered into force 1 January 1994, 32 ILM 289. The NAFTA is now known as the Agreement Between the United States of America, the United Mexican States, and Canada (signed 30 November 2018, entered into force 1 July 2020) (USMCA). The updated investment protection provisions and revamped investor–State dispute settlement mechanism in the USMCA are found in Chapter 14.

[55] Signed 17 December 1994, entered into force 16 April 1998, 2080 UNTS 95.

[56] Signed 18 May 2004, entered into force 1 January 2005.

2.1 Partial Convergence in Treaty Content

Notwithstanding some textual variation, there are similarities in the content of invest-ment protection across the thousands of investment treaties. These similarities have been attributed to 'path dependency' where treaty drafters include a provision simply because it appears in older treaties,[57] as well as to the perception that investment treaties represent 'photo opportunities' with visiting heads of States, and can be quickly reproduced from a standard template.[58] However, consequential differences among certain commonplace provisions exist, cautioning against assuming that every investment treaty is a product of cutting and pasting from earlier treaties. The following excerpts point to convergence in treaty content according investments FET, but not MFN treatment.

C. Yannaca-Small, 'Fair and Equitable Treatment Standard in International Investment Law', (2004) OECD Working Papers on International Investment Number 2004/3, 5–7 (footnotes omitted, original emphasis)

B. The current use of the standard in international agreements and state practice

– Bilateral Treaties

The influence of the OECD Draft Convention is obvious in the growing number of *bilateral investment treaties* which were negotiated between developed and developing countries beginning in the late 60s. One of the main features which gained a position of prominence was the reference to 'fair and equitable treatment'. However, while the standard appears in the majority of BITs, it is not always mentioned in treaties concluded by certain Asian countries (e.g. some treaties signed by Pakistan, Saudi Arabia and Singapore). In recent years, even countries which traditionally were in favour of national control over foreign investments and therefore favoured the use of national treatment over the fair and equitable standard have incorporated the 'fair and equitable' standard in their bilateral investment treaties. Bilateral investment treaties of Chile and China as well as between Peru and Thailand, Bulgaria and Ghana, the United Arab Emirates and Malaysia, include the fair and equitable standard. In this category it is worth noting the Latin American countries, which had embraced the Calvo doctrine since the beginning of the XXth century and had firmly avoided the terms 'fair and equitable'.

The recently concluded new generation agreements, the Free Trade Agreements between the *United States and Australia, Central America (CAFTA), Chile, Morocco,* and *Singapore,* in their Investment Chapters, provide with greater specificity that each Party has the obligation to 'accord to the covered investments treatment in accordance with customary international law, including fair and equitable treatment and full protection and security'.

---

[57] W. Alschner, 'Locked-in Language: Historical Sociology and the Path Dependency of Investment Treaty Design' in M. Hirsch and A. Lang (eds), *Research Handbook on the Sociology of International Law* (Cheltenham: Edward Elgar, 2018), 347, 348–353.

[58] L. Poulsen and E. Aisbett, 'When the Claim Hits: Bilateral Investment Treaties and Bounded Rational Learning' (2013) 65(2) *World Politics* 273, 280, 296 (Table 6).

The Free Trade Agreement between *Australia and Thailand*, in its Article 909, also provides that each Party has the obligation to 'ensure fair and equitable treatment' of foreign investment in its own territory.

– Multilateral instruments

In the multilateral context, the *Draft United Nations Code of Conduct on Transnational Corporations*, in its Article 48, stated that:

> *'Transnational corporations should receive [fair and] equitable [and non-discriminatory] treatment [under] [in accordance with] the laws, regulations and administrative practices of the countries in which they operate [as well as intergovernmental obligations to which the Governments of these countries have freely subscribed] [consistent with their international obligations] [consistent with international law]'.*

Although most of the above issues had not reached consensus in the last version of the text (1986), the negotiating States agreed that the Code should provide for 'equitable' treatment of transnational corporations.

The *1985 Convention establishing the Multilateral Investment Guarantee Agency (MIGA)* specifies in Article 12(d) that in order to guarantee an investment, MIGA must satisfy itself that fair and equitable treatment and legal protection for the investment exist in the host country concerned. This would appear to be not only a prudent standard for lowering the risk for guaranteed investments, but also one of the means by which MIGA carries out its mission under Articles 2 and 23 to promote investment flows to and among developing countries, which include promotion of investment protection.

The *1992 World Bank Guidelines on Treatment of Foreign Direct Investment* stipulate in their article III(2) that: 'each State will extend to investments established in its territory by nationals of any other State fair and equitable treatment according to the standards recommended in the Guidelines'. It then in III(3) indicates the standards of treatment which are to be accorded to foreign investors in matters such as security of person and property rights, the granting of permits and licenses, the transfer of incomes and profits, the repatriation of capital. The approach suggested is that fair and equitable treatment is an over-arching requirement.

The standard can also be found in 1990 *Lomé IV*, the Fourth Convention of the African, Caribbean and Pacific Group of States and the European Economic Community (EEC) and in the 1987 *ASEAN Treaty for the Promotion and Protection of Investments*, in its Article IV.

The *Colonia Protocol on Reciprocal Promotion and Protection of Investments* signed by MERCOSUR member States in January 1994, expressly grants to investors from each MERCOSUR country 'at any moment, fair and equitable treatment'. An additional Protocol on the Promotion and Protection of Investments from non-member States extends the same treatment to these investments.

Article 159 of the 1994 Treaty establishing the *Common Market for Eastern and Southern Africa (COMESA)* also requires COMESA member States to 'accord fair and equitable treatment to private investors'.

Article 1105(1) of the *NAFTA*, which entered into force on 1 January 1994, stipulates under the rubric 'Minimum Standard of Treatment' that:

> '*Each Party shall accord to investments of investors of another Party treatment in accordance with international law, including fair and equitable treatment and full protection and security.*'

The *Draft OECD Multilateral Agreement on Investment* (1998) in its preamble indicated that 'fair, transparent and predictable investment regimes complement and benefit the world trading system', while under the 'General Treatment' Article it stipulated that:

> '*Each contracting Party shall accord fair and equitable treatment and full and constant protection and security to foreign investments in their territories. In no case shall a contracting Party accord treatment less favourable than that required by international law.*'

The *Energy Charter Treaty* (1995) provides also that fair and equitable treatment shall be accorded at 'all times'. Although the Treaty is limited to one sector, it is significant in this context because it includes among its Parties several economies in transition which embrace the standard.

Finally, the June 2002 *Agreement between Singapore and EFTA* establishing a free-trade area among the Parties stipulates in its Article 39 that each Party shall 'accord at all times to investments of investors of another Party fair and equitable treatment'.

M.-F. Houde, 'Most-Favoured-Nation Treatment in International Investment Law', (2004) OECD Working Papers on International Investment Number 2004/2, 3–5 (footnotes omitted, original emphasis)

2.3 Examples of MFN Clauses in Investment Agreements

A stock taking of MFN clauses in investment treaties will not yield a uniform picture. In fact the universe of MFN clauses in investment treaties is quite diverse. Some MFN clauses are narrow, others are more general. Moreover, the context of the clauses varies, as does the object and the purpose of the treaties which contain them. Following is a representative sample of these clauses.

Germany has concluded the largest number of BITs. Article 3(1) and (2) of the *German 1998 Model Treaty* combines the MFN obligation with the national treatment obligation by providing that:

> '*(1) Neither Contracting State shall subject investments in its territory owned or controlled by investors of the other Contracting State to treatment less favourable than it accords to investments of its own investors or to investments of investors of any third State.*
>
> *(2) Neither Contracting State shall subject investors of the other Contracting State, as regards their activity in connection with investments in its territory, to treatment less favourable than it accords to its own investors or to investors of any third State.*'

This general MFN provision is not restricted in its scope to any particular part of the treaty containing it. It may also be noted that the 1998 German model BIT contains another MFN provision which only relates to full protection and security and to expropriation which are the matters dealt with by Article 4. Article 4(4) specifically provides that:

> *'Investors of either Contracting State shall enjoy most-favoured-nation treatment in the territory of the other Contracting State in respect of the matters provided for in this Article.'*

...

The typical formulation of an MFN clause in the *US and Canadian BITs* covers both the establishment and post establishment phases. It also lists the various operations covered and is explicit in stating that the right only applies 'in like circumstances', unlike other BITs (particularly the 'European model BIT') which make no reference to the comparative context against which treatment is to be assessed. Recent examples are to be found in the investment chapter of US–Chile Free Trade Agreement ... In the *US–Chile FTA*, Article 10.3: Most Favoured Nation Treatment reads:

> *'(1) Each Party shall accord to investors of the other Party treatment no less favourable than that it accords, in like circumstances, to investors of any non-Party with respect to the establishment, acquisition, expansion, management, conduct, operation, and sale or other disposition of investment in its territory.*
> *(2) Each Party shall accord to covered investments treatment no less favourable than that it accords, in like circumstances, to investments in its territory of investors of any non- Party with respect to the establishment, acquisition, expansion, management, conduct, operation and sale or other disposition of investments.'*

...

The texts of these agreements are alike in that they make clear that the intent to use the likeness of the circumstances in which the treatment is granted as the basis for comparison. Jurisprudence from MFN clauses with a different basis for comparison, and which focuses on categorizing industries affected by treatment, or categorizing the types of treaties that require the treatment, may be of little relevance to the analysis required by these agreements.

2.2 Claims against Host States and *Jurisprudence (In)constante*

From 1991 to 2007, 233 investor–State disputes were registered at the ICSID,[59] the vast majority of which involved claims for treaty breaches. The first investment treaty claim was registered on 2 February 1993,[60] invoking the Treaty between the United States

---

[59] 'The ICSID Caseload – Statistics' (Issue 2017–1), https://icsid.worldbank.org/sites/default/files/publications/Caseload%20Statistics/en/ICSID%20Web%20Stats%202017-1%20%28English%29%20Final%20%28Feb%209%29.pdf (accessed 31 July 2020), 7.

[60] *American Manufacturing & Trading Inc.* v. *Congo*, ICSID Case No. ARB/93/1, Award, 21 February 1997 (Sucharitkul, Golsong, Mbaye).

of America and the Republic of Zaire Concerning the Reciprocal Encouragement and Protection of Investment.[61] Many claims were to follow, with claimants invoking many different investment treaties.

Treaty claims brought by investors often alleged breaches of core treaty protection standards, such as FET and compensable expropriation, which can be found in most investment treaties. A less common but well-known treaty claim alleges a breach of an umbrella clause in the applicable treaty whenever the host State breaches a contractual obligation.[62] A typical umbrella clause obliges Contracting States to observe all obligations they may have entered into with regard to protected investors or investments, without specifying what those obligations are. The principal legal issue raised by an umbrella clause claim is whether a breach of any contractual obligation owed by the host State to a protected investor amounts to a breach of a treaty obligation. Just as how tribunals are left to determine, in accordance with the principles of treaty interpretation,[63] what the scope and content of laconic umbrella clauses are, tribunals must also define FET and deduce the method for quantifying expropriated investments. And while, as Section 2.1 shows, there is partial convergence in content across investment treaties, this has not resulted in convergence in the way this content is interpreted and understood in the growing body of arbitral awards.

J. Crawford, 'Similarity of Issues in Disputes Arising under the Same or Similarly Drafted Investment Treaties' in E. Gaillard and Y. Banifatemi (eds), *Precedent in International Arbitration* (New York: Juris Publishing, 2007), 97, 102–103 (footnotes omitted)

We do not have a *jurisprudence constante* on fair and equitable treatment, though one is perhaps starting to emerge. We do not have a *jurisprudence constante* in relation to the role of legitimate expectations. We do not have a *jurisprudence constante* in the relationship between quantification of breaches of the fair and equitable treatment standard and that of the standard for expropriation: the two tend to be conflated. And we do not have a *jurisprudence constante* in relation to umbrella clauses specifically, or more generally the relation between treaty and contract.

Crawford later explained in his 2007 Freshfields Bruckhaus Deringer Lecture why there was no '*jurisprudence constante* in relation to umbrella clauses specifically'.

---

[61] Signed 3 August 1984, entered into force 28 July 1989.
[62] See discussion in Chapter 15.
[63] These are enshrined in the Vienna Convention on the Law of Treaties (signed 23 May 1969, entered into force 27 January 1980) 1155 UNTS 331 (VCLT), Arts 31 and 32.

J. Crawford, 'Treaty and Contract in Investment Arbitration' (2008) 24(3) *Arb Int'l* 351, 366–368 (footnotes omitted)

There is neither the time nor would it be productive to go into the details of the 20 or so cases in which umbrella clauses have been discussed. It is sufficient to identify four schools of thought, if you like, four camps – though some of the dwellers in particular camps may be thought to have a nomadic attitude and to move from camp to camp as the feeling takes them.

The first camp adopts an extremely narrow interpretation of umbrella clauses, holding that they are operative only where it is possible to discern a shared intent of the parties that any breach of contract is a breach of the BIT. The second camp seeks to limit umbrella clauses to breaches of contract committed by the host state in the exercise of sovereign authority. A third view goes to the other extreme: the effect of umbrella clauses is to internationalise investment contracts, thereby transforming contractual claims into treaty claims directly subject to treaty rules.

Finally there is the view that an umbrella clause is operative and may form the basis for a substantive treaty claim, but that it does not convert a contractual claim into a treaty claim. On the one hand it provides, or at least may provide, a basis for a treaty claim even if the BIT in question contains no generic claims clause; on the other hand, the umbrella clause does not change the proper law of the contract or its legal incidents, including its provisions for dispute settlement.

The consequence of having different 'schools of thought' for almost every standard of investment protection is that none can tell, and least of all Contracting States whose compliance with treaty obligations is subject to scrutiny, when State interference crosses the line and becomes unlawful. A tribunal belonging to a certain 'school of thought' may conclude that a host State is not in breach of an umbrella clause by committing a breach of contract, while another tribunal interpreting the same treaty clause but subscribing to a different 'school of thought' can arrive at the opposite conclusion.[64] A State may have agreed to confer innocuous-sounding FET on protected investors and investments, and only realise belatedly that an extremely wide reading of what is fair and equitable by an arbitral tribunal can elevate the slightest State interferences to treaty violations, for which the State must make reparation. It should therefore come as no surprise that States grew increasingly concerned, and in some cases disenchanted, with a regime that places the burden of interpreting open-textured treaty obligations squarely on arbitrators. It is therefore arbitrators who determine, with the barest of guidance from the VCLT, the limits of sovereign authority.

The 1990s to 2007 was a period of activity, as well as awakening, for all the direct participants in the investment treaty regime. Investors brought claims and experienced the protection conferred by investment treaties in concrete terms when they prevailed on

---

[64] The presence of conflicting decisions on the same point of law has been likened to a 'legitimacy crisis': see generally S. D. Franck, 'The Legitimacy Crisis in Investment Treaty Arbitration: Privatizing Public International Law through Inconsistent Decisions' (2005) 73 *Fordham L Rev* 1521.

those claims. Counsel making submissions in and arbitrators appointed to hear investor–State disputes were instrumental in shaping international investment law through their interpretation of investment treaty obligations. And finally, States signed up for investment protection in treaties, and saw how their promises on paper bore out in practice. The investment treaty regime is one that States created. But some degree of convergence in treaty content did not ensure predictability. On the contrary, the preferred mode of dispute settlement in investment treaties – investor–State arbitration – fostered *jurisprudence inconstante*, rendering unpredictable the fault lines in investment protection. States, joined by a growing body of scholar-critics, began to resist and took steps to modify the regime that they had created.

3. 'RESISTANCE AND CHANGE': 2007 AND BEYOND

Since 2007 the investment treaty regime has been confronted by what Sornarajah terms 'resistance and change', where dissatisfaction with the status quo galvanises into positive action for the betterment or abolition of the regime.[65] It was in 2007 that Bolivia, a respondent State to several pending treaty claims submitted to ICSID arbitration, denounced the ICSID Convention. Once the denunciation takes effect, Bolivia will be neither a Contracting State to the ICSID Convention, nor obliged to submit to the jurisdiction of the ICSID.[66] As the first State to denounce the ICSID Convention, indicating serious objections to (or at the very least a change of heart regarding) the model of investment protection and investment dispute resolution that the ICSID stands for, Bolivia made a powerful political statement whose ripple effects continue to be felt today.

This section first outlines the cracks in the investment treaty regime that appeared or were perceived and commented on with greater frequency from 2007 (Section 3.1). It then outlines the changes that States and private actors are introducing to the regime, and how these changes may address inadequacies in the status quo (Section 3.2).

3.1 Cracks in the Investment Treaty Regime

Bolivia's denunciation of the ICSID Convention was one of several initiatives that revealed or led to growing disenchantment with the investment treaty regime, and fuelled fears that the regime was heavily skewed towards the benefit of foreign investors at grave expense to host States. The cracks can be broadly categorised as follows.

---

[65] With regard to this section, see also discussion in Chapter 20. The change that Sornarajah contemplates is the abolition of the investment treaty regime, since '[w]iping the slate clean seems to be the only way forward': M. Sornarajah, *Resistance and Change in the International Law on Foreign Investment* (Cambridge University Press, 2015), 408. However, the changes that have been introduced sustain the regime, albeit in a modified form, strongly suggesting that the global political will that is required for starting a clean slate is lacking.

[66] Denunciation of the ICSID Convention alone will not beget immunity from investor claims. This is because a host State's consent to ICSID arbitration with protected investors over protected investments is located in the applicable investment treaty or in the underlying investment contract. As Bolivia has not terminated its investment treaties that provide for ICSID arbitration after ceasing to be a signatory to the ICSID Convention, investor claims brought under those treaties against Bolivia can be arbitrated under the ICSID Additional Facility Rules, which apply when the respondent State is not a signatory to the ICSID Convention.

Treaty-termination. After Bolivia, Ecuador and Venezuela also denounced the ICSID Convention,[67] Ecuador followed up with the unilateral termination of nine BITs in 2008,[68] established a commission to audit the benefits other investment treaties bring to Ecuador in 2010[69] and tabled a bill to terminate its investment treaty with the United States in 2013.[70] On 16 May 2017, President Correa of Ecuador signed decrees terminating sixteen more BITs, including the one with the United States.[71] Although terminated treaties will continue to apply to investments made prior to the date of termination,[72] Ecuador's objection to investment treaties was plain to see. But barely a week later, on 24 May 2017, Ecuador had a new president and a newfound enthusiasm for investment treaties. It has since drafted a model BIT and is in the process of negotiating and concluding investment treaties based on this model. Despite Ecuador's earlier preference for treaty termination, it appears, for now, to favour treaty reform.

Other countries have also joined the termination bandwagon. Indonesia unilaterally and progressively terminated all its existing BITs starting from 2014, while India began sending out official notices of termination in 2016. Both countries have announced plans to conclude new investment treaties with their former treaty partners. Indonesia expects to release a Model BIT,[73] while the Indian Model BIT, which was published in 2015,

---

[67] See n. 12 above.

[68] 'Denunciation of the ICSID Convention and BITs: Impact on Investor-State Claims', IIA Issues Note No. 2, December 2010, http://unctad.org/en/Docs/webdiaeia20106_en.pdf (accessed 31 July 2020), n. 3.

[69] *Ibid.*

[70] 'Ecuador Seeks to End Investment Treaty Protection with U.S.', 12 March 2013, http://uk.reuters.com/article/ecuador-us-treaty-idUKL1N0C401C20130312 (accessed 31 July 2020).

[71] 'Ecuador Terminates 16 Investment Treaties', 18 May 2017, http://tni.org/en/article/ecuador-terminates-16-investment-treaties (accessed 31 July 2020).

[72] Termination clauses in investment treaties normally provide that treaty protection will continue to apply to existing investments for a period of 10 to 15 years after the date of unilateral termination of the treaty. One example is Art. 14 of the Agreement between the Government of the Republic of Finland and the Government of the Republic of Ecuador on the Promotion and Protection of Investments (signed 18 April 2001, entered into force 16 December 2001), unilaterally terminated by Ecuador on 9 December 2010:

    (1) This Agreement shall enter into force on the thirtieth day following the date of the latter notification where the Contracting Parties communicate each other in writing that the relevant constitutional requirements for the entry into force of this Agreement have been fulfilled. The Agreement shall remain in force for a period of ten years. Unless official notice of termination is given twelve months before the expiry of its period of validity, this Agreement shall be tacitly extended on the same terms for further periods of ten years.

    (2) In respect of such investments made prior to the date when the notice of expiration of this Agreement becomes effective, the provisions of Articles 1 to 13 shall remain in force for a period of ten years from the date of termination.

Investments made on or before 9 December 2010 will continue to benefit from treaty protection until 9 December 2020. It is therefore possible for a State to face treaty claims years after unilaterally terminating the treaty. Alternatively, all treaty parties can agree to terminate the treaty with immediate effect. For an overview of the implications of investment treaty termination, see T. Voon and A. Mitchell, 'Denunciation, Termination and Survival: The Interplay of Treaty Law and International Investment Law' (2016) 31(2) *ICSID Review – FILJ* 413.

[73] It was previously reported that the 'draft model BIT is scheduled to be finalised and proposed in 2016': see 'What Is Going on with Indonesia's Bilateral Investment Treaties?', 13 June 2016, http://gbgindonesia.com/en/main/legal_updates/what_is_going_on_with_indonesia_s_bilateral_investment_treaties.php (accessed 31 July 2020).

has already attracted commentary.[74] South Africa announced its intention to unilaterally terminate all existing BITs in 2013, reassuring foreign investors of adequate protection under South African legislation. Shortly after the first edition of this book was published, the Protection of Investment Act entered into force in South Africa. This piece of national legislation, which sets out standards of foreign investment protection that are compatible with South Africa's constitution, is designed to replace BITs.[75] And as the second edition of this book goes into press, the South African treaty termination process is still ongoing.

In 2013, Argentina, the respondent State to the highest number of claims in the ICSID's docket, announced its intention to denounce the ICSID Convention.[76] This announcement seemed to pave the way for the termination of Argentina's investment treaties, in the same vein as Ecuador. However, the fact that neither denunciation of the ICSID Convention nor termination of existing investment treaties have come to pass for Argentina suggests that treaty termination is not experiencing a domino effect. Sporadic withdrawal creates cracks in the investment treaty regime, but it takes mass withdrawal to shatter it.

Systemic bias. As more investors brought and prevailed on treaty claims against States, were awarded substantial damages by arbitral tribunals and actively publicised their victory, the suspicion that arbitral tribunals seemed to favour investors over States, or more specifically investors from developed States over those from developing States, grew.

However, the two leading empirical studies undertaken to test the suspicion disagree on the existence of systemic bias. Franck's 2009 study, which examines outcomes in investment treaty arbitration, suggests that there is no direct correlation between the developmental status of a respondent State and the outcome of the dispute.[77] In contrast, van Harten's 2012 study, which examines interpretive trends in arbitral awards, suggests that there is perceptible bias on the part of tribunals in favour of investors from developed States.

[74] See https://dea.gov.in/sites/default/files/ModelBIT_Annex_0.pdf (accessed 31 July 2020); G. Hanessian and K. Duggal, 'The 2015 Indian Model BIT: Is this Change the World Wishes to See?' (2015) 30(3) *ICSID Review – FILJ* 729; J. Coleman and K. Gupta, 'India's Revised Model BIT: Two Steps Forward, One Step Back?', http://ccsi.columbia.edu/files/2017/10/Investment-Claims_-India%E2%80%99s-Revised-Model-BIT_-Two-Steps-Forward-One-Step-Back_.pdf (accessed 31 July 2020).

[75] Act No. 22 of 2015, Official Gazette, Vol. 606, No. 39514.

[76] 'Argentina in the Process of Quitting from World Bank Investment Disputes Centre', 31 January 2013, http://en.mercopress.com/2013/01/31/argentina-in-the-process-of-quitting-from-world-bank-investment-disputes-centre (accessed 31 July 2020). Shortly before this announcement, the United States suspended Argentina as a beneficiary developing country under the Generalized System of Preferences (GSP) program of the World Trade Organization, in retaliation for its non-compliance with two ICSID awards, namely: *CMS Gas Transmission Co.* v. *Argentina*, ICSID Case No. ARB/01/8, Award, 12 May 2005 (Orrego Vicuña, Lalonde, Rezek); and *Azurix Corp.* v. *Argentina*, ICSID Case No. ARB/01/12, Award, 14 July 2006 (Sureda, Lalonde, Martins). The GSP program enables developed countries to accord non-reciprocal preferential treatment to developing countries of their choosing. According to the Presidential Memoranda issued by the White House, Argentina will no longer benefit from preferential treatment under the GSP program 'because it has not acted in good faith in enforcing arbitral awards in favor of US owned companies': see B. Obama, 'Presidential Memoranda – Trade Act of 1974 Argentina', 26 March 2012, www.whitehouse.gov/the-press-office/2012/03/26/presidential-memoranda-trade-act-1974-argentina (accessed 31 July 2020). This incident reveals that participation in the investment treaty regime may turn out to be costly for some countries, not only in terms of the sizeable monetary payout to a prevailing investor, but also in terms of a defaulting country's political capital.

[77] This finding was reiterated in an updated study: see S. D. Franck and L. E. Wylie, 'Predicting Outcomes in Investment Treaty Arbitration' (2015) 65 *Duke LJ* 459, 520–521.

S. D. Franck, 'Development and Outcomes of Investment Treaty Arbitration' (2009) 50(2) *Harvard ILJ* 435, 487–488 (footnotes omitted)

The statistical analyses consistently showed that, at a general level, the outcome of investment treaty arbitration was not reliably associated with the development status of the respondent state, the development status of the presiding arbitrator, or some interaction between those two variables.

The notion that outcome is not associated with arbitrator or respondent development status should be a basis for cautious optimism. It provides evidence about the integrity of arbitration and casts doubt on the assumption that arbitrators from developed states show a bias in terms of arbitration outcomes or that the development status of respondent states affect [*sic*] such outcomes. It suggests that major structural overhaul may not be necessary because it is not clear that arbitration is inherently predisposed towards particular outcomes.

The lack of a reliable relationship between development status and outcome suggests that other variables or combinations of variables may drive arbitration results. Some of these variables may be completely disassociated from the arbitration process. Possible variables could include those traditionally associated with neutral, adjudicative forums, whether courts, claims, commissions, or arbitrations, such as the quality of expert evidence, the nature and scope of legal representation, and submissions by amicus curiae. Other variables affecting results may, however, be intrinsically tied to arbitration, such as the qualities and experiences of arbitrators. Future research might usefully assess the impact of these and other variables in order to gain a more nuanced understanding of factors that are reliably associated with outcome. This could inform decisions about creating processes for managing investment treaty-related conflict.

G. van Harten, 'Arbitrator Behaviour in Asymmetrical Adjudication: An Empirical Study of Investment Treaty Arbitration' (2012) 50 *Osgoode Hall Law Journal* 211, 214, 216 (footnotes omitted)

The study is based on a systematic content analysis of all publicly available awards (i.e., decisions) dealing with jurisdictional matters in 140 known cases under investment treaties until May 2010. The awards were coded for resolutions by the arbitrators of a series of legal issues of jurisdiction and admissibility that were contested in existing awards or secondary literature. The coded data were used to test three hypotheses developed based on theoretical expectations about arbitrator interests arising from the system's structure. Two significant tendencies were observed. The first was a strong tendency toward expansive resolutions that enhanced the compensatory promise of the system for claimants and, in turn, the risk of liability for respondent states. The second was an accentuated tendency toward expansive resolutions where the claimant was from a Western capital-exporting state. This accentuated tendency was present on a statistically significant basis in cases brought by claimants from the United Kingdom, the United States, and France – with cases brought up by German claimants as a possible exception – and was supported by additional analyses of other groupings associated with Western capital-exporting states. It was most apparent in cases under a bilateral investment treaty (BIT) or the Energy Charter Treaty (ECT), for certain jurisdictional issues, and for resolutions by frequently appointed arbitrators.

...

The study found evidence of systemic bias in the case-by-case resolution by arbitrators of disputed issues of investment treaty law. If the system is meant to provide an impartial and independent adjudicative process based on principles of rationality, fairness, and neutrality, then the interpretation and application of the law should reflect a degree of evenness between claimants and respondent states in the resolution of contentious legal issues arising from ambiguous treaty texts and should be free from significant variation based on claimant nationality. However, in the resolution of the coded issues overall, arbitrators tended to favour claimants in general and claimants from major Western capital-exporting states in particular. These tendencies, especially in combination, give tentative cause for concern and provide a basis for further study and reflection on the system's design, not least because the use of investment treaty arbitration appears to be a relatively recent phenomenon.

Arbitrator appointments.[78] Closely tied to the perception of systemic bias are the predispositions, if any, of the arbitrators who are appointed to hear and decide investment treaty claims. As the number of arbitral awards multiplied and entered the public domain, it became apparent that some individuals are in high demand as arbitrators and sit on many panels. A few prominent arbitrators have developed reputations for being investor-friendly, while others come across as State-friendly. How an arbitrator leans (real or imagined) may affect the outcome of the dispute. And if a select group of individuals are repeatedly appointed to hear investment treaty disputes, there is a strong possibility that their views on how the law should be or should develop becomes the final word on what the law is and how it will develop.

In 2014, Puig published a study that mapped the degrees of connectivity between arbitrators in investment treaty disputes, showing that investment treaty arbitration is dominated by a small, highly interconnected group of 'power-brokers'. Puig's findings, which are backed by empirical data, point to a serious and disturbing diversity deficit in the investment treaty regime, which has become a cause for concern.

---

[78] See further discussion at Chapter 7.

S. Puig, 'Social Capital in the Arbitration Market' (2014) 25(2) *EJIL* 387, 403–405 (footnotes omitted)

A close look at the survey of appointments shows that 419 different arbitrators sat on ICSID tribunals and ad hoc Committees during the period analysed. However, more than half of the individuals were appointed only to a single proceeding. What is more extreme is that 10 per cent of the total pool accounts for half of the appointments.

...

Professor Stern (French) has the highest number of appointments. Her record of 48 appointments – 44 times by states – may give some insights into her political preferences. This trend of appointment by one type of litigant, more commonly observed among 'progressive' arbitrators, contrasts sharply with that of Charles N. Brower (American). Like Stern, Judge Brower accumulates an impressive record of 25 appointments. However, a reputation as a 'conservative' (or 'pro-investment', as Judge Brower would probably say) may be deduced from his 23 appointments by claimants. One decision exemplifies the potential issues that result from this growing ideological divide.

...

The size of the core of the arbitration network is small. What stands out, however, is that around 93 per cent of all the appointments are of male arbitrators, suggesting an extreme gender imbalance. It gets even worse: only two women, Professors Stern and Kaufmann-Kohler combined, held three-quarters of all female appointments, pushing the male–female composition of arbitrators in the network to an embarrassing 95 per cent to 5 per cent proportion.

In terms of nationality, the imbalance is also clear. While 87 nationalities are represented among the appointees, most arbitrators are from specific developed countries. Individuals of seven nations (New Zealand, Australia, Canada, Switzerland, France, the UK, and the US) represent almost half of total appointments. Of course, nationality requirements of arbitrators, litigation patterns, and the global trends of FDI may be implicated in this trend.

Close to 15 per cent of the appointments are of arbitrators of five Latin-American countries. This is in part thanks to the high number of appointments of single arbitrators such as Professor Orrego-Vicuña (Chilean), Eduardo Silva Romero (Colombian), Rodrigo Oreamuno (Costa Rican), Claus von Wobeser (Mexican), and Horacio Grigera (Argentinian). A quick look at the background of this sub-group of arbitrators indicates the importance of having a law degree from schools in England, France, or the US for developing a pedigree as an international arbitrator. With the exception of Oreamuno (the former First Vice-President of Costa Rica), all of them obtained an additional graduate degree in one of these countries.

3.2 Changes in the Investment Treaty Regime

The appearance of cracks elicited a number of responses from sovereign and private actors in the investment treaty regime. The key changes that have been proposed or put into action are as follows.

Treaty renegotiation, renewal. Although it has been implied that the addition of regulatory carve-outs and exceptions to investment treaties may be superfluous since general international law already recognises the right of States to regulate,[79] more States appear to favour precision over laconicism.[80] States like India who are terminating their investment treaties with a view to renegotiation, and who have published a Model BIT in recent years, are clearly hoping to base negotiations on a treaty template that bears little resemblance to the archetypal BIT of the 1990s. Newer generation investment treaties are more detailed than their predecessors, and may be construed as an attempt by States to assert interpretive control over the content and scope of their treaty obligations.[81] The contrast is illustrated by the FET and FPS clauses in the 1997 Agreement between the Government of the Republic of Croatia and the Government of Canada for the Promotion and Protection of Investments (Croatia–Canada BIT),[82] and their equivalents in the 2016 EU–Canada Comprehensive Economic and Trade Agreement (CETA) investment chapter to which both Canada and Croatia are parties.[83]

Croatia–Canada BIT, Art. II(2)

2. Each Contracting Party shall accord investments or returns of investors of the other Contracting Party
   (a) fair and equitable treatment in accordance with principles of international law, and
   (b) full protection and security.

CETA, Art. 8.10

1. Each Party shall accord in its territory to covered investments of the other Party and to investors with respect to their covered investments fair and equitable treatment and full protection and security in accordance with paragraphs 2 through 7.

---

[79] *Philip Morris Brands Sàrl and Others* v. *Uruguay*, ICSID Case No. ARB/10/7, Award, 2 July 2013 (Bernadini, Born, Crawford), para. 301. Articulating the right to regulate in investment treaties may even be counter-productive for States since the scope and manner of exercise of this right are now subject to textual constraints: see D. Davitti, J. Ho, P. Vargiu and A. Yilmaz, 'COVID-19 and the Precarity of International Investment Law', 6 May 2020, https://medium.com/iel-collective/covid-19-and-the-precarity-of-international-investment-law-c9fc254b3878 (accessed 31 July 2020).

[80] UNCTAD, 'World Investment Report 2015 – Reforming International Investment Governance', 24 June 2015, http://unctad.org/en/PublicationsLibrary/wir2015_en.pdf (accessed 31 July 2020), pp. 110–113.

[81] This was the approach of the European Commission (EC) in the abandoned negotiations over the TTIP between the European Union and the United States. In its position paper, the EC expressed confidence in the ability of 'clear and precise drafting of the substantial obligations' and 'a specific article on the right to regulate to guide the interpretation of tribunals' to counter perceived or feared investment over-protection in investment treaty arbitration: 'European Commission Services' Position Paper on the Sustainability Impact Assessment in Support of Negotiations of the Transatlantic Trade & Investment Partnership between the European Union and the United States of America', 31 March 2017, http://trade.ec.europa.eu/doclib/docs/2017/march/tradoc_155462.pdf (accessed 31 July 2020), p. 16. In view of the US' withdrawal from the Paris Climate Agreement, which was announced by President Trump on 1 June 2017, the Council of the European Union authorised a reopening of negotiations between the EU and the US with a much narrower scope than that for the TTIP, namely, the elimination of tariffs for industrial goods: see 'Council Decision authorising the opening of negotiations with the United States of America for an agreement on the elimination of tariffs for industrial goods', 9 April 2019, www.consilium.europa.eu/media/39180/st06052-en19.pdf (accessed 31 July 2020).

[82] Signed 3 February 1997, entered into force 30 January 2001.

[83] Signed 30 October 2016, not yet in force.

2. A Party breaches the obligation of fair and equitable treatment referenced in paragraph 1 if a measure or series of measures constitutes:
    (a) denial of justice in criminal, civil or administrative proceedings;
    (b) fundamental breach of due process, including a fundamental breach of transparency, in judicial and administrative proceedings;
    (c) manifest arbitrariness;
    (d) targeted discrimination on manifestly wrongful grounds, such as gender, race or religious belief;
    (e) abusive treatment of investors, such as coercion, duress and harassment; or
    (f) a breach of any further elements of the fair and equitable treatment obligation adopted by the Parties in accordance with paragraph 3 of this Article.
3. The Parties shall regularly, or upon request of a Party, review the content of the obligation to provide fair and equitable treatment. The Committee on Services and Investment, established under Article 26.2.1(b) (Specialised committees), may develop recommendations in this regard and submit them to the CETA Joint Committee for decision.
4. When applying the above fair and equitable treatment obligation, the Tribunal may take into account whether a Party made a specific representation to an investor to induce a covered investment, that created a legitimate expectation, and upon which the investor relied in deciding to make or maintain the covered investment, but that the Party subsequently frustrated.
5. For greater certainty, 'full protection and security' refers to the Party's obligations relating to the physical security of investors and covered investments.
6. For greater certainty, a breach of another provision of this Agreement, or of a separate international agreement does not establish a breach of this Article.
7. For greater certainty, the fact that a measure breaches domestic law does not, in and of itself, establish a breach of this Article. In order to ascertain whether the measure breaches this Article, the Tribunal must consider whether a Party has acted inconsistently with the obligations in paragraph 1.

Additionally, some recent treaties, such as the Indian Model BIT, refer to investor obligations and urge investors to be socially responsible corporate citizens.[84] These changes signal an awareness that both State and investor conduct merit scrutiny for propriety in the context of investment protection.[85] It remains to be see whether newer generation investment treaties can repair the cracks caused by States withdrawing from the investment

---

[84] Arts 11, 12.
[85] The turn to investor responsibility, away from the traditionally State-centric model of accountability in investment treaties, adds a substantive dimension to treaty renegotiation and renewal. For a critique on this aspect of substantive reform to the investment treaty regime, and whether investment treaties are suitable vehicles for reform, see J. Ho et al., 'Investor Responsibility: The Next Frontier in International Investment Law' (2019) *AJIL Unbound Symposium* 1–37; J. Ho, 'Hustling in International Economic Law', 21 February 2020, www.afronomicslaw.org/2020/02/21/hustling-in-international-economic-law/ (accessed 31 July 2020).

treaty regime and perceptions of systemic bias. But the emergence of these treaties shows that more States prefer to advance with a more detailed vision of investment protection through investment treaties than to turn back the clock to diplomatic protection, or retreat into the familiar province of domestic law.

Transparency. Investor–State disputes that raise issues relating to natural resource exploitation, public spending on public services and infrastructure, environmental conservation, protection of public health, and even observation of human rights, command significant public interest. Some disputes, like the challenge launched by tobacco giant Philip Morris against Australia's plain packaging rules, and by nuclear firm Vattenfall against Germany's phasing out of nuclear energy development, receive extensive coverage in mainstream media.[86] Other disputes become public knowledge when reported by specialist news agencies, or when the disputing parties consent to the publication of the award(s) rendered by the tribunal, with or without redactions. And yet other disputes, as well as their outcomes, remain confidential. Although confidentiality is prized by parties choosing to arbitrate their dispute before an international tribunal over litigating in domestic courts, it seems fitting that the level of public interest generated by investor–State disputes should be complemented by a heightened level of public access to documents on the record. Greater transparency in the arbitral process invites greater public scrutiny and public awareness, making it much harder, given the potential public backlash, for bias in decision-making to take root or flourish.

In 2013, the General Assembly adopted the UN Commission on International Trade Law Rules on Transparency in Treaty-based Investor–State Arbitration (UNCITRAL Rules on Transparency), promising enhanced public access to the arbitral process.[87] Articles 2 to 8 of this document prescribe the conditions for public access to information during the course of arbitral proceedings, and make provision for third parties to the dispute, such as non-governmental organisations or other interested organisations, to make submissions to the tribunal. Two of the more notable provisions are Article 3, which allows the public to procure documents filed by the parties to the dispute, and Article 6, which grants the public access to hearings. The UNCITRAL Rules on Transparency were applied for the first time, with the consent of the disputing parties, in *Iberdrola SA and Another* v. *Bolivia*, whose outcome is pending.[88] They have also been adopted in the CETA,[89] and credited as the model for the transparency provisions in the Comprehensive and Progressive Agreement for Trans-Pacific Partnership (CPTPP).[90]

---

[86] *Philip Morris Asia Ltd* v. *Australia*, PCA Case No. 2012–12, Award on Jurisdiction and Admissibility, 17 December 2015; *Vattenfall AB and Others* v. *Germany*, ICSID Case No. ARB/09/6, Award, 11 March 2011 (Lalonde, Berman, Kaufmann-Kohler).

[87] GA Res. 68/109, 16 December 2013. The UNCITRAL Rules on Transparency came into effect on 1 April 2014. Signatory States to the UNICTRAL Rules on Transparency wishing to apply the Rules to investments treaties concluded before 1 April 2014 can ratify the UN Convention on Transparency in Treaty-Based Investor-State Arbitration, GA Res. 69/116 (signed 10 December 2014, entry into force 18 October 2017).

[88] PCA Case No. 2015–05 (Sepúlveda-Amor, García-Valdecasas, Bottini).

[89] CETA, Art. 8.36.

[90] TPP signed 4 February 2016, CPTPP incorporating TPP signed 9 March 2018, entered into force 30 December 2018, Art. 9.24.

Alternatives and adjustments to investor–State arbitration. Concerns over the legitimacy of the investment treaty regime which is animated by investor–State arbitration have led some States to reconsider the wisdom of allowing investors to submit treaty claims to arbitral tribunals. The three proposed alternatives replace or supplement investor–State arbitration with judicial processes.

First, Australia announced in a Trade Policy Statement in 2011 that it will no longer conclude treaties providing for investor–State arbitration.[91] This promise was borne out in the Agreement between Australia and Japan for an Economic Partnership (Australia–Japan EPA),[92] which offers protected investors access to domestic courts and tribunals only.[93] However, other Australian investment treaties concluded after 2011 provide for investor–State arbitration, making the 2011 policy announcement less categorical than first impressions may suggest.[94]

Australia–Japan EPA, Art. 14.6

1. Each Party shall with respect to investment activities in its Area accord to investors of the other Party treatment no less favourable than that it accords in like circumstances to its own investors or investors of a non-Party, with respect to access to its courts of justice and administrative tribunals and agencies.
2. Paragraph 1 does not apply to treatment provided to investors of a non-Party pursuant to an international agreement concerning access to courts of justice or administrative tribunals, or judicial cooperation agreements.

Second, the European Union and some of its recent treaty partners like Canada, Singapore and Vietnam have replaced ad hoc investor–State arbitration with an ad hoc 'investment tribunal system' in their respective investment treaties. This two-tiered dispute resolution system comprises a first instance 'tribunal' and an 'appellate tribunal', whose judges will be appointed by the Contracting States.[95] The appellate tribunal can correct

---

[91] Australian Government Department of Foreign Affairs and Trade, 12 April 2011, www.dfat.gov.au (accessed 31 July 2020). This policy changed in 2013, see A. D. Mitchell et al, *Regulatory Autonomy in IEL* (EE, 2017) 176.

[92] Signed 8 July 2014, entered into force 15 January 2015.

[93] The Protocol of Cooperation and Intra-MERCOSUR Investment Facilitation, signed by Argentina, Brazil, Paraguay and Uruguay on 7 April 2017, also does not provide for recourse to investor–State arbitration. Instead, investors can bring their claims before domestic courts, or have their claims reviewed by a Joint Commission for suitability prior to submission to State-to-State arbitration. See D. Charlotin and L. E. Peterson, 'Analysis: In New MERCOSUR Investment Protocol, Brazil, Uruguay, Paraguay and Argentina Radically Pare Back Protections, and Exclude Investor-State Arbitration', www.iareporter.com/articles/analysis-in-new-mercosur-investment-protocol-brazil-uruguay-paraguay-and-argentina-radically-pare-back-protections-and-exclude-investor-state-arbitration/ (accessed 31 July 2020).

[94] Korea–Australia Free Trade Agreement (signed 8 April 2014, entered into force 12 December 2014), Art. 11.16; China–Australia Free Trade Agreement (signed 17 June 2015, entered into force 20 December 2015), Art. 9.12; CPTPP, Art. 9.19; Peru–Australia Free Trade Agreement (signed 12 February 2018, entered into force 11 February 2020), Art. 8.20; Australia–Hong Kong Investment Agreement (signed 26 March 2019, entered into force 17 January 2020), Art. 24.

[95] CETA Arts 8.27–8.28; EU–Singapore Investment Protection Agreement (15 October 2018), Arts 3.09–3.10; Vietnam-EU Investment Protection Agreement (signed 30 June 2019, not yet in force), Arts 3.38–3.39.

the first instance tribunal's erroneous interpretation of the treaty, in the same way that an appellate court corrects defective legal findings of a lower court. The objective of this partial judicialisation of investor–State dispute settlement is to ensure consistency in the interpretation of a given treaty's investment protection standards.

CETA, Arts 8.27 and 8.28

Article 8.27 Tribunal of First Instance ('Tribunal')

1. The Tribunal established under this Section shall decide claims submitted pursuant to Article 8.23.
2. The CETA Joint Committee shall, upon the entry into force of this Agreement, appoint fifteen Members of the Tribunal. Five of the Members of the Tribunal shall be nationals of a Member State of the European Union, five shall be nationals of Canada and five shall be nationals of third countries.
3. The CETA Joint Committee may decide to increase or to decrease the number of the Members of the Tribunal by multiples of three. Additional appointments shall be made on the same basis as provided for in paragraph 2.
4. The Members of the Tribunal shall possess the qualifications required in their respective countries for appointment to judicial office, or be jurists of recognised competence. They shall have demonstrated expertise in public international law. It is desirable that they have expertise in particular, in international investment law, in international trade law and the resolution of disputes arising under international investment or international trade agreements.

   ...

Article 8.28 Appeal Tribunal

1. An Appellate Tribunal is hereby established to review awards rendered under this Section.
2. The Appellate Tribunal may uphold, modify or reverse a Tribunal's award based on:
   (a) errors in the application or interpretation of applicable law;
   (b) manifest errors in the appreciation of the facts, including the appreciation of relevant domestic law;
   (c) the grounds set out in Article 52(1) (a) through (e) of the ICSID Convention, in so far as they are not covered by paragraphs (a) and (b).
3. The Members of the Appellate Tribunal shall be appointed by a decision of the CETA Joint Committee at the same time as the decision referred to in paragraph 7.

   ...

5. The division of the Appellate Tribunal constituted to hear the appeal shall consist of three randomly appointed Members of the Appellate Tribunal.

   ...

7. The CETA Joint Committee shall promptly adopt a decision setting out the following administrative and organisational matters regarding the functioning of the Appellate Tribunal:

   (a) administrative support;

   (b) procedures for the initiation and the conduct of appeals, and procedures for referring issues back to the Tribunal for adjustment of the award, as appropriate;

   (c) procedures for filling a vacancy on the Appellate Tribunal and on a division of the Appellate Tribunal constituted to hear a case;

   (d) remuneration of the Members of the Appellate Tribunal;

   (e) provisions related to the costs of appeals;

   (f) the number of Members of the Appellate Tribunal; and

   (g) any other elements it determines to be necessary for the effective functioning of the Appellate Tribunal.

Third, the European Union and its recent treaty partners have also pledged to establish a 'multilateral investment tribunal and appellate mechanism' with 'other trading partners'.[96] The projected replacement of multiple treaty-specific investment courts with a single multilateral investment court will presumably, after accounting for consequential textual differences, standardize the interpretation of various investment protection standards across treaties, ensuring both consistency and stability in the development of international investment law.

CETA, Art. 8.29

The Parties shall pursue with other trading partners the establishment of a multilateral investment tribunal and appellate mechanism for the resolution of investment disputes. Upon establishment of such a multilateral mechanism, the CETA Joint Committee shall adopt a decision providing that investment disputes under this Section will be decided pursuant to the multilateral mechanism and make appropriate transitional arrangements.

'Resistance and change' has brought the investment treaty regime to the crossroads of rejection and reform. Cracks in the regime appear in the form of treaty termination, the lingering perception of systemic bias and the inadvertent creation of an elite club of arbitrator-lawmakers. This has lent credence to calls to abandon a system which has intruded too deeply and has cost States too dearly in respect of the exercise of sovereign powers. However, the reformists outnumber the dissenters, striving to improve a flawed system rather than forsaking it altogether. The switch from laconicism in older generation treaties to precision in newer generation treaties, while less momentous for those minded to respect a State's right to regulate, is both a crucial reminder and an attempted defence of sovereignty. Moreover, the push for greater transparency in and the judicialisation of investor–State disputes, be it through limiting investor recourse to domestic courts or through instituting ad hoc or multilateral investment

---

[96] CETA, Art. 8.29; EU–Singapore IPA, Art. 3.12; Vietnam–EU IPA, Art. 3.41.

courts, represents serious attempts to address the legitimacy deficit that investor–State arbitration has incurred.

CONCLUSION

The periods of creation, proliferation and adjustment undergone by investment treaties define their metamorphosis. The investment treaties of today have evolved from brief accords containing a rudimentary framework for investment protection into complex agreements detailing the form and substance of investment protection. The evolution of investment treaties compels a corresponding evolution in the investment protection regime that derives from and is sustained by the existence of these treaties.

From 1959 to 1990, investment treaties were a novel step that a number of States took in the direction of economic betterment through foreign investment protection. The relatively smooth passage and entry into force of the ICSID Convention also marked widespread endorsement among States for the settlement of investor–State disputes through arbitration. From the 1990s to 2007, promises regarding foreign investments were, on the one hand, being made at a rapid rate in more investment treaties, while being tested, on the other hand, in the pioneering batch of investment claims. The outcomes of treaty-testing, which include expansive and conflicting interpretations of treaty obligations, and substantial payouts to investors, alarmed some States. Sporadic denunciation of the ICSID Convention and unilateral terminations of investment treaties followed.[97] The investment regime was facing a legitimacy crisis. From 2007 onwards, episodes of crisis escalation, such as empirical proof of systemic dysfunction, were countered by proposals for crisis management, such as the adoption of the UNCITRAL Rules on Transparency and the replacement of investor–State arbitration with investor–State judicial settlement.

The investment treaty regime, as it stands today, brims with uncertainty. Most States appear committed to the idea that investment treaties have a role to play in encouraging the inward flow of foreign capital. That commitment is particularly evident in States like India and Indonesia, which are terminating existing investment treaties to make way for new ones. The discernible preference among States for tweaking rather than withdrawing

---

[97] The recent decision of a majority of EU Member States to terminate intra-EU investment treaties, on the basis that such treaties and their provision for investor–State arbitration conflict with EU law, should be viewed in light of the EU's ongoing support for ad hoc two-tiered investment tribunals and a multilateral investment court in investment treaties concluded with non-EU States: see Agreement for the Termination of Bilateral Investment Treaties Between the Member States of the European Union (signed 5 May 2020, not yet in force), https://ec.europa.eu/info/sites/info/files/business_economy_euro/banking_and_finance/documents/200505-bilateral-investment-treaties-agreement_en.pdf and 'EU text proposal for the modernisation of the Energy Charter Treaty (ECT)', 29 May 2020, https://trade.ec.europa.eu/doclib/docs/2020/may/tradoc_158754.pdf (accessed 31 July 2020). As the second edition of this book goes into press, it seems likelier that the termination of intra-EU investment treaties will pave the way for the creation of an intra-EU multilateral investment court, either by conclusion of a new investment treaty between Member States or by amendment of an existing EU treaty. It would therefore be incautious to isolate and construe this episode of mass investment treaty termination as a confirmation of the EU's categorical rejection of investment treaties or withdrawal from the investment treaty regime.

completely from the investment treaty regime portends what is to come. This regime is a work-in-progress.

QUESTIONS

1. What are some possible reasons for States continuing to negotiate and conclude investment treaties, notwithstanding the tenuous link between a country's investment treaty commitments and its attraction to foreign investors (Brazil only has a handful of investment treaties currently in force, while South Africa continues to attract foreign investment), and the high cost that comes with investment treaties (Argentina being a case in point)?

2. Conflicting interpretations of similar or identical treaty obligations are a necessary by-product of investor–State arbitration because there is no binding precedent among arbitral awards. Discuss.

3. Investment treaties contain the language of political compromise. For example, the ICSID Convention does not define an 'investment' because Contracting States failed to reach consensus on this point. A treaty is thus the sum of its stipulations and non-stipulations. Is recourse to the canons of treaty interpretation in Articles 31 and 32 of the Vienna Convention on the Law of Treaties sufficient for verifying the intent of the Contracting States, or more specifically, the contours and content of their political compromise towards investment protection?

4. Consider the UNCITRAL Rules on Transparency discussed in Section 3.2. What are the potential costs to conducting an otherwise confidential investor–State arbitration along the lines of public interest litigation?

5. Consider the CETA proposal to judicialise investor–State dispute settlement through the creation of a two-tier first instance and appellate tribunal discussed in Section 3.2. Are you persuaded that these proposals can correct the perception or proven problem of bias in decision-making and arbitrator selection, or represent a superior alternative to classic investor–State arbitration? If so why, and if not, why not?

SUGGESTIONS FOR FURTHER READING

1. J. Bonnitcha, L. N. S. Poulsen and M. Waibel, *The Political Economy of the Investment Treaty Regime* (Oxford University Press, 2017), especially Chapter 1.
2. M. Sornarajah, *Resistance and Change in the International Law on Foreign Investment* (Cambridge University Press, 2015).
3. J. W. Salacuse, *The Law of Investment Treaties* (Oxford University Press, 2015).
4. A. Parra, *The History of ICSID*, 2nd edn (Oxford University Press, 2017).
5. J. Paulsson, 'Arbitration without Privity' (1995) 10(2) *ICSID Review – FILJ* 232.

4

Investment Dispute Settlement

CHAPTER OUTLINE

This chapter discusses the evolution and basis of investment arbitration against the backdrop of other means of investment dispute settlement. The introduction revisits the varieties of investment dispute settlement, of which investment arbitration is only one. Section 1 goes on to explain the notion of 'arbitration without privity'. It is that which makes non-contractually-based investment arbitration, such as treaty-based investment arbitration, distinctive. According to this idea, a claim may be brought by an investor even absent a contractual relationship between the investor and the host State. Section 2 continues this discussion by exploring the different ways in which consent to arbitration may be expressed, and the requirement that such consent should be expressed in writing. Section 3 deals with varieties of treaty clauses which provide for investment treaty arbitration, namely fork-in-the-road clauses, as well as other procedural preconditions. We continue with Section 4, which discusses the complication of contractual forum selection clauses which may exist alongside a claimant's option to choose investment arbitration – for example, contractual clauses which may choose a different means from arbitration altogether, such as those which evince the selection of a domestic court system. Finally, for the sake of completeness, Section 5 discusses inter-State (as opposed to investor–State) investment dispute settlement, with a hopefully useful summary at the end of that section. Section 6 offers – as a practical matter – a brief discussion of some of the factors which may affect the choice between ICSID and non-ICSID arbitration. It does not seek to replace more detailed comparisons in other parts of this book, but is simply intended at this juncture to draw the issue to the reader's mind.

INTRODUCTION

Recall Chapter 1. The subject of investment dispute settlement is, and ought to be, broader than investment arbitration. For decades, from around the 1950s to the 1980s, there was no effective means of adjudicating investment disputes, domestically or internationally. It was not investment arbitration which filled that gap, but the international negotiation of lump-sum settlements. Other international means of settling investment claims throughout the twentieth century included special claims commissions or tribunals, as well as State-to-State international adjudication and arbitration. Thus, the claims arising from the Mexican Revolution were addressed by a US–Mexican claims commission, while those arising from the Russian Revolution were principally addressed through diplomatic settlement. In modern times, US and Iranian claims resulting from the Iranian Revolution, which included investment claims, were settled before the Iran–US Claims Tribunal. Claims against Iraq, including investment claims, were submitted to a specialised international claims facility called the UN Compensation Commission, an ad hoc committee of the UN Security Council.[1] Some investment claims were brought before the International Court of Justice. *Barcelona Traction* and *ELSI* were two well-known inter-State, as opposed to investor–State, investment cases which were brought before the International Court of Justice.[2]

1. INVESTMENT ARBITRATION AS A PRINCIPAL MEANS OF SETTLEMENT TODAY

1.1 An Unusual Feature in Investment Arbitration

Today, investment arbitration is the principal means, and certainly the most prominent method, for settling investment disputes. An unusual feature of much investment arbitration is commonly the absence of a contractual submission to arbitration, although contractually based investment arbitration exists alongside it. In addition to a contractual agreement to arbitrate, investment arbitration may proceed from the fact that a State has stipulated in a law, treaty or investment authorisation, or any other document, that it consents to an investment claim being brought, irrespective of the fact that the investor and the host State may have no prior contract between them containing an arbitration clause.[3] Thus, depending also upon the law applying to the arbitration – typically requiring only that the disputing parties have consented in writing to submit a dispute to arbitration – a host State's legislative, treaty-based or other written 'consent' becomes perfected the moment the claimant submits a written notice of arbitration. This ex-contractual form of arbitration was most famously dubbed 'arbitration without privity' by Jan Paulsson. Steingruber adds: 'In investment arbitration there is – possibly – not only no privity, but in most cases a dissociation in the timing when consent to arbitration is expressed by the State party and the investor.'[4] Another feature is a common asymmetry of rights and

---

[1] See Chapter 1, Section 1 of this book.

[2] *Case Concerning Barcelona Traction, Light and Power Co., Ltd (Belgium v. Spain)* [1970] ICJ Rep. 3; *Elettronica Sicula SpA (ELSI) (USA v. Italy)* [1989] ICJ Rep. 15.

[3] In a sense, the question of form does not matter, as there is no universal legal definition of arbitration as such, for it is a creature of antiquity which has developed in a dynamic fashion over time. What matters is the autonomy of the parties' will – so-called 'party autonomy'. See A. M. Steingruber, *Consent in International Arbitration* (Oxford University Press, 2012), 11–12, and further, 25 et seq.

[4] *Ibid.*, 26. Another way of describing all this, as Dolzer and Stevens have, is by calling the State's consent 'advance consent', or by looking to the existence of a 'unilateral standing offer to arbitrate'; Steingruber, *Consent in International Arbitration*.

obligations; while the investor can initiate a claim under this method, the State typically or generally cannot do so.[5]

This is not to say that investment arbitration cannot be based upon a contractual submission to arbitration where there is coincidence in time of consent to arbitration and even symmetry in respective rights and obligations. Indeed, as we saw in Chapter 1, the idea that 'investment arbitration' only emerged in its full splendour in the 1990s is in a sense false. Even where that is certainly true of 'investment treaty arbitration', it is not true of investment contract arbitration which, as with international commercial arbitration, is based upon an agreement to arbitrate in a contract. Investment contract arbitration has had a longer history than investor treaty arbitration.[6]

Be that so, it is what Paulsson calls 'arbitration without privity' which makes investment arbitration unusual and notably distinct from international commercial arbitration. While this chapter focuses on investment arbitration, more specifically investment treaty arbitration because it has become the principal means today for settling investment disputes, it also serves as a reminder that investment arbitration cannot be viewed in isolation. There is currently fierce debate about whether alternative means of dispute settlement ought to be reinvigorated in light of some of the controversies surrounding investment arbitration today. That would include adjudication by judges, but as we have seen in Chapter 1, that was where the problem had begun, historically at least. The search for an effective means of settling investment disputes began as a search for an alternative to 'national' judges, arguably not only because of the risk of national bias, but also because of the risk of a different sensibility which may be precisely the sensibility sought in a return to some form of adjudicative mechanism.[7]

1.2 'Arbitration without Privity'

Here is Paulsson in his own words. The following extract illustrates, too, how commercial arbitration and investment arbitration can arise as separate, concurrent options.

---

[5] Steingruber, *Consent in International Arbitration*, 26–27. On host State counterclaims, a chief difficulty is that BITs typically provide only for claims against the host State for host State violations, even accepting that different BITs are worded differently and that remedy of this limitation is being sought in some newer BITs as a part of the broader reform of BITs worldwide (on which see Chapter 20 of this book). See, e.g., *Oxus Gold Plc* v. *Uzbekistan*, UNCITRAL, Final Award, 17 December 2015, paras 906–959, esp. 944–958 on Art. 21(3) of the UNCITRAL Arbitration Rules, as well as jurisdiction over counterclaims in the event of a close connection with the claimant's claim. The *Oxus Gold* Award also discusses *Saluka Investments BV* v. *Czech Republic*, UNCITRAL, Partial Award of 17 March 2006, paras 61, 76 and *Paushok* v. *Mongolia*, UNCITRAL, Award on Jurisdiction and Liability of 28 April 2011, paras 689, 693 among others, as well as *Spyridon Roussalis* v. *Romania*, ICSID Case No. ARB/06/1, Award, 7 December 2011 – on which see also the forceful dissent of Professor W. Michael Reisman: *ibid.*, Declaration by W. Michael Reisman, 28 November 2011, invoking Article 46 of the ICSID Convention as *Spyridon* was an ICSID arbitration.

[6] In addition to *Texaco* v. *Libya*, 19 January 1977, 17 ILM 1, discussed at length in Chapter 1 of this book, see also *Petroleum Development Ltd* v. *Sheikh of Abu Dhabi* (1951) 18 ILR 144; *Ruler of Qatar* v. *International Marine Oil Co.* (1953) 20 ILR 534; *Saudi Arabia* v. *Arabian American Oil Co.* (1958) 27 ILR 117; *Sapphire International Petroleums Ltd* v. *National Iranian Oil Co.* (1963) 35 ILR 136.

[7] On the current proposal of the European Union to create a multilateral investment court, see Chapter 20 of this book.

Jan Paulsson, 'The Pyramids Case' in *Collected Courses of the International Academy for Arbitration Law, Year 2012*, vol. 1, at 1 (2014), 1, 6–7, 10–11, 17–18, 20

I will tell you a story about a single international dispute which was resolved in a way which changed the world of arbitration.

...

The parties were SPP (the investor), on the one hand, and, on the other, the State of Egypt and EGOTH (the Egyptian General Organization for Tourism and Hotels), a State agency. The Government signed through its Minister of Tourism. The Heads of Agreement contemplated the creation of a joint venture company, fifty-fifty. That was in September 1974. A detailed agreement was then negotiated over the months that followed, and in December 1974 the final Joint Venture Agreement was concluded. It was indeed the first private foreign investment approved under the famous Law No. 43, and the Agreement specifically so stated.

...

On the Egyptian side there is also a shareholder, and it is not going to be the State; the State does not do that. We have separate State-owned organs that take shareholdings in commercial ventures. We are not going to have three shareholding parties.

Over the next couple of years, as I said, the project ran into political hot water. The Government was criticized for having agreed to these contracts. Ultimately the President concluded that the project had become too much of a controversy, and unfortunately must be cancelled.

...

Now what exactly was I to do 'to sue Egypt?' The final agreement, the December Agreement, the one which the Minister signed as 'agreed, approved, ratified' but not as a party, had an ICC clause. That clause certainly bound EGOTH. But it was not EGOTH that had cancelled the project. As SPP's joint venture partner, EGOTH adopted the position that: 'we too are sorry that our project has been cancelled, but the Government is responsible, not us.' Now, one might imagine seeking to hold EGOTH liable on some theory that it had given a warranty that the project was and would remain officially authorized, but who knows how that would work?

And if one won, would EGOTH be good for the money? You would certainly want to sue the Government too. And that is what SPP did, suing the Government and EGOTH as twin defendants, relying on the substantive unity of the two agreements and the three famous words – 'agreed, approved, ratified' – under which the Minister had signed the December Agreement.

So off we went to ICC arbitration with three arbitrators.

...

In the end, the award of the ICC tribunal was handed down against the Government, while EGOTH was absolved of liability ... the Tribunal found that EGOTH was just like SPP, powerless either to cancel the project or resist it. So force majeure worked as a defence for EGOTH, but obviously not for the Government. That was the decision, and the damages were fixed at $12.5 million dollars, with $730,000 dollars' worth of costs after half a decade of arbitral proceedings.

...

Egypt appealed. You might object that there is no appeal against arbitration awards. That is usually so, but not with respect to an issue of jurisdiction, just as though there might be an issue of violation of a fundamental rule of procedure or corruption of an arbitrator. Obviously such things may justify a challenge to the award. Of course the issue of the meaning of the Minister's signature was a matter of jurisdiction with respect to which the arbitrators' own conclusion was unlikely to be definitive; a judicial authority may feel it had the role of verifying whether the Egyptian State as an entity had indeed given valid consent to the very arbitrators who had purported to decide that question in the affirmative. The place of arbitration was Paris, and under French law the challenge to the award accordingly came before the Court of Appeal of Paris.

...

... sadly for SPP and deeply disappointingly for me, the Court of Appeal of Paris annulled the award because its judges did not believe that the Egyptian Minister's signature meant what the ICC arbitrators had said it meant. I saw the logic; if the Court of Appeal of Paris has the right to review jurisdictional decisions, it must be allowed to do that in a plenary way; and if the judges of that Court had a different opinion than that of the arbitrators, so be it. But why did they have to reach a different conclusion? They had not heard the testimony of Mr Gilmour, who had appeared for many hours before the arbitral tribunal and explained the negotiations of this particular document. That factual evidence had clearly persuaded the arbitrators. The Paris Court, to the contrary, had heard no witnesses at all and had decided on the basis of the papers before it. They were not interested in what we would today call 'jurisdictional facts', but rather affirmed the abstract view that the Minister's signature had been given only in his supervisory capacity, as what the French know as EGOTH's *autorité de tutelle*.

Well, what do I do now?

...

I had been reading this Egyptian Foreign Investment Law, Law No. 43, for five years now, and knew its substantive provisions by heart. But there was also an Article 8, which referred to the resolution of disputes. I had not really focused on it before, because the December Agreement contained the ICC clause which we had relied on successfully – until we came to the Paris Court. Article 8 established that any dispute between an investor and the State could be decided in one of four ways. Follow me now! This is key to the whole story: (1) by a complaint to the Egyptian courts; or (2) in a manner agreed between the investor and the State; or (3) in accordance with the terms of an agreement between the State of Egypt and the home State of the investor; or (4) under the ICSID Rules. For half a decade, we had been taking the position that we were under alternative (1): a specific agreement to go to the ICC. But Egypt had rejected that proposition, and now the French Court had agreed with Egypt. So – this is the beginning of the idea – let us look down the list. Having been disappointed by a promise of compensation made by the Prime Minister himself, SPP was in no frame of mind to have this controversial case heard in the Egyptian courts; the goal of arbitration in these circumstances, as famously explained by none other than the prominent Egyptian international lawyer Ibrahim Shihata, was to 'depoliticize' investment disputes by providing for a neutral international forum. So that got me thinking about alternative (3), an agreement between the investor's home State and Egypt. SPP was a Hong Kong corporate entity. There was indeed a Bilateral Investment Treaty between the United Kingdom and Egypt. Sure enough, it stipulated that in the event of a dispute as to whether the host State had respected its undertakings pursuant to the Treaty, the unhappy investor could go to arbitration. But did this treaty involving the UK extend to the UK's overseas territories? The answer turned out to be: to some, but not to others. So I had to look further. Too bad for SPP and for me: the UK had not extended this treaty to Hong Kong.

There was only one lifeboat left in the sea: alternative (4), ICSID arbitration. At that time, 1984, ICSID was known only to specialists and scholars ... The Centre had dealt with only three cases since its creation in 1965. So there were hardly any decided cases available for study, but there was much literature, technical and obscure, about how it functioned, including a number of articles written by ICSID's first Secretary-General Aron Broches, who was considered to be the father of ICSID (he had chaired the deliberations on every continent as the ICSID treaty – the Washington Convention of 1965 – was negotiated). Mr. Broches kept repeating the same thing. I saw the same sentence again and again: agreements to ICSID jurisdiction may be expressed by States in contracts – or alternatively in treaties or in laws. In laws! The investor cannot create a law, so this must be a law of the host State, expressing consent to arbitration. How exactly might an aggrieved investor rely on this consent? By accepting that expression of consent, I reckoned, as though it were an offer to the investor which becomes irrevocable as of its acceptance.

...

I went to see [Laurie Craig] ... and I explained that I had concluded that we should go to ICSID immediately, without waiting for the expected confirmation of our defeat by the French Supreme Court. Now Mr. Craig had heard of ICSID, but he did not believe that we could go there; so far all ICSID cases had been founded on a clause in an investment contract – never on a treaty or on a law. So I explained my theory, but he said, 'That's not arbitration. Arbitration is an agreement by which either side can make a claim against the other. Egypt could not sue SPP, so how can you say there is an arbitration agreement?' Now, sometimes ignorance can help, because you do not realise that what you are thinking has never been done, so you just keep questioning conventional assumptions. And indeed I insisted, 'but Mr. Broches says you can'.

The rest is history. *SPP* v. *Egypt*[8] became the first case involving 'privity without contract'.[9] *SPP* was not an investment treaty claim; it was an ICSID claim based upon Egypt's consent to investment arbitration under an Egyptian law. Sornarajah has criticised allowing the claim brought in *SPP* v. *Egypt* as 'the original sin'.

---

[8] *SPP (Middle East) Ltd and Southern Pacific Properties Ltd* v. *Egypt and Another* (ICC Arbitration No. YD/ AS NO 3493), Award, 11 March 1983.

[9] J. Paulsson, 'Arbitration without Privity' (1995) 10 *ICSID Review – FILJ* 232.

M. Sornarajah, *Resistance and Change in the International Law on Foreign Investment* (Cambridge University Press, 2015), 139–141

All arbitration depends on the consent of the parties. Consent provides legitimacy to arbitration. Unlike in the case of a judge the only condition of legitimacy of an arbitrator is the consent of the parties. It defines the extent of the powers of the arbitrators ... Early investment treaties advert to the use of arbitration as the means of settlement of disputes resulting from the alleged violations of their provisions. Some required separate agreements to arbitrate after the alleged violation had taken place. In later treaties, this requirement was dispensed with and the language used indicated that such arbitrations could take place without an intervening agreement on arbitration. The assumption is that an unilateral offer is made as to such arbitration in investment treaties; this offer is subsequently converted to an agreement when the foreign investor accepts that unilateral offer of arbitration through a request for arbitration. This is the explanation given in the different arbitral awards that have assumed jurisdiction on the basis of treaties since *AAPL* v. *Sri Lanka*, the first Award in which the technique was used. The respondent State did not challenge jurisdiction in *AAPL* v. *Sri Lanka*. Jurisdiction was simply assumed, the tribunal observing that the cooling off period in the treaty had passed and that as a result the claimant 'became entitled to institute the ICSID proceedings'. As later explained in *AMT* v. *Zaire* (1997), such jurisdiction is based on the view that the consent that is given need not be in the same Instrument. Usually, consent to arbitration is contained in a single instrument, but this is not a requirement. It could be pieced together in a series of documents. In investment treaty arbitration, a series of instruments – the unilateral offer in the treaty and the recourse to arbitration made by initiation of proceedings – are connected together in creating jurisdiction in a tribunal. Such an explanation is now commonplace. Whenever recourse was had to creating jurisdiction on the basis of treaty provisions, every effort was made to create privity through the process of creating consent through a chain of documents. Alternatively there is an exchange of consents involved in two separate documents: one a treaty expressing the state's consent, and the other the consent of the foreign investor contained in the request for [arbitration]. Later arbitrations assumed that this process was understood whenever recourse was had to an appropriately worded dispute settlement provision of an investment treaty.

...

The term ['arbitration without privity'] sacrifices accuracy for flamboyance.

...

It suggested the use of an unorthodox technique when in fact a rather conventional technique of piecing together different documents to create consent was the explanation

...

The policy justification was that in 'this new world of arbitration', the expansion of arbitral jurisdiction over foreign investment disputes was to be welcomed. The brave new world depended on the processes of globalization, which around that time had come to be spoken of as presaging significant changes.

...

Abaclat v. *Argentina* (2012) represents the most recent and damaging of the arbitral adventures. Its confirmation in *Ambiente Ufficio* v. *Argentina* (2013) compounds the problem.

As Sornarajah has explained, the first investment treaty arbitration award which had resulted from such a unilateral 'offer' contained in a treaty, rather than from an offer contained in a domestic law, was the 1987 Award in *AAPL* v. *Sri Lanka*,[10] a case involving the destruction of a shrimp farm by Sri Lankan Government security forces during an armed incident.

Investment arbitration today is dominated by the idea of such 'investment treaty' arbitration – i.e. where the host State's consent is to be found in a treaty instrument, rather than in national law or contract.[11] That has developed the idea, today, that there can be a unilateral offer to the world to accept mass, previously unidentifiable claims. *Abaclat* v. *Argentina* had raised this question of a mass investment arbitration claim. In *Abaclat*, the majority of the tribunal took the view that:

> it would be contrary to the purpose of the BIT and to the spirit of ICSID, to require in addition to the consent to ICSID arbitration in general, a supplementary express consent to the form of such arbitration. In such cases, consent to ICSID arbitration must be considered to cover the form of arbitration necessary to give efficient protection and remedy to the investors and their investments, including arbitration in the form of collective proceedings.[12]

To show how far the idea has come since, we will need to return to Mr Craig's hesitation in Paulsson's telling of the tale of *SPP* v. *Egypt*:

Jan Paulsson, 'The Pyramids Case' in *Collected Courses of the International Academy for Arbitration Law, Year 2012*, vol. 1, at 1 (2014), 20–21

Mr. Craig remained unconvinced. He pointed out that under 'my' theory Egypt might not even know who could sue it in arbitration; Egypt did not know SPP as a possible respondent for the purposes of arbitration; 'How can this be a one-way street? Have you ever heard of an arbitration where only one party can go to the arbitrators? And just how many arbitrations has Mr. Broches done anyway?' I retorted 'But why not? Once SPP accepts the offer and confirms its own consent, we have an arbitration agreement!' On and on we went, around and around, if my memory serves for several weeks, when at last I thought of a killer argument, which was simply 'So, do you have a better idea what to do now?' Now finally, being a pragmatist, and perhaps tiring of endless and inconclusive debate, he said the magic words: 'All right, young man, you try it.'

[10] *Asian Agricultural Products Ltd* v. *Sri Lanka* (1990), ICSID Case No. ARB/87/3.
[11] See Chapter 3, Section 2 of this book for the proliferation of investment treaties following the first modern bilateral investment treaty between Germany and Pakistan in 1957.
[12] *Abaclat* v. *Argentina*, ICSID Case No. ARB/07/5, Decision on Jurisdiction and Admissibility, 4 August 2011, para. 490. Professor Georges Abi-Saab dissented in *Abaclat*.

2. CONSENT TO INVESTMENT ARBITRATION

2.1 Forms of Consent and Agreement to Investment Arbitration

The notion of 'consent' deserves closer attention. Derived from Paulsson's intellectual breakthrough, the idea had become this. Consent to arbitration need not be contained in a mutual agreement to arbitrate. No arbitration agreement or arbitration clause in a contract need exist. Instead, consent can take many forms or modalities. It may even be contained in an application for investment authorisation or approval.[13] Similarly, it can flow from the host State's 'offer to arbitrate' contained in domestic legislation or in a treaty clause.[14] So long as such consent is subsequently perfected by the investor, the parties will have consented to bind themselves to arbitration. Be it contractually based or treaty-based, the suggestion which had become fully formed was that a claim advanced by an investor is the investor's own. The situation in respect of treaty-based arbitration may be more complicated as it is the home State's treaty with the host State which confers the rights in question upon the home State's investor. Thus, it may be asked if the State really has no remaining legal interest in or 'functional control' over the claim. Arguably, the answer to both is 'no' and the argument has been made at least forcefully.[15]

What is needed is an agreement to arbitrate, but the innovation in the sphere of investment arbitration is that it is unnecessary that such mutual consent or agreement should be contained in a prior binding contractual agreement. In sum, the conceptual breakthrough in Paulsson's *Pyramids* case is that the consent of the host State, directed at the world at large, is 'perfected' when the investor files a notice of or claim for arbitration regardless of the precise instrument in which the host State's 'offer to arbitrate' is contained,[16] provided only that it is in writing. Such mutual consent can also operate cumulatively; for example, where an agreement contains no arbitration clause, but incorporates a BIT which does contain such a clause, it will operate just as effectively when consent is perfected.[17] Of course, nothing prevents consent after the initiation of proceedings under the doctrine of *forum prorogatum*.

In the following extract, Churchill Mining and another company (Planet Mining) became shareholders in PT Indonesia Coal Development (PT ICD), a local Indonesian company which the former had used as a vehicle for their investment in Indonesia. The dispute concerned, in part, the consent to ICSID arbitration by the Indonesian Investment Coordinating Board (BKPM).

---

[13] See, e.g., C. Schreuer, L. Malintoppi, A. Reinisch and A. Sinclair (eds), *The ICSID Convention: A Commentary*, 2nd edn (Cambridge University Press, 2009), 194–195; citing *Amco v. Indonesia*, Decision on Jurisdiction, ICSID Case No. ARB/81/1, 25 September 1983, paras 10, 11, 25. See also *Churchill Mining Plc and Planet Mining Pty Ltd v. Indonesia*, ICSID Case No. ARB/12/14 and 12/40, Decision on Jurisdiction, 24 February 2014, esp. paras 11–13, 116–125, 142–147, 231–238, excerpted below.

[14] The example being the *Pyramids* case, discussed in Section 1.2. See *Southern Pacific Properties (Middle East) Ltd v. Egypt*, ICSID Case No. ARB/84/3, Decision on Jurisdiction and Dissenting Opinion, 14 April 1988, 3 ICSID Rep. 131 (1995).

[15] Z. Douglas, *The International Law of Investment Claims* (Cambridge University Press, 2009), 10 et seq., esp. 19.

[16] Schreuer *et al.*, *The ICSID Convention*, 202–203, 211–214, and the examples of awards cited therein.

[17] Even if the BIT itself has not yet entered into force. See *Ceskoslovenska Obchodni Banka AS v. Slovakia*, ICSID Case No. ARB/97/4, 24 May 1999, esp. paras 4, 49–55.

Churchill Mining Plc and Planet Mining Pty Ltd v. **Indonesia**, ICSID Case No. ARB/12/14 and 12/40, 24 February 2014 (Gabrielle Kaufmann-Kohler, President; Michael Hwang; Albert Jan van den Berg), paras 11–13, 116–125, 142–147, 231–238 (footnotes omitted, emphasis added)

11. On 23 November 2005, the Indonesian Investment Coordinating Board ('BKPM') delivered an authorization to PT Indonesian Coal Development ('PT ICD') to be incorporated as an Indonesian foreign direct-investment company (a so-called 'PMA') and to conduct business in the mining sector in Indonesia (the '2005 BKPM Approval'). PT ICD was initially created by Profit Point Group Ltd, a company incorporated in the British Virgin Islands, and Mr. Andreas Rinaldi, an Indonesian citizen and co-founder of the Ridlatama group. The authorized capital of PT ICD is Rupiah ('Rp.') 2,512,500,000, divided into 250,000 shares, with a nominal value of Rp. 10,050 per share. Profit Point Group Ltd acquired 237,500 shares and Mr. Andreas Rinaldi 12,500 shares.

12. According to the 2005 BKPM Approval, PT ICD could engage in general mining supporting services, i.e., 'consultancy in relation to business planning for construction of building and other facilities in the domain of general mining projects'.

13. Section IX(4) of the 2005 BKPM Approval contains a dispute settlement clause making reference to ICSID arbitration in the following terms:

> 'In the event of dispute between the company and the Government of the Republic of Indonesia which cannot be settled by consultation/deliberation, the Government of Indonesia is prepared/ready to follow settlement according to provisions of the convention on the settlement of disputes between States and Foreign Citizen regarding investment in accordance with Law Number 5 Year 1968'.

14. On 28 December 2005, PT ICD's articles of association received approval from the Indonesian Ministry of Law and Human Rights.

...

233. Section IX(4) of the 2005 BKPM approval, as translated by the Claimant, reads as follows:

> 'In the event of a dispute between the company and the Government of the Republic of Indonesia that cannot be resolved by consensus, the Government of Indonesia *[is] willing to follow* the settlement according to the provisions of the Convention on the settlement of disputes between States and Foreign Citizen regarding investments in accordance with Law Number 5 Year 1968.'

234. Indonesia's version reads:

> 'In the event of dispute between the company and the Government of the Republic of Indonesia which cannot be settled by consultation/deliberation, the Government of Indonesia *is prepared/ready to follow* settlement according to the provisions of the convention on the settlement of disputes between States and Foreign Citizen regarding investments in accordance with Law Number 5 Year 1968.'

235. In its original wording, Section IX(4) reads as follows:

'Dalam hal terjadi perselisihan antara perusahaan dengan Pemerintah Republik Indonesia yang tidak dapat diselesaikan secara musyawarah, Pemerintah Indonesia *bersedia mengikuti* penyelesaian menurut ketentuan konvensi tentang penyelesaian perselisihan antara Negara dan Warga Negara Asing mengenai penanaman modal sesuai dengan Undang-undang Nomor 5 Tahun 1968.'

236. The 2006 BKPM Approval, sanctioning the acquisition of PT ICD by Churchill and Planet incorporates by reference the content of the 2005 Approval.

237. Indonesia has essentially objected that (i) the BIT only contemplates the possibility to grant consent after the filing of a request of arbitration, (ii) that the BKPM lacks authority to grant consent to ICSID arbitration, (iii) that the word bersedia in Section IX(4) of the 2005 BKPM approval merely denotes a willingness to consider ICSID procedures, not consent, and (iv) that Section IX(4) only extends to PT ICD and not its shareholders.

238. The Tribunal finds these objections ill-founded. First, as regards the timing of consent, Article 7(1) of the BIT contains no language precluding a host State from granting its consent to ICSID arbitration prior to the filing of a dispute by an investor. Second, the Tribunal finds that the words bersedia mengikuti, correctly translated as 'readiness/ preparedness/willingness to follow' the settlement provisions of the ICSID Convention, are an expression of consent satisfying the ICSID requirement of consent in writing. Third, the Tribunal holds that Section IX(4) extends to PT ICD's shareholders because (i) PT ICD is a mere instrumentality of the Claimant, who had no choice but to structure its investment through a local vehicle, (ii) the dictionary on record does not translate the word perusahaan as company or corporation, but gives it the broader meaning of business or enterprise, (iii) the word perseroan is employed in the 2005 BKPM Approval when specifically targeting PT ICD as a corporation, while the word perusahaan is used in various contexts suggesting that it has a broader meaning, in particular in the 2006 BKPM Approval in the context of the obligation to sell shares of PT ICD to Indonesian nationals. Finally, the Tribunal is of the view that the BKPM has the power to grant consent to ICSID arbitration, since it is a government body reporting directly to the President and vested with authority to handle foreign investments. Had the President, who was copied on the 2005 BKPM Approval, deemed that the BKPM had overstepped its authority, then he would or should have intervened to rectify such mistake. Having failed to do so, Indonesia cannot now argue that the BKPM lacked authority to give consent to ICSID proceedings.

2.2 The Writing Requirement

Article 25, paragraph 1, of the ICSID Convention, reproduced below, illustrates the writing requirement under the Convention. The New York Convention, upon which reliance will have to be placed for enforcement, other than in the case of an ICSID arbitration, also stipulates a 'writing requirement'. Indeed, such a requirement is expected to be found in the rules of various arbitral institutions in the case of non-ICSID institutional arbitration.[18] It is also likely to be a requirement for a court to enforce an agreement to arbitrate. In that regard, the UNCITRAL Model Law, upon which arbitration laws in some seventy-two States have been based, is also reproduced below.

Convention on the Settlement of Investment Disputes between States and Nationals of Other States, 18 March 1965, 17 UST 1270, TIAS 6090, 575 UNTS 159, Art. 25

(1) The jurisdiction of the Centre shall extend to any legal dispute arising directly out of an investment, between a Contracting State (or any constituent subdivision or agency of a Contracting State designated to the Centre by that State) and a national of another Contracting State, which the parties to the dispute consent in writing to submit to the Centre. When the parties have given their consent, no party may withdraw its consent unilaterally.

(2) 'National of another Contracting State' means:

 (a) any natural person who had the nationality of a Contracting State other than the State party to the dispute on the date on which the parties consented to submit such dispute to conciliation or arbitration as well as on the date on which the request was registered pursuant to paragraph (3) of Article 28 or paragraph (3) of Article 36, but does not include any person who on either date also had the nationality of the Contracting State party to the dispute; and

 (b) any juridical person which had the nationality of a Contracting State other than the State party to the dispute on the date on which the parties consented to submit such dispute to conciliation or arbitration and any juridical person which had the nationality of the Contracting State party to the dispute on that date and which, because of foreign control, the parties have agreed should be treated as a national of another Contracting State for the purposes of this Convention.

(3) Consent by a constituent subdivision or agency of a Contracting State shall require the approval of that State unless that State notifies the Centre that no such approval is required.

(4) Any Contracting State may, at the time of ratification, acceptance or approval of this Convention or at any time thereafter, notify the Centre of the class or classes of disputes which it would or would not consider submitting to the jurisdiction of the Centre. The Secretary-General shall forthwith transmit such notification to all Contracting States. Such notification shall not constitute the consent required by paragraph (1).

Notice that under paragraph 4, such consent may be limited in scope. An example was the Chinese notification that only disputes over quantum (i.e. the amount of compensation) are submitted to ICSID arbitration. Earlier Chinese treaties, as with many socialist-style BITs, typically limited the scope of submission to ICSID jurisdiction in this way. Disputes concerning such clauses have, however, produced a conflicting body of jurisprudence.[19]

---

[18] See, e.g., Art. 2 of the rules of the Australian Centre for International Commercial Arbitration (ACICA).

[19] See, e.g., *Saipem v. Bangladesh*, ICSID Case No. ARB/05/7, Decision on Jurisdiction, 21 March 2007; *Telenor Mobile Communications AS v. Hungary*, ICSID Case No. ARB/04/15, Decision on Jurisdiction, 13 December

Convention on the Recognition and Enforcement of Foreign Arbitral Awards, 10 June 1958 ('New York Convention'), 330 UNTS 38 (1959), 21 UST 2517, 7 ILM 1046 (1968), Art. II

1. Each Contracting State shall recognize an agreement in writing under which the parties undertake to submit to arbitration all or any differences which have arisen or which may arise between them in respect of a defined legal relationship, whether contractual or not, concerning a subject matter capable of settlement by arbitration.
2. The term 'agreement in writing' shall include an arbitral clause in a contract or an arbitration agreement, signed by the parties or contained in an exchange of letters or telegrams.
3. The court of a Contracting State, when seized of an action in a matter in respect of which the parties have made an agreement within the meaning of this article, shall, at the request of one of the parties, refer the parties to arbitration, unless it finds that the said agreement is null and void, inoperative or incapable of being performed.

UNCITRAL Model Law on International Commercial Arbitration, 1985, with Amendments as Adopted in 2006, 64th plenary meeting, 4 December 2006[20]

Option I
Article 7. Definition and form of arbitration agreement
(As adopted by the Commission at its thirty-ninth session, in 2006)
(1) 'Arbitration agreement' is an agreement by the parties to submit to arbitration all or certain disputes which have arisen or which may arise between them in respect of a defined legal relationship, whether contractual or not. An arbitration agreement may be in the form of an arbitration clause in a contract or in the form of a separate agreement.
(2) The arbitration agreement shall be in writing.
(3) An arbitration agreement is in writing if its content is recorded in any form, whether or not the arbitration agreement or contract has been concluded orally, by conduct, or by other means.

2006; *Czech Republic* v. *European Media Ventures* [2007] EWHC 2851; *Tza Yap Shum* v. *Peru*, ICSID Case No. ARB/07/6, Decision on Jurisdiction and Competence, 19 June 2009; *Sanum Investments Ltd* v. *The Government of Laos*, Award on Jurisdiction, PCA Case No. 2013–13, 13 December 2013; *Sanum Investments Ltd* v. *Government of Laos* [2016] SGCA 57; but cf. *Berschader* v. *Russia*, SCC Case No. 080/2004, Award, 21 April 2006; *Rosinvest UK Ltd* v. *Russia*, SCC Case No. V079/2005, Award, October 2007.

[20] Previously, Art. 7(2) stated a 'writing' requirement similar to that in Art. II(2) of the New York Convention. It is now presented by UNCITRAL as 'Option 2', following the 2006 amendments. As can be seen, Option 2 omits any requirement as to form, and omits the 'writing' requirement. 'Option 1' retains the 'writing' requirement in the old Art. 7(2) (new Art. 7(2)). However, it now expressly allows the content of the agreement to be 'recorded in any form, whether or not the arbitration agreement or contract has been concluded orally, by conduct, or by other means' (new Art. 7(3)), electronic communications (new Art. 7(4)), exchanges of statements of claim and defence to constitute 'writing' (new Art. 7(5)), and reference in a contractual clause 'to any document containing an arbitration clause' to constitute 'writing' (new Art. 7(6)).

(4) The requirement that an arbitration agreement be in writing is met by an electronic communication if the information contained therein is accessible so as to be useable for subsequent reference; 'electronic communication' means any communication that the parties make by means of data messages; 'data message' means information generated, sent, received or stored by electronic, magnetic, optical or similar means, including, but not limited to, electronic data interchange (EDI), electronic mail, telegram, telex or telecopy.

(5) Furthermore, an arbitration agreement is in writing if it is contained in an exchange of statements of claim and defence in which the existence of an agreement is alleged by one party and not denied by the other.

(6) The reference in a contract to any document containing an arbitration clause constitutes an arbitration agreement in writing, provided that the reference is such as to make that clause part of the contract.

Option II
Article 7. Definition of arbitration agreement
(As adopted by the Commission at its thirty-ninth session, in 2006)

'Arbitration agreement' is an agreement by the parties to submit to arbitration all or certain disputes which have arisen or which may arise between them in respect of a defined legal relationship, whether contractual or not.

Similarly, a BIT may contain a writing requirement.

Limitations in the host State's offer to arbitrate, such as in Chinese and other socialist-style BITs discussed earlier, are also related to the topic in Chapter 5 of this book. Suffice to say that most-favoured-nation (MFN) clauses, through which a wider submission to jurisdiction may be alleged, notwithstanding a clause which limits submission of disputes to arbitration only to disputes concerning 'either the amount or payment of compensation', may be upheld.[21] Bolder attempts may be made to import a host State's consent to investment treaty arbitration under a BIT into another BIT containing no such offer at all, *via* an MFN clause which requires treatment given by the host State under the BIT to be no less favourable than that given to any other treaty partner. Such broad attempts to invoke an MFN clause are probably likely to fail.[22]

3. *ELECTA UNA VIA* ('FORK-IN-THE-ROAD') CLAUSES, 'NO U-TURN' CLAUSES AND OTHER PROCEDURAL PRECONDITIONS

3.1 Dispute Clauses and Procedural Preconditions

BITs commonly contain a whole list of arbitration options. The different arbitration options also often present a choice of ICSID and ad hoc arbitration, often stating that in the case of ad hoc arbitration the UNCITRAL Arbitration Rules will apply.[23] In other cases,

---

[21] *Rosinvest UK Ltd* v. *Russia*, SCC Case No. V079/2005, Award, October 2007.

[22] See *Plama* v. *Bulgaria*, ICSID Case No. ARB/03/24, Decision on Jurisdiction, 8 February 2005. For MFN clauses, see Chapter 13 of this book.

[23] These are model rules which therefore avoid the need to devise arbitration rules for the conduct of proceedings afresh.

a list of arbitral institutions may be named (e.g. the Regional Arbitration Centres of Cairo or Kuala Lumpur,[24] the International Arbitration Institute of the Stockholm Chamber of Commerce, and so on).[25] What might go into a choice of ICSID or non-ICSID, such as ad hoc, investment arbitration is discussed in Section 6, below.

For now, we come instead to the subject of preconditions. One possible procedural precondition to arbitration is a requirement for amicable consultations, negotiations and mediation beforehand. There may be a requirement for the exhaustion of local remedies too, or at least a requirement that there ought to be resort to local remedies for a duration (i.e. a waiting or 'cooling-off' period) regardless of whether the claimant would simply do no more than go through the motions if it has to.[26] Another is a BIT fork-in-the-road clause.[27] Typically, a fork-in-the-road clause will require choice of one dispute resolution means to preclude another for fear of the creation of parallel proceedings, the latter being a subject discussed in more detail in Chapter 5 of this book. Exhaustion of local remedies, fork-in-the-road clauses and 'no U-turn' clauses deserve some introduction in this chapter, if only to avoid any initial confusion.

3.2 Exhaustion of Local Remedies

The essential idea behind the doctrine that local remedies should, first, be exhausted is to afford the host State an opportunity and the courtesy of itself redressing the wrong alleged. The doctrine is typically expressed with the in-built flexibility that an exception ought to be made where resort to local remedies would be futile. That, at least, is the position under customary or general international law. It may be that a similar requirement under bilateral investment treaties is increasingly rare, but compare the 2018 US–Mexico–Canada Agreement (USMCA) which imposes what in effect is a treaty local remedies rule.[28] What is common is a stipulation that there should be resort to local remedies at least for a minimum duration, and USMCA stipulates 30 months, for example. In *Swissbourgh Diamond Mines (Pty) Ltd* v. *Kingdom of Lesotho*,[29] failure to exhaust local remedies was seen, perhaps unusually, to deprive the tribunal of jurisdiction rather than to make the claim merely inadmissible.[30]

---

[24] It is interesting, particularly in light of the historical differences between developing post-colonial nations and the Western industrialised nations, to note that Cairo and Kuala Lumpur are regional centres established under the auspices of the Asian–African Legal Consultative Organisation and were therefore developing country creations.

[25] C. McLachlan QC, L. Shore and M. Weiniger, *International Investment Arbitration: Substantive Principles* (Oxford University Press, 2007), 47 and the discussion of various model forms of BIT clauses therein.

[26] See, generally, G. Born and M. Šćekić, 'Pre-Arbitration Procedural Requirements: "A Dismal Swamp"' in D. D. Caron, S. W. Schill, A. Cohen Smutny and E. E. Triantafilou (eds), *Practising Virtue: Inside International Arbitration* (Oxford University Press, 2015), 227.

[27] J. Billiet, *International Investment Arbitration: A Practical Handbook* (Antwerp: Maklu, 2016), 184.

[28] 30 November 2018, revised 10 December 2019, Annex 14-D, para. 5(1)(b).

[29] *Swissbourgh Diamond Mines (Pty) Ltd and Others* v. *Kingdom of Lesotho* [2018] SGCA 81. Compare the dissent of Roberts CJ (with whom Kennedy J concurred) in *BG Group v. Republic of Argentina*, 134 SCt (2014) 1198. *Contra*: *Hochtief v. The Argentine Republic*, ICSID Case No. ARB/03/31, Decision on Jurisdiction, 24 October 2011, paras 90–91. See further, Saar A. Pauker, 'Admissibility of Claims in Investment Treaty Arbitration' (2018) 34 *Arb Int'l* 1.

[30] See further, Chapter 5 of this book.

Swissbourgh Diamond Mines (Pty) Ltd v. Kingdom of Lesotho [2018] SGCA 81 (Sundaresh Menon CJ, Andrew Phang Boon Leong JA, Judith Prakash JA, Tay Yong Kwang JA and Steven Chong JA), paras 205–208.

[Sundaresh Menon CJ (delivering the judgment of the court)]

205. While the requirement for a claimant to exhaust all of its local remedies before submitting its dispute to arbitration is not, as the amici curiae note, a common feature in most investment treaties, it is an express requirement provided for under the relevant treaty instruments here. In this regard, Art 15(2) of the SADC Treaty expressly states that '[n]o natural or legal person shall bring an action against a State unless he or she has exhausted all available remedies or is unable to proceed under the domestic jurisdiction'.

206. More relevantly for present purposes, and as we have noted earlier (at [96] above), Art 28(1) of Annex 1 also provides that investor-State disputes shall be submitted to international arbitration if either party to the dispute so wishes 'after exhausting local remedies'. In our judgment, the inclusion of the requirement that an investor must exhaust his or her local remedies in Art 28(1) as an express pre-condition for the SADC Member State's offer of consent to arbitration under Art 28(1) is significant. The failure of a claimant to exhaust local remedies has traditionally been regarded by international courts as a matter that goes towards the admissibility of the claim, and not the jurisdiction of the tribunal: see Chittharanjan Felix Amerasinghe, *Local Remedies in International Law* (Cambridge University Press, 2nd Ed, 2004) at p 294; see also *The Panevezys-Saldutiskis Railway Case (Estonia v Lithuania)* (1939) PCIJ (ser A/B) No 76 ('*The Panevezys-Saldutiskis Railway Case*') at 22 and *Interhandel Case (Switzerland v United States of America)*, Preliminary Objections [1959] ICJ 6 ('Interhandel Case') at 27. Generally, most investment arbitration tribunals also tend to regard the requirement for investors to exhaust their local remedies as a matter that concerns the admissibility of the claim brought by the investors, given that it is only a temporary obstacle to the exercise of the tribunal's jurisdiction and is a requirement that may be waived: see, for instance, *RosInvestCo UK Ltd v The Russian Federation*, SCC Case No V079/2005, Award on Jurisdiction, 1 October 2007 at [153].

207. Jurisdiction is commonly defined to refer to 'the power of the tribunal to hear a case', whereas admissibility refers to 'whether it is appropriate for the tribunal to hear it': *Waste Management, Inc v United Mexican States*, ICSID Case No ARB(AF)/98/2, Dissenting Opinion of Keith Highet, 8 May 2000 at [58]. To this, Zachary Douglas adds clarity to this discussion by referring to 'jurisdiction' as a concept that deals with 'the existence of [the] adjudicative power' of an arbitral tribunal, and to 'admissibility' as a concept dealing with 'the exercise of that power' and the suitability of the claim brought pursuant to that power for adjudication: Douglas at paras 291 and 310. Finally, in Chin Leng Lim, Jean Ho & Martins Paparinskis, *International Investment Law and Arbitration: Commentary, Awards and other Materials* (Cambridge University Press, 2018) ('Chin Leng Lim'), it is usefully observed that there are two ways of drawing the distinction between jurisdiction and admissibility (at p 118):

> ... The more conceptual reading would focus on the legal nature of the objection: is it directed against the tribunal (and is hence jurisdictional) or is it directed at the

claim (and is hence one of admissibility)? The more draftsmanlike reading would focus on the place that the issue occupies in the structure of international dispute settlement: is the challenge related to the interpretation and application of the jurisdictional clause of the international tribunal (and hence jurisdictional), or is it related to the interpretation and application of another rule or instrument (and is hence one of admissibility)?

208. The conceptual distinction between jurisdiction and admissibility is not merely an exercise in linguistic hygiene pursuant to a pedantic hair-splitting endeavour. This distinction has significant practical import in investment treaty arbitration because a decision of the tribunal in respect of jurisdiction is reviewable by the supervisory courts at the seat of the arbitration (for non-ICSID arbitrations) or before an ICSID ad hoc committee pursuant to Art 52 of the ICSID Convention (for ICSID arbitrations), whereas a decision of the tribunal on admissibility is not reviewable: see Jan Paulsson, 'Jurisdiction and Admissibility' in *Global Reflections on International Law, Commerce and Dispute Resolution, Liber Amicorum in honour of Robert Briner* (Gerald Aksen et al, eds) (ICC Publishing, 2005) at p 601, Douglas at para 307, Waibel at p 1277, paras 257 and 258, Hanno Wehland, 'Jurisdiction and Admissibility in Proceedings under the ICSID Convention and the ICSID Additional Facility Rules' in *ICSID Convention after 50 Years: Unsettled Issues* (Crina Baltag, ed) (Kluwer Law International, 2016) at pp 233–234, and Chin Leng Lim at p 124.

209. But notwithstanding the conventional understanding that the requirement of exhaustion of local remedies pertains to the question of admissibility (as explained at [206] above), it has been observed that 'States may require exhaustion of local remedies as a pre-condition for their consent to arbitration. That it is a pre-condition for consent would make it a jurisdictional requirement and not an admissibility requirement': see Waibel at pp 1283–1284, para 283. Accordingly, given the express inclusion of the exhaustion of local remedies as a pre-condition for the SADC Member State's consent to arbitration under Art 28(1) of Annex 1, we find that any failure on the part of the Appellants to exhaust their local remedies should be taken to be an issue that concerns the jurisdiction of the PCA Tribunal.

The better view may be that much yet may depend upon the proper construction of the treaty clause in question. As for a 'cooling-off' period, that too is seen typically as an issue which goes towards admissibility rather than jurisdiction.[31]

What happens if the BIT requiring a minimum cooling-off or waiting period also contains an MFN clause, and requires a longer period than that required under another BIT entered into by the host State? Can the MFN clause be invoked in order to get around the waiting period? In *Maffezini* v. *Spain*,[32] the tribunal gave an answer in the affirmative.[33]

---

[31] *Hochtief* v. *The Argentine Republic*, ICSID Case No. ARB/03/31, Decision on Jurisdiction, 24 October 2011, paras 90–91.

[32] *Emilio Agustin Maffezini* v. *Kingdom of Spain*, ICSID Case No. ARB/97/7, Decision of the Tribunal on Objections to Jurisdiction, 25 January 2000.

[33] See, further, Chapter 13 of this book.

The challenge for host States which fear being wrong-footed by an MFN clause in relation to such procedural issues is being addressed increasingly in their latest treaties, which seek to preclude the 'Maffezini problem' from arising. Below is an example of such a clause from the China–Japan–Korea Trilateral Investment Treaty of 2012, which is itself an important document as it illustrates the convergence of treaty policies between the three large North East Asian economies.[34]

> **Agreement among the Government of Japan, the Government of the Republic of Korea and the Government of the People's Republic of China for the Promotion, Facilitation and Protection of Investment, 13 May 2012, Art. 4(1) and (3) Most-Favored-Nation Treatment**
>
> 1. Each Contracting Party shall in its territory accord to investors of another Contracting Party and to their investments treatment no less favorable than that it accords in like circumstances to investors of the third Contracting Party or of a non-Contracting Party and to their investments with respect to investment activities and the matters relating to the admission of investment in accordance with paragraph 2 of Article 2.
>
> ...
>
> 3. It is understood that the treatment accorded to investors of the third Contracting Party or any non-Contracting Party and to their investments as referred to in paragraph 1 does not include treatment accorded to investors of the third Contracting Party or any non-Contracting Party and to their investments by provisions concerning the settlement of investment disputes between a Contracting Party and investors of the third Contracting Party or between a Contracting Party and investors of any non-Contracting Party that are provided for in other international agreements.

3.3 'Fork-in-the-Road' Clauses, 'No U-Turn' Clauses and the Problem of Parallel Proceedings

In the treaty context, another potential problem which could arise concerns claimants who might want a second bite at the cherry. Having first brought an ill-fated domestic claim before a municipal court, or even an unsuccessful commercial arbitration claim, the claimant now wishes to bring an investment arbitration claim. Indeed, under the exhaustion of local remedies rule it may be required to bring a municipal claim before a

---

[34] Japan and China are the second and third largest capital exporters in the world today, respectively, the United States being the largest. While the United States' treaty policies are well known and Japan has thus far had surprisingly few treaties, but is expected to conform to the United States' model (as has been shown in the currently moribund Trans-Pacific Partnership Agreement text, for which see now the investment chapter in the Comprehensive and Progressive Agreement for Trans-Pacific Partnership), questions about future Chinese treaty designs abound. Sino–Japanese treaty convergence, coupled with Japanese–American convergence and the now also moribund Sino–US bilateral investment treaty negotiations, suggest still a future possibility – hat of a convergent model between the three largest capital exporting nations in the world. Innovations such as the one discussed below are what observers are seeking out currently.

domestic court either under customary international law (e.g. in a denial of justice claim), under treaty, or indeed under both.

Investment treaties deal with this issue in various ways, but most typically by mandating that a claimant which has elected one procedure has forfeited another, and this could be stated expressly in the treaty. The clause is known as an *electa una via* (or 'fork-in-the-road') clause. A variation of this approach is a 'no U-turn' clause, which requires, as a condition of submitting an investment arbitration claim, the waiver of the right to bring some other claim in another forum. Notice that this latter type of clause applies only when the claimant submits a claim and is, in that sense, prospective. In the case of an *electa una via* clause, consent cannot be perfected despite the unilateral offer of the State to have disputes brought before investment arbitration because the treaty itself limits and conditions this offer. In the case of a 'no U-turn' clause, no claim may be submitted without the necessary waiver of a right to bring a claim elsewhere. However, this latter form does not prevent, and may indeed be used to accommodate, local remedies at least for a period beforehand, since a waiver can be offered subsequently when bringing the investment arbitration claim.

Both examples seek to prevent multiple claims, at least once investment arbitration has been initiated. In both cases, the claimant will either be precluded by treaty from bringing, or would have first been required to waive its right to bring, another set of proceedings elsewhere.

Note that the US Model BIT employs a 'no U-turn' clause. This approach was employed in the Trans-Pacific Partnership Agreement,[35] which the United States had signed under the Obama Administration before its withdrawal by the Trump Administration. A 'no U-turn' clause is also employed in the latest Indian Model BIT of 2015. This, as explained earlier, allows the Indian Model BIT nonetheless to require the exhaustion of domestic remedies, including hearings before the Indian courts, *prior* to bringing an investment treaty claim. In contrast, the China–Japan–Korea Trilateral Investment Treaty (C–J–K TIT) has a variation of an *electa una via* clause, sometimes termed a 'cafeteria-style clause', which lists a number of mutually exclusive means of dispute settlement. This nonetheless allows the treaty to require administrative hearings beforehand; it does so by using an express treaty term which simply excludes administrative hearings from the scope of the clause.[36]

---

[35] Now 'transplanted' to the Comprehensive and Progressive Agreement for Trans-Pacific Partnership (CPTPP) following the United States' withdrawal from the Trans-Pacific Partnership Agreement, which never came into force. See, for example, C. L. Lim, 'Finding a Workable Balance between Investor Protection and the Public Interest in the Trans-Pacific Partnership' in B. Kingsbury, D. Malone, R. B. Stewart and A. Sunami (eds), *Megaregulation Contested: Global Economic Ordering after TPP* (Oxford University Press, 2019), 551, 568. The TPP is not in force and had, prior to the United States' withdrawal, included twelve nations as signatories. It was until then hailed as a model for an Asia–Pacific-wide investment treaty. CPTPP is intended to consist of the remaining eleven members, and though it is in force, that aim, in terms of membership, has not yet been accomplished. At the same time, CPTPP is open to new entrants.

[36] The approach shown here in the C–J–K TIT therefore presents an alternative to the Indian Model BIT. The latter requires court hearings beforehand, which a 'no U-turn' clause would, of course, simply allow. No carve-out of such court proceedings is therefore required.

2012 US Model BIT, Art. 26(2)

2. No claim may be submitted to arbitration under this Section unless:
   (a) the claimant consents in writing to arbitration in accordance with the procedures set out in this Treaty; and
   (b) the notice of arbitration is accompanied,
       (i) for claims submitted to arbitration under Article 24(1)(a), by the claimant's written waiver, and
       (ii) for claims submitted to arbitration under Article 24(1)(b), by the claimant's and the enterprise's written waivers

       of any right to initiate or continue before any administrative tribunal or court under the law of either Party, or other dispute settlement procedures, any proceeding with respect to any measure alleged to constitute a breach referred to in Article 24.

2015 Indian Model BIT, Art. 15

15.5 In the event that the disputing parties cannot settle the dispute amicably, a disputing investor may submit a claim to arbitration pursuant to this Treaty, but only if the following additional conditions are satisfied:

...

   (iii) the disputing investor or the locally established enterprise have waived their right to initiate or continue before any administrative tribunal or court under the law of any Party, or other dispute settlement procedures, any proceedings with respect to the measure of the Defending Party that is alleged to be a breach referred to in Article 13.2.

Agreement among the Government of Japan, the Government of the Republic of Korea and the Government of the People's Republic of China for the Promotion, Facilitation and Protection of Investment, 13 May 2012, Art. 15(3) Settlement of Investment Disputes between a Contracting Party and an Investor of Another Contracting Party

3. The investment dispute shall at the request of the disputing investor be submitted to either:
   (a) a competent court of the disputing Contracting Party;
   (b) arbitration in accordance with the ICSID Convention, if the ICSID Convention is available;
   (c) arbitration under the ICSID Additional Facility Rules, if the ICSID Additional Facility Rules are available;
   (d) arbitration under the UNCITRAL Arbitration Rules; or
   (e) if agreed with the disputing Contracting Party, any arbitration in accordance with other arbitration rules, provided that, for the purposes of subparagraphs (b) through (e):
       (i) the investment dispute cannot be settled through the consultation referred to in paragraph 2 within four months from the date of the submission of the written request for consultation to the disputing Contracting Party; and

(ii) the requirement concerning the domestic administrative review procedure set
out in paragraph 7, where applicable, is met.
Note: For the purposes of subparagraph (a), this paragraph shall not be construed to prevent, where applicable, preliminary trial by administrative tribunals or agencies.

4. CONTRACTUAL FORUM SELECTION CLAUSES

A more specific problem arises where, for example, there are parallel contractual and treaty claims pursued under a contract which grants rights that are closely bound up with treaty rights, but where the contract stipulates commercial arbitration brought by either party, while the treaty grants the investor the treaty right to bring an investment treaty claim. This problem arose, famously, in the *Vivendi* case. Before the tribunal, the concession contract's choice of the Argentine administrative courts in the event of dispute was upheld as the tribunal had considered the alleged treaty breach too closely bound up with the terms of the contract. The Annulment Committee in *Vivendi* reversed this ruling of the tribunal on the basis, as shown below, that a treaty confers an independent treaty right – i.e. a right under international law – and a domestic rule, including a contractual rule, cannot operate such as to deprive an investor of such a right.

Compañia de Aguas del Aconquija SA and Vivendi Universal v. Argentina, ICSID Case No. ARB/97/3, Decision on Annulment, 3 July 2002 (Mr L. Yves Fortier, President; Professor James R. Crawford SC; Professor José Carlos Fernández Rozas), paras 95, 96

95. As to the relation between breach of contract and breach of treaty in the present case, it must be stressed that Articles 3 and 5 of the BIT do not relate directly to breach of a municipal contract. Rather they set an independent standard. A state may breach a treaty without breaching a contract, and vice versa, and this is certainly true of these provisions of the BIT. The point is made clear in Article 3 of the ILC Articles, which is entitled 'Characterization of an act of a State as internationally wrongful':

The characterization of an act of a State as internationally wrongful is governed by international law. Such characterization is not affected by the characterization of the same act as lawful by internal law.

96. In accordance with this general principle (which is undoubtedly declaratory of general international law), whether there has been a breach of the BIT and whether there has been a breach of contract are different questions. Each of these claims will be determined by reference to its own proper or applicable law – in the case of the BIT, by international law; in the case of the Concession Contract, by the proper law of the contract, in other words, the law of Tucumán. For example, in the case of a claim based on a treaty, international law rules of attribution apply, with the result that the state of Argentina is internationally responsible for the acts of its provincial authorities. By contrast, the state of Argentina is not liable for the performance of contracts entered into by Tucumán, which possesses separate legal personality under its own law and is responsible for the performance of its own contracts.

5. THE CALL FOR A RETURN TO ADJUDICATION, AND OTHER INVESTMENT DISPUTE SETTLEMENT BODIES

For the sake of completeness, it is worth emphasising the history of investment dispute settlement, which was discussed in Chapter 1. Contractually based and treaty-based investment arbitration, although popular and dominant today, were not always so, while in the future the field will continue to develop, perhaps in unexpected directions. At present, as Chapter 20 in this book will discuss, the European Union has advocated a return to investment adjudication, albeit investor–State adjudication, which could at least in principle be the next stage of evolution for investment dispute settlement.[37]

The history of the subject shows a sustained experimentation with several devices where each new device borrows or at least learns something from the past. There was diplomatic espousal in the form of diplomatic settlements. Contentious State-to-State third-party dispute settlement may of course take the form of arbitration or adjudication. That most eminent of international arbitral bodies, the Permanent Court of Arbitration, as with other arbitral institutions and the device of ad hoc arbitration, may be resorted to for inter-State disputes in the same way that they are all available to investor–State arbitration.

State-to-State investment dispute settlement today may also take place before the International Court of Justice (ICJ), as it has in the past.[38] The ICJ, unlike national courts, relies – as with arbitration – on consent for its jurisdiction. What makes it a court is that it is permanently established, with permanent judges (as well as ad hoc judges in particular cases). As has been mentioned, there may yet be a return to the idea of international adjudication, albeit that in borrowing and adapting from today's contract-based and treaty-based arbitration, the future may well see a turn to 'mixed', i.e. investor–State, adjudication instead. The idea is not novel. International human rights courts, such as the European Court of Human Rights, have already been involved in the settlement of investment claims.

In contrast, the World Trade Organization, which is said to possess a 'World Trade Court', does not strictly speaking have a court. In principle, panels and the WTO Appellate Body can make only recommendations to the WTO's Dispute Settlement Body, which chooses whether to adopt such reports. WTO panels and the WTO Appellate Body, however, do have a limited role in settling investment-related disputes, through the Trade-Related Investment Measures Agreement (TRIMS) or under the General Agreement on Trade in Services (GATS). This is because the WTO imposes certain limited investment disciplines, such as the TRIMS prohibition of performance and local content requirements – the requirement that investors should meet certain export targets or that they should

---

[37] How effective the European Union's proposal will prove to be remains to be seen. It is at least curious that EU BITs, which had helped to spread the gospel of investment arbitration, are now replacing investment arbitration with the EU's investment adjudication model, on account of the risks presented to sovereign State regulation. To the charge that this had never before been an objection when European BITs imposed investment arbitration on developing nations in order to protect European investment capital abroad, one response is that while developing nations lacked reliable legal systems and courts, Europe is replete with superior systems and courts. Whatever the merits of this retort, the proposal presently is for a multilateral investment court, as opposed to a call to fall back on European national courts. See, further, Chapter 20 of this book.

[38] See Chapter 1 of this book.

source production inputs from local host State suppliers. Another example would be the GATS regulation of services market access and services trade through the establishment of a service provider from Country A in Country B (i.e. through an investment).[39]

6. ICSID VERSUS AD HOC ARBITRATION

Finally, even in the case of investor–State arbitration, there are myriad forms. Ad hoc arbitration has infinite variety, including through the use of the UNCITRAL Arbitration Rules (UNCITRAL Rules) or institutional arbitration under the auspices of one of the well-known or even lesser-known national arbitral institutions, such as the Stockholm Chamber of Commerce, which is popular with claims against Russia. Other options are the London Court of International Arbitration, or the Kuala Lumpur or Cairo Regional Centres of Arbitration, which were established by the Asian–African Legal Consultative Organisation and enjoy the sorts of immunities enjoyed by ICSID arbitration and arbitrations administered by the Permanent Court of Arbitration, that most eminent of international arbitral bodies. The Hong Kong or Singapore international arbitration centres are commonly perceived to be efficient, neutral fora by Far Eastern parties. Since ad hoc arbitration might often employ the UNCITRAL Rules as a convenience, and the rules of the various national institutions may be too varied to be considered within the scope of this book, it may be useful at least to have a sense of the differences between ICSID arbitration, which was discussed in passing in Chapter 1 of this book, and 'UNCITRAL arbitration' (i.e. arbitration under the UNCITRAL Rules, which have been so widely used in the commercial arbitration context).

The extract from Burgstaller and Rosenberg below draws that comparison.

> **Markus Burgstaller and Charles B. Rosenberg, 'Challenging International Arbitral Awards: To ICSID or Not to ICSID?' (2011) 27 *Arb Int'l* 91, 91–93**
>
> ICSID awards are increasingly coming under tighter scrutiny. On the other hand, national courts in 'arbitration friendly' jurisdictions, such as England, France and the United States, appear to be more reluctant to set aside arbitral awards. There may, therefore, be a tendency that the non-ICSID route with the seat of arbitration in an 'arbitration friendly' country is the safer option for a claimant investor.
>
> ...
>
> Claimant investors and their counsel should carefully weigh the advantages and disadvantages of arbitration under the ICSID Convention and other arbitral rules, such as the UNCITRAL Arbitration Rules. Many differences exist between ICSID and UNCITRAL arbitration, including jurisdictional requirements, costs, and the standards for challenging arbitrators. In material terms, probably the most significant difference relates to the annulment or challenge, respectively, of arbitral awards.

[39] Referred to in WTO parlance as the supply of 'mode 3' services through the establishment of a commercial presence of the service supplier in the territory of the host State.

The following extract from *Malaysian Historical Salvors* v. *Government of Malaysia* illustrates the problem with ICSID's 'jurisdictional requirement'.

Malaysian Historical Salvors Sdn Bhd v. Government of Malaysia, ICSID No. ARB/05/10, Award on Jurisdiction, 17 May 2007, paras 75–76, 78, 84, 108, 110–114, 124 (Mr Michael Hwang) (original emphasis)

75. In Salini, the issue was whether a construction contract could be considered as an 'investment' within the meaning of Article 25(1). The Société Nationale des Autoroutes du Maroc ('ADM') was a Moroccan company which built, maintained and operated highways and various road-works, in accordance with a concession agreement (the 'Concession Agreement') concluded with the Minister of Infrastructure and Professional & Executive Training, acting on behalf of Morocco. Within the context of the Concession Agreement, ADM issued an international invitation to tender for the construction of a highway joining Rabat to Fes. The two claimants, Salini Costruttori S.p.A and Italstrade S.p.A, submitted a joint tender for the construction of a 50 km section of this highway. The joint tender was accepted, which led to a contract (the 'Construction Contract') between the two claimants and ADM. The two claimants took 36 months to complete the works, four months longer than stipulated in the Construction Contract.

76. When ADM rejected the claims of the two claimants, the latter sent a memorandum relating to the final account to the Minister of Infrastructure, in accordance with Article 51 of the Cahier des Clauses Administratives Generales (Book of General Administrative Clauses). When the two claimants did not receive any reply, they filed a Request for Arbitration against Morocco with ICSID, claiming Italian lira 132,639,617,409 as compensation for damage suffered.

...

78. The tribunal reiterated that the 'investment' requirement under the ICSID Convention is an objective condition that cannot be diluted by the consent of the parties. The tribunal held that:

> [']The doctrine **generally** considers that <u>investment infers: contributions, a certain duration of performance of the contract and a participation in the risks of the transaction ... In reading the Convention's preamble, one may add the contribution to the economic development of the host State of the investment as an additional condition.</u>
>
> In reality, these <u>various elements may be interdependent</u>. Thus, the risks of the transaction may depend on the contributions and the duration of performance of the contract. <u>As a result, these various **criteria** should be assessed globally even if, for the sake of reasoning, the Tribunal considers them individually here.</u>' (emphasis added)

...

84. ... the tribunal in *Joy Mining* (Professor Francisco Orrego Vicuna as President, Mr. William Laurence Craig and Judge C.G. Weeramantry as co-arbitrators) considered that:

> Summarizing the elements that an activity <u>must have</u> in order to qualify as an investment, both the ICSID decisions mentioned above and the commentators theron [*sic*] have indicated that the project in question <u>should have</u> a certain duration, a regularity of profit and return, an element of risk, a substantial commitment and that it should constitute a significant contribution to the host State's economy. To <u>what extent these criteria are met is of course specific to each particular case as they will normally depend on the circumstances of each case</u>. (emphasis added)...

108. The Tribunal first considers a hallmark of 'investment' cited in *Joy Mining*, which is that there must be regularity of profits and returns. This particular hallmark did not feature in the so-called Salini test, although it is mentioned in Schreuer. There is no regularity of profits and returns on the present facts. However, the Tribunal accepts the Claimant's answer in response, which is that this criterion may not always be decisive.

...

110. The Contract took almost four years to complete. Accordingly, it complies with the minimum length of time of two to five years, as discussed in Salini. However, owing to the nature of the Contract, the Claimant only managed to satisfy this factor in a quantitative sense. The original stipulated duration of the Contract was only for 18 months, which was extended by mutual consent. One might well argue that the Contract was only able to meet the minimum length of time of two years because of the element of fortuity ...

111. The ICSID tribunals in *L.E.S.I.-DIPENTA* and *Bayindir* considered that, in the context of construction contracts, one could take into consideration the time extensions that would often be required in determining whether a contract was an 'investment' within the meaning of Article 25(1). In the Tribunal's view, the key reason for ... allowing time extensions to be considered was motivated by the fact that, in *L.E.S.I.-DIPENTA*, the tribunal suggested that an assessment of the criterion of duration was linked to whether the contract was for an operation that promoted the economy and the development of the host State. Presumably, the longer the duration, the greater the economic commitment. Where the underlying contract does not promote the economy and development of the host State, there may be less justification to factor in the extensions granted under the Contract ...

112. It is not in dispute that all the risks of the Contract were borne by the Claimant. The fact that these risks were not in any way borne by the Respondent would appear to afford a stronger reason to hold that the activity is an 'investment' within the meaning of Article 25(1) as compared to an investment where the risks were shared. However, it has been conceded by counsel for the Claimant that salvage contracts are often on a 'no-finds-no-pay' [*sic*] basis. This would not necessarily mean that all salvage contracts would be an 'investment' within the meaning of Article 25(1), assuming this feature of investment to be the only factor in doubt ...

...

113. Finally, the Tribunal has to consider whether the Contract contributed to the economic development of Malaysia. There appears to be a difference in ICSID jurisprudence as to whether there is a need for a contract to make a significant contribution to the economic development of the host State. The tribunal in Salini considered that there should be a contribution to such economic development without stressing that it must be 'significant.' However, on the facts of that case, it was likely that the tribunal would have formed the view that the contribution was significant. The tribunal in *L.E.S.I.-DIPENTA* took the view that this requirement need not even be considered, because it was implicitly covered in the previous three characteristics of an 'investment.'

114. On the other hand, the tribunal in *Joy Mining* took the view that, to qualify as an 'investment,' the contribution to the economic development of the host State must be 'significant.'

...

124. In unusual situations such as the present case, where many of the typical hallmarks of 'investment' are not decisive or appear to be only superficially satisfied, the analysis of the remaining relevant hallmarks of 'investment' will assume considerable importance. The Tribunal therefore considers that, on the present facts, for it to constitute an 'investment' under the ICSID Convention, the Contract must have made a significant contribution to the economic development of the Respondent.

Mr Hwang's award was annulled.[40] Be that so, the 'Salini test' lingers.[41] Burgstaller and Rosenberg have argued that this 'Salini' problem is avoided altogether outside the ICSID context. The principal argument they have advanced is that it may be advantageous in light of such ICSID annulments for claimants to choose an arbitration seated instead in an 'arbitration friendly' jurisdiction.[42] As for costs, suffice to mention here that the loser-pays principle is explicitly recognised by the UNCITRAL Rules, at least in respect of arbitration costs, and there has been the suggestion that this could make it more likely for a tribunal to adopt the 'loser-pays' approach to costs.[43] Burgstaller and Rosenberg also discuss a lingering perception, based upon the precise wording in the ICSID Convention which requires demonstration of a 'manifest lack' of impartiality and independence,[44] that

[40] For the annulment decision, and the ICSID annulment procedure more broadly, the reader should consult Chapter 19 of this book.

[41] See also e.g. *Romak S.A. (Switzerland) v. Republic of Uzbekistan*, UNCITRAL, Award, PCA Case No. AA280, 26 November 2009 (Mantilla-Serrano, Chairman; Rubins; Molfessis) and more recently, *Capital Financial Holdings Luxembourg SA v. République du Cameroun*, ICSID Case No. ARB/15/18, Award, 22 June 2017 (Tercier, President; Mourre; Pellet), paras 419–423: notably that an investor who makes a contribution thereby participates in the risks of the transaction; through the former the investor assumes the latter.

[42] For the usual reason that courts will be slow to interfere with the findings of tribunals in such jurisdictions. See further Chapter 19 of this book.

[43] See Chapter 18 of this book.

[44] See Art. 57 of the ICSID Convention; cf. the need to show 'justifiable doubts' as to impartiality and independence under Art. 12(1) of the UNCITRAL Rules.

arbitrator challenges may be harder to establish in ICSID arbitrations. Neither the point on costs nor about arbitrator challenges[45] may be valid in the evolving, actual practice of tribunals where a convergence in approaches taken under both the ICSID and UNCITRAL regimes is just as likely. The various differences between ICSID and, by way of a common comparison, UNCITRAL arbitration may be true in principle, but one must not forget that both are simply forms of investor–State dispute settlement, and such differences which exist in detailed particulars of procedural minutiae may matter less than the fact that there is a common pool of arbitrators currently employed in respect of both ICSID and non-ICSID arbitrations. In other cases, the rules are often more similar than not. As with commercial arbitration, the Respondent has until the statement of defence in the case of UNCITRAL arbitration, and until the countermemorial in the case of ICSID arbitration, to provide particulars of its objection to the tribunal's jurisdiction.[46] In both cases, the tribunal should render an award on jurisdiction.[47]

Still, the more notable real differences may lie in the comparative regimes governing security for costs, where it may be easier to justify ordering such security, at least textually, in the case of an UNCITRAL arbitration.[48] So too with the Respondent's ease in obtaining a summary award, for that is at least made explicit in the case of an ICSID arbitration.[49]

CONCLUSION

Investment arbitration is but one of several means of investment dispute settlement. The many means available include claims commissions and inter–State adjudication. In commercial arbitration, there exists what Paulsson calls 'privity' in the form of an arbitration agreement. Investment arbitration can be different because it can take the form of a purely treaty-based arbitration – what we now call 'investment treaty arbitration' in order to distinguish it from contractually based arbitration, which is more akin to everyday international commercial arbitration.

Still, treaty clauses providing for investment treaty arbitration show a keen awareness of the variety of means available. This chapter has discussed the different forms

---

[45] See Chapter 5 of this book.

[46] ICSID Rules, Rule 41(1); Art. 23(2) of the UNCITRAL Rules.

[47] ICSID Rules, Rule 41(6); Art. 23(3) of the UNCITRAL Rules.

[48] See Art. 41 of the UNCITRAL Rules; cf. ICSID Rules, Rule 39(1), although see now *RSM Production Corp.* v. *St Lucia*, ICSID Case No. ARB/12/10, Decision on St Lucia's Request for Security for Costs, 13 August 2014. See further the discussion in Chapter 18 on costs.

[49] Art. 41(5), ICSID Convention; although UNCITRAL Rules, Rule 15(2) is said to provide a basis for a request for a hearing in this respect. See *Global Trading* v. *Ukraine*, Award, ICSID Case No. ARB/09/11, 23 November 2010; *Rachel S. Grynberg, Stephen M. Grynberg, Miriam Z. Grynberg, and RSM Production Corp.* v. *Grenada*, Award, ICSID Case No. ARB/10/6, 10 December 2010; *Trans-Global Petroleum* v. *Jordan*, ICSID Case No. ARB/07/25, Tribunal's Decision on Respondent's Objection under Rule 41(5), 12 May 2008. A respondent host State's right to seek a summary award, without prejudice to its objection to jurisdiction, and to obtain costs in the event that it succeeds in getting the claimant's claim thrown out, is seen to be an antidote to the threat of an indefinite number of unmeritorious claims: T. H. Webster, 'Efficiency in International Arbitration: Recent Decisions on Preliminary and Costs Issues' (2009) 25 *Arb Int'l* 469. This point is increasingly being addressed by investment treaty procedural rules providing for costs to be awarded against claimants who have brought frivolous claims.

and formalities of consent, as well as how the different means are sequenced or made mutually exclusive in today's treaties. In the specific context of investment treaty arbitration, if a choice between ICSID and non-ICSID arbitration is presented, this should be approached knowingly. However, it may also be useful to bear in mind that ICSID arbitration is not specific to investment treaty arbitration and that it was conceived originally as an option to be included in investment contracts. Thus, the choice between ICSID and non-ICSID arbitration is a choice which presents itself equally in the context of both investment contract arbitration and investment treaty arbitration.

QUESTIONS

1. What is the difference between investment contract arbitration and investment treaty arbitration?
2. What does 'privity without contract' refer to?
3. What are the usual ways in which consent to investment arbitration may be expressed and perfected?
4. Why might it be thought important to prevent multiple claims, and what are the ways in which a multiplicity of claims is sought to be prevented?
5. Should international adjudication be preferable? Should domestic adjudication and domestic judges be preferred?
6. What are some of the factors involved in choosing ICSID arbitration?

SUGGESTIONS FOR FURTHER READING

1. J. Paulsson, 'Arbitration without Privity' (1995) 10 *ICSID Review – FILJ* 232.
2. M. Potestá, 'The Interpretation of Consent to ICSID Arbitration Contained in Domestic Investment Laws' (2011) 27 *Arb Int'l* 149.
3. C. Schreuer, 'Consent to Arbitration' in P. Muchlinski, F. Ortino and C. Schreuer (eds), *The Oxford Handbook of International Investment Law* (Oxford University Press, 2008), 830.
4. M. Waibel, 'Coordinating Adjudication Processes' in Z. Douglas, J. Pauwelyn and J. E. Viñuales (eds), *The Foundations of International Investment Law* (Oxford University Press, 2014), 499.
5. M. Burgstaller and C. B. Rosenberg, 'Challenging International Arbitral Awards: To ICSID or Not to ICSID' (2011) 27 *Arb Int'l* 91.
6. N. Horn, 'Current Use of the UNCITRAL Arbitration Rules in the Context of Investment Arbitration' (2008) 24 *Arb Int'l* 587.

5

Jurisdiction, Admissibility and Parallel Proceedings

CHAPTER OUTLINE

This chapter addresses preliminary objections that may be made to consideration of an investment arbitration claim on its merits. The topic is addressed in five parts. Section 1 introduces the concepts of 'jurisdiction' and 'admissibility'. Section 2 discusses the practical relevance of that distinction. Section 3 sets out the procedural framework for dealing with issues of jurisdiction and admissibility. Section 4 addresses, somewhat briefly, those objections to jurisdiction and admissibility that have been most important in arbitral practice. Section 5 concludes the chapter with a deeper examination of one particular objection: an objection relating to parallel proceedings.

INTRODUCTION

International investment arbitration, just as international arbitration and international dispute settlement more generally,[1] is based on consent.[2] Various ways of granting consent to international investment arbitration were discussed in Chapter 4, including the important possibility that States may provide advance consent in an international investment treaty. The *Giovanni Alemanni and Others* v. *Argentina* (*Alemanni* v. *Argentina*) case described the manner in which consent is provided in investment treaty arbitrations.

---

[1] J. Collier and V. Lowe, *The Settlement of Disputes in International Law: Institutions and Procedures* (Oxford University Press, 1999), 198; C. Tomuschat, 'Article 36' in A. Zimmermann, C. J. Tams, K. Oellers-Frahm, C. Tomuschat (eds), *The Statute of the International Court of Justice: A Commentary*, 3rd edn (Oxford University Press, 2019), 728–729.

[2] A. M. Steingruber, *Consent in International Arbitration* (Oxford University Press, 2012), Part III.

Giovanni Alemanni and Others v. *Argentina,* ICSID Case No. ARB/07/8, Decision on Jurisdiction and Admissibility, 17 November 2014 (Berman, Böckstiegel, Thomas), paras 284, 305

284. ... the 'agreement' does not come about simultaneously, but is constructed in attenuated form out of disaggregated acts of consent by the different parties.

This is a common process which is no stranger to investment arbitration; the entire institution of dispute settlement under bilateral and multilateral investment treaties is based on a standing offer made generally by host States of investment subsequently taken up after a dispute has arisen by individual investors, the whole then being understood to constitute the necessary mutual consent to arbitration or other settlement processes.

...

305. ... What the Article [8 of the Italy–Argentina Bilateral Investment Treaty] does is to generate and record the standing offer to arbitrate ... It is trite law that the jurisdictional link is then completed by the acceptance of the offer by an investor, manifested implicitly by the investor's commencing arbitration proceedings in reliance on its terms. The process is a sequential one, but its legal effect is now universally recognized, on the basis that the claimant's acceptance of the respondent's offer brings into being the necessary legal relationship between them in the same way as if they had concluded between themselves a specific agreement to that effect.

Of course, preliminary objections relating to jurisdiction and admissibility are not limited to those arbitrations where a jurisdictional link is generated through the sequential process of States' treaty-making and the investor's commencement of arbitration. Parties may and do object to the power of the tribunal to decide a claim on its merits in international commercial arbitrations[3] and inter-State arbitrations,[4] as well as, indeed, in those international investment arbitrations where consent is expressed not in a treaty, but in a contract.[5] But the practice of investment treaty arbitration has, perhaps unsurprisingly, led respondent States to raise a particularly rich array of preliminary objections to consideration of claims on the merits, often presented under the portmanteau phrase of 'jurisdiction and admissibility'.

---

[3] Steingruber, *Consent in International Arbitration*, Part II. And consensual underpinnings of commercial arbitration may raise considerable conceptual and practical controversies, e.g. S. Brekoulakis, 'Rethinking Consent in International Commercial Arbitration: A General Theory for Non-Signatories' (2017) 8 *JIDS* 610.

[4] See in law of the sea disputes: *Duzgit Integrity Arbitration (Malta* v. *São Tomé and Principe),* PCA Case No. 2014–07, Award, 5 September 2016, Chapter V; *Dispute Concerning Coastal State Rights in the Black Sea, Sea of Azov, and Kerch Strait (Ukraine* v. *Russia),* PCA Case No. 2017–06, Award Concerning the Preliminary Objections of the Russian Federation, 21 February 2020.

[5] See *Standard Chartered Bank (Hong Kong) Limited* v. *Tanzania,* ICSID Case No. ARB/15/41, Award, 11 October 2019 (Boo, Unterhalter, Hossain), Chapter V, where the tribunal considered a number of objections to its jurisdiction, including in relation to the claimant's capacity as an assignee and *ratione personae* and *ratione materiae* elements of the ICSID Convention. For a case where the jurisdiction was not challenged, see *Grenada Private Power Limited and WRB Enterprises, Inc.* v. *Grenada,* ICSID Case No. ARB/17/13, Award, 19 March 2020 (Binnie, Adekoya, Boulton), para. 106.

1. 'JURISDICTION AND ADMISSIBILITY'

The starting point for discussion of jurisdiction and admissibility in investment arbitration is the formulation adopted in the applicable procedural rules.[6]

Convention on the Settlement of Investment Disputes between States and Nationals of Other States, 18 March 1965, 575 UNTS 159 (ICSID Convention), Art. 41(2)

Any objection by a party to the dispute that that dispute is not within the jurisdiction of the Centre, or for other reasons is not within the competence of the Tribunal, shall be considered by the Tribunal which shall determine whether to deal with it as a preliminary question or to join it to the merits of the dispute.

The ICSID Convention, as well as Rule 41 of the 2006 ICSID Arbitration Rules, employs the terms 'jurisdiction' and 'competence' – but not 'admissibility'. This drafting choice has raised questions about the place of admissibility in ICSID arbitrations and the proper interplay between these three concepts.

Giovanni Alemanni and Others v. *Argentina*, ICSID Case No. ARB/07/8, Decision on Jurisdiction and Admissibility, 17 November 2014 (Berman, Böckstiegel, Thomas), paras 258–259 (footnotes omitted)

258. The starting point is Article 41 of the ICSID Convention, read in conjunction with Rule 41 of the Arbitration Rules. Article 41, which appears at the head of the Section of the Convention dealing with the powers and functions of a tribunal, first makes the Tribunal into the judge of its own 'competence', before going on to provide for '[a]ny objection by a party to the dispute that that dispute is not within the jurisdiction of the Centre, or for other reasons is not within the competence of the tribunal'. In elaborating on the procedural aspects, Rule 41 is cast in similar terms: 'Any objection that the dispute or any ancillary claim is not within the jurisdiction of the Centre or, for other reasons, is not within the competence of the Tribunal shall be made as early as possible etc. etc. etc.' ...

259. It will be seen that the terminology is not entirely uniform, nor is it consistent as between the languages. Nevertheless, these provisions taken as a whole, and appreciated within their context, serve plainly to reflect the two types of limiting factor that go to determine whether a particular case may properly be heard by a tribunal established under the ICSID system, the first being the overall scope of ICSID arbitration, and the second being the factors germane to the seizing of a specific tribunal to hear a specific dispute. The first refers, that is to say, to Article 25 of the Washington Convention, as the foundation text, which like Article 41 is also phrased in terms of the 'competence of the Centre' ('compétence'

---

[6] Cf. the position in 2010 UNCITRAL Rules, Art. 23(1) ('The arbitral tribunal shall have the power to rule on its own jurisdiction, including any objections with respect to the existence or validity of the arbitration agreement').

and 'jurisdicción' in French and Spanish, respectively); the second, by contrast, bears primarily on factors such as the consent of the parties, the nature of the particular dispute and the like, which would normally be thought of, in common parlance in English, as the elements necessary to ground the 'jurisdiction' of the tribunal. The question that remains therefore is whether there exist other conditions, over and above these more strictly 'jurisdictional' ones, that can properly be invoked before an ICSID tribunal as grounds for it to decline to hear a case, even though the case falls within its 'jurisdiction'. Whether any such ought usefully to be given the label of 'admissibility' is open to question. The term, as Schreuer points out, is not used either in the Convention itself or in the Rules; moreover both Convention and Rules put the 'other reasons' on exactly the same footing as those relating to the Centre's 'jurisdiction', and treat both as raising issues going to the tribunal's 'competence'.

Georg Gavrilović and Gavrilović d.o.o v. Croatia, ICSID Case No. ARB/12/39, Award, 26 July 2018 (Pryles, Alexandrov, Thomas), para. 411 (footnote omitted)

... Although the ICSID Convention includes no specific reference to admissibility, investor-State jurisprudence confirms that preliminary objections based on jurisdiction and on admissibility are permissible in the ICSID context. The facts and arguments underlying these two types of objections often overlap—and they certainly do here—but admissibility is nonetheless its own species of preliminary objection, separate and apart from jurisdiction.

In practice, investment arbitration tribunals have taken the view that they may consider objections under the rubrics of both 'jurisdiction' and 'admissibility'.[7] This has been the case both in ICSID proceedings (as in the decisions by the *Alemanni* v. *Argentina* and *Gavrilović* v. *Croatia* tribunals excerpted above) and in proceedings conducted under other arbitral rules.[8] Drawing the distinction between jurisdiction and admissibility has proved to be more contentious.

[7] Heiskanen has suggested that this is the better view not only pragmatically, but also as a matter of principle, since there is no strict distinction between 'competence' and 'admissibility', V. Heiskanen, *'Ménage à trois?* Jurisdiction, Admissibility and Competence in Investment Treaty Arbitration' (2014) 29(1) *ICSID Review – FILJ* 231, 245 ('the conceptual triad of jurisdiction, admissibility and competence may be understood to consist of only two concepts – jurisdiction and competence/admissibility – or indeed of only one: jurisdiction in the broad sense (also comprehending competence/admissibility) or competence in the broad sense (also covering jurisdiction and admissibility). In any event, there is no substantive basis to draw a strict conceptual distinction between competence and admissibility – they are two sides of one and the same conceptual coin, viewed from two different perspectives, one internal to the tribunal (competence) and the other external (admissibility). Decisions on the admissibility of the claim are decisions on the tribunal's competence – and *vice versa*').

[8] For examples of investment arbitrations under various rules that have considered objections to jurisdiction and admissibility, see: 1976 UNCITRAL Rules, *WNC Factoring Ltd* v. *Czech Republic*, PCA Case No. 2014–34, Award, 22 February 2017 (Griffith, Volterra, Crawford); 2010 UNCITRAL Arbitration Rules, *Philip Morris Asia Ltd* v. *Australia*, PCA Case No. 2012–12, Award on Jurisdiction and Admissibility, 17 December 2015 (Böckstiegel, Kaufmann-Kohler, McRae); 2010 SCC Arbitration Rules, *I. P. Busta and J. P. Busta* v. *Czech Republic*, SCC Case No. V 2015/014, Final Award, 10 March 2017 (Banifatemi, Reinisch, Sands).

International investment arbitration is part and parcel of the contemporary international law of dispute settlement. It is therefore helpful to first set out the backdrop of the discussion on jurisdiction and admissibility in international dispute settlement more generally. The excerpt below is taken from Yuval Shany's 2012 Sir Hersch Lauterpacht Memorial Lectures Series.

Y. Shany, *Questions of Jurisdiction and Admissibility before International Courts* **(Cambridge University Press, 2015), 129–132 (footnotes omitted)**

Generally speaking, the literature on the jurisdiction of international courts often struggles to distinguish questions of admissibility from ones of jurisdiction. The case law on the matter has also sometimes been less than clear, and at times the very need for offering a distinction between the two concepts has been questioned ... The different provisions found in the constitutive instruments of distinct international courts that sometime [*sic*] use different labels for the same conditions further contribute to this taxonomical confusion, as they apply these labels inconsistently and, at times, interchangeably.

Still, the distinction between jurisdiction and admissibility (or between analogous concepts alluding to authority to adjudicate and power to refrain from exercising adjudicative authority) can play a useful role in practical terms and for analytical reasons. In practical terms, the distinction may help the logical sequencing of the procedure from binary questions of authority to often more complex questions of propriety, in allocating the burdens of proof between the parties, and in delineating the *proprio motu* responsibility of the relevant international court with regard to the exercise of its adjudicative powers.

In analytical terms, this distinction may help us better understand the way courts exercise judicial power and the legal interests of relevant constituencies affected as they do so.

One common denominator of many past attempts to distinguish questions of jurisdiction from questions of admissibility has been the notion that the former category addresses more fundamental issues than the latter. Hence, for example, Amerasinghe suggests that, unlike jurisdictional deficiencies, problems of inadmissibility or irreceivability are typically curable and can be waived by the parties. Fitzmaurice has claimed that questions of jurisdiction must be viewed as more fundamental than those of admissibility, as the competence of an international court to consider objections of the latter kind depends on it establishing its jurisdiction to begin with. Consequently, it has been argued that the distinction implies not only certain procedural implications (such as the order of examining preliminary objections and allocation of burdens of proof), but also a qualitative difference between jurisdiction and admissibility.

My approach to the distinction between jurisdiction and admissibility, which I elaborate later in this chapter, focuses on the difference between power to adjudicate and power not to exercise the power to adjudicate. Though articulated in rather abstract terms, it does not differ significantly in practical terms from the position expressed by Judge Fitzmaurice in his separate opinion in *Northern Cameroons* [judgment of the International Court of Justice] on the difference between jurisdiction and receivability:

> [T]he real distinction and test would seem to be whether or not the objection is based on, or arises from, the jurisdictional clause or clauses under which the jurisdiction of the tribunal is said to exist. If so, the objection is basically one of jurisdiction. If it is founded on considerations lying outside the ambit of any jurisdictional clause, and not involving the interpretation or application of such a provision, then it will normally be an objection to the receivability of the claim.
>
> ...
>
> Questions related to the interpretation and application of the jurisdictional clause or clauses touch on the international court's power to decide a dispute or apply law to a certain factual situation. And questions relating to considerations other than the scope and application of the jurisdictional clause or clauses do not challenge its legal authority to adjudicate, but rather examine whether it is proper for the court to adjudicate. In other words, questions of admissibility presume the existence of jurisdiction, but investigate whether there are valid reasons that should lead an international court to decline to exercise the power it has been entrusted with.

An influential piece by Jan Paulsson often provides the starting point for discussing the drawing of the line between jurisdiction and admissibility in international investment arbitration.

J. Paulsson, 'Jurisdiction and Admissibility' in G. Aksen and R. Briner (eds), *Global Reflections on International Law, Commerce and Dispute Resolution: Liber Amicorum in Honour of Robert Briner* (International Chamber of Commerce, 2005), 616–617 (original emphasis, some footnotes omitted)

Our lodestar takes the form of a question: is the objecting party taking aim at the tribunal or at the claim? ...

Following this lodestar will make it easy to classify objections in many cases, and it should make it *easier* in all. Timeliness issues, or conditions precedent such as participating in a conciliation attempt, pose no problem. The same goes for contentions of extinctive prescription; waiver of claims; mootness; or absence of a legal dispute or of an indispensable third party. There is even less difficulty with issues of ripeness *à la SGS v. Philippines* [see Section 2.4]. (The exhaustion of local remedies, on the other hand, goes beyond mere *ripeness*; the ICJ's treatment of exhaustion in *Ambatielos* as a matter of admissibility is subject to doubt, except in the particular area of denial of justice.)

[Footnote 46: See J. Paulsson, *Denial of Justice in International Law* (Cambridge: Cambridge University Press, 2005), c. 5. In the absence of exhaustion of local remedies, the underlying claim may still be perfectly ripe for adjudication, but not before a particular forum that requires exhaustion as precondition of access to it. The problem is one of jurisdiction. But denial of justice in international law contains a *substantive* requirement of exhaustion of local remedies, because the delict is not consummated unless it is shown that the national legal system was given a reasonable opportunity to correct it. A failure to exhaust it is therefore ordinarily fatal to the claim no matter where it might be heard.]

As for challenges of *locus standi*, the answer would depend on whether the issue was germane to the scope of jurisdiction contemplated in the relevant international instrument (e.g. the definition of an 'investor in a BIT').

[Footnote 47: For similar reasons the otherwise useful discussion of 'Admissibility' in J. Collier & V. Lowe, 'The Settlement of Dispute in International Law' (Oxford: Oxford University Press, 1999), at 155 ff., should be considered with some care because it focuses squarely on the ICJ.[9] In cases where the State parties have given broad consent to ICJ jurisdiction, arguments about nationality and exhaustion of local remedies may be classified as matters of admissibility because the Court's authority in a general sense remains. If an ephemeral arbitral tribunal is established under a treaty which contains requirements as to the nationality of private claimants, or as to their prior exhaustion of local remedies, the *claims* as such are perhaps subject to no impediment but the *forum seized* is lacking one of the elements required to give it life in the first place. For such a tribunal these are matters of jurisdiction.]

...

To understand whether a challenge pertains to jurisdiction or admissibility, one should imagine that it succeeds:

– If the reason for such an outcome would be that the claim could be brought to the particular forum seized, the issue is ordinarily one of jurisdiction and subject to further recourse.

– If the reason would be that the claim should not be heard at all (or at least not yet), the issue is ordinarily one of admissibility and the tribunal's decision is final.

---

[9] [Eds: But see S. Wordsworth, 'Case Comment: *Abaclat and Others v. Argentine Republic*: Jurisdiction, Admissibility and Pre-conditions to Arbitration' (2012) 27(2) *ICSID Review – FILJ* 255, 258 ('Given that the dispute settlement mechanism in a BIT is to be interpreted and applied as part of an instrument governed by international law, and that its application gives rise to the same question of whether consent has been given, one may expect the ICJ's approach to be seen as increasingly persuasive in BIT cases. This has been the case with respect to certain decisions on requirements to refer disputes to the domestic courts for a specific period, and it is difficult to see why obligations to negotiate should be treated any differently. Of course, in the BIT context it is a third-party investor that is invoking the mechanism agreed by the treaty parties but it is difficult to see what this changes and, if anything, it strengthens the argument that any words that circumscribe consent should be given the meaning intended by the treaty parties (one present, one not)' (footnotes omitted)).]

A similar distinction has been drawn by arbitral decisions.

Georg Gavrilović and Gavrilović d.o.o v. Croatia, ICSID Case No. ARB/12/39, Award, 26 July 2018 (Pryles, Alexandrov, Thomas), para. 412 (footnotes omitted)

The *Hochtief v Argentina* tribunal clearly and succinctly described the distinction between jurisdiction and admissibility: '[j]urisdiction is an attribute of a tribunal and not of a claim, whereas admissibility is an attribute of a claim but not of a tribunal'. This Tribunal agrees. Questions of jurisdiction relate to the tribunal, e.g., whether the tribunal is empowered to resolve the dispute. Questions of admissibility relate to the claim itself, e.g., whether the claim is timely filed, whether it is ripe for adjudication, whether the procedural requirements have been met. Tribunals have asked, in the context of admissibility, questions such as: Did the claimant provide proper notification of its claims? Did the claimant fulfil domestic litigation requirements? Are the claims based on genuine, non-fraudulent documents? These types of questions—which relate to the claim, not the tribunal—are questions of admissibility. On this point, the Tribunal also adopts the reasoning of the *Micula v Romania* tribunal, which similarly held that 'an objection to jurisdiction goes to the ability of a tribunal to hear a case while an objection to admissibility aims at the claim itself and presupposes that the tribunal has jurisdiction'.

One may read Shany, Paulsson and the arbitral practice summarised above in two ways. The more conceptual reading would focus on the legal nature of the objection: is it directed against the tribunal (and is hence jurisdictional) or is it directed at the claim (and is hence one of admissibility)? The more draftsmanlike reading would focus on the place that the issue occupies in the structure of international dispute settlement: is the challenge related to the interpretation and application of the jurisdictional clause of the international tribunal (and hence jurisdictional), or is it related to interpretation and application of another rule or instrument (and is hence one of admissibility)?[10]

The answer to these questions may, but not necessarily will, be the same.[11] A good example of this is provided by the contrast between the award of the tribunal and the partially dissenting opinion of one of the arbitrators in the *İçkale İnşaat Ltd Şirketi* v.

---

[10] The Singapore Court of Appeal quoted this paragraph from the first edition as 'usefully observ[ing] that there are two ways of drawing the distinction between jurisdiction and admissibility': *Swissbourgh Diamond Mines (PTY) Limited and Others* v. *Lesotho* [2018] SGCA 81, para. 207. See also *BBA and Others* v. *BAZ* [2020] SGCA 53, para. 75.

[11] C. Tomuschat's observation in relation to the International Court of Justice is also helpful here: 'Although in theory it may be easy to draw a distinction between jurisdiction and admissibility, in practice it may prove extremely difficult to trace such a precise line. Thus, an agreement between the parties to refer disputes arising in a specific field solely to arbitration or to use another exclusive method of dispute settlement will have to be classified as an objection challenging admissibility, while the same rule, if inserted in a declaration under the optional clause, would become relevant as a defence denying jurisdiction. .... [After discussing a number of cases, Tomuschat concludes that] [t]hese episodes show how wisely the Court acted as legislator in addressing preliminary objections *in toto* in one provision, namely Article 79 of the Rules. The Court has made clear that it does not have to follow a schematic course in examining preliminary objections. It is free to rely on those that provide the most direct and conclusive answer to whether its jurisdiction is established and whether it should exercise it in any given case. While objections related to jurisdiction have some logical priority, the Court may even, on grounds of procedural economy, reject an application for lack of admissibility before having considered all the issues relating to jurisdiction (Tomuschat, 'Article 36', 783–784 (footnotes omitted)).

Turkmenistan (*İçkale* v. *Turkmenistan*) case. The discussion in the excerpts below relates to the condition of resort to domestic courts for the period of one year. The tribunal appears to approach the issue from the first perspective outlined above, while the dissenting arbitrator appears to adopt the second perspective.

İçkale İnşaat Limited Şirketi v. *Turkmenistan*, ICSID Case No. ARB/10/24, Award, 8 March 2016 (Heiskanen, Lamm, Sands), paras 242–243, 246 (footnotes omitted, original emphasis)

242. ... it is plain that the 'provided that, if' clause does not constitute a jurisdictional requirement that delimits the scope of consent of the State parties to arbitrate; it sets out the procedure, or the step to be taken, in the event the dispute cannot be settled by way of negotiations between the parties, and thus constitutes a procedural rather than a jurisdictional requirement. The provision does not concern the issue of whether the State parties have given their consent to arbitrate – they have – but rather the issue of *how* that consent is to be invoked by a foreign investor; as an issue of 'how' rather than 'whether', it must be considered a matter of procedure and not as an element of the State parties' consent. Consequently, any objection raised on the basis of alleged non-compliance by an investor with any of the required procedural steps must be characterized as an objection to the admissibility of the claim rather than as an objection to the tribunal's jurisdiction. A claim that has not been first submitted to local courts may be said to be inadmissible before an international tribunal on grounds that it is not yet ripe for such submission as all the required procedural steps have not yet been taken.

243. ... The State's consent has been given in Article VII, and it became effective, and as such unconditional, as soon as the Treaty entered into force; there is nothing conditional about it. It is another matter that, in order for the investor to be in a position to invoke the State's consent to arbitrate in Article VII, it must first take the procedural steps set out in that Article. An investor taking these steps in order to be able to invoke the State's consent does not affect the consent itself in any way; it only affects the investor's right to invoke it. In other words, Article VII regulates the procedure for invoking consent; it does not condition the State's consent. If anything, it rather 'conditions' the investor's right to invoke the State's consent ...

...

245. [The Tribunal quoted from Jan Paulsson's chapter excerpted above.]

246. In the present case, the Respondent's objection that the Claimant has failed to comply with the domestic litigation requirement is an objection to admissibility in the sense that, if successful, the claim could 'not be heard at all (or at least not yet)', i.e., until the Claimant has taken the necessary procedural steps and complied with the domestic litigation requirement. Conversely, the Respondent's objection could not be an objection to jurisdiction since, if successful, it would not have prevented the Claimant from re-submitting the claim to another tribunal established under the BIT, once it had complied with the domestic litigation requirement. In other words, the issue is not whether the claim falls within the scope of the Treaty, but whether the proper procedure has been followed to submit the claim to a tribunal established under the Treaty.

İçkale İnşaat Limited Şirketi v. Turkmenistan, ICSID Case No. ARB/10/24, Partially Dissenting Opinion of Professor Philippe Sands QC, 10 February 2016, paras 8, 10 (excerpted, footnotes omitted, original emphasis)

8. ... Article 26 [of the ICSID Convention] provides that

'Consent of the parties to arbitration under this Convention shall, *unless otherwise stated*, be deemed consent to such arbitration to the exclusion of any other remedy. *A Contracting State may require the exhaustion of local administrative or judicial remedies as a condition of its consent to arbitration under this Convention.'* (emphasis added)

This language appears to make clear that in providing its consent for ICSID jurisdiction, a Contracting State to the ICSID Convention (such as Turkmenistan or Turkey) is free to attach as a condition the requirement that a claimant shall have prior recourse to a local judicial remedy. As set out in Article 26 – which is to be found in Chapter II of the ICSID Convention, entitled 'Jurisdiction of the Centre ... a condition of this kind forms part of the very existence of the jurisdiction of the forum that is seized, not the exercise of a jurisdiction that has been found to exist. Chapter II of the ICSID Convention is concerned with matters of jurisdiction, not admissibility: indeed, the word 'admissibility' is not to be found in that Chapter, or indeed in the Convention. Yet the majority in this case is curiously silent about Chapter II of the ICSID Convention and its Article 26, and offers no explanation as to how it justifies an alternative interpretation or reading of Article 26 and the surrounding provisions.

...

10. ... the one authority on which the majority places considerable reliance is an article by Jan Paulsson ... The majority melds together three selected passages from pages 616 and 617 of Mr Paulsson's article, but the act of melding seems to have misconstrued what the author intended. The majority omits the significant words of the text that incorporates footnote 47 [eds: excerpted above] ... Contrary to the view expressed by the majority, the plain meaning of pages 616 and 617 of the article, when read as a whole, appears to point clearly in favour of the conclusion that an 'ephemeral tribunal' such as this one will have no jurisdiction where a requirement to have recourse to national remedies has not been met.

To recap, the crux of the disagreement appears to lie in the choice of the question. If the right question is about the legal nature of the clause – as the *İçkale v. Turkmenistan* tribunal suggested – then it is one of admissibility. If the right question is about the proximity of the clause to the jurisdictional instrument – as Professor P. Sands suggested – then it is one of jurisdiction.

The distinction between jurisdiction and admissibility was also considered by the Singapore Court of Appeal regarding an atypically drafted treaty that expressly required exhaustion of local remedies.

Swissbourgh Diamond Mines (Pty) Ltd and Ors v. Kingdom of Lesotho [2018] SGCA 81, paras 205–207, 209 (original emphasis)

Whether the Appellants exhausted their local remedies

205. While the requirement for a claimant to exhaust all of its local remedies before submitting its dispute to arbitration is not, as the *amici curiae* note, a common feature in most investment treaties, it *is* an express requirement provided for under the relevant treaty instruments here. ...

206. ... Art 28(1) of Annex 1 also provides that investor-State disputes shall be submitted to international arbitration if either party to the dispute so wishes 'after exhausting local remedies'. In our judgment, the inclusion of the requirement that an investor must exhaust his or her local remedies in Art 28(1) as an express pre-condition for the SADC Member State's offer of consent to arbitration under Art 28(1) is significant. The failure of a claimant to exhaust local remedies has traditionally been regarded by international courts as a matter that goes towards the *admissibility* of the claim, and *not* the *jurisdiction* of the tribunal: see Chittharanjan Felix Amerasinghe, *Local Remedies in International Law* (Cambridge University Press, 2nd Ed, 2004) at p 294; see also *The Panevezys-Saldutiskis Railway Case (Estonia v Lithuania)* (1939) PCIJ (ser A/B) No 76 ('*The Panevezys-Saldutiskis Railway Case*') at 22 and *Interhandel Case (Switzerland v United States of America)*, Preliminary Objections [1959] ICJ 6 ('*Interhandel Case*') at 27. Generally, most investment arbitration tribunals also tend to regard the requirement for investors to exhaust their local remedies as a matter that concerns the *admissibility* of the claim brought by the investors, given that it is only a temporary obstacle to the exercise of the tribunal's jurisdiction and is a requirement that may be waived: see, for instance, *RosInvestCo UK Ltd v The Russian Federation*, SCC Case No V079/2005, Award on Jurisdiction, 1 October 2007 at [153].

207. Jurisdiction is commonly defined to refer to 'the power of the tribunal to hear a case', whereas admissibility refers to 'whether it is appropriate for the tribunal to hear it': *Waste Management, Inc v United Mexican States*, ICSID Case No ARB(AF)/98/2, Dissenting Opinion of Keith Highet, 8 May 2000 at [58]. To this, Zachary Douglas adds clarity to this discussion by referring to 'jurisdiction' as a concept that deals with 'the existence of [the] adjudicative power' of an arbitral tribunal, and to 'admissibility' as a concept dealing with 'the exercise of that power' and the suitability of the claim brought pursuant to that power for adjudication: *Douglas* at paras 291 and 310. Finally, in Chin Leng Lim, Jean Ho & Martins Paparinskis, *International Investment Law and Arbitration: Commentary, Awards and other Materials* (Cambridge University Press, 2018) ('*Chin Leng Lim*'), it is usefully observed that there are two ways of drawing the distinction between jurisdiction and admissibility (at p 118):

> ... The more conceptual reading would focus on the legal nature of the objection: is it directed against the tribunal (and is hence jurisdictional) or is it directed at the claim (and is hence one of admissibility)? The more draftsmanlike reading would focus on the place that the issue occupies in the structure of international dispute settlement: is the challenge related to the interpretation and application of the

jurisdictional clause of the international tribunal (and hence jurisdictional), or is it related to the interpretation and application of another rule or instrument (and is hence one of admissibility)?

...

209. But notwithstanding the conventional understanding that the requirement of exhaustion of local remedies pertains to the question of admissibility (as explained at [206] above), it has been observed that 'States may require exhaustion of local remedies as a pre-condition for their consent to arbitration. That it is a pre-condition for consent would make it a jurisdictional requirement and not an admissibility requirement': see *Waibel* at pp 1283–1284, para 283. Accordingly, given the express inclusion of the exhaustion of local remedies as a pre-condition for the SADC Member State's consent to arbitration under Art 28(1) of Annex 1, we find that any failure on the part of the Appellants to exhaust their local remedies should be taken to be an issue that concerns the *jurisdiction* of the PCA Tribunal. In any event, the Appellants never argued, at any point in the proceedings before us or the Judge below, that the exhaustion requirement is a question of admissibility. We are therefore satisfied that the review of the Kingdom's objections regarding the Appellants' alleged failure to exhaust their local remedies was rightly regarded by the Judge to be an issue affecting the PCA Tribunal's *jurisdiction*, and it thus fell within the court's purview.'[12]

In a later case, which dealt with commercial arbitration but involved the application of the same distinction, the Singapore Court of Appeal cited the same passage from the first edition of this book as in the *Swissbourgh* v. *Lesotho* para 207 excerpted above, and continued to apply it, as excerpted below. In investment arbitration, a similar question could be asked regarding classification of extinctive prescription under custom and a time bar in a treaty.

BBA and Others v. BAZ [2020] SGCA 53, paras 76–77, 80 (original emphasis)

76. In our judgment, the 'tribunal versus claim' test underpinned by a consent-based analysis should apply for purposes of distinguishing whether an issue goes towards jurisdiction or admissibility.

77. The 'tribunal versus claim' test asks whether the objection is targeted at the tribunal (in the sense that the claim *should not be arbitrated* due to a defect in or omission to consent to arbitration), or at the claim (in that the claim itself is defective and *should not be raised at all*). ...

---

[12] [Eds: But see also *BBA* v. *Baz*, para. 76: 'In our judgment, the "tribunal versus claim" test underpinned by a consent-based analysis should apply for purposes of distinguishing whether an issue goes towards jurisdiction or admissibility.']

...

80. Applying the 'tribunal versus claim' test, a plea of statutory time bar goes towards admissibility as it attacks the claim. It makes no difference whether the applicable statute of limitations is classified as substantive (extinguishing the claim) or procedural (barring the remedy) in the private international law sense discussed at [69] above. In both cases the complaint is that *the claim is stale and therefore defective*, and not – barring express provision in the arbitration clause (eg, 'the tribunal shall have no jurisdiction to hear claims that are time-barred under statute') – that the bringing of claims that are out of time under limitation laws *falls outside the scope of consent to arbitration*. Express provision by the parties is necessary given that statutes of limitation do not generally target or affect arbitral jurisdiction by design.

2. CONSEQUENCES OF THE DISTINCTION

What are the consequences of the distinction between jurisdiction and admissibility?

2.1 No Consequence

In many instances, there will be no obvious consequence to the distinction between jurisdiction and admissibility. Both jurisdiction and admissibility are preliminary objections to consideration of a claim on its merits for reasons unrelated to the merits. If objections to jurisdiction and admissibility are unsuccessful, the case will be considered on its merits. If objections to jurisdiction or admissibility are successful, the (part of the) case (they relate to) will not be considered on its merits. Objections to multi-party bond claims provide a good example for this proposition.

Theodoros Adamakopoulos and Others v. *Cyprus*, ICSID Case No. ARB/15/49, Decision on Jurisdiction, 7 February 2020 (McRae, Escobar, Kohen), para. 192 (footnote omitted)

The other 'mass claims' tribunals have differed over whether the issues raised by such claims go to jurisdiction or to admissibility and the *Alemanni* [v. *Argentina*] tribunal took the view that the distinction was of no particular importance for the disposition of the issues before it. This Tribunal is aware of these differences in view over the relationship between jurisdiction and admissibility but it does not find it necessary to take a position on this matter in order to reach its decision. The Tribunal will deal with the objections made by the Respondent in terms of their relevance to both jurisdiction and admissibility.

2.2 Consequence for Post-Request Developments

One possible consequence relates to the extent that it is possible for the tribunal to attribute legal significance to developments after the request for arbitration.

> **M. Waibel, 'Investment Arbitration: Jurisdiction and Admissibility' in M.**
> **Bungenberg, J. Griebel, S. Hobe and A. Reinisch (eds), *International Investment Law:***
> ***A Handbook* (Baden–Baden: C. H. Beck/Hart/Nomos, 2015), 1274**
>
> The critical date for determining whether investment tribunals have jurisdiction is the
> date of the request for arbitration (seisin). As a result, new developments after the critical
> date cannot be taken into account for purposes of assessing the tribunal's jurisdiction. In
> contrast, new developments that concern admissibility may be taken into account.

A different view appears to have been taken by the *Philip Morris* v. *Uruguay* tribunal,
which relied on the approach adopted by the International Court of Justice to take into
account post-request satisfaction of the requirement of domestic litigation.

> ***Philip Morris Brands Sàrl and Others* v. *Uruguay*, ICSID Case No. ARB/10/7, Decision**
> **on Jurisdiction, 2 July 2013 (Bernandini, Born, Crawford), para. 144 (footnotes**
> **omitted)**
>
> ... even if the requirement were regarded as jurisdictional, the Tribunal concludes that
> it could be, and was, satisfied by actions occurring after the date the arbitration was
> instituted. The Tribunal notes that the ICJ's decisions show that the rule that events
> subsequent to the institution of legal proceedings are to be disregarded for jurisdictional
> purposes has not prevented that Court from accepting jurisdiction where requirements
> for jurisdiction that were not met at the time of instituting the proceedings were met
> subsequently (at least where they occurred before the date on which a decision on
> jurisdiction is to be taken).

2.3 Consequence for Handling Objections

In international dispute settlement more generally, it is sometimes said that jurisdiction
is a concern for the court or the tribunal, while admissibility of a claim is a concern for
the parties. The international court or tribunal has to establish its jurisdiction even if no
objection to its jurisdiction has been made[13] (and, indeed, even if a disputing party does
not appear before it). Conversely, it does not need to establish admissibility of the claims
if not asked to – disputing parties may waive objections explicitly or by the necessary

---

[13] See 2006 ICSID Arbitration Rules, Rule 41(2) ('The Tribunal may on its own initiative consider, at any
stage of the proceeding, whether the dispute or any ancillary claim before it is within the jurisdiction
of the Centre and within its own competence') and *Itisaluna Iraq LLC and Others* v. *Iraq*, ICSID Case No.
ARB/17/10, Award, 3 April 2020 (Bethlehem, Peter, Stern) 151 ('legal questions going to the jurisdiction of
a tribunal ... a tribunal is required to address *proprio motu*, even if not raised by a party').

implication of not raising them.[14] While at this level of generality the proposition seems applicable to investment arbitration as well, it is buttressed by the consensual nature of arbitration that would permit variously expressed approval by disputing parties to cure many jurisdictional shortcomings.

M. Waibel, 'Investment Arbitration: Jurisdiction and Admissibility' in M. Bungenberg, J. Griebel, S. Hobe and A. Reinisch (eds), *International Investment Law: A Handbook* (Baden–Baden: C. H. Beck/Hart/Nomos, 2015), 1275

... objections to admissibility can generally be waived ... In contrast, at least some conditions for the exercise of jurisdiction contained in a multilateral treaty such as the ICSID Convention cannot be waived ... related to the question of waiver is, whether the tribunal may look at objections to jurisdiction and admissibility *proprio motu* ... host States will generally need to raise objections to admissibility for the tribunal to rule on them.

How does the general proposition that jurisdictional conditions cannot be waived square with the procedural rules that usually require all objections to be raised promptly? An extreme example of the tension played out in a recent case where the objection that the BIT had not entered into force was raised three years after the registration of the request.

Oded Besserglik v. *Mozambique*, ICSID Case No. ARB(AF)/14/2, Award, 28 October 2019 (Khan, Fortier, von Wobeser), paras 257, 311, 315–316 (footnotes omitted)

257. On July 3, 2014, the Acting Secretary-General registered the Request. On June 20, 2017, Respondent filed its Motion to Dismiss, its principal ground being that the BIT had not entered into force.

...

311. The Tribunal notes that the reaction of tribunals to jurisdictional objections filed with delay is not uniform. In some cases, tribunals have refused to take into consideration or dismissed belated jurisdictional objections. In other cases, tribunals pointed out the delay but proceeded to deal with the objections and disposed of them on the merits. In yet another line of cases, tribunals have referred to Article 41 of the Convention and Article 45(3) of the Arbitration Rules or Rule 41(2) of the ICSID Rules of Procedure for Arbitration Proceedings to conclude that the timeline specified in Article 45(2) 'cannot and does not negate the mandate of Article 41 of the Convention' which 'requires a Tribunal to determine every objection to jurisdiction'.

---

[14] For example, Japan did not raise the objection in the ICJ *Whaling* case that Australia's claim was inadmissible because of lack of legal interest (therefore, presumably, waiving the possible objection by necessary implication), and the ICJ did not address the issue of Australia's legal interest to bring the claim at all: *Whaling in the Antarctic (Australia v. Japan: New Zealand intervening)* [2014] ICJ Rep. 226.

...

315. The Tribunal would have been inclined to rule the objection out of consideration had the matter been one where Respondent by its delay had secured a procedural advantage or raised a defense of a non-fundamental nature. The objection in this case, however, is that the BIT is not in force. If that be the case, then Respondent cannot be said to have given its consent to ICSID arbitration. Without consent there can be no ICSID arbitration. The objection, therefore, goes to the very root of the jurisdiction of this Tribunal.

316. The Tribunal agrees with Professor Schreuer that, 'not all of the Convention's jurisdictional requirements are subject to the parties' disposition. The Convention also contains objective requirements [...]'. These have to be independently established. A tribunal cannot rely on a party's conduct in this regard. A treaty which is not in force cannot be deemed in force due to the delay or silence of a party in this regard.

2.4 Consequence for Stay

Another consequence may arise in cases where power to stay the proceedings is at issue. For a tribunal to have the power to stay its own proceedings, it has to possess a quantum of (jurisdictional) powers. In the *SGS* v. *Philippines* case (which J. Paulsson refers to in the excerpt of his chapter in Section 1), the tribunal concluded that it had jurisdiction over an umbrella clause claim, but that the claim was inadmissible because the investor had not pursued the claim in the contractually agreed forum; it therefore stayed the proceedings until the amount payable had been determined.[15] Conversely, in the *Kılıç İnşaat İthalat İhracat Sanayi ve Ticaret Anonim Şirketi* v. *Turkmenistan* case, the tribunal concluded that since the investor had failed to satisfy the condition of resort to domestic courts, which were characterised as jurisdictional, 'the conditions for jurisdiction not having been met, the Tribunal has no jurisdiction to suspend the proceedings'.[16]

2.5 Consequence for Challenges

A final possible consequence, noted in the concluding section of the excerpt of Jan Paulsson's chapter in Section 1, relates to review: in many instances, the authority considering challenges to arbitral decisions can – or at least should – review findings of jurisdiction, but not of admissibility (and merits).

---

[15] *SGS Société Générale de Surveillance SA* v. *Philippines*, ICSID Case No. ARB/02/6, Decision on Objections to Jurisdiction, 29 January 2004 (El-Kosheri, Crawford, Crivellaro), paras 169–176.

[16] *Kılıç İnşaat İthalat İhracat Sanayi ve Ticaret Anonim Şirketi* v. *Turkmenistan*, ICSID Case No. ARB/10/1, Award, 2 July 2013 (Rowley, Park, Sands), para. 6.4.2.

> **J. Paulsson, 'Jurisdiction and Admissibility' in G. Aksen and R. Briner (eds), *Global Reflections on International Law, Commerce and Dispute Resolution: Liber Amicorum in Honour of Robert Briner* (International Chamber of Commerce, 2005), 608**
>
> ... although the ICSID Convention does not expressly use the word 'admissibility', its all-important Article 52 mandates annulment of awards for excess of powers – and so ... it does become 'necessary' to understand the difference between objections to be finally decided by the arbitrators and objections subject to review.

A similar view has been taken by an annulment committee in the *Venezuela Holdings, BV and Others* v. *Venezuela* case[17] and the Singapore Court of Appeal.

> **Swissbourgh Diamond Mines (Pty) Ltd and Ors v. Kingdom of Lesotho [2018] SGCA 81, para. 208 (original emphasis)[18]**
>
> The conceptual distinction between jurisdiction and admissibility is not merely an exercise in linguistic hygiene pursuant to a pedantic hair-splitting endeavour. This distinction has significant practical import in investment treaty arbitration because a decision of the tribunal in respect of *jurisdiction* is reviewable by the supervisory courts at the seat of the arbitration (for non-ICSID arbitrations) or before an ICSID *ad hoc* committee pursuant to Art 52 of the ICSID Convention (for ICSID arbitrations), whereas a decision of the tribunal on *admissibility* is *not* reviewable: see Jan Paulsson, 'Jurisdiction and Admissibility' in *Global Reflections on International Law, Commerce and Dispute Resolution*, Liber Amicorum in honour of Robert Briner (Gerald Aksen *et al*, eds) (ICC Publishing, 2005) at p 601, *Douglas* at para 307, *Waibel* at p 1277, paras 257 and 258, Hanno Wehland, 'Jurisdiction and Admissibility in Proceedings under the ICSID Convention and the ICSID Additional Facility Rules' in *ICSID Convention after 50 Years: Unsettled Issues* (Crina Baltag, ed) (Kluwer Law International, 2016) at pp 233–234, and *Chin Leng Lim* at p 124.

---

[17] *Venezuela Holdings, BV* v. *Venezuela*, ICSID Case No. ARB/07/27, Decision on Annulment, 9 March 2017 (Berman, Abraham, Knieper), para. 110: 'The Committee also accepts that there is weight in the Mobil Parties' contention that questions of admissibility may require to be approached in a different way from questions of jurisdiction for the purposes of the annulment scheme laid down in Article 52 of the ICSID Convention. It is plain on the face of it that the reference in Article 52(1)(b) to a tribunal having "manifestly exceeded its powers" fits most naturally into the context of jurisdiction, in the sense that it covers the case where a tribunal exercises a judicial power which on a proper analysis had not been conferred on it (or vice versa declines to exercise a jurisdiction which it did possess). It follows that it is less easy to apply the criterion laid down in Article 52(1)(b) – and in particular when it comes to deciding whether the excess was "manifest" – when what the tribunal is doing is to make a discretionary assessment of whether, assuming the existence of its judicial power in principle, it is proper in the particular circumstances for that power to be exercised.'

[18] Full versions of the short title references are given in the excerpt of the judgment in Section 1.

3. PROCEDURE FOR ADDRESSING OBJECTIONS TO JURISDICTION AND ADMISSIBILITY

3.1 Bifurcation between Preliminary Objections and Merits

If objections to jurisdiction or admissibility are made, an important question is whether they should be disposed of before proceeding to the merits. Applicable procedural rules tend to leave considerable discretion to the investment arbitration tribunal in deciding whether preliminary objections should be considered separately before the merits ('bifurcation') or together with the merits.

ICSID Arbitration Rules 2006, Rule 41(3)

Upon the formal raising of an objection relating to the dispute, the Tribunal may decide to suspend the proceeding on the merits. The President of the Tribunal, after consultation with its other members, shall fix a time limit within which the parties may file observations on the objection.

UNCITRAL Rules 2010, Art. 23(3)

The arbitral tribunal may rule on a plea referred to in paragraph 2 either as a preliminary question or in an award on the merits ...

The broadly consistent arbitral practice has identified several considerations relevant to the exercise of this discretion.

OOO Manolium-Processing v. Belarus, PCA Case No. 2018–06, Decision on Bifurcation, 1 August 2018 (Fernández-Armesto, Alexandrov, Stern), paras 4–8

4. The Tribunal has carefully examined the Parties' arguments and, on balance, sees advantages in not bifurcating the proceedings:

   5. The Tribunal acknowledges that, if the dispute were to be bifurcated, Respondent would in the first phase avoid the need for an expert report; and that if Respondent were successful on jurisdiction or merits, no expert report would ever be required. But this advantage is off-set by the contrary scenario: if the Tribunal were to grant bifurcation and then find for Claimant on jurisdiction and merits (even if partially), the procedure would continue into a second phase, devoted exclusively to the calculation of damages. Such second phase would cause unnecessary delay and unwarranted increase in costs.

   6. The Tribunal is also not convinced by Respondent's argument that the facts and issues relevant to jurisdiction and liability are distinct from the facts and issues relevant to the quantum proceedings; as the case has been pleaded, the Tribunal sees a close relationship between both sets of facts and issues.

7. Respondent also asserts that bifurcation will foster fairness, economy and efficiency in managing these proceedings, the quantification of Claimant's damages claims being a complex and time-consuming exercise. The Tribunal is unpersuaded: the expert report submitted by Claimant is not overly complex, and is based on straightforward methodology for the calculation of damages and lost profits.

***

8. For the above reasons, and considering the principles of procedural economy and cost efficiency, the Tribunal decides not to bifurcate the proceedings.

Bay View Group LLC and The Spalena Company LLC v. Rwanda, ICSID Case No. ARB/18/21, Procedural Order No. 2 on Bifurcation, 28 June 2019 (Phillips, Bidwell Jr, Dohmann), para. 9 (excerpted, footnote omitted)

While the Parties disagree on whether Rwanda's objections to the Tribunal's jurisdiction should be decided as a preliminary question, they largely agree on the standard which the Tribunal should apply to the issue at hand. According to the Parties, tribunals have consistently applied three factors articulated in *Philip Morris* v. *Australia* to determine whether bifurcation is appropriate. They are: (i) Is the objection *prima facie* serious and substantial?; (ii) Can the objection be examined without prejudging or entering into the merits?; and (iii) Could the objection, if successful, dispose of all or an essential part of the claims raised?

3.2 Claims Manifestly without Legal Merit

By the mid-2000s, the experience of States in defending investment claims led to a call for a further – or rather anterior – layer of objections that would enable an even earlier disposal of patently unmeritorious claims. Rule 41(5) of the 2006 ICSID Arbitration Rules is set out below.[19] Special rules for an expedited procedure for making preliminary objections have also been provided in some of the newer treaties.[20]

---

[19] See also 1976 UNCITRAL Arbitration Rules, Art. 15(1) and 2010 UNCITRAL Arbitration Rules, Art. 17(1).
[20] Art. 10.20.4 of the Dominican Republic–Central America Free Trade Agreement (DR–CAFTA) provides for a special procedure of handling objections whereby 'as a matter of law, a claim submitted is not a claim for which an award in favour of the claimant may be made under Article 10.26'. The scope of this rule was considered by a tribunal in the *Renco* v. *Peru* case, which concluded that it did not cover Peru's objections to competence, *The Renco Group* v. *Peru*, ICSID Case No. UNCT/13/1, Decision as to the Scope of the Respondent's Preliminary Objections under Article 10.20.4, 18 December 2014 (Moser, Fortier, Landau), para. 213. Peru's jurisdictional objection relating to incompliance with the requirements of waivers was dealt with and accepted under the general rules on the handling of preliminary objections: *The Renco Group* v. *Peru*, ICSID Case No. UNCT/13/1, Partial Award on Jurisdiction, 15 July 2016. See also the European Union–Canada Comprehensive Economic and Trade Agreement (CETA), which has special rules for preliminary objections regarding claims manifestly without legal merit (in Art. 8.32) and unfounded as a matter of law (in Art. 8.33).

ICSID Arbitration Rules 2006, Rule 41(5)

Unless the parties have agreed to another expedited procedure for making preliminary objections, a party may, no later than 30 days after the constitution of the Tribunal, and in any event before the first session of the Tribunal, file an objection that a claim is manifestly without legal merit. The party shall specify as precisely as possible the basis for the objection. The Tribunal, after giving the parties the opportunity to present their observations on the objection, shall, at its first session or promptly thereafter, notify the parties of its decision on the objection. The decision of the Tribunal shall be without prejudice to the right of a party to file an objection pursuant to paragraph (1) or to object, in the course of the proceeding, that a claim lacks legal merit.

Respondent States have successfully made objections under Rule 41(5) in a number of cases.[21] A recent decision summarises arbitral practice and relevant considerations.

> ***Almasryia For Operating & Maintaining v. Kuwait*, ICSID Case No. ARB/18/2, Award on the Respondent's Application under Rule 41(5) of the ICSID Arbitration Rules, 1 November 2018 (Ramírez Hernández, Dévaud, Knieper), paras 28–33 (footnotes omitted, original emphasis)**
>
> 28. Rule 41(5) provides in its relevant part that: 'a party may ... file an objection that a claim is *manifestly without legal merit'* (emphasis added). At the outset, the Tribunal observes that the word 'manifestly' qualifies the term 'without legal merit'. 'Manifestly' as an adjective means: 'readily perceived by the senses and especially by the sense of sight' as well as 'easily understood or recognized by the mind: obvious'. The word 'merit' has several meanings: 'obsolete: reward or punishment due; the qualities or actions that constitute the basis of one's deserts; a praiseworthy quality: virtue; character or conduct deserving reward, honor, or esteem; spiritual credit held to be earned by performance of righteous acts and to ensure future benefits; the substance of a legal case apart from matters of jurisdiction, procedure, or form; individual significance or justification'. On the other hand, 'legal' has also several definitions: 'of or relating to law; deriving authority from or founded on law: *de jure;* having a formal status derived from law often without a basis in actual fact: titular; established by law especially: statutory; conforming to or permitted by law or established rules; recognized or made effective by a court of law as distinguished from a court of equity; of, relating to, or having the characteristics of the profession of law or of one of its members; created by the constructions of the law'.
>
> 29. The tribunal in *Trans-Global Petroleum v. Jordan* examined the ordinary dictionary meaning of 'manifestly' as well as the context provided by other provisions of the ICSID

Trans-Global Petroleum, Inc. v. *Jordan* (*Trans-Global Petroleum* v. *Jordan*), ICSID Case No. ARB/07/25, Tribunal's Decision on Respondent's Objection under Rule 41(5) of the ICSID Arbitration Rules, 12 May 2008 (Veeder, McRae, Crawford), para. 124; *Accession Mezzanine Capital LP and Another* v. *Hungary* (*Accession Mezzanine and Another* v. *Hungary*), ICSID Case No. ARB/12/3, Decision on Respondent's Objection under Arbitration Rule 41(5), 16 January 2013 (Rovine, Lalonde, McRae), para. 78; *Emmis International Holding BV and Others* v. *Hungary* (*Emmis and Others* v. *Hungary*), ICSID Case No. ARB/12/2, Decision on Respondent's Objection under ICSID Arbitration Rule 41(5), 11 March 2013 (McLachlan, Lalonde, Thomas), para. 85.

Convention and determined that: '... the ordinary meaning of the word [manifestly] requires the respondent to establish its objection *clearly and obviously, with relative ease and despatch*'. In light of this, it considered that the standard under Rule 41(5) was 'set high' and that although '[the] exercise may not always be simple ... [and] thus be complicated; [...] *it should never be difficult*' (emphasis added).

30. As to the phrase 'without legal merit' it noted the significance of the adjective 'legal' and considered that it 'is clearly used in contradistinction to "factual"', which would indicate that a tribunal is not concerned '*per se* with the factual merits'. The phrase 'legal merit' was considered in *Brandes* v. *Venezuela* as covering 'all objections to the effect that the proceedings should be discontinued at an early stage because, for whatever reason, the claim can manifestly not be granted by the Tribunal'.

31. In this regard, investment tribunals have held that Rule 41(5) concerns 'a legal impediment to a claim' (not a factual one) which can go to jurisdiction or the merits of the dispute. Nonetheless, the tribunal in *Trans-Global Petroleum* v. *Jordan* recognized that 'it is rarely possible to assess the legal merits of any claim without also examining the factual premise upon which that claim is advanced'. In that case the tribunal expressed its view that:

'[T]he tribunal need not accept at face value any factual allegation which the tribunal regards as (manifestly) incredible, frivolous, vexatious or inaccurate or made in bad faith; nor ... accept a legal submission dressed up as a factual allegation. The Tribunal does not accept, however, that a tribunal should otherwise weigh the credibility or plausibility of a disputed factual allegation.'

32. The tribunal in *Eskosol* v. *Italy* also recognized the 'level of sophistication' of investment proceedings while emphasizing that 'the Rule 41(5) procedure is not intended, nor should it be used, as the mechanism to address complicated, difficult or unsettled issues of law'. The Tribunal agrees with the interpretations provided by the aforementioned tribunals and also shares the view expressed in *Emmis* v. *Hungary*, that a tribunal:

'*must ordinarily presume the facts* which found the claim on the merits *as alleged by the claimant* to be true (*unless they are plainly without any foundation*). In the application of those presumed facts to the legal question of its jurisdiction, the tribunal must then decide whether, *as matter of law, those facts fall within or outside the scope of the consent to arbitrate*. Where the objection is taken under the procedure provided in Rule 41(5), it will decide to grant the objection if one or more of the claims *fall clearly outside the scope of its jurisdiction* so that, for the purpose of these proceedings, the claim must be treated as being "manifestly without legal merit"' (emphasis added).

33. In view of the above, our task will be to determine whether taking the facts as a given, unless they are plainly without foundation, the claims are such that they 'manifestly' (*i.e.* clearly and obviously) lack legal merit.

4. OBJECTIONS TO JURISDICTION AND ADMISSIBILITY

International investment arbitration decisions have dealt with a significant variety of objections to jurisdiction and admissibility. This section will set out, somewhat briefly, those objections to jurisdiction and admissibility that have been most important in arbitral practice. Section 5 will provide a deeper examination of one particular objection: an objection relating to parallel proceedings.

4.1 Investor

Investor–State arbitration is jurisdictionally limited, on the one side, to a peculiar procedural actor: 'an investor'. It is common for the instrument of expression of consent to provide a definition of the investor,[22] and a definition may also be contained in the rules relating to the particular forum.[23] The concept of protected investors is discussed in detail in Chapter 11, so only a few illustrative examples of objections on this basis will be noted here.

Some challenges are directed at the failure by natural persons to satisfy the definition of 'investor' in the instrument of consent or the rules of the forum. In the *Hussein Nuaman Soufraki* v. *UAE* case, the respondent State successfully objected to the tribunal's jurisdiction on the basis that the claimant was not a national of Italy, even though Italian authorities had erroneously issued a certificate of nationality to that effect.[24] In the *Micula* v. *Romania* case, the respondent State unsuccessfully objected to the tribunal's jurisdiction by relying on the genuine connection that claimants, despite their Swedish nationality, allegedly had with Romania.[25] In a number of recent cases, States have objected to double nationality of the claimants, with varied success.[26]

---

[22] For example, Art. 1(7) of the Energy Charter Treaty provides the following definition of 'Investor': '(a) with respect to a Contracting Party: (i) a natural person having the citizenship or nationality of or who is permanently residing in that Contracting Party in accordance with its applicable law; (ii) a company or other organisation organised in accordance with the law applicable in that Contracting Party; (b) with respect to a 'third state', a natural person, company or other organisation which fulfils, mutatis mutandis, the conditions specified in subparagraph (a) for a Contracting Party.' See also C. Baltag, *The Energy Charter Treaty: The Notion of Investor* (Alphen aan den Rijn: Kluwer Law International Law, 2012).

[23] For example, the Art. 25(2) of the ICSID Convention provides the following definition: '(2) "National of another Contracting State" means: (a) any natural person who had the nationality of a Contracting State other than the State party to the dispute on the date on which the parties consented to submit such dispute to conciliation or arbitration as well as on the date on which the request was registered pursuant to paragraph (3) of Article 28 or paragraph (3) of Article 36, but does not include any person who on either date also had the nationality of the Contracting State party to the dispute; and (b) any juridical person which had the nationality of a Contracting State other than the State party to the dispute on the date on which the parties consented to submit such dispute to conciliation or arbitration and any juridical person which had the nationality of the Contracting State party to the dispute on that date and which, because of foreign control, the parties have agreed should be treated as a national of another Contracting State for the purposes of this Convention.'

[24] *Hussein Nuaman Soufraki* v. *UAE*, ICSID Case No. ARB/02/7, Award, 7 July 2004 (Fortier, Schwebel, El Kholy); the particular legal issue was challenged and upheld on annulment: ICSID Case No. ARB/02/7, Decision of the Ad Hoc Committee on the Application for Annulment of Mr Soufraki, 5 June 2007 (Feliciano, Nabulsi, Stern).

[25] *Ioan Micula and Others* v. *Romania*, ICSID Case No. ARB/05/20, Decision on Jurisdiction and Admissibility, 24 September 2008 (Lévy, Alexandrov, Ehlermann).

[26] In *Ballantine* v. *Dominican Republic*, the Tribunal accepted the objection that investors were double nationals but their effective nationality was not that of the home State, as required by the Dominican Republic–Central America Free Trade Agreement, *Michael Ballantine and Lisa Ballantine* v. *Dominican Republic*, PCA Case No. 2016-17, Final Award, 3 September 2019 (Ramírez Hernández, Cheek, Vinuesa), Section X;

Many challenges are directed at the compliance by legal persons with the definition of 'investor'. In the *Rompetrol* v. *Romania* case, the tribunal rejected an objection to that effect because the claimant was a Dutch-incorporated company, and allegations that corporate control, effective seat and origin of capital linked the company to Romania had no part to play in the ascertainment of nationality under the applicable instruments.[27] In the *National Gas SAE* v. *Egypt* case, the tribunal upheld the objection that the Egypt-incorporated claimant could not be treated as a foreign investor due to the 'foreign control' clause in Article 25(2)(b) of the ICSID Convention, since, as an objective matter, it was controlled by an Egyptian national.[28] In the *CEAC* v. *Montenegro* case, the respondent State successfully objected that the claimant company did not satisfy the definition of 'investor' because it did not have a 'seat' in Cyprus, as required in the BIT.[29]

4.2 State

In terms of personal jurisdiction, investor–State arbitration is also limited to another peculiar procedural actor, usually in the capacity of the respondent: 'a State'. One type of challenge that straddles the boundaries of jurisdiction and merits raises the question of whether conduct by a State is implicated at all. In the technical parlance of public international law, this challenge relates to attribution of conduct to a State, and is to be answered by reference to secondary rules of State responsibility, which are to a considerable extent reflected in the 2001 International Law Commission's (ILC) Articles on Responsibility of States for Internationally Wrongful Acts.[30] For example, the tribunal in the *Almås* v. *Poland* case concluded that the conduct allegedly in breach of the BIT – termination of a lease agreement by the Polish Agricultural Property Agency – was not attributable to Poland, and therefore dismissed the claim.[31]

4.3 Investment

Investor–State arbitration is also jurisdictionally limited to a peculiar subject matter: 'investment'. The concept of protected investments is discussed in detail in Chapter 10, so only a few illustrative examples will be noted here.

---

cf. Partial Dissent of Arbitrator Cheek on Jurisdiction. In *Rawat* v. *Mauritius*, the Tribunal took the view that, unlike certain decisions in cases brought against Venezuela, the term 'nationals' in that particular BIT excluded double nationals, due to the somewhat peculiar context: *Dawood Rawat* v. *Mauritius*, PCA Case No. 2016–20, Award on Jurisdiction, 6 April 2018 (Reed, Honlet, Lowe).

[27] *The Rompetrol Group* v. *Romania*, ICSID Case No. ARB/06/3, Decision on Respondent's Preliminary Objections on Jurisdiction and Admissibility, 18 April 2008 (Berman, Donovan, Lalonde).

[28] *National Gas SAE* v. *Egypt*, ICSID Case No. ARB/11/7, Award, 3 April 2014 (Veeder, Fortier, Stern). See the text of Art. 25(2)(b) of the ICSID Convention at n. 22 above.

[29] *CEAC Holdings Ltd* v. *Montenegro*, ICSID Case No. ARB/14/8, Award, 26 July 2016 (Hanotiau, Park, Stern). But see Separate Opinion by Arbitrator Park, 4 July 2016. The particular legal issue was challenged and upheld on annulment: ICSID Case No. ARB/14/8, Decision on Annulment, 1 May 2018 (Greenwood, Kim, Oyekunle).

[30] See also J. Crawford, *State Responsibility: The General Part* (Cambridge University Press, 2013), Part II.

[31] The tribunal noted that the Agency was not an organ of Poland, and that the termination of the lease was neither an exercise of governmental functions nor performed on the instructions of the Polish government: *Kristian Almås and Geir Almås* v. *Poland*, PCA Case No. 2015–13, Award, 27 June 2016 (Crawford, Mestad, Reinisch).

Many challenges are directed at whether the definition of 'investment' in the instrument of consent or the rules of the forum – particularly Article 25(1) of the ICSID Convention – has been satisfied. For example, in the *Eyre* v. *Sri Lanka* case, the tribunal upheld the State's objection that the land property and plans for building a hotel upon it did not constitute an investment, either within the meaning of the applicable BIT or the ICSID Convention.[32]

Some challenges are directed at incompliance by investments with domestic law. A well-known example is *Fraport* v. *Philippines*, where the claim was dismissed because of incompliance by the investor with a constitutional rule of the Philippines that restricted operation of public utilities to Philippine citizens or Philippine corporations, 60 per cent of whose capital would have to be owned by Philippine citizens.[33] An increasing number of objections are directed at corruption.[34]

4.4 Consent and Other Issues

Many challenges may be described as directed at consent in a broad sense, suggesting from various perspectives that the State has not consented to arbitrate the particular claim in the particular manner. Some of the more important of these objections are that:

- the instrument of consent does not have legal effect (because it has not yet come into force, is not effective,[35] is no longer in force[36] or is not binding for the particular State[37]);
- while the dispute may relate to the treaty that provides the instrument of consent, consent nevertheless does not extend to it (because the dispute falls outside the scope of consent in a narrow dispute settlement clause,[38] is excluded from the scope of

---

[32] *Raymond Charles Eyre and Montrose Developments (Private) Limited* v. *Sri Lanka*, ICSID Case No. ARB/16/25, Award, 5 March 2020 (Reed, Lew, Stern). The case is currently pending before an annulment committee (Zuleta, Piracha, Sacerdoti).

[33] *Fraport AG Frankfurt Airport Services Worldwide* v. *Philippines (II)*, ICSID Case No. ARB/11/12, Award, 10 December 2014 (Bernandini, Alexandrov, van den Berg).

[34] For a successful objection on these grounds, see *Metal-Tech Ltd* v. *Uzbekistan*, ICSID Case No. ARB/10/3, Award, 4 October 2013 (Kaufmann-Kohler, Townsend, von Wobeser). For an unsuccessful objection, see *Glencore International AG and CI Prodeco SA* v. *Colombia*, ICSID Case No. ARB/16/6, Award, 27 August 2019.

[35] Regarding provisional application of the Energy Charter Treaty, see *Yukos Universal Ltd (Isle of Man)* v. *Russia*, PCA Case No. AA227, Interim Award on Jurisdiction and Admissibility, 30 November 2009 (Fortier, Poncet, Schwebel), subject to set-aside proceedings on this point in the Dutch courts, the most recent judgment by the Hague Court of Appeal reversing the initial set-aside, 18 February 2020.

[36] Regarding the effect of withdrawal by Venezuela from the ICSID Convention, see *Fábrica de Vidrios Los Andes, C.A. and Owens-Illinois de Venezuela, C.A* v. *Venezuela*, ICSID Case No. ARB/12/21, Award, 13 November 2017 (Shin, Fortier, Douglas).

[37] Regarding succession of treaties, see *World Wide Minerals* v. *Kazakhstan*, UNCITRAL Case, Decision on Jurisdiction, 19 October 2015 (Park, Berman, Crook); regarding the intra-European Union objection to the Energy Charter Treaty, see *BayWa re Renewable Energy GmbH and Other* v. *Spain*, ICSID Case No. ARB/15/16, Decision on Jurisdiction, Liability and Directions on Quantum, 2 December 2019 (Crawford, Grigera Naón, Malintoppi) paras 244–251, 262–283; for bilateral investment treaties, see *Ioan Micula and Ors* v. *Romania*, ICSID Case No. ARB/14/29, Award, 5 March 2020 (McRae, Beechey, Crook), Section V.A.

[38] A. Reinisch, 'How Narrow Are Narrow Dispute Settlement Clauses in Investment Treaties?' (2011) 2(1) *JIDS* 115.

consent because of a carve-out, usually regarding tax or financial services, or is excluded from the scope of consent because of reservations[39]);

- the dispute falls outside the territorial scope of consent;[40]
- the dispute falls outside the temporal scope of consent;[41]
- the claim brought is a contract claim, rather than a treaty claim;[42]
- the investor should have pursued the claim in the contractually agreed forum;[43]
- the investor has not satisfied the conditions of negotiations or resort to domestic judicial proceedings (discussed in Section 1);
- the investor has not properly waived access to domestic judicial proceedings[44] or has taken the wrong turn at the fork-in-the-road;[45]
- a most-favoured-nation clause cannot be relied upon to benefit the investor over more favourable rules of international dispute settlement;[46]
- the investor has waived the right to bring an investment claim;[47]
- the State has denied benefits to the investor;[48] or
- the investor has engaged in an abuse of proscess.[49]

5. PARALLEL PROCEEDINGS

It is not surprising that essentially the same conduct can give rise to responsibility under different substantive rules, implemented through different procedural regimes. But it does raise the challenge of proper coordination, which may be particularly difficult in investment arbitration, due to its decentralised character.

A famous example is provided by the duo of investment arbitrations, which are in some circles colloquially referred to as the Great Czech Cases: *Ronald S. Lauder* v. *Czech Republic*, UNCITRAL Case, Final Award, 3 September 2001 (Briner, Cutler, Klein) and *CME Czech Republic BV* v. *Czech Republic*, UNCITRAL Case, Partial Award, 13 September 2001 (Kühn, Schwebel, Hándl) (followed by its own Final Award on 14 March 2003, with Ian

---

[39] For a discussion of tax carve-outs, see *Nissan Motor Co., Ltd. (Japan)* v. *India*, PCA Case No. 2017–37, Decision on Jurisdiction, 29 April 2019 (Kalicki, Hobér, Kherar) Section X.B; *BayWa* v. *Spain*, paras 297–314.

[40] *Sanum Investments Ltd* v. *Laos*, PCA Case No. 2013–13, Award on Jurisdiction, 13 December 2013. See also the set-aside proceedings, [2016] SGCA 57.

[41] *Global Telecom Holding SAE* v. *Canada*, ICSID Case No. ARB/16/16, Award, 27 March 2020 (Affaki, Born, Lowe), paras 405–412.

[42] *Lotus Holding Anonim Şirketi* v. *Turkmenistan*, ICSID Case No. ARB/17/30, Award, 6 April 2020 (Lowe, Boykin, Stern), and generally see Chapter 4.

[43] *SGS* v. *Philippines*.

[44] *Renco* v. *Peru*.

[45] *Nissan* v. *India*, paras 208–218.

[46] *Professor Christian Doutremepuich (France) and Antoine Doutrempuich (France)* v. *Mauritius*, PCA Case No. 2018–37, Award, 23 August 2019, Section IV.C; *Itisaluna* v. *Iraq*. See also M. Paparinskis, 'MFN Clauses and International Dispute Settlement: Moving beyond Maffezini and Plama?' (2011) 26(2) *ICSID Review – FILJ* 14.

[47] Compare *SGS* v. *Philippines*, para. 154, which doubts the power of investors to waive treaty rights, with *Hochtief AG* v. *Argentina*, ICSID Case No. ARB/07/31, Decision on Liability, 29 December 2014 (Lowe, Brower, Thomas), Section IV.A, which accepts it.

[48] *Yukos* v. *Russia*.

[49] *Philip Morris* v. *Australia*, Award.

Brownlie now sitting as the State's nominated arbitrator). The backdrop for the following excerpts is that *Ronald S. Lauder* v. *Czech Republic* was brought under the US–Czech Republic BIT,[50] while *CME* v. *Czech Republic* was brought under the Netherlands–Czech BIT[51] (and Mr Lauder was a controlling shareholder of CME).

J. Crawford, 'Ten Investment Arbitration Awards That Shook the World: Introduction and Overview' (2010) 4 *Dispute Resolution Int'l* 71, 92–93 (footnotes omitted)[52]

These two decisions, lumped together as equal tenth in the list (but actually 11th and 12th), are familiar for their divergent findings in respect of the same acts. The *CME* tribunal held that the treatment of CME breached the obligation of fair and equitable treatment, the obligation not to impair investments by unreasonable and discriminatory measures, and the obligation of full security and protection. The total amount awarded in damages was US$269,814,000, roughly equivalent to the annual health budget of the Czech Republic. By contrast the primary wrong-doer, Lauder's Czech partner, was held in an ICC arbitration liable to pay a 'mere' US$20 million.

In further contrast, the *Lauder* tribunal held that there was no expropriation and no violation of the duty to provide fair and equitable treatment. It held that the Czech Republic took a discriminatory and arbitrary measure against Lauder in 1992–1993 in refusing to allowing [*sic*] an investment in CET by CEDC. But this breach was too remote to qualify as a relevant cause or the harm caused and did not itself cause any damage. No damages were awarded; each party bore their own costs and half the costs of the tribunal.

At the damages phase before the *CME* tribunal, the tribunal held that the principle of *res judicata* did not apply in favour of the London Arbitration, and even if it did, the respondent waived that defence by refusing to accept any of CME's proposals to consolidate or coordinate the two proceedings. This is fair enough – but the impression of a race to the judgment seat on the part of the two tribunals remains.

What is the best way to deal with parallel proceedings in investment arbitration? One might respond in a number of ways.

5.1 Consent by Disputing Parties

It is a trite point that arbitration is a consensual process of dispute settlement. Unless precluded by the applicable rules, disputing parties could consent to consolidate or otherwise coordinate parallel proceedings. In the *CME* v. *Czech Republic* Final Award, the tribunal

---

[50] Treaty between the United States of America and the Arab Republic of Egypt Concerning the Reciprocal Encouragement and Protection of Investments, 11 March 1986.

[51] Agreement on Encouragement and Reciprocal Protection of Investments between the Kingdom of the Netherlands and the Czech and Slovak Federal Republic, 29 April 1991.

[52] This article first appeared in the May 2010 issue of *Dispute Resolution International* 4(1), and is reproduced by kind permission of the International Bar Association, London, UK. © International Bar Association.

described how '[t]he Respondent, in the First Phase of these proceedings, expressly and repeatedly refused any coordination of the London Arbitration and this arbitration' (para. 426). The important point for the present purpose is the underlying assumption apparently shared by parties and the tribunal that consent by the Czech Republic, if provided, would have had the intended effect.

5.2 Special Treaty Rules

Applicable treaties may provide for explicit rules to coordinate proceedings by consolidating proceedings, if brought under the same treaty, or staying or otherwise coordinating proceedings, if brought under another treaty. Waivers as requirements for submission of a claim may address the same concern in prospective terms.

EU–Canada Comprehensive Economic and Trade Agreement, Art 8.22(1)(f)–(g), (2)–(3)

1. An investor may only submit a claim pursuant to Article 8.23 if the investor:

   ...

   (f) withdraws or discontinues any existing proceeding before a tribunal or court under domestic or international law with respect to a measure alleged to constitute a breach referred to in its claim; and

   (g) waives its right to initiate any claim or proceeding before a tribunal or court under domestic or international law with respect to a measure alleged to constitute a breach referred to in its claim.

2. If the claim submitted pursuant to Article 8.23 is for loss or damage to a locally established enterprise or to an interest in a locally established enterprise that the investor owns or controls directly or indirectly, the requirements in subparagraphs 1(f) and (g) apply both to the investor and the locally established enterprise.

3. The requirements of subparagraphs 1(f) and (g) and paragraph 2 do not apply in respect of a locally established enterprise if the respondent or the investor's host state has deprived the investor of control of the locally established enterprise, or has otherwise prevented the locally established enterprise from fulfilling those requirements.

EU–Canada Comprehensive Economic and Trade Agreement, Arts 8.24, 8.43

Article 8.24 (Proceedings under another international agreement)

Where a claim is brought pursuant to this Section and another international agreement and:

   (a) there is a potential for overlapping compensation; or

   (b) the other international claim could have a significant impact on the resolution of the claim brought pursuant to this Section, the Tribunal shall, as soon as possible after hearing the disputing parties, stay its proceedings or otherwise ensure that proceedings brought pursuant to another international agreement are taken into account in its decision, order or award.

...

Article 8.43 (Consolidation)

1. When two or more claims that have been submitted separately pursuant to Article 8.23 have a question of law or fact in common and arise out of the same events or circumstances, a disputing party or the disputing parties, jointly, may seek the establishment of a separate division of the Tribunal pursuant to this Article and request that such division issue a consolidation order.

5.3 No Issue

To the extent that the issue of parallel proceedings is resolved neither by special treaty rules nor by consent of disputing parties, one response to the problem of parallel proceedings is to deny its characterisation as a problem. In an important technical sense, one could then say that various proceedings are likely to be materially different from each other, and therefore principles elaborated to address parallel or repetitive proceedings do not apply. The *CME* v. *Czech Republic* tribunal made the following observations when explaining why the principle of *res judicata* did not apply to the Great Czech Cases.[53]

CME Czech Republic BV v. Czech Republic, UNCITRAL Case, Final Award, 14 March 2003 (Kühn, Schwebel, Brownlie), paras 432–436 (footnotes omitted)

432. The Tribunal further is of the view that the principle of res judicata does not apply in favour of the London Arbitration for more than one reason. The parties in the London [*Lauder* v. *Czech Republic*] Arbitration differ from the parties in this arbitration. Mr. Lauder is the controlling shareholder of CME Media Ltd, whereas in this arbitration a Dutch holding company being part of the CME Media Ltd Group is the Claimant. The two arbitrations are based on differing bilateral investment treaties, which grant comparable investment protection, which, however, is not identical. Both arbitrations deal with the Media Council's interference with the same investment in the Czech Republic. However, the Tribunal cannot judge whether the facts submitted to the two tribunals for decision are identical and it may well be that facts and circumstances presented to this Tribunal have been presented quite differently to the London Tribunal.

433. Because the two bilateral investment treaties create rights that are not in all respects exactly the same, different claims are necessarily formulated ...

434. This Tribunal decided this issue with binding effect in the Partial Award (Partial Award para. 419). This holding of the Tribunal is supported by the London Tribunal's findings, according to which the Respondent's recourse in the London Arbitration to the principle of *lis alibi pendens* was held to be of no use, since all the other court and arbitration

---

[53] The arbitrator appointed by the Czech Republic did not express a view on whether *res judicata* was applicable in principle: 'For a number of reasons this issue must be set aside. In the first place, the Respondent refused to consolidate the two arbitrations, and, secondly, the Respondent refused to adjourn the Stockholm proceedings in order to await the outcome of the London proceedings.' Separate Opinion on the Issues of Quantum Phase of *CME* v. *Czech Republic* by Arbitrator Brownlie, 14 March 2013, para. 13.

proceedings involved different parties and different causes of actions. The London Tribunal considered the risk that the two Tribunals may decide differently. It identified the risk that damages could be concurrently granted by more than one court or arbitral tribunal, in which case the amount of damages granted by the second deciding court or arbitral tribunal could take this fact into consideration when addressing the final damage (London Award para. 171–172, 174). It did not see an issue in differing decisions, which is a normal fact of forensic life, when different parties litigate the same dispute (which is not necessarily the case in all respects in this arbitration).

435. The principle of res judicata requires, for the 'same' dispute, identical parties, the same subject matter and the same cause of action. This is accepted by international tribunals. Moreover, the fact that one tribunal is competent to resolve the dispute brought before it does not necessarily affect the authority of another tribunal, constituted under a different agreement, to resolve a dispute – even if it were the 'same' dispute ...

436. Only in exceptional cases, in particular in competition law, have tribunals or law courts accepted a concept of a 'single economic entity', which allows discounting of the separate legal existences of the shareholder and the company, mostly, to allow the joining of a parent of a subsidiary to an arbitration. Also a 'company group' theory is not generally accepted in international arbitration (although promoted by prominent authorities) and there are no precedents of which this Tribunal is aware for its general acceptance. In this arbitration the situation is even less compelling. Mr. Lauder, although apparently controlling CME Media Ltd., the Claimant's ultimate parent company, is not the majority shareholder of the company and the cause of action in each proceeding was based on different bilateral investment treaties.

5.4 Sequential Proceedings: Collateral Estoppel/*Res Judicata*

The Great Czech Cases led to a considerable amount of academic reflection.[54] While generalisations do injustice to the subtlety and nuance of this discussion, the overall sense was that the Great Czech Cases may have been right *if* the tripartite definition of *res judicata* described in paragraph 435 of the Final Award in *CME* v. *Czech Republic* was the proper legal standard – but that a decent argument could be made in favour of a more flexible definition.

Hints of arbitral adoption of this approach were first glimpsed in relation to sequential proceedings. *Rachel S. Grynberg and Others* v. *Grenada* considered the issue by reference to collateral estoppel, which it took to be 'a general principle of law applicable in the international courts and tribunals such as this one' (para. 7.1.2).

---

[54] See C. Brown, *A Common Law of International Adjudication* (Oxford University Press, 2007), 245–250; H. Wehland, *The Coordination of Multiple Proceedings in Investment Treaty Arbitration* (Oxford University Press, 2013), 218–226.

Rachel S. Grynberg, Stephen M. Grynberg, Miriam Z. Grynberg and RSM Production Corp. v. Grenada, ICSID Case No. ARB/10/6, Award, 10 December 2010 (Rowley, Nottingham, Tercier), paras 7.1.4–7.1.7

7.1.4 Claimants['] only other argument against the application of the principle is that the three individual Claimants' claims cannot be affected (as regards the rights, questions and facts that were determined by the Prior Tribunal) since only RSM and Grenada were parties to the Prior Arbitration.

7.1.5 In the circumstances of this case, however, the fact the three individual Claimants were not parties to the prior arbitration does not assist. This is because they are, and were at the time of the Prior Arbitration, RSM's three Sole shareholders. They were thus privies of RSM at the time. As such, they, like RSM, are bound by those factual and other determinations regarding questions and rights arising out of or relating to the Agreement.

7.1.6 Of course, RSM is a juridical entity with a legal personality separate from its three shareholders. But this does not alter the analysis. First, the Claimant shareholders' only investment is a contract to which RSM is a party and the shareholders are not: the shareholders seek compensation for damage they allege they have suffered indirectly, 'through RSM', for violations of RSM's legal rights.

7.1.7 It is true that shareholders, under many systems of law, may undertake litigation to pursue or defend rights belonging to the corporation. However, shareholders cannot use such opportunities as both sword and shield. If they wish to claim standing on the basis of their indirect interest in corporate assets, they must be subject to defences that would be available against the corporation – including collateral estoppel.

The *Apotex Holdings Inc. and Other* v. *USA* tribunal approvingly referred to the *Rachel S. Grynberg and Others* v. *Grenada* award and applied it in relation to *res judicata*.[55]

5.5 Parallel Proceedings: Abuse of Process

The precise point of the Great Czech Cases, however, did not appear to be raised in (publicly available) awards for more than a decade. (In the view of some, this reflected a slight sense of unease on the part of practitioners that conscious parallelism, while not technically improper, was not quite a done thing.) A possibility of a second impression arose in the *Ampal-American Israel Corp. and Others* v. *Egypt* case, with a factual pattern of at least superficial similarity to the Great Czech Cases and one of the leading contributors to the academic debate as an arbitrator; an excerpt summarising his views is reproduced before the decision.

---

[55] *Apotex Holdings Inc. and Apotex Inc.* v. *USA*, ICSID Case No. ARB(AF)/12/1, Award, 25 August 2014 (Veeder, Rowley, Crook), paras 7.37–7.40.

C. McLachlan, 'Lis Pendens in International Litigation' (2009) 336 *Collected Courses of the Hague Academy of International Law* 199, 419–420

Parallel treaty arbitrations.[56] Where the same underlying dispute gives rise to claims under two different investment treaties, each tribunal is faced with a potential problem of parallel proceedings within the same legal order. To date tribunals have taken a narrow view in determining whether there is sufficient identity of parties and cause of action, upholding separate corporate personality and finding that each treaty creates separate causes of action. It is submitted that in principle a wider approach ought to be adopted in which sufficient identity of parties would be established where the claimants were in privity of interest with each other (as in the case of the shareholders in an investment company) and the identity of the cause of action is assessed substantively by reference to the nature of the right asserted, and not its source. If sufficient identity is thus established either tribunal is entitled, in the exercise of its discretion, to stay its proceedings if it [is] satisfied that it would be in the interests of justice to do so.

Ampal-American Israel Corp. and Others v. *Egypt*, ICSID Case No. ARB/12/11, Decision on Jurisdiction, 1 February 2016 (Fortier, McLachlan, Orrego Vicuña), paras 328–334 (some footnotes omitted)

328. The Tribunal agrees with the Respondent that the four parallel arbitration[s] with, essentially, the same factual matrix, the same witnesses and many identical claims may look abusive. However, subject to one important qualification in paragraphs 330–333 below, having reviewed carefully all of the Respondent's grounds invoked in support of its submission that the Claimants are not acting in good faith, the Tribunal is not persuaded that the four arbitral proceedings collectively or individually amount to an abuse of process.

329. It is possible, as a jurisdictional matter, for different parties to pursue distinct claims in different fora seeking redress for loss allegedly suffered by each of them arising out of the same factual matrix. As a matter of general principle, contract claims are distinct from treaty claims. Further, in the absence of an agreement to consolidation, two treaty tribunals may each consider claims of separate investors, each of which holds distinct tranches of the same investment. None of the four arbitrations at issue here is, per se, an abuse. It may not be a desirable situation but it cannot be characterized as abusive especially when the Respondent has declined the Claimants' offers to consolidate the proceedings.

---

[56] [Eds: See also McLachlan, '*Lis Pendens* in International Litigation', 408–415, for an extended version of the argument summarised in the excerpt.]

330. However, there is one important exception to this finding of the Tribunal. It concerns the overlap of claims by Mr. Maiman in the present case and the UNCITRAL arbitration (the two treaty cases) for the recovery of the same sum.

331. Indeed, in the present arbitration, the Claimant Ampal, controlled by Mr. Yosef Maiman, advances its claim in respect of the same 12.5% indirect interest in EMG for which Ampal's 100% subsidiary, Merhav-Ampal Group Ltd (MAGL) (and its 50% subsidiary, Merhav-Ampal Energy Holdings) claim in the parallel Maiman arbitration (together the 'MAGL portion'). This is tantamount to double pursuit of the same claim in respect of the same interest.

> [Footnote 340: *RSM Production Corporation and others* v. *Grenada*, ICSID Case No. ARB/10/6, Award, 10 December 2010, paras. 7.1.5–7.1.7; *Apotex Holdings Inc. and Apotex Inc.* v. *United States of America*, ICSID Case No. ARB(AF)/12/1, Award, 25 August 2014, para. 7.40.]
>
> In the Tribunal's opinion, while the same party in interest might reasonably seek to protect its claim in two fora where the jurisdiction of each tribunal is unclear, once jurisdiction is otherwise confirmed, it would crystallize in an abuse of process for in substance the same claim is to be pursued on the merits before two tribunals. However, the Tribunal wishes to make it very clear that this resulting abuse of process is in no way tainted by bad faith on the part of the Claimants as alleged by the Respondent. It is merely the result of the factual situation that would arise were two claims to be pursued before different investment tribunals in respect of the same tranche of the same investment.

332. On 11 December 2015, the Tribunal was provided with a copy of a letter from the Permanent Court of Arbitration in the *Maiman* arbitration, in which the Tribunal in those proceedings informed the parties therein that 'the Tribunal has now decided that it has jurisdiction *ratione personae*. The Tribunal will provide reasons for this decision subsequently, in its Award.'

333. The consequence of this finding, together with the balance of the present Decision on Jurisdiction, is that the abuse of process constituted by the double pursuit of the MAGL portion of the claim in both proceedings must now be treated as having crystallized. Both Tribunals have confirmed that they have jurisdiction. It follows from this therefore that there is no risk of a denial of justice occasioned by the absence of a tribunal competent to determine the MAGL portion of the claim. Both Tribunals are seised of the merits and neither Tribunal has yet reached a decision on the merits.

334. It lies in the power of Ampal, as 100% owner of MAGL through Ampal Energy Ltd (Israel) to cure the abuse here identified were Ampal and MAGL to elect, in light of the present Decision which has otherwise confirmed the Tribunal's jurisdiction, to submit the MAGL portion of the claim made in the *Maiman* arbitration to the exclusive jurisdiction of the present Tribunal, relinquishing that part of the claim in the *Maiman* arbitration, or conversely to pursue such claim only in the latter proceeding.

In response, the investors made an election in favour of *Ampal-American Israel Corp. and Others* v. *Egypt* proceedings, relinquishing the overlapping claim in the UNCITRAL arbitration.[57] A later decision applied the same principle more broadly, taking the view that mere *initiation* of parallel proceedings may be abusive, rather than *pursuing* parallel proceedings after jurisdiction has been confirmed in both cases. The tribunal did not comment on *Ampal-American Israel Corp. and Others.* v. *Egypt* (the State was represented by the same counsel in both cases) but did make some remarks about the Great Czech Cases.

***Orascom TMT Investments S.à r.l.* v. *Algeria*, ICSID Case No. ARB/12/35, Award, 31 May 2017 (Kaufmann-Kohler, van den Berg, Stern), paras 542–543, 547 (footnotes omitted)**

542. ... an investor who controls several entities in a vertical chain of companies may commit an abuse if it seeks to impugn the same host state measures and claims for the same harm at various levels of the chain in reliance on several investment treaties concluded by the host state. It goes without saying that structuring an investment through several layers of corporate entities in different states is not illegitimate. Indeed, the structure may well pursue legitimate corporate, tax, or pre-dispute BIT nationality planning purposes. In the field of investment treaties, the existence of a vertical corporate chain and of treaty protection covering 'indirect' investments implies that several entities in the chain may claim treaty protection, especially where a host state has entered into several investment treaties. In other words, several corporate entities in the chain may be in a position to bring an arbitration against the host state in relation to the same investment. This possibility, however, does not mean that the host state has accepted to be sued multiple times by various entities under the same control that are part of the vertical chain in relation to the same investment, the same measures and the same harm.

543. In the Tribunal's opinion, this conclusion derives from the purpose of investment treaties, which is to promote the economic development of the host state and to protect the investments made by foreigners that are expected to contribute to such development. If the protection is sought at one level of the vertical chain, and in particular at the first level of foreign shareholding, that purpose is fulfilled. The purpose is not served by allowing other entities in the vertical chain controlled by the same shareholder to seek protection for the same harm inflicted on the investment. Quite to the contrary, such additional protection would give rise to a risk of multiple recoveries and conflicting decisions, not to speak of the waste of resources that multiple proceedings involve. The occurrence of such risks would conflict with the promotion of economic development in circumstances where the protection of the investment is already triggered. Thus, where multiple treaties offer entities in a vertical chain similar procedural rights of access to an arbitral forum and comparable substantive guarantees, the initiation of multiple proceedings to recover for essentially the

---

[57] *Ampal-American Israel Corp. and Others* v. *Egypt*, ICSID Case No. ARB/12/11, Decision on Liability and Heads of Loss, 21 February 2017 (Fortier, McLachlan, Orrego Vicuña), paras 11–23.

same economic harm would entail the exercise of rights for purposes that are alien to those for which these rights were established.

...

547. It is true that tribunals in the past have adopted different approaches in relation to constellations that may show some similarities with the present case. In particular, the tribunals in *CME* v. *Czech Republic* and *Lauder* v. *Czech Republic* allowed the claims under different investment treaties to proceed, despite the fact that both sets of proceedings were based on the same facts and sought reparation for the same harm. The tribunals then reached contradicting outcomes, which was one of the reasons for which these decisions attracted wide criticism. This said, these cases should be placed in the context of their procedural history, in which the respondent had refused several offers to consolidate or otherwise coordinate proceedings. Moreover, it cannot be denied that in the fifteen years that have followed those cases, the investment treaty jurisprudence has evolved, including on the application of the principle of abuse of rights (or abuse of process), as was recalled above. The resort to such principle has allowed tribunals to apply investment treaties in such a manner as to avoid consequences unforeseen by their drafters and at odds with the very purposes underlying the conclusion of those treaties.

5.6 Remedies

Finally, parallel proceedings may also be taken into account at the remedies stage – a point alluded to in the excerpted paragraph 434 of the Final Award in *CME* v. *Czech Republic*. While it is not an issue of jurisdiction or admissibility, the remedial perspective should also be noted at this juncture because it is one of the legal tools that a tribunal may employ in dealing with parallel proceedings (more on remedies at Chapter 17). The recent decision by the annulment committee in the *Venezuela Holdings, BV and Others* v. *Venezuela* case made some critical observations about the manner of the tribunal's untangling of various rules and remedies. The passage excerpted below deals with the relevance to the investment treaty case of an International Chamber of Commerce (ICC) arbitration that one of the investors had brought against two State-owned entities of Venezuela. A reader gets a good sense of what, in the view of this annulment committee, should *not* be done (what should be done, as the committee notes at paragraph 190 excerpted below, is a different matter altogether).

***Venezuela Holdings, BV* v. Venezuela, ICSID Case No. ARB/07/27, Decision on Annulment, 9 March 2017 (Berman, Abraham, Knieper), paras 147–149, 178, 190 (footnotes omitted)**

147. The Tribunal deals with this matter (once again briefly) in Section VIII.C.5 of the Award, in which, having recalled the general principle of no *enrichissement sans cause* and recited the specific contractual provisions against it, the Tribunal notes an express statement made

by the Claimants during the proceedings (which the Tribunal says it has no reason to doubt) that, in the event of an award in their favour in the ICSID proceedings, they were willing to make the required reimbursement to PDVSA (the parent body of Lagoven). The Tribunal concludes as follows, in paragraph 381: 'Effectively, the total compensation payable to the Claimants is the amount specified in paragraph 374 above, less the amount already received by the Claimants under the ICC Award for the same damage. Double recovery will thus be avoided.' Linked to this is point (e) in the dispositive part of the Award, in which the Tribunal 'takes note ... of the Claimants' representation that, in the event of favourable award, the Claimants are willing to make the required reimbursements to PDVSA. Double recovery will thus be avoided'.

148. The Committee did its utmost to understand exactly what the Tribunal might have been intending to convey through these passages. Even after having sought the assistance of the Parties in this endeavour, the Committee remains in a state of some uncertainty. Fortunately, however, in view of what follows, the matter turns out to be immaterial to the Committee's decision on the request for annulment, and the Committee sees no need to pursue it further, on the basis that the avoidance of double recovery is, in its essence, an adjustment that might arise *ex post facto* (as the paragraphs cited above seem to imply), whereas the question raised in these annulment proceedings is one going to the basis for the assessment of the compensation due in the first place. The Committee notes simply that the conclusion is however irresistible that the Tribunal saw in its mind some sort of necessary connection, however unspecific, between the contractual liability (already met) and the compensation still to be assessed in the BIT Arbitration.

149. This conclusion is reinforced by the fact that, in a separate section of its Award, the Tribunal addresses directly what it calls 'Effects of the ICC Arbitration', and that (as paragraph 215 of the Award indicates) this was a question which the Tribunal had itself raised with the Parties. In crude terms, the Claimants' position was 'no effect at all', and the Respondent's 'full effect' (i.e. that nothing remained over for decision in the BIT arbitration). The remaining paragraphs in this section of the Award are devoted to the Tribunal's reasons for rejecting the Respondent's contention. The Tribunal points out in particular that there was no identity of parties: the State was not party to the ICC arbitration, nor was Lagoven, the respondent in the ICC proceedings, party to the BIT Arbitration. The Tribunal does, however, go on to note (in paragraph 218) that the Association Agreement limits the compensation due from PDVSA, a limitation reflected in the amount awarded by the ICC tribunal, and then adds 'No such limitation applies, however, to the State's responsibility under the BIT'; and it gives as the reasons for this that the Government of Venezuela was 'neither a party to the Association Agreement nor a third-party beneficiary', and that Venezuela had not 'advanced any relevant argument that the limitations on ... contractual liability under Clause 15 should be transmuted into limitations of the State's responsibility under international law'. The Section concludes with a forward reference to the Section of the Award dealing with quantum, to which the Committee will turn below.

...

178. The first set of reasons is to be found at paragraphs 216 and 218 of the Award. Here the Tribunal decides that the ICC arbitration and the BIT Arbitration 'concern the liability of different parties under different normative regimes'. It also decides that, while the Association Agreement does incorporate a limit on the compensation due from PDVSA, '[n]o such limitation applies ... to the State's responsibility under the BIT', and gives as the reason that the Government 'was neither a party to the CNAA nor a third-party beneficiary'. The context for these findings was (see above) the question the Tribunal had itself raised *ex officio* as to what impact (if any) the award that had in the meanwhile been issued by the ICC tribunal should have on the still pending dispute under the BIT. In this context, the decision by the Tribunal that the ICC arbitration was formally irrelevant to the issue before it is readily understandable. It is moreover a decision the Tribunal was competent to make and is not subject to appeal. What preoccupies the Committee, though, is whether a simple decision that the ICC award on the contract dispute did not in and of itself bring an end to the dispute under the BIT became transmogrified, whether consciously or not, into something much wider, and at a stage before the provisions of the BIT governing compensation had been addressed in the Award at all. Both in paragraph 216 and in paragraph 218, the Tribunal prays in aid a source of law that is not within the listing in Article 9(5), namely 'international law' *tout court* (see paragraph 155 above). That the use here of 'international law' is not merely an imprecise shorthand for the BIT appears unmistakably from the language of paragraph 216 which, as set out above, refers to responsibility for breach of the BIT 'and international law'. The same appears, though rather less explicitly, in the reference in paragraph 218 to a contractual clause becoming 'transmuted into limitations of the State's responsibility under international law'. No explanation is given of how or why a putative responsibility of the Respondent State under international law extraneous to the BIT might fall within the Tribunal's jurisdiction.

...

190. The Committee should not be understood by this Decision to be determining in what way either the Price Cap or the outcome of the ICC arbitration should be brought to bear on the assessment of compensation in the present dispute. That would lie beyond its competence, and is in any event a decision which the Committee is in no position to make. The Committee's decision is directed simply at the *a priori* exclusion in the Award of certain essential elements from the process of arriving at the compensation due pursuant to the terms of Article 6 of the BIT.

CONCLUSION

International investment arbitration is consensual. The practice of investment treaty arbitration has led respondent States to raise a particularly rich array of preliminary objections to consideration of claims on the merits, often presented under the portmanteau phrase of 'jurisdiction and admissibility'. Decisions and legal writings on jurisdiction and admissibility have grappled with both conceptual and practical issues, the former of which are convenient to address first.

What is the difference between jurisdiction and admissibility? Reasonable people and institutions have disagreed on the point, and inconsistency in the drafting of treaties and judicial and arbitral decisions has further muddied the waters. As the Singapore Court Appeal observed in *Swissbourgh* v. *Lesotho* case, with a nod to the first edition of this book, much depends on the way in which the question is posed. Some writers and tribunals consider whether the objection is directed against the tribunal (and is hence jurisdictional) or at the claim (and is hence one of admissibility). Other authorities focus on the place that the issue occupies in the structure of international dispute settlement: is the question related to the interpretation and application of the jurisdictional clause of the international tribunal (and hence jurisdictional), or is it related to interpretation and application of another rule or instrument (and is hence one of admissibility)?

Why should one care about the distinction between jurisdiction and admissibility? In many cases, one perhaps should not – other than for aesthetic reasons – since a successful invocation of either type of objection will result in the case not being considered on its merits. But there are some instances in which the distinction is important. First, perhaps there is greater flexibility for tribunals to consider developments taking place after the request for arbitration when issues of admissibility are concerned. Second, tribunals have an obligation to address possible objections to jurisdiction, while objections to admissibility are for the parties to invoke or waive, expressly or by necessary implication. Third, tribunals that uphold objections to admissibility may stay proceedings without dismissing the claim, if they have jurisdiction. Fourth, issues of jurisdiction may be (more easily) subject to review than issues of admissibility.

What is the procedure for addressing challenges to jurisdiction and admissibility? In general terms, arbitral rules leave considerable discretion to tribunals in deciding whether it is more appropriate to address preliminary objections together with the merits or separately. It bears noting that arbitral rules and treaty instruments of consent increasingly provide for special expeditious procedures for addressing preliminary objections that claims are manifestly without legal merit or unfounded as a matter of law.

What are the most important objections to jurisdiction and admissibility? The most common objections are probably those directed at the jurisdictional peculiarities that distinguish international investment arbitration from international commercial arbitration on the one hand and inter-State arbitration on the other: the peculiar procedural actor – 'investor' – and the peculiar subject matter – 'investment'. Arbitral practice has also dealt with a considerable number of other discrete objections, most of them related in one way or another to the consent by States to arbitrate a particular claim in a particular manner. Finally, what is the best legal position regarding objections to parallel proceedings, to take one particularly vexing preliminary objection? Consent by disputing parties and – increasingly – rules on consolidation or coordination in arbitral rules or the instrument of consent may resolve the issue. But often neither option is available. One response, adopted in the first great disputes, is to view parallel proceedings as reflective of the decentralised structure of international dispute settlement and, to the extent that they do not satisfy the strict criteria of traditional doctrines of *res judicata* and *lis alibi pendens*, not raising any normative eyebrows. Recent practice is more inclined to be flexible. Sequential proceedings have been addressed by reference to collateral estoppel and *res judicata*, and parallel proceedings in terms of abuse of process. And, to the extent that parallel proceedings have not been coordinated at inception, it may be possible to do that at the remedial stage – although untangling the right rights in the right order may be a challenging endeavour.

QUESTIONS

1. What is 'jurisdiction and admissibility'? How is 'jurisdiction' different from 'admissibility'? Who got the distinction right in the *İçkale İnşaat Ltd Şirketi* v. *Turkmenistan* case?
2. Distinction between jurisdiction and admissibility is, for almost all practical purposes, irrelevant. Discuss.
3. What is the procedural framework for addressing objections to jurisdiction and admissibility?
4. Practice of arbitral tribunals has shifted from insufficient to excessive willingness to accept objections to jurisdiction and admissibility. This is a particularly observable phenomenon in cases which attract public attention. Discuss.
5. Why are parallel proceedings problematic? Can the *Ampal-American Israel Corp. and Others* v. *Egypt* decision be reconciled with the *Orascom* v. *Algeria* award? If not, which is the better reading of applicable rules and principles?

SUGGESTIONS FOR FURTHER READING

1. J. Collier and V. Lowe, *The Settlement of Disputes in International Law: Institutions and Procedures* (Oxford University Press, 1999), 190–206.
2. J. Paulsson, 'Jurisdiction and Admissibility' in G. Aksen and R. Briner (eds), *Global Reflections on International Law, Commerce and Dispute Resolution: Liber Amicorum in Honour of Robert Briner* (Paris: International Chamber of Commerce, 2005), 601.
3. H. Wehland, *The Coordination of Multiple Proceedings in Investment Treaty Arbitration* (Oxford University Press, 2013).
4. M. Waibel, 'Investment Arbitration: Jurisdiction and Admissibility' in M. Bungenberg, J. Griebel, S. Hobe and A. Reinisch (eds), *International Investment Law: A Handbook* (Baden-Baden: C. H. Beck/Hart/Nomos, 2015), 1212.
5. Y. Shany, *Questions of Jurisdiction and Admissibility before International Courts* (Cambridge University Press, 2015).

6

Applicable Laws

CHAPTER OUTLINE

This chapter covers a preliminary issue that arises for consideration in investment arbitration. It can be read in conjunction with Chapter 8, which addresses another preliminary issue – the treatment of evidence. The resolution of preliminary issues should precede any attempt by an arbitral tribunal to fully evaluate the strength of each disputing party's submissions on the merits. However, excepting applicable laws governing the dispute, guiding principles on the assessment of evidence are discussed by some arbitral tribunals, but not others. This chapter focuses on the sources and interplay of laws applicable to the substance and procedure of a claim. Section 1 deals with the *lex causae*, the law applicable to the substance of the dispute. Section 2 deals with the *lex arbitri*, the law governing the arbitral process. Section 3 deals with the *lex loci arbitri*, the law of the seat of arbitration.

INTRODUCTION

Before an arbitral tribunal embarks on a thorough evaluation of the strength of a claim that culminates in a final award, it must ensure that this evaluation is conducted in accordance with the laws and principles that govern the dispute. These laws supply the juridical basis for a party's liability (*lex causae*), shape arbitral proceedings (*lex arbitri*) or belong to the seat of the arbitration (*lex loci arbitri*). Given the potential variety of laws to which a claim is subject, determining what the applicable laws are and how they interact is not always straightforward. However, the proper identification of the applicable laws by an arbitral tribunal is crucial to the finality of the ensuing award. An award premised on the erroneous identification of the applicable laws is susceptible to challenge, and may not be enforceable.[1] Determining the applicable laws is therefore one of the most vital tasks that an arbitral tribunal undertakes.

---

[1] See Section 1.3, this chapter. For awards issued pursuant to the Convention on the Settlement of Investment Disputes between States and Nationals of Other States (signed 18 March 1965, entered into force 14 October 1966) 575 UNTS 159 (ICSID Convention), the misidentification or non-application of applicable laws establishes the ground for annulment under Art. 52(1)(b), namely, 'that the Tribunal has manifestly exceeded its powers'. In *Klöckner Industrie-Anlagen GmbH and Others* v. *Cameroon and Another*, ICSID Case No. ARB/81/2, the law applicable to the substance of the dispute was 'Cameroonian law based on

Applicable laws can be substantive, procedural or both. The laws governing the merits of the dispute, namely, the *lex causae*, are substantive laws. The laws governing the arbitral process, namely, the *lex arbitri*, are procedural laws. The laws of the seat of the arbitration or the *lex loci arbitri*, particularly the mandatory rules of the forum from which parties cannot derogate or contract out of, can regulate both substantive and procedural matters. The following discussion elaborates on the identification of the standard suite of applicable laws, starting with the *lex causae*, which often derives from more than one source.

1. *LEX CAUSAE*

When a dispute arises between an investor, a traditional subject of national law, and a State, a traditional subject of international law, the *lex causae* can be national law, international law or a combination of the two.[2] Ascertaining the *lex causae* in investment arbitration involves a two-stage inquiry. The first stage pinpoints the sources of laws that have a bearing on the merits of the dispute (Section 1.1). The second stage establishes how the different laws correlate and apply when judging the merits of the dispute (Section 1.2). As the *lex causae* is central to dispute resolution, the amount of latitude arbitral tribunals possess when determining the *lex causae* is highly consequential. The final section considers the scope of arbitral mandate with regard to the choice of applicable substantive laws (Section 1.3).

1.1 Sources of Laws

There are two sources of laws that form potential bases for liability in investment arbitration. The first is national law and the second is international law. Disputing parties may agree on the source(s) of substantive laws before the dispute is heard, and in the absence of such agreement, the arbitral tribunal identifies the *lex causae*.

When national law is identified as a source of laws, this can refer to the proper law of the contract when a claim alleges the breach of contractual obligations by the host State, and/or the laws of the host State where the investment is situated. In contract-based investment disputes submitted to arbitration, parties are free to stipulate the laws of the host State or some other national law as the contractual proper law. But when the contract is silent on its governing law, tribunals normally adopt a conflict of laws approach to arrive at the host State's laws as the contractual proper law. In *SPP (Middle East) Ltd and Southern Pacific Properties Ltd* v. *Egypt and Another* (*SPP* v. *Egypt*), a contract concluded between SPP and an Egyptian State entity for the development of a touristic site on the Pyramids Plateau in Giza did not stipulate any applicable laws. In addressing

---

French law'. The tribunal made passing reference to French law in its award, but otherwise failed to connect the general principles of commercial dealings on which it based its decision with French or Cameroonian law. The award was duly annulled by the Ad Hoc Committee for the tribunal's manifest excess of powers, Decision of the Ad Hoc Committee on the Application for Annulment Submitted by Klöckner against the Arbitral Award rendered on 21 October 1983 (Lalive, El-Kosheri, Seidl-Hohenveldern), 3 May 1985, paras 57–82.

2 J. Ho, 'Unraveling the *Lex Causae* in Investment Claims' (2014) 15(3–4) *JWIT* 757, 757, 761–763.

the claim by SPP that Egypt and its State entity had breached the contract, the tribunal relied on the parties' submissions as well as the 'ordinary principles on conflict of laws' to identify Egyptian law as the applicable national law.[3]

SPP v. Egypt, ICC Arbitration No. YD/AS NO 3493, Award, 11 March 1983 (Bernini, Elghatit, Littman), para. 49

The Agreements do not provide specifically for the law which is to govern the contract. The parties have fully debated this issue coming to conclusions which only partially diverge. They both agree that in view of the circumstances of the case the relevant domestic law is that of Egypt ... May we observe, *ad abundantiam*, that failing contractual designation of the governing law the same result (i.e. reference to the law of the host country) would also normally be achieved by applying the ordinary principles on conflict of laws. In the case at issue the governing law is, in our opinion, the law of Egypt. The Agreements were both made in Egypt. The place of performance was almost entirely Egypt. There are numerous references to Egyptian law in the Agreements.

In non-contract-based investment disputes that are submitted to investment treaty arbitration, national law is a source of applicable substantive laws. This may be because the relevant investment treaty requires an investment to be admitted and established in accordance with host State laws to be eligible for treaty protection,[4] or because reference to national law is necessary to verify the ownership, content and recognition by the respondent host State of rights that the claimant investor seeks to vindicate. In both cases, the applicable national law is the host State's laws.

Agreement between the Government of the Republic of Mauritius and the Government of the Arab Republic of Egypt on the Reciprocal Promotion and Protection of Investments, 25 June 2014, Art. 1(1)

'investment' means every kind of asset that has the characteristics of an investment, such as the commitment of capital or other resources, the expectation of gain or profit, the assumption of risk, the contribution to sustainable development, and established or acquired by an investor of one Contracting Party in the territory of the other Contracting Party in accordance with the laws and regulations of the latter Contracting Party ...

---

[3] ICC Arbitration No. YD/AS NO 3493, Award, 11 March 1983 (Bernini, Elghatit, Littman), 86 International Law Reports 434.

[4] See also Agreement between the Federal Republic of Germany and the Republic of the Philippines for the Promotion and Reciprocal Protection of Investments (Germany–Philippines BIT) (signed 18 April 1997, entered into force 1 February 2000), Art. 1(1) provides in relevant part: 'For the purpose of this Agreement, the term "investment" shall mean any kind of asset accepted in accordance with the respective laws and regulations of either Contracting State.' Non-compliance with Filipino legislation rendered a German investment ineligible for the treaty's protection in *Fraport AG Frankfurt Airport Services Worldwide* v. *Philippines*, ICSID Case No. ARB/03/25, Award, 16 August 2007 (Fortier, Cremades, Reisman), paras 386–396; and again in *Fraport AG Frankfurt Airport Services Worldwide* v. *Philippines (II)*, ICSID Case No. ARB/11/12, Award, 10 December 2014 (Bernadini, Alexandrov, van den Berg), paras 442–468. The case was resubmitted after the Award of 16 August 2007 was annulled by the Decision on the Application for Annulment of Fraport AG Frankfurt Airport Services Worldwide, 23 December 2010 (Tomka, Hascher, McLachlan).

Vestey Group Ltd v. Venezuela, ICSID Case No. ARB/06/4, Award, 15 April 2016 (Kaufmann–Kohler, Grigera Naón, Dupuy), paras 251–253, 257 (footnotes omitted)

251. It is common ground between the Parties that Venezuela took over the control of Agroflora's administration and assets. The Respondent contends, however, that Vestey did not own the land of its Farms and that, therefore, it simply recovered public land for which it owes no compensation.

252. To determine whether Venezuela's taking of Agroflora's land constitutes an expropriation, the Tribunal must assess whether Vestey held a title to the land. The Parties agree that Venezuelan law governs ownership of the land. They disagree, however, on whether the Land Law, being one of the contested measures, must be taken into account when reviewing ownership.

253. As was described above, the present dispute arose when Venezuela introduced certain measures under the Land Law, starting with the adoption of the 2001 Land Law itself and culminating in the recovery proceedings in 2011. The Land Law is the very measure that Vestey is challenging before this Tribunal as one of the expropriatory acts which deprived it of its investment. The Parties are in agreement that an investor's ownership over the allegedly affected assets must be assessed immediately before the adoption of the challenged measures. Accordingly, the Tribunal will review the validity of Vestey's title just before the introduction of the Land Law, i.e. as of 13 November 2001.

...

257. ... The requirements for acquiring property rights over immovable assets situated in Venezuela are governed by specific norms of Venezuelan property law. For a private person to have a claim under international law arising from the deprivation of its property, it must hold that property in accordance with applicable rules of domestic law.

When international law is identified as a source of laws, this can refer to treaty law, customary law and/or general principles of law.[5] Investment disputes, regardless of whether they are submitted to investment treaty arbitration, may involve questions of international law. This is because one of the parties to the dispute is a State, and States bear a wide range of international obligations. And when States violate international obligations, the characterisation and consequences of the violation are governed by international law. Returning to the case of *SPP* v. *Egypt* discussed above, there was no applicable investment treaty. Apart from claiming damages from Egypt and its State entity for a

---

[5] Art. 38(1) of the Statute of the International Court of Justice sets out a widely accepted, though not necessarily exhaustive, list of sources of international law: 'The Court, whose function is to decide in accordance with international law such disputes as are submitted to it, shall apply:
    (a) international conventions, whether general or particular, establishing rules expressly recognized by the contesting states;
    (b) international custom, as evidence of a general practice accepted as law;
    (c) the general principles of law recognized by civilized nations;
    (d) subject to the provisions of Article 59, judicial decisions and the teachings of the most highly qualified publicists of the various nations, as subsidiary means for the determination of rules of law.'

breach of contract, SPP requested, in the alternative, just compensation in accordance with international law, for the expropriation by Egypt of its contractual rights. The tribunal agreed with SPP that in addition to Egyptian law, general principles of law are a source of *lex causae*.

SPP v. Egypt, ICC Award (Bernadini, Elghatit, Litman), para. 49

The claimants, however, contend that no rules and/or principles drawn from the body of domestic Egyptian law should be allowed to override the principles of international law applicable to international investment projects of this kind (Final Submission, pages 24–7; Statement of Argument, pages 65–778). The defendants refute 'the claimants' argument in favour of the so-called "denationalization" of the applicable law', coming to the conclusion that 'the law governing the substantive issues could be nothing but the Egyptian legal system' (Government's Supplementary Statement of Argument, page 13, referring to Government's Rejoinder and Statement of Argument, pages 104–30).

...

Claimants' arguments in the affirmative are supported by the opinion of Egyptian law specialists aimed at demonstrating that principles of international law such as '*pacta sunt servanda*' and 'just compensation for expropriatory measures' are not incompatible with the Egyptian legal system.

...

The impact of Law No 43 of 1974 upon the Egyptian legal system is a further decisive element in support of Claimants' contention. This law makes specific reference to the ICSID Convention, signed and ratified by Egypt on 11 February 1972 and 3 May 1972 respectively, and entered into force for Egypt as of 2 June 1972.

We have found that international law principles such as '*pacta sunt servanda*' and 'just compensation for expropriatory measures' can be deemed as part of Egyptian Law. The adherence to the ICSID Convention should then be treated as conclusive evidence of Egypt's declared intent to abide by these principles, which indeed represent the basic philosophy adopted by the Convention's drafters.[6]

Last but not least, art. 13(5) of the ICC rules unequivocally states that 'in all cases the arbitrator shall take into account the provisions of the contract and the relevant trade usages['] ...

For the foregoing reasons we find that references to Egyptian law must be construed so as to include such principles of international law as may be applicable and that the national laws of Egypt can be relied upon only in as much as they do not contravene said principles.

If an investor brings a treaty claim, treaty law becomes the principal source of *lex causae*. Unless an aspect of the treaty claim is unregulated by treaty, the general rule of thumb is that treaty law as *lex specialis* will prevail over any conflicting customary law or general

---

[6] [Eds: Convention on the Settlement of Investment Disputes between States and Nationals of Other States (signed 18 March 1965, entered into force 14 October 1966), 575 UNTS 159.]

principles of law as *lex generalis*.[7] In *CMS Gas Transmission Co.* v. *Argentina*,[8] Argentina argued that the devaluation of the peso, which damaged US investments, was a necessary measure taken in response to an economic crisis, and precluded Argentina's liability for a breach of its treaty obligations by virtue of Article XI of the Treaty between the United States of America and the Argentine Republic Concerning the Reciprocal Encouragement and Protection of Investment (US–Argentina BIT).[9] The tribunal assessed Argentina's defence of necessity with reference to the conditions for a state of necessity to accrue under customary international law, as codified in Article 25 of the International Law Commission (ILC) Articles on State Responsibility.[10]

In its application for an annulment of the award, Argentina objected to the conflation of the treaty and customary position on a defence of necessity by the tribunal, calling this a manifest excess of the tribunal's powers.[11] The Ad Hoc Committee agreed with Argentina that the tribunal erred in law, but disagreed that this was a manifest excess of powers. In dismissing Argentina's application to annul this portion of the award, the Ad Hoc Committee confirmed that Article XI as *lex specialis* takes precedence over Article 25 as *lex generalis*.[12]

1.2 Interplay of Laws

To the extent that the *lex causae* in investment arbitration is a mix of national and international law,[13] the second stage of the inquiry examines how these laws interact. There are three possible configurations. The first is the application of national law to the head(s)

---

[7] J. Crawford (ed.), *Brownlie's Principles of Public International Law*, 8th edn (Oxford University Press, 2012), 22.

[8] ICSID Case No. ARB/01/8, Decision of the Ad Hoc Committee on the Application for Annulment of the Argentine Republic, 25 September 2007 (Guillaume, Elaraby, Crawford).

[9] Signed 14 November 1991, entered into force 20 October 1994. Art. XI. It provides: 'This Treaty shall not preclude the application by either Party of measures necessary for the maintenance of public order, the fulfillment of its obligations with respect to the maintenance or restoration of international peace or security, or the Protection of its own essential security interests.'

[10] Articles on Responsibility of States for Internationally Wrongful Acts, UN Doc. A/56/83 (2001). Art. 25 provides:
  1. Necessity may not be invoked by a State as a ground for precluding the wrongfulness of an act not in conformity with an international obligation of that State unless the act:
     (a) is the only way for the State to safeguard an essential interest against a grave and imminent peril; and
     (b) does not seriously impair an essential interest of the State or States towards which the obligation exists, or of the international community as a whole.
  2. In any case, necessity may not be invoked by a State as a ground for precluding wrongfulness if:
     (a) the international obligation in question excludes the possibility of invoking necessity; or
     (b) the State has contributed to the situation of necessity.

[11] Convention on the Settlement of Investment Disputes between States and Nationals of Other States, 18 March 1965 (ICSID Convention), Art. 52.

[12] Decision of the Ad Hoc Committee on the Application for Annulment of the Argentine Republic, paras 128–136.

[13] The interplay of national and international law in investment arbitration was not always a given. As Ho explains in 'Unraveling the *Lex Causae* in Investment Claims', 761–762 (footnotes omitted): '[d]iscussions on the identification of the *lex causae* in international claims often revisit the contested order of priority in which national law or international law applies, otherwise known as the debate between monism and dualism. Monism asserts the superiority of international law over national law so that international law

of claim that engage a State's liability under national law, and the application of international law to the head(s) of claim that engage a State's liability under international law. The second is the application of national law to determine if rights which can only be conferred by the host State, and for which the investor seeks treaty protection, exist. The third, lesser-known configuration is the merged application of national and international law whenever an investor alleges that the host State has violated an umbrella clause. Each of these configurations will be explained in turn.

1.2.1 Configuration 1 – Matching Each Head of Claim to Its Governing Law

The first configuration divides an investment claim into parts which should be governed by national law and parts which should be governed by international law. An investment claim that lends itself to such a division tends to be contractual in origin. When a foreign investor alleges that a host State is liable for damages for breaching a contract or concession, it is making a contract claim that falls to be determined in accordance with the proper law of the contract, which is often host State law, or national law. When the investor further alleges that the State, by breaching the contract or concession, is simultaneously in breach of a treaty obligation, it is making a treaty claim that has to be determined in accordance with international law. The distinction between a contract claim and a treaty claim, and the resulting distinction between the substantive laws applicable to each claim, was set out by the Ad Hoc Committee in *Compañia de Aguas del Aconquija SA and Vivendi Universal* v. *Argentina* (*Vivendi Universal and Another* v. *Argentina*).[14] Here, the US claimants requested a partial annulment of an award on the basis that the tribunal manifestly exceeded its powers by declining to consider whether the activities of the provincial Tucumán government in relation to a concession were in breach of the US–Argentina BIT.

> **Vivendi Universal and Another v. Argentina, ICSID Case No. ARB/97/3, Decision on Annulment, 3 July 2002 (Fortier, Crawford, Fernández Rozas), paras 95–96 (footnotes omitted)**
>
> 95. As to the relation between breach of contract and breach of treaty in the present case, it must be stressed that Articles 3 and 5 of the BIT do not relate directly to breach of a municipal contract. Rather they set an independent standard. A state may breach a treaty without breaching a contract, and vice versa, and this is certainly true of these provisions of the BIT. The point is made clear in Article 3 of the ILC Articles [on State Responsibility], which is entitled 'Characterization of an act of a State as internationally wrongful':

as the ultimate *lex causae* always trumps national law. Dualism, in contrast, maintains that national law applies only to disputes between private persons while international law applies only to disputes between States. Depending on who the parties to the dispute are, the *lex causae* can only be national law, or international law, but never both. However, the proliferation of investment treaties which pair traditional subjects of national law (investors) who pursue investment claims, with traditional subjects of international law (States) who defend investment claims, contextualises the difficulty of reducing the *lex causae* to a stark choice between utter supremacy or separation. New developments call for new perspectives.'

[14] ICSID Case No. ARB/97/3, Decision on Annulment, 3 July 2002 (Fortier, Crawford, Fernández Rozas).

The characterization of an act of a State as internationally wrongful is governed by international law. Such characterization is not affected by the characterization of the same act as lawful by internal law.

96. In accordance with this general principle (which is undoubtedly declaratory of general international law), whether there has been a breach of the BIT and whether there has been a breach of contract are different questions. Each of these claims will be determined by reference to its own proper or applicable law – in the case of the BIT, by international law; in the case of the Concession Contract, by the proper law of the contract, in other words, the law of Tucumán. For example, in the case of a claim based on a treaty, international law rules of attribution apply, with the result that the state of Argentina is internationally responsible for the acts of its provincial authorities. By contrast, the state of Argentina is not liable for the performance of contracts entered into by Tucumán, which possesses separate legal personality under its own law and is responsible for the performance of its own contracts.

1.2.2 Configuration 2 – *Renvoi* to National Law

The second configuration applies national law to determine an investor's eligibility for treaty protection. Eligibility depends on the investor's nationality, the legality of the investment and existence of the right(s) that the investor asserts. Whether an investor possesses the nationality of the other Contracting State to an investment treaty, thereby qualifying as a protected investor under that treaty, falls to be determined by the laws of its identified home State.[15] Whether an investment satisfies the admissibility and establishment requirements laid down by the host State can only be answered by returning to host State laws.[16] And whether the investor possesses the right(s) which it claims and whether such right(s) are capable of treaty protection are again questions for the laws of the host State. This configuration of the interplay between national and international law is commonly seen in expropriation claims, where tribunals must ascertain that the investor has, in the first place, rights which can be expropriated.

In *Accession Mezzanine Capital LP and Another v. Hungary*,[17] the tribunal applied Hungarian law – the host State's law – to ascertain if the claimants held rights recognised under Hungarian law that could form the object of an expropriation claim brought under Article 6 of the Agreement between the Government of the United Kingdom of Great Britain and Northern Ireland and the Government of the Hungarian People's Republic for the Promotion and Reciprocal Protection of Investments.[18]

[15] See Chapter 11, Section 2.1.
[16] See Section 1.1 and n. 7 above.
[17] ICSID Case No. ARB/12/3, Award, 17 April 2015 (Rovine, Lalonde, Douglas).
[18] Signed 9 March 1987, entered into force 28 August 1987. Art. 6 provides:
    1.   Neither Contracting Party shall nationalise, expropriate or subject to measures having effect equivalent to nationalisation or expropriation (hereinafter referred to as 'expropriation') the investments of investors of the other Contracting Party in its territory unless the following conditions are complied with:

Accession Mezzanine and Another v. Hungary, ICSID Case No. ARB/12/3, Award, 17 April 2015 (Rovine, Lalonde, Douglas), para. 75 (footnotes omitted)

The question of whether the Claimants had any right to broadcast over a radio frequency in Hungary at the critical point in 2009 can only be answered by reference to Hungarian law. Hence the first and second steps of the Claimants' reasoning as summarised above must be assessed in accordance with Hungarian law. Upon the ascertainment of the existence of such rights under Hungarian law as well as their nature and scope, it then falls to consider whether they are capable of constituting a protected investment for the purposes of Article 1 of the BIT and Article 25 of the ICSID Convention. This question must be resolved by reference to those treaty provisions as interpreted against the background of general international law. This corresponds to the third step in the Claimants' reasoning. Finally, the question of whether a protected investment with the characteristics previously ascertained is capable of being expropriated must be answered by reference to Article 6 of the BIT and the general international law on expropriation.

1.2.3 Configuration 3 – Composite National–International Law

The third configuration proposes the merged application of national and international law whenever an investor pleads violation of an umbrella clause. An archetype umbrella clause provides that the host State shall observe any commitment undertaken towards protected investments.[19] An umbrella clause, when present in the applicable investment treaty, is most often invoked by investors whose disputes with the host States are contractual in origin.[20] As umbrella clauses tend not to specify the genre or nature of obligations that host States have to respect, contractual obligations owed by host States arguably fall within the purview of an archetypal umbrella clause and benefit from treaty protection. According to one author, the merged application of national and international law in umbrella clause claims occurs in three stages.

(a) the expropriation is for a public purpose related to the internal needs of that Party and is subject to due process of law;
(b) the expropriation is non-discriminatory; and
(c) the expropriation is followed by the payment of prompt, adequate and effective compensation. Such compensation shall amount to the market value of the investment expropriated immediately before the expropriation or impending expropriation became public knowledge, shall include interest at a normal commercial rate until the date of payment, shall be made without delay, be effectively realisable and be freely transferable. The investor shall have a right, under the law of the Contracting Party making the expropriation, to prompt review, by a judicial or other independent authority of that Party, of his or its case and of the valuation of his or its investment in accordance with the principles set out in this paragraph.

2. Where a Contracting Party expropriates the assets of a company which is constituted or incorporated under the law in force in any part of its own territory, and in which investors of the other Contracting Party own shares, it shall ensure that the provisions of paragraph 1 of this Article are applied to the extent necessary to guarantee prompt, adequate and effective compensation in respect of their investment to such investors of the other Contracting Party who are owners of those shares.

[19] One example of an archetypal umbrella clause is Art. II(2)(c) of the US–Argentina BIT: 'Each Party shall observe any obligation it may have entered into with regard to investments.'
[20] See, for instance, *SGS Société Générale de Surveillance v. Pakistan*, ICSID Case No. ARB/01/13, Decision on Objections to Jurisdiction, 6 August 2003 (Feliciano, Faurès, Thomas).

H. E. Kjos, *Applicable Law in Investor-State Arbitration: The Interplay between National and International Law* (Oxford University Press, 2013), 248, 251–252 (footnotes omitted)

More specifically, it is argued that tribunals should follow a three-step process with respect to 'umbrella' clauses. First, since the clause is inserted in a treaty, tribunals should interpret the scope of the clause by international rules of treaty interpretation, such as articles 31 and 32 of the Vienna Convention on the Law of Treaties. A textual interpretation of various clauses supports the view that they create an international cause of action for investors, especially in view of the mandatory language and the principle of effectiveness.

...

Secondly, tribunals should construe the rights and obligations of the parties in accordance with the proper law of the source of the obligation, most likely the national law of the host state. Hence, the ICSID Tribunal in *SGS* v. *Philippines* (2004) correctly noted that the 'umbrella' clause at issue does not convert investment contracts into treaties by way of 'instant transubstantiation'; and, in particular, it does not change the proper law of the investment contract from the law of the Philippines to international law. Stated differently, the 'umbrella' clause does not address 'the scope of the commitments entered into with regard to the specific investments but the performance of these obligations, once they are ascertained'. In similar language, ICSID ad hoc committee in *CMS Gas Transmission Company* v. *Argentine Republic* (2007) held:

> In speaking of 'any obligations it may have entered into with regard to investments', it seems clear that Article II(2)(c) is concerned with consensual obligations arising independently of the BIT itself (i.e. under the law of the host State or possibly under international law) ... The effect of the umbrella clause is not to transform the obligation which is relied on into something else; the content of the obligation is unaffected, as is its proper law.

Next to scholarship, also the award and the decision on annulment in *MTD Equity* (2004/07) support this interpretation. The claimants argued that because a breach of the foreign investment contracts was internationalized by reason of the 'umbrella' clause in the BIT at hand, the contracts themselves were governed by international law. The ICSID Tribunal rejected this argument: 'The Tribunal has to apply the BIT. The breach of the BIT is governed by international law. However, to establish the facts of the breach, it will be necessary to consider the contractual obligations undertaken by the Respondent and the Claimants and what their scope was under Chilean law.'

...

Would the contract appear to have been violated, though, this would mean a violation of the 'umbrella' clause as well, and the investor accordingly has an international remedy. Thus, the third step to be taken is for tribunals to apply rules of state responsibility and to grant the investor a remedy pursuant to international law.

Unlike the first and second configurations on the interplay between national and international laws, the third configuration is a recent innovation that has yet to be tested by any tribunal. However, putting this configuration into practice may be problematic, due to the improbability of national and international laws applying simultaneously to the same head of claim.

J. Ho, 'Unraveling the *Lex Causae* in Investment Claims' (2014) *JWIT* 757, 767–768 (footnotes omitted)

At first glance, this approach, where both national law and international law feature as the *lex causae*, neatly complements the interplay between the two laws that Kjos depicts. On second thought, one may reasonably ask if the interpretation of umbrella clauses is being contorted to fit in with Kjos' broader vision. As umbrella clauses are treaty provisions, the relevance of Articles 31 and 32 of the [Vienna Convention on the Law of Treaties] as interpretive canons is a given. Kjos' contribution lies in the second and third prongs of her approach, which are akin to supplementary interpretive guides, and invite careful reflection. Umbrella clauses may not be free from textual ambiguity, but they are not such unusual treaty provisions that recourse to established rules of treaty interpretation will not suffice. Even if they are, any supplementary interpretive guide ought to clarify that which a textual reading does not illuminate, namely, the nature and the content of the obligation protected. When the source of an obligation is national law, the *lex causae* is national law.

Kjos admits that '[i]n the context of investment arbitration, one substantive area that, as a rule, is governed by national law concerns contracts' (p. 171). As umbrella clauses are most frequently invoked by investors seeking redress from investment treaty tribunals for breached investment contracts, Kjos' identification of national law as the default *lex causae* for national obligations is notable. It also removes the need to refer to the rules on State responsibility as a final step in a tribunal's finding on liability. State responsibility can only be engaged when an international obligation is breached. Unless the breach of a contractual obligation is being characterised as the breach of an international obligation, the issue of State responsibility simply does not arise. Moreover, it is unclear what international law remedies Kjos had in mind for the violation of obligations governed by national law. Either national law applies to breached contractual obligations and affixes the amount of damages as a contractual remedy, or international law applies to breached international obligations and affixes the quantum of compensation or type of restitution due for violating international law. The present reviewer is unaware of any mixed national–international obligation that warrants the application of national law as the proper law and international law as the remedial law.

1.3 Arbitral Mandate and Choice-of-Laws

The source of an arbitral tribunal's mandate is the agreement of the parties who have consented to submit their disputes to arbitration. When that agreement covers applicable laws, the tribunal's choice-of-laws ought to conform to what the parties agreed. In contract-based investment arbitration, any provision for applicable laws will normally be found in the contract, or in the institutional rules under which the arbitration is conducted.[21] In treaty-based arbitration, any provision for applicable laws may be found either in the relevant treaty or in the institutional rules under which the arbitration can be conducted. When an applicable laws clause directs a tribunal to apply a specific law, such as the laws of State X or international law, without making allowance for the tribunal to derogate from, modify or supplement the parties' choice of applicable laws, the tribunal is ostensibly bound by the parties' choice. A tribunal that disregards this choice when judging the dispute arguably exceeds the mandate that has been conferred on it by the parties, and may imperil the enforceability of the resulting award.[22] If there is no applicable laws clause, or if an applicable laws clause expressly defers to the tribunal's choice-of-laws, then tribunals may decide what the applicable laws are. The applicable laws clause that frequently arises for consideration in investment arbitration is Article 42(1) of the ICSID Convention. Article 42(1) sets out the methodology for tribunals to follow when identifying the applicable laws. However, according to the Convention's chief architect, Aron Broches, Article 42(1) leaves open the question of whether tribunals can apply international law if the parties have identified only national law as the *lex causae*.[23] In other words, Article 42(1) neither insists on the application of both national and international law in investment disputes, nor does it express a preference for a particular configuration on the interplay of laws.

> **Convention on the Settlement of Investment Disputes between States and Nationals of Other States, 18 March 1965 (ICSID Convention), Art. 42(1)**
>
> The Tribunal shall decide a dispute in accordance with such rules of law as may be agreed by the parties. In the absence of such agreement, the Tribunal shall apply the law of the Contracting State party to the dispute (including its rules on the conflict of laws) and such rules of international law as may be applicable.

---

[21] See, e.g., *SPP* v. *Egypt*, ICC Award, para. 49, where the tribunal followed the applicable laws provision in the then ICC Rules of Arbitration. In the most recent update, the applicable laws provision of the 2012 ICC Rules of Arbitration is set out in Art. 21:
   (1) The parties shall be free to agree upon the rules of law to be applied by the arbitral tribunal to the merits of the dispute. In the absence of any such agreement, the arbitral tribunal shall apply the rules of law which it determines to be appropriate.
   (2) The arbitral tribunal shall take account of the provisions of the contract, if any, between the parties and of any relevant trade usages.
   (3) The arbitral tribunal shall assume the powers of an amiable compositeur or decide ex aequo et bono only if the parties have agreed to give it such powers.
[22] On the potential non-enforceability of ICSID awards for excess of arbitral mandate, see, e.g., *Klöckner and Others* v. *Cameroon and Another*, Decision of the Ad Hoc Committee, paras 57–82.
[23] A. Broches, 'The Convention on the Settlement of Investment Disputes between States and Nationals of Other States' (1972) 136 *RCADI* 331, 381.

When an applicable laws clause is, like Article 42(1) of the ICSID Convention, open to interpretation, then arbitral tribunals tasked with interpretation will, in all likelihood, have the final say on what the applicable laws are. Although provocative at first glance, the observation that arbitral tribunals enjoy 'broad discretion' in the identification of the *lex causae*[24] is, on further reflection, a candid statement of practice.

2. *LEX ARBITRI*

The *lex arbitri* refers to procedural rules that govern how an arbitration unfolds. These rules can be located in institutional rules for parties who opt to arbitrate under the auspices of a certain arbitral institution such as the Permanent Court of Arbitration (PCA), the ICC, the International Centre for Settlement of Investment Disputes (ICSID), the London Court of International Arbitration (LCIA), the Singapore International Arbitration Center (SIAC), the Stockholm Chamber of Commerce (SCC) or the Hong Kong International Arbitration Center (HKIAC), or in the UN Commission on International Trade Law (UNCITRAL) Arbitration Rules (UNCITRAL Arbitration Rules) for parties who opt for non-institutional arbitration.[25] They address a range of matters, including the composition of the arbitral tribunal,[26] the different steps to take and the corresponding time limits in an arbitration,[27] and the form and finality of the award.[28]

Given the discrete bodies of *lex arbitri*, differences in the stipulations, the text, the level of detail and even the number of provisions governing an aspect of the arbitration are inevitable. These variations may motivate the claimant to request arbitration in accordance with one set of *lex arbitri* and not another (when election is possible), but it does not necessarily imply the categorical superiority of the chosen *lex arbitri*. Instead, it suggests that the choice of *lex arbitri*, exercised by the claimant, reflects the claimant's preferences. The following example illustrates.

When Hungary decided to privatise its energy sector in the 1990s, it concluded power purchase agreements (PPAs) with foreign investors. Under these agreements, investors will construct and operate electricity plants, and then sell the generated electricity to the government at an agreed rate. Upon Hungary's accession to the European Union in 2004, the European Commission began investigating the compatibility of these PPAs with EU laws.[29] The EC concluded that the PPAs amounted to illegal State aid to the foreign

---

[24] G. Kaufmann-Kohler, 'Arbitral Precedent: Dream, Necessity or Excuse?' (2007) 23(3) *Arb. Int'l* 357, 364.

[25] UN Doc. A/RES/31/98. The UNCITRAL Arbitration Rules were first made available in 1976, and amended in 2010 and 2013. The latest amendment incorporates the UNCITRAL Rules on Transparency in Treaty-based Investor-State Arbitration (UNCITRAL Transparency Rules) into the 2010 UNCITRAL Arbitration Rules. Although parties are free to design a set of procedural rules unique to their arbitration, the ready availability of institutional or ad hoc *lex arbitri* removes any compelling need for parties to create their own. Party-created *lex arbitri* is a theoretical possibility, but unlikely to gain traction in practice. Parties are also free to adopt national laws as *lex arbitri*, but once again, the ready availability of compact institutional or ad hoc *lex arbitri* is a far more convenient option than adapting litigation-oriented procedural rules for arbitration.

[26] See, e.g., 2010 UNCITRAL Arbitration Rules, Arts 7–16.

[27] See, e.g., *ibid.*, Arts 18–32.

[28] See, e.g., *ibid.*, Arts 33–43.

[29] Commission of the European Communities, 'Commission Decision on the State Aid awarded by Hungary through Power Purchase Agreements', 2008 (Doc. No. C 41/05), paras 1–29.

investors and ordered Hungary to terminate them.[30] Two of the affected investors were Electrabel SA, a Belgian company, and EDF International SA, a French company.

Electrabel and EDF each brought a claim in arbitration against Hungary.[31] Electrabel had the option of bringing its claim under the BLEU (Belgium–Luxembourg–Economic Union)–Hungary BIT or the Energy Charter Treaty (ECT),[32] while EDF had the option of bringing its claim under the France–Hungary BIT or the ECT.[33] The BLEU–Hungary BIT, France–Hungary BIT and ECT all give claimant investors a choice of *lex arbitri*, which in most cases refers to the rules of the chosen arbitral institution. The relevant provisions are reproduced below.

BLEU–Hungary BIT, Art. 9(2)

(2) If the dispute cannot be settled within a period of six months from the date of the written notification in accordance with paragraph (1), it will be submitted to arbitration conducted under one of the institutions designed below, as chosen by the investor:

(a) The Arbitration Institute of the Stockholm Chamber of Commerce;

(b) The Arbitral Tribunal of the International Chamber of Commerce in Paris;

(c) The International Centre for the Settlement of Investment Disputes.[34]

France–Hungary BIT, Art. 9(2)

If a dispute cannot be settled amicably within a period of six months from the date on which either party to the dispute requested amicable settlement, it will be submitted at the request of one of the parties to arbitration. It will be finally resolved, in conformity with the Arbitration Rules of the United Nations Commission on International Trade Law, which was adopted by the United Nations General Assembly in Resolution 31–98 of 15 December 1976.

In the event that each of the Contracting Parties becomes a party to the Convention for the Settlement of Investment Disputes between States and Nationals of Other States, concluded in Washington on 18 March 1965, a dispute, if it cannot be settled amicably within a period of six months from the date on which either party to the dispute requested amicable settlement, will be submitted to the International Centre for the Settlement of Investment Disputes for resolution through arbitration.[35]

---

[30] *Ibid.*, para. 468.

[31] *Electrabel SA* v. *Hungary*, ICSID Case No. ARB/07/19, Decision on Jurisdiction, Applicable Law and Liability, 30 November 2012 (Kaufmann-Kohler, Stern, Veeder); *Electricité de France (EDF) International SA* v. *Hungary*, UNCITRAL-PCA, Award (not public), 4 December 2014 (Böckstiegel, Dupuy, van den Berg).

[32] Accord entre l'Union Economique Belgo-Luxembourgeoise et le Gouvernement de la République Populaire Hongroise, Concernant l'Encouragement et la Protection Réciproque des Investissements (signed 14 May 1986, entered into force 23 September 1988); (signed 17 December 1994, entered into force 16 April 1998), 2080 UNTS 95.

[33] Accord entre le gouvernement de la République Française et le Gouvernement de la République Populaire Hongroise sur l'Encouragement et la Protection Réciproque des Investissements (signed 6 November 1986, entered into force 30 September 1987).

[34] The full title of the BLEU–Hungary BIT is: Accord entre le gouvernement de la République Française et le Gouvernement de la République Populaire Hongroise sur l'Encouragement et la Protection Réciproque des Investissements (signed 6 November 1986, entered into force 30 September 1987).

[35] Translation from the original French.

ECT, Arts 26(2)(c), 26(4)

(2) If such disputes cannot be settled according to the provisions of paragraph (1) within a period of three months from the date on which either party to the dispute requested amicable settlement, the Investor party to the dispute may choose to submit it for resolution: in accordance with any applicable, previously agreed dispute settlement procedure ...

    (c) in accordance with the following paragraphs of this Article.

    ...

(4) In the event that an Investor chooses to submit the dispute for resolution under subparagraph (2)(c), the Investor shall further provide its consent in writing for the dispute to be submitted to:

    (a) (i) The International Centre for Settlement of Investment Disputes, established pursuant to the Convention on the Settlement of Investment Disputes between States and Nationals of other States opened for signature at Washington, 18 March 1965 (hereinafter referred to as the 'ICSID Convention'), if the Contracting Party of the Investor and the Contracting Party party to the dispute are both parties to the ICSID Convention; or

       (ii) The International Centre for Settlement of Investment Disputes, established pursuant to the Convention referred to in subparagraph (a)(i), under the rules governing the Additional Facility for the Administration of Proceedings by the Secretariat of the Centre (hereinafter referred to as the 'Additional Facility Rules'), if the Contracting Party of the Investor or the Contracting Party party to the dispute, but not both, is a party to the ICSID Convention;

    (b) a sole arbitrator or ad hoc arbitration tribunal established under the Arbitration Rules of the United Nations Commission on International Trade Law (hereinafter referred to as 'UNCITRAL'); or

    (c) an arbitral proceeding under the Arbitration Institute of the Stockholm Chamber of Commerce.

From the foregoing, Electrabel had a choice of the SCC Arbitration Rules, the ICC Arbitration Rules and the ICSID Arbitration Rules as the *lex arbitri* if it sued under the BLEU–Hungary BIT, and a choice of the ICSID Arbitration Rules, the UNCITRAL Arbitration Rules and the SCC Arbitration Rules as the *lex arbitri* if it sued under the ECT. EDF, on the other hand, could choose between the UNCITRAL Arbitration Rules and the ICSID Arbitration Rules if it sued under the France–Hungary BIT, and had the same choices as Electrabel if it proceeded under the ECT. Eventually, both Electrabel and EDF elected to bring their claims under the ECT. However, Electrabel chose the ICSID Arbitration Rules as the *lex arbitri*, while EDF chose the UNCITRAL Arbitration Rules as the *lex arbitri*.

Claimants are not required to explain or justify their choice of *lex arbitri*, so inferring Electrabel's preferences from its choice of the ICSID Arbitration Rules and EDF's preferences from its choice of the UNCITRAL Arbitration Rules should be appreciated in that light. Depending on the claimant's needs, the ICSID Arbitration Rules and the UNCITRAL Arbitration Rules have their respective strengths and shortcomings.

If the claimant's principal concern is the ease of enforceability and finality of an award rendered by the tribunal, the ICSID Arbitration Rules, applied in conjunction with the ICSID Convention, offer greater certainty than the UNCITRAL Arbitration Rules. This is because the ICSID Arbitration Rules and Convention establish a self-contained enforcement regime, whereby a Contracting State to the ICSID Convention is obliged to enforce an ICSID award 'as if it were a final judgment of a court of that State'.[36] Challenges to the finality of an award are strictly and exclusively regulated by the ICSID Arbitration Rules[37] and the Convention.[38] In contrast, the UNCITRAL Arbitration Rules do not deal with award enforcement. Awards issued by tribunals applying the UNCITRAL Arbitration Rules as the *lex arbitri* are usually enforced pursuant to the Convention on the Recognition and Enforcement of Foreign Arbitral Awards ('New York Convention') if the enforcing State is a party,[39] or, on the rare occasion where the enforcing State is not a party to the New York Convention, pursuant to national laws. As courts in different States have disagreed on whether a New York Convention ground for setting aside is met by the same set of facts,[40] there is a known risk that an award may be enforceable in one jurisdiction, but not in another.

If the claimant's pressing concern is obtaining interim relief, the UNCITRAL Arbitration Rules are more accommodating than the ICSID Arbitration Rules, because the requirements for the award of provisional measures are less stringent in the former. For example, Article 26 of the UNCITRAL Arbitral Rules permit the award of provisional measures *ex parte*, whereby only the party applying for relief is heard by the tribunal, but this is not available under Rule 39 of the ICSID Arbitration Rules. Urgent applications for interim relief benefit from quicker processing under the UNCITRAL Arbitration Rules than under the ICSID Arbitration Rules. Furthermore, a disputing party can seek interim relief from national courts under the UNCITRAL Arbitration Rules without the prior agreement of the other disputing party. This is not possible under the ICSID Arbitration Rules. The greater flexibility that tribunals have when ordering provisional measures under Article 26 of the UNCITRAL Arbitration Rules is evident when juxtaposed against Rule 39 of the ICSID Arbitration Rules.

---

[36] ICSID Convention, Art. 54(1): 'Each Contracting State shall recognize an award rendered pursuant to this Convention as binding and enforce the pecuniary obligations imposed by that award within its territories as if it were a final judgment of a court in that State. A Contracting State with a federal constitution may enforce such an award in or through its federal courts and may provide that such courts shall treat the award as if it were a final judgment of the courts of a constituent state.'

[37] ICSID Arbitration Rules, Rules 50–4.

[38] ICSID Convention, Art. 52.

[39] Signed 10 June 1958, entered into force 7 June 1959, 330 UNTS 3.

[40] *Dallah Real Estate and Tourism Holding Co. v. Ministry of Religious Affairs of the Government of Pakistan* [2011] 1 AC 763 (decision of the UK Supreme Court holding that the facts did not disclose a valid agreement to arbitrate, thereby justifying non-enforcement pursuant to Art. V(1)(a) of the New York Convention), cf. *Gouvernement du Pakistan* v. *Société Dallah Real Estate and Tourism Holding Co.*, Cour d'Appel de Paris, No. 09/28533, 17 February 2011 (decision of the Paris Court of Appeal holding that the facts did disclose a valid agreement to arbitrate).

UNCITRAL Arbitration Rules, Art. 26

(1) At the request of either party, the arbitral tribunal may take any interim measures it deems necessary in respect of the subject-matter of the dispute, including measures for the conservation of the goods forming the subject-matter in dispute, such as ordering their deposit with a third person or the sale of perishable goods.

(2) Such interim measures may be established in the form of an interim award. The arbitral tribunal shall be entitled to require security for the costs of such measures.

(3) A request for interim measures addressed by any party to a judicial authority shall not be deemed incompatible with the agreement to arbitrate, or as a waiver of that agreement.

ICSID Arbitration Rules, Rule 39

(1) At any time after the institution of the proceeding, a party may request that provisional measures for the preservation of its rights be recommended by the Tribunal. The request shall specify the rights to be preserved, the measures the recommendation of which is requested, and the circumstances that require such measures.

(2) The Tribunal shall give priority to the consideration of a request made pursuant to paragraph (1).

(3) The Tribunal may also recommend provisional measures on its own initiative or recommend measures other than those specified in a request. It may at any time modify or revoke its recommendations.

(4) The Tribunal shall only recommend provisional measures, or modify or revoke its recommendations, after giving each party an opportunity of presenting its observations.

(5) If a party makes a request pursuant to paragraph (1) before the constitution of the Tribunal, the Secretary-General shall, on the application of either party, fix time limits for the parties to present observations on the request, so that the request and observations may be considered by the Tribunal promptly upon its constitution.

(6) Nothing in this Rule shall prevent the parties, provided that they have so stipulated in the agreement recording their consent, from requesting any judicial or other authority to order provisional measures, prior to or after the institution of the proceeding, for the preservation of their respective rights and interests.

3. LEX LOCI ARBITRI

The laws of the place where the arbitration is seated, when neither identified as the *lex causae* nor the *lex arbitri*, are nonetheless relevant when they are mandatory laws from which no derogation is permitted. Mandatory laws vary from country to country, but one matter often subject to mandatory rules is the non-arbitrability of certain genres of disputes like anti-trust, tort and crime. The importance of mandatory rules of the forum is highlighted in the 1980 Rome Convention on the Law Applicable to Contractual Obligations (Rome Convention), which is part of EU law.[41]

---

[41] [1980] Official Journal of the European Communities C027/34.

Rome Convention, Art. 7

(1) When applying under this Convention the law of a country, effect may be given to the mandatory rules of the law of another country with which the situation has a close connection, if and in so far as, under the law of the latter country, those rules must be applied whatever the law applicable to the contract. In considering whether to give effect to these mandatory rules, regard shall be had to their nature and purpose and to the consequences of their application or non-application.

(2) Nothing in this Convention shall restrict the application of the rules of the law of the forum in a situation where they are mandatory irrespective of the law otherwise applicable to the contract.

Where there is little or no connection between the arbitral seat and either party to an investment dispute, the *lex loci arbitri* tends not to feature in the arbitral discourse on applicable laws. However, where there is a likelihood of seeking enforcement of the final award at the arbitral seat under the New York Convention, there is a need to ensure that the award does not run afoul of the mandatory rules of the forum. This is because an award that deals with a non-arbitrable subject matter as defined in the *lex loci arbitri* can be denied enforcement, as can an award that contravenes other mandatory rules and is as such contrary to the public policy of the enforcing State.[42] The refusal of the courts of the arbitral seat to recognise the award may have a knock-on effect. It gives rise to a separate ground for setting aside that can be pleaded in all future enforcement proceedings brought under the New York Convention.

New York Convention, Arts V(1)(e), V(2)

1. Recognition and enforcement of the award may be refused, at the request of the party against whom it is invoked, only if that party furnishes to the competent authority where the recognition and enforcement is sought, proof that:

   ...

   (e) The award has not yet become binding on the parties, or has been set aside or suspended by a competent authority of the country in which, or under the law of which, that award was made.

2. Recognition and enforcement of an arbitral award may also be refused if the competent authority in the country where recognition and enforcement is sought finds that:

   (a) The subject matter of the difference is not capable of settlement by arbitration under the law of that country; or

   (b) The recognition or enforcement of the award would be contrary to the public policy of that country.

---

[42] See generally D. Otto and O. Elwan, 'Article V(2)' in H. Kronke, P. Nacimiento, D. Otto and N. C. Port (eds), *Recognition and Enforcement of Foreign Arbitral Awards: A Global Commentary on the New York Convention* (Alphen aan den Rijn: Kluwer Law International, 2010), 345.

Applicable laws potentially raise the most complex preliminary issue faced by arbitral tribunals. From unravelling the *lex causae* through the identification of the sources and content of national and international law, and determining how these substantive laws interact, to ensuring that arbitral procedure follows the stipulations in the *lex arbitri*, a correct decision on applicable laws steers the tribunal towards an enforceable final award. Arbitral tribunals hearing investment disputes rarely discuss the *lex loci arbitri*, since the laws of the forum only come into play in select circumstances, and since claimants (and their legal counsel) are unlikely to bring claims that are prohibited by or might offend the mandatory rules of the arbitral seat. Awareness of these rules is nonetheless advisable, because when the New York Convention applies to the enforcement of an arbitral award, non-compliance with mandatory rules gives rise to three out of seven potential grounds for denying enforcement.

CONCLUSION

The principal applicable laws in investment arbitration are the *lex causae*, the *lex arbitri* and the *lex loci arbitri*. The *lex causae*, which can include national and international law, governs the substance of the dispute. The *lex arbitri*, which is found in party-agreed institutional or ad hoc rules, governs the arbitral procedure. The *lex loci arbitri*, in particular the mandatory rules of the forum of arbitration, is a body of laws against which the resulting arbitral award should be checked to ensure enforceability. Of the three principal applicable laws, the identification and interplay of the *lex causae* may pose the biggest challenge. This is because many investment claims will involve questions that may fall within the exclusive purview of national law, the exclusive purview of international law or the joint purview of national and international law. Deciding which law applies, and which provisions of that law apply to determine the existence, content and holder of the rights for which protection is sought, is a task that every tribunal must perform.

QUESTIONS

1. What are the different stages of the inquiry when ascertaining the *lex causae* for an investment dispute?
2. Recall Configurations 1–3 on the interplay of applicable substantive laws. Accepting that the *lex causae* can be a mix of national and international laws, do these configurations clarify when national laws apply and when international laws apply? If so, why, and if not, why not?
3. Recall Configuration 2 on the interplay of applicable substantive laws. When, if ever, is *renvoi* to national law impermissible or unnecessary?
4. How is the scope of an arbitral tribunal's mandate determined? In other words, if there are limits to a tribunal's authority to hear and decide the dispute at hand, where are these limits located?
5. Under what circumstances, if at all, can or should an arbitral tribunal override the parties' express choice of applicable laws?

SUGGESTIONS FOR FURTHER READING

1. J. W. Salacuse, *The Three Laws of International Investment: National, Contractual, and International Frameworks for Foreign Capital* (Oxford University Press, 2013).
2. H. E. Kjos, *Applicable Law in Investor-State Arbitration: The Interplay between National and International Law* (Oxford University Press, 2013).
3. M. Sasson, *Substantive Law in Investment Treaty Arbitration: The Unsettled Relationship between International and Municipal Law* (Leiden: Kluwer Law International, 2010).
4. J. Ho, 'Unraveling the *Lex Causae* in Investment Claims' (2014) 15(3–4) *JWIT* 757.
5. Y. Banifatemi, 'The Law Applicable in Investment Treaty Arbitration' in K. Yannaca-Small (ed.), *Arbitration under International Investment Agreements: A Guide to the Key Issues* (Oxford University Press, 2010), 191.

7

Arbitrators

CHAPTER OUTLINE

In a decentralised dispute settlement system such as international investment arbitration, the choice of arbitrators and the ethical standards to which they can be held become crucial, both in systemic terms and for the resolution of particular disputes. Section 1 introduces the key figures in investment arbitration. Section 2 deals with the appointment process, considering in a comparative manner ICSID and non-ICSID arbitrations. Sections 3 and 4 address the process and substantive standards for challenging arbitrators in a similar manner. Section 5 addresses in more detail selected grounds of challenge. The connection between arbitrator conflicts and the proposal to replace investment treaty arbitration with a Multilateral Investment Court is discussed in Chapter 20 of this book.

INTRODUCTION

Arbitrators are key figures in arbitration. The importance, and generally the very high quality, of investment arbitrators is an important systemic characteristic. However, that is also reflective, perhaps paradoxically, of international investment law's weaknesses rather than its strengths. Joost Pauwelyn has argued that the role of arbitrators in international investment law is explicable not by what this field has but what it does not have: first, strong secretariats that contribute to the decision-making process; second, appellate or indeed any standing adjudicative institutions; third, embeddedness within a formalised or informalised political community.[1] Investment law has none of these. Unless and until the field of international investment law undergoes significant changes in terms of its institutions and dispute settlement mechanisms, of the kind being discussed in UNCITRAL Working Group III, arbitrators will retain a systemically crucial role.[2] This chapter will consider the role of arbitrators in four parts. Section 1 introduces the key actors. Section 2 discusses the selection process, with an eye to the important

---

[1] J. Pauwelyn, 'The Rule of Law without the Rule of Lawyers? Why Investment Arbitrators Are from Mars, Trade Adjudicators from Venus' (2015) 109 *AJIL* 761. Not everybody will agree with everything that Pauwelyn argued (see the Symposium (2016) 109 AJIL Unbound 277), but the basic claim is sound.

[2] https://uncitral.un.org/en/working_groups/3/investor-state (accessed 26 September 2020).

role of appointing institutions. Sections 3 and 4 address the flipside of appointments – challenges brought against arbitrators – considering in turn procedural and substantive issues, while Section 5 contains selected case studies of particularly common and important grounds of challenge. The conclusion offers thoughts on future directions, taken up in greater detail in Chapter 20 of this book.

1. WHO ARE THE ARBITRATORS?

A glimpse of who the arbitrators in international investment law are is provided by flicking through five of the most 'Recently Constituted' tribunals (or committees) on the ICSID webpage. It is likely that at least one person will be a repeat appointment, at least ten of the fifteen positions will be filled by men and representatives of Western Europe and North America, and a brief Google search will lead you to profiles of senior practitioners of international arbitration and senior academics of public international law. For a less anecdotal inquiry, a helpful starting point is a classic work by Yves Dezalay and Bryant Garth on the sociology of international arbitration published 25 years ago.[3] Dezalay and Garth focused on commercial arbitration because investment arbitration was not a significant enough field for practitioners to market themselves in those terms – but many of the leading figures in commercial arbitration in the 1990s are now (also) leading investment arbitrators, so the book's argument, summarised in the excerpt below, is of considerable interest. What sort of people, by their lights, become successful arbitrators?

T. Schultz and R. Kovacs, 'The Rise of a Third Generation Arbitrators? Fifteen Years after Dezalay and Garth' (2012) 28 _Arb Int'l_ 161, 161–162 (footnotes omitted)

[Dezalay and Garth] made their answer succinct, and rather compelling. The main result of their research was the identification of two quite different generations of arbitrators. The first they called the 'Grand Old Men' (no misogyny here, they really were males). They represented the past generation. They were people who had risen to the top of their national legal professions, but had not specialized in the field of arbitration; men whose general legal and social aura made them credible arbitrators. These men typically developed 'platforms' outside of arbitration and then entered the field at a very high level. The second generation, which prevailed at the time of Dezalay and Garth's study, were assigned the name of 'Technocrats' by the authors. ('Technocrats' was meant as technical experts, not proponents of technocracy.) Successful arbitrators of that generation typically acquired their credentials through activities in the field of international arbitration. They usually had a career almost entirely dedicated to arbitration. In 1996, the Dezalay and Garth study suggested that the principal quality, almost necessary and sufficient in terms of logic, required to be a successful arbitrator was a great command of the technicalities of arbitration.

[3] Y. Dezalay and B. Garth, _Dealing in Virtue: International Commercial Arbitration and the Construction of a Transnational Legal Order_ (University of Chicago Press, 1996).

That evolution in profile, they thought, was merely a reflection of arbitration's own evolution: arbitration had simply become much more technical, and mere grandeur was no longer a sufficient competitive advantage. It took a proper technician to master arbitration proceedings.

In a recent review essay, Garth has reflected on how the arguments of his co-authored book could apply to investment arbitration.

B. Garth, 'One Window into the State of Insiders' Arbitration Scholarship' (2018) 19 JWIT 155, 160–162 (footnotes omitted)

One way to approach the current notions of crisis and reform is to draw on history mentioned in our book [Dezalay and Garth, *Dealing in Virtue*] twenty years ago. The first big wave of commercial arbitrations came in the 1980s and typically involved states on one side and corporations on the other. The states had been persuaded to go along with arbitration clauses and had some faith in the system. This was the era of the *lex mercatoria*. But the developing states, according to what we were told through our interviews, tended to lose these arbitrations and one of the complaints was that the *lex mercatoria* served as a way to discount local laws and state activities.

It appears in retrospect that a 'generational battle' at that time in the arbitration community helped to keep the developing world invested in arbitration. Our contention in the book that the younger generation promoted more formal and rational law versus the grand old men's *lex mercatoria* is well-noted. What is less noted is that the younger generation also suggested that the transformation would help developing countries and give them more favorable outcomes. Jan Paulsson's articles about ICSID and relegitimation in the 1980s along with his representation in ICSID proceedings make this point. He and others were pushing the older generation, defended by Pierre Lalive, and that push might have helped keep the system open enough to survive what might have been a crisis. The younger generation and their allies offered arbitrators and counsel that made the system friendlier to developing states. I do not see the same level of generational conflict today. There may be some generational conflict not apparent to outsiders, however ... Any such generational division is more muted than in the 1980s and 1990s. One reason is that the most important arbitrators in investor arbitration now are the very same people who led the field twenty years ago, except now the young generation has matured as well. There is not as much space for newcomers in the major investment arbitrations as there was in the past. The crisis would look very different if there was an important and identifiable group or generation that, again, challenged the system but also invested in the overall maintenance of the system.

International investment arbitration is a deeply decentralised mechanism of dispute settlement, even by the generally decentralised standards of international law. Unsurprisingly, it is hard to take stock of the general characteristics of arbitrators, particularly when appreciating the varied but often significant length of proceedings as well as the limited availability of information about many non-ICSID arbitrations. An important contribution to the discussion was made by Sergio Puig, who explains the systemic dimension through the lens of social network analysis (the excerpt below omits the technical details and tables).

S. Puig, 'Social Capital in the Arbitration Market' (2014) 25 *EJIL* 387, 411–412, 416–419 (footnotes omitted, original emphasis)

... the core of the network as represented in Figure 4 ... depict[s] the 25 most central arbitrators (using degree centrality) in a *circular graph*. The graph also represents the number of total connections by calibrating the size of the node and indicates the number of internal connections with the core ... the core shows a high proportion of European nationals as well as nationals of countries that share history, culture, and traits in their legal systems, i.e. the UK, US, New Zealand, and Canada, but partially defies the explanation of

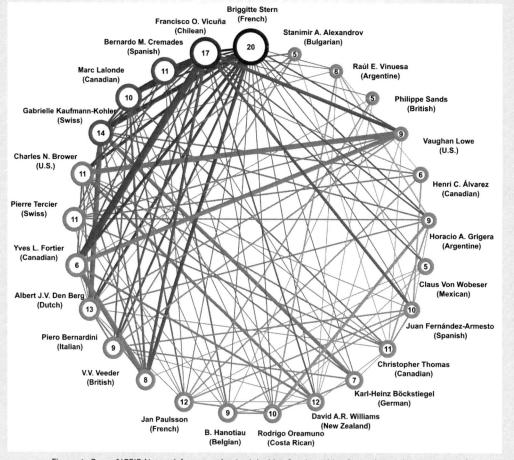

Figure 4: *Core of ICSID Network (representing both inside of and outside of core ties, and common cases).*

Garth and Dezaley. Francisco Orrego-Vicuna (Chilean) is at the centre of the social structure and some Latin-American arbitrators also stand out, perhaps as a consequence of the high number of claims against countries of that region (including Mexico, claims against which represent more than 40 per cent of cases) under ICSID.

...

By any measure, Professors Stern, Orrego-Vicuna, Tercier, and Kaufmann-Kohler, as well as Bernardo Cremades, Yves Fortier, Albert Jan Van Den Berg, and Judge C. N. Brower (to mention just a few), are at the core of the social structure of investor–state arbitrators ... 18 arbitrators – according to this analysis – dominate ICSID and thus may play an important role in the field of international arbitration more broadly. Of course, some are more important than others, as is the case with Professor Stern, who is at the centre ... The different measures also help to identify arbitrators who, like Professor Bernardini (Italian), owe their centrality to their number of appointments, and others like Professor El-Kosheri (Egyptian), who owe their centrality not to the number of cases, but to the ties shared with central figures in the field ... With the information analysed, it is impossible to ascertain the reason for these observed trends, but future research can test how background variables such as education, professional memberships, or the quality of legal reasoning may affect arbitrators' positions within the investor–state arbitration network. Centrality ranks could be used as outcome variables for a more nuanced understanding of the role of sharing a case with valuable ties in future appointments or the spread of specific ideas embedded in legal analysis.

The betweenness list, on the other hand, highlights arbitrators who link different clusters or groups of arbitrators. Bernardo Cremades (Spaniard) appears as the most important 'bridge'; he links a high number of professionals, serving as a key link in the connectivity of the network. Interestingly, the betweenness list also shows arbitrators who do not appear on the other lists. Some of these arbitrators participated in disputes in the 1990s such as Judge Kéba Mbaye (e.g., *American Manufacturing & Trading, Inc. v. Republic of Zaire*), Ibrahim Fadlallah (e.g., *Wena Hotels v. Egypt*), Andrea Giardina (e.g., *Tradex Hellas S.A. v. Albania*), and Professor Elihu Lauterpacht (e.g., *Compañia del Desarrollo de Santa Elena S.A. v. Republic of Costa Rica*).[4] While they play a less prominent role within today's social structure, from this analysis it is clear that at one point these arbitrators served as important intergenerational links or 'transmission belts' within the network ... The closeness scores of the core are also revealing. Stern and Orrego-Vicuña connect with almost all the core of the network.

Professor Kaufmann-Kohler [is confirmed] as the 'most "highly regarded" figure in arbitration' ... . Professors Orrego-Vicuña and Tercier – stand-outs in the four centrality scores – are also probably in influential authorities within the hierarchy. Related to the authority scores, the hub top scorers are arbitrators appointed only or predominantly by one type of litigant: for example, Thomas (only) or Rezek and Stern (predominantly) appointed

---

[4] [Eds: The late Francisco Orrego-Vicuña (1942–2018), Ahmed El-Kosheri (1932–2019), Kéba Mbaye (1924–2017), Elihu Lauterpacht (1928–2017).]

by states, or Hober and Faures (only) or Brower and Lalonde (predominantly) appointed by claimants. This confirms other important ties of the network such as Professor Gaillard, a top practitioner in the arbitration field, and Professor Bockstiegel, the past president of the Iran–United States Claims Tribunal (1984–1988).

...

By relying on social network analysis, this article has ... provided a more nuanced picture of the arbitration network, which can be summarized as follows:

(a) *Small World Properties:* the arbitrator network is dominated by a small, dense and interconnected group, where members at the core are unlikely to escape the observation of other members of the core, but may remain insulated from outside influence.

(b) *Exceptional Professionals:* the arbitrator network is dominated by arbitrators from Europe as well as Anglo-American professionals; however, Latin-American arbitrators trained in Europe, the UK and the US play a fundamental role in the social structure.

(c) *Formidable Women:* the arbitrator network remains male-dominated; however, Brigitte Stern and Gabrielle Kaufmann-Kohler are at the core of the structure. While there are different reasons for the centrality of the two top female arbitrators, the distribution of female appointments is consistent with the behaviour of the network.

(d) *Political Signalling as a Source of Capital:* party appointments play a fundamental role in propelling arbitrators' centrality, based in part on effective means to signal identifiable preferences detectable to litigants.

Most of the arbitrators that Puig mentions remain important actors (it would be extraordinary if none of their names came up in a survey of the latest tribunals on the ICSID webpage), but seven passing years have inevitably wrought change.[5] Some leading figures have passed away, others have gradually stopped appearing as arbitrators, yet others (like judges of the International Court of Justice) have been excluded by their own institutions.[6] Also, new figures have entered the world of arbitration: retired

---

[5] Other writers identify different key actors, e.g. in a more recent piece that considers the influence in roles not limited to arbitrators: M. Langford, D. Behn and R.H. Lie, 'The Revolving Door in International Investment Arbitration' (2017) 20 *J Int'l Econ L* 301, 319–320 ('we provide a new and alternative picture of the most powerful actors. For certain actors, there is a clear jump up the ladder. Arbitrators that have worn multiple hats or individuals with other hats constitute this surging group. They have served as both legal counsel and arbitrator (e.g., Alexandrov, Crawford, Price, Paulsson, Gailliard, and Schwebel); both expert witness and arbitrator (e.g., Reisman); or frequently as tribunal secretaries (e.g., Alvarez-Avila and Flores)').

[6] Speech by HE Mr Abdulqawi A. Yusuf, President of the International Court of Justice, on the Occasion of the Seventy-Third Session of the United Nations General Assembly (25 October 2018) www.icj-cij.org/files/press-releases/0/000-20181025-PRE-02-00-EN.pdf (accessed 3 September 2020), 12 ('Members of the Court have come to the decision, last month, that they will not normally accept to participate in international arbitration. In particular, they will not participate in investor-State arbitration or in commercial arbitration').

judges of domestic and (some) international courts, eminent academics, practitioners of commercial arbitration as well as the first generation of 'genuine' investment arbitration practitioners who do not need to justify the contiguity of their experience or reputation in investment law because they have practised just that for the last two decades.

A broader normative question one might reflect upon is whether the body of arbitrators deciding the cases in 2021 is reflective of the community of relevant actors and interests, with gender, geographical and development-related diversity the more prominent but certainly not the only relevant topics in the discussion (disability is an important but overlooked factor). To take one example from ICSID as the most transparent appointing institution, what should one make of the contrast between the geographic distribution of appointments in 2019, with Western European and Northern American arbitrators comprising around two thirds of the total number (44% and 22% respectively), while just 15% of cases were instituted against States in these regions?[7] Appointments of adjudicators raise hard political and normative questions even in centralised and permanent international institutions (think the World Trade Organization and the International Court of Justice), so it not surprising that they raise even thornier ones in the decentralised and de-institutionalised field of international investment arbitration. A key question now faced in UNCITRAL Working Group III's deliberations, discussed in Chapter 20 of this book, is whether having a permanent body of a set number of adjudicators will address these concerns.

2. APPOINTMENT OF ARBITRATORS

A starting point in discussions of arbitrator appointments is provided by the applicable rules in the particular international arbitration. ICSID will be considered first, and the Permanent Court of Arbitration (PCA), mostly operating regarding arbitration under UNCITRAL Rules, after that. When reading these sections, consider the cross-cutting elements in a comparative manner. What are the similarities and differences regarding:

- deadlines,
- involvement of party-appointed arbitrators and parties in appointment of the presiding arbitrator,
- the manner in which the appointing authority engages parties in appointment of the presiding arbitrator, and
- the extent to which the appointing authority is restricted in choosing the presiding arbitrator in the absence of agreement between the parties?

---

[7] ICSID, *The ICSID Caseload – Statistics* (Issue 2020–1) https://icsid.worldbank.org/sites/default/files/publications/Caseload%20Statistics/en/The%20ICSID%20Caseload%20Statistics%20%282020-1%20Edition%29%20ENG.pdf (accessed 3 September 2020), 24, 28–29.

2.1 ICSID

Convention on the Settlement of Investment Disputes between States and Nationals of Other States, 18 March 1965 (ICSID Convention), Arts 37–40

Section 2 Constitution of the Tribunal

Article 37

(1) The Arbitral Tribunal (hereinafter called the Tribunal) shall be constituted as soon as possible after registration of a request pursuant to Article 36.

(2) (a) The Tribunal shall consist of a sole arbitrator or any uneven number arbitrators appointed as the parties shall agree.

    (b) Where the parties do not agree upon the number of arbitrators and method of their appointment, the Tribunal shall consist of three arbitrators, one arbitrator appointed by each party and the third, who shall be the president of the Tribunal, appointed by agreement of the parties.

Article 38

If the Tribunal shall not have been constituted within 90 days after notice of registration of the request has been dispatched by the Secretary-General [of ICSID] in accordance with paragraph (3) of Article 36, or such other period as the parties may agree, the Chairman [of the Board of Directors of the World Bank] shall, at the request of either party and after consulting both parties as far as possible, appoint the arbitrator or arbitrators not yet appointed. Arbitrators appointed by the Chairman pursuant to this Article shall not be nationals of the Contracting State party to the dispute or of the Contracting State whose national is a party to the dispute.

Article 39

The majority of the arbitrators shall be nationals of States other than the Contracting State party to the dispute and the Contracting State whose national is a party to the dispute; provided, however, that the foregoing provisions of this Article shall not apply if the sole arbitrator or each individual member of the Tribunal has been appointed by agreement of the parties.

Article 40

(1) Arbitrators may be appointed from outside the Panel of Arbitrators, except in the case of appointments by the Chairman pursuant to Article 38.

(2) Arbitrators appointed from outside the Panel of Arbitrators shall possess the qualities stated in paragraph (1) of Article 14.

The key procedural dynamic takes place in Articles 37(2)(b) and 38. Unless otherwise agreed (very rarely in practice), 'the Tribunal shall consist of three arbitrators' and 'one arbitrator [shall be] appointed by each party'. What about 'the third, who shall be the president of the Tribunal'? They may be 'appointed by agreement of the parties' (Article 37(2)(b)) or by the President of the World Bank, 'at the request of either party and after consulting both parties as far as possible' (Article 38). (The latter procedure also applies to the rare but not unheard of dispute where one of the parties has not appointed an arbitrator.[8])

Note as well Article 40(1), with an important restriction for appointments *not* by the agreement of the parties: 'in the case of appointments by the Chairman pursuant to Article 38 ... [a]rbitrators may [not] be appointed from outside the Panel of Arbitrators'. What is the Panel of Arbitrators?

ICSID Convention Articles 12–14

Article 12
The Panel of Conciliators and the Panel of Arbitrators shall each consist of qualified persons, designated as hereinafter provided, who are willing to serve thereon.

Article 13
(1) Each Contracting State may designate to each Panel four persons who may but need not be its nationals.
(2) The Chairman may designate ten persons to each Panel. The persons so designated to a Panel shall each have a different nationality.

Article 14
(1) Persons designated to serve on the Panels shall be persons of high moral character and recognized competence in the fields of law, commerce, industry or finance, who may be relied upon to exercise independent judgment. Competence in the field of law shall be of particular importance in the case of persons on the Panel of Arbitrators.
(2) The Chairman, in designating persons to serve on the Panels, shall in addition pay due regard to the importance of assuring representation on the Panels of the principal legal systems of the world and of the main forms of economic activity.

ICSID maintains a list of current designees to the ICSID Panels of Arbitrators and of Conciliators on its website.[9] The reader may consult the relevant national procedure.[10] The procedure for the appointment of arbitrators is further elaborated in the ICSID Arbitration

---

[8] *Axiata Investments (UK) Limited and Ncell Private Limited* v. Nepal, ICSID Case No. ARB/19/15, https://icsid.worldbank.org/en/Pages/cases/casedetail.aspx?CaseNo=ARB%2f19%2f15 (accessed 3 September 2020) ('The Tribunal is constituted in accordance with Article 37(2)(b) of the ICSID Convention. Its members are: Joongi Kim (Korean), President, appointed by the Chairman of the Administrative Council in accordance with Article 38 of the ICSID Convention; Albert Jan van den Berg (Dutch), appointed by the Claimants; and Paul Friedland (U.S.), appointed by the Chairman of the Administrative Council in accordance with Article 38 of the ICSID Convention').

[9] ICSID, Panels of Conciliators and Arbitrators, ICSID/10 https://icsid.worldbank.org/en/Pages/icsiddocs/Panels-of-Arbitrators-and-Conciliators.aspx (accessed 3 September 2020). Note also that only members of the Panel of Arbitrators can be appointed to *ad hoc* annulment committees: ICSID Convention Article 52(3). On ICSID annulment, see Chapter 19.

[10] E.g. UK Department for International Trade, Appointments to ICSID Panels: call for expression of interest (19 March 2020) https://www.gov.uk/government/publications/appointments-to-icsid-panels-call-for-expressions-of-interest (accessed 3 September 2020).

Rules Chapter I (Establishment of the Tribunal), where Rule 4 addresses the procedure of appointment under Article 38 of the ICSID Convention.

ICSID Arbitration Rules 2006, Rule 4

Appointment of Arbitrators by the Chairman of the Administrative Council

(1) If the Tribunal is not constituted within 90 days after the dispatch by the Secretary-General of the notice of registration, or such other period as the parties may agree, either party may, through the Secretary-General, address to the Chairman of the Administrative Council a request in writing to appoint the arbitrator or arbitrators not yet appointed and to designate an arbitrator to be the President of the Tribunal.

(2) The provision of paragraph (1) shall apply mutatis mutandis in the event that the parties have agreed that the arbitrators shall elect the President of the Tribunal and they fail to do so.

(3) The Secretary-General shall forthwith send a copy of the request to the other party.

(4) The Chairman shall use his best efforts to comply with that request within 30 days after its receipt. Before he proceeds to make an appointment or designation, with due regard to Articles 38 and 40(1) of the Convention, he shall consult both parties as far as possible.

(5) The Secretary-General shall promptly notify the parties of any appointment or designation made by the Chairman.

How does the appointment process work in 'the real world'? The most important procedural innovation, introduced in 2009 and drawing to some extent upon elements of Articles 37(2)(b) and 38 (referred to by an OECD paper as ICSID's 'quasi-appointing authority') is the ballot procedure.[11]

ICSID website, Selection and appointment of tribunal members[12]

When a party makes ... a request [to appoint the arbitrator(s) not yet appointed (Article 38)] in respect of the Sole Arbitrator or President of the Tribunal, ICSID first conducts a ballot procedure:

- ICSID provides the parties with a ballot form containing the names of several candidates, who may or may not be members of the ICSID Panel of Arbitrators.
- Each party is given a short time limit to return its completed ballot form, indicating the candidates it accepts or rejects.
- A party is not required to share its ballot with the other party.
- If the parties agree on a candidate from the ballot, that person will be deemed to have been appointed by agreement of the parties.

[11] D. Gaukrodger, 'Appointing Authorities and the Selection of Arbitrators in Investor-State Dispute Settlement: An Overview' (Consultation Paper, 2018) https://www.oecd.org/investment/investment-policy/ISDS-Appointing-Authorities-Arbitration-March-2018.pdf (accessed 3 September 2020), para. 151.

[12] https://icsid.worldbank.org/en/Pages/process/Selection-and-Appointment-of-Tribunal-Members-Convention-Arbitration.aspx (accessed 30 September 2020).

- If the parties agree on more than one proposed candidate, ICSID selects one of them and informs the parties of the selection.

A successful ballot is considered an appointment by agreement of the parties under the established method of constituting the Tribunal.

D. Gaukrodger, 'Appointing Authorities and the Selection of Arbitrators in Investor-State Dispute Settlement: An Overview' (Consultation Paper, 2018), paras 154–155 (footnotes omitted)[13]

154. ... The ICSID Secretary General has described the rationale, emphasising both the ability for the Secretariat to go 'off-roster' and the greater degree of disputing party consent than under the formal procedure:

> Under the Convention, you're basically meant to go to the roster for appointments. Where the ICSID Secretary is asked to appoint, we didn't have the ability to appoint what we would call 'off roster' or 'off panel'. So we thought about it, and we have a part of the ICSID Convention that says that if there's consent by the parties, any arbitrator can be named. So we developed a system where, because both parties consented to a non-panel name, we would have the legal authority to appoint. We thought there was a lot to commend this approach, because at the end of the day, having a consensually appointed nominee, even if it's from a smaller list provided by the Secretariat, is probably a better thing than just imposing an arbitrator on the candidates.

155. Describing the procedure of finding ballot candidates, the ICSID Secretary General stated in 2010 that '[w]e look to see what the parties need, whether it's a Spanish or Bulgarian speaker, or even immediate availability – all of the things that you might need. And then you say, "Who are the people out there who might be able and willing to meet those qualifications?" We'll contact them and say, "Would you be willing to have us propose your name to the parties?" And we always ask specifically, "Are you immediately available?" Because this is one of those time concerns, so this is a very particular issue that we check.' A conflicts check will be done before arbitrators are proposed in the ballot-procedure. The ICSID Secretary General has stated that whenever possible ICSID tries to include at least one female arbitrator on the ballot and to ensure regional diversity.

---

[13] In response to the OECD Consultation Paper, ICSID noted, among other things, that '[t]he usual number of ballot candidates is 5, but we have done more where parties have asked for it. We have also done two rounds of ballots if requested by the parties. ... The success rate of the ballots has varied from year to year, but has averaged 27% in the last 4 years. This means 27% of the time the ballot results in a consensus candidate. Anecdotally, parties have advised ICSID that they appreciate the ballot process, even where it does not result in an appointment. ... The ICSID ballot does not circumscribe choice; it adds the potential for choice where the parties have not agreed to a nomination. If the parties do not agree on a ballot candidate, the usual choice from the ICSID Panel will be applied. As a result, a ballot is an additional layer of choice rather than going straight to a direct appointment from the Panel': OECD, 'Appointing Authorities and the Selection of Arbitrators in Investor-State Dispute Settlement: An Overview' (Compilation of Initial Comments Received, March 2018) https://www.oecd.org/investment/investment-policy/ISDs-Appointing-Authorities-Arbitration-Compilation-March-2018.pdf (accessed 3 September 2020), 7.

Since 2018 ICSID has been engaged in a Rules and Regulations Amendment Process.[14] In Working Paper #4, the most recent version at the time of writing, the current Rule 4 has been renumbered, partially split into a number of separate Rules, and stylistically redrafted, but is essentially unchanged in substance.[15] (Just as with other aspects of the ICSID Rules, comments to the Working Papers are invaluable for appreciating the legal and policy tensions underpinning seemingly technical drafting choices.[16])

---

[14] https://icsid.worldbank.org/resources/rules-and-regulations/icsid-rules-and-regulations-amend-ment-working-papers (accessed 26 September 2020).

[15] Rule 18 Appointment of Arbitrators by the Chair in accordance with Article 38 of the Convention
    (1) If the Tribunal has not been constituted within 90 days after the date of registration, or such other period as the parties may agree, either party may request that the Chair appoint the arbitrator(s) who have not yet been appointed pursuant to Article 38 of the Convention.
    (2) The Chair shall appoint the President of the Tribunal after appointing any members who have not yet been appointed.
    (3) The Chair shall consult with the parties as far as possible before appointing an arbitrator and shall use best efforts to appoint any arbitrator(s) within 30 days after receipt of the request to appoint, ICSID.

ICSID, 'Proposals for Amendment of the ICSID Rules', Working Paper #4, Volume 1 (February 2020) https://icsid.worldbank.org/en/Documents/WP4Vol1En.pdf (accessed 3 September 2020), 296.

[16] ICSID, 'Proposals for Amendment of the ICSID Rules', Working Paper #2, Volume 1 (March 2019) https://icsid.worldbank.org/en/Documents/Vol1.pdf 296: '153. One State suggested that proposed AR 17(3) require the Chair to provide the parties with information about the candidates and the criteria used to select arbitrators. The Chair appoints from the ICSID Panel of Arbitrators, an identified group, and the criteria considered are in Art. 14(1) of the Convention. The parties are provided with the candidate's CV, nationality information and any disclosures made, as part of the consultation in Art. 38 of the Convention.'

ICSID, 'Proposals for Amendment of the ICSID Rules', Working Paper #3, Volume 1 (August 2019) https://icsid.worldbank.org/en/Documents/WP3VOLUME1ENGLISH.pdf 296: '64. Two Member States and another commentator suggested that proposed AR 18(3) explicitly state that the Chair shall strive to achieve gender and geographical diversity in appointments. Geographical diversity is expressly mandated in appointments to the Panel by the Chair pursuant to Art. 14 of the Convention. Further, gender and geographical diversity are among the many factors routinely considered in appointments by the Chair under Art. 38 of the Convention, and they are embodied in the notion that such appointments are to be made from the Panel, a defined and necessarily diverse body of individuals designated by the Member States themselves.'

ICSID, Working Paper #4, 297: '58. A State reiterated a suggestion to codify in AR 18 the current practice to strive for more gender and geographical balance in appointments. The Secretariat refers to the observations in WP #3, ¶ 64.

59. Another State observed that language capability should be considered in appointments by the Chair. In practice, language capability is among the factors routinely considered to the extent possible, bearing in mind other factors including candidate availability and conflicts.

60. One State suggested amendment of AR 18(3) to delete the consultation requirement for appointment of a co-arbitrator by the Chair. Two other States reiterated a suggestion to amend AR 18(3) to eliminate the words "as far as possible". No further amendment has been made in either regard, as this language rule originates in Article 38 of the Convention (WP #3, ¶ 65).

61. One State reiterated the suggestion that AR 18 be amended to specify that parties shall be informed of the selection criteria for appointments by the Chair under Article 38 of the Convention. The Secretariat refers to the observations at WP #2, ¶ 153.

62. One State suggested favouring mechanisms to facilitate arbitrator selection by the parties, rather than by the Chair. The AR do so. AR 15 expressly envisages that the parties may agree on a method of constitution of the Tribunal, and the default method of constitution in Article 37(2)(b) of the ICSID Convention and AR 16 contemplate the appointment of one arbitrator by each party. Moreover, in practice, when the Chair is requested to appoint a presiding arbitrator under Article 38 of the ICSID Convention, the parties are invited to state whether they want ICSID to first conduct a ballot or list process to assist them in selecting a mutually agreeable candidate.'

2.2 UNCITRAL/Permanent Court of Arbitration

UNCITRAL Arbitration Rules 2010, Arts 8–10

Article 8

1. If the parties have agreed that a sole arbitrator is to be appointed and if within 30 days after receipt by all other parties of a proposal for the appointment of a sole arbitrator the parties have not reached agreement thereon, a sole arbitrator shall, at the request of a party, be appointed by the appointing authority.

2. The appointing authority shall appoint the sole arbitrator as promptly as possible. In making the appointment, the appointing authority shall use the following list-procedure, unless the parties agree that the list-procedure should not be used or unless the appointing authority determines in its discretion that the use of the list-procedure is not appropriate for the case:

    (a) The appointing authority shall communicate to each of the parties an identical list containing at least three names;

    (b) Within 15 days after the receipt of this list, each party may return the list to the appointing authority after having deleted the name or names to which it objects and numbered the remaining names on the list in the order of its preference;

    (c) After the expiration of the above period of time the appointing authority shall appoint the sole arbitrator from among the names approved on the lists returned to it and in accordance with the order of preference indicated by the parties;

    (d) If for any reason the appointment cannot be made according to this procedure, the appointing authority may exercise its discretion in appointing the sole arbitrator.

Article 9

1. If three arbitrators are to be appointed, each party shall appoint one arbitrator. The two arbitrators thus appointed shall choose the third arbitrator who will act as the presiding arbitrator of the arbitral tribunal.

2. If within 30 days after the receipt of a party's notification of the appointment of an arbitrator the other party has not notified the first party of the arbitrator it has appointed, the first party may request the appointing authority to appoint the second arbitrator.

3. If within 30 days after the appointment of the second arbitrator the two arbitrators have not agreed on the choice of the presiding arbitrator, the presiding arbitrator shall be appointed by the appointing authority in the same way as a sole arbitrator would be appointed under article 8.

Article 10

1. For the purposes of article 9, paragraph 1, where three arbitrators are to be appointed and there are multiple parties as claimant or as respondent, unless the parties have agreed to another method of appointment of arbitrators, the multiple parties jointly, whether as claimant or as respondent, shall appoint an arbitrator.

2. If the parties have agreed that the arbitral tribunal is to be composed of a number of arbitrators other than one or three, the arbitrators shall be appointed according to the method agreed upon by the parties.

3. In the event of any failure to constitute the arbitral tribunal under these Rules, the appointing authority shall, at the request of any party, constitute the arbitral tribunal and, in doing so, may revoke any appointment already made and appoint or reappoint each of the arbitrators and designate one of them as the presiding arbitrator.

The Permanent Court of Arbitration explained its practice in a submission to UNCITRAL Working Group III.

Permanent Court of Arbitration, Mechanisms for Selection and Appointment of Presiding Arbitrators or Sole Arbitrators (Submitted on 11 May 2020), paras 4–7, 20–21 (footnotes omitted)

4. When asked to appoint a presiding arbitrator or a sole arbitrator, the PCA Secretary-General will ordinarily follow a list-procedure, as envisaged by the UNCITRAL Arbitration Rules or the PCA Arbitration Rules 2012.
5. Typically, the Secretary-General initially consults the disputing parties with regard to the desired arbitrator profile. The Secretary-General then compiles a list of potential arbitrators that reflects the disputing parties' preferences to the extent possible, having verified with each candidate that no conflicts of interest exist. Second, each disputing party may strike any number of proposed names and establish an order of preference between the remaining names. Third, a selection is made by the Secretary-General on the basis of the candidates' rankings on the returned lists. In the event that no candidate who is acceptable to both sides emerges, the Secretary-General may decide to proceed to a direct appointment without use of a list.
6. The Secretary-General will also regularly enquire with the disputing parties whether they agree to a modified list-procedure, pursuant to which the number of strikes by each side is limited to '50 percent minus one'. This approach ensures that at least one common candidate will remain on the list.
7. The combination of consulting the disputing parties in respect of the composition of the list and enabling them to rank and strike candidates on the list is intended to lead to an appointment that corresponds closely to the joint preferences of the disputing parties.

...

20. ... the Secretary-General, when asked to appoint a presiding arbitrator or sole arbitrator, will typically take account of the following factors, subject to any specific requirements that the treaty parties or disputing parties may have identified:
    - the nationalities of the parties,
    - the place of arbitration,
    - the language(s) of the arbitration,
    - the amount claimed, and
    - the subject-matter and complexity of the dispute;
and, with respect to any prospective arbitrator:
    - nationality,
    - qualifications,
    - experience,

- place of residence,
- language abilities, and
- availability.

21. Attention to geographic and gender diversity of appointments is also given in each case.

These seemingly technical procedural details are very important, both in the practice of dispute settlement and for the broader conceptual discussion of systemic pressure points in international investment law. In practical terms, it matters a great deal whether the appointing authority uses the ICSID ballot procedure (acceptance/rejection indicated), UNCITRAL/PCA list procedure (acceptance/rejection/order of preference indicated), the PCA modified list procedure (number of rejections limited) or one of the many imaginable alternative possibilities, which may be provided in the applicable rules or agreed to by the parties.[17] The broader point worth emphasising, because the commonplace practice in

---

[17] The PCA submission to UNCITRAL Working Group III lists the following appointment procedures:

9. *List-procedure excluding 'strikes'*: The disputing parties are limited to ranking candidates on the list and/or commenting on the relative qualifications and suitability of candidates. This procedure allows the Secretary-General to take the disputing parties' views, in terms of ranking, and – as the case may be – comments, in respect of each candidate into account.

10. *List-procedure involving nomination by the disputing parties*: The list-procedure is conducted on the basis of names supplied separately (*i.e.* without copying the other disputing party) by each disputing party as well as names identified by the Secretary-General. The disputing parties are not made aware whether candidates have been proposed by the other disputing party or by the Secretary-General.

11. *List-procedure on the basis of a list composed by the co-arbitrators*: A list-procedure is conducted by the PCA on the basis of names identified by the co-arbitrators.

12. *Appointment in consultation with the party-appointed arbitrators*: In the event that a list-procedure conducted on the basis of names identified by the co-arbitrators fails, the Secretary-General appoints the presiding arbitrator in consultation with the party-appointed arbitrators.

13. *List-procedure on the basis of an open (recommendatory) list*: In the composition of a list of candidates, regard may be had to a recommendatory list of arbitrators possessing special expertise in the subject-matter of the dispute, which may be based on nominations by States. The Secretary-General will in this case send a list containing an uneven number of candidates.

14. *Appointment on the basis of matching proposals by the disputing parties*: The disputing parties separately submit lists of candidates ranked in order of preference. In the event of matches of names on the disputing parties' lists, the disputing parties are deemed to have agreed on the candidate with the best joint ranking.

15. *Appointment based on proposals from the disputing parties*: Each disputing party nominates an agreed number of candidates, accompanied by written observations. The Secretary-General then selects one candidate for appointment, taking the disputing parties' views into account.

16. *Appointment based on names jointly submitted by the disputing parties*: Following direct consultations, the disputing parties jointly submit the names of (two or more) candidates to the Secretary-General, without disclosing which candidate is preferred by one or other party. The Secretary-General will then select a candidate for appointment from that joint list.

17. *Appointment on the basis of a closed (mandatory) roster constituted by the treaty parties*: All arbitrators, including the presiding arbitrator, must be appointed from a closed list (roster) of arbitrators, constituted by the treaty parties on the basis of criteria identified in the treaty.

18. *Appointment at the discretion of the Secretary-General*: The selection of the sole or presiding arbitrator (or, indeed, all arbitrators) is placed in the hands of the Secretary-General. While the disputing parties are invited to provide general comments on the required profile of the arbitrator, they have no role in proposing, or commenting on, any specific candidates for appointment.

19. *Appointment by agreement of the disputing parties, based on suggestions from the Secretary-General*: The Secretary-General conveys a list of suitable candidates to the disputing parties, who then directly consult with each other with a view to reaching agreement on the appointment of the presiding arbitrator.

investment arbitration may obscure its peculiarity, is how exceptional the broad power of appointing authorities in choosing arbitrators is in the comparative setting of international dispute settlement. States take the appointment of international adjudicators very seriously indeed, and it is common for the process of appointment to be either the stuff of the highest politics, as in the International Court of Justice and the World Trade Organization's Appellate Body (of yesteryear), technocracy (Court of Justice of the European Union) or a mixture of both (International Criminal Court and European Court of Human Rights).[18] It is unusual, at least in modern international dispute settlement, for States to entrust such broad powers to an independent institution. Sometimes treaties set out standards and considerations that appointing authorities have to take into account, usually expertise in investment law and international law.

Comprehensive and Progressive Agreement for Trans-Pacific Partnership, 9 March 2018, Arts 9.22(5), 9.25(2) (footnote omitted)

Article 9.22: Selection of Arbitrators
5. ... If the parties fail to agree on the appointment of the presiding arbitrator, the Secretary-General [of ICSID] shall also take into account the expertise or relevant experience of particular candidates with respect to the relevant governing law under Article 9.25.2.

Article 9.25: Governing Law
2. ... the tribunal shall apply:
   (a) the rules of law applicable to the pertinent investment authorisation or specified in the pertinent investment authorisation or investment agreement, or as the disputing parties may agree otherwise; or
   (b) if, in the pertinent investment agreement the rules of law have not been specified or otherwise agreed:
       (i) the law of the respondent, including its rules on the conflict of laws; and
       (ii) such rules of international law as may be applicable.

But mostly there are no explicit standards or criteria for guiding the appointment. To be clear: it is not a criticism of appointing institutions which exercise functions that are entrusted to them by international treaties, and are doing so in what appears to be, overall, a transparent and good-faith manner. But the policy question to consider, with an eye to the reform of investment dispute settlement, is whether all appointing institutions as currently constituted and operating are always well placed to exercise such functions without further guidance in the applicable rules.[19]

---

[18] Generally see R. Mackenzie, K. Malleson, P. Martin and P. Sands, *Selecting International Judges: Principle, Process and Politics* (Oxford University Press, 2010), and with an eye to investment law, G. Kaufmann-Kohler and M. Potestà, 'The Composition of a Multilateral Investment Court and of an Appeal Mechanism for Investment Awards', CIDS Supplemental Report (15 November 2017) https://uncitral.un.org/sites/uncitral.un.org/files/media-documents/uncitral/en/cidssupplementalreport.pdf (accessed 3 September 2020).

[19] In response to the OECD Consultation Paper, one of us noted that '[i]t would be helpful for stakeholders to consider whether appointing authorities, as currently constituted, are best placed to decide these questions. ... perhaps these are functions that no appointing authorities should be exercising; perhaps some appointing authorities are better suited for engaging with these issues than others; or perhaps the

3. CHALLENGE BROUGHT AGAINST ARBITRATORS: PROCEDURE

Section 2 addressed appointments of arbitrators by comparing the ICSID and non-ICSID approaches. This section and Section 4 will approach challenges brought against arbitrators in the same comparative manner, dealing with the procedure of challenge (this section) and then the substantive standards for challenge (Section 4). Section 5 will consider in more detail selected case studies.

3.1 ICSID

Chapter 4 of this book introduced the distinction between ICSID and non-ICSID investment arbitration. This is relevant for multiple issues discussed throughout the book, including this topic. Challenge of arbitrators in ICSID proceedings is an outlier from general practice in two ways, which will be addressed in turn: in terms of the procedure for bringing a challenge and the standard to be applied in a challenge. When reading the excerpt below, consider in particular the decision tree for determining who decides on the challenge.

ICSID Convention, Arts 57–58

Article 57
A party may propose to a Commission or Tribunal the disqualification of any of its members on account of any fact indicating a manifest lack of the qualities required by paragraph (1) of Article 14. A party to arbitration proceedings may, in addition, propose the disqualification of an arbitrator on the ground that he was ineligible for appointment to the Tribunal under Section 2 of Chapter IV.

Article 58
The decision on any proposal to disqualify a conciliator or arbitrator shall be taken by the other members of the Commission or Tribunal as the case may be, provided that where those members are equally divided, or in the case of a proposal to disqualify a sole conciliator or arbitrator, or a majority of the conciliators or arbitrators, the Chairman [of the Administrative Council of ICSID] shall take that decision. If it is decided that the proposal is well-founded the conciliator or arbitrator to whom the decision relates shall be replaced in accordance with the provisions of Section 2 of Chapter III or Section 2 of Chapter IV.

ICSID Arbitration Rules 2006, Rule 9 (Disqualification of Arbitrators)

(1) A party proposing the disqualification of an arbitrator pursuant to Article 57 of the Convention shall promptly, and in any event before the proceeding is declared closed, file its proposal with the Secretary-General, stating its reasons therefor.

delegation of hard policy calls to appointing authorities is entirely proper, accurately reflecting the underlying political disagreement among the stakeholders': OECD, Compilation of Initial Comments Received, 45 para. 15. See further, Note by the Secretariat, 'Possible reform of investor-State dispute settlement (ISDS): Arbitrators and decision makers: appointment mechanisms and related issues' (30 August 2018) UN Doc. A/CN.9/WG.III/WP.152.

(2) The Secretary-General shall forthwith:
   (a) transmit the proposal to the members of the Tribunal and, if it relates to a sole arbitrator or to a majority of the members of the Tribunal, to the Chairman of the Administrative Council; and
   (b) notify the other party of the proposal.
(3) The arbitrator to whom the proposal relates may, without delay, furnish explanations to the Tribunal or the Chairman, as the case may be.
(4) Unless the proposal relates to a majority of the members of the Tribunal, the other members shall promptly consider and vote on the proposal in the absence of the arbitrator concerned. If those members are equally divided, they shall, through the Secretary-General, promptly notify the Chairman of the proposal, of any explanation furnished by the arbitrator concerned and of their failure to reach a decision.
(5) Whenever the Chairman has to decide on a proposal to disqualify an arbitrator, he shall use his best efforts to take that decision within 30 days after he has received the proposal.
(6) The proceeding shall be suspended until a decision has been taken on the proposal.

A number of points may be noted. First, unlike in most other procedural settings, there are two bodies that may take the decision on a proposal to disqualify an arbitrator (or a member of an ad hoc Annulment Committee: see Article 52(4) of the ICSID Convention). The default body is the other (two unchallenged) members of the Tribunal or the Committee. The second body, which acts where those members are equally divided, or in the case of a proposal to disqualify a sole arbitrator, or a majority (or all) of the arbitrators, is the chairman of the Administrative Council of ICSID (the president of the World Bank). In practice, a third setting has emerged where challenges may be considered, as it were, indirectly: annulment.

Victor Pey Cassado and President Alliende Foundation v. Chile (II), ICSID Case No. ARB/98/2, Decision on Annulment, 8 January 2020 (Knieper, Angelet, Zhang), para. 564 (footnotes omitted)

... *ad hoc* committees cannot, in principle, address the independence and impartiality of an arbitrator *de novo* in disregard of the proceedings that have taken place pursuant to Articles 57 and 58 of the ICSID Convention. They may only address the issue *de novo* if the decision taken pursuant to Articles 57 and 58 of the ICSID Convention was so plainly unreasonable that no reasonable decision-maker could have reached it. This is the approach taken in *EDF v. Argentina* and *Suez v. Argentina*. The same position was taken by the *ad hoc* committee in *Mobil v. Argentina*. As the Respondent argues, the *Mobil* committee expressly adhered to the two abovementioned decisions. While the Applicants correctly observe that the *Mobil* decision recognized further powers of annulment committees, this was to the effect that annulment committees can evaluate an arbitral tribunal's impartiality on the basis of the decisions taken by the tribunal (or by the majority of the arbitrators) regarding a challenge brought against one of them. The Committee agrees with the *Mobil* committee in this respect and will proceed accordingly, but observes that this is not concerned with the circumstances under which an annulment committee can address *de novo* a challenge decided upon by the Chairman, rather than by the remaining arbitrators.

Another annulment committee considered the challenge through the lens of an improper constitution of the tribunal.

Eiser Infrastructure Limited and Energía Solar Luxembourg S.à r.l. v. Spain, ICSID Case No. ARB/13/36, Decision on Annulment, 11 June 2020 (Hernández, Khan, Hascher), para. 178

... this Committee concludes that, for purposes of determining whether the Tribunal was properly constituted [under Article 52(1)(a) of the ICSID Convention], it has the authority to examine whether the members of the Tribunal were and remained (and were seen to be/remain) impartial and independent throughout the proceedings. The role of an *ad hoc* committee is to ensure that the integrity of the proceedings and the legitimacy of the award was not undermined. The impartiality and independence of the arbitrators, being an essential requirement for a valid and legitimate award, can, therefore, be assessed in the context of annulment proceedings.

Second, ICSID is an outlier in investment arbitration in that the default body for making decisions on challenges consists of the two unchallenged arbitrators. On one view, that is an undesirable position, particularly in terms of its perception.

A. Sheppard, 'Arbitrator Independence in ICSID Arbitration' in C. Binder and others (eds), *International Investment Law for the 21st Century: Essays in Honour of Christoph Schreuer* (Oxford University Press, 2009), 155, 156

[A] notable or unusual feature of ICSID is that challenges are decided by the other two arbitrators (unless they disagree). It is inevitable that a challenging party will have further doubts as to whether the remaining arbitrators will have a conflict of interest themselves when determining a challenge, in that they may have been or might expect one day to be challenged themselves, and may have a (subliminal) desire to set the test at a high level.
    ... Accordingly, I recommend that the ICSID rules and procedures be changed such that:
  • challenges should be decided by an independent ad hoc challenge committee.

It also leaves open the possibility of an unpleasant tribunal dynamic. If the unchallenged members are divided and the president of the World Bank rejects the challenge, the challenged arbitrator continues to be in place but is aware that a co-arbitrator considers them to be manifestly lacking in independence or impartiality. (Reportedly, some arbitrators finding themselves in such a situation have found it untenable and have resigned, either before or after the decision by the president of the World Bank.) It is also sometimes said that the president of the World Bank is more likely to uphold challenges than are co-arbitrators. (Again, reportedly, some of the challenges are framed as relating to more than one arbitrator because of this perception, to trigger the fall-back mechanism.) The number of challenges upheld is too limited for generalisations to be particularly helpful, but there is no obvious tendency in that direction; from the five challenges upheld, three decisions were taken by the president and two by the unchallenged arbitrators (and indeed the two most recent decisions in 2014 and 2018 fall into the latter category).[20] The 2020 decision in *Eiser* v. *Spain* effectively upheld the challenge by annulling the award as having been rendered by an improperly constituted tribunal.

It is also worth noting the comparative perspective: while the position is indeed unusual if investment arbitration is taken as the benchmark, it is entirely in line with the practice of inter-State dispute settlement, and the ICSID Convention was drafted firmly with an eye to the public international law framework (despite occasional anachronistic nods in recent writings to investment arbitration as a hybrid between commercial and international law).[21] And if there is sufficient political support, the Article 58 mechanism can be addressed by way of treaty amendment.[22]

Finally, one point that has arisen in practice picks on the 'provided that where those members are equally divided' proviso in Article 58. Does this apply only where the two unchallenged arbitrators are divided on the merits of the challenge, or would it also cover the situation where one or both are unable to decide for some other reason? The president of the World Bank has considered challenges where the unchallenged arbitrators indicate that they are unable to decide for reasons unrelated to the merits,[23] and one annulment committee endorsed this practice by the president.

---

[20] ICSID, Decisions on Disqualification https://icsid.worldbank.org/cases/content/tables-of-decisions/disqualification (accessed 3 September 2020).

[21] E.g. *Legal Consequences of the Construction of a Wall in the Occupied Palestinian Territory* (Order of 30 January 2004) [2004] ICJ Rep 3.

[22] 'The Centre received numerous comments from States and the public that favoured repeal of the portion of Art. 58 of the Convention conferring a decision on a challenge to co-arbitrators unless they are "equally divided" on the matter. This change would require an amendment to Art. 58 of the Convention, and may be suitable for consideration by Member States in the future': ICSID, 'Proposals for Amendment of the ICSID Rules' Working Paper #1, Volume 3 (2 August 2018), para. 333, https://icsid.worldbank.org/sites/default/files/publications/WP1_Amendments_Vol_3_WP-updated-9.17.18.pdf (accessed 26 September 2020).

[23] *Raiffeisen Bank International AG and Other* v. *Croatia*, ICSID Case No. ARB/17/34, Decision on the Proposal to Disqualify Stanimir Alexandrov, 17 May 2018 (Yong Kim) para. 10 ('By letter of April 6, 2018, Mr. Lazar Tomov informed the Centre that, for reasons explained in his letter, he could not decide the Proposal, recusing himself. A copy of Mr. Tomov's letter was transmitted to the Parties on that same date indicating that the proposal would be decided by the Chairman of the ICSID Administrative Council (the "Chairman"). No comments were received from the Parties on this issue').

Victor Pey Cassado and President Alliende Foundation v. Chile (II), ICSID Case No. ARB/98/2, Decision on Annulment, 8 January 2020 (Knieper, Angelet, Zhang), paras 579–580 (footnotes omitted)

579. Article 58 of the ICSID Convention does not specifically address the situation when one of the remaining arbitrators declines (or for that matter, both arbitrators decline) to take part in the challenge procedure. However, Article 58 addresses a series of hypotheses where the decision shall be made by the Chairman, namely 'where those [remaining] members are equally divided, or in the case of a proposal to disqualify a sole [...] arbitrator, or a majority of [...] arbitrators'. These hypotheses taken together make it clear that when the decision cannot be made by consensus between the two remaining arbitrators, it is for the Chairman to decide. This solution is also bound to apply where one or both of the remaining arbitrators, decline to make a decision. This has the consequence that the remaining arbitrators do not reach a consensual decision either in favour or against the challenge, which according to the terms of Article 58 triggers the Chairman's decision-making power.

580. The Committee agrees with the *ad hoc* committee in *EDF v. Argentina* that through Article 58 of the ICSID Convention the 'machinery' for a challenge was put in place to allow 'swift' solutions. The provision breathes fair and rational procedural economy and the intention to limit the loss of time and the possibility of obstruction to a minimum, as specified in ICSID Arbitration Rule 9. Even assuming that the abstention of President Berman to decide were unjustified, a swift and procedurally economical solution was called for, which for the reasons set out above clearly consisted in having the decision made by the Chairman.

In the Rules Amendment process, ICSID has similarly suggested, without being challenged by States, a need to 'clarif[y] that the co-arbitrators need not be divided on the merits of the challenge for the purposes of Art. 58 of the Convention. Instead, their lack of consensus may be caused by any reason that leads to their inability to decide it. This reflects case practice.'[24]

The third broader point is that the role of ICSID regarding challenges cannot be fully appreciated by examining only the ICSID Convention and Arbitration Rules. The complicated network of interactions between appointing authorities is not the topic here but three examples should suffice to illustrate the complexities: different institutions interact in different capacities under different rules in different situations. In the first case, a treaty designated the ICSID Secretary-General as the appointing authority, who is also authorised to decide on challenges (note that in the excerpt below it is the Secretary-General of ICSID, rather than the president of the World Bank, who is deciding the challenge, and by application of UNCITRAL, rather than ICSID standards).

---

[24] Working Paper #1, para. 337. In Working Paper #2, '[o]ne commentator suggested that arbitrators provide reasons explaining why they are equally divided when giving notice under proposed AR 22(2)(a). This has not been adopted because it would delay determination of the challenge to allow for preparation of reasons that have no dispositive effect and because *the Convention does not require such reasons*', para. 180 (emphasis added).

Vito G Gallo v. *Canada*, NAFTA/UNCITRAL Case No. 55798, Decision on the Challenge to Mr J Christopher Thomas, QC, 14 October 2009 (Ziadé), paras 2, 19

2. NAFTA Article 1124(1) provides that the ICSID Secretary-General shall serve as appointing authority for arbitration under Section B of NAFTA Chapter 11. NAFTA Article 1120(2) indicates that the applicable arbitration rules, i.e., in this case the UNCITRAL Arbitration Rules, shall govern the arbitration. Article 12(1) of the UNCITRAL Arbitration Rules provides that the decision on a challenge shall be made by the appointing authority.

...

19. The applicable standard for deciding whether to sustain a challenge to an arbitrator in the present case is set out in Article 10(1) of the UNCITRAL Arbitration Rules, which provides that an 'arbitrator may be challenged if circumstances exist that give rise to justifiable doubts as to the arbitrator's impartiality or independence'.

The second example is *Vattenfall AB and Others* v. *Germany*. ICSID asked the Secretary-General of the PCA to provide a recommendation on Germany's proposal to disqualify all the members of the tribunal in the ICSID proceedings, the Secretary-General recommended a rejection of the proposal, and the Acting Chairman of the Administrative Council of ICSID did so.[25] (It is not entirely clear in what circumstances ICSID would ask for a recommendation from the PCA: in another case where the challenging party asked for the challenge to be referred to the PCA, 'the Centre [ICSID] informed the Parties that there were no circumstances justifying referral of the Berman Proposal to the Permanent Court of Arbitration'.[26])

The third case is slightly more controversial: can the disputing parties agree to a non-ICSID mechanism and non-ICSID standards for decisions on challenges? In one case, disputing parties did exactly that (reportedly, the legal effectiveness of the parties' opt-out of the ICSID Convention was received more favourably in The Hague than in Washington DC).[27] Note that, despite apparent similarities, *Perenco* is different from *Vattenfall*. In the former, the disputing parties opt out of the ICSID procedure and standards and the PCA decides by reference to non-ICSID standards; in the latter, ICSID asks the PCA for a recommendation on how ICSID should decide a challenge under ICSID's own procedure and standards.

[25] *Vattenfall AB and Others* v. *Germany*, PCA Case No. IR-2019/01, ICSID Case No. ARB/12/12, Recommendation Pursuant to the Request by ICSID Dated 24 January 2019 on the Respondent's Proposal to Disqualify all Members of the Arbitral Tribunal Dated 12 November 2018, 4 March 2019 (Siblesz); *Vattenfall AB and Others* v. *Germany*, ICSID Case No. ARB/12/12, Decision of the Acting Chairman of the Administrative Council, 6 March 2019.

[26] *Victor Pey Cassado and President Allende Foundation* v. *Chile (II)*, ICSID Case No. ARB/98/2, Decision on the Proposals to Disqualify Mr VV Veeder QC and Sir Franklin Berman QC, 13 April 2017 (Yong Kim) para. 9.

[27] The lack of enthusiasm in Working Paper #2 is clear: 'Some commentators suggested that ... the parties be able to agree on a different decision-maker. These proposals have not been adopted because Art. 58 of the Convention mandates who decides a disqualification and Convention amendment would be required to effect these changes': para. 184.

Perenco Ecuador Limited v. Ecuador, PCA Case No. IR-2009/01, *In the Matter of a Challenge to be Decided by the Secretary-General of the Permanent Court of Arbitration Pursuant to an Agreement Concluded on October 2, 2008 in ICSID Case No. ARB/08/6*, Decision on Challenge to Arbitrator, 8 December 2009 (Kröner), paras 1–2, Section V

1. This challenge procedure arises out of a pending International Centre for Settlement of Investment Disputes ('ICSID') arbitration between a French company, Perenco Ecuador Limited ('Perenco' or 'Claimant') and the Republic of Ecuador ('Ecuador') and its state-owned oil company, Empresa Estatal Petroleos del Ecuador ('Petroecuador', together with Ecuador, 'Respondents').

2. Claimant and Respondents (the 'Parties') had, in October 2008, agreed that any arbitrator challenges in this case would be resolved by the Secretary-General of the Permanent Court of Arbitration ('PCA'), applying the International Bar Association Guidelines on Conflicts of Interest in International Arbitration ('IBA Guidelines').

...

V. Decision

NOW THEREFORE, I, Christiaan M.J. Kröner, Secretary-General of the Permanent Court of Arbitration, having considered the comments submitted by the Parties and by Judge Brower, and having established to my satisfaction my competence to decide this challenge applying the IBA Guidelines in accordance with the October 2008 Agreement between the Parties ...

As noted in Section 2.1 regarding appointments, the Rules Amendment process is invaluable for appreciating the legal and policy tensions underpinning the seemingly technical drafting choices. Comparison of the current Rule 9, quoted above, and the corresponding provisions in Working Paper #4 is instructive, particularly regarding the level of detail with which the vague temporal benchmark of 'promptly' in current Rule 9(1) has been replaced.[28] The one issue that is worth noting separately is currently reflected in Rule

---

[28] Working Paper #4: Rule 22 Proposal for Disqualification of Arbitrators

  (1) A party may file a proposal to disqualify one or more arbitrators ('proposal') in accordance with the following procedure:

    (a) the proposal shall be filed after the constitution of the Tribunal and within 21 days after the later of:

      (i) the constitution of the Tribunal; or

      (ii) the date on which the party proposing the disqualification first knew or first should have known of the facts on which the proposal is based;

    (b) the proposal shall include the grounds on which it is based, a statement of the relevant facts, law and arguments, and any supporting documents;

    (c) the other party shall file its response and supporting documents within 21 days after receipt of the proposal;

    (d) the arbitrator to whom the proposal relates may file a statement that is limited to factual information relevant to the proposal. The statement shall be filed within five days after receipt of the response referred to in paragraph (1)(c); and

    (e) each party may file a final written submission on the proposal within seven days after the earlier of receipt of the statement or expiry of the time limit referred to in paragraph (1)(d).

9(6) ('The proceeding shall be suspended until a decision has been taken on the proposal'), since its practice of application has raised concerns about strategic use of multiple consecutive challenges to delay proceedings. Despite that, the default non-suspension subject to agreement otherwise, initially suggested in Working Paper #1, was eventually rejected in favour of default suspension subject to agreement otherwise in Working Papers #2–4.

ICSID, 'Proposals for Amendment of the ICSID Rules' Working Paper #2, Volume 1 (March 2019), para. 174 (footnotes omitted)[29]

... numerous comments were received both in favor of and against the proposal to eliminate the automatic suspension of the proceeding. Some commentators expressed hesitation that the challenged arbitrator would continue to participate in decision-making, particularly if a hearing or a decision on substantive matters was pending. Others supported this change as it would discourage strategic challenges and increase efficiency. Some comments offered alternatives to address these concerns, for example, suggesting that having the Chair or the non-challenged arbitrators decide whether to suspend the proceeding; suspending the proceeding only as regards Tribunal decisions but not as regards the filing of parties' submissions; or suspending the proceeding for only 60 days. AR 21(2) proposes to maintain the automatic suspension upon the filing of a challenge until a decision on the proposal has been made, but allows the parties to agree not to suspend portions of the arbitration, or the entire arbitration. This would allow the parties to agree to continue with all or part of the case schedule, and hopefully to ensure that a challenge has minimal impact on the overall time to complete the arbitration.

ICSID, 'Proposals for Amendment of the ICSID Rules' Working Paper #4, Volume 1 (February 2020), paras 73–74 (footnotes omitted)[30]

73. Whether the suspension of the proceeding should operate automatically was again raised by various States, but there was no consensus on this question, and hence WP #4 retains the automatic suspension of the proceeding.

---

(2) The proceeding shall be suspended upon the filing of the proposal until a decision on the proposal has been made, except to the extent that the parties agree to continue the proceeding.

Rule 23 Decision on the Proposal for Disqualification

(1) The decision on a proposal shall be made by the arbitrators not subject to the proposal or by the Chair in accordance with Article 58 of the Convention.

(2) For the purposes of Article 58 of the Convention:
  (a) if the arbitrators not subject to a proposal are unable to decide the proposal for any reason, they shall notify the Secretary-General and they shall be considered equally divided;
  (b) if a subsequent proposal is filed while the decision on a prior proposal is pending, both proposals shall be decided by the Chair as if they were a proposal to disqualify a majority of the Tribunal.

(3) The arbitrators not subject to the proposal and the Chair shall use best efforts to decide any proposal within 30 days after the later of the expiry of the time limit referred to in Rule 22(1)(e) or the notice in Rule 23(2)(a).

[29] https://icsid.worldbank.org/sites/default/files/amendments/Vol_1.pdf (accessed 30 September 2020).
[30] https://icsid.worldbank.org/sites/default/files/amendments/WP_4_Vol_1_En.pdf (accessed 30 September 2020).

74. One State suggested dispensing with the automatic suspension if the proceeding was in a phase that does not require Tribunal involvement. While the parties to a particular proceeding remain free to agree to this, it is not incorporated in AR 22(2) as the need to involve the Tribunal at any stage of the proceeding cannot generally be anticipated with certainty.

3.2 Non-ICSID

The procedure for challenges in non-ICSID arbitrations varies, depending on applicable rules. Sometimes, applicable institutional rules will set out the procedure and designate the authority to decide on the challenge. For example, in Stockholm Chamber of Commerce proceedings, the decision will be taken by the Board of the Stockholm Chamber of Commerce, as it was in the challenge of Kaj Hober in *FREIF Eurowind Holdings Ltd. v. Kingdom of Spain.*[31]

Stockholm Chamber of Commerce Arbitration Rules 2017, Art. 19 (Challenge to arbitrators)

(1) A party may challenge any arbitrator if circumstances exist that give rise to justifiable doubts as to the arbitrator's impartiality or independence or if the arbitrator does not possess the qualifications agreed by the parties.

(2) A party may challenge an arbitrator it has appointed, or in whose appointment it has participated, only for reasons it becomes aware of after the appointment was made.

(3) A party wishing to challenge an arbitrator shall submit a written statement to the Secretariat stating the reasons for the challenge, within 15 days from the date the circumstances giving rise to the challenge became known to the party. Failure to challenge an arbitrator within the stipulated time constitutes a waiver of the party's right to make the challenge.

(4) The Secretariat shall notify the parties and the arbitrators of the challenge and give them an opportunity to submit comments.

(5) If the other party agrees to the challenge, the arbitrator shall resign. In all other cases, the Board shall take the final decision on the challenge.

In most other non-ICSID cases where challenges have been considered, the arbitrations are ad hoc and the applicable rules are UNCITRAL Arbitration Rules, in either their 1976 or 2010 incarnations. The excerpt below is from the 2010 Rules (the 1976 Rules do not differ in material respects in a manner relevant for this discussion). Note the standard of challenge in Article 12(1) – 'justifiable doubts as to the arbitrator's impartiality or independence' – which will be further addressed in Section 4.2.

---

[31] SCC Arbitration V2017/060 (December 2019, January 2020), not currently publicly available.

UNCITRAL Arbitration Rules 2010, Arts 12–13

Article 12

1. Any arbitrator may be challenged if circumstances exist that give rise to justifiable doubts as to the arbitrator's impartiality or independence.
2. A party may challenge the arbitrator appointed by it only for reasons of which it becomes aware after the appointment has been made.
3. In the event that an arbitrator fails to act or in the event of the de jure or de facto impossibility of his or her performing his or her functions, the procedure in respect of the challenge of an arbitrator as provided in article 13 shall apply.

Article 13

1. A party that intends to challenge an arbitrator shall send notice of its challenge within 15 days after it has been notified of the appointment of the challenged arbitrator, or within 15 days after the circumstances mentioned in articles 11 and 12 became known to that party.
2. The notice of challenge shall be communicated to all other parties, to the arbitrator who is challenged and to the other arbitrators. The notice of challenge shall state the reasons for the challenge.
3. When an arbitrator has been challenged by a party, all parties may agree to the challenge. The arbitrator may also, after the challenge, withdraw from his or her office. In neither case does this imply acceptance of the validity of the grounds for the challenge.
4. If, within 15 days from the date of the notice of challenge, all parties do not agree to the challenge or the challenged arbitrator does not withdraw, the party making the challenge may elect to pursue it. In that case, within 30 days from the date of the notice of challenge, it shall seek a decision on the challenge by the appointing authority.

The key concept is found in the final words of the above provision: the decision on the challenge will ultimately be taken 'by the appointing authority'. What (who) is the appointing authority? Under Article 6 of the 2010 UNCITRAL Rules, the appointing authority may either be agreed upon by the parties or, in the absence of such agreement and upon any party's request, is designated by the Secretary-General of the PCA (Article 6 of the 1976 Rules, applicable in the following examples, does not differ in material respects). The agreement may be given by the disputing parties. For example, in *Nord Stream 2 AG* v. *the European Union* the parties agreed that the Secretary General of the PCA shall act as the appointing authority.[32] Agreement may also be given in the investment treaty. In *Vito Gallo* v. *Canada*, excerpted at Section 3.1, the NAFTA provided that the ICSID Secretary-General would be the appointing authority, while in *CC/Devas* v. *India*, considered in Section 5.2, the treaty provided that the president of the International Court of Justice would be the appointing authority.[33]

---

[32] *Nord Stream 2 AG* v. *the European Union*, PCA Case No. AA761, Decision on Challenge to Mr Peter Rees QC, 9 December 2019 (Siblesz) paras 6–8.

[33] *CC/Devas (Mauritius) Ltd. and Others* v. *India*, PCA Case No. 2013/09, Decision on the Respondent's Challenge to Hon. Marc Lalonde as Presiding Arbitrator and Prof. Francisco Orrego Vicuña as Co-Arbitrator, 30 September 2013 (HE Judge Tomka) para. 1.

4. CHALLENGES BROUGHT AGAINST ARBITRATORS: SUBSTANCE

It is a cliché that substance and procedure cannot be neatly delineated from each other. In this setting, the connection between substance and procedure is particularly worth keeping in mind, especially when reflecting on ICSID as the apparent outlier on both substance and procedure. With that caveat, this section will consider the substantive standards involved in a challenge, dealing in turn with ICSID and non-ICSID arbitrations.

4.1 ICSID

ICSID Convention, Arts 57, 14(1)

Article 57
A party may propose to a Commission or Tribunal the disqualification of any of its members on account of any fact indicating a manifest lack of the qualities required by paragraph (1) of Article 14. A party to arbitration proceedings may, in addition, propose the disqualification of an arbitrator on the ground that he was ineligible for appointment to the Tribunal under Section 2 of Chapter IV.

Article 14
(1) Persons designated to serve on the Panels shall be persons of high moral character and recognized competence in the fields of law, commerce, industry or finance, who may be relied upon to exercise independent judgment. Competence in the field of law shall be of particular importance in the case of persons on the Panel of Arbitrators.

Three points may be noted about the substantive aspects of ICSID's challenge regime. First, the peculiar way of drafting by reference: the standard of challenge in Article 57 is 'a manifest lack of the qualities required by paragraph (1) of Article 14', which in turn sets out the requirements not for arbitrators but for members of the Panels of Arbitrators and Conciliators (on which, see Section 2.1). Second, leaving aside the 'high moral character and recognized competence in the fields of law, commerce, industry or finance' proviso, which has not played a significant role in practice, the phrase '[p]ersons ... who may be relied upon to exercise independent judgment' seems to omit an important term: impartiality. At this point, it is worth recalling that the three authentic languages of the ICSID Convention are English, French and Spanish.

Canepa Green Energy Opportunities I, S.à.r.l. and Other v. *Spain,* ICSID Case No. ARB/19/4, Decision on the Second Proposal to Disqualify Mr Peter Rees QC, 10 February 2020 (Murphy, González Napolitano), paras 51, 53 (footnotes omitted)

51. While the English version of Article 14 of the ICSID Convention refers to 'independent judgment' (and the French version to 'toute garantie d'indépendance dans l'exercice de leurs fonctions'), the Spanish version requires '*imparcialidad de juicio*' (impartiality of judgment).

Given that all three versions are equally authentic, the Unchallenged Arbitrators agree with earlier decisions that arbitrators must be both independent and impartial.

...

53. As for what is meant by the allied concepts of 'independence' and of 'impartiality', the former concept speaks principally to the absence of external control, while the latter concept relates to the absence of bias or predisposition towards a party. Both concepts seek to protect the parties from having arbitrators who are influenced by factors unrelated to the merits of the case.

The more controversial question is the meaning of 'a manifest lack of the qualities' in Article 57.[34] A key text, which clearly identifies two possible approaches, is excerpted below. Note that, first, the author was one of the unchallenged members of the annulment committee in *Vivendi* v. *Argentina (I)*, also noted in this excerpt and excerpted after it, and second, this (widely read) paper was originally delivered at the PCA Peace Palace Centenary Seminar on 11 October 2013; therefore, all subsequent decisions have to be read against its background.

J. Crawford, 'Challenges to Arbitrators in ICSID Arbitration' in David Caron and Others (eds), *Practising Virtue: Inside International Arbitration* (Oxford University Press, 2015), 597, 602, 605–606 (footnotes omitted, original emphasis)

Some tribunals have asked whether an arbitrator who has been challenged manifestly lacks independence, in the same way that one might ask whether an arbitrator manifestly lacks high moral character or competence. Other tribunals have asked whether a challenged arbitrator can be 'relied upon to exercise independent judgment'. The second approach is preferable, since it takes into account the different character of a judgment of independence.

But even if we accept this second approach, there remains a further question: the meaning of 'manifest'. Some tribunals have considered the pertinent enquiry to be whether the *evidence* of unreliability is manifest, meaning that it is *clear*. Others have considered the enquiry to be whether the *degree* of the unreliability is manifest: here 'manifest' means *serious*.

The remaining members of the ad hoc committee in *Vivendi* [v. *Argentina (I)*] in 2001 took the former approach – that 'manifest' applies to the evidence ......

Two trends are evident from the more recent decisions. The first is the interpretation of the requirement that a lack of independence be 'manifest' as permitting disqualification

---

[34] Would having attended a law school together count? See *Alpha Projektholding GmbH* v. *Ukraine*, ICSID Case No. ARB/07/16, Decision on Respondent's Proposal to Disqualify Arbitrator Dr Yoram Turbowicz, 19 March 2010 (Robinson, Alexandrov) para. 83.

only when a certain or almost certain lack of independence is proved. The second is the explicit affirmation that the standard of 'reasonable doubt' (for example, in the UNCITRAL Rules and the IBA Guidelines) is not applicable in ICSID disqualification cases.

...

The compatibility of the 'reasonable doubt' test for the disqualification of arbitrators with the provisions of the ICSID Convention is still an open question. One could take the view – consistent with the *Vivendi* decision – that the word 'manifest' in Article 57 does not substantially raise the threshold for disqualification. That would suggest that the integrity of proceedings and the independence of arbitrators will receive no less attention in an ICSID arbitration than they would in, for example, proceedings under the UNCITRAL Rules. But given the relatively low proportion of challenges to ICSID arbitrators that have led to disqualification, the threshold in ICSID does indeed appear to be higher. There is a discernible trend, at least since 2008, away from the 'reasonable doubt' test and towards a more onerous test of a 'certain or almost certain lack of independence'. Studies comparing the disqualification procedures in various arbitral regimes have questioned this trend, which draws on Schreuer's remarks. One thing is clear: disqualification in ICSID is in need of greater conceptual clarity.

The unchallenged members of the annulment committee in *Vivendi* v. *Argentina (I)* had approached 'manifest' in the following terms.

Compañía de Aguas del Aconquija S.A. & Vivendi Universal v. Argentina, ICSID Case No. ARB/97/3, Decision on the Challenge to the President of the Committee, 3 October 2001 (Crawford, Rozas), paras 20, 25 (footnotes omitted)

20. ... a question arises with respect to the term 'manifest lack of the qualities required' in Article 57 of the Convention. This might be thought to set a lower standard for disqualification than the standard laid down, for example, in Rule 3.2 of the IBA Code of Ethics, which refers to an 'appearance of bias'. The term 'manifest' might imply that there could be circumstances which, though they might appear to a reasonable observer to create an appearance of lack of independence or bias, do not do so manifestly. In such a case, the arbitrator might be heard to say that, while he might be biased, he was not manifestly biased and that he would therefore continue to sit. As will appear, in light of the object and purpose of Article 57 we do not think this would be a correct interpretation.

...

25. It is not necessary to consider the implications of the term 'manifest' in Article 57 for cases in which there is any dispute over the facts, since there is none in the present case. On the one hand it is clear that that term cannot preclude consideration of facts previously undisclosed or unknown, provided that these are duly established at the time the decision is made. On the other hand, the term must exclude reliance on speculative assumptions or

arguments – for example, assumptions based on prior and in themselves innocuous social contacts between the challenged arbitrator and a party. But in cases where (as here) the facts are established and no further inference of impropriety is sought to be derived from them, the question seems to us to be whether a real risk of lack of impartiality based upon those facts (and not on any mere speculation or inference) could reasonably be apprehended by either party. If (and only if) the answer is yes can it be said that the arbitrator may not be relied on to exercise independent judgment. That is to say, the circumstances actually established (and not merely supposed or inferred) must negate or place in clear doubt the appearance of impartiality. If the facts would lead to the raising of some reasonable doubt as to the impartiality of the arbitrator or member, the appearance of security for the parties would disappear and a challenge by either party would have to be upheld. Once the other arbitrators or Committee members had become convinced of this conclusion, there would no longer be room for the view that the deficiency was not 'manifest'.

Conversely, as Crawford noted in the chapter excerpted above, '[t]he second *Suez* [v. *Argentina*] decision, from 2008, seems to suggest that a standard of "reasonable doubt" is incompatible with the requirement of a "manifest lack" in Article 57.'[35] Note the different way in which the standard for deciding upon the same challenge is formulated under UNCITRAL and ICSID rules.

Suez, Sociedad General de Aguas de Barcelona SA and InterAguas Servicios Integrales del Agua SA v. Argentina, ICSID Case No. ARB/03/17, and *Suez, Sociedad General de Aguas de Barcelona SA and Vivendi Universal SA* v. Argentina, ICSID Case No. ARB/03/19, Decision on a Second Proposal for the Disqualification of a Member of the Arbitral Tribunal, and *AWG Group Limited* v. Argentina, Decision on a Second Proposal for Disqualification of a Member of the Arbitral Tribunal, 12 May 2008 (Salacuse, Nikken), paras 22, 29 (footnotes omitted, original emphasis)

22. Under Article 10(1) of the UNCITRAL Arbitration Rules: 'An arbitrator may be challenged if circumstances exist that give rise to justifiable doubts as to the arbitrator's impartiality or independence' ... The application of such standard in the particular case requires an answer to the following question: Would a reasonable, informed person viewing the facts be led to conclude that there is a justifiable doubt as to the challenged arbitrator's independence and impartiality?

...

29. ... in this Second Proposal to Disqualify Professor Kaufmann-Kohler, the Respondent to succeed must prove such facts that would lead an informed reasonable person to

---

[35] Crawford, 'Challenges to Arbitrators in ICSID Arbitration', 599.

conclude that Professor Kaufmann-Kohler *clearly* or *obviously* lacks the quality of being able to exercise independent judgment and impartiality in the two above entitled ICSID cases. It is important to emphasize that the language of Article 57 places a heavy burden of proof on the Respondent to establish facts that make it obvious and highly probable, *not just possible*, that Professor Kaufmann-Kohler is a person who may not be relied upon to exercise independent and impartial judgment.

Have the last eight years satisfied the need for greater clarity? To some extent. For some, the IBA Guidelines on Conflict of Interests in International Arbitration (IBA Guidelines) offer exactly that: they may be only guidelines in the technical sense but are relevant in practice. For others, the trend today is that they are almost invariably invoked only to be laid aside politely.[36] Be that as it may, and returning to the key question about greater clarity, not obviously so. As a recent decision noted, '[t]he unchallenged members are aware that the term "manifest" has been interpreted to mean "obvious" or relate to the "seriousness" of the allegations.'[37] And it is probably not surprising that the issue is not settled: recall that the procedural framework of ICSID challenges, discussed at Section 3.1, has as the default (and by far the more common) decision-maker the truncated body of two arbitrators chosen by the sole merit of not being challenged. Having said that, it does seem that practice has become unenthusiastic about the 'seriousness' school of thought: most recent decisions either explicitly adopt the 'obviousness' approach or essentially leave the choice open, as in *Italba Corporation* v. *Uruguay*: 'The unchallenged members coincide with the view of the unchallenged arbitrators in *Saint-Gobain* that "*there is no clear-cut guideline as to the degree to which the facts invoked by the challenging party must substantiate the alleged lack of qualification.*" A decision has to be made on facts sufficiently proven for a reasonable person to be convinced that it is possible that the challenged member manifestly lacks the qualities required by Article 14(1) of the ICSID Convention'.[38] The institutional practice in particular seems to have endorsed the Crawford/*Vivendi* 'obviousness' approach, as in the two recent decisions by the president of the World Bank and the Secretary General of the PCA.

---

[36] *Raiffeisen Bank*, para. 85 ('The Parties have referred to IBA Guidelines on Conflicts of Interest in International Arbitration in their arguments. While these rules or guidelines may serve as useful references, the Chairman is bound by the standard set forth in the ICSID Convention. Accordingly, this decision is made in accordance with Articles 57 and 58 of the ICSID Convention'). Compare e.g. *Eiser Infrastructure Limited and Energía Solar Luxembourg S.à r.l.* v. *Spain*, ICSID Case No. ARB/13/36, Decision on Annulment, 11 June 2020 (Hernández, Khan, Hascher) para. 223 ('As the IBA Guidelines state, "[a]ny doubt as to whether an arbitrator should disclose certain facts or circumstance should be resolved in favour of disclosure"'), also excerpted further below.

[37] *Italba Corporation* v. *Uruguay*, ICSID Case No. ARB/16/19, Decision on the Proposal to Disqualify Mr Gabriel Bottini, 29 October 2019 (Rigo Sureda, Pinto) para. 37.

[38] *Ibid*, original emphasis.

Vattenfall AB and Others v. *Germany*, PCA Case No. IR-2019/01, ICSID Case No. ARB/12/12, Recommendation Pursuant to the Request by ICSID Dated 24 January 2019 on the Respondent's Proposal to Disqualify all Members of the Arbitral Tribunal Dated 12 November 2018, 4 March 2019 (Siblesz), paras 48–50 (footnotes omitted)

48. I note that the standard imposed by Articles 14 and 57 has been considered in a number of prior decisions. It has been held that 'manifest' in Article 57 of the ICSID Convention means 'evident' or 'obvious' and relates to 'the ease with which the alleged lack of the required qualities can be perceived'.

49. The Parties appear to be largely in agreement with respect to the applicable legal standard. I note that both accept the interpretation of Article 57 and 14(1) set out in *Interocean Oil Development Company and Interocean Oil Exploration Company v. Federal Republic of Nigeria*, namely that:

Articles 57 and 14(1) of the ICSID Convention do not require proof of actual dependence or bias; rather it is sufficient to establish the appearance of dependence or bias. The legal standard applied to a proposal to disqualify an arbitrator is an 'objective standard based on a reasonable evaluation of the evidence by a third party'. As a consequence, the subjective belief of the party requesting the disqualification is not enough to satisfy the requirements of the Convention.

50. In sum, the applicable legal principles are as follows. Pursuant to Article 57 of the ICSID Convention, the challenging party carries the burden to establish, first, the existence of facts on the basis of which a 'manifest' lack of the qualities of an arbitrator can be inferred. Second, the challenging party must establish that such inference is reasonable, considering the circumstances of the case. Article 57 of the ICSID Convention contains an objective standard. Subjective perceptions or beliefs of the challenging party are insufficient to disqualify an arbitrator.

KS Invest GmbH and TLS Invest GmbH v. *Spain*, ICSID Case No. ARB/15/25, Decision on the Proposal to Disqualify Prof. Kaj Hobér, 15 May 2020 (Malpass), paras 77–78 (footnotes omitted)

77. Articles 57 and 14(1) of the ICSID Convention do not require proof of actual dependence or bias; rather, it is sufficient to establish the appearance of dependence or bias.

78. The legal standard applied to a proposal to disqualify an arbitrator is an 'objective standard based on a reasonable evaluation of the evidence by a third party'. Therefore, the subjective belief of the party requesting the disqualification is not enough to satisfy the requirements of the Convention.

4.2 Non-ICSID

We have already encountered the substantive standards of challenge in non-ICSID arbitrations during the discussion of procedure at Section 3.2 and in the comparative discussion from the perspective of ICSID at Section 4.1. The key recurring phrase is 'justifiable doubts as to the arbitrator's impartiality or independence'.

Stockholm Chamber of Commerce Arbitration Rules 2017, Art. 19(1) (Challenge to arbitrators)

A party may challenge any arbitrator if circumstances exist that give rise to justifiable doubts as to the arbitrator's impartiality or independence or if the arbitrator does not possess the qualifications agreed by the parties.

UNCITRAL Arbitration Rules 2010, Art. 12(1)

Any arbitrator may be challenged if circumstances exist that give rise to justifiable doubts as to the arbitrator's impartiality or independence.

As Judge Peter Tomka put it in his role as the appointing authority in the *CC/Devas* v. *India* UNCITRAL case, '[t]he standard to be applied here evaluates the objective reasonableness of the challenging party's concern'.[39] One document that is often invoked in discussing the application of this vague standard is the IBA Guidelines – note that they exist in 2004 and 2014 incarnations, and the references in pre-2014 cases would not be made to the current version. That is because the 'justifiable doubts' standards also appear in the Guidelines. General Standard 2 explains the application of the 'justifiable doubts' test,[40] similar to that under the UNCITRAL Rules.

IBA Guidelines on Conflicts of Interest in International Arbitration, adopted by resolution of the IBA Council on Thursday 23 October 2014, updated 2015, Part I(2)

(2) Conflicts of Interest
   (a) An arbitrator shall decline to accept an appointment or, if the arbitration has already been commenced, refuse to continue to act as an arbitrator, if he or she has any doubt as to his or her ability to be impartial or independent.
   (b) The same principle applies if facts or circumstances exist, or have arisen since the appointment, which, from the point of view of a reasonable third person having

---

[39] *CC/Devas* v. *India*, para. 64.

[40] The other General Standards are not reproduced here, and the IBA Guidelines should be consulted in full – General Standards 1 (the general principle of independence and impartiality), 3 (disclosure), 4 (waiver), 6 (governing relationships, for example with a law firm or one of the parties), and 7, which concerns parties' and the arbitrator's duties, such as the duty of a party to disclose a relationship with an arbitrator or with its counsel (for example, by virtue of the two being in the same set of barristers' chambers).

knowledge of the relevant facts and circumstances, would give rise to justifiable doubts as to the arbitrator's impartiality or independence, unless the parties have accepted the arbitrator in accordance with the requirements set out in General Standard 4.

(c) Doubts are justifiable if a reasonable third person, having knowledge of the relevant facts and circumstances, would reach the conclusion that there is a likelihood that the arbitrator may be influenced by factors other than the merits of the case as presented by the parties in reaching his or her decision.

(d) Justifiable doubts necessarily exist as to the arbitrator's impartiality or independence in any of the situations described in the Non-Waivable Red List.

Explanation to General Standard 2:

(a) If the arbitrator has doubts as to his or her ability to be impartial and independent, the arbitrator must decline the appointment. This standard should apply regardless of the stage of the proceedings. This is a basic principle that is spelled out in these Guidelines in order to avoid confusion and to foster confidence in the arbitral process.

(b) In order for standards to be applied as consistently as possible, the test for disqualification is an objective one. The wording 'impartiality or independence' derives from the widely adopted Article 12 of the United Nations Commission on International Trade Law (UNCITRAL) Model Law, and the use of an appearance test based on justifiable doubts as to the impartiality or independence of the arbitrator, as provided in Article 12(2) of the UNCITRAL Model Law, is to be applied objectively (a 'reasonable third person test'). Again, as described in the Explanation to General Standard 3(e), this standard applies regardless of the stage of the proceedings.

(c) Laws and rules that rely on the standard of justifiable doubts often do not define that standard. This General Standard is intended to provide some context for making this determination.

(d) The Non-Waivable Red List describes circumstances that necessarily raise justifiable doubts as to the arbitrator's impartiality or independence. For example, because no one is allowed to be his or her own judge, there cannot be identity between an arbitrator and a party. The parties, therefore, cannot waive the conflict of interest arising in such a situation.

The key added value of the IBA Guidelines lies in Part II, 'Practical Application of the General Standards', divided into the Red List (circumstances which give rise to justifiable doubts, some but not all of which can be subject to a waiver), the Orange List (circumstances which may give rise to justifiable doubt and need to be disclosed) and the Green List (circumstances which do not give rise to justifiable doubt and need not be disclosed).

IBA Guidelines on Conflicts of Interest in International Arbitration, adopted by resolution of the IBA Council on Thursday 23 October 2014, updated 2015

Page i

While the Guidelines were originally intended to apply to both commercial and investment arbitration, it was found in the course of the review process that uncertainty lingered as to their application to investment arbitration. Similarly, despite a comment in the original version of the Guidelines that their application extended to non-legal professionals serving as arbitrator, there appeared to remain uncertainty in this regard as well. A consensus emerged in favour of a general affirmation that the Guidelines apply to both commercial and investment arbitration, and to both legal and non-legal professionals serving as arbitrator.

Introduction

(5) The Guidelines apply to international commercial arbitration and investment arbitration, whether the representation of the parties is carried out by lawyers or non-lawyers, and irrespective of whether or not non-legal professionals serve as arbitrators.

While often invoked, one view is that the IBA Guidelines have not played a major role in recent practice. In rare cases, such as *Perenco v. Ecuador*, they were specifically agreed by the disputing parties as providing the standard.[41] In the early ICSID cases, where the IBA Guidelines were taken more seriously (reflecting, perhaps, the comparative dearth of directly relevant practice), the attitude by tribunals differed. In *Urbaser v. Argentina*, where the arbitrator's academic work became an issue, the unchallenged arbitrators were 'not convinced that distinctions like the one based on the notion of "general opinion" as it is used to define the attitudes to be put on the "green list" according to the IBA Guidelines makes much sense'.[42] In two cases that dealt with challenges regarding multiple appointments, the *Tidewater v. Venezuela* tribunal downplayed the IBA Guidelines as 'no more than a rule of thumb', while the *OPIC v. Venezuela* tribunal noted that despite all the caveats '[t]he IBA Guidelines do, however, indicate that multiple appointments represent an issue relevant to impartiality and independence and, in our opinion, are correct in so doing'.[43] The recent *Eiser v. Spain* annulment decision illustrates the ambivalence: IBA Guidelines are cited regarding the general approach to disclosure but were found to be unhelpful for the particular substantive issue, as resolving it in neither positive nor negative terms.[44]

---

[41] *Perenco v. Ecuador*, para. 2.

[42] *Urbaser SA and Other v. Argentina*, ICSID Case No. ARB/07/26, Decision on Claimant's Proposal to Disqualify Professor Campbell McLachlan, Arbitrator, 12 August 2010 (Bucher, Martinez-Fraga) para. 52.

[43] *Tidewater Inc. and Others v. Venezuela*, ICSID Case No. ARB/10/05, Decision on the Claimant's Proposal to Disqualify Professor Brigitte Stern, Arbitrator, 23 December 2010 (McLachlan, Rigo Sureda) para. 59; *OPIC Karimum Corporation v. Venezuela*, ICSID Case No. ARB/10/14, Decision on the Proposal to Disqualify Professor Philippe Sands, Arbitrator, 5 May 2011 (Jones, Santiago Tawil) para. 48.

[44] *Eiser and Energía Solar v. Spain*, paras 223, 226, excerpted further below.

5. CHALLENGES BROUGHT AGAINST ARBITRATORS: ISSUES

How do the standards discussed in Section 4, vague in the technical sense of the word, apply in practice? Two points in particular complicate this area of law: first, uncertainty as to whether the 'manifest lack' in the ICSID Convention ('obviousness' v. 'seriousness', discussed in Section 4.1) and 'justifiable doubt' in other settings reflect the same or different standards; second, the apparent novelty of challenges arising in investment arbitration, without obvious analogies either in commercial arbitration or public international law dispute settlement (e.g. 'issue conflict'). These considerations ought to be kept in mind when reflecting on whether the decisions are coherent and consistent. This section addresses challenges brought against arbitrators in three loosely delineated subject-areas, of which the first category is very broad indeed: arbitrators and parties (Section 5.1), arbitrators encountering déjà vu (Section 5.2) and arbitrators and double-hatting (Section 5.3).

5.1 Arbitrators and Parties

Arbitration is, famously, a party-driven dispute settlement mechanism. It is therefore unsurprising that the influence of parties in shaping the process and influencing the choice of adjudicators raises particularly hard questions about the boundaries of independence and impartiality. The various permutations may be sliced and divided into different categories, but it is proposed to consider three particular lines of tension: counsel work, appointments and relationship with the parties.

First, can the work for or against a party, or a type of party, be a ground of challenge? The very first ICSID challenge considered the simplest version of the situation – legal advice by an arbitrator given to a party – in a quaint decision that has not aged well at all.

Compañía de Aguas del Aconquija S.A. & Vivendi Universal v. Argentina, ICSID Case No. ARB/97/3, Decision on the Challenge to the President of the Committee, 3 October 2001 (Crawford, Rozas), paras 21–22 (footnotes omitted)

21. ... In the *Amco Asia* [v. *Indonesia (I)*] case, the Respondent challenged the Claimant's party-appointed arbitrator, Mr. Rubin, on a number of grounds. Prior to his appointment as arbitrator (but after the commencement of the arbitration) Mr. Rubin had personally given a limited amount of tax advice to the principal shareholder in the Claimant company. His law firm had also, prior to the commencement of the arbitration, had a profit sharing arrangement with the lawyers acting for the Claimants. During the period of that arrangement neither the shareholder nor the Claimant had been clients of either law firm. In their unpublished decision of 14 June 1982, the other two arbitrators (Professors Goldman and Foighel) ... sa[id] that this requirement did not preclude the appointment as an arbitrator of a person who has had, before his appointment, some relationship with a party, unless this appeared to create a risk of inability to exercise independent judgment.

In this context, in their view, the existence of some prior professional relationship in and of itself did not create such a risk 'whatever the character – even professional – or the extent of said relations'. As to Article 57, they laid stress on the term 'manifest', which in their view required 'not a possible lack of the quality, but ... a highly probable one'. On this basis they rejected the challenge. In their view, legal advice (with a fee, in 1982, of Can$450) given by someone who had never been 'regular counsel of the appointing party' was minor and had no bearing on the reliability of the arbitrator; nor could the links between the two law firms 'create any psychological risk of partiality'. Thus Mr. Rubin's lack of reliability was not manifest; indeed, in their view, it was not even reasonably apprehended.

22. The decision has been strongly criticized. To the extent that it concerned a personal relationship of legal advice given by the arbitrator to a party or to a related person after the dispute in question had arisen, it can in our view only be justified under the *de minimis* exception. That the advice was given on an unrelated matter, though a relevant factor, can hardly be sufficient. The fact remains that a lawyer-client relationship existed between the claimant and the arbitrator personally during the pendency of the arbitration; this must surely be a sufficient basis for a reasonable concern as to independence, unless the extent and content of the advice can really be regarded as minor and wholly discrete.

What about the reverse situation, legal advice *against* a party? Note the complicating modern elements, such as the structure of international law firms and the similarity of claims brought by different (States') investors against the same (measures by the) State. Would any of the elements listed in paragraphs 67 and 68 of the extract below be problematic on their own?

Blue Bank International & Trust (Barbados) Ltd v. Venezuela, ICSID Case No. ARB/12/20, Decision on the Parties' Proposals to Disqualify a Majority of the Tribunal, 12 November 2013 (Kim), paras 66–69

66. The following facts are undisputed: (i) Mr. Alonso is a partner in Baker & McKenzie Madrid; (ii) Baker & McKenzie New York and Baker & McKenzie Caracas represent the claimant in a parallel proceeding against the Respondent *(Longreef v. Venezuela)*; (iii) Mr. Alonso has no direct involvement in the parallel *Longreef v. Venezuela* case; and (iv) Mr. Alonso is a member of Baker & McKenzie's International Arbitration Steering Committee.

67. The sharing of a corporate name, the existence of an international arbitration steering committee at a global level, and Mr. Alonso's statement that his remuneration depends 'primarily' but not exclusively on the results achieved by the Madrid firm imply a degree of connection or overall coordination between the different firms comprising Baker & McKenzie International.

68. In addition, given the similarity of issues likely to be discussed in *Longreef v. Venezuela* and the present case and the fact that both cases are ongoing, it is highly

probable that Mr. Alonso would be in a position to decide issues that are relevant in *Longreef v. Venezuela* if he remained an arbitrator in this case.

69. In view of the above, the Chairman concludes that it has been demonstrated that a third party would find an evident or obvious appearance of lack of impartiality on a reasonable evaluation of the facts of this case. Accordingly, the Chairman finds that Mr. Alonso manifestly lacks one of the qualities required by Article 14(1) of the ICSID Convention in this particular case.

The *Blue Bank* decision concerned current representation by a firm connected with the arbitrator against the same State. Consider the flipside: historical representation against the State by the arbitrator.

Fernando Fraiz Trapote v. *Venezuela*, PCA Case No. AA737, Decision on the Disqualification of Arbitrator Oscar Garibaldi, 19 June 2019 (Siblesz), paras 53–54 (footnotes omitted, authors' translation from Spanish)

53. Mr. Garibaldi's performance as counsel for plaintiffs in arbitrations against the Respondent or PDVSA [Petróleos de Venezuela, S.A.] deserves different consideration ... the performance of an arbitrator in an adverse position to that of a party in separate proceedings, even in proceedings that bear no relation to that in which he or she acts as arbitrator, has been considered as a circumstance capable of raising justified doubts about the impartiality and independence of an arbitrator. And, when examining the frequency and magnitude of Mr. Garibaldi's performance on behalf of adverse parties to Venezuela, I must conclude that there is a risk that the impressions formed in the course of his participation in said procedures influence his assessment of the merits of the present controversy.

54. Mr. Garibaldi has continuously represented adverse parties to Venezuela or PDVSA from a pre-eminent position. In at least two of these arbitrations, Mr. Garibaldi acted as lead counsel (lead attorney, team leader, first chair), or, what is the same, as the main definer of the legal strategy of the case and ultimately responsible to the client for the result of the procedure. Mr. Garibaldi emphasizes that in these cases he fulfilled 'his professional function of representing the interests of [his] clients', and nothing leads me to think otherwise. But the direct, habitual involvement of Mr. Garibaldi in a position of leadership in cases against Venezuela would lead a reasonable third party to consider whether there is a risk that Mr. Garibaldi has come to share, or identify with, the positions that he has constantly and habitually defended against Venezuela, or even to develop animosity towards it, in such a way that it cannot decide this controversy impartially. In light of the high frequency and intensity of Mr. Garibaldi's participation in the aforementioned procedures, and despite the time that has elapsed since he ceased to be a member of Covington, I consider that this risk cannot be ruled out, and this is sufficient to generate justified doubts about his impartiality and independence.

The cases considered thus far address historical or current involvement with actors adverse to a party (i.e. the State). It could be that the relationship impugned is that with an 'adverse' third party,[45] one said to have an interest in the outcome which is somehow adverse to the challenging party. It could be a law firm acting against that party with whom the arbitrator is said to have or have had a professional relationship, including in parallel, even unrelated, proceedings,[46] e.g. a non-direct past or other special relationship such as some form of continued relationship with a former law firm.[47]

Vito Gallo v. *Canada*, already discussed in Section 3.1 and which is further discussed below, complicates the picture even more: what about *potential* advice to a *non*-disputing party? Note paragraph 32 in the excerpt below: while *Amco* v. *Indonesia* is not specifically mentioned and the substantive standard is UNCITRAL, the decision (by the Deputy Secretary-General of ICSID) must suggest a rejection of the *Amco* approach, even on its charitable reading in para. 22 of the *Vivendi* decision.

Vito G. Gallo v. Canada, NAFTA/UNCITRAL, PCA Case No. 55798, Decision on the Challenge to Mr J Christopher Thomas, QC, 14 October 2009, paras 30–36

30. The real issue is that Mr. Thomas is presently advising Mexico, a State Party to the NAFTA and a potential participant in this case pursuant to NAFTA Article 1128. In his letter of June 22, 2009, Mr. Thomas stated that he had not since March 2009 represented Mexico 'in respect of the interpretation or application of the provisions of NAFTA Chapter 11 or similar provisions in Mexico's Bilateral Investment Treaties', but has done 'a small amount of work for BLG on Mexico-related matters, consisting principally of reviewing its advice in respect of matters that fall within the rubric of international trade and investment law'.

31. In the particular context of NAFTA Article 1128, this is too fine a distinction to dispel doubt. By serving on a tribunal in a NAFTA arbitration involving a NAFTA State Party, while simultaneously acting as an advisor to another NAFTA State Party which has a legal right to participate in the proceedings, an arbitrator inevitably risks creating justifiable doubts as to his impartiality and independence.

32. The Respondent opines that there can be no conflict of interest since the amount of legal advice provided by Mr. Thomas to Mexico is *de minimis.* The Respondent misses the point, however. Where arbitral functions are concerned, any paid or *gratis* service provided to a third party with a right to intervene can create a perception of a lack of impartiality.

---

[45] According to the terminology in M. N. Cleis, *The Independence and Impartiality of ICSID Arbitrators* (Leiden: Brill/Nijhoff, 2017), 73–82.

[46] *CEMEX Caracas Investments B.V. and CEMEX Caracas ii Investments B.V.* v. *Bolivarian Republic of Venezuela*, ICSID Case No. ARB/08/15, Decision on the Respondent's Proposal to Disqualify a Member of the Tribunal, 6 November 2009 (parallel proceedings). In one unsuccessful challenge the arbitrator's firm was seeking to merge with a firm which was advising the other party in separate cases: see *ConocoPhillips Petrozuata B.V., ConocoPhillips Hamaca B.V. and ConocoPhillips Gulf of Paria B.V.* v. *Bolivarian Republic of Venezuela*, ICSID Case No. ARB/07/30, Decision on the Proposal for the Disqualification of L. Yves Fortier, Q.C., 27 February 2012 (Keith, Abi-Saab).

[47] *CEMEX* v. *Venezuela*, note 38.

The amount of work done makes no difference. What matters is the mere fact that work is being performed.

33. Mr. Thomas' personal integrity is unquestioned, and he is to be commended for disclosing his advisory services to Mexico in a forthright manner. Nevertheless, in an arrangement like the one presently at issue, the arbitrator could be perceived as attentive to the interests of the advised State Party. His judgment may appear to be impaired by the potential interest of the advised State Party in the proceedings. Moreover, if the advised State Party were formally to intervene under Article 1128, this would necessarily lead to the reconstitution of the tribunal. In any event, the arbitrator's involvement is problematic.

34. The Claimant demands Mr. Thomas' disqualification on the basis that 'there is no way to "un-ring" the bell'. But the bell has not yet actually been rung. Mexico has not stated an interest in this case by participating under Article 1128, or otherwise. Had Mexico intervened, this would have required Mr. Thomas' immediate disqualification. The fact is, however, that Mexico has not yet done so. The Claimant's request must therefore be rejected.

35. Nevertheless, because Mexico has the immanent right under Article 1128 formally to state its interest by participating in the case, an apparent conflict of interest is perceptible. Even if Mexico were not in the end to intervene, the arbitration would have had to proceed under the shadow of this possibility. The parties would inevitably be in a distracting and unsettled situation. It would be next to impossible for Mr. Thomas to avoid altogether, in his work as an arbitrator, the appearance of an inability to distance himself fully from the interests of Mexico, the advised NAFTA State Party and a potential participant in the present case.

36. ... Mr. Thomas must therefore now choose whether he will continue to advise Mexico, or continue to serve as an arbitrator in this case.

In response, Arbitrator Thomas resigned from the tribunal.[48]

A peculiar aspect of investment law is that even though the disputes are different, the characters of the two parties are fixed: investors on the one side, and States[49] on the other. If long-term high-level representation against (as well as, presumably, in favour of) a party could become problematic, as in *Fernando Fraiz Trapote*, how should one approach such conduct in respect of a different party but having the same character, i.e. either as investors or States as two broad categories? Challenges in investment arbitration on this point appear to be different from those in international commercial arbitration, due to the inquiry into whether a potential arbitrator is appointed by States or claimants.

---

[48] *Vito G Gallo* v. *Canada*, NAFTA/UNCITRAL Case 55798, Resignation letter of Arbitrator Thomas, 21 October 2009.
[49] But see ICSID Convention, Art. 25(1).

Saint-Gobain Performance Plastics Europe v. *Venezuela*, ICSID Case No. ARB/12/13, Decision on Claimant's Proposal to Disqualify Mr. Gabriel Bottini from the Tribunal under Article 57 of the ICSID Convention, 27 February 2013 (Sachs, Brower), paras 80–82

80. Even if one assumes *arguendo* that Mr. Bottini did in fact vigorously advocate Argentina's positions in other investment treaty arbitrations, the Arbitral Tribunal cannot see why Mr. Bottini would be locked in to the views he presented at the time. It is at the core of the job description of legal counsel – whether acting in private practice, in-house for a company, or in government – that they present the views which are favorable to their instructor and highlight the advantageous facts of their instructor's case. The fact that a lawyer has taken a certain stance in the past does not necessarily mean that he will take the same stance in a future case.

81. There is no indication in the file, or otherwise, why this should be any different for Mr. Bottini or why he should not be in a position to freely form a view on the merits presented to him in this arbitration. Absent any specific facts which indicate that Mr. Bottini is not able to distance himself in a professional manner from the cases in which he was acting as counsel, Mr. Bottini has the assumption in his favor that he is a legal professional with the ability to keep a professional distance. The same assumption is granted in favor of many arbitrators who today sit as arbitrators in ICSID cases but who started their career as counsel or who still act as counsel in such cases.

82. The Arbitral Tribunal also notes that Mr. Bottini has stated that he has not only advised Argentina, but also other parties, including investors.

Second, can multiple appointments by the same actor be a ground for challenge? Note in particular the relevant considerations identified in paragraph 50 of the extract below.

Elitech BV and Razvoj Golf DOO v. *Croatia*, ICSID Case No. ARB/17/32, Decision on the Proposal to Disqualify Professor Brigitte Stern, 23 April 2018 (Kim), paras 49–51 (footnotes omitted)

49. With respect to Professor Stern's prior nominations by Croatia in other investor-state arbitrations, reference can be made to the *Tidewater* [v. *Venezuela*] decision. In that case, it was held that 'the question of whether multiple appointments to arbitral tribunals may impugn the independence or impartiality of an arbitrator is a matter of substance, not of mere mathematical calculation'. Furthermore, the 'starting-point is that multiple appointments as arbitrator by the same party in unrelated cases are neutral, since in each case the arbitrator exercises the same independent arbitral function'.

50. In this case, the Claimants have not pointed to any circumstance related to Professor Stern's other appointments by the Respondent that would call into question her

impartiality or independence. First, as explained below, the Claimants have not established that a problematic overlap in terms of factual or legal issues of the cases exists at this time. Second, no evidence has been presented to show that a relationship of dependence, financial or otherwise, exists between Professor Stern and the Respondent or its counsel. Third, no evidence has been presented which could give rise to the inference that Professor Stern's decisions would be influenced in any way by the fact of such multiple appointments by one party; the evidence on the record would tend to support the opposite inference. Finally, the Chairman notes that the facts underlying the Claimants' proposal are not dissimilar to those underlying the challenge to Professor Stern in *Universal Compression*, in which the challenge in question was also rejected.[50]

51. In the Chairman's view, a third party undertaking a reasonable evaluation of Professor Stern's appointments by Croatia would not conclude that this evidences a manifest lack of the qualities required under Article 14(1) of the ICSID Convention at this time.

What about multiple appointments and engagements by the same counsel rather than a party?

Merck Sharp & Dohme (IA) Corporation v. *Ecuador*, PCA Case No. AA442, Decision on Challenge to Arbitrator Judge Stephen M. Schwebel, 8 August 2012 (Siblesz), paras 87–89, 92

87. The issue of multiple appointments involves, but is not limited to, a consideration of financial dependence arising from the significance of the multiple appointments – and expectation of future appointments – to the arbitrator's income. The issue of multiple appointments also engages the question of an affinity developed by the arbitrator for the party or the counsel that has repeatedly appointed him or her. It should therefore not be limited to an examination of financial dependence arising from the arbitrator's income from the appointments. The question remains: do the number and significance of the appointments considered in context, and in light of the period of time over which the appointments were made, raise justifiable doubts in the eyes of a reasonable and fair-minded third person as to the arbitrator's independence or impartiality?

88. The previous appointments of Judge Schwebel as arbitrator on behalf of parties represented by counsel for the Claimant occurred in 1997 and 2008, and those as expert in 2005 and 2008, approximately fifteen, seven, and three and a half years prior to his appointment in this case.

---

[50] [Eds: *Universal Compression International Holdings SLU* v. *The Bolivarian Republic of Venezuela*, ICSID Case No. ARB/10/9, Decision on the Proposal to Disqualify Professor Brigitte Stern and Professor Guido Santiago Tawil, Arbitrators, 20 May 2011 (Zoellick) paras 24–27, 31, 38–47, 76–79.]

89. Considered in the context of Judge Schwebel's total number of publicly known appointments as arbitrator or expert, the four prior appointments on behalf of parties represented by counsel for the Claimant do not give rise to justifiable doubts as to Judge Schwebel's financial independence. In terms of the potential effect that the appointments might hold for an appearance of bias on the part of Judge Schwebel, a closer look is warranted.

...

92. Taking all relevant circumstances into account, the prior appointments of Judge Schwebel – while relevant disclosure items – do not give rise to justifiable doubts in the eyes of a reasonable and fair-minded third person. The earlier appointments are limited in number and were spread over a significant period. They do not support the inference that Judge Schwebel has developed a particular affinity or close professional relationship with the counsel for the Claimant.

What about multiple appointments by parties who may be in a relationship of adversity *against* the same actor, or the same type of actor in general? The decision excerpted below on a challenge by Croatia shows the same polite scepticism as in the *Elitech* v. *Croatia* decision on the challenge of the Croatia-appointed arbitrator, rendered in the same spring.

Raiffeisen Bank International AG and Other v. Croatia, ICSID Case No. ARB/17/34, Decision on the Proposal to Disqualify Stanimir Alexandrov, 17 May 2018 (Kim), paras 87–89 (footnotes omitted)

87. The first ground of the Respondent's proposal concerns Dr. Alexandrov's multiple appointments by claimants generally and by other claimants in cases against Croatia in particular ...

88. The decisions in *Tidewater* and *Vivendi I* are instructive in this regard. In *Tidewater*, the unchallenged arbitrators stated that 'multiple appointments as arbitrator by the same party in unrelated cases are neutral, since in each case the arbitrator exercises the same independent function'. The Chairman finds that the same principle applies in this case to multiple appointments by different claimants, even if they are in cases against the same respondent. In *Vivendi I*, the unchallenged arbitrators stated that a finding that a lack of impartiality or independence is manifest 'must exclude reliance on speculative assumptions or arguments' and that 'the circumstances actually established ... must negate or place in clear doubt the appearance of impartiality'.

89. The Chairman finds that the Respondent has not submitted any evidence of Dr. Alexandrov's bias beyond allegations of unconscious bias nor has the Respondent submitted evidence of financial dependence. The Respondent's allegations of unconscious bias and

financial dependence are the kind of speculative assumptions or arguments that would not lead a third party undertaking a reasonable evaluation of Dr. Alexandrov's appointments by claimants to conclude that the alleged lack of impartiality or independence is manifest. As a result, the Chairman rejects the Respondent's Proposal based on this ground.

Third, can a relationship between arbitrators and parties or counsel to the parties be a ground for challenges? As a matter of first principles, independence and impartiality impose significant limitations on the relationship between an adjudicator and a disputing party. The application of these principles in practice, often against the background of the complicated web woven by the modern economic order and the many hats worn by arbitrators, is fact-specific and the decisions deserve to be read in their entirety. The following examples serve to illustrate the variety of factors that have been raised and considered in practice.

Some challenges relate, as it were, to positive connections that the arbitrator has. For example, in *Canepa* v. *Spain* multiple appointments by the counsel of a party, reliance on the counsel of the party for transactional advice in a previous capacity as the legal director of Shell, and involvement with a third-party litigation fund did not support a challenge under the ICSID rules.[51] Conversely, in *Nord Stream 2* v. *the European Union* the former professional connections of the (same) arbitrator with Shell, an investor in the Nord Stream 2 project, as well as ongoing connections via shareholdings and pensions, were found to have been sufficient to raise justifiable doubts.[52] In *Raiffeisen Bank* v. *Croatia*, a history of 'cross-appointments' between an arbitrator and a partner of a law-firm acting for a party did not, without more, constitute grounds for an ICSID challenge,[53] nor did the use by a party adverse to the interests of the challenging party in another case of experts allegedly having close links with the arbitrator.[54] (Note, as well, the flipside of this challenge: asking the tribunal to exclude counsel because of their connection with the arbitrators.[55]) Other challenges upheld have been more focused on the confrontational elements, as in *Perenco* v. *Ecuador*, discussed in Section 3.1.

In the recent *Eiser* v. *Spain* case, the annulment committee found that multiple connections between an arbitrator and a valuation expert of a party reached the standard for a successful challenge.

---

[51] *Canepa Green Energy Opportunities I, S.á. r.l. and Other* v. *Spain*, ICSID Case No. ARB/19/4, Decision on the Proposal to Disqualify Mr Peter Rees QC, 19 November 2019 (Murphy, González Napolitano).

[52] *Nord Stream 2 AG* v. *EU*, paras 31–34.

[53] *Raiffeisen Bank* v. *Croatia*, paras 93–95.

[54] *Ibid.*, paras 96–97.

[55] See endorsement of such powers, *Hrvatska Elektroprivreda, dd* v. *Slovenia*, ICSID Case No. ARB/05/24, Tribunal's Ruling regarding the participation of David Mildon QC in further stages of proceedings, 6 May 2008 (Williams, Brower, Paulsson), and significantly more lukewarm reaction, *Rompetrol Group BV* v. *Romania*, ICSID Case No. ARB/06/3, Decision of the Tribunal on the Participation of a Counsel, 14 January 2010 (Berman, Donovan, Lalonde) paras 14–27.

Eiser Infrastructure Limited and Energía Solar Luxembourg S.à r.l. v. *Spain*, ICSID Case No. ARB/13/36, Decision on Annulment, 11 June 2020 (Hernández, Khan, Hascher), paras 217–219 (footnotes omitted)

217. The Committee has carefully reviewed the uncontested facts, as well as other decisions in such cases. As pointed out in the *Suez* [v. *Argentina*] case, it is true that arbitrators, lawyers and experts doing investment arbitrations live on the same planet. Some interaction is, therefore, inevitable. Nevertheless, it is obvious and it is to be expected that the more 'connections' there are between them, across cases and, particularly, in different roles, the more chances there are that these may give rise to conflicts. For the sake of the fair and objective conduct of the arbitral proceedings, these should, therefore, be declared and specifically brought to the attention of the parties and other arbitrators.

218. The Committee finds that this case does not bring forth merely an isolated instance of Mr. Lapuerta and Dr. Alexandrov working together. In addition to the several past and present professional connections and interactions between them, the Committee has taken particular note of four instances where Dr. Alexandrov and Mr. Lapuerta worked for the same party, as counsel and expert respectively. In two of those cases, Dr. Alexandrov, as counsel, was interacting with Mr. Lapuerta as expert, at the same time that he was acting in this case as an arbitrator and Mr. Lapuerta as a damages expert of one of the parties. This was in addition to the longstanding relationship between the Brattle Group and Dr. Alexandrov's the then law firm, Sidley Austin, and included another concurrent case – *Bear Creek* – in which Dr. Alexandrov was working as counsel with Brattle Group experts (Prof. Davis).

219. Arbitrators should either not sit in cases or be prepared to be challenged and/or disqualified where, on an objective assessment of things, assessed by a fair minded and informed third party observer, they may not be perceived as independent and impartial. The role of a third party observer, when these matters are challenged, in annulment proceedings, is performed by annulment committees. It matters not that Dr. Alexandrov may not even have been conscious of the insidious effects of this association. What matters is that an independent observer, on an objective assessment of all the facts, would conclude that there was a manifest appearance of bias on the part of Dr. Alexandrov.

5.2 Arbitrators and Déjà Vu

Very few things are entirely new, even in international law. Arbitrators are not blank sheets, and it is likely that they have articulated an opinion on the same or an analogous issue in their pre-arbitral life, whether as arbitrators, counsel, experts or academics, particularly taking into account the boiler-plate character of many rules in investment law.

First, consider earlier legal writings on an issue likely to arise in an arbitration. The decision in *Urbaser* v. *Argentina* usually provides the starting point for discussion.

Report of the ASIL–ICCA Joint Task Force on Issue Conflicts in Investor–State Arbitration (The ICCA Reports No. 3) 17 March 2016, paras 108–110 (footnotes omitted)

108. With one possible recent exception discussed below, challenges involving arbitrators' past expressions of general views on substantive legal issues, either in scholarly or professional writings or in lectures or remarks at professional meetings, have not been accepted. (Writings taking positions regarding the specific case at issue are another matter; such writings seem likely to be found disqualifying.)

109. Probably the best known such challenge occurred in *Urbaser SA v. Argentine Republic*, an ICSID case. In a 2010 decision, the two unchallenged arbitrators rejected a challenge by claimants based on two of Professor Campbell McLachlan's scholarly writings claimed to favor the respondent's positions on important issues in the pending case, application of most-favored-nation (MFN) clauses and the defense of necessity. In a 2007 treatise, Professor McLachlan strongly criticized what he characterized as the 'heretical' earlier decision in *Maffezini v. Spain*, holding that the MFN provision in the bilateral investment treaty between Argentina and Spain served to import the more liberal dispute settlement provisions of the corresponding treaty between Chile and Spain. The second challenged writing, an article in the *International and Comparative Law Quarterly*, involved the necessity defense. Professor McLachlan there applauded the CMS Annulment Committee's discussion of the necessity defense, writing that 'the eminent experience in public international law of the [Annulment] Committee, suggest that great weight should be given to the Committee's categorical views on the central issues confronted in these cases'.

110. The unchallenged arbitrators rejected the contention that their colleague 'lacks the freedom to give his opinion and to make a decision with respect to the facts and circumstances of this case because he already had prejudged those facts and circumstances, issued his opinion, and made it known'. Instead:

> What matters is whether the opinions expressed by Prof. McLachlan on the two issues qualified as crucial by Claimants are specific and clear enough that a reasonable and informed third party would find that the arbitrator will rely on such opinions without giving proper consideration to the facts, circumstances, and arguments presented by the Parties in this proceeding ...
>
> ... [T]he mere showing of an opinion, even if relevant in a particular arbitration, is not sufficient to sustain a challenge for lack of independence or impartiality of an arbitrator. For such a challenge to succeed there must be a showing that such opinion or position is supported by factors related to and supporting a party to the arbitration (or a party closely related to such party), by a direct or indirect interest of the arbitrator in the outcome of the dispute, or by a relationship with any other individual involved, such as a witness or arbitrator.

The key authority for a successful challenge partly on the basis of academic writings is *CC/Devas v. India*, noted earlier in this chapter.

Report of the ASIL–ICCA Joint Task Force on Issue Conflicts in Investor–State Arbitration (The ICCA Reports No. 3) 17 March 2016, paras 118, 120–121 (footnotes omitted)

118. In *CC/Devas (Mauritius) Ltd. et al. v. India*, the respondent challenged two members of an arbitral panel constituted to hear a large telecommunications-related claim against India. Judge Peter Tomka, then President of the International Court of Justice, the appointing authority under the India-Mauritius bilateral investment treaty, decided the challenge. India challenged both the presiding arbitrator, Hon. Marc Lalonde, and the arbitrator appointed by the claimants, Professor Orrego Vicuña, because they had served together on two tribunals (*CMS* and *Sempra*) that took a position on a legal issue ('essential security interests') expected to arise in the current proceedings. The respondent also cited Professor Orrego Vicuña's participation in a third award addressing the same issue and in a later article defending his views on the issue. The respondent emphasized that all three arbitral decisions were later annulled or annulled in part.

...

120. Judge Tomka accepted the challenge Prof. Orrego Vicuña, but rejected the challenge to Mr. Lalonde, although he had joined with Orrego Vicuña on two of the three Argentine cases involving the 'necessity' issue cited in the challenge. In doing so, Judge Tomka recalled that prior decisions had not found scholarly publication to be reason for disqualification. However, in his view, when taken together with other relevant circumstances, published views could indicate unacceptable pre-judgment.

> The conflict is based on a concern that an arbitrator will not approach an issue impartially, but rather with a desire to conform to his or her own previously expressed view. In this respect ... some challenge decisions and commentators have concluded that knowledge of the law or views expressed about the law are not per se sources of conflict that require removal of an arbitrator; likewise, a prior decision in a common area of law does not automatically support a view that an arbitrator may lack impartiality. Thus, to sustain any challenge brought on such a basis requires more than simply having expressed any prior view; rather, I must find, on the basis of the prior view and any other relevant circumstances, that there is an appearance of pre-judgment of an issue likely to be relevant to the dispute on which the parties have a reasonable expectation of an open mind.

121. Judge Tomka clearly saw Prof. Orrego Vicuña's vigorous published defense of his views as a contributing factor in allowing the challenge.

> In my view, being confronted with the same legal concept in this case arising from the same language on which he has already pronounced on the four aforementioned occasions could raise doubts for an objective observer as to Professor Orrego Vicuña's ability to approach the question with an open mind. The later article in particular suggests that, despite having reviewed the analyses of three different annulment committees, his view remained unchanged. Would

a reasonable observer believe that the Respondent has a chance to convince him to change his mind on the same legal concept? Professor Orrego Vicuna is certainly entitled to his views, including to his academic freedom. But equally the Respondent is entitled to have its arguments heard and ruled upon by arbitrators with an open mind. Here, the right of the latter has to prevail.

What is the rationale of *CC/Devas*? At its narrowest, that decision is limited to the peculiar situation of a line of consistent decisions by tribunals chaired by the same arbitrator, all set aside or otherwise heavily criticised, taken together with an academic defence of the original arbitral position, with the challenge considered under UNCITRAL Rules. At its broadest, it is a significant qualification to *Urbaser*, articulated by a (*the*) pre-eminent international lawyer and standing for the proposition that repeated firm expression of opinion, including (and perhaps even solely) in the academic format, suggests an unchanged and unchangeable view that could sustain a challenge in any setting.

The Joint Task Force certainly preferred a narrow reading,[56] and the absence of any successful challenge of this character since 2015 could support the approach. Yet the real effect of *CC/Devas* may lie in self-restraint by arbitrators, which is harder to ascertain (dare one mention 'regulatory chill'?). It would be unkind to say that no leading arbitrator since 2012 has said or written anything of the slightest interest or possible controversy in actual disputes – but there does seem to have been a watershed in 2013 regarding the willingness of leading figures to venture too deeply and clearly into such debates.

Second, consider decisions on similar legal or factual issues in earlier cases. If *CC/Devas* is the rare successful challenge to an arbitrator's academic writings, *Caratube* v. *Kazakhstan* plays the same role for challenges relating to other arbitral proceedings.

---

[56] Task Force Report, paras 172–173: '172. Challenges based on prior scholarship or expressions of views appear to have been much more common than those involving concurrent service as counsel and arbitrator. Even these challenges, however, have been almost entirely unsuccessful, save for the CC/Devas case (which, as noted above, appeared to rely on additional circumstances taken together with public expressions of views). Decision makers have generally recognized not only that arbitrators are entitled to form academic and doctrinal views on general legal topics, but also that arbitrators can and do change their positions in light of evolving circumstances, new information, or further reflection.

173. This is as it should be. Members of the Task Force from all perspectives urged that international arbitration benefits significantly from vigorous and open discussion of contemporary legal issues by knowledgeable persons. In the Task Force's view, scholarly or professional publications addressing issues at a general level (but not discussing details of a particular dispute in which they have been named) should not be seen as impairing impartiality. It would be a significant loss for such informed commentary to be chilled by fear of a possible future challenge to the author on account of the views expressed. Opinion in the Task Force thus mirrored the approach of the 2014 IBA Guidelines on Conflicts of Interest, which consider that no disclosure is required where the arbitrator "has previously published a legal opinion (such as a law review article or public lecture) concerning an issue that also arises in the arbitration...." In this sense, the challenge in the CC/Devas case could be understood as illustrating – and not departing from – the general recognition that doctrinal views are not problematic based on the assumption that the arbitrator can be convinced to take a different view.'

Caratube International Oil Company LLP & Mr Devincci Salah Hourani v. *Kazakhstan*, ICSID Case No. ARB/13/13, Decision on the Proposal for Disqualification of Mr Bruno Boesch, 20 March 2014 (Lévy, Aynès), paras 87–89, 93–94 (footnotes omitted)

87. Having determined that the facts underlying the *Ruby Roz* [v. *Kazakhstan*] case are at a minimum similar to the facts alleged in the present arbitration, the Unchallenged Arbitrators now turn to the question whether these facts are potentially relevant for the determination of the legal issues in the present arbitration. In both the *Ruby Roz* case and the present arbitration the Claimants argue that the acts and omissions of the Respondent against the Claimants were in violation of Kazakhstan's legal obligations, in particular its obligations under customary international law and Kazakhstan's Foreign Investment Law. It is observed that some of the breaches listed in the Claimants' Request of Arbitration are the same as those invoked in the *Ruby Roz* arbitration ...

88. As a result of this overlap in facts and legal issues, the Unchallenged Arbitrators find that the facts of which Mr. Boesch has gained knowledge (or been able to gain knowledge) through his serving as arbitrator in the *Ruby Roz* case are also relevant for the determination of some of the legal issues in the present arbitration.

89. The Unchallenged Arbitrators have carefully considered Mr. Boesch's Explanations of 13 February 2014, in particular his assurances that he 'consider[s] that it would be improper for [him] to discuss or disclose anything that transpired in the Ruby Roz Agricol LLP case, and [he] will not do so' and that he 'consider[s] it improper to form any opinion based upon external knowledge including in particular what may be found in the public media, and [he] will not do so'. However, the Unchallenged Arbitrators agree with the tribunal in *EnCana Corporation v. Republic of Ecuador* in that Mr. Boesch 'cannot reasonably be asked to maintain a "Chinese wall" in his own mind: his understanding of the situation may well be affected by information acquired in the [Ruby Roz] arbitration'. That Mr. Boesch would consider it improper to form any opinion based upon external knowledge is not to be doubted and neither is his intention not to do so: it remains that Mr. Boesch is privy to information that would possibly permit a judgment based on elements not in the record in the present arbitration and hence there is an evident or obvious appearance of lack of impartiality as this concept is understood without any moral appraisal: a reasonable and informed third party observer would hold that Mr. Boesch, even unwittingly, may make a determination in favor of one or as a matter of fact the other party that could be based on such external knowledge.

...

93. For the same reasons as those set forth in section A.1., namely the significant overlap in the underlying facts between the *Ruby Roz* case and the present arbitration, the Unchallenged Arbitrators find that a reasonable and informed third party would find it highly likely that, due to his serving as arbitrator in the *Ruby Roz* case, Mr. Boesch has benefitted from knowledge of facts on the record in that case which may not be

available to the two other arbitrators in the present arbitration (or even be incompatible or contradictory with some facts on the record of the present arbitration), thereby giving rise to a manifest imbalance within the Tribunal to the disadvantage of the Claimants.

94. This finding is corroborated by the fact that the claimants in both sets of proceedings are not the same, albeit that they are closely related. Therefore, it cannot be excluded that the Parties in the present arbitration do not have access to or, for example for reasons of confidentiality, cannot use all the information or documents available to the parties in the *Ruby Roz* case, even though such information or documents would be relevant for the determination of the legal issues in the present arbitration.

In all the publicly available decisions since *Caratube*, challenges of this kind have been rejected. A recent example is provided by a challenge in one of the many Spanish renewable energy arbitrations, where emphasis was placed on a dissenting opinion by the challenged arbitrator.[57]

KS Invest GmbH and TLS Invest GmbH v. *Spain*, ICSID Case No. ARB/15/25, Decision on the Proposal to Disqualify Prof. Kaj Hobér, 15 May 2020 (Malpass), paras 87, 89–92 (footnotes omitted)

87. The Respondent's position is that because Prof. Hobér expressed his views [in the Dissenting Opinion he issued in *Stadtwerke* v. *Spain*] on many 'key issues' at stake in this case, and did so in a way that, according to the Respondent, 'leaves no room for a different decision in this arbitration', he can no longer sit in this arbitration without 'depriving the Respondent of an arbitrator that will exercise an independent judgment'.

...

89. *First*, it should be noted that the circumstance that an arbitrator has expressed views on issues of law or fact common to two or more parallel arbitrations in which that arbitrator is involved is not – without more – evidence of partiality or appearance thereof.

90. *Second*, the two cases at stake involve investments in Spain by unrelated companies, made at different times, and in different sectors. These are not distinctions without relevance in the context of renewable energy cases against Spain, as decisions of ICSID tribunals have shown. Even in cases where issues could be similar, the arguments and the manner in which they are presented by different parties could differ depending on the particularities of each case.

---

[57] *FREIF* v. *Spain* is another example of a successful challenge, but is not publicly available at the time of writing. It is summarised in the following terms by Spain: '36. ... the Respondent brought to the attention of the Tribunal a challenge that it filed against Prof. Hobér in an SCC arbitration "for exactly the same reasons as those presented in this arbitration". This challenge was upheld by the SCC Board in a decision dated January 7, 2020.

37. In its comments on the SCC Decision, the Respondent points out that ... [t]his decision concludes that "the *Stadtwerke* arbitration includes issues of fact and law which overlap with the present arbitration".'

91. Finally, *Stadtwerke* and the present arbitration commenced within six months of each other, in January and June 2015, respectively. In *Stadtwerke*, the claimants appointed Prof. Hobér on April 15, 2015. In the present case, the Claimants appointed Prof. Hobér on August 12, 2018, following Mr. Born's resignation.

92. The parties could anticipate at the time of Prof. Hobér's appointment that both cases would deal with similar issues of fact and law. They also knew that one of the cases could be decided in advance of the other; yet neither party asked that the two cases be decided simultaneously. Spain did not raise concerns upon the appointment of Prof. Hobér in this case, and, it should be noted, has appointed the same individuals in several other investor-State arbitrations.

5.3 Arbitrators and Double-Hatting

The challenges discussed so far are not unique to investment arbitration, although its peculiar dynamic brings the issues out particularly clearly. But one challenge that is often posed in terms of first impressions (even though, as the first excerpt shows, is not entirely without analogy), is sartorial in character: can the same (one-headed) person simultaneously wear the hat of counsel and arbitrator?[58] Note three points: first, this is not a (boilerplate) challenge of a relationship between an arbitrator and a party in the same case (see *Amco* v. *Indonesia* at Section 5.1) but a more fundamental critique of the propriety of arguing, say, an MFN clause case in the morning and deciding the same question of principle in an unrelated case in the afternoon. Second, this is a point on which reasonable (great and good) people disagree: a quick survey of the recent ICSID cases, as the opening of the chapter suggested, is likely to reveal that a plurality of arbitrators do not argue investment cases in parallel, but a respectable minority of arbitrators do. Some (practitioners) will say that a career often does not begin or end by proceeding directly towards becoming an arbitrator, and the survival of a legal career often requires the supplement of counsel work. Others, as in the excerpt below, strongly disagree. Also note that reasonable people may change their minds. A leading figure in the field is reported to have observed a marked decrease in their tolerance for double-hatting after becoming a judge of a permanent international tribunal. Is a Multilateral Investment Court therefore the answer?[59]

---

[58] See https://en.wikipedia.org/wiki/Zaphod_Beeblebrox (accessed 3 September 2020).
[59] See the discussion in Chapter 20 of this book. One counter-argument is that parties should be able to choose their arbitrators. Some, even many, may prefer the practitioner rather than the tenured professional academic, retired diplomat or national court judge, who is elevated by national appointment to an international bench. A second argument is that the current system was intended to depoliticise investment disputes, for which see Aron Broches' views which are reproduced in Chapter 1 of this book. As Brigitte Stern has put it: 'This [the proposal for a Multilateral Investment Court] is not at all a step forward and certainly introduces again politics ... who will be the nominees of the States? Probably retired diplomats, retired judges, civil servants that have the State and have always been on good terms with the State. I think it might be re-politicised': B. Stern, 'Appointment of Arbitrators and Related Issues' in *Proceedings of the ISDS Reform Conference 2019* (Hong Kong: AAIL/HKSAR DOJ, 2019), 193–194, and more generally 190–201. Of course, whether depoliticisation is a helpful perspective is a separate debate; for a sceptical view by one of the authors, see M. Paparinskis, 'The Limits of Depoliticisation in Contemporary Investor-State Arbitration' (2012) 3 *Selected Proceedings of ESIL* 271.

The usual starting point for such a discussion is Professor Philippe Sands' paper, published a decade ago, which makes a powerful argument against double-hatting. It discusses the (2000s) practice in investment law and analogous fields and deserves to be read in its entirety; the excerpt below is of key passages from the introduction and conclusion.

P. Sands, 'Conflict and Conflicts in Investment Treaty Arbitration: Ethical Standards for Counsel' in C. Brown and K. Miles (eds), *Evolution in Investment Treaty Law and Arbitration* (Cambridge University Press, 2011), 23–24, 29–30 (footnotes omitted)

The issue that arises seems reasonably clear: it is possible to recognise the difficulty that may arise if a lawyer spends a morning drafting an arbitral award that addresses a contentious legal issue, and then in the afternoon as counsel in a different case drafts a pleading making arguments on the same legal issue. Can that lawyer, while acting as arbitrator, cut herself off entirely from her simultaneous role as counsel? The issue is not whether she thinks it can be done, but whether a reasonable observer would so conclude. Speaking for myself, I find it difficult to imagine that I could do so without, in some way, potentially being seen to run the risk of allowing myself to be influenced, however subconsciously. That said, a number of my closest colleagues and friends take a different view.

...

We are bound to recognise that at the heart of many investment treaty cases, the outcome will turn on the same issues: expropriation, fair and equitable treatment, full protection and security, the effect of MFN clauses, of 'umbrella clauses' and so on. This feature distinguishes the field of investment treaty arbitration from commercial arbitration: in the latter, the same legal issues do not come out with such regularity or frequency, in part because the applicable law will often differ. Special attention is required in investment treaty arbitration because of particular features of this area, including the fact that the applicable law is invariably the same set of rules of public international law, coupled with the point that investment arbitration cases often raise issues that are of particular political sensitivity to the States involved whilst directly affecting the economic interests of the investor. Both constitute legitimate concerns that require protection and special prudence in the field of investment treaty arbitration, an area that cannot be characterised as being exclusively commercial in character: investment treaty arbitration also has a core public law function.

...

... two fundamental objections were raised with regard to the imposition of the same restrictions upon investment treaty arbitration as are in place at the ICJ [International Court of Justice][60] and the CAS [Court of Arbitration for Sports]. The first argument that the pool

---

[60] [Eds: ICJ, Practice Directions (adopted 7 February 2002), https://www.icj-cij.org/en/practice-directions (accessed 3 September 2020): 'Practice Direction VII: The Court considers that it is not in the interest of the sound administration of justice that a person sit as judge *ad hoc* in one case who is also acting or has recently acted as agent, counsel or advocate in another case before the Court. Accordingly, parties, when choosing a judge *ad hoc* pursuant to Article 31 of the Statute and Article 35 of the Rules of Court, should refrain from nominating persons who are acting as agent, counsel or advocate in another case before the Court or have acted in that capacity in the three years preceding the date of the nomination. Furthermore,

of individuals who are capable of serving as high-class international arbitrators is small, and the system could not sustain a change. I do not buy this argument as being dispositive: there are many individuals who are capable of acting as arbitrators – and just as the ICJ was able to carry on with its work unaffected by the change in rules,[61] so will investment treaty arbitrations. In this respect, it may be helpful to have another look at the book by Yves Dezalay – *Dealing in Virtue* – which describes a community of able lawyers driven by a particular perception of what is in the public good that appears to be closely connected to perception of what is in the interest of the members of the community.

The second objection is that not everyone is in a financial position such as to be able to opt to be arbitrator rather than counsel. This argument is essentially an economic one, recognising that appointments as arbitrator are not guaranteed and, having elected to discard appointments as counsel, the individual exposes himself to a risk of economic uncertainty. The argument is not an attractive one, in the sense that it might be seen by some as giving greater weight to economic interests than to an issue of principle. Moreover, I am not persuaded that the pool of possible candidates is as small as some would suggest; it is an expanding group, and over time it will grow even more, which must be a good thing in enriching the pool of lawyers who make the arguments. Beyond that, it seems inappropriate to allow what should be an issue of principle underpinning the legitimacy and effectiveness of the system to be driven by the particular economic considerations of individuals or law firms: given the parties involved, investment treaty arbitration has of necessity a public component and, relatedly, a public-service component: it is not a purely commercial activity (even if it is the case that this field has become an enormously lucrative area of international law, in which the costs of litigation have now risen very significantly). We need to keep our eye on the big picture: the system exists to protect the interests of investors and of States and to provide for efficient and effective means for resolving disputes when they arise.

In short, I believe there is a large and able pool of men and women from jurisdictions around the world who are perfectly well qualified to serve as arbitrators in investment treaty arbitrations, and who do not feel impelled to act both as counsel and arbitrator in investment treaty disputes. Future decision-making should be driven by principle and not by other factors.

parties should likewise refrain from designating as agent, counsel or advocate in a case before the Court a person who sits as judge *ad hoc* in another case before the Court.

Practice Direction VIII: The Court considers that it is not in the interest of the sound administration of justice that a person who until recently was a Member of the Court, judge *ad hoc*, Registrar, Deputy-Registrar or higher official of the Court (principal legal secretary, first secretary or secretary), appear as agent, counsel or advocate in a case before the Court. Accordingly, parties should refrain from designating as agent, counsel or advocate in a case before the Court a person who in the three years preceding the date of the designation was a Member of the Court, judge *ad hoc*, Registrar, Deputy-Registrar or higher official of the Court.']

[61] [Eds: But see *Application of the Convention on the Prevention and Punishment of the Crime of Genocide (Bosnia and Herzegovina* v. *Serbia and Montenegro)* [2007] ICJ Rep. 43 para. 29 ('By a letter dated 22 February 2002 to the President of the Court, Judge *ad hoc* Lauterpacht resigned from the case'); *Certain Property (Liechtenstein* v. *Germany)* [2005] ICJ Rep. 6 para. 4 ('Liechtenstein ... first chose Mr. Ian Brownlie, who resigned on 25 April 2002').]

Perhaps surprisingly, not too many decisions tackle the point directly. The two key decisions are *Ghana* v. *Malaysia Telekom* (rendered by the District Court of The Hague)[62] and *Saint Gobain* v. *Venezuela*.

Saint-Gobain Performance Plastics Europe v. *Venezuela*, ICSID Case No. ARB/12/13, Decision on Claimant's Proposal to Disqualify Mr. Gabriel Bottini from the Tribunal under Article 57 of the ICSID Convention, 27 February 2013 (Sachs, Brower), paras 77, 81, 83–85

77. The Arbitral Tribunal notes that Claimant has not alleged that Mr. Bottini is subject to any current control by either the Argentine or the Venezuelan Government. Claimant's concerns are entirely based on the issue of so-called abstract 'issue conflict', *i.e.* on the assumption that there is a danger that Mr. Bottini will decide a certain issue in favor of Venezuela because he has argued the same, or similar, issues in favor of Argentina in the past and potentially in the future, and in doing so, that he will not have sufficient regard to the merits of this case.

...

81. ... Absent any specific facts which indicate that Mr. Bottini is not able to distance himself in a professional manner from the cases in which he was acting as counsel, Mr. Bottini has the assumption in his favor that he is a legal professional with the ability to keep a professional distance. The same assumption is granted in favor of many arbitrators who today sit as arbitrators in ICSID cases but who started their career as counsel or who still act as counsel in such cases.

...

83. Further, the present case is distinguishable from the case *Republic of Ghana v. Telekom Malaysia Berhard [sic.]*,[63] Decision of the District Court of the Hague (Civil Law Section), 18 October 2004, on which Claimant relies.

84. In the cited case, Prof. Gaillard was acting simultaneously as counsel for a party in one arbitration [*RFCC* v. *Morocco* annulment] and as arbitrator in another case. The Arbitral Tribunal agrees that this constellation can potentially raise doubts as to the impartiality and independence of the concerned individual in his role as arbitrator. It seems possible that the arbitrator in such a case could take a certain position on a certain issue, having in mind that if he took a different position as arbitrator, he could undermine his credibility as counsel as which he is arguing on the same, or very similar, issue.

85. However, this case is different. The Arbitral Tribunal has no present information that Mr. Bottini currently is advocating for or advising Argentina in any way. Doubtless Mr. Bottini is aware of the obligation of someone in his position to make appropriate disclosures as needed of any potential conflict of interest, including an issue conflict, for which process the IBA Guidelines on Conflicts of Interest in International Arbitration provide widely accepted guidance.

---

[62] *Republic of Ghana* v. *Telekom Malaysia Berhad*, Decision of the District Court of The Hague (Civil Law Section), 18 October 2004.

[63] [Eds: 'Berhad'.]

Are *Malaysia Telekom* and *Saint Gobain* compatible? Are they to be explained by the temporal overlap, present in the former but not the latter, or by differences in the applicable standard? Note also the point assumed in both cases: if the challenge of double-hatting is directed at the propriety of arguing and deciding similar issues, are all investment arbitrations to be treated as raising similar issues for the purposes of this challenge? In a recent decision, the president of the World Bank suggested a narrower approach, focused on factual and legal issues in particular cases.

KS Invest GmbH and TLS Invest GmbH v. Spain, ICSID Case No. ARB/15/25, Decision on the Proposal to Disqualify Prof. Kaj Hobér, 15 May 2020 (Malpass), paras 80–84 (footnotes omitted)

80. The first ground upon which Spain is seeking to disqualify Prof. Hobér as an arbitrator in this case relates to his involvement as counsel in the Nord Stream Arbitration.

81. Spain contends that because of the similarities between the Nord Stream Arbitration and the present case, Prof. Hobér will be unable to exercise independent and impartial judgment in this case.

82. Spain explains that in both cases the respondent's right to regulate is contested. Spain also notes that 'in both arbitrations claimants have submitted their claims under Articles 10(1) and 13 of the ECT'.

83. It is to be noted that the present arbitration and the Nord Stream Arbitration concern (i) different claimants; (ii) different respondents; (iii) different subsectors of the energy industry; and (iv) different measures. As Prof. Hobér indicated in his October 27, 2019 letter, the claimant in the Nord Stream Arbitration is the Swiss owner and operator of a gas pipeline; the respondent is the European Union. The energy subsector involved is the transportation of natural gas, and the measures challenged are European EU directives which are not at stake in the present ICSID proceeding.

84. Given the multiple differences between the two cases, a third party undertaking a reasonable evaluation of the facts would not conclude that there is evidence: (i) that Prof. Hobér manifestly appears to lack the qualities required under Article 14(1) of the ICSID Convention, or (ii) that Prof. Hobér breached his duty to disclose a circumstance that might call into question his ability to exercise independent and impartial judgement.

It is not easy to take stock of the current state of affairs. It is clear that many arbitrators do and many do not engage in double-hatting. Langford, Behn and Lie suggested in 2017 'that there has not been a significant decrease (or increase) over time', and that the decrease in particular cases may be driven by retirement age, the sheer number of arbitrations that can no longer be combined with other work, or appointment to judicial institutions,[64] rather than concerns about challenges. The practice of authorities considering

---

[64] Langford *et al.*, The Revolving Door in International Investment Arbitration', 326.

challenges has not moved beyond where it was when Sands surveyed the field a decade ago either. Treaty-makers can, of course, explicitly exclude double-hatting in the relevant rules. Some influential actors in the field disapprove of the practice, with the European Union as the more obvious example (that it is 'only by moving away from appointment by the disputing parties to a system of adjudicators on long, non-renewable terms that the concerns on independence and impartiality can be definitively addressed. This will bring double-hatting (i.e. acting as counsel and arbitrator) to an end').[65] But most States do not seem to feel as strongly, as is reflected in the absence of such language in most recent treaties that do not involve the EU or its Member States.

The 2020 Draft Code of Conduct prepared by ICSID and UNCITRAL is helpful in putting specific language on the table, highlighting the variety of shapes that a prohibition of double-hatting may take, and also for identifying counter-arguments for some, broader forms of prohibition. Note in particular the argument about diversity: if the current cohort of counsel is more diverse than the current cohort of arbitrators, and greater diversity of the latter is accepted as a normatively desirable goal, would complete exclusion of double-hatting have the undesirable effect of precluding the accretion of arbitrators' profile and experience by the new entrants?

Code of Conduct for Adjudicators in Investor-State Dispute Settlement (Draft Text, 1 May 2020) Art. 6, Commentaries 66–68

Article 6
Limit on Multiple Roles
Adjudicators shall [refrain from acting]/[disclose that they act] as counsel, expert witness, judge, agent or in any other relevant role at the same time as they are [within X years of] acting on matters that involve the same parties, [the same facts] [and/or] [the same treaty].

Commentary
66. Double-hatting is usually understood as the practice by which one individual acts simultaneously as an international arbitrator and as a counsel in separate ISDS proceedings. However, there is no comprehensive definition of double-hatting and, for the purpose of the code, there would be a need to better delineate its scope. For example, is double-hatting limited to overlaps between counsel and adjudicator work, or should it also include overlaps between counsel work and serving as an expert or as a mediator? Similarly, should double-hatting arise only out of proceedings under the same treaty or with respect to all ISDS proceedings? Should all international counsel work be prohibited or only investment dispute work? For some, any concurrent representation creates a possible conflict of interest and should therefore be prohibited. Others consider double-hatting problematic only in certain circumstances, for example where

[65] 'Possible reform of investor-State dispute settlement (ISDS): Submission from the European Union and its Member States', UN Doc. A/CN.9/WG.III/WP.159/Add.1 (24 January 2019), para. 47.

the facts or parties are related. As a result, a clear understanding of what double-hatting encompasses is important to determine how it should be regulated in a code of conduct.

67. Regulating double-hatting raises many interconnected questions. First, it is important to determine whether a code should create an outright ban on double-hatting or, conversely, whether it should create an obligation to disclose the overlapping roles and allow the parties to challenge the adjudicator if they find the overlapping roles objectionable. An outright ban is easier to implement, by simply prohibiting any participation by an individual falling within the scope of the prohibition. It also avoids the burden of having to challenge a person who is playing another role and having to determine whether the double roles create a real or perceived conflict in the particular case.

68. On the other hand, an outright ban may exclude a greater number of persons than necessary to avoid conflicts of interest and would interfere with the freedom of choice of adjudicators and counsel by States and investors. A ban on double-hatting also constrains new entrants to the field, as few counsel are financially able to leave their counsel work upon receiving their first adjudicator nomination. Indeed, many arbitrators receive only one ISDS case in their career and requiring them to abandon their other sources of income to accept a case would be a barrier to entry. This may be especially relevant for younger arbitrators (new entrants) and arbitrators who bring gender and regional diversity. A possible way to address this concern would be to introduce a phased approach so that an adjudicator may overlap in a small number of cases at the start of their adjudicator career. However, even a phased approach is hard to justify if the mere fact of double-hatting is considered as creating a conflict of interest.

Finally, the recent *Eiser* v. *Spain* annulment decision made the following broadly phrased observation (note that the issue in this case was not double-hatting as discussed in this section so far, but connections between a particular arbitrator and a particular expert).

Eiser Infrastructure Limited and Energía Solar Luxembourg S.à r.l. v. *Spain,* ICSID Case No. ARB/13/36, Decision on Annulment, 11 June 2020 (Hernández, Khan, Hascher), para. 223 (footnotes omitted)

The ongoing obligation to disclose cannot be construed narrowly in favor of the arbitrator. It must be approached from the point of view of a party. Disclosure inoculates arbitrators from the possibility of any, real or perceived, conflict of interest. As the IBA Guidelines state, '[a]ny doubt as to whether an arbitrator should disclose certain facts or circumstance should be resolved in favour of disclosure.' There are multiple ways in which a conflict of interest may arise when an arbitrator also acts or has acted as counsel, in another dispute, albeit between different parties. The risks and possibilities of conflict of interest, inherent in double-hatting, dictate caution.

CONCLUSION

International investment arbitration is, as the title of this book does not really hide, to a considerable extent about arbitrators. The situation may change in the future, if investment law either eliminates formalised investor–State dispute settlement entirely or moves towards a permanent judicial model. There may also be scope for rethinking the dispute settlement models, whether by moving beyond formalised dichotomies in line with other fields of international law ('mechanisms' of criminal law, 'review panels' of fisheries law or 'implementation committees' of environmental law) or by tackling the basic assumptions of how international arbitration works. Sergio Puig's recent argument for blinding international justice by withholding information about which party makes which appointments is an important contribution to that line of scholarship.[66] Future developments in international investment law and dispute settlement, discussed in Chapter 20, may well lead to such changes. But we are not there yet, as the ever-changing 'Recently Registered' rubric on the mid-left of the ICSID webpage suggests. For now, this decentralised, de-institutionalised and essentially de-politicised field will turn to a large degree on arbitrators.

Who are the arbitrators? Section 1 set out the terrain. Dezalay and Garth's 'Grand Old Men' and 'Technocrats' of the 1990s – respectively senior academics/former judges and leading practitioners of commercial arbitration – are certainly there, but the complicated world of twenty-first-century investment law also has Puig's category of 'Formidable Women' (if still too few of them), as well as the first generation of true investment law practitioners. Whether the cohort of investment arbitrators is a fair representation of the broader community presents a thorny political and normative debate, particularly when the current focus on gender and regional diversity is expanded to finer-grained discussion of other, often overlooked topics, such as disability. If long(er)-standing tribunals have taught us anything, it is that discussion of the representativeness and qualities of adjudicators touches upon the deeper strands of institutional legitimacy and is unlikely to be solved to everybody's satisfaction, whatever the institutional frame for that discussion. The OECD Freedom of Investment Roundtables and UNCITRAL Working Group III would be the fora to watch for future developments.

How does one get arbitrators? Section 2 set out the procedural decision tree for appointments, dealing in turn with ICSID and non-ICSID cases. The most important feature is the appointment of the presiding arbitrator, who holds the formal deciding vote in almost all cases where unanimity is lacking, and who is likely to be highly influential in shaping the discussion even where such unanimity is present. In that process, explicit limitations in institutional rules are important, such as the exclusionary role that the Panel of Arbitrators plays in ICSID *ex officio* appointments. But possibly more turns on the practical arrangements that appointing authorities take to implement their authority, such as the ballot procedure at ICSID and UNCITRAL's (mandated) list approach. A basic tension between a party-driven perspective, which prioritises path dependence, and broader normative considerations favouring qualitative change is likely to remain salient.

[66] S. Puig, 'Blinding International Justice' (2016) 56 *Virginia J Int'l L* 647.

How does one get rid of an arbitrator? Section 3 addressed the procedure of challenges, dealing in a comparative manner with both ICSID and non-ICSID approaches, with a particular eye to the ICSID default rule for the decision to be made by the unchallenged arbitrators. The 2020 decision in *Eiser* v. *Spain* to annul the underlying award in its entirety for improper constitution because of undisclosed impartiality concerns introduces a third institutional player. Section 4 shifted the focus to substantive standards, and discussed in turn ICSID's 'manifest lack of' and UNCITRAL's 'justifiable doubt' standards concerning arbitrator independence and impartiality. The key question, formulated by Judge James Crawford, is whether both standards are the same ('obviousness') or ICSID calls for a different and higher benchmark ('seriousness'). Both approaches are, in their own way, unattractive, suggesting either a laxer standard of propriety in one part of the investment law universe ('what is a little partiality amongst friends?') or requiring the creative application of principles of treaty interpretation, downplaying a usual preference for ordinary meaning. Treaty-makers can, of course, regulate explicitly the procedural and substantive aspects in a prospective manner – but that is not always done with sufficient attention to technical detail.

Section 5 considered the application of these standards to three categories of challenges. One line of practice has explored the limits of propriety for various connections between arbitrators and parties, where the *Eiser* v. *Spain* decision has sent a shock wave through the practitioners' community. Another line of practice has struggled with drawing the line regarding previous expressions of views, in academic as well as practitioner guise: the *CC/Devas* v. *India* and *Caratube* v. *Kazakhstan* decisions are the leading authorities, with much turning on how narrowly or broadly their shadow falls. The final challenge relates to the permissibility of combining the hat of an advocate with that of an arbitrator. *Eiser* v. *Spain* urged caution through proactive disclosure, even if turning on connections peculiar to the particular case rather than broader issues of principle. Unsurprisingly, vague rules, complicated facts and decentralised decision-makers do not always lead to bright lines – but, at the very least, areas of certainty and uncertainty can be identified by reference to practice, and they can always be clarified by States if they wish.

QUESTIONS

1. The dominance of North American and Western European arbitrators of the first three decades of investment law is no longer fit for the 2020s. Discuss, with practical suggestions for change.
2. Should treaty parties restrict the freedom of disputing parties and arbitral institutions to choose arbitrators, either by reference to lists of potential arbitrators or to clear and specific criteria?
3. '[A] notable or unusual feature of ICSID is that challenges are decided by the other two arbitrators (unless they disagree). It is inevitable that a challenging party will have further doubts as to whether the remaining arbitrators will have a conflict of interest

themselves when determining a challenge' (A. Sheppard, 'Arbitrator Independence in ICSID Arbitration'). Discuss, with practical suggestions for change.

4. 'Some tribunals have considered the pertinent enquiry to be whether the *evidence* of unreliability is manifest, meaning that it is *clear*. Others have considered the enquiry to be whether the *degree* of the unreliability is manifest: here "manifest" means *serious*' (J. Crawford, 'Challenges to Arbitrators in ICSID Arbitration', original emphasis). Which is the better reading of the ICSID standard of challenge?

5. By the standard applied in *Eiser* v. *Spain*, is any double-hatting permissible?

SUGGESTIONS FOR FURTHER READING

1. J. Crawford, 'Challenges to Arbitrators in ICSID Arbitration' in David D. Caron, *et al.* (eds), *Practising Virtue: Inside International Arbitration* (Oxford University Press, 2015).
2. Report of the ASIL-ICCA Joint Task Force on Issue Conflicts in Investor-State Arbitration (The ICCA Reports No. 3) 17 March 2016.
3. S. Puig, 'Blinding International Justice' (2016) 56 *Virginia J Int'l L* 647.
4. M. N. Cleis, *The Independence and Impartiality of ICSID Arbitrators* (Leiden: Brill/Nijhoff, 2017), chapter 2.
5. ICSID and UNCITRAL Draft Code of Conduct for Adjudicators in Investor-State Dispute Settlement (with annotations) (1 May 2020).

8

Evidence

CHAPTER OUTLINE

This chapter covers another preliminary issue that arises for consideration in investment arbitration. It can be read in conjunction with Chapter 6, which deals with applicable laws. Section 1 examines how the burden of proof is allocated in investor–State disputes, while Section 2 examines how the standard of proof is articulated and applied by investment arbitration tribunals.

INTRODUCTION

The treatment of evidence is a topical concern of arbitral tribunals. Unlike national courts which are bound by national laws, international courts and tribunals are unfettered by any hard and fast rules in their assessment of evidence tendered by the disputing parties. There is an overwhelming tendency to admit and assess all evidence. Earlier investment arbitration tribunals rarely discussed how evidence presented by the parties should be assessed.[1] In contrast, modern-day investment arbitration tribunals articulate thresholds on the strength of submitted evidence that parties need to meet to prevail.

There is often a voluminous amount of evidence that is submitted by the parties, analysed by counsel and arbitrators, and cited in support of the tribunal's decision in investment arbitration. Yet there are no hard and fast rules governing the assessment of evidence. National laws on evidence do not apply unless the disputing parties make provision for this, and they are not binding in the way that mandatory rules of the forum are. Additionally, there is no international law, customary or treaty, on how evidence should be assessed. Moreover, most institutional rules are silent on the matter.[2] Investment arbitration tribunals have embraced the ability to assess evidence absent applicable laws. However, this has not stopped tribunals from proffering some general guiding principles on the allocation of the burden of proof and the standard of proof.

---

[1] One exception is *Asian Agricultural Products Ltd (AAPL)* v. *Sri Lanka*, ICSID Case No. ARB/87/3, Final Award, 27 June 1990 (El-Kosheri, Goldman, Asante (dissenting)), paras 55–65.

[2] One exception is 1976 UNCITRAL Arbitration Rules, Art. 24(1): 'Each party shall have the burden of proving the facts relied on to support his claim or defence.' A related document is the 2010 IBA Rules on the Taking of Evidence in International Arbitration, which parties and arbitral tribunals are free to adopt, in whole or in part, at or after the commencement of the arbitration, and regardless of whether the arbitration is conducted pursuant to institutional rules.

1. THE BURDEN OF PROOF

The burden of proof is a legal term of art that denotes the duty to persuade a court or a tribunal. A party that bears the burden of proof on a given matter is the party that must adduce evidence to persuade a court or a tribunal of the truth or falsity of that matter. In other words, the burden of proof is a tie-breaker in contentious proceedings. When evidence adduced by the party bearing the burden of proof on a given matter, and conflicting evidence adduced by the party disputing that position, is equivocal, the party bearing the burden of proof loses because it has failed to persuade. Investment arbitration tribunals generally agree that a party bears the burden of proving the truth of its assertions (Section 1.1). However, the discretionary assessment of evidence has led to varying degrees of adherence to this guiding principle. Two notable variations on the traditional allocation of the burden of proof are the 'vanishing' burden (Section 1.2) and the 'shifting' burden (Section 1.3).

1.1 *Onus Probandi Actori Incumbit*

There is frequent endorsement by international courts and tribunals, including investment arbitration tribunals, for the Latin maxim that allocates the burden of proof on the party making the assertion.[3] Therefore, when an investor claims that a State has violated certain treaty obligations owed to protected investments, it is for the investor to prove that those violations occurred. Conversely, when the State raises a defence that denies, precludes or mitigates the wrongfulness of its conduct, it is for the State to prove that it is entitled to rely on that defence.[4]

This otherwise straightforward allocation of the burden of proof,[5] which is regarded as a basic evidential principle in international dispute settlement,[6] is not always recommended in investor–State dispute settlement. Unlike traditional dispute settlement between private litigants or between sovereign litigants on symbolically equal footing, the modern phenomenon of dispute settlement between private investors and States is, on the face of it, asymmetrical. The non-sovereign investor, so the argument goes, has fewer resources and capabilities at its disposal than its sovereign opponent, placing it at a disadvantage when proving its claim. This, as Wälde explained, poses a threat to the 'equality of arms' in international adjudication, which arbitral tribunals should try to defuse.

---

[3] C. Brown, *A Common Law of International Adjudication* (Oxford University Press, 2007), 94–95.

[4] *William Ralph Clayton and Others* v. *Government of Canada*, NAFTA-UNCITRAL, PCA Case No. 2009–04, Award on Jurisdiction and Liability, 17 March 2015 (Simma, McRae, Schwartz), paras 717–723.

[5] See, e.g., *Vigotop Ltd* v. *Hungary*, ICSID Case No. ARB/11/22, Award, 1 October 2014 (Sachs, Bishop, Heiskanen), para. 544.

[6] D. V. Sandifer, *Evidence before International Tribunals*, rev. edn (Charlottesville, VA: University Press of Virginia, 1975), 127; M. Kazazi, *Burden of Proof and Related Issues: A Study on Evidence before International Tribunals* (The Hague: Kluwer Law International, 1995), 85; C. F. Amerasinghe, *Evidence in International Litigation* (Leiden: Martinus Nijhoff, 2005), 62; A. Riddell and B. Plant, *Evidence before the International Court of Justice* (London: British Institute of International and Comparative Law, 2009), 87.

> **T. W. Wälde, 'Procedural Challenges in Investment Arbitration under the Shadow of the Dual Role of the State – Asymmetries and Tribunals' Duty to Ensure, Pro-actively, the Equality of Arms' (2010) 26(1) *Arb Int'l* 3, 6, 28–29 (footnotes omitted)**
>
> [p. 6] That attitude of state 'superiority' or supremacy – of the location of the state on a higher level than private actors, domestic or foreign – consciously or instinctively still often underlies the reactions of the state to challenges by investor-initiated international arbitration. The state (and the politicians, media, civil servants, lawyers and the political constituencies of the state) tends to resist the notion that the state can be challenged before an international adjudicatory process which is not, as domestic courts ultimately are, under the political control of the state and exposed to the domestic political process. That resistance exists even where the state (usually through a prior government) has formally and legally, through its legitimate agents and constitutional procedures, accepted international accountability ...
>
> ...
>
> [pp. 28–29] Intimidation directly or indirectly by the respondent state is difficult for the tribunal to deal with. First, full evidence will be hard to come by; few witnesses for example, that have been intimidated will want to come forward to prove it. The tribunal in such cases will need to follow the example of the [European Court of Human Rights], the world's most experienced international court in this field, and operate a system of adverse inferences and reversal of the burden of proof. It cannot expect the claimant, in the face of indications of at least a reasonable probability of intimidation by the state, to provide full proof.

Eagerness to uphold or restore the 'equality of arms' may have prompted some tribunals to accept *onus probandi actori incumbit* in principle, but to depart from it in practice. It is to these departures that the discussion now turns.

1.2 The 'Vanishing' Burden

The 'vanishing' burden can be found in a string of awards in the Yukos saga, where the tribunals accepted that the investors bore the burden of proving their claim that Russia had unlawfully expropriated their investment, but eventually appeared to relieve the investors from proving unlawfulness.

The Yukos saga originated in a series of measures taken by Russia in the name of taxation that precipitated the bankruptcy of oil giant Yukos. Minority and majority shareholders of Yukos commenced five separate arbitrations against Russia, seeking reparation under the applicable investment treaty for the unlawful expropriation of their investments. Each tribunal had to determine whether the Russian measures complained of were expropriatory, and if so, whether the expropriation was unlawful. Notably, every tribunal found Russia liable for unlawful expropriation. Other than the tribunal in *Quasar de Valores SA and Others* v. *Russia,*[7] which did not examine the burden of proof when dealing with the evidentiary record in its award, the tribunal in *RosInvestCo UK Ltd* v. *Russia,*[8] as well as the identically constituted tribunals in *Hulley Enterprises Ltd (Cyprus)* v. *Russia, Yukos Universal Ltd (Isle of Man)* v. *Russia* and *Veteran Petroleum Ltd (Cyprus)* v. *Russia* did.[9] While broadly in agreement with *onus probandi actori incumbit*, the tribunals in *RosInvestCo* v. *Russia, Hulley* v. *Russia, Yukos* v. *Russia* and *Veteran Petroleum* v. *Russia* did not insist on its strict application. As a result, the investor's burden of proving an unlawful expropriation appears at the outset of the award, but seemingly vanishes over the course of the award.

1.2.1 The *RosInvestCo* Arbitration

The *RosInvestCo* arbitration was conducted in accordance with the 2007 Stockholm Chamber of Commerce (SCC) Arbitration Rules. These Rules offer no guidance on how the burden of proof should be allocated in a claim for unlawful expropriation, leaving the tribunal free to decide for itself.[10] The tribunal commenced its analysis of Russia's liability by pointing out that 'the burden of proof generally lies with the Claimant to establish the facts on which the claim is based'.[11] Here, the investor contended that the Russian measures were expropriatory, and in violation of the Agreement between the Government of the United Kingdom of Great Britain and Northern Ireland and the Government of the Union of Soviet Socialist Republics for the Promotion and Reciprocal Protection of Investments (UK–Soviet BIT),[12] because none of the conditions for a lawful expropriation was met.

> **UK–Soviet BIT, Art. 5.1 (emphasis added)**
>
> Investments of investors of either Contracting Party shall not be nationalised, expropriated or subjected to measures having effect equivalent to nationalisation or expropriation (hereinafter referred to as 'expropriation') in the territory of the other Contracting Party except for *a purpose which is in the public interest* and is *not discriminatory* and *against the payment, without delay, of adequate and effective compensation.*

The tribunal was persuaded that the investor had discharged its burden of proving the existence of an expropriation, but it was the tribunal's findings on unlawfulness that point to a vanishing burden of proof.

---

[7] SCC Case No. 24/2007, Award, 20 July 2012 (Paulsson, Landau, Brower).
[8] SCC Arbitration V (079/2005), Final Award, 12 September 2010 (Böckstiegel, Steyn, Berman).
[9] *Hulley Enterprises Ltd (Cyprus)* v. *Russia,* PCA Case No. AA226, Final Award, 28 July 2014 (Fortier, Poncet, Schwebel); *Yukos Universal Ltd (Isle of Man)* v. *Russia,* PCA Case No. AA227, Final Award, 28 July 2014 (Fortier, Poncet, Schwebel); *Veteran Petroleum Ltd (Cyprus)* v. *Russia,* PCA Case No. AA228, Final Award, 18 July 2014 (Fortier, Poncet, Schwebel).
[10] 2007 SCC Arbitration Rules, Art. 26(1): 'The admissibility, relevance, materiality and weight of evidence shall be for the Arbitral Tribunal to determine.'
[11] Final Award, para. 250.
[12] Signed 6 April 1989, entered into force 3 July 1991.

RosInvest Co v. Russia, SCC Arbitration No. V079/2005, Final Award, 12 September 2010 (Böckstiegel, Steyn, Berman), paras 567–568, 556–567, 580–581 (excerpted)

[On whether there was public purpose, or 'bona fide']

567–568. [T]he application of the tax law, the tax assessments on Yukos and the conduct of the auctions must be seen as a treatment which can hardly be accepted as bona fide ... [W]hether this, by itself, would be sufficient to find a breach of Article 5 ... must not be decided by the Tribunal here ... [D]oubts must be taken into account in the context of the examination later in this award regarding the question whether the cumulative [e]ffect of the totality of Respondent's conduct is a breach of Article 5 ...

[On whether there was discrimination]

556–567. Yukos was treated by Respondent quite different to the treatment accorded to its competitors and other comparable tax payers and no convincing reasons have been shown by Respondent for this differentiation ... [W]hether this, by itself, would be sufficient to find a breach of Article 5 ... must not be decided here by the Tribunal ... [D]oubts ... must be taken into account in the context of the examination later in this award regarding the question whether the cumulative [e]ffect of the totality of Respondent's conduct is a breach of the [treaty].

[On whether there was prompt, adequate and effective compensation]

580–581. It is undisputed that Respondent did not offer or pay any compensation to Yukos or its shareholders for the measures which resulted in the deprivation of Yukos' assets ... [W]hether this, by itself, would be sufficient to find a breach of Article 5 ... by expropriation without compensation ... must not be decided here by the Tribunal ... [T]his qualification must be taken into account in the context of the examination later in this award regarding the question whether the cumulative [e]ffect of the totality of Respondent's conduct is a breach of Article 5.

The tribunal's refrain that the 'cumulative effect of the totality of Respondent's conduct' determines unlawfulness is puzzling for two reasons. First, according to Article 5.1 of the UK–Soviet BIT, the conditions for an unlawful expropriation are non-cumulative. If the tribunal accepts that the investor bears the burden of proving its claim, then the investor needs to show that there is an expropriation, and that one of the three Article 5.1 conditions for a lawful expropriation have not been met. This can mean the absence of public purpose, or the presence of discrimination, or the absence of prompt, adequate and effective compensation. If the tribunal is not persuaded that the non-satisfaction of a given Article 5.1 condition amounts in and of itself to unlawfulness, then multiplying its doubts by the number of unmet conditions hardly justifies a finding of unlawfulness. Second, focusing on the legality of the 'cumulative effect of the totality of Respondent's conduct' suggests that the investor only bears the burden of proving the existence of an expropriation, while Russia bears the burden of proving lawfulness. This allows the investor to allege unlawfulness without having to prove it. Notably, the tribunal did not object to Russia's submission that the burden of proving unlawfulness fell squarely on the investor.[13]

However, by basing its finding of unlawfulness on the 'cumulative effect of the totality of Respondent's conduct', it appears that the tribunal in the *RosInvestCo* arbitration resolved any doubts over the legality of the expropriation in favour of the investor.

1.2.2 The *Hulley*, *Yukos* and *Veteran Petroleum* Arbitrations

The *Hulley*, *Yukos* and *Veteran Petroleum* arbitrations were borne from the same factual matrix as the *RosInvestCo* arbitration. Unlike the *RosInvestCo* arbitration, though, the applicable treaty here was not the UK–Soviet BIT, but the Energy Charter Treaty (ECT). The *Hulley*, *Yukos* and *Veteran Petroleum* tribunals, which were identically constituted, made only sporadic references to the burden of proof throughout their lengthy awards, which were identical in respect of liability. Two of these references indicated that the tribunals were in general agreement with *onus actori probandi incumbit*. First, in verifying the investors' assertion that the tax assessments carried out by Russia were calculated to harass, the tribunals held that '[t]he crucial question ... is whether Claimants have discharged their burden of proof and established that the tax assessments, and the enforcement processes of the Russian Federation which followed, are more consistent with the conclusion that they evidence a punitive campaign against Yukos and its principal beneficial owners'.[14] Second, in accepting the investors' explanation that their costs outstripped those of Russia because the burden of proof usually falls on claimants,[15] the tribunals held that 'it is not surprising that Claimants' costs in this case should be higher than those of Respondent since they bore the burden of proof for their claims under the ECT and produced many fact witnesses in the Hearing on the Merits whereas Respondent produced no fact witness'.[16]

One of the claims brought by the investors against Russia was a claim for unlawful expropriation pursuant to Article 13 of the ECT. And notwithstanding their general agreement with *onus probandi actori incumbit*, it is debatable if the investors prevailed because they discharged the burden of proving unlawfulness, or because Russia failed to prove lawfulness.

---

[13] Final Award, para. 188.
[14] *Hulley* v. *Russia*, Final Award, para. 514; *Yukos* v. *Russia*, Final Award, para. 514; *Veteran Petroleum* v. *Russia*, Final Award, para. 514.
[15] *Hulley* v. *Russia*, Final Award, para. 1852; *Yukos* v. *Russia*, Final Award, para. 1852; *Veteran Petroleum* v. *Russia*, Final Award, para. 1852.
[16] *Hulley* v. *Russia*, Final Award, para. 1882; *Yukos* v. *Russia*, Final Award, para. 1882; *Veteran Petroleum* v. *Russia*, Final Award, para. 1882.

Energy Charter Treaty, 17 December 1994, 2080 UNTS 100, Art. 13(1)

(1) Investments of Investors of a Contracting Party in the Area of any other Contracting Party shall not be nationalized, expropriated or subjected to a measure or measures having effect equivalent to nationalization or expropriation (hereinafter referred to as 'Expropriation') except where such Expropriation is:

    (a) for a purpose which is in the public interest;

    (b) not discriminatory;

    (c) carried out under due process of law; and

    (d) accompanied by the payment of prompt, adequate and effective compensation.

Article 13, which couches the prospect of expropriation in negative terms ('shall not ... except where ...'), characterises expropriation as a prohibited act.[17] Article 5 of the UK–Soviet BIT, which formed the legal basis for liability in the *RosInvestCo* arbitration, also characterises expropriation as a prohibited act. When a treaty provision like Article 13 of the ECT is invoked by an investor, how should the burden of proof for a claim for unlawful expropriation be allocated? The weight of opinion favours the investor bearing the burden of proving unlawfulness, despite the wording of the treaty provision, because States have an indelible sovereign right to expropriate property.[18] As Lowe explains, investment treaties do not remove the sovereign right to expropriate property because they were not concluded 'to guarantee the success of investments, or even to guarantee that investors will suffer no loss ... and by no means deprive[d] the host State of the right to exercise its regulatory powers'.[19] Reinisch goes further. He opines that the expropriation clauses in investment treaties 'are based on the assumption that expropriations of the property of nationals of the other Contracting Party or Parties are, in principle, permissible'.[20] In short, the investor who alleges unlawfulness should bear the burden of proving unlawfulness.

Departing from the established view, the *Hulley*, *Yukos* and *Veteran Petroleum* tribunals appear undecided on investors bearing the burden of proving unlawfulness. The section heading to the tribunals' analysis on the legality of expropriation under Article 13 of the ECT reads: 'If Respondent's Actions Constitute Expropriation, Has Respondent Met the Criteria for a Lawful Expropriation under Article 13(1) of the ECT?' By requiring Russia to

---

[17] UNCTAD 2007 study on BIT provisions.

[18] Permanent Sovereignty over Natural Resources, UNGA Res. 1803 (XVIII) (14 December 1962) GAOR Supp. 17, 15; Declaration on the Establishment of a New International Economic Order, UNGA Res. A/Res/3201 (S-VI) (9 May 1974); Programme of Action on the Establishment of a New International Economic Order, UNGA Res. A/Res/3202 (S-VI) (15 May 1974); UN General Assembly Resolution on a Charter of Economic Rights and Duties of States, UNGA Res. A/Res/3281(XXIX) (12 December 1974), Report of the Working Group of the Trade and Development Board (1 August 1974), TD/B/AC.12/4, partially reproduced in J. Kuusi, *The Host State and the Transnational Corporation* (Farnborough: Saxon House, 1979), 131–135; also A. P. Fachiri, 'Expropriation and International Law' (1925) 6 *BYbIL* 159, 170; R. Higgins, 'The Taking of Property by the State' (1982) 176 *RCADI* 263, 275.

[19] V. Lowe, 'Regulation or Expropriation?' (2002) 55 *Curr Leg Probl* 447, 450.

[20] A. Reinisch, *Standards of Investment Protection* (Oxford University Press, 2008), 177.

meet the criteria for lawfulness, the tribunals appear to have relieved the investors from proving unlawfulness. However, when assessing if the criteria for lawfulness have been met, the tribunals do not specify which party bears the burden of proof and the corresponding risk of failure if there are doubts or gaps in the evidential record.[21] Instead, the tribunals found Russia liable for unlawful expropriation 'on the totality of the extensive evidence'.[22] So, while the tribunals accept that investors bear 'the burden of proof for their claims under the ECT',[23] it is questionable if the tribunals actually held the investors to the burden of proving unlawfulness in their expropriation claims.

1.3 The 'Shifting' Burden

Some tribunals have held that the burden of proof can shift from one party to another. The notion of a shifting burden originated in the adversarial litigation process in common law jurisdictions, where the disputing parties, or their counsel, are expected to take the initiative and take turns adducing evidence that helps their case. What a 'shifting' burden means in investment arbitration is neatly summed up by the tribunal in *Apotex Holdings Inc. and Apotex Inc. v. USA.*

Apotex and Apotex Inc. v. United States of America, ICSID Case No. ARB(AF)/12/1, Award, 25 August 2014 (Veeder, Rowley, Crook), para. 8.8

The Tribunal considers such a distinction exists between the legal burden of proof (which never shifts) and the evidential burden of proof (which can shift from one party to another, depending upon the state of the evidence). In the *Pulp Mills* case, the ICJ noted that: '... in accordance with the well-established principle of *onus probandi incumbit actori*, it is the duty of the party which asserts certain facts to establish the existence of such facts. This principle which has been consistently upheld by the Court applies to the assertions of fact both by the Applicant and the Respondent.'

Most tribunals that refer to a 'shifting' burden appear to share the view of the *Apotex* tribunal that the shift represents the volleying between the parties on the production of evidence, and does not affect the allocation of the burden of proof.[24] However, a 'shifting'

---

[21] *Hulley* v. *Russia*, Final Award, paras 1581–1584; *Yukos* v. *Russia*, Final Award, paras 1581–1584; *Veteran Petroleum* v. *Russia*, Final Award, paras 1581–1584.

[22] *Hulley* v. *Russia*, Final Award, para. 1585; *Yukos* v. *Russia*, Final Award, para. 1585; *Veteran Petroleum* v. *Russia*, Final Award, para. 1585.

[23] *Hulley* v. *Russia*, Final Award, para. 1882; *Yukos* v. *Russia*, Final Award, para. 1882; *Veteran Petroleum* v. *Russia*, Final Award, para. 1882.

[24] *Marvin Roy Feldman Karpa* v. *Mexico*, ICSID Case No. ARB(AF)/99/1, Award, 16 December 2002 (Kerameus, Covarrubias Bravo (dissenting), Gantz), para. 177; *International Thunderbird Gaming Corp.* v. *United Mexican States*, NAFTA-UNCITRAL, Arbitral Award, 26 January 2006 (van den Berg, Ariosa, Wälde), para. 95; *Bayindir Insaat Turizm Ticaret Ve Sanayi AS* v. *Pakistan*, ICSID Case No. ARB/03/29, Award, 27 August 2009 (Kaufmann-Kohler, Berman, Böckstiegel), para. 419; *Les Laboratoires Servier, SAS and Others* v. *Poland*, PCA-UNCITRAL, Award (Redacted), 14 February 2012 (Park, Hanotiao, Lalonde); see also *Tokios Tokelés* v. *Ukraine*, ICSID Case No. ARB/02/18, Award, 26 July 2007 (Mustill, Bernadini, Price (dissenting)),

burden may also refer to the burden of proof. This occurs when the tribunal takes the view that the respondent should disprove the claimant's assertions. It does not mean that the claimant adduces no evidence whatsoever in support of its assertions. The claimant is deemed to have proven, to a large extent, the truth of its assertions. The burden of proof then shifts to the respondent to disprove the truth of those very assertions. The legal burden originally borne by the claimant is essentially reversed, and placed on the respondent. When the burden of proof is reversed, the claimant prevails because it has proven the truth of its assertions, and also because the respondent has failed to discharge the burden of disproving the truth of those assertions.

According to the tribunal in *Waguih Elie George Siag and Clorinda Vecchi* v. *Egypt* (*Siag and Another* v. *Egypt*), reversing the burden of proof may be necessary if there are 'special circumstances or good reasons'.[25] Here, Egypt alleged that the investor had obtained his Lebanese nationality by fraud and submitted that the tribunal should, on account of the evidence tendered by Egypt, hold that 'the burden has shifted' to the investor to disprove fraud. The tribunal rejected this submission, but accepted that the burden of proof can be a 'shifting' burden in 'special circumstances' or for 'good reasons'.

Waguih Elie George Siag and Clorinda Vecchi v. Egypt, ICSID Case No. ARB/05/15, Award, 1 June 2009 (Williams, Pryles, Orrego Vicuña), para. 317

For its part, Egypt asserted that it had proved Mr Siag's non-Lebanese nationality and that accordingly 'the burden has shifted'. The Tribunal does not accept this latter submission. Because negative evidence is very often more difficult to assert than positive evidence, the reversal of the burden of proof may make it almost impossible for the allegedly fraudulent party to defend itself, thus violating due process standards. It is for this reason that Tribunals have rarely shifted the burden of proof. The Tribunal considers that the burden of proof in respect of all jurisdictional objections and substantive defences lies with Egypt. The Tribunal concurs with the opinion of Professor Reisman, that it is a widely-accepted principle of law that the party advancing a claim or defence bears the burden of establishing that claim or defence. There are no special circumstances or good reasons for doing so in this case.

While *onus probandi actori incumbit* could have been an effective guiding principle for tribunals sifting through and weighing voluminous evidence, tribunals tend to struggle with the terminology and theory of a 'shifting' burden. Recourse by investment arbitration tribunals to the shifting burden to inject some order and structure into their assessment

Dissenting Opinion of Daniel Price, para. 19. Cf. *RosInvestCo* v. *Russia*, Final Award, para. 250 and *Vito G. Gallo* v. *Government of Canada*, NAFTA-UNCITRAL, PCA Case No. 55798, Award (Redacted), 15 September 2011 (Fernández-Armesto, Castel, Lévy), para. 277, where the tribunals likened the shift in the phase of the proceedings from the claimant investor presenting its claim to the respondent State presenting its defence to a 'shifting' burden. In substance, this is no different from saying that the investor bears the burden of proving its claim, while the State bears the burden of proving its defence.

[25] ICSID Case No. ARB/05/15, Award, 1 June 2009 (Williams, Pryles, Orrego Vicuña), para. 318.

of the evidence on the record is suboptimal if there is no uniform understanding of what a 'shifting' burden is or entails. In this regard, the call by one tribunal to abandon references to 'shifting' burdens is appealing.[26]

The Rompetrol Group NV v. Romania, ICSID Case No. ARB/06/3, Award, 6 May 2013 (Berman, Donovan, Lalonde), para. 178

Operating within an international system characterised by principle rather than procedural formality, the Tribunal is not enamoured of arguments setting out to show that a burden of proof can under certain circumstances shift from the party that originally bore it to the other party, and then perhaps in appropriate circumstances shift back again to the original party. To the mind of the Tribunal, arguments of that kind confuse, unhelpfully, the separate questions of who has to prove a particular assertion and whether that assertion has in fact been proved on the evidence.

---

2. THE STANDARD OF PROOF

Closely connected to the burden of proof is the standard of proof. While the former expresses what a claimant has to prove, the latter represents the evidential threshold that a claimant needs to meet in order to prove the truth of its assertions. Although 'there is a general lack of consensus on the appropriate standard of proof in international adjudication',[27] investment arbitration tribunals, like a considerable number of international courts and tribunals,[28] adopt a 'preponderance of evidence', otherwise known as 'balance of probabilities', threshold (Section 2.1).[29] To meet the adopted standard of proof, evidence has to be of a certain quantity, as well as a certain quality. As the factual matrix of each investment dispute is different, it is not possible to predetermine the exact quantity and quality of submitted evidence that satisfies a 'balance of probabilities'. However, in situations where only indirect or no evidence is submitted by one party, arbitral *jurisprudence* on the weight accorded to circumstantial evidence (Section 2.2), and the drawing of adverse inferences from the non-production of evidence (Section 2.3), offer some general pointers on the possibility of lowering the standard of proof for the other party.

---

[26] See also *Tethyan Copper Company Pty Limited* v. *Islamic Republic of Pakistan*, ICSID Case No. ARB/12/1, Decision on Respondent's Application to Dismiss the Claims (With Reasons), 10 November 2017 (Sachs, Alexandrov, Hoffmann), para. 318.

[27] Brown, *A Common Law of International Adjudication*, 102.

[28] K. Highet, 'Evidence, the Chamber and the ELSI Case' in R. B. Lillich (ed.), *Fact-Finding before International Tribunals* (Ardsley, NY: Transnational, 1992), 70; Amerasinghe, *Evidence in International Litigation*, 245; R. Pietrowski, 'Evidence in International Arbitration' (2006) 22(3) *Arb Int'l* 373, 409; Brown, *A Common Law of International Adjudication*, 102; M. T. Grondo, *Evidence, Proof, and Fact-Finding in WTO Dispute Settlement* (Oxford University Press, 2009), 130; also M. Benzing, 'Evidentiary Issues' in A. Zimmerman, K. Oellers-Frahm, C. Tomuschat *et al.* (eds), *The Statute of the International Court of Justice: A Commentary*, 2nd edn (Oxford University Press, 2012), 1265.

[29] See for example *Bernhard von Pezold and Others* v. *Zimbabwe*, ICSID Case No. ARB/10/15, Award, 28 July 2015 (Fortier, Williams, Hwang), para. 177.

2.1 Balance of Probabilities

The 'balance of probabilities' is not an exigent standard of proof. If this standard is translated into percentage ratios, then a likely ratio will be 51:49. So long as the claimant adduces enough evidence to tilt the balance of truth in its favour, it will prevail. That said, arbitral tribunals are well aware that the question of whether the submitted evidence proves a claim or a defence on a balance of probabilities cannot be answered with scientific precision, and much depends on the circumstances of each case. Allegations of serious wrongdoing such as fraud or corruption may motivate tribunals to hold the evidence produced to a higher standard.[30] On other occasions, probative evidence may, for one reason or another, be unavailable. When one party relies on less probative evidence to prove the truth of its assertions, and when the tribunal is nonetheless satisfied that the standard of proof is met, the standard of proof applied is arguably lower. The 'balance of probabilities' in investment arbitration may therefore be akin to a floating standard, whose threshold varies according to context and across cases.

2.2 Circumstantial Evidence

In *Amco Asia Corp. and Others* v. *Indonesia*,[31] a US investor concluded a 'Lease and Management Agreement' with an Indonesian company to complete the construction and undertake the management of a hotel. A dispute arose over the investor's performance of the agreement. The Indonesian company convinced the Indonesian militia to forcibly reclaim control of the hotel, as well as the Indonesian Government to revoke the investment licence previously granted to the investor's local subsidiary. The Indonesian company also obtained a court order in Indonesia, affirming the validity of the licence revocation because the US investor's capital outlay fell short of the contractually agreed amount. The US investor instituted arbitration proceedings under the ICSID Convention against Indonesia, challenging the validity of the revocation order which it construed as an illegal deprivation of its management rights.

The tribunal reiterated in its award that both parties referred to, but did not produce, relevant documentary evidence to back up their account of the facts.[32] Yet the tribunal ultimately found for the investor because Indonesia failed to adduce 'direct evidence' to rebut the 'correctness' of documents submitted by the investor. Given the patchy evidential record, the documents submitted by the investor were more likely circumstantial evidence pertaining to the alleged invalidity of the revocation order. The reasoning of the tribunal suggests either that circumstantial evidence suffices to prove an assertion on a balance of probabilities, or that in situations where only circumstantial evidence is available, the party submitting the evidence benefits from a floating standard of proof.[33]

---

[30] *The Rompetrol Group N.V.* v. *Romania*, ICSID Case No. ARB/06/3, Award, 6 May 2013 (Berman, Donovan, Lalonde), paras 181–183; see below n. 36.
[31] ICSID Case No. ARB/81/1, Award on the Merits, 20 November 1984 (Goldman, Foighel, Rubin).
[32] *Ibid.*, paras 25, 116, 123.
[33] *Ibid.*, para. 236.

Amco Asia Corporation and Others v. *Indonesia*, ICSID Case No. ARB/81/1, Award on the Merits, 20 November 1984 (Goldman, Foighel, Rubin), para. 236

[I]t is difficult to strictly share, in the instant case, the *onus probandi* in respect of the amount of the investment realized. The insufficiency of the investment is relied on by Respondent, to justify the revocation of the licence, so that it could be said that it is to it to prove said insufficiency, and indeed, Respondent did its best to assist the Tribunal in this respect. On their side, Claimants were obligated to invest a certain amount of capital, so that they had to contribute as well to the Tribunal's investigations as to the effective realization of the promised investment, and so they did. In the circumstances, the Tribunal is bound to utilize documents provided their alleged incorrectness is not established merely by general rules of accountancy, but by factual evidence directly applicable to them. The Tribunal does not find that such direct evidence of incorrectness was brought by Respondent[.]

Indonesia subsequently applied to have the award annulled pursuant to Article 52(1) of the ICSID Convention. Indonesia argued that the tribunal had manifestly exceeded its powers, seriously departed from a fundamental rule of procedure and failed to state the reasons for its decision, for deeming the investment shortfall immaterial to the revocation of the licence, and for holding that the licence revocation was invalid.[34] Indonesia added that the tribunal treated the parties unequally, allowing the investor to prevail when it had not put forward sufficient evidence to prove its claim that the revocation order was invalid.[35]

The Ad Hoc Committee annulled the portion of the award on the investment shortfall and the validity of the revocation order. However, the Ad Hoc Committee found that there was no unequal treatment of the parties. Rather, the tribunal had erred because it had not applied Indonesian law. Had it done so, it would have found that there was a shortfall in investment which rendered the revocation order valid. Agreeing with Indonesia that the evidential record before the tribunal was incomplete, the Ad Hoc Committee pointed out that both the investor and Indonesia, due to their respective institutional inadequacies, failed to produce relevant and material documentary evidence which would normally be in their possession. In the circumstances, the tribunal's willingness to give the investor the benefit of the doubt on some matters did not evince 'systematic favour[ing]' of the investor by the tribunal. The Ad Hoc Committee seemed to share the tribunal's view that the circumstances warranted a floating standard of proof for the US investor.[36]

---

[34] ICSID Case No. ARB/81/1, Decision of the Ad Hoc Committee on Annulment, 16 May 1986 (Hohenveldern, Feliciano, Giardina), para. 4(a).

[35] *Ibid.*

[36] See also A. Reiner, who endorses the tribunal's and Ad Hoc Committee's approach in 'Burden and General Standards of Proof' (1994) 10(3) *Arb Int'l* (Special Section) 328, 333–334. In cases involving allegations of corruption, circumstantial evidence usually does not suffice to persuade the tribunal of the truth of the allegation. However, direct evidence of corruption is uncommon. This suggests a higher evidential

Amco Asia Corporation and Others v. Indonesia, ICSID Case No. ARB/81/1, Decision of the Ad Hoc Committee on Annulment, 16 May 1986 (Hohenveldern, Feliciano, Giardina), paras 90–91

90. The Tribunal undertook the task of determining the amount invested by P.T. Amco in the construction, outfitting and furnishing of the Hotel. This task was rendered difficult by the incompleteness of the evidence submitted by Amco as well as that submitted by Indonesia. The Tribunal did not find that P.T. Amco's records and accounts were stolen as P.T. Amco had claimed (Award, para. 104) but the fact remains that P.T. Amco was expelled from its business premises under circumstances imposing at least the risk of loss of records. Thus, documents which in the ordinary course of business should have been in the possession of P.T. Amco and presented by it to the Tribunal, were submitted by Indonesia instead. At the same time, however, important documents such as those relating to the registration or the registerability of foreign exchange supposedly infused into the project were not submitted to the Tribunal by P.T. Amco; a reasonably prudent foreign non-resident investor may be expected in the ordinary course of business to keep copies of such documents outside the host State. The incomplete character of the evidence submitted by Indonesia – e.g., the lack of copies of complete tax returns and financial statements by P.T. Wisma (a company wholly owned by Inkopad, itself controlled by the Government) and of investment reports of P.T. Amco – may also be noted. The relatively low capability of an administrative agency efficiently to store and monitor and enforce the submission of formally required documentation is commonly a reflection of the realities of developing countries, and not an indication of bad faith towards investors, domestic or foreign. It seems to the ad hoc Committee that the Tribunal was aware of all these difficulties and took them into account in distributing the burden of proof between the parties (Award, para. 236).

91. Thus, the ad hoc Committee does not consider the claim of Indonesia (Reply, p. 31) of unequal treatment of the parties in the allocation of the burden of proof as successfully established and therefore does not regard annulment as justified in this respect.

threshold that claimants have to cross before the standard of proof, be it 'balance of probabilities' or 'clear and convincing evidence' (*EDF (Services) Limited v. Romania*, ICSID Case No. ARB/05/13, Award, 8 October 2009 (Bernadini, Rovine, Derains), para. 221), is met. The tribunal in *Spentex Netherlands, B.V. v. Republic of Uzbekistan*, ICSID Case No. ARB/13/26, Award, 27 December 2016 (Reinisch, Alexandrov, Stern) (not public) attempted to mitigate the uncertainty of deciding when circumstantial evidence proves corruption by deeming the accumulation of unrebutted circumstantial 'red flags', such as the payment of astronomical consultancy fees to unqualified personnel, as evidence of corruption. This decision has been labelled a 'milestone' as it is a rare example of a corruption allegation proved solely by circumstantial evidence: see K. Betz, *Proving Bribery, Fraud and Money Laundering in International Arbitration: On Applicable Criminal Law and Evidence* (Cambridge University Press, 2017), 132–135; see also a later decision where corruption was proved by circumstantial evidence in *Chevron Corporation and Texaco Petroleum Corporation v. The Republic of Ecuador*, UNCITRAL, PCA Case No. 2009–23, Second Partial Award on Track II, 30 August 2018 (Veeder, Grigera Naón, Lowe), paras 2.4, 4.405–4.408, 5.12, 5.144–5.145, 5.147, 5.161, 5.231, 8.16.

In contrast, there is considerable resistance to a floating standard of proof by the Iran–United States Claims Tribunal (IUSCT). The IUSCT was established in the aftermath of the diplomatic crisis between Iran and the United States, which saw the storming of the US Embassy in Tehran and the taking of US hostages by Iranian student revolutionaries in 1979. The US government responded by freezing all Iranian assets located in the United States. The IUSCT supplied a détente to strained bilateral ties by hearing claims of US nationals against Iran and of Iranian nationals against the United States.[37] The bulk of the claims heard by the IUSCT were brought by US nationals against Iran for the alleged expropriation of their investment in Iran. Evidential records were often incomplete because revolutionary activity in Iran destroyed direct evidence, while revolutionary fervour deterred witnesses from coming forward to testify for fear of political reprisals by the Iranian government. Absent direct documentary evidence and direct witness testimony, US investors often had to resort to circumstantial evidence to prove expropriation. The IUSCT exhibited great reluctance to give the investor the benefit of the doubt when there were gaps in the evidential record. The expectation that claimants prove their claims on a preponderance of evidence, notwithstanding the destruction of probative evidence which the claimants were helpless to prevent,[38] has prompted one dissenting arbitrator to observe that the claimant is held to a standard of proof that is 'virtually impossible' to meet.[39]

2.3 No Evidence

It is not standard practice among international courts and tribunals to draw adverse inferences against a party who absents itself from proceedings, or who elects to remain silent when called to give evidence.[40] There are usually extenuating circumstances

[37] 1981 Claims Settlement Declaration of the Iran–United States Claims Tribunal, www.iusct.net/General%20 Documents/2-Claims%20Settlement%20Declaration.pdf (accessed 31 July 2020).

[38] *Houston Contracting Co.* v. *Iran and Others* (1988) 20 Iran–USCTR 3, pp. 124–125; *Leonard and Mavis Daley* v. *Iran* (1988) 18 Iran–USCTR 232, pp. 237–241.

[39] *Houston Contracting Co.* v. *Iran and Others*, Concurring and Dissenting Opinion of Judge Brower, pp. 147–150. See also *Leonard and Mavis Daley* v. *Iran*, Concurring and Dissenting Opinion of Assadollah Noori, pp. 263–268.

[40] Brown, *A Common Law of International Adjudication*, 109; Riddell and Plant, *Evidence before the ICJ*, 121; H. von Mangoldt and A. Zimmerman, 'Article 53' in A. Zimmerman, K. Oellers-Frahm, C. Tomuschat and C. J. Tams (eds), *The Statute of the International Court of Justice: A Commentary*, 2nd edn (Oxford University Press, 2012), 1346–1347; note, however, T. W. Wälde, 'Procedural Challenges in Investment Arbitration under the Shadow of the Dual Role of the State – Asymmetries and Tribunals' Duty to Ensure, Pro-actively, the Equality of Arms' (2010) 26(1) *Arb Int'l* 3, 29, where he argued that tribunals can in appropriate situations treat the drawing of adverse inferences as a 'sanction'; and Pietrowski, 'Evidence in International Arbitration', 405, who observes that in international commercial disputes, the party 'who refuses to produce evidence on the ground that it would disclose proprietary or confidential business information risks an adverse inference'. For ICSID arbitrations, Art. 45(1) of the ICSID Convention (adopted 18 March 1965, entered into force 14 October 1966) 575 UNTS 159 provides that the '[f]ailure of a party to appear or to present his case shall not be deemed an admission of the other party's assertions'. From the drafting history on Art. 45(1), there was no indication from any of the delegates who commented on this provision that the non-appearance of a host State at the proceedings could, in some cases, lessen the claimant's burden of proof: see generally ICSID, *History of the ICSID Convention* (Washington, DC: ICSID, 1968), vols II-1 and II-2, 215, 332, 421, 572–573, 807, 809, 939, 986. ICSID tribunals are unlikely to draw adverse inferences from silence when 'the general principle in ICSID proceedings, and in international adjudication generally, [is] that who asserts must prove, and that in order to do so, the party which asserts must itself obtain and present the necessary evidence in order to prove what it asserts': see *Azurix Corp.* v. *Argentina*, ICSID Case

accompanying an adverse inference from absence or silence,[41] such as when the State is believed to withhold information which might corroborate the investor's claim. A tribunal that draws an adverse inference from a party's absence or silence construes the absence or silence against that party. In investment arbitration, an adverse inference drawn against an absent or silent State may lower the evidential threshold for the investor whose assertions are strengthened by lack of challenge. Existing commentaries on the use of adverse inferences rely predominantly on the decisions of the IUSCT to illustrate that the drawing of adverse inferences by tribunals in investment arbitration is the exception, not the norm.[42]

The low incidence of adverse inferences being drawn from non-appearance or silence in investment arbitration reflects circumspect decision-making. Non-appearance is ambiguous. It can stem from any number of reasons, including mistrust of the impartiality of the proceedings launched by the investor,[43] conviction that highly political disputes cannot be resolved by judicial settlement[44] or even forced submission to arbitration that is founded on voluntary and consensual participation.[45] Silence is also ambiguous. It

No. ARB/01/12, Decision on the Application for Annulment by the Argentine Republic, 1 September 2009 (Griffith, Ajobola, Hwang), para. 215. Furthermore, Art. 34 of the ICSID Arbitration Rules empowers the tribunal to order the production of evidence by the parties, but the provision is silent on the imposition of sanctions by the tribunal for non-compliance. The tribunal in *Churchill Mining PLC and Planet Mining Pty Ltd* v. *Republic of Indonesia*, ICSID Case No. ARB/12/14 and 12/40, Award, 6 December 2016 (Kaufmann-Kohler, Hwang, van den Berg), paras 247–248, held that an adverse inference should not be automatically drawn against a party for non-compliance with an order made pursuant to Art. 34. The infrequency of ICSID tribunals drawing adverse inferences is confirmed in a concise review of recent ICSID awards: see M. Polkinghorne and C. R. Rosenberg, 'The Adverse Inference in ICSID Practice' (2015) 3(3) *ICSID Review – FILJ* 741, 751.

[41] Highet, 'Evidence, the Chamber and the ELSI Case', 36.

[42] G. H. Aldrich, 'What Constitutes a Compensable Taking of Property? – The Decisions of the Iran–United States Claims Tribunal' (1994) 88 *AJIL* 585, 605; J. K. Sharpe, 'Drawing Adverse Inferences from the Non-Production of Evidence' (2006) 22(4) *Arb Int'l* 549, 551.

[43] The President of the Russian delegation to the 1922 Hague Conference, Maxim Litvinov, announced that his government did not trust arbitral tribunals constituted to hear disputes between foreign investors and held the Soviet government to be impartial: see 'The Hague Failure', 1 August 1922, *Western Argus* 19. The Russian boycott of the arbitration commenced by English company Lena Goldfields in the late 1920s was a manifestation of this distrust.

[44] The United States famously withdrew from the proceedings in the *Case Concerning Military and Paramilitary Activities in and Against Nicaragua* (*Nicaragua* v. *USA*), claiming that the ICJ lacked 'jurisdiction and competence' over the dispute: 'US Withdrawal from the Proceedings Initiated by Nicaragua in the ICJ', Department Statement, 18 January 1985, Department State Bulletin, No. 2096 (March 1985), 64. Commentators broadly agree that the ICJ should be wary of admitting into its docket claims that lack from the outset any genuine prospect of enforceability: see W. M. Reisman, 'Has the International Court Exceeded Its Jurisdiction?' (1986) 80 *AJIL* 128, 132; J. Charney, 'Disputes Implicating the International Credibility of the Court: Problems of Non-Appearance, Non-Participation, and Non-Performance' in L. F. Damrosch (ed.), *The International Court of Justice at a Crossroads* (Ardsley, NY: Transnational, 1987), 297; C. Paulson, 'Compliance with Final Judgments of the International Court of Justice since 1987' (2004) 98 *AJIL* 434, 437–452.

[45] *Société des Grands Travaux Marseille* v. *East Pakistan Industrial Development Corp.*, ICC Case No. 1803, Award Procedural Order, 12 December 1972, (1980) V Yearbook of Commercial Arbitration 177, pp. 179–185; *Westland Helicopters* v. *Arab Organization for Industrialization and Others*, ICC Case No. 3879, Interim Award, 5 March 1984, (1984) 23 ILM 1071; *NTA* v. *Municipality Jabal Al Akhdar*, ICC Case No. 7245, Interim Award, 28 January 1994, unpublished, summarised in M. Blessing, 'State Arbitrations: Predictably Unpredictable Solutions?' (2005) 22(6) *J Int'l Arb* 435, 463–464; *Dallah Real Estate and Tourism Holding Co.* v. *The Ministry of Religious Affairs, Government of Pakistan*, ICC Case No. (unknown), Final Award, 23 June 2006, unpublished, excerpted in [2010] UKSC 46.

cannot illuminate when the interpreter does not 'know the will or belief which prompted the silence in the first place'.[46]

***

The allocation of the burden of proof on the party who asserts a fact or legal position and the affixing of the standard of proof at the 'balance of probabilities' are the key guidelines for the assessment of evidence by investment arbitration tribunals. However, tribunals have either departed from or stretched them. Tribunals that allow a claimant to prevail not because it has proven all the elements of its claim, but because the respondent has failed to disprove some of those elements, circumvent *onus probandi actori incumbit*, whether or not this is expressly admitted in the award. Tribunals that resolve significant gaps in the evidential record in favour of the party reliant on missing evidence to prove its claim or defence appear to apply a floating standard of proof where the evidential threshold that must be met for proving an allegation on 'balance of probabilities' can be raised or lowered depending on context. Variety in arbitral approaches towards the assessment of evidence in investment disputes is not surprising in a system of international adjudication with no binding precedent. But it means that disputing parties cannot take for granted that the burden of proof will always fall on the party who asserts. Nor can disputing parties take for granted that the evidential threshold attached to the standard of proof in a given case is readily discernible. The lack of clarity, certainty and consistency in the treatment of evidence in investment arbitration may be inimical to the correctness and legitimacy of decided outcomes.

CONCLUSION

Preliminary issues precede the tribunal's consideration of the merits of the dispute, but determinations on preliminary issues are no less important than determinations on the merits found in the operative part of the award. Applicable laws, which were discussed in Chapter 6, establish the legal boundaries within which arbitral analysis of the merits takes place. International practice and trends on evidence in investment dispute settlement, discussed in this chapter, guide arbitral tribunals in verifying whether the disputing parties have discharged their respective duties of evidence production. Preliminary issues are thus akin to the foundations on which a determination on the merits should be made.

As there are no applicable laws on evidence, the allocation of the burden of proof and the setting of the standard of proof in investment arbitration may be steered by guidelines generated by accumulated international practice, but is ultimately a matter for arbitral discretion. It is generally accepted that the burden of proof should be borne by the party making an assertion, and that the burden is discharged when the party proves its assertion to the satisfaction of the tribunal on a 'balance of probabilities'. However, instances of a tribunal refusing to rule out the possibility of burden reversal

---

[46] M. Koskienniemi, *From Apology to Utopia* (Cambridge University Press, 2005), 437.

in unspecified circumstances, and of tribunals appearing to accept a floating standard of proof, are a recipe for unchecked diversity in the way investment arbitration tribunals assess evidence.

QUESTIONS

1. What are some possible reasons for the divergent approaches to how the burden of proof should be allocated in investment arbitration?
2. Can and should investment arbitration accommodate a floating standard of proof? For example, parties alleging fraud or corruption may be required to meet a higher evidential threshold by producing more and better quality evidence in order to prevail on their allegation. If so, why, and if not, why not?
3. Investment arbitration will benefit from common rules on the treatment of evidence. Discuss.
4. Refer to Chapter 6. In *SPP* v. *Egypt*, *Vestey Group* v. *Venezuela* and *Accession Mezzanine* v. *Hungary* there was extensive reference in the awards to the laws of the host State as the *lex causae*, which not all, or even none of the arbitrators are familiar with. In the event of conflicting expert testimony on the content or interpretation of a national law, and in the absence of binding rules on evidence tendered by expert witnesses, how should arbitral tribunals determine which account of national law and the outcome it dictates is more persuasive?

SUGGESTIONS FOR FURTHER READING

1. D. V. Sandifer, *Evidence before International Tribunals*, rev. edn (Charlottesville, VA: University Press of Virginia, 1975).
2. T. W. Wälde, 'Procedural Challenges in Investment Arbitration under the Shadow of the Dual Role of the State – Asymmetries and Tribunals' Duty to Ensure, Pro-actively, the Equality of Arms' (2010) 26(1) *Arb Int'l* 3.
3. C. Brown, *A Common Law of International Adjudication* (Oxford University Press, 2007), chapter 3.
4. J. K. Sharpe, 'Drawing Adverse Inferences from the Non-Production of Evidence' (2006) 22(4) *Arb Int'l* 549.

9

Provisional Measures

CHAPTER OUTLINE

This chapter discusses interim, provisional or conservatory measures which may be sought by the claimant in order to preserve the status quo pending the dispute's resolution. Such relief may be sought from the tribunal, from national courts or both. Section 1 explains some of the special considerations which may apply in the case of an interim measure against a sovereign State or other investment dispute party which exercises sovereign powers. Should a tribunal order a sovereign State to halt criminal proceedings against the investor, for example? Should a tribunal order a sovereign not to move the investor's money from a bank account in a certain location to another place, indeed more broadly from disposing of or dealing in any way with those assets? This section describes the power of the ICSID and other tribunals to grant – or in the curious language of the ICSID Convention, 'recommend' – such provisional measures. Section 2 uses a well-known English case to illustrate recourse to a national court where an ICSID arbitration is already underway. It draws the reader's mind to the potential role of national courts, albeit using as its example an instance of national deference to the exclusive authority of an ICSID tribunal. Section 3 in turn discusses potential limits, be they legal or simply practical, to the types of measures which a tribunal might order. It discusses, in particular, the power of the tribunal to require security for costs (i.e. to assure the respondent that its legal costs will be met in the event that it prevails over the claimant), as well as a well-known line of awards concerning the circumstances in which a tribunal will seek to halt criminal proceedings against the claimant, at least while the arbitration is still in progress. Section 4 compares the test adopted by an ICSID tribunal to that of a well-known tribunal applying the UNCITRAL Arbitration Rules in evaluating requests for interim relief. Together, they offer the reader a sense of some key factors which will matter to tribunals. Perhaps there is already a good degree of consistency in the ICSID jurisprudence, without denying that tribunals will differ in their approach as an increasingly mature body of jurisprudence and opinion continues to develop.

INTRODUCTION

Interim, provisional or conservatory measures are sought, typically, to preserve the position of the parties pending the resolution of the dispute or prevent harm to arbitration of the dispute. In practice, when representing a client in bringing an arbitration claim and in seeking enforcement of a foreign arbitral award, one might ask whether a bank account in the jurisdiction needs to be 'frozen' without giving notice to, and thereby alerting, the party against whom a claim or enforcement proceedings are to be brought. The aim, ultimately, is to seize those assets in order to preserve the status quo or to satisfy the award. In the enforcement example, the dispute has been disposed of in arbitration and the only question that remains is that of enforcement of the award, and execution by way of attachment of the losing party's assets.

However, what if those assets are sought to be attached prior to the dispute being heard by the tribunal – in other words as an interim or provisional measure so as to conserve those assets in the meantime? Can the tribunal itself or a court make an appropriate order? It may be, to think of a different and more common example, that the host State in an investment dispute has interfered and continues to interfere with the use and enjoyment of the investment, and that indeed was what triggered the dispute. Can the host State be prevented from continuing with its alleged interference in the meantime, pending that very issue being heard and decided by the tribunal? Suppose that there is a risk that the host State might destroy or alter the evidence. Can it be ordered to desist from doing so pending the dispute being heard and decided by the tribunal?

Whether or not a tribunal can make a variety of orders for interim relief, can the claimant pursue interim, provisional or conservatory measures in a domestic court as a matter of real urgency (for example, before the arbitration tribunal is constituted)? Will that prejudice the arbitral process itself (for example, by prejudicing one's consent to arbitration)? The tribunal's power to order interim relief is what this chapter is concerned with. Relief by domestic courts will depend ultimately upon domestic law, and although we will necessarily have to understand how curial assistance relates to investment arbitration, it is not the primary subject of this chapter.[1] A distinction may also need to be drawn between the ICSID and other forms of arbitration. This chapter contains by way of illustration an English case in which there was refusal to order interim relief where an ICSID tribunal was already seised of the issue. That case also illustrates the interaction, in practice, between requests for interim relief before a local court and an ongoing investment arbitration.[2]

There is also the question of the power on the part of arbitration tribunals to order interim relief against a sovereign State specifically. Today, it is often said that consent to arbitration by itself lifts immunity, including immunity against the attachment of

---

[1] One would have to turn to the specialist works on the civil procedure rules and the arbitration law in that domestic jurisdiction.

[2] *ETI Euro Telecom International NV* v. *Bolivia and Another* [2008] EWCA Civ. 880, below.

sovereign assets, and there are many examples of modern legal systems which take that view.[3] Yet, even if the tribunal can make an order against a sovereign State because immunity is somehow lifted, there may be other limitations, including practical limitations, on its power to do so. Provisional measures quite often involve questions about the need to conserve assets or evidence until arbitration has concluded. A freezing order – one which seeks to freeze the assets of the respondent State for fear that they may be dissipated or removed from the particular jurisdiction – is a typical measure that can be taken. But can investment tribunals enforce a request for provisional measures against a sovereign State? In some situations, the assistance of the courts is unavoidable. Of course, in practice, no respondent should wish to be seen to disobey a tribunal order wilfully, at least while the tribunal proceedings are still ongoing for fear of prejudicing its case in the tribunal's eyes.

In general, however, if investment arbitration is treated as being no different from commercial arbitration, then there is no reason to think that a tribunal should not order relief in the same way that it might in relation to a private respondent. This, predictably, is the approach under the UNCITRAL Arbitration Rules, which are widely applied in ad hoc investment arbitration.

1. INTERIM MEASURES AND SOVEREIGN RESPONDENTS

The difficulty with interim measures in investment arbitration is that arbitration involves a sovereign party whose assets may not always be treated, at least ordinarily in our commercial legal imagination, in the same way as the assets of a garden variety private commercial party.[4] Is this difference reflected in ICSID arbitration, which is designed specifically with respondent host States in mind, and arbitration adopting the UNCITRAL Rules of Arbitration?

A country's warship docked in a harbour is not to be treated in the same manner as a private company's bank account. To draw a domestic analogy, domestic courts are typically prevented from attaching foreign warships under their domestic law, at least not without the foreign sovereign's express and specific consent. In some jurisdictions, military assets may simply be immune and the foreign sovereign's alleged consent to lift immunity will have nothing to do with the matter.[5] Even where the immunity of foreign sovereign assets from attachment is lifted by law, the ability to make a freezing order as an interim or conservatory measure would typically require a 'separate' act of consent of the foreign sovereign because of the intrusive nature of interim measures.[6]

---

[3] This is discussed further in Chapter 19 of this book. See also C. L. Lim, 'Worldwide Litigation over Foreign Sovereign Assets' (2016) 10 *Dispute Resolution Int'l* 145, 154. One must be careful to distinguish between the post-award attachment of assets and an application for freezing order as a form of interim relief only; as the US court pointed out in *NML Capital Ltd* v. *Argentina*, 699 F3d 246, 261–263 (2nd Cir. 2012), an injunction operates merely *in personam* and is no 'attachment' of assets at all, and that may matter in respect of the scope of a foreign sovereign's immunity, which may only extend to immunity from pre-judgment 'attachment' absent an express waiver of immunity.
[4] Foreign State or sovereign immunity is discussed further in Chapter 19 of this book.
[5] Such appears to be the case under the United States' Foreign Sovereign Immunities Act 1976, s. 1611(b)(2).
[6] See, e.g., Lim, 'Worldwide Litigation', 148 (on the Anglo-American requirement of a 'separate waiver').

At a broader level, one might tend to think that an arbitration involving a foreign sovereign automatically deserves some degree of special consideration, precisely because foreign sovereigns possess sovereign rights. Consider, for example, criminal proceedings that are being brought against the investor in the host State. Can such proceedings be halted by the tribunal? This goes to the heart of the issue today, which is discussed in Chapter 19 of this book, about the proper extent of tribunal powers vis-à-vis the sovereign authority of the host State. Another example might be a request for an order to require the host State to desist from the imposition or collection of a tax pending the outcome of the dispute.

This is not to say that allowing interim relief will always put the host State at a disadvantage as against the investor. Interim measures are not solely the weapons of claimants. From the investor's viewpoint, should the claimant, assuming that it may at the end of the proceedings find itself being ordered to pay the legal costs of a winning host State,[7] be required to provide security in the meantime for such costs as a condition for its claim to go forward? It is sometimes said that an order for security prejudices the position of claimants since they have a 'right' to bring an investment claim, while it is also said that orders to secure costs will guard against the risk of frivolous claims.[8] Similar issues about striking the right balance between the respondent State's rights and the claimant's rights could arise when considering whether a tribunal should have the power to restrain the claimant from continuing with other proceedings; although, having said that, it is probably the more widely held view today that the respondent State should not have to face a multiplicity of proceedings over the same claim. These issues are discussed elsewhere in this book.[9]

To all these questions, the 2010 version of the UNCITRAL Arbitration Rules which are widely used in international commercial arbitration, state, simply, that a tribunal itself may grant interim measures and that the claimant may also turn to the local courts for interim relief without prejudicing the arbitration. Of course, it will be up to domestic law when and in what circumstances a domestic court will be permitted to 'intervene' by rendering curial assistance to an arbitration tribunal and its proceedings. In situations where the tribunal has not yet been constituted, it might be thought that the assistance of the courts will be most valuable in filling a gap. In other cases, it may be impractical not to seek judicial assistance (for example, in order to freeze a bank account operated by a bank which is a non-party to the arbitration proceedings).

UNCITRAL Arbitration Rules 2010, Art. 26

1. The arbitral tribunal may, at the request of a party, grant interim measures.
2. An interim measure is any temporary measure by which, at any time prior to the issuance of the award by which the dispute is finally decided, the arbitral tribunal orders a party, for example and without limitation, to:
   (a) Maintain or restore the status quo pending determination of the dispute;

---

[7] The apportionment of legal costs is discussed further in Chapter 18 of this book.
[8] See Chapter 18 of this book on costs.
[9] For parallel proceedings, see Chapter 5 of this book. For dissatisfaction over multiple claims stirring a 'backlash' against investment arbitration, see Chapter 20 of this book.

(b) Take action that would prevent, or refrain from taking action that is likely to cause,
   (i) current or imminent harm or (ii) prejudice to the arbitral process itself;
(c) Provide a means of preserving assets out of which a subsequent award may be
   satisfied; or
(d) Preserve evidence that may be relevant and material to the resolution of the dispute.
   ...

9. A request for interim measures addressed by any party to a judicial authority shall not
be deemed incompatible with the agreement to arbitrate, or as a waiver of that agreement.
Note in particular the words 'for example and without limitation, to'. Much then is left in
the hands of the tribunal, not just in deciding upon the appropriateness of relief but also in
deciding upon the form of relief.

The equivalent provision in the case of an ICSID Arbitration is Article 47 of the ICSID
Convention, and the rule is elaborated upon further in Rule 39 of the ICSID Arbitration
Rules. One difficulty, it has been noticed, involves Article 47's language. It states that the
tribunal may 'recommend' provisional measures, and so it has been asked whether the
tribunal has the power to make an 'order'. It is probably true to say that the word 'recommend' is not typically seen to preclude an ICSID tribunal's power to make an 'order'.[10]

**Convention on the Settlement of Investment Disputes between States and Nationals
of Other States, 18 March 1965, 575 UNTS 159, Art. 47**

Except as the parties otherwise agree, the Tribunal may, if it considers that the
circumstances so require, recommend any provisional measures which should be taken to
preserve the respective rights of either party.

The ICSID Arbitration Rules provide further elaboration.

**ICSID Rules of Procedure for Arbitration Proceedings (Arbitration Rules), in
effect from 10 April 2006, reprinted in ICSID Convention, Regulations and Rules
(Washington, DC: ICSID, April 2006), Rule 39 Provisional Measures**

(1) At any time after the institution of the proceeding, a party may request that provisional
   measures for the preservation of its rights be recommended by the Tribunal. The request
   shall specify the rights to be preserved, the measures the recommendation of which is
   requested, and the circumstances that require such measures.
(2) The Tribunal shall give priority to the consideration of a request made pursuant to
   paragraph (1).
(3) The Tribunal may also recommend provisional measures on its own initiative or
   recommend measures other than those specified in a request. It may at any time modify
   or revoke its recommendations.

---

[10] The distinction between a power to recommend or order provisional measures was described as being more
apparent than real in *Maffezini v. Spain*, ICSID Case No. ARB/97/7, Decision on Provisional Measures
(Procedural Order No. 2), 28 October 1999, para. 9. There are similar statements by other tribunals.

(4) The Tribunal shall only recommend provisional measures, or modify or revoke its recommendations, after giving each party an opportunity of presenting its observations.

(5) If a party makes a request pursuant to paragraph (1) before the constitution of the Tribunal, the Secretary-General shall, on the application of either party, fix time limits for the parties to present observations on the request, so that the request and observations may be considered by the Tribunal promptly upon its constitution.

(6) Nothing in this Rule shall prevent the parties, provided that they have so stipulated in the agreement recording their consent, from requesting any judicial or other authority to order provisional measures, prior to or after the institution of the proceeding, for the preservation of their respective rights and interests.

When it comes to recourse to domestic courts, the words 'provided that they have so stipulated in the agreement recording their consent', contained in Rule 39(6) of the ICSID Rules, mean that ordinarily the power for a domestic court to order interim relief will not have been consented to by the parties to an ICSID arbitration. Once dispute erupts, why then should the respondent State in investment arbitration agree to it? As one commentator has remarked, from the claimant's viewpoint, consent to judicial interim relief should therefore make its way into an investment contract at the outset.[11] This was the issue in *ETI Euro Telecom NV v. Bolivia and Another,*[12] reproduced in part in Section 2.

2. RECOURSE TO NATIONAL COURTS AND THE POWER OF ICSID TRIBUNALS

The English decision excerpted below relates to whether interim relief ought, at least ordinarily, to be granted by an English court where an ICSID arbitration is involved.[13] The question arises in light of the common view that an ICSID arbitration, unlike an ad hoc arbitration, is typically 'self-contained' under the so-called 'exclusivity clause' in Article 26 of the ICSID Convention – namely, that the parties have agreed not to seek relief in the domestic courts. Lord Justice Collins, as he then was, delivering the leading judgment, adopted the view that the English courts should desist, ordinarily, from granting such relief in respect of an ICSID arbitration on the ground of 'inexpediency' in the language of the Civil Jurisdiction and Judgments Act of 1992. Nonetheless, as the extract below shows, the Court of Appeal took the view that the word 'recommend' in Article 47 of the ICSID Convention by itself presents no bar to the view that the ICSID tribunal can order interim relief. There is also a useful review of the ICSID authorities on this point.

---

[11] See A. Carlevaris, 'Preliminary Matters: Objections, Bi-furcation, Request for Provisional Measures' in C. Giorgetti (ed.), *Litigating International Investment Disputes* (Leiden: Brill/Nijhoff, 2014), 173, 195, 196, who also observes that most arbitration rules operate differently, including under ICSID's Additional Facility Rules, to which Art. 26 of the ICSID Convention is inapplicable; see ICSID's Additional Facility Arbitration Rules, Art. 46(4).

[12] [2008] EWCA Civ. 880.

[13] For the test applied in applications for interim relief in England and Wales and in the Anglo-Commonwealth more widely, see *American Cyanamid Co. v. Ethicon Ltd* [1975] AC 396 and the line of authorities associated with it.

ETI Euro Telecom International NV v. Bolivia and Another [2008] EWCA Civ. 880, paras 1, 29–42, 99–102 (Lord Justice Lawrence Collins)

1. This is an urgent appeal brought by permission of this court from a decision of Andrew Smith J given on July 11, 2008, in which he set aside freezing orders granted in favour of ETI Euro Telecom International NV ('ETI'), the appellant, against the Republic of Bolivia ('Bolivia') and Empresa Nacional de Telecomunicaciones Entel SA ('Entel'), the respondents. It concerns an attempt by ETI to use national courts to secure its position in an international arbitration arising out of the nationalisation of its interests in Bolivia.

...

99. The respondents' position is that it will always be inexpedient to grant interim relief in aid of an ICSID arbitration because the rules governing such arbitration exclude the possibility of such relief unless the parties have agreed otherwise, and those rules form part of the arbitration agreement to which the court will always wish to give effect. A 'highly material' consideration was 'the likely reaction of the court which is seised of the substantive dispute': *Credit Suisse Fides Trust v Cuoghi* [1998] QB 818 at 829; *Refco Inc v Eastern Trading Co* [1999] 1 Lloyds Rep 159 at 174; *Motorola Credit Corp v Uzan* (No. 2) [2003] EWCA Civ 752, [2004] 1 WLR 113 at [72].

100. My conclusions on the inapplicability of section 25 to arbitration make it unnecessary to decide the question of inexpediency, which simply cannot arise if section 25 is inapplicable. But since the point was argued, I will set out the relevant considerations.

101. Section 25(2) of the 1982 Act provides that on an application for interim relief under section 25(1) the court may refuse to grant that relief, if, in the opinion of the court, the fact that the court has no jurisdiction apart from section 25 in relation to the subject matter of the proceedings in question 'makes it inexpedient for the court to grant it'. The Court of Appeal in *Motorola Credit Corp v Uzan* (No.2) [2003] EWCA Civ 752, [2004] 1 WLR 113, at [115] said that, among the considerations which had to be borne in mind in relation to the question whether it was inexpedient to make an order under section [25] were (adapting the language to a case such as the present) (1) whether the making of the order would interfere with the management of the case in the foreign tribunal; (2) whether it was the policy of the foreign tribunal not itself to make orders of the type sought in England; and (3) whether, in a case where jurisdiction was resisted and disobedience was to be expected, the court would be making an order which it could not enforce.

102. I have set out above verbatim the provisions of Articles 26 and 47 of the ICSID Convention. The effect of Article 26 is that consent to ICSID arbitration is 'deemed consent to such arbitration to the exclusion of any other remedy'. Article 47 gives an ICSID tribunal the power to 'recommend any provisional measures which should be taken to preserve the respective rights of either party'. Although Article 47 uses the word 'recommend' there is no doubt that 'according to a well-established principle laid down by the jurisprudence of the ICSID tribunals, provisional measures "recommended" by an ICSID tribunal are legally compulsory; they are in effect "ordered" by the tribunal, and the parties are under a legal obligation to comply with them': *Tokios Tokeles v Ukraine* (2007) 11 ICSID Rep 307, para 4;

also *Casado v Chile* (2001) 8 ICSID Rep 373, 380–382; *Occidental Petroleum Corp v Republic of Ecuador* (2007), para 58. *Cf LaGrand Case (Germany v United States)* 2001 ICJ Rep 3, at paras 98 et seq (binding character of orders made under Article 41 of the Statute of the International Court of Justice, which gives the Court power to 'indicate' provisional measures).

103. There is some doubt whether an order designed to have a similar effect to an attachment or freezing order is a provisional measure for the purposes of Article 47. In *Tanzania Electric Supply Co v Independent Power Tanzania Ltd* (1999) in (2005) 8 ICSID Rep 226 it was said by the tribunal (para 14) that provisional measures under Article 39 should not be recommended in order, in effect, to give security for the claim. Schreuer, *The ICSID Convention: A Commentary* (2001), p 777 seems to take the same view, but Friedland, *ICSID and Court-Ordered Provisional Remedies: An Update* (1988) 4 Arb Int 161, 164–165 suggests that an ICSID tribunal might recommend a freeze on transfers in exceptional circumstances.

104. It would certainly be surprising if such an order could be made against a State solely as security for a claim in the arbitration. Mr Moss QC pointed to the broad language used by the tribunal in *Casado v Chile* (2001) 8 ICSID Rep 373, para 26: '... provisional measures are principally aimed at preserving or protecting the efficiency of the decision that is given on the merits; they are intended to avoid prejudicing the execution of judgment, or prevent a party, by unilateral act or omission, infringing the rights of the opposing party'. But that was not a case in which the order sought bore any resemblance to an attachment or freezing order. It is not, however, necessary to express even a provisional view on this question in the present case. The tribunal has not been constituted and no request for a recommendation has therefore been made.

105. Rule 39 of the ICSID Arbitration Rules deals with the provisional measures procedure, and Rule 39(6) provides:

> '(6) Nothing in this Rule shall prevent the parties, provided that they have so stipulated in the agreement recording their consent, from requesting any judicial or other authority to order provisional measures, prior to or after the institution of the proceeding, for the preservation of their respective rights and interests.'

106. What is now Rule 39(6) was introduced in 1984 as Rule 39(5). Prior to that date the prevailing view had been that the effect of Article 26 was that it was not possible for a private party to obtain an attachment in a national court in aid of an ICSID arbitration: see decisions in Belgium and Switzerland cited in Collins, *Essays in International Litigation and the Conflict of Laws* (1994), p 76; and Schreuer, *The ICSID Convention: A Commentary* (2001), pp 376 et seq. In *MINE v Guinea* (1986) 1 ICSID Review – FILJ 383, at 390), the Geneva court said:

> 'Recourse to ICSID arbitration should be considered as an implied waiver of all other means of settlement ... the state should not be exposed to other means of pressure or to other remedies.'

107. But in 1986 the French Cour de Cassation decided (in a case where the attachment pre-dated what is now Rule 39(6)) that Article 26 was not intended to prevent recourse to

a judge for conservatory measures designed to secure the eventual execution of an award. The court held that the power to order conservatory measures could only be excluded by express consent of the parties, or by implied agreement resulting from the adoption of arbitral rules which required such a waiver, and the ICSID Convention and Rules did not amount to such a waiver: *Guinea and Soguipeche v Atlantic Triton Co* (1987) 26 ILM 373, 1987 Rev Crit 760, 1987 Clunet 125. The decision has been the subject of criticism: e.g. Collins, op cit, p 78.

108. But the effect of Rule 39(6) is that provisional measures may be sought only from the ICSID tribunal itself, and not from national courts, unless the parties agree otherwise: Shihata (who was the former Secretary-General of ICSID) and Parra (the former deputy Secretary-General), *The Experience of the International Centre for Settlement of Investment Disputes* (1999) ICSID Rev 299, 324; Schreuer, op cit, p 384; Dicey, Morris & Collins, *Conflict of Laws* (14th ed 2006), para 16–179; Fouchard, Gaillard, Goldman, *International Commercial Arbitration* (1999, ed Gaillard and Savage), paras 1309 and 1319–20.

109. Mr Moss QC suggested that Articles 26 and 47 of the ICSID Convention and Rule 39(6) had no application in England because the ICSID Convention was not incorporated in United Kingdom law. It is true that the Convention is not part of United Kingdom law, but in a case such as this the effect of these provisions taken together is that the parties have agreed not to seek interim measures in a national court. Although there may be exceptional circumstances which might justify a national court in disregarding the agreement of the parties, in my judgment that agreement pursuant to the Convention and the Rules would of itself normally make an interim order under section 25 inexpedient, and also make it unnecessary to consider all the other circumstances.

The clarity of this judgment should not mask a history of contentiousness regarding the issue of the ICSID's self-contained regime.[14]

3. OTHER TYPES OF RELIEF

We have already seen freezing orders in *ETI Euro Telecom*. In practice, such orders may not practicably be sought from the tribunal itself where the order is directed at a third party, and thus the question falls, as indeed it did in *ETI*, to domestic courts from whom relief is sought instead.

The Award in *RSM* v. *St Lucia* excerpted below is discussed later in the present book in the context of a more comprehensive discussion of the issue of costs.[15] It is worth noting

---

[14] Carlevaris, 'Preliminary Matters', 196–197.
[15] See Chapter 18 of this book.

in this context, however, that the *RSM* tribunal's order to secure costs, in particular its view that the power of an ICSID tribunal to order interim relief includes the power to order security, has been controversial.

RSM Production Corp. v. *St Lucia*, ICSID Case No. ARB/12/10, Decision on St Lucia's Request for Security for Costs, 13 August 2014 (Professor Siegfried H. Elsing, President; Dr Gavan Griffith QC; Judge Edward W. Nottingham (dissenting)), paras 54–56, 83–84 (original emphasis)

54. The Tribunal, by majority, agrees with the general proposition that security for costs can be ordered based on Article 47 ICSID Convention and ICSID Arbitration Rule 39. The fact that ordering security for costs is not expressly provided for in those provisions does not exclude the Tribunal's jurisdiction to issue such measure. Rather, such provisions are phrased broadly and encompass '*any provisional measures*' the Tribunal, after carefully balancing the Parties' interests deems appropriate '*to preserve the respective right of either party*' under the given circumstances. The fact that other sets of arbitration rules (such as Art. 25.2 of the London Court of International Arbitration Rules) expressly provide for the possibility to order security for costs does not lead to a different conclusion: The broad wording does not address any particular measure but rather leaves it entirely to the Tribunal's discretion which measure it finds necessary and appropriate under the circumstances of the individual case.

55. The fact that Article 47 ICSID Convention and ICSID Arbitration Rule 39 do not expressly make reference to security for costs in particular – nor to any other particular measure – can easily be explained by the time at which the ICSID Convention was drafted. In 1965, issues such as third party funding and thus the shifting of the financial risk away from the claiming party were not as frequent, if at all, as they are today. Hence, the omission does not allow any negative inference.

56. Moreover, the reference to other arbitration rules such as Art. 25.2 of the LCIA Rules and the explicit mention of security for costs as a provisional measure does not provide a valid argument against ordering such measure under the ICSID regime. Institutional arbitration rules are constantly subject to review and modernization as deemed necessary by the drafters. By contrast, there is no comparable mechanism with regard to the ICSID Convention. Amending the ICSID Convention in general and in particular to the effect that security for costs as a provisional measure is expressly dealt with would require considerably more effort. Hence, stating that such amendment has not been made cannot serve as a ground for assuming that the drafters of the ICSID Convention intended to exclude security for costs.

So far as other types of relief are concerned, originally the issue which drew attention to provisional measures had concerned the not uncommon spectre of an investor, its executives, legal advisers or witnesses being prosecuted in the courts of the host nation.[16] The first such case in the ICSID jurisprudence was *Tokios Tokelés* v. *Ukraine.*[17]

Henry G. Burnett and Jessica Beess und Chrostin, 'Interim Measures in Response to the Criminal Prosecution of Corporations and Their Employees by Host State in Parallel with Investment Arbitration Proceedings' (2015) 30 *Maryland J Int'l L* 31, 40 (original emphasis, footnotes omitted)

Tribunals in at least seven ICSID and two UNCITRAL cases have addressed requests for protection in the face of a Host State's pursuit of criminal charges.

A. *Tokios Tokelés v. Ukraine*

The arbitral tribunal in *Tokios Tokelés* was the first tribunal to hold that it had authority to grant a provisional measures request to enjoin a Host State from continuing criminal prosecution of an investor's corporate executives. In this case, the claimant was an investor company that carried on a 'business in Ukraine in the advertising, printing, publishing and allied trades, under the control and management of two brothers, Mr. Oleksandr V. Danylov

---

[16] The immunity of arbitration participants from legal process is typically insufficient even where certain forms of arbitration enjoy such immunity in order to protect the integrity of the arbitration. For example, in a Permanent Court of Arbitration (PCA)-administered arbitration, parties, counsel and witnesses may be extended such immunity. For ICSID arbitration, see Arts 21 and 22 of the ICSID Convention, and C. H. Schreuer, L. Malintoppi, A. Reinisch and A. Sinclair (eds), *The ICSID Convention: A Commentary*, 2nd edn (Cambridge University Press, 2009), 62–66. In cases involving criminal prosecution in the host State, such immunity will, however, be ineffective. In the case of ICSID arbitrations, immunity for participants is limited to immunity from travel to and from, and their presence in, the place of arbitration, whereas in a typical case where a provisional measure is sought, the question involved is not one connected to the need for a travel immunity. For the PCA, see B. W. Daly, E. Goriatcheva and H. Meighen, *A Guide to the PCA Arbitration Rules* (Oxford University Press, 2014), 62–63, which discusses immunity under the headquarters agreement with the Netherlands and under various host country agreements into which the PCA has entered. Such host country agreements also extend immunity to arbitration participants, but, again, such immunity will typically be limited to 'words spoken or written and all acts performed by them in the course of their participation in PCA Proceedings or PCA Meetings', the 'inviolability of all papers, documents in whatever form and materials relating to their participation in PCA Proceedings or PCA Meetings', their communications in respect of the proceedings, and of course travel and immigration restrictions. Such immunity will likely be insufficient or unsatisfactory from the claimant's viewpoint. See Art. 8 of the Schedule to Hong Kong's International Organizations (Privileges and Immunities) (Permanent Court of Arbitration) Order, LN 26 of 2016, by way of example. At present, the PCA's Headquarters Agreement operates more widely following an Exchange of Notes in 2012 between the PCA and the Government of the Netherlands, and extends immunity to witnesses in relation to acts or even convictions prior to their entry into the Netherlands; Daly *et al.*, *A Guide to the PCA Arbitration Rules*, 62–63. The more basic difficulty is that protection is required to restrain the host country within its own territory, and the host State need not, indeed will not usually, be the headquarters or country having a host country agreement with the PCA. That will usually be some other neutral forum instead. Other types of arbitration to bear in mind in this respect include arbitrations administered by the Kuala Lumpur Regional Centre for Arbitration and the Cairo Regional Centre for Arbitration, for these too are inter-governmental organisations established by agreement between the Asian–African Legal Consultative Organisation (AALCO) and the Governments of Malaysia and Egypt.

[17] *Tokios Tokelés* v. *Ukraine*, ICSID Case No. ARB/02/18, Order No. 1, Claimant's Request for Provisional Measures, 1 July 2003.

and Mr. Serhiy V. Danylov'. Among other things, the claimant alleged that its company was the subject of a targeted and long-running campaign of oppression by State agencies, ultimately culminating in a wrongful expropriation of the claimant's investment. During the pendency of the investment arbitration, the claimant filed a request for provisional measures, requesting the tribunal to order the respondent to 'refrain from, suspend, and discontinue: (i) the criminal proceedings against O.V. Danylov, General Director of Claimant's subsidiaries in Ukraine; (ii) the arrest of assets of Claimant's subsidiaries in Ukraine; and (iii) tax investigations of Claimant's subsidiaries in Ukraine'.

...

In its Order No. 3, the tribunal discussed Article 47 of the ICSID Convention and Arbitration Rule 39, as well as prior investor-state arbitrations addressing requests for interim relief. The tribunal concluded that: '[t]he circumstances under which provisional measures are required under Article 47 are those in which the measures are necessary to preserve a party's rights and that need is urgent'. IMs are necessary 'where the actions of a party are capable of causing or of threatening irreparable prejudice to the rights invoked', and they are urgent where 'action prejudicial to the rights of either party is likely to be taken before such final decision is taken'. The tribunal proceeded to note that the respondent was incorrect in arguing that criminal proceedings against an employee of the investor cannot be the subject of a provisional measure because such proceedings are not part of a legal dispute arising directly out of the claimant's investment. The tribunal stated that:

> It is not necessary for a tribunal to establish that the actions complained of in a request for provisional measures meet the jurisdictional requirements of Article 25 [of the ICSID Convention]. A tribunal may order a provisional measure if the actions of the opposing party 'relate to the subject matter of the case before the tribunal and not to separate, unrelated issues or extraneous matters'.

Having established that criminal proceedings may properly be the subject of IMs, however, the tribunal ultimately concluded that the request for IMs should not be granted in this instance to enjoin the criminal proceedings against O.V. Danylov. The tribunal reasoned that the claimant had failed to show that a provisional measure was either necessary or urgent to protect its rights.

Importantly, the tribunal looked to the timing of the institution of the criminal proceedings and noted that they were initiated nine months before the claimant registered its ICSID claim, yet the claimant did not include the criminal proceedings in its prior request for provisional measures. Consequently, the claimant could not now credibly claim that IMs were urgent.

B. City Oriente v. Ecuador

In *City Oriente*, the claimant initiated ICSID arbitration proceedings against Ecuador following amendments to the Hydrocarbon Law purporting to unilaterally modify the parties' hydrocarbon production-sharing contract. City Oriente refused to comply with the amended law, and in response, the State Attorney General of Ecuador announced that a criminal complaint against City Oriente's representatives and managers would be filed on the basis of the investor's non-compliance with the new Hydrocarbon Law. City Oriente requested interim measures to maintain the *status quo ante* after the State Attorney General of Ecuador made this announcement. And in fact, during the pendency of the IM request, two criminal complaints were filed against the claimant's executives. In its Decision on Provisional Measures, the tribunal stated that a tribunal determining applications for IMs may and should take into consideration whether the adoption of the IMs is necessary to preserve the petitioner's rights, whether their ordering is urgent, and whether each party has been afforded an opportunity to raise observations.

The tribunal looked at each of these factors in turn and granted City Oriente's IM request, finding that City Oriente met all three considerations. More specifically, the tribunal found that the main purpose of provisional measures in ICSID arbitrations is to preserve the *status quo ante*, and that this was precisely what the claimant sought to do:

> In other words, it is the Tribunal's view that Article 47 of the Convention provides authorization for the passing of provisional measures prohibiting any action that affects the disputed rights, aggravates the dispute, frustrates the effectiveness of the award or entails having either party take justice into their own hands. Where there is an agreement in place between the parties that has so far defined the framework of their mutual obligations, then the rights to be preserved are, precisely, those that were thereby agreed upon.

...

C. Caratube v. Kazakhstan

In *Caratube*, the claimant initiated ICSID arbitration proceedings against Kazakhstan after that State unilaterally terminated a contract for the exploration and production of hydrocarbons. Despite the termination, Caratube continued to operate certain oil wells to avoid adverse technical consequences, and, in response, Kazakhstan initiated criminal proceedings against Caratube and its directors for the unlawful continued operation of the wells. The claimant requested interim measures ordering Kazakhstani authorities to refrain from acting upon any existing criminal complaints or to file any new criminal complaints against the claimant. In its Decision Regarding Claimant's Application for Provisional Measures, the tribunal cited *Tokios Tokelés* with approval and pointed to the language of ICSID Article 47 and Rule 39, stating that the rule does not indicate that any specific state action must be excluded from the scope of possible provisional measures. Rather, 'this broad language can be interpreted to the effect that, in principle, criminal investigations may not be totally excluded from the scope of provisional measures in ICSID proceedings'. However, in recognition of the state's sovereign right to prosecute crime, 'a particularly high threshold must be overcome before an ICSID tribunal can indeed recommend provisional measures regarding criminal investigations conducted by a state'. The tribunal held that the claimant did not meet this particularly high threshold. The claimant failed to show, according to the tribunal, that its procedural right to continue with the ICSID arbitration would be precluded by the criminal investigation, and further, since the claimant sought monetary damages rather than injunctive relief, any additional harm to the claimant could be examined and determined at a later stage in the proceedings. For these reasons there was neither necessity nor urgency supporting the claimant's IM application.

D. Quiborax v. Bolivia

In *Quiborax v. Bolivia*, Quiborax, alongside Non Metallic Minerals (NMM) and Allan Fosk Kaplún, instituted ICSID arbitration proceedings against Bolivia, seeking compensation for damages following the Host State's revocation of eleven mining concessions. Bolivia initiated criminal proceedings against the coclaimants and other related individuals on the ground that they had allegedly forged a document establishing that Quiborax and Mr. Fosk were NMM shareholders and thus protected investors under the Bolivia–Chile BIT.

Although the subject matter of the criminal proceedings was the prosecution of the investors' alleged crimes of forgery and fraud, the tribunal found that the criminal proceedings could properly be the subject of IMs since the crimes at issue were directly related to the arbitration. The subject matter of the criminal proceedings could be outcome determinative for the investors' access to the arbitration, and, in fact, 'this access to ICSID arbitration is expressly deemed to constitute the harm caused to Bolivia that is required as one of the constituent elements of the crimes prosecuted'.

...

Importantly, the tribunal expressly declared that it had full respect for Bolivia's sovereign right to prosecute crimes committed in its territory, but also found that the criminal prosecutions appeared to target the claimants in the arbitration *because* they had initiated the arbitration ... the tribunal ordered Bolivia to take appropriate measures to suspend the criminal proceedings, finding that they threatened the procedural integrity of the arbitration.

The four disputes discussed in the above extract were all submitted to ICSID arbitration.[18]

4. THE TEST APPLIED BY TRIBUNALS

In *Quiborax*, the ICSID tribunal considered that the appropriate test for ordering interim relief involves consideration of whether such measures are 'urgent and necessary', provided a protected right exists.

[18] *Tokios Tokelés* v. *Ukraine*, Order No. 1, Claimant's Request for Provisional Measures, 1 July 2003; *City Oriente Ltd* v. *Ecuador and Empresa Estatal Petróleos del Ecuador (Petroecuador)*, ICSID Case No. ARB/06/21, Decision on Provisional Measures, November 2007; *Caratube International Oil Co. LLP* v. *Kazakhstan*, ICSID Case No. ARB/08/12, Decision Regarding Claimant's Application for Provisional Measures, 31 July 2009; *Quiborax SA, Non Metallic Minerals SA and Allan Fosk Kaplún* v. *Bolivia*, ICSID Case No. ARB/06/2, Decision on Provisional Measures, 26 February 2010. Other tribunal decisions discussed by Burnett and Beess und Chrostin, but which are not reproduced here, include *Lao Holdings NV* v. *Laos*, ICSID Case No. ARB(AF)/12/6, Ruling on Motion to Amend the Provisional Measures Order, 30 May 2014; and *Churchill Mining Plc and Planet Mining Pty Ltd* v. *Indonesia*, ICSID Case No. ARB/12/14 and 12/40, Procedural Order No. 9, Provisional Measures, 8 July 2014. *Sergei Paushok, CJSC Golden East Co. and CJSC Vostokneftegaz Co.* v. *Mongolia*, UNCITRAL, Order on Interim Measures, 2 September 2008 is excerpted in Section 4 in the context of the threshold test to be met by an application for provisional measures. *Paushok* illustrates a request for provisional measures under the UNCITRAL Rules.

Quiborax SA, Non Metallic Minerals SA and Allan Fosk Kaplún v. *Bolivia,* ICSID Case No. ARB/06/2, Decision on Provisional Measures, 26 February 2010 (Professor Gabrielle Kauffman-Kohler, President; Hon. Marc Lalonde; Prof. Brigitte Stern) (footnotes omitted), paras 113–114, 126, 139, 149–160, 163–165

IV Discussion

A. Applicable Standards

...

3. Requirements for provisional measures

113. There is no disagreement between the Parties, and rightly so, that provisional measures can only be granted under the relevant rules and standards, if rights to be protected do exist (Section B below), and the measures are urgent (Section C below) and necessary (Section D below), this last requirement implying an assessment of the risk of harm to be avoided by the measures. By contrast, the Parties disagree on the type and existence of the rights to be protected. The Parties further disagree on whether the measures are urgent and/or necessary. The Tribunal will now review the different requirements for provisional measures set out and the Parties' divergent positions in this respect.

B. Existence of Rights Requiring Preservation

114. Claimants allege that the following three rights need preservation by way of provisional measures: (i) the right to preservation of the status quo and non-aggravation of the dispute; (ii) the right to the procedural integrity of the arbitration proceedings, and (iii) the right to exclusivity of the ICSID proceedings in accordance with Art. 26 of the ICSID Convention.

...

126. Claimants argue that the criminal proceedings are aimed at destroying their status as foreign investors under the Bolivia–Chile BIT and thus constitute 'other remedy' for purposes of Art. 26 of the ICSID Convention. Bolivia rejects this argument by pointing out that the subject matter of the ICSID proceeding (determining whether Bolivia has breached its obligations under the BIT and Claimants are entitled to the relief sought) is distinct from the subject matter of the criminal proceedings (prosecuting and punishing crimes in accordance with Bolivian law).

...

139. Claimants assert that the criminal proceedings impair their right to the procedural integrity of the arbitration proceedings, in particular with respect to their access to evidence and the integrity of the evidence. Specifically, Claimants claim that through the criminal proceedings Respondent has obstructed their access to indispensable evidence by sequestering their corporate records and alienating potential witnesses; that Respondent has fabricated *ex post facto* evidence by forcing false confessions out of a potential witness and thus making him unavailable to testify, and seeks to do the same with other

potential witnesses; and that Respondent attempts to destroy the probative value of certain documents ...

...

C. Urgency

149. The Parties agree that there is urgency when there is a need to safeguard rights that are in imminent danger of irreparable harm before a decision is made on the merits. They disagree, however, on whether the present facts meet the urgency requirement.

150. The Arbitral Tribunal agrees with Claimants that the criterion of urgency is satisfied when 'a question cannot await the outcome of the award on the merits' [Eds: citing Professor Schreuer]. This is in line with the practice of the International Court of Justice ('ICJ'). The same definition has also been given in *Biwater Gauff v. Tanzania*:

> In the Arbitral Tribunal's view, the degree of 'urgency' which is required depends on the circumstances, including the requested provisional measures, and may be satisfied where a party can prove that there is a need to obtain the requested measures at a certain point in the procedure before the issuance of an award.

151. Claimants argue that the requirement of urgency is met in this case. Specifically, Claimants contend that because the measures are intended to protect against the aggravation of the dispute and to safeguard the jurisdictional powers of the Tribunal and the integrity of the arbitration, they are urgent by definition.

152. By contrast, Respondent argues that there is no imminent threat to any of Claimants' rights because the alleged harm to such rights is mere speculation.

153. The Tribunal agrees with Claimants that if measures are intended to protect the procedural integrity of the arbitration, in particular with respect to access to or integrity of the evidence, they are urgent by definition. Indeed, the question of whether a Party has the opportunity to present its case or rely on the integrity of specific evidence is essential to (and therefore cannot await) the rendering of an award on the merits.

D. Necessity

154. The Tribunal has found that the criminal proceedings threaten the procedural integrity of the ICSID proceeding, and that provisional measures are urgent. The Tribunal will now examine if provisional measures such as those requested by Claimants are necessary.

155. The Parties agree that provisional measures must be necessary, in other words, that they must be required to avoid harm or prejudice being inflicted upon the applicant. However, they disagree on the qualification of the harm, whether serious or irreparable, and also whether the criminal proceedings present a harm to Claimants' rights that requires avoidance by granting provisional measures.

156. The Tribunal considers that an irreparable harm is a harm that cannot be repaired by an award of damages. Such a standard has been adopted by several ICSID tribunals

and embodied in Art. 17A of the UNCITRAL Model Law. That provision requires the party requesting an interim measure to satisfy the tribunal that:

> Harm not adequately repaired by an award of damages is likely to result if the measure is not ordered, and such harm substantially outweighs the harm that is likely to result to the party against whom the measure is directed if the measure is granted.

157. Following this standard, Claimants submit that the provisional measures requested are necessary because the harm caused would not be adequately repaired by an award of damages. The Tribunal agrees with Claimants in this respect: any harm caused to the integrity of the ICSID proceedings, particularly with respect to a party's access to evidence or the integrity of the evidence produced could not be remedied by an award of damages.

158. However, Claimants have accurately pointed out that the necessity requirement requires the Tribunal to consider the proportionality of the requested provisional measures. The Tribunal must thus balance the harm caused to Claimants by the criminal proceedings and the harm that would be caused to Respondent if the proceedings were stayed or terminated.

159. Respondent claims that its sovereignty would be harmed if the Tribunal orders the provisional measures sought by Claimants, as this would unduly interfere with its right to prosecute crimes committed on its territory. Respondent also argues that the criminal proceedings may provide evidence that it could present in the ICSID proceedings, and that granting the measures requested by Claimants would prevent such evidence from ever reaching the Tribunal and would thus affect its right to present its case.

160. In addition, Respondent has committed to collaborate with Claimants' access to documentary evidence and witnesses. Specifically, it has committed to:

(a) 'obtain from the Prosecutor's Office certified copies of any documents identified by the Claimants, if they should have any difficulty in doing so';

(b) 'cooperate as necessary so that [the persons charged in the criminal proceedings] could offer their testimony to the Tribunal'.

...

163. The Tribunal takes due notice of Respondent's commitments set out in paragraph 160 above. Nonetheless, the Tribunal agrees with Claimants that in the particular circumstances of this case the commitment with respect to witnesses is insufficient. Regardless of whether the criminal proceedings have a legitimate basis or not (an issue which the Tribunal is not in a position to determine), the direct relationship between the criminal proceedings and this ICSID arbitration is preventing Claimants from accessing witnesses that could be essential to their case. No assurance of cooperation from Respondent can guarantee that persons who are being prosecuted for having allegedly caused harm to Respondent by permitting Claimants to present this arbitration will be willing to participate as witnesses in this very same arbitration. Under these circumstances, the Tribunal considers that Claimants' access to witnesses may improve if the criminal proceedings are stayed until this arbitration is finalized or this decision is reconsidered.

164. The Tribunal has given serious consideration to Respondent's argument that an order granting the provisional measures requested by Claimants would affect its sovereignty. In this respect, the Tribunal insists that it does not question the sovereign right of a State to conduct criminal cases. As mentioned in paragraph 129 above, the international protection granted to investors does not exempt suspected criminals from prosecution by virtue of their being investors. However, the situation encountered in this case is exceptional. The Tribunal has been convinced that there is a very close link between the initiation of this arbitration and the launching of the criminal cases in Bolivia. It has become clear to the Tribunal that one of the Claimants is being subjected to criminal proceedings precisely because he presented himself as an investor with a claim against Bolivia under the ICSID/BIT mechanism. Likewise, the Tribunal has been convinced that the other persons named in the criminal proceedings are being prosecuted because of their connection with this arbitration (be it as Claimants' business partners or counsel, or as authors of a report ordered by a state agency). Although Bolivia may have reasons to suspect that the persons being prosecuted could have engaged in criminal conduct, the facts presented to the Tribunal suggest that the underlying motivation to initiate the criminal proceedings was their connection to this arbitration, which has been expressly deemed to constitute the harm caused to Bolivia that is required as one of the constituent elements of the crimes prosecuted.

165. In addition, the Tribunal is of the opinion that a mere stay of the criminal proceedings would not affect Respondent's sovereignty nor require conduct in violation of national law ... Once this arbitration is finalized, Respondent will be free to continue the criminal proceedings, subject to the Tribunal terminating or amending this Decision prior to the completion of this arbitration.

As for the test under the UNCITRAL Arbitration Rules, the provisions of the 2010 Rules are as follows.

UNCITRAL Arbitration Rules 2010, Art. 26(3)–(8)

3. The party requesting an interim measure under paragraphs 2(a) to (c) shall satisfy the arbitral tribunal that:
   (a) Harm not adequately reparable by an award of damages is likely to result if the measure is not ordered, and such harm substantially outweighs the harm that is likely to result to the party against whom the measure is directed if the measure is granted; and
   (b) There is a reasonable possibility that the requesting party will succeed on the merits of the claim. The determination on this possibility shall not affect the discretion of the arbitral tribunal in making any subsequent determination.
4. With regard to a request for an interim measure under paragraph 2(d), the requirements in paragraphs 3(a) and (b) shall apply only to the extent the arbitral tribunal considers appropriate.

5. The arbitral tribunal may modify, suspend or terminate an interim measure it has granted, upon application of any party or, in exceptional circumstances and upon prior notice to the parties, on the arbitral tribunal's own initiative.

6. The arbitral tribunal may require the party requesting an interim measure to provide appropriate security in connection with the measure.

7. The arbitral tribunal may require any party promptly to disclose any material change in the circumstances on the basis of which the interim measure was requested or granted.

8. The party requesting an interim measure may be liable for any costs and damages caused by the measure to any party if the arbitral tribunal later determines that, in the circumstances then prevailing, the measure should not have been granted. The arbitral tribunal may award such costs and damages at any point during the proceedings.

There is a constant struggle between a host State's search for a 'fair' share of profits derived from resource extraction and the investor's search for certainty and stability in royalty or other means of payment. Taxation is merely a form of payment to the host State, yet it can also amount to expropriation. In other words, disputes over what essentially might be considered payment terms do become wrapped up in the language of expropriation by way of taxation measures. The dispute in *Paushok*, which applied the UNCITRAL Rules, involved a Mongolian profit tax law.

Sergei Paushok, CJSC Golden East Co. and CJSC Vostokneftegaz Co. v. Government of Mongolia, UNCITRAL, Order on Interim Measures, 2 September 2008 (Marc Lalonde, President; Brigitte Stern; Horacio A. Grigera Naón) (footnotes omitted), paras 45–48, 55–62, 64–70, 78–79, 81–82, 84–90

45. It is internationally recognized that five standards have to be met before a tribunal will issue an order in support of interim measures. They are (1) prima facie jurisdiction, (2) prima facie establishment of the case, (3) urgency, (4) imminent danger of serious prejudice (necessity) and (5) proportionality.

46. In addressing the first two criteria, the Tribunal wishes to make it clear that it does not in any way prejudge the issues of fact or law which may be raised by the Parties during the course of this case concerning the jurisdiction or competence of the Tribunal or the merits of the case.

1– Prima facie jurisdiction

47. The International Court of Justice described the interpretation to be given to this standard in the *Case Concerning Military and Paramilitary Activities in and Against Nicaragua*:

> '(O)n a request for provisional measures the Court need not, before deciding whether or not to indicate them, finally satisfy itself that it has jurisdiction on the merits of the case, or, as the case may be, that an objection to jurisdiction is well founded, yet it ought not to indicate such measures unless the provisions invoked

by the applicant appear, prima facie, to afford a basis on which the jurisdiction of the court might be founded;'

48. The Tribunal is of the view that, in their Notice of Arbitration and their submissions in connection with their Request, Claimants have established such a basis upon which the jurisdiction of the Tribunal might be founded.

...

2– Prima facie establishment of the case

55. At this stage, the Tribunal need not go beyond whether a reasonable case has been made which, if the facts alleged are proven, might possibly lead the Tribunal to the conclusion that an award could be made in favor of Claimants. Essentially, the Tribunal needs to decide only that the claims made are not, on their face, frivolous or obviously outside the competence of the Tribunal. To do otherwise would require the Tribunal to proceed to a determination of the facts and, in practice, to a hearing on the merits of the case, a lengthy and complicated process which would defeat the very purpose of interim measures.

56. In the present circumstances, the Tribunal concludes that Claimants have succeeded in a prima facie establishment of the case. In so ruling, the Tribunal wishes to stress that in no way does that ruling imply that the Tribunal would reach a similar conclusion on the merits of the case, once it has received submissions and heard witnesses and experts from each side on their respective allegations.

3– Urgency

57. From the evidence submitted, it appears that the WPT Law has had a major negative impact on the gold mining industry in Mongolia. Ms. S. Oyun, the President of the Mongolian Geologists Association and a Member of the Mongolian Parliament declared in September 2007 that, subsequently to the adoption of that Law, some 93 gold mining companies discontinued their operations, most of them declaring bankruptcy. This would represent a reduction by more than 50% of the previous number of firms in the industry.

58. The Government of Mongolia itself recognized the critical situation resulting from its legislation and proposed in 2007 major amendments which it did not succeed in getting enacted. And, according to information transmitted to the press service of the Mongolian Government and contained in an undated press release submitted to the Tribunal, the Government decided on May 7, 2008, to propose to Parliament a new law reducing very substantially the tax rates established under the WPT Law. As an explanation, the Government said that the changes were proposed '(w)ith the purpose of easing the tax burden on the mining companies, increasing the amount of gold deliveries and consolidating all of the tax payment on sold gold and gold-related royalties in the national budget and harmonizing the royalty payments with the international standards'. The use of the expression 'standards' and its interpretation by Claimants were contested by Respondent, but, even accepting Respondent's translation of the appropriate Mongolian word into

English, it is clear that the Mongolian Government has realized for quite some time that its taxation regime had led its gold mining industry into a crisis.

59. The Tribunal is not called upon to rule on that overall situation but taking cognizance of it helps the Tribunal in understanding whether the condition of urgency alleged by Claimants can be met in the present case.

60. From the evidence submitted by the Parties and taking into account the very specific features of this case, it appears to the Tribunal that urgent action in the form of interim measures is justified.

61. Respondent claims that over US$41 million is currently owed by GEM, under the WPT Law. It appears from the financial statements and taxation reports submitted to the Tribunal that GEM could not proceed to the immediate payment of this total sum out of its own resources. The only alternatives would be either loans from financial institutions or a large equity infusion by shareholders. It has been established to the satisfaction of the Tribunal that, in the current fiscal conditions, no financial institution would consider lending such an amount of money to GEM. And, assuming that Respondent is right in stating that GEM's net book value assets are worth less than 50% of the amount of WPT owing and the possibility that the Mongolian Parliament would again refuse to amend the WPT Law, it would be very presumptuous for any investor to make additional equity investment in that company. The likelihood of GEM's bankruptcy in such a context therefore becomes very real.

62. The Tribunal is aware of preceding awards concluding that even the possible aggravation of a debt of a claimant did not ('generally' says the *City Oriente* case cited below) open the door to interim measures when, as in this case, the damages suffered could be the subject of monetary compensation, on the basis that no irreparable harm would have been caused. And, were it not for the specific characteristics of this case, the Tribunal might have reached the same conclusion, although it might have expressed reservations about the concept that the possibility of monetary compensation is always sufficient to bar any request for interim measures under the UNCITRAL Rules. But those specific features point not only to the urgency of action by the Tribunal but also to the necessity of such action in the face of an imminent danger of serious prejudice.

4- Imminent danger of serious prejudice (necessity)

...

64. Respondent, citing ICSID awards, contends that provisional measures are limited to situations where specific performance is requested and that such a request for specific performance could only occur when the dispute is based on a contractual relationship. Respondent further argues that when the dispute only relates to a claim for damages, as in this case, there is no place for provisional measures, as damages can always be compensated, with the payment of money. Moreover, says Respondent, the only remedy available under Article 6 the BIT is monetary compensation.

65. Respondent refers in particular to the following cases. In *Occidental Petroleum*, the Tribunal says that 'provisional measures should only be granted in situations of necessity

and urgency in order to protect legal rights that could, absent such measures, be definitely lost' and in paragraph 98, it adds: 'The harm in this case is only "more damages", and this is harm of a type which can be compensated by monetary compensation, so there is neither necessity nor urgency to grant a provisional measure to prevent such harm.' Respondent also refers to the Decision on revocation of provisional measures in *City Oriente* where the Tribunal states that 'a possible aggravation of a debt does not generally warrant the ordering of provisional measures'. Respondent also relies on *Plama Consortium United v. Bulgaria* where the Tribunal says that '(t)he Tribunal accepts Respondent's argument that harm is not irreparable if it can be compensated for by damages, which is the case in the present arbitration and which, moreover is the only remedy Claimant seeks'.

66. Claimants, for their part, argue that their right to interim measures is not excluded in the case of a claim for damages only and that, in any event, their request for relief is not only for damages but also for declaratory relief under the provisions of the Treaty.

67. They refer in particular to the *Behring International, Inc. v. Islamic Republic Iranian Air Force* case where the Iran–U.S. Claims Tribunal states that 'the concept of irreparable prejudice in international law arguably is broader than the Anglo-American concept of irreparable injury. While the latter formulation requires a showing that the injury complained of is not remediable by an award of damages (...), the former does not necessarily so require'. Claimants also mention *Saipem SpA v. The People's Republic of Bangladesh* where the Tribunal found that Saipem was facing a risk of irreparable damage if it had to pay the amount of a bond.

68. The Tribunal does not agree with Respondent that Claimants are merely requesting damages, as is clearly demonstrated by the text of their request for relief. Moreover, the possibility of monetary compensation does not necessarily eliminate the possible need for interim measures. The Tribunal relies on the opinion of the Iran–U.S. Claims Tribunal in the *Behring* case to the effect that, in international law, the concept of 'irreparable prejudice' does not necessarily require that the injury complained of be not remediable by an award of damages. To quote K.P. Berger who refers specifically to Article 26 of the UNCITRAL Rules:

> 'To preserve the legitimate rights of the requesting party, the measures must be "necessary". This requirement is satisfied if the delay in the adjudication of the main claim caused by the arbitral proceedings would lead to a "substantial" (but not necessarily "irreparable" as known in common law doctrine) prejudice for the requesting party.'

69. The Tribunal shares that view and considers that the 'irreparable harm' in international law has a flexible meaning. It is noteworthy in that respect that the UNCITRAL Model Law in its Article 17A does not require the requesting party to demonstrate irreparable harm but merely that '(h)arm not adequately reparable by an award of damages is likely to result if the measure is not ordered, and such harm substantially outweighs the harm that is likely to result to the party against whom the measure is directed if the measure is granted'.

70. Whatever the situation under the ICSID Convention, the Tribunal does not support the contention that such measures can only be issued, under the UNCITRAL Rules, when specific

performance is requested in connection with a contractual relationship. No such restriction is implied under the broad language of Article 26(1) of the UNCITRAL Rules. The specific examples mentioned in that Article, on the contrary, point to a wide discretion in the hands of the Tribunal.

...

78. While it is true that Claimants would still have a recourse in damages and that other arbitral tribunals have indicated that debt aggravation was not sufficient to award interim measures, the unique circumstances of this case justify a different conclusion. In particular, while not putting in doubt the value of the undertaking of Respondent not to seize or put a lien on GEM's assets, the Tribunal believes that it is preferable to formalize that commitment into an interim measures order.

5- Proportionality

79. Under proportionality, the Tribunal is called upon to weigh the balance of inconvenience in the imposition of interim measures upon the parties.

...

81. In its consideration of this criterion with regard to Respondent, the Tribunal does not question in any way the sovereign right of a State to enact whatever tax measures it deems appropriate at any particular time. Every year, governments around the world propose the adoption of tax measures which constitute either new initiatives or amendments to existing fiscal legislation. There is a presumption of validity in favor of legislative measures adopted by a State and the burden of the proof is upon those who challenge such measures to demonstrate their invalidity. Moreover, a government is generally entitled to demand immediate payment of taxes owing, even if there is a dispute with a taxpayer about them. Finally, the fact that a particular level of taxation would appear excessive to some taxpayers does not make it illegal per se, even though it may open the door to contestation, including by foreign investors under a relevant BIT.

82. However, in the present instance, the Government itself has recognized that the WPT Law was not achieving the objectives it had in mind when it was adopted in 2006. This is quite apparent in its attempts, both in 2007 and 2008, to repeal that Law and to replace it with a much more modest taxation regime; similarly with the more recent undertaking made by Respondent not to seize or put a lien upon GEM's assets until a final award has been rendered in this case.

...

84. If Respondent were to prevail, it would be in a position to obtain payment of the full amount owing to it, specially taking into account the security in favor of Respondent to be provided by Claimants according to directions further issued under this Order. If, on the other hand, Claimants were to prevail, Respondent would probably face a claim for lower damages than if GEM's activities had been terminated; this is not an insignificant factor, considering Respondent's tight budgetary constraints.

85. On balance, the Tribunal concludes that there is considerable advantage for both parties in the issuance of interim measures of protection.

86. However, while granting Claimants the requested protection from immediate payment of the WPT and from seizure of or liens upon GEM's assets, the Tribunal also understands Respondent's concern that, at the end of the process, it should not be 'thrown the keys' of GEM with assets worth significantly less than the amount of the WPT owing. Hence, its request that, if Claimants' request for interim measures were to be accepted, an escrow account should be established where the full amount of the WPT owing would be deposited until a final award.

87. The Tribunal finds that the Respondent's concern underlying its request in that regard is legitimate but not that setting up an escrow account is the only alternative to address it.

88. If Respondent were to prevail, it would not find itself without possibility of realizing at least part of its tax claim upon GEM's assets, if that company would not be able to pay the whole sum out of its own liquidities. Respondent itself has recognized that GEM's assets currently represent close to 50% of its tax claim, Claimants arguing that those assets are worth significantly more. The present Order provides that those assets and the revenues from future production should remain in Mongolia until a final award has been rendered.

89. In those circumstances, taking into account the value of GEM's assets inside Mongolia, the restrictions in that regard imposed by the Tribunal in the present Order and that GEM's business prospects are likely to improve since it will be free from the WPT burden so long as the present Order remains in place, it does not appear necessary that the security to be provided by Claimants should cover the full value of the claimed WPT thus, limiting it to about 50% of that amount would be sufficient. At the same time, taking into account GEM's inability to pay the full amount immediately, a schedule of monthly payments by Claimants into the escrow account would be a reasonable solution. Moreover, such payments could be reduced or increased depending on reasonable proof as to the evolution of GEM's business.

90. Article 26 of the UNCITRAL Rules does not mandate any specific type of security. An escrow account is not the exclusive measure of protection from which Respondent could benefit. Different measures with equivalent results can also be considered. The Tribunal is retaining one such measure: the provision of a bank guarantee having the same effect.

The tribunal in *Paushok* v. *Mongolia* may have considered its approach to have been an 'internationally recognised' one. Yet the absence of any further explanation for how it arrived at the test which it adopted has drawn comment.

J. Matthews and K. Stewart, 'Time to Evaluate the Standards for Issuance of Interim Measures of Protection in International Investment Arbitration' (2009) 25 *Arb. Int'l* 529, 544, 546, 551

The authors disagree with the learned tribunal in *Paushok* v. *Mongolia* in respect of the proper measure of likely success on the merits as a factor in determining whether to grant interim measures. That tribunal asserted that it needed 'to decide only that the claims made are not, on their face, frivolous or obviously outside the competence of the Tribunal' (Interim Order, para. 9). Whether or not it came to the correct conclusion in the case before it, this standard introduces far too much opportunity for inappropriate and premature interference by a panel of international arbitrators in the public affairs of sovereign nations. Now that this Interim Order is in the public domain, this loose language should not be relied upon by other parties or tribunals.

...

The authors contend that a better standard was actually set forth in the holding of the Occidental decision on provisional measures. After an exhaustive analysis of Occidental's claim for specific performance, that tribunal's holding was as follows ... :

> 86. In conclusion, it is the Tribunal's view that the Claimants have not established a strongly arguable case that there exists a right to specific performance where a natural resources concession agreement has been terminated or cancelled by a sovereign State. The view of the Tribunal at this stage of the proceedings is that no such right exists. As a result, the Claimants have failed to establish that it would be appropriate for the Tribunal to grant a provisional measure such as the one sought by the Claimants pursuant to their 'third-party notice' request.

The authors believe that before the tribunal entered an interim award that deprived Mongolia, a functioning democracy, of critical tax revenues from one of the largest mining companies in the country, for an indeterminate length of time, claimants should have been obligated to prove at least a strongly arguable case.

...

Some jurisdictions require the posting of adequate security by the party seeking interim relief as a condition to granting the relief. Although not specifically listing it as one criterion it considered, the tribunal in *Paushok* v. *Mongolia* was clearly influenced by the need to make certain there was adequate security to protect both parties as it fashioned the complicated escrow procedures.

CONCLUSION

The law on provisional measures will no doubt continue to evolve. That evolution will be watched closely due to the practical importance of the subject. Part of the current uncertainty may be due, ultimately, to differences in national approach as well as an acceptable degree of divergence between tribunals dealing with the individual facts before them, but it is important to keep in mind that there are also differences which lie plainly in the rules applied by investment tribunals. A major difference in particular between ICSID and other forms of investment arbitration ought to be mentioned in closing. An ICSID tribunal may grant interim relief on its own initiative. While Article 26(1) of the UNCITRAL Arbitration Rules states that the tribunal may only grant relief 'at the request of a party', Article 47 of the ICSID Convention states that: 'Except as the parties otherwise agree, the Tribunal may, if it considers that the circumstances so require, recommend any provisional measures.' When such points are considered, it becomes difficult to say that the ICSID regime is necessarily more sensitive to the concerns of host States.

QUESTIONS

1. Assume that *ETI Euro Telecom* had concerned not an ICSID arbitration, but an arbitration applying the UNCITRAL Arbitration Rules. Should the Court of Appeal have decided differently?
2. What factors have tribunals taken into account in deciding whether to grant interim measures to halt criminal prosecution by the host State against the claimant? In this regard, do ICSID tribunals differ from tribunals applying the UNCITRAL Arbitration Rules?
3. The tribunal in *Paushok* v. *Mongolia* considered that '[i]t is internationally recognized that five standards have to be met before a tribunal will issue an order in support of interim measures'. Has this view been adopted by ICSID arbitral tribunals? Should it be?
4. Can an ICSID tribunal grant relief merely in the form of an Order, or can it make an Award to that effect in keeping with most other arbitration rules? What is the difference, at least in terms of legal effect, between an 'Order' and an 'Award'?

SUGGESTIONS FOR FURTHER READING

1. A. Carlevaris, 'Preliminary Matters: Objections, Bi-furcation, Request for Provisional Measures' in C. Giorgetti (ed.), *Litigating International Investment Disputes* (Leiden: Brill/ Nijhoff, 2014), 173.
2. C. H. Schreuer, L. Malintoppi, A. Reinisch and A. Sinclair (eds), *The ICSID Convention: A Commentary*, 2nd edn (Cambridge University Press, 2009), 757–804.
3. C. Croft, C. Kee and J. Waincymer, *A Guide to the UNCITRAL Arbitration Rules* (Cambridge University Press, 2013), 266–297.
4. J. Matthews and K. Stewart, 'Time to Evaluate the Standards for Issuance of Interim Measures of Protection in International Investment Arbitration' (2009) 25 *Arb Int'l* 529.

10

Protected Investments

CHAPTER OUTLINE

This chapter, which should be read in conjunction with Chapter 11, addresses the first of two principal criteria for a dispute to enter the scope of submission to investment treaty arbitration – the existence of a protected investment. Whether an investment qualifies for treaty protection depends on the definition of a protected investment. This definition can be drawn from the terms of the applicable investment treaty (subjective) and/or from the typical features of investment projects (objective). Section 1 explores the rationale for relying solely on treaty terms to define protected investments. Section 2 considers the basis for and attempts to impart an objective definition, located outside the boundaries of the applicable treaty, to protected investments. Section 3 demonstrates how tribunals eschew voting for subjectivity or objectivity by examining both the treaty and non-treaty definitions of protected investments, eventually arriving at a dual meaning.

INTRODUCTION

In order for a tribunal to establish jurisdiction over a claim brought under an investment treaty, it must be satisfied that the claim concerns a protected investment (the subject matter of this chapter) brought by a protected investor (the subject matter of Chapter 11). Ascertaining the existence of a protected investment becomes one of the earliest and most critical tasks that any arbitral tribunal constituted pursuant to an investment treaty performs. While defining 'investment', by no means a legal term of art, may seem straightforward, reality tells a different story. Disagreement among arbitral tribunals and academic commentators over where the definition of a protected investment is located has led to divergent definitional approaches.

One approach locates the definition of protected investments in the applicable investment treaty. Barring the rare outlier,[1] the majority of investment treaties that are currently in force supply an asset-based definition of investments that qualify for treaty protection.

---

[1] Convention between the Government of the French Republic and the Government of the Federal Socialist Republic of Yugoslavia on the Protection of Investments (signed 28 March 1974, entered into force 3 March 1975).

According to this approach, the definition of protected investments is subjective to the Contracting States to an investment treaty. What a protected investment is under an investment treaty is determined by following the basic canons of treaty interpretation found in Articles 31 and 32 of the Vienna Convention on the Law of Treaties (VCLT).[2] As different Contracting States can agree on different definitions of protected investments in different investment treaties, an investment that may qualify for protection under one treaty may not qualify under another.

A second approach, which is less commonly seen, locates the definition of protected investments exclusively in traits that large-scale investments typically bear. These include significant capital contribution, a certain duration of performance, the assumption of risk and, more controversially, contribution to the host State's economic development. As an investment was first tested against a list of objective criteria in *Salini Costruttori SpA and Another* v. *Morocco*,[3] these criteria have since been labelled 'the *Salini* test'.[4] Investments that do not satisfy one or more prongs of the *Salini* test will not qualify for treaty protection, regardless of what the treaty definition of protected investments stipulates. Under this approach, the tribunal will not even consider the treaty definition of protected investments.

A third approach combines both the subjective and objective definitional approaches to propose a 'dual test' for ascertaining if an investment qualifies for treaty protection.[5] Despite its apparent popularity, the propriety of ascribing a dual meaning to protected investment is debatable. Unless the terms of the applicable investment treaty are deficient for the purpose of determining whether a protected investment exists, there may be little justification for venturing beyond the four corners of the treaty to supplement or suppress the subjective meaning of a protected investment.

1. THE SUBJECTIVE MEANING OF PROTECTED INVESTMENTS

States are at liberty to agree on a bilateral or multilateral basis the genres of investments on which they wish to confer treaty protection, and correspondingly the types of disputes they consent to submit to arbitration.[6] If the investment in question is not recognised as a protected investment under the treaty, consent to arbitrate a dispute arising from the investment is not established.

Additionally, States often agree in their investment treaties to arbitrate disputes arising from protected investments under the auspices of the International Centre for the Settlement of Investment Disputes (ICSID). When a tribunal is appointed in accordance

---

[2] Signed 23 May 1969, entered into force 27 January 1980, 1155 UNTS 331.
[3] ICSID Case No. ARB/00/4, Decision on Jurisdiction, 23 July 2001 (Briner, Cremades, Fadlallah), para. 52.
[4] See below, Sections 2.1, 3.1 and 3.2.
[5] C. H. Schreuer, L. Malintoppi, A. Reinisch and A. Sinclair (eds), *The ICSID Convention: A Commentary*, 2nd edn (Cambridge University Press, 2009), para. 124.
[6] See, generally, J. D. Mortenson, 'The Meaning of "Investment": ICSID's *Travaux* and the Domain of International Investment Law' (2010) 51 *Harvard ILJ* 257.

with the provisions in the underlying treaty and the ICSID Convention,[7] its jurisdictional competence is set out in the underlying treaty's scope of submission to arbitration, *as well as* in Article 25(1) of the ICSID Convention. One example of a bilateral investment treaty (BIT) whose arbitration clause refers to ICSID is the 1981 Agreement between the Government of the United Kingdom of Great Britain and Northern Ireland and the Government of Malaysia for the Promotion and Protection of Investments (UK–Malaysia BIT).[8]

UK–Malaysia BIT, Art. 7(1) (emphasis added)

Each Contracting Party hereby consents to submit to the International Centre for the Settlement of Investment Disputes (hereinafter referred to as 'the Centre') for settlement by conciliation or arbitration under the Convention on the Settlement of Investment Disputes between States and Nationals of Other States opened for signature at Washington on 18 March 1965 any legal dispute arising between that Contracting Party and a national or company of the other Contracting Party concerning *an investment* of the latter in the territory of the former.

ICSID Convention, Art. 25(1) (emphasis added)

The jurisdiction of the Centre shall extend to any legal dispute arising directly out of *an investment*, between a Contracting State (or any constituent subdivision or agency of a Contracting State designated to the Centre by that State) and a national of another Contracting State, which the parties to the dispute consent in writing to submit to the Centre. When the parties have given their consent, no party may withdraw its consent unilaterally.

Although both Article 7(1) of the UK–Malaysia BIT and Article 25(1) of the ICSID Convention list the existence of 'an investment' as a condition precedent to a tribunal's exercise of jurisdiction over a dispute, only the UK–Malaysia BIT articulates what an 'investment' is. The Contracting States to the ICSID Convention considered but were unable to reach a consensus on a definition of 'investment'.[9] The eventual decision to omit any definition of 'investment' from Article 25(1) by a 'very substantial majority' of delegates[10] paved the way for a plurality of definitions of 'investment', depending on what Contracting States deemed worthy of protection in a given treaty.

---

[7] Signed 18 March 1965, entered into force 14 October 1966, 575 UNTS 159.

[8] Signed 21 May 1981, entered into force 21 October 1988, footnote omitted.

[9] A. Broches, *Selected Essays: World Bank, ICSID, and Other Subjects of Public and Private International Law* (The Hague: Martinus Nijhoff, 1995), 168; ICSID, 'Legal Committee on Settlement of Investment Disputes: Definition of "Investment", November 27, 1964' in *History of the ICSID Convention* (Washington, DC: ICSID, 1968), 843–844; and ICSID, 'Memorandum of the Meeting of the Committee of the Whole, February 16, 1965' in *History of the ICSID Convention*, para. 65.

[10] Broches, *Selected Essays*, 168.

UK–Malaysia BIT, Art. 1(1)(a)

[E]very kind of asset and in particular, though not exclusively, includes:

(i)   movable and immovable property and any other property rights such as mortgages, liens or pledges;

(ii) shares, stock and debentures of companies or interests in the property of such companies;

(iii) claims to money or to any performance under contract having a financial value;

(iv) intellectual property rights and goodwill; business concessions conferred by law or under contract, including concessions to search for, cultivate, extract or exploit natural resources.

Whether a tribunal can or should be guided exclusively by the definition of protected investments found in Article 1(1)(a) of the UK–Malaysia BIT when establishing its jurisdiction over a dispute was analysed at length in *Malaysian Historical Salvors Sdn Bhd v. Government of Malaysia* (*MHS* v. *Malaysia*). Malaysia challenged the jurisdiction of the tribunal constituted to hear a claim brought by a UK investor for payment due under a marine salvage contract, on the ground that the contract did not qualify as a protected investment under Article 1(1)(a). In the Award on Jurisdiction, the sole arbitrator dismissed the claim for lack of jurisdiction.[11] Without referring to Article 1(1)(a) of the UK–Malaysia BIT, he found that the marine salvage contract did not exhibit any of the 'hallmarks' that protected investments ought to possess.[12]

The investor applied to annul the Award on Jurisdiction pursuant to Article 52(1) of the ICSID Convention.[13] The majority of the Ad Hoc Committee agreed with the investor that the award should be annulled, on the ground that the sole arbitrator had manifestly exceeded his powers by failing to exercise jurisdiction over the dispute (Article 52(1)(b)).[14] In particular, the majority of the Ad Hoc Committee highlighted the sole arbitrator's failure to consider the definition of protected investments under Article 1(1)(a) of the UK–Malaysia BIT. They explained why, notwithstanding the applicability of Article 25(1) of the ICSID Convention, Article 1(1)(a) of the UK–Malaysia BIT remains the first and only port of call for determining if the marine salvage contract was a protected investment.

---

[11] ICSID Case No. ARB/05/10, Award on Jurisdiction, 17 May 2007 (Hwang), para. 146.

[12] These 'hallmarks' are regularity of returns and profits, capital outlay, duration, the assumption of risk and contribution to the economic development of the host State: see *ibid.*, Award on Jurisdiction, paras 108–123.

[13] Article 52(1) provides: 'Either party may request annulment of the award by an application in writing addressed to the Secretary-General on one or more of the following grounds: (a) that the Tribunal was not properly constituted; (b) that the Tribunal has manifestly exceeded its powers; (c) that there was corruption on the part of a member of the Tribunal; (d) that there has been a serious departure from a fundamental rule of procedure; or (e) that the award has failed to state the reasons on which it is based.'

[14] *MHS* v. *Malaysia*, Decision on the Application for Annulment, 16 April 2009 (Schwebel, Tomka, Shahabuddeen (dissenting)), para. 80.

Malaysian Historical Salvors Sdn Bhd v. Malaysia, ICSID Case No. ARB/05/10, Decision on the Application for Annulment, 16 April 2009 (Schwebel, Tomka, Shahabuddeen (dissenting)), paras 58–62, 71, 73–74 (footnotes omitted)

58. At issue in this case is the meaning of the treaty term 'investment' as that term is used in Article 25(1) of the ICSID Convention – but also in Article 1 of the Agreement between the Government of the United Kingdom of Great Britain and Northern Ireland and the Government of Malaysia for the Promotion and Protection of Investments because that instrument is the medium through which the Contracting States involved have given their consent to the exercise of jurisdiction of ICSID.

59. Article 1 of that Agreement defines 'investment' capaciously.

For the purpose of this Agreement

(1) (a) 'investment' means every kind of asset and in particular, though not exclusively, includes:

...

    (ii) shares, stock and debentures of companies or interests in the property of such companies;

    (iii) claims to money or to any performance under contract having a financial value;

    (iv) intellectual property rights ... ;

    (v) business concessions conferred ... under contract ...

60. The Contract between the Government of Malaysia and Malaysian Historical Salvors is one of a kind of asset; what is precisely at issue between the Government and the Salvor is a claim to money and to performance under a contract having financial value; the contract involves intellectual property rights; and the right granted to salvage may be treated as a business concession conferred under contract.

61. It follows that, by the terms of the Agreement, and for its purposes, the Contract is an investment. There is no room for another conclusion. The Sole Arbitrator did not reach another considered conclusion in respect of the Agreement. He rather chose to examine, virtually exclusively, the question of whether there was an investment within the meaning of Article 25(1) of the ICSID Convention. Finding that there was not, he found that 'it is unnecessary to discuss whether the Contract is an "investment" under the BIT'. Nevertheless the Sole Arbitrator observed that, 'while the Contract did provide some benefit to Malaysia', there was not 'a sufficient contribution to Malaysia's economic development to qualify as an "investment" for the purposes of Article 25(1) or Article 1(a) of the BIT'. He provided an extensive analysis in support of his conclusion in respect of the ICSID Convention, but none in respect of his conclusion in respect of the BIT. The Committee is unable to see what support the Sole Arbitrator could have mustered to sustain the conclusion that the Contract and its implementation did not constitute an investment within the meaning of that Agreement ... it is clear that the Contract and its performance by the Salvor constitute an investment as that term is defined by the Agreement.

62. Under Article 7 of the Agreement, the sole recourse in the event that a legal dispute between the investor and the host State should arise which is not settled by

agreement between them through pursuit of local remedies or otherwise is reference to the International Centre for Settlement of Investment Disputes. Unlike some other BITs, no third party dispute settlement options are provided in the alternative to ICSID. It follows that, if jurisdiction is found to be absent under the ICSID Convention, the investor is left without international recourse altogether. That result is difficult to reconcile with the intentions of the Governments of Malaysia and the United Kingdom in concluding their Agreement, as those intentions are reflected by the terms of Article 7 as well as the Agreement's inclusive definition of what is an investment. It cannot be accepted that the Governments of Malaysia and the United Kingdom concluded a treaty providing for arbitration of disputes arising under it in respect of investments so comprehensively described, with the intention that the only arbitral recourse provided between a Contracting State and a national of another Contracting State, that of ICSID, could be rendered nugatory by a restrictive definition of a deliberately undefined term of the ICSID Convention, namely, 'investment', as it is found in the provision of Article 25(1). It follows that the Award of the Sole Arbitrator is incompatible with the intentions and specifications of the States immediately concerned, Malaysia and the United Kingdom.

...

71. The preparatory work of the Convention as well as the Report of the Executive Directors thus shows that: (a) deliberately no definition of 'investment' as that term is found in Article 25(1) was adopted; (b) a floor limit to the value of an investment was rejected; (c) a requirement of indefinite duration of an investment or of a duration of no less than five years was rejected; (d) the critical criterion adopted was the consent of the parties. By the terms of their consent, they could define jurisdiction under the Convention. Paragraph 23 of the Report provides that: '[c]onsent of the parties is the cornerstone of the jurisdiction of the Centre. ...' Paragraph 27 imports that the term 'investment' was left undefined 'given the essential requirement of consent by the parties'. It continues that 'States can make known in advance ... the classes of disputes which they would or would not submit to the Centre', i.e., they could specify particularities of their consent.

...

73. While it may not have been foreseen at the time of the adoption of the ICSID Convention, when the number of bilateral investment treaties in force were few, since that date some 2800 bilateral, and three important multilateral, treaties have been concluded, which characteristically define investment in broad, inclusive terms such as those illustrated by the above-quoted Article 1 of the Agreement between Malaysia and the United Kingdom. Some 1700 of those treaties are in force, and the multilateral treaties, particularly the Energy Charter Treaty, which are in force, of themselves endow ICSID with an important jurisdictional reach. It is those bilateral and multilateral treaties which today are the engine of ICSID's effective jurisdiction. To ignore or depreciate the importance of the jurisdiction they bestow upon ICSID, and rather to embroider upon questionable interpretations of the term 'investment' as found in Article 25(1) of the Convention, risks crippling the institution.

74. In the light of this history of the preparation of the ICSID Convention and of the foregoing analysis of the Report of the Executive Directors in adopting it, the Committee finds that the failure of the Sole Arbitrator even to consider, let alone apply, the definition of investment as it is contained in the Agreement to be a gross error that gave rise to a manifest failure to exercise jurisdiction.

The rationale proffered by the majority in *MHS* v. *Malaysia* for according a subjective meaning to protected investments was rejected by the dissenting member of the Ad Hoc Committee. Judge Shahabuddeen opined that there are 'outer limits' to the definition of protected investments that cannot be deduced by looking at the text of the treaty alone.[15] These 'outer limits' ensure that the notion of protected investments is not rendered 'meaningless' by an overly capacious treaty definition.[16] However, as Ho observes below, it is questionable whether the 'outer limits' of protected investments can, as Judge Shahabuddeen claims, be read into Article 25(1) of the ICSID Convention. Moreover, even if treaty definitions of protected investments are indeed overly capacious, Judge Shahabuddeen's concern appears to be addressed by newer generation treaties. For example, the 2009 Association of South East Asian Nations (ASEAN) Comprehensive Investment Agreement (ACIA),[17] to which Malaysia is a party, contains a definition of protected investments that is noticeably more precise than that in the 1981 UK–Malaysia BIT.

J. Ho, 'The Meaning of "Investment" in ICSID Arbitrations' (2010) 26(4) *Arb. Int'l* 633, 642–643 (footnotes omitted)

Judge Shahabuddeen took the 'view that outer limits' to the meaning of 'investment' in Article 25(1) of the ICSID Convention were necessary, despite the inability of the delegates to agree on a single definition, in order to preserve 'fundamental, if residual, ideas' that were subscribed to at the drafting phase of the ICSID Convention. These ideas represent 'ultimate boundaries' within which contracting states can exercise their prerogative to define 'investment'. The extent to which this view appeals is contingent on the articulation of a 'core meaning' of 'investment' that distinguishes an 'investment' from an ordinary commercial transaction ... One commentator has argued that the refusal of the ICSID Secretary-General to register a request for arbitration, when the cause of action arose from a contract for the sale of goods, is proof that 'investment' in Article 25(1) of the ICSID Convention has what is akin to a 'core meaning'. That the claim was refused registration,

---

[15] Dissenting Opinion of Judge Mohamed Shahabuddeen, 16 April 2009 (Schwebel, Tomka, Shahabuddeen (dissenting)), paras 7–8.

[16] *Ibid.*

[17] Signed 29 February 2009, entered into force 29 March 2012.

despite the fact that the contract of sale could have constituted an 'investment' according to the BIT, confirms this theory. However, it is one thing to observe that an aggrieved national of a contracting state is not entitled to submit any dispute it pleases to ICSID arbitration, and another to surmise from a refusal on the part of ICSID to register a claim that a definition of 'investment', capable of general application, was intended and readily ascertainable. All that can be said of the refusal to register is that the ICSID Secretary-General considered the request for arbitration to be 'manifestly outside the jurisdiction of the Centre'; it does not as a result enumerate what an 'investment' is nor give rise to a 'core meaning' of 'investment'. The fact remains that 'no explanation of the concept of investment' is offered in the ICSID Convention, which makes reasoning from silence speculative.

ACIA, Art. 4(a) and (c)

(a) 'covered investment' means, with respect to a Member State, an investment in its territory of an investor of any other Member State in existence as of the date of entry into force of this Agreement or established, acquired or expanded thereafter, and has been admitted according to its laws, regulations, and national policies, and where applicable, specifically approved in writing[1] by the competent authority of a Member State;

[Fn 1: For the purpose of protection, the procedures relating to specific approval in writing shall be specific as in Annex 1 (Approval in Writing).]

...

(c) 'investment'[2] means every kind of asset, owned or controlled, by an investor, including but not limited to the following:

[Fn 2: Where an asset lacks the characteristics of an investment, that asset is not an investment regardless of the form it may take. The characteristics of an investment include the commitment of capital, the expectation of gain or profit, or the assumption of risk.]

   (i) movable and immovable property and other property rights such as mortgages, liens or pledges;

   (ii) shares, stocks, bonds and debentures and any other forms of participation in a juridical person and rights or interest derived therefrom;

   (iii) intellectual property rights which are conferred pursuant to the laws and regulations of each Member State;

   (iv) claims to money or to any contractual performance related to a business and having financial value;[3]

[Fn 3: For greater certainty, investment does not mean claims to money that arise solely from:

   (a) commercial contracts for sale of goods or services; or

   (b) the extension of credit in connection with such commercial contracts.]

    (v) rights under contracts, including turnkey, construction, management, production or revenue-sharing contracts; and

    (vi) business concessions required to conduct economic activities and having financial value conferred by law or under a contract, including any concessions to search, cultivate, extract or exploit natural resources.

The term 'investment' also includes amounts yielded by investments, in particular, profits, interest, capital gains, dividend, royalties and fees. Any alteration of the form in which assets are invested or reinvested shall not affect their classification as investment.

The subjective meaning of protected investments is found in the applicable investment treaty, usually presented as a non-exhaustive list of forms that investments can take. The generality of treaty definitions has given rise to the concern that the qualifying threshold for protected investments may be too low. This concern was amply fleshed out in *MHS* v. *Malaysia*, which saw disagreement between the majority of the Ad Hoc Committee and the sole arbitrator, as well as within the Ad Hoc Committee, over the sufficiency of relying on the treaty definition of protected investments to establish a tribunal's jurisdictional competence. The sharp division of views calls for a serious look at the trend of defining protected investments independently of the text of the underlying treaty.

2. THE OBJECTIVE MEANING OF PROTECTED INVESTMENTS

Given the potential for over-inclusiveness when a treaty's definition of protected investments appears extremely broad, arbitral tribunals have seen fit to develop, propose and apply tests to determine if the dispute concerns a protected investment. These tests, of which the *Salini* test is the forerunner and the most well known, are designed to sift out the kinds of investments which are the proper beneficiaries of treaty protection from all other types of transactions that may nominally satisfy the treaty definition, but actually fall outside treaty coverage. Although the tribunal in *MHS* v. *Malaysia* was not the first to find that protected investments have an objective meaning, it remains the first and only tribunal to base the existence of a protected investment purely on a set of objective criteria. In the words of the tribunal, '[h]aving concluded that the Contract is not an "investment" within the meaning of Article 25(1) of the ICSID Convention ... it is unnecessary to discuss whether the Contract is an "investment" under the BIT'.[18]

    Attempts at devising an objective meaning of protected investments are not limited to tribunals obliged to apply Article 25(1) of the ICSID Convention. Even tribunals unfettered by Article 25(1) have tried to impart an objective meaning to protected investments. In this section, we will first examine the various tests proposed in the context of ICSID arbitrations by *Salini* v. *Morocco*, *Consorzio Groupement LESI Dipenta* v. *République Algérienne Démocratique et Populaire* and *LESI SpA et Astaldi SpA* v. *République*

---

[18] *MHS* v. *Malaysia*, Award on Jurisdiction (Hwang), para. 148.

Algérienne Démocratique et Populaire (*LESI Astaldi v. Algeria*),[19] and *Phoenix Action, Ltd v. Czech Republic* (Section 2.1),[20] followed by the test proposed in the context of non-ICSID arbitrations by *Romak SA (Switzerland) v. Uzbekistan* (Section 2.2).[21]

The following awards are presented in chronological order. To better appreciate if subsequent tests modify or are merely updated expressions of the classic *Salini* test, we recommend reading the excerpts of these awards in the order that they are presented.

2.1 The ICSID Tests

> ### *Salini Costruttori SpA and Italstrade S.p.A. v. Kingdom of Morocco*, ICSID Case No. ARB/00/4, Decision on Jurisdiction, 23 July 2001 (Briner, Cremades, Fadlallah), para. 52 (emphasis added)
>
> The Tribunal notes that there have been almost no cases where the notion of investment within the meaning of Article 25 of the Convention was raised. However, it would be inaccurate to consider that the requirement that a dispute be 'in direct relation to an investment' is diluted by the consent of the Contracting Parties ...
>
> The doctrine generally considers that investment infers: [i] *contributions*, [ii] *a certain duration of performance of the contract and* [iii] *a participation in the risks of the transaction* ... In reading the Convention's preamble, one may add [iv] *the contribution to the economic development of the host State of the investment* as an additional condition.

In reality, these various elements may be interdependent. Thus, the risks of the transaction may depend on the contributions and the duration of performance of the contract. As a result, these various criteria should be assessed globally even if, for the sake of reasoning, the Tribunal considers them individually here.

> ### *Consorzio Groupement LESI Dipenta v. République Algérienne Démocratique et Populaire*, ICSID Case No. ARB/03/8, Sentence, 10 January 2005 (Tercier, Faurès, Gaillard), Part II, paras 13(ii), (iii) and (iv)
>
> ### *LESI SpA and Astaldi SpA v. Algeria*, ICSID Case No. ARB/05/3, Decision, 12 July 2006 (Tercier, Hanotiau, Gaillard), paras 72(ii), (iii) and (iv)
>
> 13(ii)/72(ii). Both Parties cite the *Salini* decision. Contrary to what the Respondent claims, this is not at all an isolated decision; it is situated amongst other contemporary arbitral awards which have adopted a relatively generous definition of [protected] investments

---

[19] ICSID Case No. ARB/03/8, Sentence, 10 January 2005 (Tercier, Faurès, Gaillard); ICSID Case No. ARB/05/3, Decision, 12 July 2006 (Tercier, Hanotiau, Gaillard).

[20] ICSID Case No. ARB/06/5, Award, 15 April 2009 (Stern, Bucher, Fernández-Armesto).

[21] *Romak SA (Switzerland) v. Uzbekistan*, PCA Case No. AA280, Award, 26 November 2009 (Mantilla-Serrano, Rubins, Molfessis).

(*Fedax N.V.* v. *The Republic of Venezuela*, Decision of the Tribunal on Objections to Jurisdiction, 11 July 1997, JDI 1999.278[;] *CSOB* v. *The Slovak Republic*, Decision of the Tribunal on Objections to Jurisdiction, 24 May 1999, ICSID Rev. 1999, p. 251; *SGS* v. *Islamic Republic of Pakistan*, Decision of the Tribunal on Objections to Jurisdiction, 6 August 2003, 19 Int'l Arb. Rep. C1 (February 2004)).

13(iii)/72(iii). These decisions do not provide any clear guidelines, but appear, on the contrary, to have been decided on a case by case basis. The arbitral tribunal observes that these decisions generate several objective criteria, of a nature that can offer legal stability.

13(iv)/72(iv). Though it appears consistent with the objective of the [ICSID] Convention, that a contract, in order to constitute an investment for the purpose of treaty protection, must meet the following conditions:

(a) that the contracting party must make a contribution in the host State,

(b) that this contribution must be for a certain duration,

(c) that the contribution poses a certain risk for the contributor.

However, it does not appear necessary for the contribution to meet any special requirement of aiding the economic development of the host State, a condition which is in any case difficult to establish and implicitly covered by the three conditions above.[22]

Phoenix Action Ltd v. *Czech Republic*, ICSID Case No. ARB/06/5, Award, 15 April 2009 (Stern, Bucher, Fernández-Armesto), paras 83–85, 101, 106–107, 114 (footnotes omitted)

83. ICSID case law has developed various criteria in order to identify the pertinent elements of the notion of investment. The definition most frequently referred to relies on what has come to be known as the '*Salini* test', according to which the notion of investment implies the presence of the following elements: (i) a contribution of money or other assets of economic value, (ii) a certain duration, (iii) an element of risk, and (iv) a contribution to the host State's development ...

84. There are some divergent approaches concerning the fourth criterion of the definition of an investment (i.e., the contribution to the host State's development). Some tribunals, adopting the '*Salini* test', insist on its importance, even if analyzing it with flexibility. Some tribunals have shown scepticism toward this criterion. For example, in *L.E.S.I. S.p.A. et ASTALDI S.p.A.* v. *Algeria*, the tribunal ignored this element as a separate condition, considering it inherent in the other criteria ...

85. It is the Tribunal's view that the contribution of an international investment to the development of the host State is impossible to ascertain – the more so as there are highly

---

[22] Authors' translation from the original French.

diverging views on what constitutes 'development'. A less ambitious approach should therefore be adopted, centered on the contribution of an international investment to the economy of the host State, which is indeed normally inherent in the mere concept of investment as shaped by the elements of contribution/duration/risk, and should therefore in principle be presumed ...

...

101. In the Tribunal's view, States cannot be deemed to offer access to the ICSID dispute settlement mechanism to investments made in violation of their laws. If a State, for example, restricts foreign investment in a sector of its economy and a foreign investor disregards such restriction, the investment concerned cannot be protected under the ICSID/BIT system. These are illegal investments according to the national law of the host State and cannot be protected through an ICSID arbitral process. And it is the Tribunal's view that this condition – the conformity of the establishment of the investment with the national laws – is implicit even when not expressly stated in the relevant BIT ...

...

106. In the Tribunal's view, States cannot be deemed to offer access to the ICSID dispute settlement mechanism to investments not made in good faith. The protection of international investment arbitration cannot be granted if such protection would run contrary to the general principles of international law, among which the principle of good faith is of utmost importance.

107. The principle of good faith has long been recognized in public international law, as it is also in all national legal systems. This principle requires parties 'to deal honestly and fairly with each other, to represent their motives and purposes truthfully, and to refrain from taking unfair advantage ...' This principle governs the relations between States, but also the legal rights and duties of those seeking to assert an international claim under a treaty. Nobody shall abuse the rights granted by treaties, and more generally, every rule of law includes an implied clause that it should not be abused ...

...

114. To summarize all the requirements for an investment to benefit from the international protection of ICSID, the Tribunal considers that the following six elements have to be taken into account:

    1 – a contribution in money or other assets;
    2 – a certain duration;
    3 – an element of risk;
    4 – an operation made in order to develop an economic activity in the host State;
    5 – assets invested in accordance with the laws of the host State;
    6 – assets invested *bona fide*.

2.2 The Non-ICSID Test

Romak SA (Switzerland) v. Uzbekistan, PCA Case No. AA280, Award, 26 November 2009 (Mantilla-Serrano, Rubins, Molfessis), paras 205–207 (footnotes omitted, original emphasis)

205. There is some debate as to whether, from a purely subjective perspective – and by analogy to the freedom of contract normally enjoyed by private parties – an investment will consist of whatever the contracting States have decided to label as such in the treaty they have concluded. Operating under the UNCITRAL Rules, this Arbitral Tribunal does not need to engage in a discussion of the interplay of the ICSID Convention and the instrument providing consent to arbitration. However, we are of the view that contracting States are free to deem any kind of asset or economic transaction to constitute an investment as subject to treaty protection. Contracting States can even go as far as stipulating that a 'pure' one-off sales contract constitutes an investment, even if such a transaction would not normally be covered by the ordinary meaning of the term 'investment'. However, in such cases, the wording of the instrument in question must leave no room for doubt that the intention of the contracting States was to accord to the term 'investment' an extraordinary and counterintuitive meaning. As explained above, the wording of the BIT does not permit the Arbitral Tribunal to infer such an intent in the present case.

206. The point of departure for the Arbitral Tribunal remains the ordinary meaning of the term 'investment' (see, *supra*, ¶177), which entails expenditure or contribution, as well as the purpose of obtaining an economic benefit the existence and extent of which is, by definition, uncertain. However, as stated above (see, *supra*, ¶¶ 181, 188 and 189), the Arbitral Tribunal needs to construe the term 'investments' in its context and in light of the object and purpose of the BIT. In this regard, the Arbitral Tribunal attaches importance to the BIT's preamble (see, *supra*, ¶¶ 181 and 189), and also to the definition of the term 'returns' (Article 1(3)), the repeated references to 'territory' in relation with the investment (particularly at Article 2), and the description of the protection offered at Article 3(1), all of which denote an economic activity involving some permanence or duration in relation to the host State.

207. The Arbitral Tribunal therefore considers that the term 'investments' under the BIT has an inherent meaning (irrespective of whether the investor resorts to ICSID or UNCITRAL arbitral proceedings) entailing a *contribution* that extends over a *certain period of time* and that involves some *risk*. The Arbitral Tribunal is further comforted in its analysis by the reasoning adopted by other arbitral tribunals (see, *supra*, ¶¶ 198 – 204) which consistently incorporates contribution, duration and risk as hallmarks of an 'investment'. By their nature, asset types enumerated in the BIT's non-exhaustive list may exhibit these hallmarks. But if an asset does not correspond to the inherent definition of 'investment', the fact that it falls within one of the categories listed in Article 1 does not transform it into an 'investment'. In the general formulation of the tribunal in *Azinian*, '*labeling ... is no substitute for analysis*'.

The foregoing excerpts permit four observations. First, tribunals proposing objective criteria for protected investments in ICSID arbitrations seem to treat these criteria as self-evident. Given how these very tribunals simultaneously emphasise the lack of a sizeable body of arbitral awards from which these criteria can be distilled, the assured deductions from silence are remarkable.

Second, dissatisfaction with the *Salini* test has been directed at the criterion of 'contribution to the economic development of the host State'. The tribunals in the two *LESI* awards abandoned this criterion altogether, whereas the tribunal in *Phoenix* v. *Czech Republic* watered down the criterion to one of 'develop[ing] an economic activity in the host State'. Although subsequent tribunals have not always adopted the *Salini* test in full, constant reference to the criteria laid down by the tribunal in *Salini* v. *Morocco*, in order to subtract from (the *LESI* awards) or supplement them (the *Phoenix* award), reflects the usefulness of the *Salini* test as a basic, modifiable template. There is arguably some common ground, even if tribunals partial to an objective meaning of protected investments do not agree on the importance of each and every criterion.

Third, although the tribunal in *Romak* v. *Uzbekistan* did not formally apply the *Salini* test in its final analysis, it made extensive reference to the *Salini* test in its award.[23] The eventual three-prong test constructed by the tribunal from the text of the underlying investment treaty, namely contribution, duration and risk, mirrors the three-prong test in the *LESI* awards. The latter is a progeny of *Salini* minus the criterion of 'contribution to the economic development of the host State'. This suggests that although the *Salini* test was developed to define 'investment' in Article 25(1) of the ICSID Convention, its components are arguably sufficiently generic to guide tribunals in non-ICSID arbitrations.[24]

Fourth, and finally, unlike the tribunal in *MHS* v. *Malaysia*, the tribunals in *Salini* v. *Morocco*, *LESI Dipenta* v. *Algeria* and *LESI Astaldi* v. *Algeria*, *Phoenix* v. *Czech Republic* and *Romak* v. *Uzbekistan* verified the existence or non-existence of a protected investment against the treaty definition, as well as their preferred test of objective criteria. In some cases, the subjective meaning was overridden by the objective meaning of a protected investment. An investment that was eligible for protection according to the treaty definition was deemed ineligible after applying a variant of the *Salini* test. For example, a one-off wheat supply contract failed to meet the criteria of contribution, duration and risk in *Romak* v. *Uzbekistan*. Additionally, the calculated acquisition of Israeli nationality in order for an investment to benefit from protection under the Czech Republic–Israel BIT[25] ran afoul of the criterion of good faith in *Phoenix* v. *Czech Republic*. As Section 3 will demonstrate in

---

[23] *Romak* v. *Uzbekistan*, Award, 26 November 2009 (Mantilla-Serrano, Rubins, Molfessis), paras 193–204.

[24] Cf. *Anatolie Stati and Others* v. *Kazakhstan*, SCC Arbitration V (116/2010), Award, 19 December 2013 (Böckstiegel, Haigh, Lebedev), para. 806. The source treaty of a tribunal's obligation to discern the 'ordinary meaning' of an 'investment' (Art. 31(1) of the VCLT) is different in ICSID and non-ICSID arbitrations. In ICSID arbitrations, the source treaty is the ICSID Convention. In non-ICSID arbitrations, the source treaty is the applicable investment treaty. This is why the tribunal in *Romak* v. *Uzbekistan* developed its own test with reference to the text of the Switzerland–Uzbekistan BIT, rather than simply modifying and applying the *Salini* test, which was developed to define 'investment' in Art. 25(1) of the ICSID Convention.

[25] Agreement between the Government of the Czech Republic and the Government of the State of Israel for the Reciprocal Promotion and Protection of Investments, 23 September 1997.

greater detail, pairing the subjective treaty definition with an objective test appears to plug any loopholes that a typically capacious treaty definition of protected investments may present, and has gained considerable traction in investment treaty arbitration.

The *Salini* test, developed to define 'investment' in Article 25(1) of the ICSID Convention, is not set in stone. Subsequent tribunals have seen fit to modify it, resulting in variants on a classic. The criteria that tribunals partial to an objective meaning of protected investments generally agree on are contribution, duration and risk. The criterion that has divided tribunals is the requirement that an investment contributes to the economic development of the host State. Regarded as indispensable by Judge Shahabuddeen in his sharp dissent in *MHS* v. *Malaysia*, this criterion has been largely sidelined by other tribunals due to difficulty of proof.

3. THE DUAL MEANING OF PROTECTED INVESTMENTS

Although the propriety of checking a treaty definition of protected investments with a test that originates outside the treaty is debatable in principle, it appears to be taken for granted by many arbitral tribunals in practice. However, there is uneven commitment to a dual meaning of protected investments. A number of tribunals, like the *Phoenix* v. *Czech Republic* tribunal, regard the so-called objective criteria as binding. Accordingly, an investment that does not meet the cumulative objective criteria is ineligible for treaty protection even if it meets the treaty definition of a protected investment (Section 3.1). Other tribunals regard a given set of objective criteria as illustrative, rather than binding. If an investment does not display any of the illustrative traits of protected investments, it may, but will not automatically, be denied treaty protection (Section 3.2).

There is admittedly a fine line separating the analyses of tribunals which regard objective criteria as binding and those which regard the same as illustrative. As the choice of one or the other is rarely made explicit, much has to be inferred from the manner in which a tribunal discusses objective characteristics of protected investments. The difficulty of this task is enhanced in the wake of *Salini* v. *Morocco* because tribunals have the convenience of adopting or adapting the *Salini* test, which has become synonymous with a standard checklist. From the vast pool of arbitral awards to date, the following six excerpted awards have been selected for their ability to convey, in as precise a manner as possible, the distinction between relying on objective criteria of protected investments as non-derogable jurisdictional requirements, and for illustrative purposes.

3.1 Binding Objective Criteria

Ioannis Kardassopoulos v. *Georgia*, ICSID Case No. ARB/05/18, Decision on Jurisdiction, 6 July 2007 (Fortier, Orrego Vicuña, Watts), paras 116, 122, 124 (emphasis added)

116. The ICSID Convention does not define the term 'investment'. ICSID tribunals have, however, developed a set of conjunctive criteria to determine whether an investment was

made within the meaning of the Convention. There *must* be: (i) a contribution, (ii) a 'certain duration of performance of the contract', (iii) a 'participation in the risks of the transaction', and (iv) a contribution to the host State's economic development [referencing *Salini Costrutorri S.p.A. and Italstrade S.p.A. v. Morocco*, ICSID Case No. ARB/00/4, Decision on Jurisdiction, 23 July 2001 (Briner, Cremades, Fadlallah), para. 52, and *Fedax NV v. Republic of Venezuela*, ICSID Case No. ARB/96/3, Decision on Objections to Jurisdiction, 11 July 1997 (Orrego Vicuña, Heth, Owen), para. 43.].

...

121. The Tribunal recalls that Article 1(6) of the ECT defines investment as follows:
"'Investment' means every kind of asset, owned or controlled directly or indirectly by an Investor and includes:

...

(b) a company or business enterprise, or shares, stock or other forms of equity participation in a company or business enterprise, and bonds and other debt of a company or business enterprise."

122. As for the BIT, Article 1 thereof defines investment as follows:
"'Investment' means every kind of asset and in particular, though not exclusively, includes:

...

(b) shares in and stock and debentures of a company and any other form of participation in a company.'

...

124. The Tribunal is of the view that, in the present case, the indirect ownership of shares by Claimant constitutes an 'investment' under the BIT and the ECT.

Toto Costruzioni Generali SpA v. Lebanon, ICSID Case No. ARB/07/12, Decision on Jurisdiction, 11 September 2009 (van Houtte, Feliciani, Moghaizel), paras 66, 69, 81, 84–85 (footnotes omitted)

66. ... [T]he Tribunal agrees with Lebanon that, for this Tribunal to have jurisdiction, it is not sufficient that the dispute arises out of an investment as per the meaning of 'investment' given by the parties in the Treaty, but also as per the meaning of 'investment' under the ICSID Convention.

...

69. The notion of 'investment' under the ICSID system has been clarified by legal scholars and jurisprudence. A number of legal scholars and some ICSID Tribunals follow the four criteria to be found in *Salini Costruttori S.p.A. and Italstrade S.p.A. v. Kingdom of Morocco* to determine whether a transaction qualifies as an 'investment' in the sense of the ICSID Convention. These four criteria, sometimes called the *Salini* test, comprise a) duration, b) a contribution on the part of the investor, c) a contribution to the development of the host state, and d) some risk taking.

...

81. The Tribunal finds that, regarding the issue of investment, the requirements for jurisdiction under the ICSID Convention are fulfilled in this case. However, the Tribunal wishes to make clear that it does not reach this conclusion strictly on the basis of the *Salini* test, even if it agrees with Toto that in the present case that test is met, as demonstrated above. The Tribunal deviates from this commonly followed test in a desire to delineate the necessary features of an investment in a way that it considers more appropriate to the present case.

...

84. In the absence of specific criteria or definitions in the ICSID Convention, the underlying concept of investment, which is economical in nature, becomes relevant: it implies an economical operation initiated and conducted by an entrepreneur using its own financial means and at its own financial risk, with the objective of making a profit within a given period of time. It has been argued that 'investment' should include some duration, e.g., a minimum duration of two years, although a shorter duration also may be conceivable, or that the investment should serve the public interest.

85. Additional criteria have been applied in some cases, for example, in *Phoenix v. Czech Republic*, in which the Tribunal added two criteria to have an 'investment' under the ICSID Convention: that assets be invested in accordance with the laws of the host state and that they be invested bona fide. These two criteria, however, are not relevant to the case at hand.

Bernhard Friedrich Arnd Rüdiger von Pezold and Others v. Zimbabwe, ICSID Case No. ARB/10/15, Award, 28 July 2015 (Fortier, Williams, Hwang), paras 284–285, 309, 327 (emphasis added)

284. There is considerable jurisprudence to support the proposition that, although the primary task of an ICSID tribunal is to establish whether an investment exists in accordance with the specific words of the relevant treaty, there may nonetheless be certain inherent characteristics of an investment which assist a tribunal in this task. This is so whether under the ICSID Convention or otherwise.

285. Whatever the position may be on *Salini* as regards the elements to be satisfied, the Tribunal finds that it is rather less clear that the *Salini* test is the authoritative statement on those characteristics. Indeed, there seems to be a move away from *Salini* to a simpler test involving contribution, duration and risk. *All of these characteristics are satisfied in the present case* ...

...

309. Article 11 of the German BIT provides that only disputes 'concerning an investment of [a] national or company [of a Contracting Party] in the territory of the [other] Contracting Party' are protected. Similarly, Article 10 of the Swiss BIT provides that only

disputes 'with respect to investments between a Contracting Party and an investor of the other Contract Party' are protected. The issue here is whether the Claimants' investments satisfy the definition of 'investment' in each respective BIT.

...

327. Based on the foregoing, the Tribunal finds that it has jurisdiction *ratione materiae* under the ICSID Convention, and the relevant BITs.

3.2 Illustrative Objective Criteria

Fedax NV v. Venezuela, ICSID Case No. ARB/96/3, Decision of the Tribunal on Objections to Jurisdiction, 11 July 1997 (Orrego Vicuña, Heth, Owen), paras 30–31, 34 (footnotes omitted)

30. The Tribunal considers that the broad scope of Article 25(1) of the Convention and the ensuing ICSID practice and decisions are sufficient, without more, to require a finding that the Centre's jurisdiction and its own competence are well-founded. In addition, as explained above, loans qualify as an investment within ICSID's jurisdiction, as does, in given circumstances, the purchase of bonds. Since promissory notes are evidence of a loan and a rather typical financial and credit instrument, there is nothing to prevent their purchase from qualifying as an investment under the Convention in the circumstances of a particular case such as this. This conclusion, however, has to be examined next in the context of the specific consent of the parties and other provisions which are controlling in the matter.

31. The Tribunal turns now to a consideration of the relevant terms and provisions of the Agreement between the Kingdom of the Netherlands and the Republic of Venezuela, which is the specific bilateral investment treaty governing the consent to arbitration by the latter Contracting Party ...

...

34. A broad definition of investment such as that included in the Agreement is not at all an exceptional situation. On the contrary, most contemporary bilateral treaties of this kind refer to 'every kind of asset' or to 'all assets', including the listing of examples that can qualify for coverage; claims to money and to any performance having a financial value are prominent features of such listings. This broad approach has also become the standard policy of major economic groupings such as the European Communities. In providing for the protection of investments the EC have included 'all types of assets, tangible and intangible, that have an economic value, including direct or indirect contributions in cash, kind or services invested or received'. Among the transactions listed as investments are 'stocks, bonds, debentures, guarantees or other financial instruments of a company, other firm, government or, other public authority or an international organization; claims to money, goods, services or other performance having economic value'. Since the Kingdom of the Netherlands is a prominent member of the European Communities, it is hardly surprising

that a similar approach has been followed in its bilateral investment treaties. Indeed, only very exceptionally do bilateral investment treaties explicitly relate the definition of the assets or transactions included in this concept to questions such as the existence of a lasting economic relation, or specifically associate titles to money and similar transactions strictly to a concept of investment.

Ceskoslovenska Obchodni Banka AS v. *Slovakia*, ICSID Case No. ARB/97/4, Decision of the Tribunal on Objections to Jurisdiction, 24 May 1999 (Buerganthal, Bernadini, Bucher), paras 76, 78, 90–91 (footnotes omitted)

76. The Slovak Republic submits that loans as such do not qualify as investments under Article 25(1) of the Convention, nor under Article 1 of the BIT. It contends further that the loan in the instant case is not an investment because it did not involve a transfer of resources in the territory of the Slovak Republic. As to the first point, the Tribunal considers that the broad meaning which must be given to the notion of an investment under Article 25(1) of the Convention is opposed to the conclusion that a transaction is not an investment merely because, as a matter of law, it is a loan. This is so, if only because under certain circumstances a loan may contribute substantially to a State's economic development. In this connection, Claimant correctly points out that other ICSID Tribunals have affirmed their competence to deal with the merits of claims based on loan agreements.

...

78. The Slovak Republic contends that the CSOB loan does not constitute an investment. It defines an investment essentially as the acquisition of property or assets through the expenditure of resources by one party (the 'investor') in the territory of a foreign country (the 'host State'), which is expected to produce a benefit on both sides and to offer a return in the future, subject to the uncertainties of the risk involved. While the Slovak Republic argues that the CSOB loan does not meet any elements of the above definition, CSOB submits that its loan qualifies as an investment thereunder. The Tribunal notes, in this connection, that while it is undisputed that CSOB's loan did not cause any funds to be moved or transferred from CSOB to the Slovak Collection Company in the territory of the Slovak Republic, a transaction can qualify as an investment even in the absence of a physical transfer of funds.

...

90. Finally, applying the definition of an investment proffered by the Slovak Republic (para. 78, *supra*), it would seem that the resources provided through CSOB's banking activities in the Slovak Republic were designed to produce a benefit and to offer CSOB a return in the future, subject to an element of risk that is implicit in most economic activities. The Tribunal notes, however, that these elements of the suggested definition, while they tend as a rule to be present in most investments, are not a formal prerequisite for the finding that a transaction constitutes an investment as that concept is understood under the Convention.

91. The Tribunal concludes, accordingly, that CSOB's claim and the related loan facility made available to the Slovak Collection Company are closely connected to the development of CSOB's banking activity in the Slovak Republic and that they qualify as investments within the meaning of the Convention and the BIT.

Biwater Gauff (Tanzania) Ltd v. *Tanzania*, ICSID Case No. ARB/05/22, Award, 24 July 2008 (Hanotiau, Born, Landau), paras 312, 314–316 (footnotes omitted)

312. In the Tribunal's view, there is no basis for a rote, or overly strict, application of the five *Salini* criteria in every case. These criteria are not fixed or mandatory as a matter of law. They do not appear in the ICSID Convention. On the contrary, it is clear from the *travaux préparatoires* of the Convention that several attempts to incorporate a definition of 'investment' were made, but ultimately did not succeed. In the end, the term was left intentionally undefined, with the expectation (*inter alia*) that a definition could be the subject of agreement as between Contracting States. Hence the following oft-quoted passage in the Report of the Executive Directors:

> 'No attempt was made to define the term 'investment' given the essential requirement of consent by the parties, and the mechanism through which Contracting States can make known in advance, if they so desire, the classes of disputes which they would or would not consider submitting to the Centre (Article 25(4)).'

...

314. Further, the *Salini Test* itself is problematic if, as some tribunals have found, the 'typical characteristics' of an investment as identified in that decision are elevated into a fixed and inflexible test, and if transactions are to be presumed excluded from the ICSID Convention unless each of the five criteria are satisfied. This risks the arbitrary exclusion of certain types of transaction from the scope of the Convention. It also leads to a definition that may contradict individual agreements (as here), as well as a developing consensus in parts of the world as to the meaning of 'investment' (as expressed, e.g., in bilateral investment treaties). If very substantial numbers of BITs across the world express the definition of 'investment' more broadly than the *Salini Test*, and if this constitutes any type of international consensus, it is difficult to see why the ICSID Convention ought to be read more narrowly.

315. Equally, the suggestion that the 'special and privileged arrangements established by the Washington Convention can be applied only to the type of investment which the Contracting States to that Convention envisaged' does not, in this Arbitral Tribunal's view, lead to a fixed or autonomous definition of 'investment' which must prevail in all cases, for the 'type of investment' which the Contracting States to the Convention in fact envisaged was an intentionally undefined one, which was susceptible of agreement.

316. The Arbitral Tribunal therefore considers that a more flexible and pragmatic approach to the meaning of 'investment' is appropriate, which takes into account the features identified in *Salini*, but along with all the circumstances of the case, including the nature of the instrument containing the relevant consent to ICSID.

While tribunals in ICSID arbitrations are undoubtedly correct to establish jurisdiction over the dispute at hand under both the applicable treaty as well as the ICSID Convention, it is far less certain if a *Salini*-esque test should supply the controlling definition for protected investments. The hesitation of tribunals in awards like *Biwater Gauff* v. *Tanzania* in deeming any particular set of criteria binding underscores the dilemma faced by arbitrators when searching for legitimate 'outer limits' to the meaning of protected investments. If the meaning of 'investment' in Article 25(1) of the ICSID Convention is to be found in the applicable investment treaty, there is no need to resort to external criteria, binding or otherwise. If the meaning of 'investment' in Article 25(1) of the ICSID Convention is autonomous from any treaty definition, and there is to date no authoritative statement to this effect, then the definition obtained by applying a *Salini*-esque test is controlling. However, articulating *Salini*-esque criteria, but relegating them to illustrative status, tends to obfuscate the issue of whether there are 'outer limits' to the meaning of protected investments, and if there are, where such 'outer limits' should be found. If 'outer limits' are merely illustrative, they become an open list subject to constant change. Flexibility, prized by the *Biwater Gauff* v. *Tanzania* tribunal, can be a double-edged sword. A capacious treaty definition of protected investments has, at the very least, the benefit of certainty. Objective criteria that are tacked onto the treaty definition but applied in an unpredictable, non-committal fashion risk turning the existence of a protected investment into anyone's guess.

When arbitral tribunals ascertain the existence of a protected investment against the treaty definition as well as a set of objective criteria, they assign a dual meaning to protected investments. Of the tribunals that adopt this interpretive logic, some regard the objective criteria (usually a variant of the *Salini* test) as binding, while others regard them as illustrative. The former approach, which is most often seen in ICSID arbitrations, is defensible if 'investment' in Article 25(1) of the ICSID Convention has a meaning that has to be determined separately from 'investment' in the underlying investment treaty. The latter approach is more problematic because it generates considerable uncertainty. Illustrative criteria may sketch a protected investment in the abstract, but there is no way to foretell if a particular criterion suffices to confirm or disqualify an investment as a protected investment.

CONCLUSION

The current weight of arbitral jurisprudence leans in favour of a dual meaning of protected investments, where both the subjective meaning derived from the treaty definition and the objective meaning derived from the application of a *Salini*-esque test are considered. As there is no doctrine of binding precedent in investment arbitration, no tribunal is bound by the *Salini* test or a particular iteration of it. This has resulted in tribunals revisiting the individual prongs of the *Salini* test and revising it, to purportedly better suit contemporary circumstances. Drawing on the awards excerpted in this chapter, the following are possible, although by no means permanent, prongs of a *Salini*-esque test:

(1) capital contribution;[26]
(2) a certain duration of performance;
(3) risk;
(4) the availability of profits;
(5) contribution to the economic development, an economic activity or the public interest of the host State;
(6) compliance with the laws of the host State;
(7) good faith in the making of the investment.

Amid continuing efforts by tribunals to come up with the next best test, the emergence of newer generation investment treaties that contain more restrictive and precise definitions of protected investments cast doubt on the justifiability of relying on a set of criteria that does not account for the text of the applicable investment treaty. The future of defining protected investments is more likely to lie in a return to the basic canons of investment treaty interpretation than in further renditions of the *Salini* test.

QUESTIONS

1. Are asset-based laundry-list definitions of protected investments in investment treaties well suited for their purpose? If so, why, and if not, why not?
2. Is the prevailing approach among arbitral tribunals on how protected investments are defined principled? If so, why, and if not, why not?
3. If you were a treaty drafter, how would you define a protected investment?

---

[26] The prong of 'capital contribution' is the subject of ongoing controversy as the findings on jurisdiction in a number of arbitral awards have turned on the presence or absence of an 'active' contribution (*Alapli Elektrik B.V.* v. *Republic of Turkey*, ICSID Case No. ARB/08/13, Award, 16 July 2012 (Park, Lalonde (dissenting), Stern), para. 350; *Standard Chartered Bank* v. *The United Republic of Tanzania*, ICSID Case No. ARB/10/12, Award, 2 November 2012 (Park, Pryles, Legum), para. 230), or an 'action in investing' by the claimant investor (*Quiborax S.A., Non Metallic Minerals S.A. and Allan Fosk Kaplún* v. *Plurinational State of Bolivia*, ICSID Case No. ARB/06/2, Decision on Jurisdiction, 27 September 2012 (Kaufmann-Kohler, Lalonde, Stern), para. 233; *Clorox Spain S.L.* v. *Bolivarian Republic of Venezuela*, PCA Case No. 2015–30, Award, 20 March 2019 (Derains, Hanotiau, Vinuesa), paras 782–836). Moreover, tribunals are divided on whether an 'active' contribution or an 'action in investing' is a trait of a protected investment (this chapter) or of a protected investor (Chapter 11), both jurisdictional conditions inviting the application of different criteria, and calling for distinct lines of inquiry and analysis. Perhaps a compromise can be found in *Anglo-Adriatic Group Limited* v. *Republic of Albania*, ICSID Case No. ARB/17/6, Award, 7 February 2019 (Fernández-Armesto, Stern, von Segesser), paras 207, 210, where the tribunal held that jurisdiction can still be lacking even if there is a protected investment and a protected investor if there is no link between the two. In order words, an 'active' contribution or an 'action in investing' may be that crucial link on which jurisdiction ultimately rests.

4. A standard, but often neglected, requirement of a protected investment is its location within the territory of a Contracting State to the investment treaty.[27] When an investment does not take the form of physical property, but, rather, is embodied by a financial instrument, such as a sovereign bond that can be bought and sold in foreign markets, should investment treaty protection extend to investments arising from transactions that did not take place within the territory of the host State?[28]

5. Is the monetary value of an investment relevant to the determination of whether that investment qualifies for treaty protection? Should the understanding of protected investments be construed to include 'microinvestments'?[29]

SUGGESTIONS FOR FURTHER READING

1. C. H. Schreuer, L. Malintoppi, A. Reinisch and A. Sinclair (eds), *The ICSID Convention: A Commentary*, 2nd edn (Cambridge University Press, 2009), 114–143.

2. J. Ho, 'The Meaning of "Investment" in ICSID Arbitrations' (2010) 26(4) *Arb Int'l* 633.

3. J. D. Mortenson, 'The Meaning of "Investment": ICSID's *Travaux* and the Domain of International Investment Law' (2010) 51 *Harvard ILJ* 257.

4. A. Mills, 'Rethinking Jurisdiction in International Law' (2014) 84 *BYbIL* 187.

5. M. Waibel, 'Investment Arbitration: Jurisdiction and Admissibility' in M. Bungenberg, J. Griebel, S. Hobe and A. Reinisch (eds), *International Investment Law: A Handbook* (Oxford: Hart/C. H. Beck, 2015), 1212.

---

[27] According to the UK–Malaysia BIT, Art. 1(1)(b), a protected investment is made '(i) ... in the territory of –the United Kingdom of Great Britain and Northern Ireland ... [and] in accordance with its legislation, and (ii) ... in the territory of Malaysia ... in projects classified by the appropriate Ministry of Malaysia [and] in accordance with its legislation and administrative practice as an "approved project"'.

[28] For divided views on whether the territoriality requirement for investments that take the form of financial instruments is better met by identifying the destination to which the benefit has flowed or by the physical location of the disbursed funds, see the majority and dissenting holdings in *Abaclat and Others* v. *Argentine Republic*, ICSID Case No. ARB/07/5 (formerly *Giovanna a Beccara and Others* v. *The Argentine Republic*), Decision on Jurisdiction and Admissibility, 4 August 2011 (Tercier, van den Berg, Abi-Saab (dissenting)), paras 373–378, cf. Dissenting Opinion, paras 78–119; and *Ambiente Ufficio S.p.A. and others* v. *Argentine Republic*, ICSID Case No. ARB/08/9 (formerly *Giordano Alpi and others* v. *Argentine Republic*), Decision on Jurisdiction and Admissibility, 8 February 2013 (Simma, Böckstiegel, Torres Bernádez), paras 498–508, cf. Dissenting Opinion, paras 298–317.

[29] P. S. Bechky, 'Microinvestment Disputes' in T. Rensmann (ed.), *Small and Medium-Sized Enterprises in International Economic Law* (Oxford University Press, 2017), 267, 269–270.

11

Protected Investors

CHAPTER OUTLINE

This chapter, which should be read in conjunction with Chapter 10, addresses the second of two principal criteria for a dispute to enter the scope of submission to investment treaty arbitration – the existence of a protected investor. Whether an investor qualifies for treaty protection depends on its nationality. Essentially, only investors who are nationals of the other or another Contracting State to an investment treaty are eligible to seek treaty protection from a Contracting State. Arbitral tribunals are thus tasked with verifying if an investor is in possession of the nationality that it claims to have. Section 1 outlines the centrality of a determination on an investor's nationality to its status as a protected investor, and the implications of the premium placed on nationality. Section 2 explores in greater detail the process of determining the nationality of individual investors, while Section 3 is devoted to the nationality of corporate investors. Section 4 touches on the emerging phenomenon of 'divisible' investors, whereby duplicate claims are launched against a host State by an investor through or in conjunction with close affiliates bearing different nationalities. The result is parallel or multiple proceedings.

INTRODUCTION

The majority of investment treaties empower foreign investors to bring claims against host States for breaches of the latter's treaty obligations.[1] Direct access to international dispute resolution was not unknown before the advent of investment treaties, but it was limited to those foreign investors who could rely on an arbitration clause in a contract concluded with the host State.[2] Other contractual claims had to be presented by the home State through diplomatic channels. Satisfaction was both uncertain and heavily dependent

---

[1] 'Introduction' in UNCTAD, 'Dispute Settlement: Investor-State' (2003) UNCTAD Series on Issues in International Investment Agreements, http://unctad.org/en/Docs/iteiit30_en.pdf (accessed 31 July 2020).

[2] See, for instance, the oil concessions awarded by Libya to US investors in the 1950s and which formed the basis of three notable investor-State arbitrations, namely, *British Petroleum Exploration Co.* v. *Libya*, 53 ILR 297, Award, 10 October 1973 (Lagergren); *Texaco Overseas Petroleum Co./California Asiatic Oil Co.* v. *Libya*, 53 ILR 389, Award on the Merits, 19 January 1977 (Dupuy); and *Libyan American Oil Co.* v. *Libya*, 62 ILR 140, Award, 12 April 1977 (Mahmassani).

on the discretion of the investor's home State in extending diplomatic support.[3] What contract-based arbitration envisaged on a case-by-case basis in the past, treaty-based arbitration allows on a much larger scale in the present. The standing offer made by host States in investment treaties to arbitrate qualifying disputes with an unidentified number of protected investors in the absence of an underlying contract opened a 'new world of arbitration'.[4] And the deciding factor in this new order on an investor's eligibility to claim treaty protection is the investor's nationality.

Investment treaties, both bilateral and multilateral, define protected investors as nationals of another or other Contracting State(s). The following provisions are illustrative.

2012 US Model BIT, Art. 1 (emphasis added)

'enterprise' means any entity constituted or organized under applicable law, whether or not for profit, and whether privately or governmentally owned or controlled, including a corporation, trust, partnership, sole proprietorship, joint venture, association, or similar organization; and a branch of an enterprise.

'investor of a Party' means a Party or state enterprise thereof, or *a national or an enterprise of a Party*, that attempts to make, is making, or has made an investment *in the territory of the other Party*; provided, however, that a natural person who is a dual national shall be deemed to be exclusively a national of the State of his or her dominant and effective nationality.

'national' means:

(a) for the United States, a natural person who is a national of the United States as defined in Title III of the Immigration and Nationality Act; and

(b) for [Country], [_____].

Association of South East Asian Nations (ASEAN) Comprehensive Investment Agreement (ACIA) 26 February 2009, Art. 4(d), (e), (g) (emphasis added)

(d) 'investor' means a *natural person* or a Member State or a *juridical person* of a Member State that is making, or has made an investment *in the territory of any other Member State*;

(e) 'juridical person' means any legal entity duly constituted or otherwise organized under the applicable law of a Member State, whether for profit or otherwise, and whether privately-owned or governmentally-owned, including any enterprise, corporation, trust, partnership, joint venture, sole proprietorship, association, or organization;

...

(g) 'natural person' means any natural person possessing the nationality or citizenship of, or right of permanent resident in the Member State in accordance with its laws, regulations and national policies.

---

[3] For a historical overview, see J. Ho, 'The Evolution of Contractual Protection in International Law: Accessing Diplomatic Archives, Discovering Diplomatic Practice, and Constructing Diplomatic History' in S. Schill, C. J. Tams and R. Hofmann (eds), *International Investment Law and History* (Cheltenham: Edward Elgar, 2017), 213, 218–224.

[4] J. Paulsson, 'Arbitration without Privity' (1995) *ICSID Review – FILJ* 232, 232.

The above provisions outline three key considerations of every discussion on protected investors. The first and foremost is the nationality requirement (addressed in Section 1), which delimits the scope of application of the treaty. In investment treaties, the nationality requirement confers treaty protection on nationals of the Contracting States, but bars any national from seeking treaty protection against its home State.[5] Under the US Model BIT and the ACIA, a US investor cannot seek protection against the United States under an investment treaty to which the United States is a party, just as a Singaporean investor cannot seek protection against Singapore under the ACIA, to which Singapore is a party. Disputes between States and their nationals are domestic disputes, and should be settled before domestic courts.[6] The prohibition has prompted some local investors, otherwise ineligible for treaty protection, to acquire a nationality that may transform them into protected foreign investors.

The second consideration (addressed in Sections 2 and 3) is the possibility for a protected investor to be a natural or juridical person. With the possible exception of dual nationals, determining the nationality of an individual is usually more straightforward than determining the nationality of a company. The former calls for proof of citizenship, which can be regulated by legislation, as indicated in Article 1 of the US Model BIT. The latter may be determined by the company's place of incorporation, or follow the nationality of the company's ultimate owners or controllers. The more complex the corporate structure and shareholding, the more difficult it is at times to pinpoint a company's nationality. Due to the adoption of different tests for determining the nationality of natural and juridical persons, these two categories of protected investors will be discussed separately.

The third consideration (addressed in Section 4) is the absence of limits on the number of protected investors who can bring claims against a host State. Again, with the possible exception of dual nationals, the nationality requirement guards against host States being sued by their own nationals under any given treaty. However, it does not stop the *same* protected foreign investor bringing multiple claims against the *same* State under *different* investment treaties. This is done by suing in the name of affiliates with different nationalities. Recent examples of this aggressive and possibly abusive litigation strategy mark the unsettling rise of 'divisible' investors.

1. NATIONALITY-BASED ELIGIBILITY FOR PROTECTION

The nationality requirement in many investment treaties limits the personal jurisdiction of arbitral tribunals to investors who are nationals of a Contracting State other than the respondent State to the dispute. This requirement is also found in Article 25(2) of the Convention on the Settlement of Investment Disputes between States and Nationals of Other States (ICSID Convention).[7] The nationality requirement comprises a formal and a

---

[5] Dual nationals, discussed at Section 2.2. below, are a possible exception to this rule.
[6] *Phoenix Action, Ltd* v. *Czech Republic*, ICSID Case No. ARB/06/5, Award, 15 April 2009 (Stern, Bucher, Fernández-Armesto), paras 97, 141–144.
[7] Signed 18 March 1965, entered into force 14 October 1966, 575 UNTS 159.

substantive component. The formal component refers to the possession of the required nationality on a critical date(s) (Section 1.1), while the substantive component refers to the propriety of circumstances leading to the acquisition of the required nationality (Section 1.2). The non-satisfaction of either component will likely result in the tribunal finding that it has no jurisdiction over the dispute.

1.1 Form – Critical Date(s) of Nationality Possession

Investment treaties, as well as Article 25(2) of the ICSID Convention, set out the critical dates, often explicitly, on which an investor claiming treaty protection must possess the requisite nationality.

Starting with Article 1 of the US Model BIT, which was excerpted in the Introduction, a protected investor is a national 'that [i] attempts to make, [ii] is making, or [iii] has made an investment in the territory of the other Party', while a claimant is 'an investor of a Party that is a party to an investment dispute with the other Party'. Therefore, an investor invoking the US Model BIT as a US national in a dispute is only eligible for treaty protection if it possessed US nationality on two critical dates. The first is when the investment was being made, regardless of whether the investment is at a pre- or post-establishment stage when treaty protection is sought. The second is when the claim for treaty protection is submitted to arbitration in accordance with the provisions in Section B of the US Model BIT. The critical dates for nationality acquisition under the ACIA are the same.

Investors submitting claims to ICSID arbitration are also required to satisfy the critical dates for nationality possession.

ICSID Convention, Art. 25(1), (2) (emphasis added)

(1) The jurisdiction of the Centre shall extend to any legal dispute ... between a Contracting State ... and a national of another Contracting State ...

(2) 'National of another Contracting State' means:

(a) any natural person who had the nationality of a Contracting State other than the State party to the dispute on the date on which the parties consented to submit such dispute to conciliation or arbitration as well as on the date on which the request was registered pursuant to paragraph (3) of Article 28 or paragraph (3) of Article 36 ...; and

(b) any juridical person which had the nationality of a Contracting State other than the State party to the dispute *on the date on which the parties consented to submit such dispute to conciliation or arbitration.*

The critical date for nationality possession that satisfies the nationality requirement in Article 25(2) of the ICSID Convention is the date on which the disputing parties consent to submit to arbitration. As investment treaties contain the consent of Contracting States to arbitrate with protected investors writ large, the consent of a protected investor to arbitrate is always given later in time. Mutual consent to arbitrate is established when the investor 'accepts' the 'offer' of the State to arbitrate, usually by indication in a request for arbitration. Article 25(2)(a) refers to two dates – the 'date on which the parties consented to submit such dispute to conciliation or arbitration' and the 'date on which the request was registered'. However, the tendency for claimants to express consent in a request for arbitration which is registered on the day the request is made points to one critical date for nationality possession for both natural and juridical persons. This date, set out in Articles 25(2)(a) and (b), is 'the date on which the parties consented to submit such dispute to conciliation or arbitration'.

1.2 Substance – Circumstances of Nationality Acquisition

Possession of the requisite nationality on a critical date or critical dates may not suffice to render an investor a protected investor. Some arbitral tribunals exhibit willingness to scrutinise the circumstances giving rise to an investor's professed nationality. In many cases, the circumstances of nationality acquisition are innocuous and routine. For example, a parent company which is a long-time national of its home State may claim treaty protection for losses suffered by a locally incorporated subsidiary or investment vehicle from the host State. The flurry of claims brought by US investors against Argentina for severely devalued investments in the wake of Argentina's economic collapse in the 2000s fall into this category. In some cases, however, the method or timing of nationality acquisition may give pause for thought. Arguably suspicious circumstances tend to originate from investors seeking treaty protection from their *home* State, contrary to the rule against nationals suing their home States under investment treaties (Section 1.2.1),[8] and from investors shopping for treaty protection shortly before a dispute with a host State is submitted to arbitration (Section 1.2.2).

1.2.1 'Round-Tripping'

Some investors attempt to hold their home States to the protection standards found in investment treaties concluded by their home State, using a technique called 'round-tripping'. 'Round-tripping' injects a foreign element into a local investor, enabling the otherwise local investor to sue the State as a foreign investor. As Sornarajah explains, there is much a local investor stands to gain by 'round-tripping'.

> **M. Sornarajah, *The International Law on Foreign Investment*, 3rd edn (Cambridge University Press, 2010), 329 (footnotes omitted)**
>
> 'Round-tripping' is a technique which nationals of a state use in order to protect their investments from interference by their own states. It involves an investor transferring funds to another state and then redirecting the funds into his own home state, thus securing the protection as well as the advantageous treatment that may be given by the law of the home state to foreign investors. One such advantage is that the funds, when vested in companies incorporated in the host state, may become entitled to the diplomatic protection of that state as well as to the protection of its investment treaties.

---

[8] It bears repeating that dual nationals, discussed at Section 2.2 below, are a possible exception to this rule.

A classic example of 'round-tripping' is a national of State A incorporating a company in State B, both States having concluded an investment treaty. The company, the majority of whose shares are held by nationals of State A, then proceeds to invest in State A. In the event of a dispute between the company and State A, the company seeks treaty protection as a national of State B.

Despite the possibly negative connotations of 'round-tripping', tribunals are generally untroubled when a claimant's nationality is the product of 'round-tripping'. In a trio of claims brought by UK and Cypriot claimants against Russia under the Energy Charter Treaty (ECT),[9] the tribunal found that incorporation according to the laws of the home State was all that mattered for nationality determination. The fact that the claimants were shell companies wholly owned and controlled by Russian nationals did not, in and of itself, disqualify the claimants from treaty protection.[10] By this token, 'round-tripping' appears to be a legitimate technique for circumventing the general prohibition against nationals bringing investment treaty claims against their home States.

Hulley Enterprises Ltd (Cyprus) v. Russia; Yukos Universal Ltd (Isle of Man) v. Russia; Veteran Petroleum Ltd (Cyprus) v. Russia, PCA Case Nos AA 226, 227 and 228, Interim Award on Jurisdiction and Admissibility, 30 November 2009 (Fortier, Poncet, Schwebel), paras 413, 415 (footnote omitted)

413. The Tribunal is bound to interpret the terms of the ECT, including Article 1(7), not as they might have been written but as they were actually written ... Article 1(7) provides that, 'Investor' means:

(a) with respect to a Contracting Party:

...

(ii) a company or other organization organized in accordance with the law applicable in that Contracting Party;

Claimant was organized 'in accordance with the law applicable' in a Contracting Party. Claimant accordingly qualifies as a company so organized in the instant case. The Tribunal is not entitled, by the terms of the ECT, to find otherwise.

...

415. The Tribunal knows of no general principles of international law that would require investigating how a company or another organization operates when the applicable treaty

---

[9] Signed 17 December 1994, entered into force 16 April 1998, 2080 UNTS 95.

[10] See also *Tokios Tokelés* v. *Ukraine*, ICSID Case No. ARB/02/18, Decision on Jurisdiction, 29 April 2004 (Weil (dissenting), Bernadini, Price). In this case, the claimant is a company incorporated in Lithuania, but 99 per cent owned and predominantly controlled by two Ukrainian nationals. The majority of the tribunal rejected Ukraine's contention that the claimant was not a 'genuine entity' of Lithuania (para. 21) because '[u]nder the well established presumption *expressio unius est exclusio alterius*, the state of incorporation, not the nationality of the controlling shareholders or *siège social*, thus defines "investors" of Lithuania under Article 1(2)(b) of the [Lithuania–Ukraine] BIT' (para. 30). The majority of the tribunal added that '[t]he object and purpose of the Treaty likewise confirm that the control-test should not be used to restrict the scope of "investors" in Article 1(2) (b)' (para. 31).

simply requires it to be organized in accordance with the laws of a Contracting Party. The principles of international law, which have an unquestionable importance in treaty interpretation, do not allow an arbitral tribunal to write new, additional requirements – which the drafters did not include – into a treaty, no matter how auspicious or appropriate they may appear.

1.2.2 Litigation-Oriented Nationality Acquisition

Although tribunals appear to accommodate 'round-tripping', nationality acquisition in potential pursuit of an investment treaty claim is usually frowned upon. The giveaway in this situation is invariably the timely acquisition of a nationality that gives an investor standing to sue under a particular investment treaty.

In *Philip Morris Asia Ltd* v. *Australia*[11] the claimant, a Hong Kong incorporated company, acquired 100 per cent of the shares of Philip Morris (Australia) Ltd, which was in turn the sole shareholder of Australian tobacco giant Philip Morris Ltd. The share transfer was part of a corporate restructuring effort which took place weeks after the Australian government announced the imminent implementation of plain-packaging regulations on tobacco products. Barely a year after the restructuring, the claimant challenged Australia's plain-packaging legislation for violating Australia's foreign investment protection obligations under the Hong Kong–Australia BIT.[12] After examining the chronology of events, the tribunal concluded that the so-called corporate restructuring was in fact calculated litigation-oriented nationality acquisition. This amounted to an 'abuse of rights' which rendered the claimant ineligible for treaty protection.[13]

Philip Morris Asia Ltd v. *Australia*, PCA Case No. 2012–12, Award on Jurisdiction and Admissibility, 17 December 2015 (Böckstiegel, Kaufmann-Kohler, McRae), paras 586–588

586. In the present case, the Tribunal has found that the adoption of the Plain Packaging Measures was foreseeable well before the Claimant's decision to restructure was taken (let alone implemented). On 29 April 2010, Australia's Prime Minister Kevin Rudd and

---

[11] PCA Case No. 2012–12, Award on Jurisdiction and Admissibility, 17 December 2015 (Böckstiegel, Kaufmann-Kohler, McRae).

[12] Agreement between the Government of Hong Kong and the Government of Australia for the Promotion and Protection of Investments (signed 15 September 1993, entered into force 15 October 1993).

[13] See also *Phoenix Action* v. *Czech Republic*, Award, 15 April 2009 (Stern, Bucher, Fernández-Armesto), paras 135–144, where the tribunal declined to exercise jurisdiction over the dispute because the investment was not made in good faith by the claimant. The tribunal concluded that the Israeli claimant's purchase of two Czech companies (all three companies having the same ultimate owner, a former Czech national who subsequently acquired Israeli citizenship), thus becoming the assignee of their claims against the Czech Republic, evinced 'the sole purpose of bringing international litigation against the Czech Republic' (para. 142). As '[t]he unique goal of the "investment" was to transform a pre-existing domestic dispute into an international dispute subject to ICSID arbitration under a bilateral investment treaty', the investment 'is not a *bona fide* transaction and cannot be a protected investment under the ICSID system' (para. 142).

Health Minister Roxon unequivocally announced the Government's intention to introduce Plain Packaging Measures. In the Tribunal's view, there was no uncertainty about the Government's intention to introduce plain packaging as of that point. Accordingly, from that date, there was at least a reasonable prospect that legislation equivalent to the Plain Packaging Measures would eventually be enacted and a dispute would arise. Political developments after 29 April 2010 did not involve any change in the intention of the Government to introduce Plain Packaging Measures and, thus, were not such as to change the foreseeability assessment.

587. The Tribunal's conclusion is reinforced by a review of the evidence regarding the Claimant's professed alternative reasons for the restructuring. The record indeed shows that the principal, if not sole, purpose of the restructuring was to gain protection under the Treaty in respect of the very measures that form the subject matter of the present arbitration. For the Tribunal, the adoption of the Plain Packaging Measures was not only foreseeable but actually foreseen by the Claimant when it chose to change its corporate structure.

588. In light of the foregoing discussion, the Tribunal cannot but conclude that the initiation of this arbitration constitutes an abuse of rights, as the corporate restructuring by which the Claimant acquired the Australian subsidiaries occurred at a time when there was a reasonable prospect that the dispute would materialise and as it was carried out for the principal, if not sole, purpose of gaining Treaty protection. Accordingly, the claims raised in this arbitration are inadmissible and the Tribunal is precluded from exercising jurisdiction over this dispute.

***

Whether a tribunal can establish personal jurisdiction over an investor bringing an investment treaty claim depends on the nationality of the investor. As a rule, protected investors under investment treaties are those bearing the nationality of a Contracting State other than their home State on the critical date(s) stipulated in the treaty or any other relevant instrument. In other words, and with the possible exception of dual nationals, nationals cannot claim investment treaty protection from their home State. However, this rule can be circumvented by using the technique of 'round-tripping', which has passed muster with arbitral tribunals. In contrast, nationality acquisition for the dominant purpose of commencing investment treaty arbitration has been called an 'abuse of process' which will deprive the investor of treaty protection.

2. INDIVIDUAL INVESTORS

The avenues available to an individual in becoming a national of a particular State are closely governed by domestic law. For example, Title III of the US Immigration and Nationality Act, which is referred to in Article 1 of the US Model BIT, is the controlling domestic legislation that defines a US national. Comprising sixty-one provisions, the Immigration and Nationality Act exhaustively identifies the various ways in which US nationality can be acquired and lost. Due to the relative ease with which an individual's nationality can be verified, such as through the production of a valid passport or other standard citizenship certification, an individual investor's professed nationality is seldom contested in investment treaty arbitration. But when disagreements arise, they tend to centre around the authentication of nationality (Section 2.1) and dual nationality (Section 2.2).

2.1 Authentication of Nationality

Whether an individual investor is a national of a particular State is a question for domestic law. In disputes where the respondent State queries the professed nationality of the claimant investor, arbitral tribunals have turned to the applicable domestic law for answers.

In *Hussein Nuaman Soufraki* v. *United Arab Emirates* (*Soufraki* v. *UAE*) and *Waguih Elie George Siag & Clorinda Vecchi* v. *Egypt* (*Siag* v. *Egypt*), the respondent States challenged the professed nationality of the individual investor. Mr Soufraki, who sought protection under the Italy–United Arab Emirates BIT,[14] had supposedly lost his Italian nationality by becoming a naturalised Canadian citizen,[15] while Mr Siag, who sought protection under the Italy–Egypt BIT,[16] was purportedly an Egyptian national.[17]

Notably, the tribunal in *Soufraki* v. *UAE* did not accept the Certificates of Nationality issued by the Italian Ministry of Foreign Affairs as conclusive proof of Mr Soufraki's Italian nationality. Instead, it regarded these Certificates as rebuttable evidence of nationality while conducting an independent examination of Italian nationality laws to establish if Mr Soufraki had managed to maintain his Italian nationality despite living abroad most of the time.[18] As the facts revealed that Mr Soufraki did not meet the residency requirement under Italian law, he did not possess Italian nationality when the dispute was submitted to investment treaty arbitration. In *Siag* v. *Egypt*, the tribunal found, by a majority, that since Mr Siag was obliged under Egyptian law to make a formal declaration to retain his Egyptian nationality after acquiring a foreign nationality (first Italian, then Lebanese), but had failed to do so, his Egyptian nationality had lapsed by operation of law.[19] The dissenting arbitrator objected to this finding in the strongest terms, arguing that the prohibition against nationals suing their own States in Article 25(2) of the ICSID Convention will be meaningless if individual investors can, like Mr Siag, simply secure

---

[14] Agreement between the Government of the United Arab Emirates and the Government of the Italian Republic for the Promotion and Protection of Investments (signed 22 January 1995, entered into force 29 April 1997).

[15] ICSID Case No. ARB/02/7, Award, 7 July 2004 (Fortier, Schwebel, El Kholy), para. 26.

[16] Agreement for the Promotion and Protection of Investments between the Republic of Italy and the Arab Republic of Egypt (signed 2 March 1989, entered into force 1 May 1994).

[17] ICSID Case No. ARB/05/15, Decision on Jurisdiction, 11 April 2007 (Williams, Pryles, Orrego Vicuña (partially dissenting)), paras 27–32.

[18] Award, paras 53–84.

[19] Decision on Jurisdiction, paras 154–173.

and shed nationalities when it suited them. While there may have been a compelling policy reason for denying Mr Siag treaty protection, there appears to be little doubt from the analysis of the majority of the tribunal that Egyptian law dictated the loss of Mr Siag's Egyptian nationality. To nonetheless deem Mr Siag an Egyptian national arguably jettisons the long-standing rule in general international law that questions of nationality fall within the 'reserved domain' of States.[20]

Waguih Elie George Siag and Clorinda Vecchi v. Egypt, ICSID Case No. ARB/05/15, Partially Dissenting Opinion of Professor Francisco Orrego Vicuña, 11 April 2007, p. 63

The drafting history of Article 25(2)(a) is unequivocal about the concern expressed by many countries that did not want to be taken to international arbitration by investors who were their nationals, even if holding the nationality of another Contracting Party as well.

...

It is in this context that the situation of Waguih appears to be at odds with the meaning of the [ICSID] Convention. The investor was Egyptian at the time the investment was made, benefited from Egyptian legislation granting exclusive rights to Egyptian citizens and was at all times considered to be Egyptian, not just by the Egyptian Government but this was also his own understanding and that of his family ...

The fact that Waguih later acquired a different nationality (Italy) and allegedly lost his original nationality (Egypt) because of acquiring that of a third State (Lebanon), cannot in my view prevail over the precise prohibition of the Convention. It is on this point where I believe the Convention goes beyond the strict technical situation of dual nationals and the dates used to this effect and covers additional situations that could contradict the prohibition in question, not to mention the fact that otherwise there could be uncontrollable abuse arising from acquisition or loss of nationalities.

2.2 Dual Nationality and Permanent Residents

The possession of dual nationality by individual investors is a potential complication when ascertaining eligibility for treaty protection, especially when the investor is also, allegedly, a national of the host State. Recalling the case of *Siag* v. *Egypt* discussed above, Mr Siag made an investment in Egypt for which he subsequently sought protection under the Italy–Egypt BIT as an Italian national. However, Egypt contended that Mr Siag was also an Egyptian national, and was therefore barred from claiming treaty protection against his home State, Egypt. After considering the evidential record and the position under Egyptian nationality laws, the tribunal found that Mr Siag was not an Egyptian

---

[20] *Case of Nationality Decrees Issued in Tunis and Morocco (France v. Great Britain)* (Request for an Advisory Opinion) (1923) PCIJ Rep. Series B No. 4, p. 24.

national on the date that he consented to submit the dispute to arbitration. If, hypothetically, the tribunal had found that Mr Siag was a dual national of Italy and Egypt, then it would have been necessary for the tribunal to determine, somewhat artificially, if Mr Siag was more an Italian national or an Egyptian national, in accordance with the principle of effective nationality.

The principle of effective nationality requires proof of a 'predominant' connection between the individual investor and the State of the investor's professed nationality.[21] In concrete terms, the strength of a dual national's ties with a particular State of nationality may depend on factors as varied as 'habitual residence; ... employment and financial interests; ... family ties in each country; participation in social and public life; ... taxation[;] bank account[;] social security insurance' and more.[22] This principle is rarely applied by investment arbitration tribunals, which are more often confronted with single nationality, instead of actual dual or multiple nationality fact patterns.[23] However, its recent application in *Michael Ballantine and Lisa Ballantine* v. *The Dominican Republic* (*Ballantine* v. *Dominican Republic*) demonstrates the challenge of determining an investor's effective and dominant nationality by feeding factual circumstances into a multi-factorial test.[24]

The claimants in *Ballantine* v. *Dominican Republic* were originally US-based US nationals who decided to develop a luxury residential housing project in the Dominican Republic. They subsequently relocated to the Dominican Republic and voluntarily acquired Dominican Republic citizenship, making them dual nationals. The claimants challenged the compatibility of certain environmental regulations passed by the Dominican Republic which derailed their project, with the latter's obligations towards protected investors under the Dominican Republic–Central America–United States Free Trade Agreement (DR–CAFTA).[25] According to Article 10.28, dual nationals like the claimants can sue the host State provided that they have 'dominant and effective nationality' of *another* State Party to the DR–CAFTA.[26] The point of contention was whether the claimants' 'dominant

---

[21] The requirement of 'predominance' developed in the context of diplomatic protection in the event of multiple nationality. It is codified in Art. 7 of the International Law Commission's (ILC) Draft Articles on Diplomatic Protection, UN Doc. A/61/10, which provides: 'A State of nationality may not exercise diplomatic protection in respect of a person against a State of which that person is also a national unless the nationality of the former State is predominant, both at the date of injury and at the date of the official presentation of the claim.' This requirement was also endorsed in dicta by the International Court of Justice in the *Nottebohm Case* (*Liechtenstein* v. *Guatemala*) (Second Phase) [1955] ICJ Rep. 4, at p. 23, although the case did not involve any question of multiple nationality.

[22] ILC, 'Draft Articles on Diplomatic Protection with Commentaries' (2006) *Yearbook of the International Law Commission*, vol. II, Part Two, 46.

[23] Tribunals have expressly rejected a test for effective nationality when only one nationality is in issue: see *Ioan Micula and Others* v. *Romania*, ICSID Case No. ARB/05/20, Decision on Jurisdiction and Admissibility, 24 September 2008 (Lévy, Alexandrov, Ehlermann), paras 98–100; and *Mr. Franck Charles Arif* v. *Moldova*, ICSID Case No. ARB/11/23, Award, 8 April 2013 (Cremades, Hanotiau, Knieper), para. 359.

[24] PCA Case No. 2016–17 (UNCITRAL), Final Award, 3 September 2019 (Ramírez Hernández, Cheek (partially dissenting), Vinuesa (partially dissenting)), paras 529–600 and Partial Dissent of Ms Cheek on Jurisdiction, paras 4–29.

[25] Signed 5 August 2004, entered into force 1 March 2007.

[26] DR-CAFTA Art. 10.28 provides: 'investor of a Party means a Party or state enterprise thereof, or a national or an enterprise of a Party, that attempts to make, is making, or has made an investment in the territory of another Party; provided, however, that a natural person who is a dual national shall be deemed to be exclusively a national of the State of his or her dominant and effective nationality.'

and effective nationality' was that of the US or that of the Dominican Republic. If the latter, the claimants would not qualify as protected investors under the DR–CAFTA. And although both purported to apply the various factual circumstances surrounding the claimants' dual nationality to the multi-factorial test in a 'holistic' manner,[27] the majority and partially dissenting arbitrators reached opposite conclusions on the country of the claimants' 'dominant and effective nationality'.

Michael Ballantine and Lisa Ballantine v. *The Dominican Republic*, PCA Case No. 2016–17 (UNCITRAL), Final Award, 3 September 2019 (Ramírez Hernández, Cheek (partially dissenting), Vinuesa (partially dissenting)), paras. 559, 566, 573, 576, 584, 599–600 (footnotes omitted)

559. The Tribunal considers that the factors mentioned by the Parties can be analyzed within the criteria indicated in Procedural Order No. 2, *i.e.* (a) habitual residence, (b) the individual's personal attachment for a particular country, (c) the center of the person's economic, social and family life, and (d) the circumstances in which the second nationality was acquired, bearing in mind the specific context of this dispute. Additionally, we are called upon to examine the nationality of each Claimant, Mr. and Ms. Ballantine. While the evaluation must be made in relation to each of them, the Tribunal considers that it can be addressed in the specific section of each criterion making the distinction when necessary. We turn now to our examination of the criteria mentioned above in light of the facts of the case.

1. Habitual Residence

...

566. Although the number of days spent in each country may confirm that the Claimants split significant amounts of time between two countries and consequently resided at times in both countries, their legal status, at least from 2008 until the moment they became Dominican nationals in 2010 was as permanent residents of the Dominican Republic and being nationals from 2010 to 2014, most of their time was spent in that country. We view this evidence as confirming the legal status the Claimants voluntarily chose to acquire. Consequently, although the Claimants maintained ties with the United States, their permanent residence at the relevant time was centered in the Dominican Republic.

2. The Individual's Personal Attachment for a Particular Country

...

573. The Tribunal considers that the Claimants had personal connections or attachment to both the United States and the Dominican Republic during the relevant period. We are aware that the extent of such connections is difficult to measure objectively, particularly

---

[27] PCA Case No. 2016–17 (UNCITRAL), Final Award, para. 556, 558; Partial Dissent of Ms Cheek on Jurisdiction, paras 13, 18, 21, 24, 29.

to the extent there have been some contradictory statements. In terms of professional relations, the Claimants seem to have been more connected to the Dominican Republic by virtue of their investment, however, it appears to this Tribunal that, although the Claimants had personal and professional attachments to the Dominican Republic, the attachments to the U.S. seem to be of equal force.

3. The Center of the Person's Economic Social and Family Life

...

576. Regarding where the center of the Claimants economic, social and family life was, this Tribunal is of the view that during the relevant time such center was in the Dominican Republic. According to the facts of the case, the Claimants moved to the Dominican Republic in 2006 and made a significant investment creating Jamaca de Dios, a luxury residential community; in order to do this, they sold two of their homes and commercial real estate. Therefore, the reason for moving to the Dominican Republic was to establish Jamaca de Dios and although they maintained connections to the United States, it seems to the Tribunal that from 2006 to the moment the claim was submitted, the Claimants had moved or relocated their economic center and their family center to the country where they resided permanently, independently of the fact that they often visited the United States, that their children continued their education in the U.S or that they kept social relations in the U.S. The fact is that the Claimants established what appeared to be their 'main' business in the Dominican Republic and reorganized their way of living in the Dominican Republic for several years around the investment. In consequence, this Tribunal is of the view that the Dominican Republic was the center of their economic, family and social life, despite maintaining ties with the U.S.

...

4. Naturalization

...

584. Whilst the Claimants have mentioned that discriminatory treatment was one of the reasons for becoming Dominican, the Claimants have expressed that their motives were for protection of the investment, as a business decision for commercial aspects, an economic decision. The sole reason for becoming Dominican and domestic investors was the investment. The Tribunal finds trouble reconciling the fact that the Claimants' desire was to be viewed as Dominicans for purposes of bolstering their investment and yet, regarding the application of the protections designed for foreign investors, they contend such nationality is not as important.

...

599. In sum, the Claimants' motivation for taking on the Dominican nationality was said to be economic and commercial in nature, for their business and the substantial investment they had made. During that relevant period of time, they lived, ran a business and accepted to be viewed as Dominicans. Nationality was not forced upon them, it was requested and

accepted by them. It is not the intention of this Tribunal to assert that the Claimants ceased to be Americans or that they did not have connections to that country. As already indicated, acquired dual-nationality is not about renouncing one nationality or ceasing to have connections with one's country of origin.

600. Thus, the Tribunal considers that their Dominican nationality took precedence during the relevant times, i.e., at the time the alleged measures were taken and at the time of the submissions of the claim. Therefore, the Claimants do not qualify as investors of a Contracting Party in accordance to the definition set forth in Article 10.28 of DR-CAFTA.

Michael Ballantine and Lisa Ballantine v. *The Dominican Republic*, PCA Case No. 2016–17 (UNCITRAL), Partial Dissent of Ms Cheek on Jurisdiction, 3 September 2019, paras 13–14, 25–29 (footnotes omitted)

13. While the Majority and I agree that the Claimants' entire lifetime is relevant to the dominant and effective nationality inquiry, we diverge where the Majority also focuses on what it deems the specific context of DR-CAFTA for the dominant and effective nationality test. The Majority 'considers that the investment itself, the status of investor as well as other circumstances surrounding those elements may be relevant factors for assessing nationality and its dominance and effectiveness within Article 10.28 of DR-CAFTA'. This appears to go beyond an examination of the Claimants' economic ties to both countries over their lifetimes. The Majority concludes that 'a claimant's entire life is relevant but not dispositive' and examines whether the Claimants' Dominican nationality 'was strong enough to take precedence over their U.S. nationality and it was producing effects or was operative during the relevant time in order to determine whether they were investors under DR-CAFTA'. The result of this approach, which the Majority describes elsewhere as 'temporal context in which the terms of Article 10.28 shall be interpreted', is to give greater weight to the Claimants' investment-related contacts as of the date the claim arose and the date the claim was submitted, rather than engaging in a truly holistic inquiry of the Claimants' entire lifetimes on each of those dates.

14. The proper inquiry should examine the Claimants' ties to the United States and the Dominican Republic over the course of their lifetimes to determine whether, at the time of the alleged breach (i.e., 12 September 2011) and at the time of the submission of the claim to arbitration (i.e., 11 September 2014), the dominant and effective nationality of each Claimant was that of the United States or the Dominican Republic.

...

25. With regard to bad faith or abuse of rights, both Parties agree that the Ballantines did not acquire a second nationality as a form of treaty shopping to gain access to a dispute settlement mechanism. In fact, their Dominican nationality had the potential to defeat their ability to bring a claim. Claimants did not take steps to avail themselves of a second

nationality so they could gain protections under DR-CAFTA or bring a claim they would not otherwise have been entitled to bring. They made their investments as U.S. nationals, and the steps they took to become Dominican nationals involved a risk that they would jeopardize their ability to bring a potential future investment claim against the Dominican Republic.

26. On these facts, the Dominican Republic chose not to allege bad faith or abuse of rights in this case, and rightly so.

27. It is commonplace for a U.S. corporation to incorporate a wholly-owned subsidiary abroad in order to do business. In the typical case, the U.S. corporation would have created a Dominican corporation for the ease of doing business – for buying property, paying employees, etc. – and the U.S. company would maintain ownership over its subsidiary and manage it from afar. There is no question that the U.S. company could bring a claim on behalf of that U.S.-owned Dominican enterprise under DR-CAFTA.

28. The difference between the Ballantines and this hypothetical U.S. corporation is that the Ballantines were small business owners, and while they created a Dominican corporation for the ease of doing business, they decided not to manage it from afar. Instead, they moved to the Dominican Republic and chose to directly manage and run their investments with personal devotion and commitment.

29. In this case, these two U.S. nationals acquired a second nationality in 2010 in an effort to help their investments thrive. Under those circumstances, the second nationality does not become the dominant one by virtue of the investment-related motivations of the Claimants. Instead, the test for dominant and effective nationality remains a holistic one that focuses on the totality of one's personal, familial, economic, and civic ties over a lifetime. Under that test, both Lisa and Michael Ballantine are U.S. nationals who qualified as U.S. investors under the DR-CAFTA at the time of the alleged breach and at the time they submitted their claims against the Dominican Republic.

Apart from being dual nationals, individual investors can also be nationals of one State and permanent residents of another. There is generally no prohibition against a permanent resident seeking treaty protection for his investment against the State of his permanent residency. This is so even if the applicable investment treaty equates permanent residents with citizens in its definition of a national of a Contracting State. Article 201 of the North American Free Trade Agreement (NAFTA),[28] and its interpretation by a majority of the tribunal in *Marvin Roy Feldman Karpa* v. *Mexico* (*Karpa* v. *Mexico*),[29] illustrate how a permanent resident of Mexico can nonetheless qualify for protection under the NAFTA against Mexico.

---

[28] Signed 17 December 1992, entered into force 1 January 1994, 32 ILM 289. Since the publication of the first edition of this book, the NAFTA has been updated and renamed the Agreement Between the United States of America, the United Mexican States, and Canada (signed 30 November 2018, entered into force 1 July 2020) (USMCA).

[29] ICSID Case No. ARB(AF)/99/1, Interim Decision on Preliminary Jurisdiction Issues, 6 December 2000 (Kerameus, Gantz, Bravo (dissenting)).

NAFTA, Art. 201

...

national means a natural person who is a citizen or permanent resident of a Party and any other natural person referred to in Annex 201.1

Marvin Roy Feldman Karpa v. *Mexico*, ICSID Case No. ARB(AF)/99/1, Interim Decision on Preliminary Jurisdiction Issues, 6 December 2000 (Kerameus, Gantz, Bravo (dissenting)), paras 33–36

33. ... As already indicated (supra, para. 24), NAFTA Article 201 in its relevant part defines 'national' as 'a natural person who is a citizen or permanent resident of a Party'. It has accordingly been argued that this Article makes permanent residence tantamount to nationality for all purposes, and therefore, in the present case, an instance of dual nationality arises which would call for a determination of the dominant or effective one.

34. The Tribunal cannot adopt such interpretation for two reasons. The first one relates to the very structure of NAFTA Article 1117(1)(a), which is here the applicable provision concerning an investor of a State Party having standing (cf. supra para 23).[30] This provision is supplemented by the definition in NAFTA Article 1139, according to which '"investor of a Party" means, among other persons, "a national or an enterprise of such Party, that seeks to make, is making or has made an investment"' (cf. supra, para. 24). In the framework of the above mentioned and reproduced provisions, it appears that the concept of 'national', as defined in NAFTA Article 201, becomes relevant here only with respect to a State Party other than the one in which the investment is made. In fact, Article 1117(1) literally addresses '[a]n investor of a Party, on behalf of an enterprise of another Party'. Thus, the definition of 'national' as 'a natural person who is a citizen or permanent resident of a Party' is needed in this context to complement the definition in Article 1139 of the 'investor of a Party' which, in the scope of application of Article 1117(1), refers to an investor of a Party other than the one in which the investment is made. Such contextual interpretation of an equal treatment of nationals and permanent residents leads to the result that permanent residents are treated like nationals in a given State Party only if that State is different from the State where the investment is made.

35. This result is further corroborated by the very purpose of NAFTA itself. Article 102(1) (c) and (e) have been pointed to, according to which '[t]he objectives of this Agreement, as elaborated more specifically through its principles and rules', are to 'increase substantially investment opportunities in the territories of the Parties' and to 'create effective procedures for the implementation and application of this Agreement, for its

---

[30] [Eds: Art. 1117(1)(a) NAFTA provides: 'An investor of a Party, on behalf of an enterprise of another Party that is a juridical person that the investor owns or controls directly or indirectly, may submit to arbitration under this Section a claim that the other Party has breached an obligation under Section A or Article 1503(2) (State Enterprises).']

joint administration and for the resolution of disputes'. Such increase of both investment opportunities and their effective protection is also supported by enlarging the circle of investors to be protected, beyond nationals of another State Party, to permanent residents therein as well. Thus, e.g., an investor of a Party, entitled to seek arbitration under Chapter Eleven can be not only a U.S. citizen but a French citizen as well, provided he is a permanent resident of the United States. This is, in the opinion of the Tribunal, the proper meaning and function of the definition of 'national[s]' in NAFTA Article 201.

36. Under the interpretation elaborated above (paras. 33–35), which concurs with general principles of international law (see supra, paras. 30–32), the Claimant in this case, being a citizen of the United States and of the United States only, and despite his permanent residence (*inmigrado status*) in Mexico, has standing to sue in the present arbitration under Chapter Eleven of NAFTA. Indeed, the Claimant as a citizen of the United States should not be barred from the protection provided by Chapter Eleven just because he is also a permanent resident of Mexico.

The tribunal in *Karpa* v. *Mexico* placed citizens and permanent residents on equal footing in the home State, but not in the host State of the investment. In the latter, permanent residents could claim treaty protection under NAFTA from their State of residence, but citizens of that State could not.

***

Ascertaining the nationality of an individual investor is usually uncontroversial, unless the investor happens to possess multiple nationalities, one of which is the nationality of the host State. In this situation, the principle of effective or dominant nationality has a role to play. This principle calls for an examination of ties an individual investor maintains with States of which he is a national in order to determine if he is eligible for treaty protection. While the application of this principle seems straightforward in theory, the weight accorded to certain factual circumstances, which in turn affects the perceived strength of certain ties, invites disagreement. Many investment treaties, as well as Article 25(2)(a) of the ICSID Convention, disallow nationals from claiming treaty protection from their home States. This restriction does not extend to some dual nationals and permanent residents, who may be eligible under both older and newer generation investment protection agreements to seek treaty protection from the State where they are not deemed to possess effective nationality, or the State of their permanent residency.

3. CORPORATE INVESTORS

Due to variety in corporate structures and shareholding patterns, determining the nationality of a corporate investor can be more challenging than that of an individual investor. While questions over an individual investor's nationality can usually be squarely settled by reference to the relevant domestic laws, questions over a corporate investor's nationality usually involve a mix of legal and factual considerations. Turning to the domestic law of a corporate investor's professed nationality alone may not yield a conclusive answer to a question over that investor's true nationality. This situation arises because, unlike in the case of individual investors, there is no single way of determining the nationality of a corporate investor; different methods beget different outcomes. Also, unlike individuals who assume the same human form, corporations assume a variety of different forms, one of which in particular – the shell or holding company – may impact eligibility for treaty protection.

In this section we examine two critical factors that assist the determination of a corporate investor's nationality – the place of incorporation (Section 3.1) and the presence of foreign control (Section 3.2). Where a particular corporate form has the potential to negate eligibility for treaty protection, the implications of a corporate investor assuming such a corporate form will also be discussed.

3.1 Place of Incorporation

Under customary international law, a corporation's nationality is usually identified by its place of incorporation. The *locus classicus* is the *Case Concerning the Barcelona Traction, Light and Power Co., Ltd* (the *Barcelona Traction Case*).[31] The issue here was whether Belgium, the State of nationality of shareholders in Barcelona Traction, or Canada, the State of incorporation of Barcelona Traction, was entitled to exercise diplomatic protection for damage suffered by the company. The claim was brought by Belgium, arguing that shareholders can vindicate a company's rights on behalf of the company. The International Court of Justice (ICJ) rejected this argument and ruled that diplomatic protection can only be exercised by the State where the company was incorporated, which in this case was Canada, not Belgium.[32] As a result, Belgium had no standing to bring the claim.

Case Concerning Barcelona Traction, Light and Power Co., Ltd (Belgium v. Spain) [1970] ICJ Rep. 3 (Second Phase), paras 70–71, 77–79

70. In allocating corporate entities to States for purposes of diplomatic protection, international law is based, but only to a limited extent, on an analogy with the rules governing the nationality of individuals. The traditional rule attributes the right of diplomatic protection of a corporate entity to the State under the laws of which it

---

[31] (*Belgium v. Spain*) (Second Phase) [1970] ICJ Rep. 3.
[32] See also Separate Opinion of Sir Gerald Fitzmaurice in the *Barcelona Traction Case*, para. 33 (footnote omitted): 'There has, doctrinally, been much discussion and controversy as to what is the correct test to apply in order to determine the national status of corporate entities; and although the better view is that (at least for public as opposed to private international law and some other purposes) the correct test is that of the State of incorporation, there is equally no doubt that different tests have been applied for different purposes, and that an element of fluidity is still present in this field.'

is incorporated and in whose territory it has its registered office. These two criteria have been confirmed by long practice and by numerous international instruments. This notwithstanding, further or different links are at times said to be required in order that a right of diplomatic protection should exist. Indeed, it has been the practice of some States to give a company incorporated under their law diplomatic protection solely when it has its seat (*siège social*) or management or centre of control in their territory, or when a majority or a substantial proportion of the shares has been owned by nationals of the State concerned. Only then, it has been held, does there exist between the corporation and the State in question a genuine connection of the kind familiar from other branches of international law. However, in the particular field of the diplomatic protection of corporate entities, no absolute test of the 'genuine connection' has found general acceptance. Such tests as have been applied are of a relative nature, and sometimes links with one State have had to be weighed against those with another. In this connection reference has been made to the *Nottebohm* case. In fact the Parties made frequent reference to it in the course of the proceedings. However, given both the legal and factual aspects of protection in the present case the Court is of the opinion that there can be no analogy with the issues raised or the decision given in that case.

71. In the present case, it is not disputed that the company was incorporated in Canada and has its registered office in that country. The incorporation of the company under the law of Canada was an act of free choice. Not only did the founders of the company seek its incorporation under Canadian law but it has remained under that law for a period of over 50 years. It has maintained in Canada its registered office, its accounts and its share registers. Board meetings were held there for many years; it has been listed in the records of the Canadian tax authorities. Thus a close and permanent connection has been established, fortified by the passage of over half a century. This connection is in no way weakened by the fact that the company engaged from the very outset in commercial activities outside Canada, for that was its declared object. Barcelona Traction's links with Canada are thus manifold.

...

77. It is true that at a certain point the Canadian Government ceased to act on behalf of Barcelona Traction, for reasons which have not been fully revealed, though a statement made in a letter of 19 July 1955 by the Canadian Secretary of State for External Affairs suggests that it felt the matter should be settled by means of private negotiations. The Canadian Government has nonetheless retained its capacity to exercise diplomatic protection; no legal impediment has prevented it from doing so: no fact has arisen to render this protection impossible. It has discontinued its action of its own free will.

78. The Court would here observe that, within the limits prescribed by international law, a State may exercise diplomatic protection by whatever means and to whatever extent it thinks fit, for it is its own right that the State is asserting. Should the natural or legal persons on whose behalf it is acting consider that their rights are not adequately protected, they have no remedy in international law. All they can do is to resort to

municipal law, if means are available, with a view to furthering their cause or obtaining redress. The municipal legislator may lay upon the State an obligation to protect its citizens abroad, and may also confer upon the national a right to demand the performance of that obligation, and clothe the right with corresponding sanctions. However, all these questions remain within the province of municipal law and do not affect the position internationally.

79. The State must be viewed as the sole judge to decide whether its protection will be granted, to what extent it is granted, and when it will cease. It retains in this respect a discretionary power the exercise of which may be determined by considerations of a political or other nature, unrelated to the particular case. Since the claim of the State is not identical with that of the individual or corporate person whose cause is espoused, the State enjoys complete freedom of action. Whatever the reasons for any change of attitude, the fact cannot in itself constitute a justification for the exercise of diplomatic protection by another government, unless there is some independent and otherwise valid ground for that.

The ICJ reiterated the identification of corporate nationality with the place of incorporation in the *Case Concerning Ahmadou Sadio Diallo* (the *Diallo Case*).[33] However, conferring treaty protection on a corporate investor by virtue of its place of incorporation may be inappropriate in some cases. For example, an investor of nationality C decides to invest in State B by channelling funds through a company incorporated in State A, so as to take advantage of the investment protection provisions found in a treaty concluded between States B and A.[34] The company has no business activities in State A and no assets to its name. Such a company is also known as a holding company or a shell company. In the event of a dispute arising from the investment made in State B, the investor brings a treaty claim against State B in the name of the company. Is this holding or shell company – the corporate investor bearing the nationality of the State of its incorporation – eligible for treaty protection?

The answer is found in the applicable investment treaty. Some treaties, like the 1991 US–Argentina BIT, do not expressly address the eligibility of holding or shell companies for treaty protection,[35] while other treaties, like the ECT, do.

---

[33] (*Guinea* v. *Congo*) (Preliminary Objections, Judgment) [2007] ICJ Rep. 582, paras 59–64.

[34] An alternative explanation for the incorporation of an offshore company to make investments is tax avoidance: see generally G. Zucman, *The Hidden Wealth of Nations: The Scourge of Tax Havens* (University of Chicago Press, 2015). This may enable the ultimate investor to avail itelf not only of the investment protection agreements concluded by its home State, but also of the investment protection agreements concluded by the various tax havens where the holding company or companies are incorporated; see also discussion at Section 4 below.

[35] Treaty between United States of America and the Argentine Republic Concerning the Reciprocal Encouragement and Protection of Investment (signed 14 November 1991, entered into force 20 October 1994).

US–Argentina BIT, Arts I(1)(b), VII(1)

I(1)(b). 'company' of a Party means any kind of corporation, company, association, state enterprise, or other organization, legally constituted under the laws and regulations of a Party or a political subdivision thereof whether or not organized for pecuniary gain, and whether privately or governmentally owned;

...

VII(1). For purposes of this Article, an investment dispute is a dispute between a Party and a national or company of the other Party arising out of or relating to (a) an investment agreement between that Party and such national or company; (b) an investment authorization granted by that Party's foreign investment authority (if any such authorization exists) to such national or company; or (c) an alleged breach of any right conferred or created by this Treaty with respect to an investment.

ECT, Art. 17(1)

Each Contracting Party reserves the right to deny the advantages of this Part to a legal entity if citizens or nationals of a third state own or control such entity and if that entity has no substantial business activities in the Area of the Contracting Party in which it is organized.

The difficulty with conferring treaty protection on holding or shell companies lies in their inherent inability to meet the aims of States in concluding investment treaties. Such companies will not 'stimulate the flow of private capital and the economic development of the [Contracting] Parties' (US–Argentina BIT, Preamble), or 'catalyse economic growth' (ECT, Preamble), as their non-integration into the economy of the State of incorporation means that profits from the investment are unlikely to be repatriated to that State.

Yet the presence of cumulative conditions for the denial of benefits in Article 17(1) of the ECT makes it possible for treaty protection to be conferred on shell companies, *so long as* they are owned or controlled by nationals of a Contracting Party other than the host State of the investment. In *Plama Consortium Ltd* v. *Bulgaria*, the claimant corporate investor admitted that it had no 'substantial business activities' in Cyprus, the place of incorporation and a Contracting State to the ECT.[36] However, the claimant was able to prove that it was owned and controlled by a French national before the dispute was submitted to arbitration.[37] Since France is a Contracting State to the ECT, and not a 'third [S]tate', the claimant, a shell company, was eligible for treaty protection.[38]

---

[36] ICSID Case No. ARB/03/24, Decision on Jurisdiction, 8 February 2005 (Salans, van den Berg, Veeder), para. 74; Award, 27 August 2008 (Salans, van den Berg, Veeder), para. 81.

[37] Award, paras 91–95.

[38] However, the tribunal found that the French owner of the Claimant procured governmental authorisation for the investment through fraudulent misrepresentation. By giving or failing to correct the impression that the investment had the financial backing of a consortium, instead of an individual with limited financial resources, 'this behavior is contrary to other provisions of Bulgarian law and to international law and that it, therefore, precludes the application of the protections of the ECT' (Award, para. 135, also 96–124, 138–48). The tribunal concluded that it 'cannot lend its support to Claimant's request and cannot, therefore, grant the substantive protections of the ECT'.

3.2 Foreign Control

In addition to the place of incorporation, the ICJ in the *Barcelona Traction Case* referred to an alternative test for corporate nationality, namely the place where a corporation has 'its seat (*siège social*) or management or centre of control'. As the ICJ opted to identify corporate nationality with the place of incorporation (Canada), the fact that Barcelona Traction was a company largely owned and controlled by non-Canadian shareholders (Belgian) was irrelevant. As the company was Canadian, only Canada was entitled to exercise diplomatic protection as the State of nationality. The Belgian shareholders, and by extension Belgium, had no standing to sue to recover damage inflicted on the value of the company's shares. What the ICJ left open in the *Barcelona Traction Case*,[39] but subsequently confirmed in the *Diallo Case*,[40] was the possibility for shareholders to vindicate infringement of their direct rights against a foreign State (such as management rights in a company), but not rights which belong to the company (such as rights pertaining to share value). Under customary international law, therefore, shareholders have no standing to bring a claim if State measures adversely impact the value of their shares. Their only recourse in this circumstance is against the company.

Under Article 25(2)(b) of the ICSID Convention, however, corporate nationality is determined by looking at the place of incorporation *and* the nationality of the controllers of the company. As many States require foreign capital to be injected through a locally incorporated company, pegging corporate nationality solely to the place of incorporation to determine eligibility for treaty protection becomes a zero-sum game for foreign investors. This defeats the reciprocal promotion and protection of foreign investment that investment treaties stand for. Therefore, for the purpose of establishing the jurisdiction of an ICSID tribunal over a claimant investor, Article 25(2)(b) permits a local corporation to assume the nationality of its foreign controllers.

In addition to the existence of foreign control, Article 25(2)(b) also requires the disputing parties to agree that a local corporation 'should be treated as a national of another Contracting State'.[41] However, this requirement has since been eclipsed by the requirement for foreign control. As succinctly explained by one tribunal, 'the virtually insurmountable burden of proof in showing what motivated a government's actions might well frustrate

---

[39] [1970] ICJ Rep. 3, paras 47–49.

[40] [2007] ICJ Rep. 582, paras 60–66.

[41] Agreement is usually explicit and can find expression in investment treaties (see, e.g., Art. VII(8) of the US–Argentina BIT, which provides 'For purposes of an arbitration held under paragraph 3 of the Article, any company legally constituted under the applicable laws and regulations of a Party or a political subdivision thereof but that, immediately before the occurrence of the event or events giving rise to the dispute, was an investment of nationals or companies of the other Party, shall be treated as a national or company of such other Party in accordance with Article 25(2)(b) of the ICSID Convention'), or in a contract for a specific investment (see, e.g., ICSID Model Clause 7, which provides 'It is hereby agreed that, although the Investor is a national of the Host State, it is controlled by nationals of name(s) of other Contracting State(s) and shall be treated as a national of [that]/[those] State[s] for the purposes of the Convention': http://icsidfiles.worldbank.org/icsid/icsid/staticfiles/model-clauses-en/9.htm#c (accessed 31 July 2020)). States can also pass legislation recognising a locally incorporated company subject to foreign control as a foreign national. For examples of domestic legislation that recognise foreign control as the determinant of corporate nationality, see C. H. Schreuer, L. Malintoppi, A. Reinisch and A. Sinclair (eds), *The ICSID Convention: A Commentary*, 2nd edn (Cambridge University Press, 2009), 310, §806.

the purpose of the [ICSID] Convention', and therefore, 'unless circumstances clearly indicate otherwise, it must be presumed that where there exists foreign control, the agreement to treat the company in question as a foreign national is "because" of this foreign control'.[42] Conversely, the absence of foreign control, in fact, cannot be swept aside by the disputing parties' agreement on foreign nationality.[43] Ascribing a foreign nationality to a local corporation under Article 25(2)(b) of the ICSID Convention thus turns on the presence or absence of foreign control.

ICSID Convention, Art. 25(2)(b)

'National of another Contracting State' means: any juridical person which had the nationality of a Contracting State other than the State party to the dispute on the date on which the parties consented to submit such dispute to conciliation or arbitration and any juridical person which had the nationality of the Contracting State party to the dispute on that date and which, because of foreign control, the parties have agreed should be treated as a national of another Contracting State for the purposes of this Convention.

Foreign control over a local corporation can be direct or indirect,[44] absolute or partial, exercised by a majority or minority shareholder. The exercise and extent of control is a question of fact that has to be answered on a case-by-case basis. To date, no tribunal has attempted to formulate a comprehensive test for foreign control. What emerges from arbitral jurisprudence instead are factors that are or may be indicative of foreign control; a non-binding, non-exhaustive checklist that can guide future arbitral tribunals in their factual determinations. Foreign control is likely in the following situations:

(1) where a foreign national(s) is/are the sole or majority shareholder(s) in the local corporation;[45]

(2) where a foreign national(s) has/have significant decision-making or veto power through voting rights;[46] and

(3) where a foreign national(s) has/have significant influence over the appointment and direction of managerial personnel.[47]

---

[42] *Liberian Eastern Timber Corp.* v. *Liberia* (*LETCO* v. *Liberia*), ICSID Case No. ARB/83/2, Award, 31 March 1986 (Cremades, Pereira, Redfern), p. 8.

[43] *Vacuum Salt Products Ltd* v. *Ghana*, ICSID Case No. ARB/92/1, Award, 16 February 1994 (Jennings, Brower, Hossain), para. 38.

[44] This usually refers to the proximity of the foreign national to the local company through its shareholding. Direct control is present when the foreign national is the immediate, sole shareholder of the local company, whereas indirect control can manifest itself through sole or substantial shareholdings in companies that are in turn sole or substantial shareholders in the local company: see *Aguas del Tunari, SA* v. *Bolivia*, ICSID Case No. ARB/02/3, Decision on the Respondent's Objections to Jurisdiction, 21 October 2005 (Caron, Alberro-Semerena, Alvarez), paras 318–319.

[45] *Klöckner Industrie-Anlagen GmbH and Others* v. *Cameroon and Another*, ICSID Case No. ARB/81/2, Award, 21 October 1983 (de Arechaga, Schmidt, Rogers) (51 per cent shareholding); *LETCO* v. *Liberia* (100 per cent shareholding); *Cable Television of Nevis Ltd and Another* v. *Federation of St Kitts and Nevis*, ICSID Case No. ARB/95/2, Award, 13 January 1997 (David, Maynard, McKay) (99 per cent shareholding); *Aguas del Tunari* v. *Bolivia* (55 per cent shareholding).

[46] *Vacuum Salt* v. *Ghana*, at para. 53, where the tribunal observed that a minority shareholding is not the antithesis to control, so long as it can be established that a minority shareholder was nonetheless able to 'steer, through positive or negative action, the fortunes of [the company]'.

[47] *Ibid.*

In addition to embracing a concept of corporate nationality that is more flexible than customary international law, investment treaty law is more generous with shareholder claims. Departing from the position in the *Barcelona Traction Case*, where shareholders could only enforce their direct rights against a host State, investment treaties often permit shareholders to enforce rights belonging to the company. As a result, shareholders can and often do challenge State measures which devalue their shareholding. The claims brought by US investors against Argentina in the wake of Argentina's economic collapse in the early 2000s are cases in point.[48] The investment, whether in the electricity, water or sewage disposal industry, was invariably made through an Argentinian company where the US investor was a shareholder. Measures taken by the Argentinian government in response to the economic crises caused share values to plunge, effectively wiping out the original investment. The claims were brought under the US–Argentina BIT, which includes 'shares of stock or other interests in a company' in its definition of a protected investment,[49] and 'any kind of corporation ... legally constituted under the laws and regulations of a Party' as a protected investor.[50]

Other investment protection agreements, such as the ACIA and the Comprehensive Economic and Trade Agreement (CETA),[51] expressly empower protected investors, including shareholders, to bring claims on behalf of a company that they own or control.

ACIA, Art. 28(b)

'disputing investor' means an investor of a Member State that makes a claim on its own behalf under this Section, and where relevant, includes an investor of a Member State that makes a claim on behalf of a juridical person of the other Member State that the investor owns or controls.

CETA, Art. 8.1, 8.18(1)

8.1 **covered investment** means, with respect to a Party, an investment:

...

(c) directly or indirectly owned or controlled by an investor of the other Party ...

investor means a Party, a natural person or an enterprise of a Party, other than a branch or a representative office, that seeks to make, is making or has made an investment in the territory of the other Party ...

...

8.18(1) Without prejudice to the rights and obligations of the Parties under Chapter Twenty-Nine (Dispute Settlement), an investor of a Party may submit to the Tribunal

---

[48] See, for instance, *CMS Gas Transmission Co.* v. *Argentina*, ICSID Case No. ARB/01/8; *Azurix Corp.* v. *Argentina*, ICSID Case No. ARB/01/12; *LG&E Energy Corp. and Others* v. *Argentina*, ICSID Case No. ARB/02/1; *Sempra Energy International* v. *Argentina*, ICSID Case No. ARB/02/16; *Pan American Energy LLC and Another* v. *Argentina*, ICSID Case No. ARB/03/13; and *El Paso Energy International Co.* v. *Argentina*, ICSID Case No. ARB/03/15. For more claims brought against Argentina by US investors, see http://italaw.com (accessed 31 July 2020).

[49] Art. I(1)(a)(ii).

[50] Art. I(1)(b).

[51] Signed 30 October 2016, not yet in force.

constituted under this Section a claim that the other Party has breached an obligation under:

(a) Section C, with respect to the expansion, conduct, operation, management, maintenance, use, enjoyment and sale or disposal of its covered investment; or

(b) Section D, where the investor claims to have suffered loss or damage as a result of the alleged breach.

***

The nationality of a corporate investor can either be determined by its place of incorporation or by the nationality of its foreign controller(s). The latter method of determining corporate nationality, which is activated if the applicable treaties make provision for it, responds to the widespread practice of injecting foreign capital through a locally incorporated company. Identifying corporate nationality solely with the place of incorporation will bar foreign investors who choose or are compelled by domestic laws to invest through a local vehicle from seeking treaty protection from the host State in the name of the local entity. Allowing a corporate investor's nationality to follow that of its foreign controller(s), often its majority shareholder(s), ensures that eligibility for treaty protection turns on nationality in substance (control), rather than nationality in form (incorporation).

4. 'DIVISIBLE' INVESTORS

There is no rule requiring foreign shareholders to bring a claim against a host State on behalf of the local company when seeking treaty protection. Shareholders can and often do sue in their own name. Shares fall within the stock treaty definition of protected investments, and when the shareholder possesses the nationality of the other Contracting State to the treaty, it qualifies as a protected investor. As a soured investment venture can affect more than one foreign shareholder, there are times when each foreign shareholder of the embattled local company brings a treaty claim against the host State, resulting in multiple claims which share a factual core. In the interests of minimising cost and time expenses, disputing parties may confer,[52] or be compelled by the relevant treaty,[53] to consolidate proceedings. This means that separate claims will be heard at the same time by the same tribunal. Parallel proceedings are neither uncommon in investment treaty arbitration, nor unseemly when the claimant investors are unrelated but for their

---

[52] *Suez, Sociedad General de Aguas de Barcelona and Another* v. *Argentina* and *AWG Group Ltd* v. *Argentina*, ICSID Case No. ARB/03/19 and UNCITRAL respectively, Decision on Jurisdiction, 3 August 2006 (Salacuse, Kaufmann-Kohler, Nikken), paras 1–6. Suez's claim was brought under the France–Argentina BIT, while AWG's claim was brought under the UK–Argentina BIT.

[53] For instance, Art. 1126(2) NAFTA provides: 'Where a Tribunal established under this Article is satisfied that claims have been submitted to arbitration under Article 1120 that have a question of law or fact in common, the Tribunal may, in the interests of fair and efficient resolution of the claims, and after hearing the disputing parties, by order: (a) assume jurisdiction over, and hear and determine together, all or part of the claims; or (b) assume jurisdiction over, and hear and determine one or more of the claims, the determination of which it believes would assist in the resolution of the others.' Art. 14.D.12(6) USMCA retains the substance of Art. 1126(2) NAFTA.

participation in a joint investment venture. However, parallel proceedings can also be launched by a foreign corporate investor(s) and its/their shareholder(s), seeking virtually identical relief under different investment treaties.

One example of a 'divisible' investor is found in *CME Czech Republic BV* v. *Czech Republic*[54] and *Ronald S. Lauder* v. *Czech Republic*.[55] CME, a Dutch company, was the majority shareholder in a Czech broadcasting company, while Mr Lauder, a US national, was an indirect shareholder through his controlling shareholding in CME. The dispute arose from the termination of a broadcasting licence. Both CME and Mr Lauder sought relief as protected investors for the Czech Republic's violations of treaty obligations owed to their protected investment in the Czech broadcasting company. CME brought its claim under the Netherlands–Czech Republic BIT,[56] while Mr Lauder brought his claim under the US–Czech Republic BIT.[57] Although CME and Mr Lauder possessed separate legal personalities, it would have been improbable for CME to bring a claim against the Czech Republic without the assent of its controlling shareholder, Mr Lauder. What could have been one claim brought by Mr Lauder was divided into two. The strong connection between CME and Mr Lauder made Mr Lauder – the ultimate, controlling shareholder in the Czech broadcasting company – a 'divisible' investor. The Czech Republic argued in both proceedings that this was an 'abuse of process'. The tribunals disagreed.

CME Czech Republic BV v. Czech Republic, UNCITRAL, Partial Award, 13 September 2001 (Kühn, Schwebel, Hándl), para. 412

There is also no abuse of the Treaty regime by Mr. Lauder in bringing virtually identical claims under two separate Treaties. The Czech Republic views it as inappropriate that claims are brought by different claimants under separate Treaties. The Czech Republic did not agree to consolidate the Treaty proceedings, a request raised by the Claimant (again) during these arbitration proceedings. The Czech Republic asserted the right to have each action determined independently and promptly. This has the consequence that there will be two awards on the same subject which may be consistent with each other or may differ. Should two different Treaties grant remedies to the respective claimants deriving from the same facts and circumstances, this does not deprive one of the claimants of jurisdiction, if jurisdiction is granted under the respective Treaty. A possible abuse by Mr. Lauder in pursuing his claim under the US Treaty as alleged by the Respondent does not affect jurisdiction in these arbitration proceedings.

---

[54] UNCITRAL, Partial Award, 13 September 2001 (Kühn, Schwebel, Hándl).
[55] UNCITRAL, Final Award, 3 September 2001 (Briner, Cutler, Klein).
[56] Agreement on Encouragement and Reciprocal Protection of Investments between the Kingdom of the Netherlands and the Czech and Slovak Federal Republic (signed 29 April 1991, entered into force 1 October 1992).
[57] Treaty with the Czech and Slovak Federal Republic Concerning the Reciprocal Encouragement and Protection of Investment (signed 22 October 1991, entered into force 19 December 1992).

> **Ronald S. Lauder v. Czech Republic, UNCITRAL, Final Award, 3 September 2001 (Briner, Cutler, Klein), para. 174**
>
> Finally, there is no abuse of process in the multiplicity of proceedings initiated by Mr. Lauder and the entities he controls. Even assuming that the doctrine of abuse of process could find application here, the Arbitral Tribunal is the only forum with jurisdiction to hear Mr. Lauder's claims based on the Treaty. The existence of numerous parallel proceedings does in no way affect the Arbitral Tribunal's authority and effectiveness, and does not undermine the Parties' rights. On the contrary, the present proceedings are the only place where the Parties' rights under the Treaty can be protected.

According to the *CME* v. *Czech Republic* and *Lauder* v. *Czech Republic* tribunals, 'divisible' investors are worthy of treaty protection. However, the observation by the *CME* v. *Czech Republic* tribunal that the Czech Republic should have opted to consolidate proceedings sidesteps the issue raised by the Czech Republic – the *propriety* of Mr Lauder launching parallel proceedings. Consolidation merges separate claims into a single hearing; it does not merge several claimants into one. The *Lauder* v. *Czech Republic* tribunal, in contrast, directly addressed the issue of *propriety*, explaining why parallel proceedings are permitted within the investment treaty framework. So long as an investor meets the nationality requirement in a given treaty, that investor is a protected investor.

It is notable how provision is made (in investment treaties and Article 25(2)(b) of the ICSID Convention) to disregard the separate legal personalities of corporations and their controllers for the purpose of nationality determination, but not in the context of parallel proceedings. While the piercing of the corporate veil in the former situation is justified by the concern for investor underprotection, the refusal to pierce in the latter may precipitate investor overprotection.[58] The danger with extending treaty protection to 'divisible' investors is the risk of double recovery. Double recovery is objectionable because it denotes the unjust enrichment of an undeserving party at the expense of another party.[59] If an investor brings multiple proceedings in his own name and in the names of entities he controls, suing under a different treaty in each proceeding, the host State may end up paying the same debt more than once, thereby unjustly enriching that investor. And even if the host State is not subjected to double recovery, it still incurs considerable expense defending multiple proceedings against an investor hedging its bets. This may explain why later parallel proceedings involving closely connected claimants have received closer scrutiny by arbitral tribunals.

---

[58] M. Waibel, 'Coordinating Adjudication Processes' in Z. Douglas, J. Pauwelyn and J. E. Viñuales (eds), *The Foundations of International Investment Law* (Oxford University Press, 2014), 513, 530. Not all are perturbed by signs of investor over-protection; see, e.g. V. V. Veeder, 'Issue Estoppel, Reasons for Awards and Transnational Arbitrations' (2003) 14 *ICC Bulletin* (Special Supplement) 72, 78: 'the practical lesson to be learnt from the CME case must lead to carefully structured investments to ensure that the ultimate investor can take advantage of as many BITs (and BIT arbitrations) as possible, thereby ensuring multiple bites at the cherry until success is ensured.'

[59] C. Schreuer, 'Unjustified Enrichment in International Law' (1974) 22 *Am J Comp L* 281, 288–297, 301.

In 2012, two separate claims were brought against Egypt concerning the termination of a gas supply contract concluded with a local company. One claim was brought by Ampal-American Israel Corp. and its affiliates, who were shareholders in the local company, under the US–Egypt BIT.[60] Another claim was brought by the CEO of Ampal, Mr Maiman, and two subsidiaries of Ampal under the Poland–Egypt investment treaty.[61] Both claims sought to recover damages from Egypt for the loss caused to Ampal's shareholding in the local company by the contractual termination. Like the Czech Republic in the CME/Lauder claims, Egypt argued that the bringing of 'duplicative claims' by the direct and indirect shareholders of the local company was an abuse of process.[62] Unlike the *CME* v. *Czech Republic* and *Lauder* v. *Czech Republic* tribunals, the *Ampal-American* v. *Egypt* tribunal appeared to be more wary of 'divisible' investors.

Ampal-American v. Egypt, ICSID Case No. ARB/12/11, Decision on Jurisdiction, 1 February 2016 (Fortier, McLachlan, Orrego Vicuña), paras 331, 334 (footnotes omitted)

331. Indeed, in the present arbitration, the Claimant Ampal, controlled by Mr. Yosef Maiman, advances its claims in respect of the same 12.5% indirect interest in EMG for which Ampal's 100% subsidiary, Merhav-Ampal Group Ltd (MAGL) (and its 50% subsidiary, Merhav-Ampal Energy Holdings) claim in the parallel Maiman arbitration (together the 'MAGL portion'). This is tantamount to double pursuit of the same claim in respect of the same interest. In the Tribunal's opinion, while the same party in interest might reasonably seek to protect its claim in two fora where the jurisdiction of each tribunal is unclear, once jurisdiction is otherwise confirmed, it would crystallize in an abuse of process for in substance the same claim is to be pursued on the merits before two tribunals. However, the Tribunal wishes to make it very clear that this resulting abuse of process is in no way tainted by bad faith on the part of the Claimants as alleged by the Respondent. It is merely the result of the factual situation that would arise were two claims to be pursued before different investment tribunals in respect of the same tranche of the same investment.

...

334. It lies in the power of Ampal, as 100% owner of MAGL through Ampal Energy Ltd (Israel) to cure the abuse here identified were Ampal and MAGL to elect, in light of the present Decision which has otherwise confirmed the Tribunal's jurisdiction, to submit the MAGL portion of the claim made in the Maiman arbitration to the exclusive jurisdiction of the present Tribunal, relinquishing that part of the claim in the Maiman arbitration, or conversely to pursue such claim only in the latter proceeding.

---

[60] *Ampal-American Israel Corp. and Others* v. *Egypt*, ICSID Case No. ARB/12/11, Decision on Jurisdiction, 1 February 2016 (Fortier, McLachlan, Orrego Vicuña).

[61] *Yousef Maiman and Others* v. *Egypt*, UNCITRAL, pending (McRae, Reisman, Thomas); Agreement between the Arab Republic of Egypt and the Republic of Poland for the Reciprocal Promotion and Protection of Investments, 1 July 1995.

[62] *Ampal-American* v. *Egypt*, Decision on Jurisdiction, paras 312–313.

By directing the Ampal group to discontinue one proceeding on the merits, the tribunal tried to alleviate the problem of 'divisible' investors. While this is a welcome development, it arguably does not go far enough. Host States remain exposed to multiple jurisdictional proceedings orchestrated by the same investor. And although only a handful of States so far have been sued by 'divisible' investors,[63] the trend will catch on if more investors perceive that the benefit of bringing multiple jurisdictional proceedings outweighs its cost. The *CME v. Czech Republic/Lauder v. Czech Republic* outcome taught investors to adopt the aggressive strategy of bringing multiple claims, and to aim for multiple recovery for loss suffered. The *Ampal-American v. Egypt* decision checks, to some extent, the abuse of process by 'divisible' investors, by allowing the main claimant to proceed to the merits phase under only one investment treaty.

Doubt surrounds the eligibility of 'divisible' investors for treaty protection. As a 'divisible' investor orchestrates the bringing of multiple treaty claims against the same host State for the same dispute for the sole objective of boosting his/its chances of success, the risk of double recovery is troublingly high. Although earlier arbitral tribunals did not consider the bringing of multiple treaty claims by a 'divisible' investor an abuse of process, modern-day tribunals may gravitate towards the opposite view.

CONCLUSION

Protected investors include individual investors, corporate investors and, for some tribunals, 'divisible' investors. The third category of investors, which can be made up of individuals or corporations and is characterised by the bringing of multiple claims under multiple investment treaties by closely connected claimants, pushes the limits of treaty protection. The test for determining whether individual or corporate investors are eligible for treaty protection centres around their nationality. This calls for an examination of

[63] Other than the Czech Republic and Egypt, Laos has also been sued by a 'divisible' investor. In two Notices of Arbitration filed on the same day, Laos was named as the respondent in *Lao Holdings NV v. Laos*, ICSID Case No. ARB(AF)/12/6 (*Lao Holdings v. Laos*) (Laos–Netherlands investment treaty) and *Sanum Investments Ltd v. Laos*, UNICTRAL, PCA Case No. 2013-13 (*Sanum Investments v. Laos*) (China–Laos investment treaty). The investment in gaming projects in Laos, and the object of the dispute, was made by Sanum Investments, a Macanese company. Lao Holdings, a Dutch company, acquired Sanum Investments several months before it commenced arbitration against Laos. The 'divisible' investor is Lao Holdings, the owner of Sanum Investments. Both arbitral tribunals established jurisdiction over the dispute under the respective treaties, in full awareness of an existing parallel proceeding (*Lao Holdings v. Laos*, Decision on Jurisdiction, 21 February 2014 (Binnie, Hanotiau, Stern), para. 19; *Sanum Investments v. Laos*, Award on Jurisdiction, 13 December 2013 (Hanotiau, Stern, Rigo Sureda), para. 41). Neither tribunal considered the propriety of Lao Holdings running parallel proceedings or recommended the discontinuation of one proceeding at the merits phase. And although both suits were dismissed on the merits for lack of evidence (*Lao Holdings v. Laos*, Award, 6 August 2019, para. 293; *Sanum Investments v. Laos*, Award, 6 August 2019, para. 264), the tribunals' willingness to hear both Lao Holdings' and Sanum Investments' expropriation claims against Laos, brought under different investment treaties, regarding the *same* slot club engenders a real risk of double recovery: see *Lao Holdings v. Laos*, Award, paras 172–190; *Sanum Investments v. Laos*, Award, paras 178–196. Apart from declaring that Sanum Investments and Lao Holdings were distinct claimants bringing distinct claims (*Lao Holdings v. Laos*, Award, para. 3; *Sanum Investments v. Laos*, Award, para. 3), neither tribunal appeared in the least concerned that all of the claims shared a factual core wholly shaped by the activities of Sanum Investments.

the date(s) and circumstances of nationality acquisition. A protected investor is normally expected to bear the nationality of another Contracting State to an investment treaty when the investment was made, and when the dispute is being submitted to arbitration. An investor will likely be denied treaty protection if it acquired a particular nationality shortly before and with the objective of bringing a treaty claim. As a general rule, disputes between nationals and their home States do not fall within the purview of investment treaties. These disputes should be settled before domestic courts.

The nationality of an individual investor is determined by verifying the requirements under the laws of the State where nationality is claimed. A valid passport or official certification of citizenship are common modes of proof. An individual's nationality can change over time, for example by the acquisition of the nationality of the State of present domicile and the loss of the nationality of the State of previous domicile. An individual can also possess more than one nationality. So long as the individual investor is not adjudged to be a national of the State against whom a treaty claim is being brought, dual nationals are just as eligible for treaty protection as single nationals. Some individual investors are nationals of one State and permanent residents of another. Whether permanent residents are eligible for treaty protection from the State of residence depends on the wording of the relevant investment protection agreement.

The nationality of a corporate investor is identified either by its place of incorporation or, in the case of certain investment treaties and Article 25(2)(b) of the ICSID Convention, by the nationality of its controllers. Relying solely on the place of incorporation to ascertain the nationality of a corporate investor may disqualify many corporate investors from seeking treaty protection. This is because it is common practice for foreign investment to enter a State through a locally incorporated company with foreign shareholders. Under customary international law, injury to the company, such as loss of share value, can only be vindicated by the company or the company's State of incorporation – not by its shareholders or the shareholders' home State. There are no such restrictions in investment treaty law. To facilitate the reciprocal promotion and protection of investments and investors, and to ensure that treaty protection is not unduly circumscribed by form, claims can be brought by locally incorporated companies subject to foreign control against host States. Telling factors of foreign control include majority shareholding, significant voting rights and appreciable influence over corporate management.

QUESTIONS

1. What is the difference between 'round-tripping' and litigation-oriented nationality acquisition? What are some possible reasons for tribunals recognising the former as a legitimate way to acquire nationality, but not the latter? Are these reasons sound?
2. Consider the excerpted reasoning of the tribunal in *Philip Morris* v. *Australia*. What is an 'abuse of rights'? Why is Philip Morris' corporate restructuring for the sole purpose of securing treaty protection so objectionable that it amounts to an 'abuse of rights'?
3. Is the current test for individual nationality driven by form, substance or both? Is this test satisfactory?

4. With the rise of 'divisible' investors, what are the options available to host States for countering aggressive litigation strategies?

5. Some consider international investment law to date to be overprotective of shareholders and corporations. Do you agree with this assessment and why?

SUGGESTIONS FOR FURTHER READING

1. E. C. Schlemmer, 'Investment, Investor, Nationality and Shareholders' in P. Muchlinski, F. Ortino and C. Schreuer (eds), *The Oxford Handbook of International Investment Law* (Oxford University Press, 2008), 51.

2. C. Schreuer, L. Malintoppi, A. Reinisch and A. Sinclair (eds), *The ICSID Convention: A Commentary*, 2nd edn (Cambridge University Press, 2009), 263–337.

3. C. McLachlan, '*Lis Pendens* in International Litigation' (2008) 336 *RCADI* 199.

4. M. Waibel, 'Coordinating Adjudication Processes' in Z. Douglas, J. Pauwelyn and J. E. Viñuales (eds), *The Foundations of International Investment Law* (Oxford University Press, 2014), 499.

12

Fair and Equitable Treatment, and Full Protection and Security

CHAPTER OUTLINE

This chapter discusses two important 'absolute' standards of treaty protection – fair and equitable treatment (FET) and full protection and security (FPS). Section 1 explains the idea of an international minimum standard of treatment (MST) for the protection of foreign-owned property, and its oft-perceived relationship with both FET and FPS treaty clauses. Section 2 contains excerpts of some well-known arbitral awards discussing both FET and FPS. Section 2.1 describes the most common heads of claim under the general rubric of FET. Section 2.2 reproduces tribunal awards which discuss the precise standard of treatment under FPS. Thereafter, Section 2.3 discusses some of the complexities faced today in the growing interrelationship between FET and FPS. Section 3 reproduces two of the latest treaty clauses, including an attempt to enumerate and particularise the contents of the FET obligation, while Section 4 contains an expanded discussion of a possible key difference between 'qualified' and 'unqualified' treaty clauses – i.e. a difference which turns upon whether the treaty language stipulates or suggests a connection with customary international law standards of protection. Notwithstanding particular forms of treaty language, might there be a latent and even more complex conceptual interaction between custom and treaty? That issue might perhaps be distilled into a single question – with the many thousands of bilateral investment treaties which have come into being, has not the customary international law standard of protection risen over time on the back of such treaty practice?

INTRODUCTION

The standards discussed in this chapter are referred to as 'absolute', the reason being that unlike the most-favoured-nation standard, which requires all foreign investors to be treated equally favourably, or the national treatment standard, which requires foreign and domestic investors to be treated equally favourably,[1] fair and equitable treatment (FET) and full protection and security (FPS) are not measured against – i.e. they are *not* 'relative

---

[1] For which, see Chapter 13 of this book.

to' – the nature of treatment given elsewhere. It is also to be noted that a FET claim is the most popular head of claim today, by reason of the fact that it may be easier to establish than an expropriation claim.

1. RELATIONSHIP WITH AN INTERNATIONAL MINIMUM STANDARD OF TREATMENT

1.1 The 'Minimum Standard' of Treatment

We begin with the perspective most commonly associated with contemporary US treaties. According to this view, both FET and FPS are only expressions or mere components of an international minimum standard of treatment (MST) of foreign-owned property. The classic proposition that there is an international MST was reflected in the famous correspondence, in 1938, between US Secretary of State Cordell Hull and the Mexican government following the Mexican Revolution, in which Mexico had instituted agrarian reforms that the United States alleged to be the expropriation of agrarian properties owned by US nationals. Mexico in turn claimed that the treatment of foreign nationals and their property according to the standard applied by Mexico to its own nationals was simply an expression of national treatment and of equality of treatment. Mexico intimated in its correspondence with Secretary Hull that, as such, the United States could hardly object. Secretary Hull replied that the United States had no objection to such principles provided that they were not distorted by deviating from an international MST.[2] The international MST is thus an absolute, minimum standard; absolute in the sense that it depends not on the national standards and laws applied by the host State,[3] and a minimum standard in the sense that no lesser standard of treatment ought to be accepted by foreign investors regardless of how Mexico might choose to treat the property rights of its own nationals. The United States was alleging an international consensus which Mexico was at pains to deny. The idea that there is an international MST for foreign-owned property has been central to the development of the international law on foreign investment and the practice of investment arbitration.

The diplomatic exchange between the United States and Mexico concerned the appropriate standard of compensation for Mexican expropriations of American-owned property. Thus, the international MST has been said to comprise three elements: first, the standard of compensation for the expropriation of foreign-owned property; second, a rule against denial of justice; and third, the responsibility of the host State for violence and the destruction of foreign-owned property.[4] Expropriation is dealt with in Chapter 14 of this book. This chapter is concerned with denials of justice to foreign property owners,

---

[2] See US Secretary of State to Mexican Ambassador, 22 August 1938, reproduced in A. Lowenfeld, *International Economic Law*, 2nd edn (Oxford University Press, 2008), 478–479.

[3] For a contemporary statement of this position, see the US Rejoinder of 15 March 2007, 144, in *Glamis Gold, Ltd v. USA*, UNCITRAL (NAFTA) Arbitration, available at www.state.gov.

[4] M. Sornarajah, *The International Law on Foreign Investment*, 3rd edn (Cambridge University Press, 2010), 346, who doubts the application of the MST outside these areas.

which today is discussed under the rubric of FET, and international responsibility for the destruction of foreign-owned property, which today falls under the rubric of FPS.[5]

1.2 Fair and Equitable Treatment

Some key characteristics of the FET treaty standard today, characteristics which have attracted considerable attention, are its flexibility, its apparently broad scope and its continued expansion and popularity as a head of claim in investment arbitration. Today, it is said that overly broad readings of FET clauses by tribunals in recent years is one of the principal elements fuelling a backlash against investment arbitration.[6] There is truth in that observation, but the criticism that some of these tribunal pronouncements have been capricious,[7] or that there have been clear examples of overt law-creation on the part of investment arbitration tribunals,[8] should not cloud the fact that any intrinsic breadth or capaciousness of the FET notion had long ago been remarked upon by the late F. A. Mann[9] almost two decades before the first investment tribunal pronouncements which have been the cause of contemporary controversy. The current controversy concerns allegedly overbroad readings of the FET standard, initially by pitching that standard as one which is autonomous of and independent from the international law MST,[10] and subsequently by extending the scope of protection beyond situations involving a denial of justice to those which, as the *Waste Management* tribunal had put it, involve 'arbitrary, grossly unfair, unjust or idiosyncratic' treatment, terms which moreover are to be interpreted flexibly.[11] Such flexibility has been defended by other writers as a necessary requirement of the need to treat each case on its own facts.[12]

One could do worse than to begin with Dr F. A. Mann. Commenting in the early 1980s on the FET clause in the UK–Philippines BIT, where the British treaties since 1975 had

---

[5] It is also worth mentioning that 'North American' investment treaties reflect, in a way, the approach taken in this chapter by expressly subsuming FET and FPS (but not the rule against uncompensated expropriation) under the clause which states that the MST applies.

[6] The authors observe that this sentence was relied upon by the Colombian Constitutional Court, Judgment C-252/19. For the backlash, see Chapter 20 of this book.

[7] M. Sornarajah, 'The Fair and Equitable Standard of Treatment: Whose Fairness? Whose Equity?' in F. Ortino, L. Liberti, A. Sheppard and H. Warner (eds), *Investment Treaty Law, Current Issues II: Nationality and Investment Treaty Claims and Fair and Equitable Treatment* (London: BIICL, 2007); cf. R. Dolzer and C. Schreuer, *Principles of International Investment Law*, 2nd edn (Oxford University Press, 2012), 139.

[8] M. Sornarajah, 'A Coming Crisis: Expansionary Trends in Investment Treaty Arbitration' in K. Sauvant (ed.), *Appeals Mechanism in International Investment Disputes* (Oxford University Press, 2008), 39–77.

[9] F. A. Mann, 'British Treaties for the Promotion and Protection of Investments' (1981)52 *BYbIL* 241, 243.

[10] See *S. D. Myers, Inc. v. Government of Canada*, UNCITRAL (NAFTA) Arbitration, Partial Award, 13 November 2000, para. 266; cf. NAFTA Free Trade Commission, Notes of Interpretation of Certain Chapter 11 Provisions (Washington, DC, 31 July 2001), clarifying that the standard is not higher than the customary minimum standard of Treatment. This clarification has been reflected in successive US Model BITs, beginning with the 2004 US Model BIT and most recently in the 2012 US Model BIT, Art. 5(2); in the Trans-Pacific Partnership Agreement 2016 and now in the Comprehensive Agreement for Trans-Pacific Partnership 2018, Art. 9.6(2); and also in Canada's recent China–Canada BIT 2012, Art. 4(2).

[11] *Waste Management Inc. v. Mexico ('No. 2')*, ICSID Case No. ARB(AF)00/3, Award, 30 April 2004, paras 98, 99. See further, D. Schneiderman, 'The Paranoid Style of Investment Lawyers and Arbitrators: Investment Law Norm Entrepreneurs and Their Critics' in C. L. Lim (ed.), *Alternative Visions of the International Law on Foreign Investment: Essays in Honour of Muthucumaraswamy Sornarajah* (Cambridge University Press, 2016), 131, 136–137.

[12] Dolzer and Schreuer, *Principles of International Investment Law*, 139.

also borne striking similarities in their nature, content and structure to German, Swiss and French treaties, Mann had proposed that inequitable treatment is a concept which is broader than simply unfair treatment.

F. A. Mann, 'British Treaties for the Promotion and Protection of Investments' (1981) 52 *BYbIL* 241, 243

The overriding obligation is that investments 'shall at all times be accorded fair and equitable treatment and shall enjoy full protection and security' ... Although these are very familiar terms they have hardly ever been judicially considered. Thus, while it may be suggested that arbitrary, discriminatory or abusive treatment is contrary to customary international law, unfair and inequitable treatment is a much wider conception which may readily include such administrative measures in the field of taxation, licences and so forth, as are not plainly illegal in the accepted sense of international law ... So general a provision is likely to be almost sufficient to cover all conceivable cases, and it may well be that other provisions of the Agreements affording substantive protection are no more than examples or specific instances of this overriding duty.

That was a potent prophecy. Today, we ask how far the notion of FET should extend beyond Mann's categories of 'arbitrary, discriminatory and abusive' treatment. While the United States still tends to employ a broad formulation,[13] the rising trend in recent treaties has been to confine the notion of FET to only the above-mentioned forms of specific ill-treatment and to do so in express terms.[14] Other recent examples of the struggle of treaty draftsmen with the drafting of suitably circumscribed FET clauses omit reference to the troublesome notion of FET altogether, merely stating the wrongfulness of those specific categories of treatment.[15] Yet other examples can be shown which carve out

---

[13] According to Art. 5(2)(a) of the 2012 US Model BIT: '"fair and equitable treatment" includes the obligation not to deny justice in criminal, civil, or administrative adjudicatory proceedings in accordance with the principle of due process embodied in the principal legal systems of the world', and this is reflected, for example, in the Trans-Pacific Partnership Agreement, 24 February 2016, and now in the Comprehensive Agreement for Trans-Pacific Partnership, 8 March 2018, Art. 9.6(2)(a).

[14] Article 8.10(2) of legally reviewed text of the EU–Canada Comprehensive Economic Trade Agreement, 29 February 2016, now exemplifies this: 'A Party breaches the obligation of fair and equitable treatment referenced in paragraph 1 if a measure or series of measures constitutes: (a) denial of justice in criminal, civil or administrative proceedings; (b) fundamental breach of due process, including a fundamental breach of transparency, in judicial and administrative proceedings; (c) manifest arbitrariness; (d) targeted discrimination on manifestly wrongful grounds, such as gender, race or religious belief; (e) abusive treatment of investors, such as coercion, duress and harassment; or (f) a breach of any further elements of the fair and equitable treatment obligation adopted by the Parties in accordance with paragraph 3 of this Article.'

[15] The India Model BIT 2016 makes no mention of 'fair and equitable treatment' in Art. 3(1), but states that: 'Each Party shall not subject Investments of Investors of the other Party to Measures which constitute: (i) Denial of justice under customary international law; (ii) Un-remedied and egregious violations of due process; or (iii) Manifestly abusive treatment involving continuous, unjustified and outrageous coercion or harassment.'

particular matters such as taxation from the scope of the FET clause,[16] or seek to limit the extension of the FET clause to such matters.[17]

It is important to be mindful, therefore, of differences in treaty language. Perhaps the most basic difference to consider, which has already been mentioned, is the difference in a 'North American' approach, exemplified by NAFTA[18] and the US Model BITs today, in which the FET and FPS standards are subsumed under the MST, and where the appropriate treaty clause 'qualifies' the MST standard by stating that it amounts to no more than the standard available under customary international law. We will come back to the difference between 'qualified' and 'unqualified' types of FET and FPS clauses. But as to the question 'Why has FET become so controversial?', the answer lies ultimately in its success as a basis for investor claims before investment tribunals.

1.3 Full Protection and Security

The classic example of the FPS standard in operation may be found in the unanswered killing of an American mine superintendent in Mexico in the *Neer* claim. In *Neer*, the United States had brought a claim against Mexico on behalf of the deceased's widow and daughter for Mexico's failure to meet its FPS obligation by failing to capture the killer.[19] A key feature was the fact that although the killer was well known, he remained at liberty and thus there was, it was alleged, a shocking and egregious quality to Mexico's breach of its duty to afford full protection and security. The US–Mexican Claims Commission had held that 'the propriety of governmental acts should be put to the test of international standards', and that the wrong 'should amount to an outrage, to bad faith, to willful neglect of duty, or to an insufficiency of governmental action so far short of international standards' that every reasonable person would recognise that insufficiency. Much of the difficulty involves agreement on whether, as the *Neer* tribunal had put it, the conduct of the host State should amount to 'outrage, to bad faith, to willful neglect',[20] or whether responsibility should attach notwithstanding the absence of any fault on the part of the host State.[21] The former is usually termed the 'subjective' theory and the latter the 'objective' theory of responsibility.

As we have also seen, there may always have been a historical association between FET and FPS. That association has only become more, not less, pronounced as we began to see modern cases which extended the FPS standard beyond physical protection. Once

---

[16] See, e.g., India Model BIT 2016.

[17] For an illuminating comparison, see Art. 29.4(8) of the Trans-Pacific Partnership Agreement, and now the Comprehensive Agreement for Trans-Pacific Partnership, in force 30 December 2019 following the sixth ratification, under which, if both home and host States agree that a tax measure is not expropriatory, no expropriation claim brought on the basis of that measure will survive. Notice in particular how this clause applies only to expropriation, but not to an FET claim.

[18] North American Free Trade Agreement (NAFTA), 17 December 1992.

[19] *Neer Case (USA v. Mexico)*, 4 RIAA 60 (1926); 3 ILR 213.

[20] *Ibid.* Other famous examples are *Home Frontier Missionary Society (USA v. Britain)* (1920) VI RIAA 42, and Judge Krylov's dissenting opinion in the *Corfu Channel Case* [1949] ICJ Rep. 1, at 72.

[21] *Estate of Jean-Baptiste Caire (France v. Mexico)*, (1929) V RIAA 516.

that began to occur, the line between 'destruction and violence' and 'denials of justice' became uncertain, if not confused.

2. THE HEADS OF CLAIM UNDER FET AND FPS, THEIR EVOLUTION AND INTERRELATIONSHIP

The excerpts below are intended to illustrate the application of the FET (Section 2.1) and FPS (Section 2.2) standards by modern tribunals, as well as the modern overlap and interrelationship between FET and FPS (Section 2.3). That overlap is sometimes said to result from the extension of FPS beyond protection against physical harm or violence, but it will also be seen below that FET itself had begun to be extended towards protecting the stability of the business or legal environment in which an investment operates.

2.1 Heads of Claim under FET

At its core, the FET rule, or the old standard of 'denial of justice' under the MST, is about unfair treatment, however variously described over the years. There has admittedly been a preoccupation with formulations. Mann considered that 'arbitrary, discriminatory or abusive treatment is contrary to customary international law', but added that 'unfair and inequitable treatment is a much wider conception'.[22] The tribunal in *Waste Management*, referred to earlier and which we will go on to discuss below, adopted a different tack by referring to 'arbitrary, grossly unfair, unjust or idiosyncratic' conduct, adding crucially that each of these is to be interpreted 'flexibly'. Even so, the 'sub-heads' of FET claims are today broadly discernible from the patterns of available tribunal jurisprudence. At its core, FET consists of arbitrary and discriminatory treatment and denials of justice and due process. However, new heads of claim have arisen, not least in claims that there had been a violation of the legitimate expectations of the investor,[23] including its expectation of business and legal stability.

2.1.1 Arbitrary and Discriminatory Treatment

This is perhaps the clearest example of a FET violation. Here are two Argentinian disputes for the purpose of comparison. Both involved the privatisation of services in Argentina. In *CMS*, the US company held a 30 per cent share in an Argentine gas transportation company. Its right to calculate tariffs in US dollars for transporting gas was abrogated following a sharp depreciation in the Argentinian peso. In *LG&E*, the claimant had bought stakes in three Argentinian gas transportation and gas distribution companies, and the claim arose in similar circumstances as the claim in *CMS* following Argentina's 'pesoisation' policy.

---

[22] Mann, 'British Treaties for the Promotion and Protection of Investments', 243.
[23] This new head is not limited to FET claims only, but also extends to developments in indirect expropriation claims. Notice that in *Metalclad v. Mexico*, Award, 30 August 2000 (ICSID Case No. ARB(AF)/97/1), a short extract from which appears in this chapter, violation of investor expectations led to a finding of indirect expropriation. See further, S. Fietta, 'Expropriation and the "Fair and Equitable Treatment Standard"' in Ortino *et al.*, *Investment Treaty Law, Current Issues II*, 183.

CMS Gas Transmission Co. v. *Argentina*, ICSID Case No. ARB/01/8, Award, 12 May 2005 (Professor Francisco Orrego-Vicuña, President; Hon. Marc Lalonde PC, OC QC; HE Judge Francisco Rezek), para. 290

The standard of protection against arbitrariness and discrimination is related to that of fair and equitable treatment. Any measure that might involve arbitrariness or discrimination is in itself contrary to fair and equitable treatment. The standard is next related to impairment: the management, operation, maintenance, use, enjoyment, acquisition, expansion, or disposal of the investment must be impaired by the measures adopted.[24]

LG&E Energy Corp. and Others v. *Argentina*, ICSID Case No. ARB/02/1, Decision on Liability, 3 October 2006 (Dr Tatiana B. de Merkelt, President; Judge Francisco Rezek; Professor Albert Jan van den Berg), para. 162

While Claimants have alleged Argentina's political motivation to use foreign investors in the public utility sector as an excuse to justify the economic mistakes committed in the country, Argentina has explained that the Government's motivation was its desire to avoid its full economic collapse. To this end, it entered into agreements with the licensees in 2001, in addition to other actions taken. Bearing in mind the Tribunal's analysis, characterizing the measures as not arbitrary does not mean that such measures are characterized as fair and equitable or regarded as not having affected the stability of the legal framework under which gas transportation companies in Argentina operated. On the contrary, this means that Argentina faced severe economic and social hardships from 2001 onwards and had to react to the circumstances prevailing at the time. Even though the measures adopted by Argentina may not have been the best, they were not taken lightly, without due consideration. This is particularly reflected in the PPI adjustments which, before deciding on their postponement, Argentina negotiated with the investors. The Tribunal concludes that the charges imposed by Argentina to Claimants' investment, though unfair and inequitable, were the result of reasoned judgment rather than simple disregard of the rule of law.

---

[24] Unlike the *Enron* and *Sempra* Awards, discussed in Section 4.2, the *CMS* Award was not annulled despite a finding by the Ad Hoc Committee that there was a manifest error of law. The Award was upheld on the basis that this did not amount to a manifest excess of powers. *CMS* v. *Argentina*, ICSID Case No. ARB/01/8, Decision on Annulment, 25 September 2007, paras 130, 136, 158–159; for a discussion of this, and also of the *Enron* and *Sempra* annulments, see E. A. Martinez, 'Understanding the Debate over Necessity: Unanswered Questions and Future Implications of Annulment in the Argentine Gas Cases' (2012) 23 *Duke J Int'l Comp L* 149, 151, 169, and generally.

2.1.2 Violation of Due Process and Lack of Transparency

'Due process' is US treaty terminology,[25] and unsurprisingly is found in American FET clauses. The NAFTA tribunal jurisprudence is therefore instructive, subsuming notions such as a lack of transparency on the part of the host State under that term, in addition to arbitrary, unfair and 'unjust or idiosyncratic' conduct by the host State. That jurisprudence has also seen a rejection of any requirement of bad faith on the part of the host State. The cases reproduced below all involved denials of operating licences. In *Waste Management*, the investor had been granted an exclusive waste disposal concession. The local mayor had intervened following public unrest, and the investor failed to receive payments due under a credit line in its favour.

> *Waste Management Inc. v. Mexico ('No. 2')*, ICSID Case No. ARB (AF)/00/3, Award, 30 April 2004 (Professor James Crawford, President; Benjamin R. Civiletti; Mr Eduardo Magallón Gómez), para. 98
>
> The search here is for the [NAFTA] Article 1105 standard of review, and it is not necessary to consider the specific results reached in the cases discussed above. But as this survey shows, despite certain differences of emphasis a general standard for Article 1105 is emerging. Taken together, the *S.D. Myers, Mondev, ADF* and *Loewen* cases suggest that the minimum standard of treatment of fair and equitable treatment is infringed by conduct attributable to the State and harmful to the claimant if the conduct is arbitrary, grossly unfair, unjust or idiosyncratic, is discriminatory and exposes the claimant to sectional or racial prejudice, or involves a lack of due process leading to an outcome which offends judicial propriety – as might be the case with a manifest failure of natural justice in judicial proceedings or a complete lack of transparency and candour in an administrative process. In applying this standard it is relevant that the treatment is in breach of representations made by the host State which were reasonably relied on by the claimant.

For the transparency requirement under FET, another notable case, of which there are many, was *Metalclad* v. *Mexico*, which had involved the difficulty faced by the investor in obtaining, and ultimately being denied, a local licence permit for a waste landfill notwithstanding the Mexican federal government's prior assurance that 'all' necessary permits had been obtained. The violation of the transparency requirement was considered to be a violation of the FET standard. We will come back to the link between transparency and an investor's legitimate expectations, which is also referred to in *Metalclad* below.

---

[25] The Fifth and Fourteenth Amendments of the US Constitution state, respectively, 'nor shall any person ... be deprived of life, liberty, or property, without due process of law ...' and 'nor shall any State deprive any person of life, liberty, or property, without due process of law'. The phrase, however, derives from the confirmation of Magna Carta. See P. Millett, *As in Memory Long* (London: Wildy, 2015), 186 for the recent observation that 'it protected the subject from absolute monarchy and the exercise of arbitrary executive power ... But such expressions mean different things in different ages'.

Metalclad Corp. v. Mexico, ICSID Case No. ARB (AF)/97/1, Award, 30 August 2000 (Professor Sir Elihu Lauterpacht QC CBE, President; Mr Benjamin R. Civiletti; Mr José Luis Siqueiros), paras 49, 76

49. Metalclad asserts that SLP was invited to participate in the process of negotiating the Convenio, but that SLP declined. The Governor of SLP denounced the Convenio shortly after it was publicly announced.

...

76. Prominent in the statement of principles and rules that introduces the Agreement is the reference to 'transparency' (NAFTA Article 102(1)). The Tribunal understands this to include the idea that all relevant legal requirements for the purpose of initiating, completing and successfully operating investments made, or intended to be made, under the Agreement should be capable of being readily known to all affected investors of another Party. There should be no room for doubt or uncertainty on such matters. Once the authorities of the central government of any Party (whose international responsibility in such matters has been identified in the preceding section) become aware of any scope for misunderstanding or confusion in this connection, it is their duty to ensure that the correct position is promptly determined and clearly stated so that investors can proceed with all appropriate expedition in the confident belief that they are acting in accordance with all relevant laws.

...

99. Mexico failed to ensure a transparent and predictable framework for Metalclad's business planning and investment. The totality of these circumstances demonstrates a lack of orderly process and timely disposition in relation to an investor of a Party acting in the expectation that it would be treated fairly and justly in accordance with the NAFTA.

2.1.3 Is There a Requirement of 'Bad Faith' on the Part of the Host State?

American notions of due process require no showing of bad faith. Procedural irregularity itself may be sufficient. Compare the following cases. The first case, *Genin*, involved shareholders in a financial institution which had its licence cancelled by the Central Bank of Estonia. The second, *Loewen*, involved a Canadian investor's complaint that US anti-trust laws which required payment of treble (i.e. punitive) damages was a violation of FET. *Azurix* and *CMS* were a part of the proliferation of Argentinian cases following the Argentinian crisis. Except for *Genin*, all the tribunals in the other cases excerpted below rejected any requirement of bad faith.

Alex Genin, Eastern Credit Ltd, Inc. and AS Baltoil v. Estonia, ICSID Case No. ARB/99/2, Award, 25 June 2001 (Mr L. Yves Fortier CC QC, President; Professor Meir Heth; Professor Albert Jan van den Berg), para. 371

It is also relevant that the Tribunal, having regard to the totality of the evidence, regards the decision by the Bank of Estonia to withdraw the license as justified. In light of this conclusion, in order to amount to a violation of the BIT, any procedural irregularity that may have been present would have to amount to bad faith, a wilful disregard of due process of law or an extreme insufficiency of action. None of these are present in the case at hand. In sum, the Tribunal does not regard the license withdrawal as an arbitrary act that violates the Tribunal's 'sense of juridical propriety.' Accordingly, the Tribunal finds that the Bank of Estonia's actions did not violate Article II(3)(b) of the BIT.

Loewen Group, Inc. and Raymond L. Loewen v. USA, ICSID Case No. ARB (AF)/98/3, Award, 26 June 2003 (Sir Anthony Mason, President; Judge Abner J. Mikva; Lord Mustill), para. 132

Neither State practice, the decisions of international tribunals nor the opinion of commentators support the view that bad faith or malicious intention is an essential element of unfair and inequitable treatment or denial of justice amounting to a breach of international justice. Manifest injustice in the sense of a lack of due process leading to an outcome which offends a sense of judicial propriety is enough, even if one applies the Interpretation according to its terms.

Azurix Corp. v. Argentina, ICSID Case No. ARB/01/12, Award, 14 July 2006 (Dr Andrés Rigo Sureda, President; Hon. Marc Lalonde PC, OC QC; Dr Daniel Hugo Martins), paras 366, 372

366. The parties have interpreted differently how arbitral tribunals have understood this standard. We will turn to the cases discussed. Argentina has placed particular emphasis on *Genin*. In that case, the tribunal had to decide on whether the investor had been treated fairly and equitably in the context of the revocation of a banking license. The tribunal found no breach of the standard because there were ample grounds for the action taken by the Bank of Estonia. The tribunal in considering the meaning of fair and equitable did not engage in a textual analysis of the fair and equitable treatment clause in the US–Estonia BIT but simply referred to how this requirement has been generally understood under international law, namely, an international minimum standard separate from domestic law but 'that is, indeed, a minimum standard'. According to the same tribunal, for State conduct to breach such standard, it would need to reflect 'a willful neglect of duty, an insufficiency of action falling far below international standards, or even subjective bad faith'.

...

372. Except for *Genin*, there is a common thread in the recent awards under NAFTA and *Tecmed* which does not require bad faith or malicious intention of the recipient State as a necessary element in the failure to treat investment fairly and equitably. As recently stated in *CMS*, it is an objective standard 'unrelated to whether the Respondent has had any deliberate intention or bad faith in adopting the measures in question. Of course, such intention and bad faith can aggravate the situation but are not an essential element of the standard'. It is also understood that the conduct of the State has to be below international standards but those are not at the level of 1927. A third element is the frustration of expectations

that the investor may have legitimately taken into account when it made the investment. The standards of conduct agreed by the parties to a BIT presuppose a favorable disposition towards foreign investment, in fact, a pro-active behavior of the State to encourage and protect it. To encourage and protect investment is the purpose of the BIT. It would be incoherent with such purpose and the expectations created by such a document to consider that a party to the BIT has breached the obligation of fair and equitable treatment only when it has acted in bad faith or its conduct can be qualified as outrageous or egregious.

CMS Gas Transmission Co. v. *Argentina,* ICSID Case No. ARB/01/8, Award, 12 May 2005 (Professor Francisco Orrego-Vicuña, President; Hon. Marc Lalonde PC, OC QC; HE Judge Francisco Rezek), paras 274, 280

274. The Treaty Preamble makes it clear, however, that one principal objective of the protection envisaged is that fair and equitable treatment is desirable 'to maintain a stable framework for investments and maximum effective use of economic resources'. There can be no doubt, therefore, that a stable legal and business environment is an essential element of fair and equitable treatment.

...

280. The Tribunal believes this is an objective requirement unrelated to whether the Respondent has had any deliberate intention or bad faith in adopting the measures in question. Of course, such intention and bad faith can aggravate the situation but are not an essential element of the standard.

2.1.4 Recent Developments in the Scope of the FET Rule: Protecting Investors' Legitimate Expectations, and the Stability of the Business and Legal Environment Surrounding the Investment

The more dramatic development in the FET standard of protection in recent years has been its extension, by way of an administrative law analogy, to situations where (1) there has been an alleged violation of an investor's legitimate expectations. Possibly related as well is (2) the protection of investors and investments under the sheltering scope of FET against the failure of host States to ensure a stable business or legal environment for the investment. There are fears that 'legitimate expectations' might be taken to replace the actual terms of the treaty,[26] or result in upholding the subjective expectations of the investor.[27]

In respect of legitimate investor expectations, *International Thunderbird Gaming* v. *Mexico,* excerpted below, concerned the denial of a Mexican gaming licence. A licence would not have been granted for the operation of games of risk and chance. The investor

---

[26] A. R. Sureda, *Investment Treaty Arbitration: Judging under Uncertainty* (Cambridge University Press, 2012), 77.

[27] J. Crawford, 'Treaty and Contract Claims in Investment Arbitration – 22nd Freshfields Lecture' (2008) 24 *Arb Int'l* 351, 372; cited in Sureda, *Investment Treaty Arbitration,* 77.

gaming operator claimed that it operated games of 'skill'. In the event, the licensing application was denied and the investor brought an unsuccessful claim before an investment
arbitral tribunal. Of interest in particular is the late Thomas Wälde's dissent in which he
viewed the protection of an investor's reasonable and justifiable expectations as having
taken the transparency requirement a step further. It is one thing to show that an investor
lost or was never granted a licence due to intransparent regulations. It is another to argue
that the investor reasonably expected to have the licence. In any case, this may be easier
to prove than an indirect expropriation.

In the second extract, *Saluka* v. *Czech Republic*, the tribunal cites the *Tecmed* award in
which intransparency had also featured prominently. *Saluka* had involved the Japanese
financial firm Nomura's investment in the Czech Republic's privatisation of its banking
sector. While other failing Czech banks were bailed out following a banking crisis, there
were those in the Czech government who intended Nomura, as a strategic investor, to
assist in the crisis by injecting capital into IPB, which Nomura owned as the largest shareholder through Saluka. Nomura's intention, however, was to locate a strategic partner or
to pursue a bail-out, which from the Czech government's viewpoint would be conditioned
upon Nomura injecting further capital into IPB. In any event, either option would have
required the support of the Czech government. Various attempts to achieve a satisfactory
solution came to naught amid several runs on IPB. Ultimately, IPB was allowed to fail.
Saluka alleged that a meeting had taken place in Paris in which a conspiracy had been
hatched between the Czech authorities and another competitor bank, CSOB, in which the
latter had been forewarned that the Saluka-owned bank, IPB, would fail to meet its capital adequacy requirements and thus revocation of IPB's banking licence was imminent.
However, if CSOB bought out Saluka's interest, which ultimately it did for one Czech
koruna, IPB would receive a bail-out from the Czech government, which indeed it did
receive.[28] According to the *Saluka* tribunal:[29]

> A foreign investor whose interests are protected under the Treaty is entitled to
> expect that the [host State] will not act in a way that is manifestly inconsistent,
> non-transparent, unreasonable (i.e. unrelated to some rational policy), or
> discriminatory (i.e. based on unjustifiable distinctions).

Compare the third extract from *Tecmed*, where the tribunal's view was that FET requires
the host State to accord treatment which does not 'affect the basic expectations that were
taken into account by the foreign investor to make the investment'.[30] That case concerned
the non-renewal of a permit to operate an investor's landfill site following community
opposition and proposals for its relocation.

Turning to the concept of a stable business and legal framework, treaty clauses may also
contain such an explicit assurance. Putting such situations aside, *Occidental* v. *Ecuador*,

---

[28] See further G. S. Georgiev, 'The Award in *Saluka Investments v. Czech Republic*' in G. A. Alvarez and W.
M. Reisman (eds), *The Reasons Requirement in International Investment Arbitration: Critical Case Studies*
(The Hague: Brill, 2008), 149.

[29] *Saluka* v. *Czech Republic*, Partial Award, 17 March 2006, UNCITRAL, PCA, para. 309.

[30] *Tecnicas Medioambientales Tecmed SA* v. *Mexico*, Case No. ARB(AF)/00/2, Award, 29 May 2003, para. 154.

excerpted below, involved a contract for oil exploration and production into which the investor had entered with Petroecuador. The dispute involved the denial by Ecuador of an application for VAT refunds, where Ecuador also required the investor to return previous tax reimbursements. As the *Occidental* extract below also shows, protection against host State failure to ensure a stable business or legal environment may also be related to the requirement discussed earlier, that host State laws and procedures should be sufficiently transparent. *Occidental* cites *Metalclad*, which is discussed in Section 2.1.2.[31] *Occidental* also cites[32] *Tecmed* v. *Mexico*, where linkages were, in turn, drawn between the investor's legitimate expectations, the transparency requirement and the stability requirement (for the purposes of business planning) – the *Tecmed* Award had spoken in the same breath of 'basic expectations', 'total transparency' and the ability of the investor to 'plan its investment'.[33]

CMS v. *Argentina*, also extracted below, is in keeping with a line of Argentinian awards in which the stability requirement is teased out of the preambular language of investment treaties,[34] but in this passage we see the tribunal equating the stability requirement with the customary international law standard.

International Thunderbird Gaming Corp. v. Mexico, UNCITRAL (NAFTA), Award, 26 January 2006 (Professor Dr Albert Jan van den Berg, President; Lic. Agustin Portal Ariosa; Professor Thomas W. Wälde (dissenting)), para. 147

Having considered recent investment case law and the good faith principle of international customary law, the concept of 'legitimate expectations' relates, within the context of the NAFTA framework, to a situation where a Contracting Party's conduct creates reasonable and justifiable expectations on the part of an investor (or investment) to act in reliance on said conduct, such that a failure by the NAFTA Party to honour those expectations could cause the investor (or investment) to suffer damages.

International Thunderbird Gaming Corp. v. *Mexico*, UNCITRAL (NAFTA), Separate Opinion of Thomas Wälde, 1 December 2005, para. 37

The most relevant NAFTA (and ICSID) awards have translated these authoritative objectives and instruments provided by the NAFTA and similar investment treaties into an

---

[31] *Occidental Exploration and Production Co.* v. *Ecuador* (LCIA Case No. UN 3467), Final Award, 1 July 2004 277, para. 185, excerpted below.

[32] *Ibid.*

[33] *Tecmed*, para. 154; also *Saluka*, paras 348, 360. See also *Eiser Infrastructure Limited and Energía Solar Luxembourg S.à.r.l.* v. *Kingdom of Spain*, ICSID Case No. ARB/13/36, Award, 4 May 2017 (Crook, President; Alexandrov, McLachlan), in particular the Claimants' argument at paras 357–358, para 379 for the tribunal linking the stability and transparency requirements in its interpretation of the Energy Charter Treaty, and para. 382 for the tribunal linking the stability requirement and investors' legitimate expectations. Note that the Award in *Eiser* has since been annulled, albeit on the unrelated grounds of improper constitution of the tribunal and for 'serious' departure from a fundamental rule of procedure: see *Eiser Infrastructure Limited and Energía Solar Luxembourg S.à r.l.* v. *Spain*, ICSID Case No. ARB/13/36, Decision on Annulment, 11 June 2020 (Hernandéz, President; Khan, Hascher).

[34] See further, M. Potesta, 'Legitimate Expectations in Investment Treaty Law: Understanding the Roots and the Limits of a Controversial Concept' (2013) 28 *ICSID Review* 88, who attempts to analyse the awards according to their different factual settings – contractual situations, situations where a representation has been made by the host State, and licensing situations.

emphasis on 'transparency' and a concept of 'legitimate expectation' that takes up, but further develops the meaning of this concept in conventional international, comparative contract, administrative and European and WTO law jurisprudence. One can observe over the last years a significant growth in the role and scope of the legitimate expectation principle, from an earlier function as a subsidiary interpretative principle to reinforce a particular interpretative approach chosen, to its current role as a self-standing subcategory and independent basis for a claim under the 'fair and equitable standard' as under Art. 1105 of the NAFTA. This is possibly related to the fact that it provides a more supple way of providing a remedy appropriate to the particular situation as compared to the more drastic determination and remedy inherent in concept [*sic*] of regulatory expropriation. It is probably partly for these reasons that 'legitimate expectation' has become for tribunals a preferred way of providing protection to claimants in situations where the tests for a 'regulatory taking' appear too difficult, complex and too easily assailable for reliance on a measure of subjective judgment.

Saluka Investments BV v. *Czech Republic,* Partial Award, 17 March 2006, UNCITRAL, PCA (Sir Arthur Watts, Chairman; Maitre L. Yves Fortier CC QC; Professor Dr Peter Behrens), paras 302–311, 347–349, 360–361, 407, 498–502 (footnotes omitted)

302. The standard of 'fair and equitable treatment' is therefore closely tied to the notion of legitimate expectations which is the dominant element of that standard. By virtue of the 'fair and equitable treatment' standard included in Article 3.1 the Czech Republic must therefore be regarded as having assumed an obligation to treat foreign investors so as to avoid the frustration of investors' legitimate and reasonable expectations. As the tribunal in *Tecmed* stated, the obligation to provide 'fair and equitable treatment' means:

> to provide to international investments treatment that does not affect the basic expectations that were taken into account by the foreign investor to make the investment.

Also, in *CME*, the tribunal concluded that the Czech authority

> breached its obligation of fair and equitable treatment by evisceration of the arrangements in reliance upon which the foreign investor was induced to invest.

The tribunal in *Waste Management* equally stated that:

> In applying [the 'fair and equitable treatment'] standard it is relevant that the treatment is in breach of representations made by the host State which were reasonably relied on by the claimant.

303. The expectations of foreign investors certainly include the observation by the host State of such well-established fundamental standards as good faith, due process, and nondiscrimination. And the tribunal in *OEPC* went even as far as stating that

> [t]he stability of the legal and business framework is thus an essential element of fair and equitable treatment.

304. This Tribunal would observe, however, that while it subscribes to the general thrust of these and similar statements, it may be that, if their terms were to be taken too literally, they would impose upon host States' [sic] obligations which would be inappropriate and unrealistic. Moreover, the scope of the Treaty's protection of foreign investment against unfair and inequitable treatment cannot exclusively be determined by foreign investors' subjective motivations and considerations. Their expectations, in order for them to be protected, must rise to the level of legitimacy and reasonableness in light of the circumstances.

305. No investor may reasonably expect that the circumstances prevailing at the time the investment is made remain totally unchanged. In order to determine whether frustration of the foreign investor's expectations was justified and reasonable, the host State's legitimate right subsequently to regulate domestic matters in the public interest must be taken into consideration as well. As the *S.D. Myers* tribunal has stated, the determination of a breach of the obligation of 'fair and equitable treatment' by the host State must be made in the light of the high measure of deference that international law generally extends to the right of domestic authorities to regulate matters within their own borders.

306. The determination of a breach of Article 3.1 by the Czech Republic therefore requires a weighing of the Claimant's legitimate and reasonable expectations on the one hand and the Respondent's legitimate regulatory interests on the other.

307. A foreign investor protected by the Treaty may in any case properly expect that the Czech Republic implements its policies bona fide by conduct that is, as far as it affects the investors' investment, reasonably justifiable by public policies and that such conduct does not manifestly violate the requirements of consistency, transparency, even-handedness and nondiscrimination. In particular, any differential treatment of a foreign investor must not be based on unreasonable distinctions and demands, and must be justified by showing that it bears a reasonable relationship to rational policies not motivated by a preference for other investments over the foreign-owned investment.

308. Finally, it transpires from arbitral practice that, according to the 'fair and equitable treatment' standard, the host State must never disregard the principles of procedural propriety and due process and must grant the investor freedom from coercion or harassment by its own regulatory authorities.

(iv) Conclusion

309. The 'fair and equitable treatment' standard in Article 3.1 of the Treaty is an autonomous Treaty standard and must be interpreted, in light of the object and purpose of the Treaty, so as to avoid conduct of the Czech Republic that clearly provides disincentives to foreign investors. The Czech Republic, without undermining its legitimate right to take measures for the protection of the public interest, has therefore assumed an obligation to treat a foreign investor's investment in a way that does not frustrate the investor's underlying legitimate and reasonable expectations. A foreign investor whose interests are protected under the Treaty is entitled to expect that the Czech Republic will not act in a way that is manifestly inconsistent, non-transparent, unreasonable (i.e. unrelated to some

rational policy), or discriminatory (i.e. based on unjustifiable distinctions). In applying this standard, the Tribunal will have due regard to all relevant circumstances.

2. Application of the Standard

310. In applying Article 3 of the Treaty to the present case, the Claimant contends that the Czech Republic has violated the 'fair and equitable treatment' standard in Article 3.1 of the Treaty in a number of ways. The Claimant principally contends that

(a) the Czech Republic gave a discriminatory response to the systemic bad debt problem in the Czech banking sector, especially by providing State financial assistance to the other Big Four banks to the exclusion of IPB, and thereby created an environment impossible for the survival of IPB;

(b) the Czech Republic failed to ensure a predictable and transparent framework for Saluka's investment;

(c) the Czech Republic's refusal to negotiate with IPB and its shareholders in good faith prior to the forced administration was unreasonable and discriminatory;

(d) the provision by the Czech Republic of massive financial assistance to IPB's business, once the beneficiary of such assistance had become CSOB following the forced administration, was unfair and inequitable; and

(e) the Czech Republic's failure to prevent the unjust enrichment of CSOB at the expense of the IPB shareholders, including Saluka, upon the transfer of IPB's business to CSOB and the aforementioned State aid following the forced administration was equally unfair and inequitable.

311. The Tribunal will examine each of these claims separately.

(a) The Czech Republic's Discriminatory Response to the Bad Debt Problem...

347. The Tribunal ... finds that the Respondent has not offered a reasonable justification for IPB's differential treatment. Consequently, the Czech Republic is found to have given a discriminatory response to the bad debt problem in the Czech banking sector, especially by providing state financial assistance to three of the Big Four banks to the exclusion of IPB, and thereby created an environment impossible for the survival of IPB.

(b) Failure to Ensure a Predictable and Transparent Framework

348. The Czech Republic has failed to ensure a predictable and transparent framework for Saluka's investment, if it has frustrated Saluka's legitimate expectations regarding the treatment of IPB without reasonable justifications.

349. The Claimant argues that the Czech Republic has frustrated Saluka's expectations

(a) by contradictory and misleading declarations about its policy towards the banking sector in crisis and by justifying IPB's exclusion from the State aid granted to save the other banks on the grounds that it had already been fully privatised;

(b) by the unpredictable increase of the provisioning burden for non-performing loans; and

(c) by leaving the banks with no effective mechanisms to enforce loan security.

...

360. ... the Tribunal is unable to find that the Czech Republic has frustrated Nomura's legitimate and reasonable expectations and violated the 'fair and equitable treatment' standard by its failure to improve the legal framework within a timescale of help to Nomura.

(c) Refusal to Negotiate in Good Faith

361. The Claimant contends that, whereas Saluka and Nomura as well as IPB were actively engaged in seeking a solution to IPB's financial problems, the Czech Government refused to negotiate in good faith on the proposals made by IPB and its shareholders.

...

407. In light of all the factual elements relating to the Czech Government's role in CSOB's successful acquisition of IPB's business, and IPB's as well as Saluka's/Nomura's unsuccessful attempts to find a cooperative solution, the Tribunal finds ... that the Czech Republic's conduct towards IPB and Saluka/Nomura in respect of Saluka's investment in IPB shares was unfair and inequitable. In particular, the Ministry of Finance and the CNB unreasonably frustrated IPB's and its shareholders' good faith efforts to resolve the bank's crisis. The Czech Government failed to deal with IPB's as well as Saluka's/Nomura's proposals in an unbiased, even-handed, transparent and consistent way and it unreasonably refused to communicate with IPB and Saluka/Nomura in an adequate manner.

...

498. The Respondent has violated the 'fair and equitable treatment' obligation by responding to the bad debt problem in the Czech banking sector in a way which accorded IPB differential treatment without a reasonable justification. The Big Four banks were in a comparable position regarding the bad debt problem. Nevertheless, the Czech Republic excluded IPB from the provisioning of financial assistance. Only in the course of CSOB's acquisition of IPB's business during IPB's forced administration was considerable financial assistance from the Czech Government forthcoming. Nomura (and subsequently Saluka) was justified, however, in expecting that the Czech Republic would provide financial assistance in an even-handed and consistent manner so as to include rather than exclude IPB. That expectation was frustrated by the Respondent. The Tribunal finds that the Respondent has not offered a reasonable justification for IPB's differential treatment.

499. The Czech Republic has furthermore violated its 'fair and equitable treatment' obligation by unreasonably frustrating IPB's and its shareholders' good faith efforts to resolve the bank's crisis. Saluka was entitled to expect that the Czech Republic took seriously the various proposals that may have had the potential of solving the bank's problem and that these proposals were dealt with in an objective, transparent, unbiased and even-handed way. The fundamentally different approach of the Czech Government towards CSOB's acquisition of IPB, on the one hand, and towards IPB's and Saluka's/Nomura's attempts to negotiate a cooperative solution, on the other, frustrated Saluka's legitimate expectations. The Czech Government's conduct lacked even-handedness, consistency and

transparency and the Czech Government has refused adequate communication with IPB and its major shareholder, Saluka/Nomura. This made it difficult and even impossible for IPB and Saluka/Nomura to identify the Czech Government's position and to accommodate it. The Respondent has not offered a reasonable justification for its treatment of Saluka.

500. The Tribunal does not find, however, that the Respondent has violated its 'fair and equitable treatment' obligation by a failure to ensure a predictable and transparent framework for Saluka's investment. Neither was the increase of the provisioning burden for nonperforming loans unpredictable for Saluka/Nomura, nor could Saluka/Nomura legitimately expect that the Czech Republic would fix the legal shortcomings regarding the protection of creditor's rights and the enforcement of loan security within a timescale of help to Nomura.

501. Nor does the Tribunal find that the Respondent has violated its 'fair and equitable treatment' obligation by providing financial assistance to CSOB after its acquisition of IPB. At the time the financial assistance was implemented, IPB had already lost its banking business to CSOB. Therefore, IPB and its shareholders could no longer have suffered harm in addition to the harm that had already been caused by the forced administration and the subsequent loss of the banking business. After the takeover of IPB's banking business by CSOB, IPB was no longer a competitor of CSOB whose competitive position could be undermined by the State aid provided by the Czech Government.

502. The Tribunal also cannot find that the Respondent has violated its 'fair and equitable treatment' obligation by a failure to prevent the unjust enrichment of CSOB at the expense of the IPB shareholders, including Saluka, upon the transfer of IPB's business to CSOB and the provision of State aid following forced administration. For there to be an actionable, unjust enrichment as between the parties, the Respondent must have received something at the expense of the Claimant. It was not the Respondent which received the banking business from IPB, but rather CSOB, nor was it the Claimant's banking business that was transferred to CSOB, but rather IPB's.

Tecnicas Medioambientales Tecmed SA v. Mexico, ICSID Case No. ARB(AF)/00/2, Award, 29 May 2003 (Dr Horacio A. Grigera Naon, President; Professor José Carlos Fernandez Rozas; Mr Carlos Bernal Verea), paras 152–156 (footnotes omitted)

II. Fair and Equitable Treatment

152. According to Article 4(1) of the Agreement:

> Each Contracting Party will guarantee in its territory fair and equitable treatment, according to International Law, for the investments made by investors of the other Contracting Party.

153. The Arbitral Tribunal finds that the commitment of fair and equitable treatment included in Article 4(1) of the Agreement is an expression and part of the bona fide principle

recognized in international law, although bad faith from the State is not required for its violation:

> To the modern eye, what is unfair or inequitable need not equate with the outrageous or the egregious. In particular, a State may treat foreign investment unfairly and inequitably without necessarily acting in bad faith.

154. The Arbitral Tribunal considers that this provision of the Agreement, in light of the good faith principle established by international law, requires the Contracting Parties to provide to international investments treatment that does not affect the basic expectations that were taken into account by the foreign investor to make the investment. The foreign investor expects the host State to act in a consistent manner, free from ambiguity and totally transparently in its relations with the foreign investor, so that it may know beforehand any and all rules and regulations that will govern its investments, as well as the goals of the relevant policies and administrative practices or directives, to be able to plan its investment and comply with such regulations. Any and all State actions conforming to such criteria should relate not only to the guidelines, directives or requirements issued, or the resolutions approved thereunder, but also to the goals underlying such regulations. The foreign investor also expects the host State to act consistently, i.e. without arbitrarily revoking any preexisting decisions or permits issued by the State that were relied upon by the investor to assume its commitments as well as to plan and launch its commercial and business activities. The investor also expects the State to use the legal instruments that govern the actions of the investor or the investment in conformity with the function usually assigned to such instruments, and not to deprive the investor of its investment without the required compensation. In fact, failure by the host State to comply with such pattern of conduct with respect to the foreign investor or its investments affects the investor's ability to measure the treatment and protection awarded by the host State and to determine whether the actions of the host State conform to the fair and equitable treatment principle. Therefore, compliance by the host State with such pattern of conduct is closely related to the above-mentioned principle, to the actual chances of enforcing such principle, and to excluding the possibility that state action be characterized as arbitrary; i.e. as presenting insufficiencies that would be recognized '... by any reasonable and impartial man', [Eds citing *Neer*[35]] or, although not in violation of specific regulations, as being contrary to the law because:

> ... (it) shocks, or at least surprises, a sense of juridical propriety.[36]

155. The Arbitral Tribunal understands that the scope of the undertaking of fair and equitable treatment under Article 4(1) of the Agreement described above is that resulting from an autonomous interpretation, taking into account the text of Article 4(1) of the Agreement according to its ordinary meaning (Article 31(1) of the Vienna Convention), or from international law and the good faith principle, on the basis of which the scope of the

---

[35] 4 RIAA 60 (1926); 3 ILR 213, discussed in Section 1.3.
[36] [Eds citing *Case Concerning Elettronica Sicula SpA (ELSI) (USA* v. *Italy)* [1989] ICJ Rep. 15, discussed in Chapter 1 of this book.]

obligation assumed under the Agreement and the actions related to compliance therewith are to be assessed.

156. If the above were not its intended scope, Article 4(1) of the Agreement would be deprived of any semantic content or practical utility of its own, which would surely be against the intention of the Contracting Parties upon executing and ratifying the Agreement since, by including this provision in the Agreement, the parties intended to strengthen and increase the security and trust of foreign investors that invest in the member States ...

Occidental Exploration and Production Co. v. *Ecuador*, LCIA No. UN 3467, Final Award, 1 July 2004 (Professor Francisco Orrego Vicuna, President; Hon. Charles N. Brower; Dr Patrick Barrera Sweeney), paras 183–186

183. Although fair and equitable treatment is not defined in the Treaty, the Preamble clearly records the agreement of the parties that such treatment 'is desirable in order to maintain a stable framework for investment and maximum effective utilization of economic resources'. The stability of the legal and business framework is thus an essential element of fair and equitable treatment.

184. The Tribunal must note in this context that the framework under which the investment was made and operates has been changed in an important manner by the actions adopted by the SRI. It was explained above that the Contract has been interpreted by the SRI in a manner that ended up being manifestly wrong as there is no evidence that VAT reimbursement was ever built into Factor X. The clarifications that OEPC sought on the applicability of VAT by means of a 'consulta' made to the SRI received a wholly unsatisfactory and thoroughly vague answer. The tax law was changed without providing any clarity about its meaning and extent and the practice and regulations were also inconsistent with such changes.

185. Various arbitral tribunals have recently insisted on the need for this stability. The Tribunal in Metalclad held that the Respondent 'failed to ensure a transparent and predictable framework for Metalclad's business planning and investment. The totality of these circumstances demonstrate[s] a lack of orderly process and timely disposition in relation to an investor of a Party acting in the expectation that it would be treated fairly and justly ...'. Also the Tribunal in Tecnicas Medioambientales,[37] as recalled by the Claimant, has held:

> The foreign investor expects the host State to act in a consistent manner, free from ambiguity and totally transparently in its relations with the foreign investor, so that it may know beforehand any and all rules and regulations that will govern its investments, as well as the goals of the relevant policies and administrative

---

[37] [Eds. *Tecmed* v. *Mexico*, Award, para. 154, reproduced above.]

practices or directives, to be able to plan its investment and comply with such regulations ...

186. It is quite clear from the record of this case and from the events discussed in this Final Award that such requirements were not met by Ecuador.

CMS Gas Transmission Co. v. *Argentina*, ICSID Case No. ARB/01/8, Award, 12 May 2005 (Professor Francisco Orrego-Vicuña, President; Hon. Marc Lalonde PC, OC QC; HE Judge Francisco Rezek), para. 284

While the choice between requiring a higher treaty standard and that of equating it with the international minimum standard might have relevance in the context of some disputes, the Tribunal is not persuaded that it is relevant in this case. In fact, the Treaty standard of fair and equitable treatment and its connection with the required stability and predictability of the business environment, founded on solemn legal and contractual commitments, is not different from the international law minimum standard and its evolution under customary law.

2.2 Full Protection and Security

The first modern BIT arbitration, *AAPL* v. *Sri Lanka*, involved an allegation of a FPS violation due to the failure of Sri Lanka to protect the Hong Kong investor's shrimp farm from action taken by the Sri Lankan armed forces against rebel forces.[38] The tension between the subjective and objective theories of responsibility for violation of the FPS standard has already been mentioned. The first thing to notice is that responsibility may attach not through commission, but through failure or omission of the host State to act so as to protect the investor's investment against the actions of third parties. This is illustrated in the *Eurotunnel* arbitration,[39] excerpted below, where illegal migrants trespassing on a construction site had caused damage, delay, losses and expenses, against which the investor (the concessionaire under the Eurotunnel project) claimed protection from the Principals – namely, Britain and France. Likewise, with *Wena* v. *Egypt*. That case concerned an investor's rights under two leases of the Luxor and El Nile hotels in Cairo, where the Egyptian counterparty had stormed the hotels. The tribunal considered that responsibility attaches even if Egypt itself had not instigated the actions or participated in them.[40]

Ultimately, the issue comes down to one concerning the appropriate standard of liability for a failure to afford full protection and security. Is it a matter of strict liability?

---

[38] *Asian Agricultural Products Ltd (AAPL)* v. *Sri Lanka*, ICSID Case No. ARB/87/3, 27 June 1990.

[39] *Channel Tunnel Group and Another* v. *UK Secretary for Transport and Another*, Partial Award, 30 January, 2007, PCA, para. 305 (responsibility for 'situations of disorder').

[40] *Wena Hotels Ltd* v. *Egypt*, ICSID Case No. ARB/98/4, Award, 8 December 2000.

Is it perhaps a failure to exercise vigilance or due diligence? Or, as was unsuccessfully argued by the Respondents in the *Eurotunnel* arbitration, is it merely about the violation of a lower standard on the part of the host State to endeavour to do its best to protect the investor or investment? The *Eurotunnel* tribunal was clear that the obligation was not simply a 'best endeavours' obligation or an 'obligation of means'. Rather, the FPS standard imposes an 'obligation of conduct' on the host State. However, as the extract from *Tecmed* suggests, this standard is not one of strict liability either. It is rather one of vigilance or due diligence, as is illustrated in the extracts from *AAPL v. Sri Lanka* and *Saluka* below. The oft-quoted statement from the tribunal in *AAPL* is that the guarantee of FPS is not absolute. It is not a 'warranty' that the investor's property will suffer no disturbance or interference.

Channel Tunnel Group and Another v. UK Secretary for Transport and Another, **Partial Award, 30 January 2007, PCA (Professor James Crawford SC, Chairman; Maître L. Yves Fortier CC QC; HE Judge Gilbert Guillaume; The Rt Hon. Lord Millett; Mr Jan Paulsson), paras 314, 319**

314. It is argued by the Respondents that the relevant obligations under the Concession Agreement to cooperate and coordinate their policies were obligations of means, not result. But the general classification of obligations, useful though it may be for various purposes, is no substitute for their application in the concrete circumstances of a given case. Under the Concession Agreement the Concessionaires were not required to bear the risk of a failure of coordinated action when serious threats to the security of the Fixed Link, and of the United Kingdom's immigration controls, were occurring at times on a nightly basis.

...

319. ... the Tribunal concludes that in the circumstances of the clandestine migrant problem as it existed in the Calais region in the period from September 2000, it was incumbent on the Principals, acting through the IGC and otherwise, to maintain conditions of normal security and public order in and around the Coquelles terminal; that they failed to take appropriate steps in this regard, and thereby breached Clauses 2.1 and 27.7 of the Concession Agreement, and that the Claimants are entitled to recover the losses directly flowing from this breach.

Tecnicas Medioambientales Tecmed SA v. Mexico, **ICSID Case No. ARB(AF)/00/2, Award, 29 May 2003 (Dr Horacio A. Grigera Naon, President; Professor José Carlos Fernandez Rozas; Mr Carlos Bernal Verea), paras 176–177**

176. The Arbitral Tribunal considers that the Claimant has not furnished evidence to prove that the Mexican authorities, regardless of their level, have encouraged, fostered, or contributed their support to the people or groups that conducted the community and

political movements against the Landfill, or that such authorities have participated in such movement. Also, there is not sufficient evidence to attribute the activity or behavior of such people or groups to the Respondent pursuant to international law.

177. The Arbitral Tribunal agrees with the Respondent, and with the case law quoted by it, in that the guarantee of full protection and security is not absolute and does not impose strict liability upon the State that grants it.

As the tribunal in *AAPL* had quoted Commissioner Zuloaga in the earlier *Sambiaggo* case so memorably: 'Governments are constituted to afford protection, not to guarantee it.'

Asian Agricultural Products Ltd v. *Sri Lanka*, ICSID Case No. ARB/87/3, Award, 27 June 1990 (Dr Ahmed Sadek El-Kosheri, President; Professor Berthold Goldman; Dr Samuel K. B. Asante), paras 48–49

48. The arbitral Tribunal is not aware of any case in which the obligation assumed by the host State to provide the nationals of the other Contracting State with 'full protection and security' was construed as an absolute obligation which guarantees that no damages will be suffered, in the sense that any violation thereof creates automatically a 'strict liability' on behalf of the host State. *Sambiaggo* case seems to be the only reported case in which such argument was voiced, but without success. The Italian Commissioner AGNOLI, referred in his Report to:

The protection and security ... which the Venezuelan Government explicitly guarantees by Article 4 of the Treaty of 1861 to Italians residing in Venezuela (U.N. Report, *op. cit.*, p. 502 – underlining added). The Venezuelan Commissioner ZULOAGA responded by indicating that: Governments are constituted to afford protection, not to guarantee it (*Ibid.*, p. 511).

...

49. In the recent case concerning *Elettronica Sicula S.P.A.(ELSI)* between the U.S.A. and Italy adjudicated by a Chamber of the International Court of Justice, the U.S.A. Government invoked Article V(1) of the Bilateral Treaty which established an obligation to provide 'the most constant protection and security', but without claiming that this obligation constitutes a 'guarantee' involving the emergence of a 'strict liability' (Section 2 – Chapter V of the U.S.A. Memorial dated May 15, 1987, where reference is made, on the contrary at page 135 to the: 'One well-established aspect of the international standard of treatment ... that States must use "due diligence" to prevent wrongful injuries to the person or property of aliens within their territory'). In its Judgment of July 20, 1989, the ICJ Chamber clearly stated that:

The reference in Article V to the provision of 'constant protection and security' cannot be construed as the giving of a warranty that property shall never in any circumstances be occupied or disturbed (CIJ, *Recueil*, 1989, 108, p. 65).

Consequently, both the oldest reported arbitral precedent and the latest I.C.J. ruling confirms that the language imposing on the host State an obligation to provide 'protection and security' or 'full protection and security required by international law' (the other expression included in the same Article V) could not be construed according to the natural and ordinary sense of the words as creating a 'strict liability'.

Saluka Investments BV v. Czech Republic, Partial Award, 17 March 2006, UNCITRAL, para. 484 (footnotes omitted)

The standard does not imply strict liability of the host State however. The *Tecmed* tribunal held that 'the guarantee of full protection and security is not absolute and does not impose strict liability upon the State that grants it'. The host State is, however, obliged to exercise due diligence. As the tribunal in *Wena*, quoting from *American Manufacturing and Trading*, stated,

> The obligation incumbent on the [host State] is an obligation of vigilance, in the sense that the [host State] shall take all measures necessary to ensure the full enjoyment of protection and security of its investments and should not be permitted to invoke its own legislation to detract from any such obligation.

Accordingly, the standard obliges the host State to adopt all reasonable measures to protect assets and property from threats or attacks which may target particularly foreigners or certain groups of foreigners.

2.3 Interrelationship of FET and FPS beyond Physical Security

We have seen how FET extends to an assurance, at least to a degree, of business and legal stability. Is this not, however, a matter of FPS? The answer, traditionally, would have been that FPS reflects protection against physical injury to the investor, or damage or destruction of foreign-owned property. Yet here are two examples of tribunal pronouncements which suggest, as one writer puts it, an increasingly large area of modern overlap between the FET and FPS standards. This, in turn, is explained by the extension of FPS beyond physical protection.[41] Observe that in *Occidental* the tribunal had turned to the Preamble of the BIT in interpreting the meaning of the FET clause, while in *Azurix* the tribunal reached a similar conclusion about the assurance of business and legal stability by pointing to the word 'full' (i.e. including both physical and non-physical protection) in

---

[41] G. C. Moss, 'Full Protection and Security' in A. Reinisch (ed.), *Standards of Investment Protection* (Oxford University Press, 2008), 131, 132. See further, *Anglo American plc* v. *Bolivarian Republic of Venezuela*, ICSID Case No. ARB(AF)/14/1, Award, 18 January 2019, para. 482, which also contains a useful review of the relevant authorities.

the treaty phrase 'full protection and security'. Both tribunals perceived an 'interrelationship' between the FET and FPS standards of protection. The *Occidental* tribunal appears to have reached this conclusion by assuming that a breach of FET automatically entails a breach of FPS.[42]

***Occidental Exploration and Production Co. v. Ecuador*, LCIA No. UN 3467, Final Award, 1 July 2004 (Professor Francisco Orrego-Vicuña, President; Hon. Charles N. Brower; Dr Patrick Barrera Sweeney), paras 183–184, 187**

183. Although fair and equitable treatment is not defined in the Treaty, the Preamble clearly records the agreement of the parties that such treatment 'is desirable in order to maintain a stable framework for investment and maximum effective utilization of economic resources'. The stability of the legal and business framework is thus an essential element of fair and equitable treatment.

184. The Tribunal must note in this context that the framework under which the investment was made and operates has been changed in an important manner by the actions adopted by the SRI.

...

187. The Tribunal accordingly holds that the Respondent has breached its obligations to accord fair and equitable treatment under Article II(3)(a) of the Treaty. In the context of this finding the question of whether in addition there has been a breach of full protection and security under this Article becomes moot as a treatment that is not fair and equitable automatically entails an absence of full protection and security of the investment.

***Azurix Corp. v. Argentina*, ICSID Case No. ARB/01/12, Award, 14 July 2006 (Dr Andrés Rigo Sureda, President; Hon. Marc Lalonde PC, OC QC; Dr Daniel Hugo Martins), para. 408**

The Tribunal is persuaded of the interrelationship of fair and equitable treatment and the obligation to afford the investor full protection and security. The cases referred to above show that full protection and security was understood to go beyond protection and security ensured by the police. It is not only a matter of physical security; the stability afforded by a secure investment environment is as important from an investor's point of view. The Tribunal is aware that in recent free trade agreements signed by the United States, for instance, with Uruguay, full protection and security is understood to be limited to the level of police protection required under customary international law. However, when the terms 'protection and security' are qualified by 'full' and no other adjective or explanation, they extend, in their ordinary meaning, the content of this standard beyond physical security. To conclude,

---

[42] This has not been shown to be necessarily so in other awards and while it is an interesting proposition (that a breach of FET automatically entails a breach of FPS), it cannot be easily taken for granted.

> the Tribunal, having held that the Respondent failed to provide fair and equitable treatment to the investment, finds that the Respondent also breached the standard of full protection and security under the BIT.

Imagine, therefore, a case where there is no protection, for whatever reason, available under the FET clause in the treaty.[43] Might one then be able to assert an obligation to ensure a stable business and legal environment under the FPS clause? In some instances, treaty clauses may provide explicitly for 'legal stability'. For example, the Germany–Argentina BIT[44] cited in *Siemens* contained the words 'full legal protection and full legal security'.[45]

At its core then, the old rule against denials of justice, which we today call the FET standard, was clear. That rule sought to address situations where foreign-owned property or their owners were subjected to arbitrary, discriminatory or abusive treatment. This may be distinguished from cases involving allegations of destruction of foreign-owned property, the domain of the FPS standard. However, the scope of FET has evolved and expanded to new categories of 'abuse', not least when legitimate investor expectations are said to have been violated. This has encroached upon the domain of FPS where both the FET and FPS standards have on occasion been extended to the assurance of a (relatively) stable business and legal environment.

3. 'NARROWING DOWN' FET: SOME RECENT EXAMPLES OF TREATY CLAUSES

The shifting meaning of the FET standard has caused some of the latest treaties to endeavour to pin down the scope of protection under it. The following section deals with two examples of the latest treaty clauses. Neither is in force at the time of writing. Observe the highly particularised approach in the EU–Canada clause below and compare it to the clause in the Trans-Pacific Partnership (TPP) Agreement 2016,[46] which embodies the sort of open-ended approach which is characteristic of US FET treaty clauses,[47] being content – as we will see below – to link what FET means to the standard under customary international law. Compare, too, in respect of violation of an investor's expectations, Article 8.10(4) of EU–Canada Comprehensive Economic and Trade Agreement 2016

---

[43] What if the preambular words in the BIT discussed in *Occidental* did not exist, but that protection under the FPS standard is described as 'full' protection?

[44] Vertrag zwischen der Bundesrepublik Deutschland und der Argentinischen Republik über die Förderung und den gegenseitigen Schutz von Kapitalanlagen, 9 April 1991.

[45] Signed 9 April 1991, Art. 4(1). See *Siemens* v. *Argentina*, ICSID Case No. ARB/02/8, Award, 6 February 2007.

[46] Following the withdrawal of the US, the TPP is now adopted almost wholly by the remaining countries in the Comprehensive and Progressive Agreement for Trans-Pacific Partnership (CPTPP), 9 March 2018.

[47] For the high degree of textual similarity between the TPP's investment chapter and other US BITs, such as the investment chapter of the US–Colombia FTA (US–Colombia Trade Promotion Agreement, 22 November 2006): see W. Alschner and D. Skugarievskiy, 'The New Gold Standard? Empirically Situating the TPP in the Investment Treaty Universe', Graduate Institute of Geneva and Centre for Trade and Economic Integration, Working Paper No. IHEIDCTEI2015-08, 30.

(CETA) with the TPP's Article 9.6(4). In short, the US treaty approach tends to 'delegate' to tribunals what might be provided for explicitly in other treaty approaches.[48]

CETA, Art. 8.10(2)–(4)

(2) A Party breaches the obligation of fair and equitable treatment referenced in paragraph 1 if a measure or series of measures constitutes:

(a) denial of justice in criminal, civil or administrative proceedings;

(b) fundamental breach of due process, including a fundamental breach of transparency, in judicial and administrative proceedings;

(c) manifest arbitrariness;

(d) targeted discrimination on manifestly wrongful grounds, such as gender, race or religious belief;

(e) abusive treatment of investors, such as coercion, duress and harassment; or

(f) a breach of any further elements of the fair and equitable treatment obligation adopted by the Parties in accordance with paragraph 3 of this Article.

(3) The Parties shall regularly, or upon request of a Party, review the content of the obligation to provide fair and equitable treatment. The Committee on Services and Investment, established under Article 26.2.1(b) (Specialised committees), may develop recommendations in this regard and submit them to the CETA Joint Committee for decision.

(4) When applying the above fair and equitable treatment obligation, a Tribunal may take into account whether a Party made a specific representation to an investor to induce a covered investment, that created a legitimate expectation, and upon which the investor relied in deciding to make or maintain the covered investment, but that the Party subsequently frustrated.

Trans-Pacific Partnership Agreement/Comprehensive and Progressive Agreement for Trans-Pacific Partnership, Art. 9.6(2)–(4)

2. For greater certainty, paragraph 1 prescribes the customary international law minimum standard of treatment of aliens as the standard of treatment to be afforded to covered investments. The concepts of 'fair and equitable treatment' and 'full protection and security' do not require treatment in addition to or beyond that which is required by that standard, and do not create additional substantive rights. The obligations in paragraph 1 to provide:

(a) 'fair and equitable treatment' includes the obligation not to deny justice in criminal, civil or administrative adjudicatory proceedings in accordance with the principle of due process embodied in the principal legal systems of the world ...

...

---

[48] See further C. L. Lim, 'Finding a Workable Balance between Investor Protection and the Public Interest in the Trans-Pacific Partnership' in B. Kingsbury *et al.* (eds), *Megaregulation Contested: Global Economic Ordering after TPP* (Oxford University Press, 2019), 551.

3. A determination that there has been a breach of another provision of this Agreement, or of a separate international agreement, does not establish that there has been a breach of this Article.

4. For greater certainty, the mere fact that a Party takes or fails to take an action that may be inconsistent with an investor's expectations does not constitute a breach of this Article, even if there is loss or damage to the covered investment as a result.

4. 'QUALIFIED' AND 'UNQUALIFIED' TREATY CLAUSES, AND THE INTERACTION OF TREATY AND CUSTOM

4.1 NAFTA and the 'North American' Model of 'Qualified' Treaty Clauses

The North American approach of linking the MST, which encompasses both FET and FPS, as exemplified by NAFTA, the US Model BIT and the TPP, is distinctive.[49] Some of the circumstances surrounding its origins are shown in *Mondev* v. *USA*, excerpted below, a case which was brought in 2002 after certain Awards prompted the NAFTA Free Trade Commission (FTC), a body which comprises the three NAFTA parties, to issue a binding interpretation.[50] That interpretation states that the FET clause in NAFTA's Article 1105(1) reflects only the customary international law standard – i.e. it sets a customary 'ceiling' to the protection granted by the treaty clause. One difficulty which this created in part was that there were ongoing cases like *Mondev*. Another difficulty had to do with whether the binding 'interpretation' was in effect a legislative instrument which effectively trimmed down the protection under NAFTA's FET clause, such that NAFTA's FET clause would accord no higher protection than the MST applicable at the time of the 1926 *Neer* claim (the '1927 standard').

Mondev v. USA, ICSID Case No. ARB(AF)/99/2, Award, 11 October 2002 (Sir Ninian Stephen, President; Professor James Crawford; Judge Stephen M. Schwebel), para. 125

For the purposes of this Award, the Tribunal need not pass upon all the issues debated before it as to the FTC's interpretations of 31 July 2001. But in its view, there can be no doubt that, by interpreting Article 1105(1) to prescribe the customary international law minimum standard of treatment of aliens as the minimum standard of treatment to be afforded to investments of investors of another Party under NAFTA, the term 'customary international law' refers to customary international law as it stood no earlier than the

---

[49] The terminology of 'qualified' and 'unqualified' treaty clauses is Dumberry's: see P. Dumberry, 'The Emergence of a Consistent Case Law: How NAFTA Tribunals Have Interpreted the Fair and Equitable Treatment Standard', *Kluwer Arbitration Blog*, 30 October 2013.

[50] See, e.g., R. Dolzer and A. von Walter, 'Fair and Equitable Treatment – Lines of Jurisprudence on Customary Law' in Ortino *et al.*, *Investment Treaty Law, Current Issues II*, 99, 100–103.

time at which NAFTA came into force. It is not limited to the international law of the 19th century or even of the first half of the 20th century, although decisions from that period remain relevant. In holding that Article 1105(1) refers to customary international law, the FTC interpretations incorporate current international law, whose content is shaped by the conclusion of more than two thousand bilateral investment treaties and many treaties of friendship and commerce. Those treaties largely and concordantly provide for 'fair and equitable' treatment of, and for 'full protection and security' for, the foreign investor and his investments. Correspondingly the investments of investors under NAFTA are entitled, under the customary international law which NAFTA Parties interpret Article 1105(1) to comprehend, to fair and equitable treatment and to full protection and security.

ADF v. *USA*, ICSID Case No. ARB(AF)/00/1, Final Award, 9 January 2003 (Judge Florentino P. Feliciano; Professor Armand deMestral; Ms Carolyn B. Lamm), para. 179

In considering the meaning and implications of the 31 July 2001 FTC Interpretation, it is important to bear in mind that the Respondent United States accepts that the customary international law referred to in Article 1105(1) is not 'frozen in time' and that the minimum standard of treatment does evolve. The FTC Interpretation of 31 July 2001, in the view of the United States, refers to customary international law 'as it exists today'. It is equally important to note that Canada and Mexico accept the view of the United States on this point even as they stress that 'the threshold [for violation of that standard] remains high'. Put in slightly different terms, what customary international law projects is not a static photograph of the minimum standard of treatment of aliens as it stood in 1927 when the Award in the *Neer* case was rendered. For both customary international law and the minimum standard of treatment of aliens it incorporates, are constantly in a process of development.

A later tribunal in *Anglo American* v. *Venezuela* referred to the question of linking the FET standard to a minimum customary standard as 'sterile', taking a position similar to that in *Mondev* and *ADF*: namely, that the MST under customary international law has evolved.[51] A key case which took a different view and which is often cited precisely for that fact is *Glamis Gold* v. *USA*.

---

[51] *Anglo American* v. *Venezuela*, Award (Derain, President; Tawil; Vinuesa), paras 439–442.

Glamis Gold v. USA, UNCITRAL (NAFTA) Arbitration, Award, 8 June 2009 (Mr Michael K. Young, President; Professor David D. Caron; Mr Kenneth D. Hubbard), paras 600–601, 604 (footnotes omitted)

600. The question thus becomes: what does this customary international law minimum standard of treatment require of a State Party vis-à-vis investors of another State Party? Is it the same as that established in 1926 in *Neer* v. *Mexico*? Or has Claimant proven that the standard has 'evolved'? If it has evolved, what evidence of custom has Claimant provided to the Tribunal to determine its current scope?

601. As a threshold issue, the Tribunal notes that it is Claimant's burden to sufficiently answer each of these questions. The State Parties to the NAFTA (at least Canada and Mexico) agree that 'the test in *Neer* does continue to apply', though Mexico 'also agrees that the standard is relative and that conduct which may not have violated international law [in] the 1920's might very well be seen to offend internationally accepted principles today'. If, as Claimant argues, the customary international law minimum standard of treatment has indeed moved to require something less than the 'egregious', 'outrageous', or 'shocking' standard as elucidated in *Neer*, then the burden of establishing what the standard now requires is upon Claimant.

...

604. The Tribunal notes that, although an examination of custom is indeed necessary to determine the scope and bounds of current customary international law, this requirement – repeatedly argued by various State Parties – because of the difficulty in proving a change in custom, effectively freezes the protections provided for in this provision at the 1926 conception of egregiousness.

An important factor in the *Glamis* tribunal's reasoning was that arbitral pronouncements do not constitute state practice and therefore do not, at least by themselves, make new customary international law.[52] Scholars who criticise a perceived expansion by tribunals of the scope of protection given by FET clauses in recent years, an expansion which might have been expected under the *Waste Management* tribunal's exhortation to interpret the requirements of FET case by case in a 'flexible' manner, often point to *Glamis* for support instead. Perhaps the difference between the two views is exaggerated, as the following extract might be taken to suggest.

---

[52] *Glamis Gold* v. *USA*, para. 605. One wrinkle is that even the *Glamis* tribunal had accepted that the pleadings of the parties may be relevant to proving custom. If so, then what of the fact that parties in investment disputes plead past tribunal awards? See further, *RDC* v. *Guatemala*, ICSID Case No. ARB/07/23, Award, 29 June 2012, para. 217 (accepting, therefore, that tribunal awards make new customary law); N. Bernasconi-Osterwalder, 'Giving Arbitrators Carte Blanche – Fair and Equitable Treatment in Investment Treaties' in Lim, *Alternative Visions*, 324, 331–336.

International Thunderbird Gaming Corp. v. *Mexico*, UNCITRAL (NAFTA), Award, 26 January 2006 (Professor Dr Albert Jan van den Berg, President; Lic. Agustin Portal Ariosa; Professor Thomas W. Wälde), para. 194 (footnotes omitted)

The content of the minimum standard should not be rigidly interpreted and it should reflect evolving international customary law. Notwithstanding the evolution of customary law since decisions such as *Neer Claim* in 1926, the threshold for finding a violation of the minimum standard of treatment still remains high, as illustrated by recent international jurisprudence. For the purposes of the present case, the Tribunal views acts that would give rise to a breach of the minimum standard of treatment prescribed by the NAFTA and customary international law as those that, weighed against the given factual context, amount to a gross denial of justice or manifest arbitrariness falling below acceptable international standards.

However, the tribunal in *Bilcon* v. *Canada* more recently had not only relied upon NAFTA tribunal awards for evidence of the customary rule in order to support a view that the international minimum standard had evolved, but also rejected the *Neer* standard on the basis that '[m]any NAFTA tribunals' have done so. The tribunal did, however, concede that a new consensus has yet to emerge 'on a formulation' of the minimum standard of treatment 'that best suits the modern evolution of the standard'.[53]

4.2 'Unqualified' FET Treaty Clauses and Their Relationship with International Custom

There are numerous examples of FET treaty clauses which, unlike the American and NAFTA clauses, make no explicit mention of custom or general international law, and are on their face 'unqualified' by any customary international law standard. This, however, does not mean that a tribunal will not refer to international custom in interpreting such clauses.[54]

Siemens v. *Argentina*, ICSID Case No. ARB/02/8, Award, 6 February 2007 (Dr Andrés Rigo Sureda, President; Judge Charles N. Brower; Professor Domingo Bello Janeiro), para. 291

The specific provision of the Treaty on fair and equitable treatment is found also in Article 2(1) after the commitment to promote and admit investments in accordance with the law and regulations and as an independent sentence: 'In any case [the parties to the

---

[53] *Bilcon of Delaware and Others* v. *Canada*, UNCITRAL (NAFTA) Arbitration, Award on Jurisdiction and Liability, 17 March 2015, paras 435, 440. See further, Bernasconi-Osterwalder, 'Giving Arbitrators Carte Blanche', 337–338.

[54] See further, Dolzer and Walter, 'Fair and Equitable Treatment', 108–112; K. Yannaca-Small, 'Fair and Equitable Treatment Standard' in Reinisch, *Standards of Investment Protection*, 113–118.

Treaty] shall treat investments justly and fairly ('En todo caso tratará las inversiones justa y equitativamente')! There is no reference to international law or to a minimum standard. However, in applying the Treaty, the Tribunal is bound to find the meaning of these terms under international law bearing in mind their ordinary meaning, the evolution of international law and the specific context in which they are used.

Other tribunals may consider that while the treaty clause may be given its own 'autonomous' meaning, in the end the standard both under treaty and custom is the same.[55]

Tecnicas Medioambientales Tecmed SA v. Mexico, ICSID Case No. ARB (AF)/00/2, Award, 29 May 2003 (Dr Horacio A. Grigera Naon, President; Professor José Carlos Fernandez Rozas; Mr Carlos Bernal Verea), para. 155

The Arbitral Tribunal understands that the scope of the undertaking of fair and equitable treatment under Article 4(1) of the Agreement described above is that resulting from an autonomous interpretation, taking into account the text of Article 4(1) of the Agreement according to its ordinary meaning (Article 31(1) of the Vienna Convention), or from international law and the good faith principle, on the basis of which the scope of the obligation assumed under the Agreement and the actions related to compliance therewith are to be assessed.

In yet other cases there has been the suggestion, as in *Enron* v. *Argentina*, that the treaty language may be more precise and that is why such clauses should be given an autonomous meaning. In this vein, the treaty standard may therefore be higher than the customary international law standard. If, however, customary international law is relevant to how we read treaty rules on investment protection, how is that so? There has been the suggestion, as in *Sempra* v. *Argentina*, that customary international law fills in any gaps which may exist in the treaty definition. Without necessarily being inconsistent with both these views, the tribunal in *Azurix* v. *Argentina* considered that the customary international law standard sets at least a *minimum* standard of treatment. *Enron, Sempra, Azurix* and *Vivendi* v. *Argentina* (which is considered below) were all cases which had involved the disruption of various investment agreements in the wake of the Argentine financial crisis. As a crisis measure, Argentina mandated through its 'pesoisation' or 'pesification' policy that contractual payments originally denominated in US dollars should henceforth be payable only in the Argentinian peso. This had the effect of diminishing the returns of investors who had invested in the privatisation of Argentinian utilities.

---

[55] Dolzer and Walter, 'Fair and Equitable Treatment', 109.

Enron v. *Argentina*, ICSD Case No. ARB/01/3, Award, 22 May 2007 (Professor Francisco Orrego-Vicuña, President; Professor Albert Jan van den Berg; Mr Pierre-Yves Tschanz) (Annulled), para. 258

It might well be that in some circumstances where the international minimum standard is sufficiently elaborate and clear, fair and equitable treatment might be equated with it. But in other more vague circumstances, the fair and equitable standard may be more precise than its customary international law forefathers. This is why the Tribunal concludes that the fair and equitable standard, at least in the context of the Treaty applicable to this case, can also require a treatment additional to, or beyond that of, customary law. The very fact that recent FTC interpretations or investment treaties have purported to change the meaning or extent of the standard only confirms that those specific instruments aside, the standard is or might be a broader one.[56]

Sempra Energy International v. *Argentina*, Case No. ARB/02/16, 28 September 2007 (Professor Francisco Orrego-Vicuña, President; Hon. Marc Lalonde PC, OC QC; Dr Sandra Morelli Rico) (Annulled), paras 291–292, 294, 302 (footnotes omitted)

291. The Claimant explains that while this particular standard originates in the obligation of good faith under international law, it has gradually acquired a specific meaning in the light of decisions and treaties, and requires, inter alia, a treatment compatible with the expectations of foreign investors, the observance of arrangements. on which the investor has relied in making the investment, and the maintenance of a stable legal and business framework.

292. The Respondent's argument on this point is based on the premise that fair and equitable treatment is a standard indistinguishable from the customary international minimum standard, and that it is not for tribunals to set out its meaning and even less to legislate on the matter. The Respondent asserts that this view is confirmed by the practice of a number of governments, NAFTA and ICSID decisions, and opinions of learned writers.

...

294. The Respondent maintains in particular that devaluation was the result of market decisions, and that the consistent decisions of courts in other crises have reaffirmed the

---

[56] This Award, as with the *Sempra* Award, was subsequently annulled under Art. 52 of the ICSID Convention due to the tribunal's conflation of the treaty's non-precluded measures clause with the stricter customary international law defence of necessity. The ICSID annulment committee reasoned that the tribunal may have decided differently had it admitted Argentina's defence of necessity under the lower treaty standard. The tribunal's annulled Award is nonetheless illustrative of the trend of tribunal jurisprudence. See *Enron* v. *Argentina*, ICSID Case No. ARB/01/3, Decision on Annulment, 30 July 2010. The *Sempra* Award was subsequently annulled in its entirety by reason of the tribunal having manifestly exceeded its powers by equating the defence under the non-precluded measures clause in the BIT with the customary international law defence of necessity. *Sempra* v. *Argentina*, Case No. ARB/02/16, Decision on Annulment, 29 June 2010.

constitutionality of such a measure, most notably in the context of the Great Depression in the U.S. The *Thunderbird v. Mexico* decision has also been invoked by the Respondent in support of its view that the standard of fair and equitable treatment does not include the protection of legitimate expectations, and it is no different from the international minimum standard.

...

302. It might well be that in some circumstances in which the international minimum standard is sufficiently elaborate and clear, the standard of fair and equitable treatment might be equated with it. But in other cases, it might as well be the opposite, so that the fair and equitable treatment standard will be more precise than its customary international law forefathers. On many occasions, the issue will not even be whether the fair and equitable treatment standard is different or more demanding than the customary standard, but only whether it is more specific, less generic and spelled out in a contemporary fashion so that its application is more appropriate to the case under consideration. This does not exclude the possibility that the fair and equitable treatment standard imposed under a treaty can also eventually require a treatment additional to or beyond that of customary law. Such does not appear to be the case with the present dispute, however.

Azurix Corp. v. Argentina, ICSID Case No. ARB/01/12, Award, 14 July 2006 (Dr Andrés Rigo Sureda, President; Hon. Marc Lalonde PC, OC QC; Dr Daniel Hugo Martins), para. 361

Turning now to Article II.2(a), this paragraph provides: 'Investment shall at all times be accorded fair and equitable treatment, shall enjoy full protection and security and shall in no case be accorded treatment less than required by international law.' The paragraph consists of three full statements, each listing in sequence a standard of treatment to be accorded to investments: fair and equitable, full protection and security, not less than required by international law. Fair and equitable treatment is listed separately. The last sentence ensures that, whichever content is attributed to the other two standards, the treatment accorded to investment will be no less than required by international law. The clause, as drafted, permits to interpret fair and equitable treatment and full protection and security as higher standards than required by international law. The purpose of the third sentence is to set a floor, not a ceiling, in order to avoid a possible interpretation of these standards below what is required by international law. While this conclusion results from the textual analysis of this provision, the Tribunal does not consider that it is of material significance for its application of the standard of fair and equitable treatment to the facts of the case. As it will be explained below, the minimum requirement to satisfy this standard has evolved and the Tribunal considers that its content is substantially similar whether the terms are interpreted in their ordinary meaning, as required by the Vienna Convention, or in accordance with customary international law.

Finally, turning to *Vivendi* v. *Argentina*, it cannot be assumed that the potential relevance of customary international law to the interpretation of FET treaty clauses is necessarily confined to consideration of what the international minimum standard of treatment requires. There may be other relevant and applicable standards of international law which go beyond or even exist in a state of tension with the international protection of foreign-owned property. Precisely because international investment agreements are a part of international law more broadly, human rights, environmental and other international norms could enter into the equation.

Compañia de Aguas del Aconquija SA and Vivendi Universal v. Argentina v. Argentina, ICSID Case No. ARB/97/3, Award, 20 August 2007 (J. William Rowley QC, President; Professor Gabrielle Kaufmann–Kohler; Professor Carlos Bernal Verea), para. 7.4.7

The Tribunal sees no basis for equating principles of international law with the minimum standard of treatment. First, the reference to principles of international law supports a broader reading that invites consideration of a wider range of international law principles than the minimum standard alone. Second, the wording of Article 3 requires that the fair and equitable treatment conform to the principles of international law, but the requirement for conformity can just as readily set a floor as a ceiling on the Treaty's fair and equitable treatment standard. Third, the language of the provision suggests that one should also look to contemporary principles of international law, not only to principles from almost a century ago.

The view in *Vivendi* v. *Argentina* is consistent with the principle of interpretation in the Vienna Convention on the Law of Treaties that *any* relevant rules of international law applicable to the relationship between the parties shall in the course of the interpretation of the investment treaty be taken into account, together with the context of the investment treaty.[57]

CONCLUSION

There is perhaps no more controversial issue in investment arbitration than the current popularity of FET as a head of claim. Investment claims against host States were once framed as expropriation claims, but notwithstanding expansive developments in

---

[57] See further the so-called 'systemic integration clause' in Art. 31(3)(c) of the Vienna Convention on the Law of Treaties 1969. The reference to the 'context' of the treaty refers, in the usual way, to the requirement that, in addition to the ordinary meaning of the treaty's terms, the 'internal' context (e.g. the preambles, annexures and so on) as well as the 'external' context of the treaty (e.g. any subsequent agreements, and subsequent practice which establishes an agreement, between the investment treaty parties) should also be taken into account.

that area too, the hurdle for establishing an indirect expropriation remains forbidding. Pleading a breach of FET presents an attractive alternative. This, it has been suggested, is what explains the inclusion of a FET claim in pleadings almost as a matter of course, thereby making breach of FET a form of 'expropriation light' in the eyes of claimants.[58] The resultant controversy is neither purely jurisprudential nor academic. The backlash against investment arbitration may in large part be explained by the expansion of FET claims.[59] Perhaps this was inevitable with the explosion of investment arbitration claims. The potential broadness of FET protection, as Mann explained so many decades ago, had offered great promise even early on. Mann's own expansive view was cited approvingly by a tribunal in one of the earliest controversial Awards involving a FET claim.[60] Yet, for critics, part of the FET standard's potential breadth of application, indeed its flexibility, is simply the result of an unacceptable degree of vagueness in the notion.

Today, States negotiating investment treaties have sought to narrow down the concept of FET with more precisely formulated clauses. Whether such attempts to manage FET as a bloated concept will succeed still remains to be seen. Increasingly, the controversy over FET has turned to the very way in which we think about FET claims; namely, whether an exercise of balancing the rights of host states against investor rights is involved. It is said that the principle of proportionality or necessity presents the best tool for such an exercise in balancing competing rights.[61] Typically, a proportionality test might ask if the host State measure pursues a legitimate aim, whether the measure in question is rationally connected to and advances that aim and whether the actual design of the measure is proportionate to or no more restrictive of investors' rights than is necessary. Tribunals which apply a proportionality analysis or some version of it would have to make judgments of fact, degree and value. Critics would argue that this entrusts too much authority to arbitrators, who will be tasked to assess the validity and legitimacy of host State measures, not least when we consider that a proportionality analysis is normally applied under the colour of national judicial authority. Others argue that tribunals are precisely the agents to whom we should entrust the task.[62]

---

[58] Yannaca-Small, 'Fair and Equitable Treatment Standard', 111, 112.

[59] Beginning with the kind of 'clarification' we saw in the case of the NAFTA parties' binding interpretation, see further Bernasconi-Osterwalder, 'Giving Arbitrators Carte Blanche', 328.

[60] See *S. D. Myers* v. *Government of Canada* (2001) 40 ILM 1408, paras 265–266.

[61] See further, H. Xiuli, 'On the Application of the Principle of Proportionality in ICSID Arbitration and Proposals to Government of the People's Republic of China' (2006) 13 *JCULR* 223; B. Kingsbury and S. Schill, 'Investor-State Arbitration as Governance: Fair and Equitable Treatment, Proportionality and the Emerging Global Administrative Law', IILJ Working Paper 2009/6, NYU School of Law, 21; C. Henckels, *Proportionality and Deference in Investor-State Arbitration: Balancing Investment Protection and Regulatory Autonomy* (Cambridge University Press, 2015); V. Vadi, *Analogies in Investment Law and Arbitration* (Cambridge University Press, 2016), 203; G. Bücheler, *Proportionality in Investor State Arbitration* (Oxford University Press, 2015).

[62] For an example of this last argument, see, e.g., A. Stone Sweet, 'Investor-State Arbitration: Proportionality's New Frontier' (2010) 4 *LEHR* 47. For criticism of proportionality analysis, see, e.g., M. Sornarajah, *Resistance and Change in the International Law on Foreign Investment* (Cambridge University Press, 2015), 371 et seq.

QUESTIONS

1. What is the relationship between the idea of an international minimum standard of treatment (MST) on the one hand, and, on the other, full protection and security (FPS) and fair and equitable treatment (FET)?
2. In what way have FET and FPS become more closely interrelated?
3. How have recent treaties sought to define the meaning of FET and FPS more closely?
4. What is the relationship, if any, between treaty standards and the standard of protection under customary international law? Is this simply a matter of what particular treaty clauses say?

SUGGESTIONS FOR FURTHER READING

1. S. Vasciannie, 'The Fair and Equitable Treatment Standard in International Investment Law and Practice' (1999) 70 *BYbIL* 99.
2. G. C. Moss, 'Full Protection and Security' in A. Reinisch (ed.), *Standards of Investment Protection* (Oxford University Press, 2008), 131.
3. C. Schreuer, 'Full Protection and Security' (2010) 1 *JIDS* 353.
4. M. Paparinskis, *The International Minimum Standard and Fair and Equitable Treatment* (Oxford University Press, 2013).
5. R. Dolzer, 'Fair and Equitable Treatment: Today's Contours' (2014) 12 *Santa Clara J Int'l L* 7.
6. N. Bernasconi-Osterwalder, 'Giving Arbitrators Carte Blanche – Fair and Equitable Treatment in Investment Treaties' in C. L. Lim (ed.), *Alternative Visions of the International Law on Foreign Investment: Essays in Honour of Muthucumaraswamy Sornarajah* (Cambridge University Press, 2016), 324.

13

Contingent Standards: National Treatment and Most-Favoured-Nation Treatment

CHAPTER OUTLINE

This chapter addresses two obligations commonly included in investment protection treaties and drafted in a contingent manner: national treatment and most-favoured-nation (MFN) treatment. The topic is addressed in four parts: Sections 1 and 2 deal with national treatment, and Sections 3 and 4 deal with most-favoured-nation treatment. Section 1 sets the scene, outlining how national treatment may be expressed in various primary obligations of investment protection law. Section 2 analyses various legal issues that arise in the application of national treatment, dealing in turn with the accepted categories of 'like circumstances' and 'distinctions with treatment', as well as the less settled issue of 'justification'. Sections 3 and 4 deal with the MFN treatment obligation, and also consider its application to primary obligations and to rules of international dispute settlement.

INTRODUCTION

At one point in time, non-discrimination was *the* issue in the international law on treatment of aliens and foreign investment.[1] In the late nineteenth and early twentieth centuries, this body of law was shaped primarily by contestation between non-discrimination and the international minimum standard[2] – or, as modern international lawyers would put it, between primary obligations of international law that only require States to conform with internal law, and primary obligations that require States to (also) engage in other conduct.

---

[1] The Colombian Constitutional Court quoted this sentence from the first edition to support the argument that 'the substantive provisions of IIAs and, in general, international investment law, arise to protect the foreign investor against discriminatory treatment in favor of the national investor, and not vice versa', Sentencia C-252/19, Judgment of 2 June 2019, para. 112, www.corteconstitucional.gov.co/relatoria/2019/c-252-19. htm (accessed 18 September 2020) (authors' translation from Spanish).

[2] See M. Paparinskis, *The International Minimum Standard and Fair and Equitable Treatment* (Oxford University Press, 2013), chapter 2.

2001 International Law Commission (ILC) Articles on Responsibility of States for Internationally Wrongful Acts (2001 ILC Articles), Art. 3, Commentary 7

The rule that the characterization of conduct as unlawful in international law cannot be affected by the characterization of the same act as lawful in internal law makes no exception for cases where rules of international law require a State to conform to the provisions of its internal law, for instance by applying to aliens the same legal treatment as to nationals. It is true that in such a case, compliance with internal law is relevant to the question of international responsibility. But this is because the rule of international law makes it relevant, e.g. by incorporating the standard of compliance with internal law as the applicable international standard or as an aspect of it. Especially in the fields of injury to aliens and their property and of human rights, the content and application of internal law will often be relevant to the question of international responsibility. In every case it will be seen on analysis that either the provisions of internal law are relevant as facts in applying the applicable international standard, or else that they are actually incorporated in some form, conditionally or unconditionally, into that standard.

It is fair to say that non-discrimination has lost its central role in the practice of international investment law, and international arbitral tribunals are more likely to determine responsibility arising out of breach of primary obligations of fair and equitable treatment – discussed in Chapter 12 – and expropriation – discussed in Chapter 14.

Investor–State Dispute Settlement: Review of Developments in 2015 (June 2016) IIA Issues Note No. 2, p. 6

... in 2015: ... In the decisions holding the State liable, tribunals most frequently found breaches of the fair and equitable treatment (FET) provision and the expropriation provision.

Investor–State Dispute Settlement: Review of Developments in 2016 (May 2017) IIA Issues Note No. 1, p. 4

In the decisions [rendered in 2016] holding the State liable, tribunals most frequently found breaches of the FET provision and the expropriation provision.

Investor–State Dispute Settlement: Review of Developments in 2017 (June 2018) IIA Issues Note No. 2, p. 5

In the decisions [rendered in 2017] holding the State liable, tribunals most frequently found breaches of the expropriation and the fair and equitable treatment (FET) provisions.

Fact Sheet of Investor–State Dispute Settlement Cases in 2018: (May 2019) IIA Issues Note No. 2, p. 4

In the decisions [rendered in 2018] holding the State liable, tribunals most frequently found breaches of the fair and equitable treatment provision.

But this does not mean that rules on non-discrimination are irrelevant. Some cases do turn on non-discrimination, and disputes about interpretation and application of non-discrimination have raised important legal questions. Non-discrimination has been most important, as it were, incidentally: as a contested element of fair and equitable treatment, as a criterion of lawfulness for expropriation and as a conduit for more favourable primary obligations and rules of international dispute settlement in third-party treaties.

1. NINE LIVES OF NATIONAL TREATMENT

National treatment requires States, to borrow the phrase from the Commentary to the 2001 ILC Articles excerpted in the Introduction, to apply 'to aliens the same legal treatment as to nationals' (Art. 3, Commentary 7). It is useful to begin the discussion by identifying various ways in which national treatment may be expressed in investment protection law. The excerpted treaty provisions come from the North American Free Trade Agreement (NAFTA), because, even though it is no longer in force, many of the early, important cases were decided on its basis; in addition, the Comprehensive and Progressive Agreement for Trans-Pacific Partnership (CPTPP) reflects careful thinking and provides an extensive note on interpretation that is of direct relevance for this chapter.[3]

1.1 National Treatment

The first example, unsurprisingly, is the obligation of national treatment as such.

> **North American Free Trade Agreement, Art. 1102 (National Treatment)**
>
> 1. Each Party shall accord to investors of another Party treatment no less favorable than that it accords, in like circumstances, to its own investors with respect to the establishment, acquisition, expansion, management, conduct, operation, and sale or other disposition of investments.
> 2. Each Party shall accord to investments of investors of another Party treatment no less favorable than that it accords, in like circumstances, to investments of its own investors with respect to the establishment, acquisition, expansion, management, conduct, operation, and sale or other disposition of investments.
> 3. The treatment accorded by a Party under paragraphs 1 and 2 means, with respect to a state or province, treatment no less favorable than the most favorable treatment accorded, in like circumstances, by that state or province to investors, and to investments of investors, of the Party of which it forms a part.
> 4. For greater certainty, no Party may:
>   (a) impose on an investor of another Party a requirement that a minimum level of equity in an enterprise in the territory of the Party be held by its nationals, other than nominal qualifying shares for directors or incorporators of corporations; or

---

3 Drafters' Note on Interpretation of 'In Like Circumstances' under Article 9.4 (National Treatment) and Article 9.5 (Most-Favoured-Nation Treatment), https://www.mfat.govt.nz/assets/Trans-Pacific-Partnership/Other-documents/Interpretation-of-In-Like-Circumstances.pdf (accessed 1 July 2020), excerpted in Section 3.

(b) require an investor of another Party, by reason of its nationality, to sell or otherwise dispose of an investment in the territory of the Party.

Comprehensive and Progressive Agreement for Trans-Pacific Partnership, Art. 9.4 (National Treatment)

[Fn 14: For greater certainty, whether treatment is accorded in 'like circumstances' under Article 9.4 (National Treatment) or Article 9.5 (Most-Favoured-Nation Treatment) depends on the totality of the circumstances, including whether the relevant treatment distinguishes between investors or investments on the basis of legitimate public welfare objectives.]

1. Each Party shall accord to investors of another Party treatment no less favorable than that it accords, in like circumstances, to its own investors with respect to the establishment, acquisition, expansion, management, conduct, operation, and sale or other disposition of investments in its territory.

2. Each Party shall accord to covered investments treatment no less favorable than that it accords, in like circumstances, to investments in its territory of its own investors with respect to the establishment, acquisition, expansion, management, conduct, operation, and sale or other disposition of investments.

3. For greater certainty, the treatment to be accorded by a Party under paragraphs 1 and 2 means, with respect to a regional level of government, treatment no less favorable than the most favourable treatment accorded, in like circumstances, by that regional level of government to investors, and to investments of investors, of the Party of which it forms a part.

Note the key role that 'in like circumstances' and 'like situations' plays in the structure of the obligation in all three treaties. Also, consider the added value that footnote 14 in CPTPP plays in broadening the spectrum of relevant considerations, including 'legitimate public welfare objectives'. Note also that another way of expressing an obligation with a similar structure would be by prohibiting 'discrimination', which does not explicitly bring likeness of circumstances and situations at play (for an example, see Section 1.3).

1.2 Expropriation

The second example of non-discrimination in treaty obligations is as a criterion of lawfulness for expropriation that includes national treatment, but is not limited to it.

North American Free Trade Agreement, Art. 1110(1)(b) (Expropriation and Compensation)

1. No Party may directly or indirectly nationalize or expropriate an investment of an investor of another Party in its territory or take a measure tantamount to nationalization or expropriation of such an investment ('expropriation'), except:

   ...

   (b) on a non-discriminatory basis;

The importance of criteria of lawfulness of expropriation is discussed, from the perspective of expropriation in Chapter 14 and from the perspective of remedies in Chapter 17. It suffices to note here that a number of arbitral decisions have drawn the distinction between compensation as an element of the primary obligation of expropriation and compensation as a secondary rule of State responsibility for internationally wrongful acts, which may differ regarding standards and date of valuation. For example, the arbitral tribunal in the *ADC* v. *Hungary* case found that expropriation had been unlawful because, among other reasons, it was discriminatory, and therefore awarded market value at the date of the award, rather than at the date of expropriation.[4] A more recent example of a finding of discriminatory expropriation is the award in the *Quiborax* v. *Bolivia* case, discussed in Section 2.[5]

1.3 Fair and Equitable Treatment

The third example is the international minimum standard and fair and equitable treatment. There is some disagreement between States and tribunals whether an obligation of non-discriminatory treatment is implicit in obligations to provide the international minimum standard and fair and equitable treatment (or, perhaps more accurately, whether it is a relevant consideration in the application of the treaty or customary rule). The NAFTA Free Trade Commission's 2001 interpretation suggested that '[a] determination that there has been a breach of another provision of the NAFTA, or of a separate international agreement, does not establish that there has been a breach of Article 1105(1)'[6] – a point not limited to national treatment, but thought to have been particularly motivated by suggestions to that effect in some early decisions. The US has been one prominent critic of efforts to read general non-discrimination into customary law.

Elliot Associates, LP v. *Republic of Korea*, PCA Case No. 2018–51, Submission of the US, 7 February 2020, para. 19 (footnotes omitted)

The customary international law minimum standard of treatment set forth in Article 11.5.1 [of the United States–Korea Free Trade Agreement] does not incorporate a prohibition on economic discrimination against aliens or a general obligation of non-discrimination. As a general proposition, a State may treat foreigners and nationals differently, and it may also treat foreigners from different States differently. To the extent that the customary international law minimum standard of treatment incorporated in Article 11.5 prohibits discrimination, it does so only in the context of other established customary international

---

[4] *ADC Affiliate Ltd and Other* v. *Hungary*, ICSID Case No. ARB/03/16, Award, 2 October 2006 (Kaplan, Brower, van den Berg), paras 441–443, 479–499.

[5] *Quiborax SA, Non Metallic Minerals SA and Allan Fosk Kaplún* v. *Bolivia*, ICSID Case No. ARB/06/2, Award, 16 September 2015 (Kaufmann-Kohler, Lalonde, Stern), paras 246–254.

[6] NAFTA Free Trade Commission, Notes of Interpretation of Certain Chapter 11 Provisions, 31 July 2001, www.sice.oas.org/tpd/nafta/Commission/CH11understanding_e.asp (accessed 26 September 2020).

law rules, such as prohibitions against discriminatory takings, access to judicial remedies or treatment by the courts, or the obligation of States to provide full protection and security and to compensate aliens and nationals on an equal basis in times of violence, insurrection, conflict or strife. Moreover, general investor-State claims of nationality-based discrimination are governed exclusively by the provisions of Chapter Eleven that specifically address that subject, and not Article 11.5.1.

Other authorities are more receptive to non-discrimination in relation to fair and equitable treatment. The EU–Canada Comprehensive Economic and Trade Agreement (CETA) points to 'targeted discrimination on manifestly wrongful grounds, such as gender, race or religious belief' as one example of conduct that may breach the obligation of fair and equitable treatment (Art. 8.7); and the tribunal in the *Crystallex* v. *Venezuela* award described non-discrimination as one of the 'central components of FET'.[7] Finally, while the particular formulation has faded somewhat in recent treaty practice, some treaties explicitly connect discrimination with (what many people would characterise as) the core of fair and equitable treatment: the Article 10(1) of the Energy Charter Treaty, to take perhaps the most important example, prohibits 'unreasonable or discriminatory measures'. The more general response to the US position excerpted above is that the focus on 'other established customary international law rules' misses the wood for the trees: the better reading of non-discrimination is as a *de minimis* element of custom in the area, and to the extent that the modern international standard is capable of having more general application, it also necessarily carries with it this *de minimis* obligation.

1.4 Other Examples

The final category of examples includes obligations that have not, so far, led to significant disputes.

EU–Canada Comprehensive Economic and Trade Agreement, Chapter 8

Article 8.8 Senior management and boards of directors
A Party shall not require that an enterprise of that Party, that is also a covered investment, appoint to senior management or board of director positions, natural persons of any particular nationality.

...

---

[7] *Crystallex International Corp.* v. *Venezuela*, ICSID Case No. ARB(AF)/11/2, Award, 4 April 2016 (Lévy, Gotanda, Boisson de Chazournes), para. 615.

Article 8.11 Compensation for losses

Notwithstanding Article 8.15.5(b), each Party shall accord to investors of the other Party, whose covered investments suffer losses owing to armed conflict, civil strife, a state of emergency or natural disaster in its territory, treatment no less favourable than that it accords to its own investors or to the investors of a third country, whichever is more favourable to the investor concerned, as regards restitution, indemnification, compensation or other settlement.

...

Article 8.13 Transfers

...

3. Nothing in this Article shall be construed to prevent a Party from applying in an equitable and non-discriminatory manner and not in a way that would constitute a disguised restriction on transfers, its laws relating to ...

2. INTERPRETATION AND APPLICATION OF NATIONAL TREATMENT

Tribunals tend to approach claims of national treatment by asking three questions: (1) are the circumstances like, (2) is the treatment different, and (3) is there a reasonable justification for that? The excerpt below is taken from a recent decision that summarises arbitral jurisprudence on the matter. Note, though, that the treaty language in which the obligation is expressed may itself contain important qualifiers, which should not necessarily be brushed aside by excessive reliance on arbitral decisions that interpret and apply differently worded treaties.

Quiborax SA, Non Metallic Minerals SA and Allan Fosk Kaplún v. Bolivia, ICSID Case No. ARB/06/2, Award, 16 September 2015, para. 247

To determine whether the Revocation Decree discriminated against NMM, the Tribunal will apply the three-pronged test formulated in *Saluka*, cited by the Respondent: 'State conduct is discriminatory, if (i) similar cases are (ii) treated differently (iii) and without reasonable justification.'

[Footnote 272: *Saluka v. Czech Republic*, Partial Award of 17 March 2006, 313. Other tribunals (whether dealing with the prohibition of discriminatory treatment, or with national treatment provisions, which prohibit nationality-based discrimination), have applied a similar standard. See, e.g., *Joseph C. Lemire v. Ukraine*, ICSID Case No. ARB/06/18 ('*Lemire v. Ukraine*'), Decision on Jurisdiction and Liability of 21 January 2010, ¶ 261 (footnotes omitted) ('Discrimination, in the words of pertinent precedents, requires more than different treatment['. To amount to discrimination, a case must be treated differently from similar cases without justification; a measure must be 'discriminatory and expose[s] the claimant to sectional or racial prejudice'; or a measure must 'target[ed] [sic] Claimant's investments specifically as foreign investments'); *Champion Trading Company and Ameritrade International, Inc. v. Arab Republic of Egypt*, ICSID Case No. ARB/02/9, Award of 27 October 2006, ¶ 130 ('The national treatment obligation does not generally prohibit a State from adopting measures that constitute a difference in treatment. The obligation only prohibits a State from taking measures resulting in different treatment in like circumstances'); *Total S.A. v. Argentine Republic*, ICSID Case No. ARB/04/01 ('*Total v. Argentina*'), Decision on Liability of 27 December 2010, ¶ 344 ('This standard requires, as a rule, a comparison between the treatment of different investments, usually within a given sector, of different national origin or ownership ... The purpose is to ascertain whether the protected investments have been treated worse without any justification, specifically because of their foreign nationality. The similarity of the investments compared and of their operations is a precondition for a fruitful comparison').]

As to the third element, the Tribunal agrees with *Parkerings* that there are situations that may justify differentiated treatment, a matter to be assessed under the specific circumstances of each case.

[Footnote 273: *Parkerings-Compagniet AS v. Republic of Lithuania*, ICSID Case No. ARB/05/8, Award of 11 September 2007, ¶ 368 ('Discrimination is to be ascertained by looking at the circumstances of the individual cases. Discrimination involves either issues of law, such as legislation affording different treatments in function of citizenship, or issues of fact where a State unduly treats differently investors who are in similar circumstances. Whether discrimination is objectionable does not in the opinion of this Tribunal depend on subjective requirements such as the bad faith or the malicious intent of the State: at least, Article IV of the Treaty does not include such requirements. However, to violate international law, discrimination must be unreasonable or lacking proportionality, for instance, it must be inapposite or excessive to achieve an otherwise legitimate objective of the State. An objective justification may justify differentiated treatments of similar cases. It would be necessary, in each case, to evaluate the exact circumstances and the context').].

Following this approach, the next subsection will consider whether (1) circumstances are like, (2) treatment is different and (3) there is a reasonable justification for that.

2.1 Like Circumstances

What (type of) considerations are relevant for determining the presence or absence of likeness? One point of contention in arbitral decisions is whether a competitive relationship is relevant for the inquiry into likeness. Two early awards from the mid-2000s were sceptical about the relevance of the competitive relationship. In the *Occidental* v. *Ecuador* case, an investor in the oil production sector argued that Ecuador had acted in breach of national treatment by not permitting a VAT refund, while permitting it to companies involved in the export of flowers, and mining and seafood products. The State responded that '"in like situations" can only mean that all companies in the same sector are to be treated alike and this happens in respect of all oil producers'.[8] The tribunal, however, accepted the investor's approach, and found a breach of national treatment.

Occidental Exploration and Production Co. v. Ecuador, LCIA Case No. UN 3467, Final Award, 1 July 2004 (Orrego Vicuña, Brower, Barrera Sweeney), para. 173

The Tribunal is of the view that in the context of this particular claim the Claimant is right and its arguments are convincing. In fact, 'in like situations' cannot be interpreted in the narrow sense advanced by Ecuador as the purpose of national treatment is to protect investors as compared to local producers, and this cannot be done by addressing exclusively the sector in which the particular activity is undertaken.

In the *Methanex* v. *US* case, the tribunal rejected the investor's argument that it – a Canadian methanol producer – was in like circumstances with US ethanol producers due to the competitive relationship between ethanol and methanol products, since an identical comparator existed: US methanol producers. The challenged measure did not distinguish between Canadian and US methanol producers, therefore the national treatment claim failed.

Methanex Corp. v. *US,* UNCITRAL Case, Final Award of the Tribunal on Jurisdiction and Merits, 3 August 2005 (Veeder, Rowley, Reisman), Part IV – Chapter B, paras 16–17, 19 (footnotes omitted)

16. The major distinction between the two proposed methodologies is in the specific method of selecting what the USA called the 'comparator' for purposes of determining like circumstances. In the formula quoted above, Methanex's methodology begins by assuming that its comparator is the ethanol industry, while the USA proposes a procedure in which the comparator that is to be selected is that domestic investor or domestically-owned investment which is like or, if not like, then close to the foreign investor or investment in all relevant respects, but for nationality of ownership. Despite the difference in approach, it is clear that if the result of the application of the US procedure were to identify the ethanol industry as the comparator, Methanex's methodology would simply be the final sequence in the US methodology.

17. The key question is: who is the proper comparator? Simply to assume that the ethanol industry or a particular ethanol producer is the comparator here would beg that question.

---

[8] *Occidental Exploration and Production Co. v. Ecuador,* LCIA Case No. UN 3467, Final Award, 1 July 2004, para. 171.

Given the object of Article 1102 and the flexibility which the provision provides in its adoption of 'like circumstances', it would be as perverse to ignore identical comparators if they were available and to use comparators that were less 'like', as it would be perverse to refuse to find and to apply less 'like' comparators when no identical comparators existed. The difficulty which Methanex encounters in this regard is that there are comparators which are identical to it.

...

19. In this respect, the NAFTA award in *Pope & Talbot v. Canada* is instructive. There, a US investor in Canada, which was obliged to pay export fees, alleged that it was in like circumstances with Canadian producers in other provinces that were not subject to export fees. The tribunal, however, rejected the claim for there were more than 500 Canadian producers in other provinces which were subject to the fees. That is, the tribunal selected the entities that were in the most 'like circumstances' and not comparators that were in less 'like circumstances'. It would be a forced application of Article 1102 if a tribunal were to ignore the identical comparator and to try to lever in an, at best, approximate (and arguably inappropriate) comparator. The fact stands – Methanex did not receive less favourable treatment than the identical domestic comparators, producing methanol.

The apparent width of divergence in approaches to determination of likeness has raised concerns in legal writings.

A. Reinisch, 'National Treatment' in M. Bungenberg, J. Griebel, S. Hobe and A. Reinisch (eds), *International Investment Law: A Handbook* (Baden–Baden: C. H. Beck/Hart/Nomos, 2015), 859 (footnotes omitted)

... the *Occidental* and *Methanex* cases demonstrate quite well that the breadth of the scope of likeness is indeed remarkable and may lead to unpredictable outcomes, depending upon whether a tribunal intends to take into account only identical comparators (*Methanex*), those that are in a competitive relationship (most cases) or, even broader, all those that operate commercially (*Occidental*).

Reasonable people may disagree on whether it is possible to identify *jurisprudence constante* in recent arbitral decisions in relation to likeness. In the *Bilcon v. Canada* case, where the investor challenged the environmental assessment regulatory process, the tribunal chose to compare the treatment of the investment to those mining projects that were 'sufficiently' similar to it.[9] In the *Quiborax* v. *Bolivia* case, where the investor challenged

---

[9] *William Ralph Clayton and Others* v. *Government of Canada*, PCA Case No. 2009–04, Award on Jurisdiction and Liability, 17 March 2015 (Simma, McRae, Schwartz), para. 696 (more commonly known as *Bilcon* v. *Canada*) ('The actual comparison cases brought forward by the Investors in the present case generally

the loss of its concession, the tribunal referred to treatment applied to other investors that had operated in the same area, had also been fined and had lost environmental licences.[10] In the *Mercer* v. *Canada* case, the tribunal emphasized the importance of determining 'like circumstances' with respect to particular measures, rather than in abstract, and while accepting certain self-generating pulp mills to be ostensibly comparators, ultimately found them not to be in like circumstances with respect to load displacement services.[11] In the *Marfin* v. *Cyprus* case, where the investor challenged the conduct regarding the Laiki Bank in the context of financial crisis, the tribunal found that Laiki was in similar circumstances to the Bank of Cyprus in terms of size, systemic importance, exposure and need for capitalization.[12] The *Archer Daniels Midland and Other* v. *Mexico* (*ADM* v. *Mexico*) decision may provide a starting point for formulating a generally applicable approach of treating the competitive relationship as a relevant consideration, at least in the absence of identical comparators. Note that the drafters of the CPTPP (excerpted further below) explicitly referred to this case when postulating that tribunals should 'follow the existing approach'.

Archer Daniels Midland Co. and Tate & Lyle Ingredients Americas, Inc. v. Mexico, ICSID Case No. ARB(AF)/04/05, Award, 21 November 2007 (Cremades, Rovine, Siqueiros), paras 199, 201–202, 204

199. Considering the object of Article 1102 – to ensure that a national measure does not upset the competitive relationship between domestic and foreign investors – other tribunals convened under Chapter Eleven have focused mainly on the competitive relationship between investors in the marketplace.

...

201. ALMEX and the Mexican sugar industry are in like circumstances. Both are part of the same sector, competing face to face in supplying sweeteners to the soft drink and processed food markets. The competitive relationship between them was confirmed by Mexico's administrative and judicial authorities, when the Government initiated

---

involve federal Canada or JRP [Joint Review Panel] assessments of mining projects, including oil and gas exploration, accompanied by exports that involve sea routes. A number of them specifically involved quarry and marine terminal export projects that had the potential to affect a local community. At least three of them involved assessments that included the marine terminal component of a project that was connected to a quarry and took place in an ecologically sensitive coastal area'). While the approach appears similar to *Methanex* v. *USA* and *ADM* v. *Mexico*, excerpted below, the tribunal explicitly referred to the investor's invocation of *Occidental* v. *Ecuador*, para. 693.

[10] *Quiborax* v. *Bolivia*, para. 247 ('In this case, other mining companies operating in the Río Grande Delta were audited under Law 2,564. Other mining companies, such as Copla and Tecno Química, were fined for alleged errors in their export declarations, like NMM. Additionally, Copla obtained and lost its environmental license at the same time as NMM').

[11] *Mercer International Inc.* v. *Canada*, ICSID Case No. ARB(AF)/12/3, Award, 6 March 2018 (Veeder, Orrego Vicuña, Douglas) paras 7.18–7.41.

[12] *Marfin Investment Group Holdings SA, Alexandros Bakatselos and Others* v. *Cyprus*, ICSID Case No. ARB/13/27, Award, 26 July 2018 (Hanotiau, Edward, Price) para. 1241.

anti-dumping investigations in 1997 on HFCS, based on a petition filed by the Sugar Chamber. In addition, Mexico's Federal Competition Commission has confirmed that HFCS is a substitute of sugar and that both products compete in the same market (Comisión Federal de Competencia, Informe Anual 1993–94).

202. Notwithstanding the fact that fructose and cane sugar producers are not identical comparators, even though they compete face-to-face in the same market, it is the Tribunal's view that when no identical comparators exist, the foreign investor may be compared with less like comparators, if the overall circumstances of the case suggest that they are in like circumstances. This was the specific situation in *Methanex*, where the State of California issued an order that banned the use of the gasoline additive methyl tertiary-butyl ether (MTBE). Methanex does not manufacture MTBE, but it is one of [the] world's largest producers and marketers of methanol, the principal ingredient of MTBE. The gist of Methanex's Article 1102 claim was that California intended to favor domestic producers of ethanol by discriminating against foreign producers of methanol; and that the two products should be considered 'like' because they both compete in the oxygenate market. After considering the arguments of both Parties, the Arbitral Tribunal determined that Methanex was not in like circumstances as domestic producers of ethanol, because there were also identical comparators in the United States (other producers of methanol) which were subject to the same treatment as Methanex. Furthermore, looking at the 'circumstances' of competition between methanol and ethanol in the market for fuel additives, the tribunal found the circumstances of methanol and ethanol to be different because unlike ethanol, methanol itself is not usable as a gasoline additive.

...

204. Accordingly, the appropriate subjects for comparison in the present case are the Mexican cane sugar producers, as they compete face-to-face with the Claimants in supplying sweeteners to the industry producing beverages and syrups subject to the Tax.

CPTPP Drafters' Note on Interpretation of 'In Like Circumstances' under Article 9.4 (National Treatment) and Article 9.5 (Most-Favoured-Nation Treatment)

1. The TPP Investment Negotiating Group and the Chief Negotiators discussed the interpretation of 'in like circumstances' under Article 9.4 (National Treatment) and Article 9.5 (Most-Favoured-Nation Treatment) and confirmed the shared intent of the Parties, as reflected in the text of these articles and the relevant footnote, to ensure that tribunals follow the existing approach set out below.

2. When a claimant challenges a measure as inconsistent with Article 9.4 (National Treatment) or Article 9.5 (Most-Favoured-Nation Treatment), the claimant bears the burden to prove that the respondent failed to accord to the claimant or the claimant's covered investment treatment no less favourable than it accords, in like circumstances, (a) to its own investors, or their investments, in its territory (Article 9.4), or (b) to investors of any other Party or of any non-Party, or their investments, in its territory

(Article 9.5). Articles 9.4 and 9.5 do not prohibit all measures that result in differential treatment. Rather, they seek to ensure that foreign investors or their investments are not treated less favourably on the basis of their nationality.

3. The phrase 'in like circumstances' ensures that comparisons are made only with respect to investors or investments on the basis of relevant characteristics. This is a fact-specific inquiry requiring consideration of the totality of the circumstances, as reflected in paragraphs 4 and 5. Such circumstances include not only competition in the relevant business or economic sectors, but also such circumstances as the applicable legal and regulatory frameworks and whether the differential treatment is based on legitimate public welfare objectives. Accordingly, the Parties agreed to include a new footnote in the text: 'For greater certainty, whether treatment is accorded in "like circumstances" depends on the totality of the circumstances, including whether the relevant treatment distinguishes between investors or investments on the basis of legitimate public welfare objectives.'

4. In considering the phrase 'in like circumstances', NAFTA tribunals have held that investors or investments that are 'in like circumstances' based on the totality of the circumstances have been discriminated against based on their nationality. See, e.g., *Archer Daniels Midland, et al, v. United Mexican States*, ICSID Case No. ARB(AF)/04/05, Award, (21 November 2007), para. 197 (finding a breach of the national treatment obligation after taking into account 'all "circumstances" in which the treatment was accorded ... in order to identify the appropriate comparator').

2.2 Distinctions in Treatment

In most cases, determination of distinction in treatment between comparators in like circumstances does not give rise to particular controversy. Consider the cases referred to so far as examples. In *Occidental* v. *Ecuador*, the investor, unlike other companies, was not entitled to receive a VAT refund.[13] In *Methanex* v. *US*, the investor's claim failed because ethanol producers were not in like circumstances, and the treatment of all methanol producers was the same[14] – but, had that part of the claim succeeded, the tribunal would presumably have found that the lack of prohibition of ethanol products had constituted distinctions in treatment. In *ADM* v. *Mexico*, the investment was taxed in excess of like domestic products.[15] In *Quiborax* v. *Bolivia*, the investor, but not other mining companies, had lost its concession.[16] In *Bilcon* v. *Canada*, the tribunal took the view that the investor's investment, but not other comparable investments, had been subject to a harsher standard of review.[17] In *Mercer* v. *Canada*, the investor was treated differently from its ostensible comparators, but that was due to different and individual circumstances that rendered circumstances not 'like'.[18]

[13] *Occidental* v. *Ecuador*, para. 177.
[14] *Methanex* v. USA, Part IV, Chapter B, para. 19.
[15] *ADM* v. *Mexico*, para. 206.
[16] *Quiborax* v. *Bolivia*, para. 247.
[17] *Bilcon* v. *Canada*, paras 696–716.
[18] *Mercer* v. *Canada*, para. 7.45.

There are three broader questions that may be convenient to note here. First, is distinction in treatment limited to de jure discrimination (openly linked to foreign nationality) or is it also applicable to de facto discrimination (that disadvantages foreign investors as a practical matter, even though it may be neutral on its face)?[19] Tribunals have accepted that the obligation of national treatment applies to distinctions in treatment in both kinds of situations;[20] indeed, in none of the cases noted in the previous paragraph were the challenged measures explicitly linked to foreign nationality.

Second, is it relevant that, while some domestic investments are treated better than the foreign investment, others are treated in the same manner (or indeed worse)? Tribunals tend to focus on those domestic investments that do receive better treatment, and the question posed by the *ADM* v. *Mexico* tribunal – whether foreign investors 'receive the best treatment which was accorded' to the domestic investors[21] – seems representative of the general outlook. This also appears to be in line with the formulation adopted in national treatment provisions in NAFTA and CPTPP (excerpted at Section 1), which use the terminology of 'treatment no less favourable than the most favourable treatment accorded' when explaining the treatment to be accorded by sub-federal entities.

Third, what is the role of discriminatory intent for finding distinctions in treatment? The better view is that intent is neither sufficient nor necessary. Responsibility of a State arises from a breach of a primary obligation by conduct attributable to the State;[22] therefore mere intentions that do not lead to any conduct would not make the State responsible.[23] Similarly, most authority supports the proposition that discriminatory intent is not necessary. The prevailing view is that the tripartite test, as the *Bilcon* v. *Canada* tribunal put it, 'does not require a demonstration of discriminatory intent'.[24] For example, in *Occidental* v. *Ecuador*, the tribunal was 'convinced that [application of treatment less favourable] has not been done with the intent of discriminating against foreign-owned companies'.[25] In the *ADM* v. *Mexico* case, where the tribunal did find that the challenged measure had both discriminatory effect and intent, it approvingly referred to the tendency of tribunals to focus on a measure's adverse effects, rather than intent.[26] (*South American Silver Ltd.* v. *Bolivia* may seem an outlier by suggesting a focus on discriminatory intent, but that was due to the way in which the investor had argued its case, and in any event the issue was not decisive because no entity receiving more favourable treatment could be identified.[27]) Overall, the better view is that discriminatory intent is neither necessary nor sufficient for a finding of a breach. At the same time, intentional discrimination is

---

[19] Reinisch, 'National Treatment', 862.

[20] *ADM* v. *Mexico*, para. 193.

[21] *Ibid.*, paras 196, 211.

[22] 2001 ILC Articles, Art. 2.

[23] For a possible example, see *Crystallex* v. *Venezuela*, para. 616, where the tribunal noted 'the repeated and rather derogatory references to "transnationals" and "transnational companies" in the President's and some Ministers' statements', but found that discriminatory conduct had not been proven.

[24] *Bilcon* v. *Canada*, para. 719.

[25] *Occidental* v. *Ecuador*, para. 177.

[26] *ADM* v. *Mexico*, para. 209.

[27] *South American Silver Limited (Bermuda)* v. *Bolivia*, PCA Case No. 2013–15, Award, 22 November 2018 (Zuleta, Orrego Vicuña, Guglielmino), paras 716–722.

important for providing a central example of the type of conduct that the obligation of national treatment seeks to discipline. The Declaration by the United States and Canada to the Energy Charter Treaty is suggestive of this line of thought.

Final Act of the European Energy Charter Conference, Declaration 4

... In determining whether a differential treatment of Investors and Investments is consistent with Article 10,13 two basic factors must be taken into account....[28]

The second factor is the extent to which the measure is motivated by the fact that the relevant Investor or Investment is subject to foreign ownership or under foreign control. A measure aimed specifically at Investors because they are foreign, without sufficient countervailing policy reasons consistent with the preceding paragraph, would be contrary to the principles of Article 10. The foreign Investor or Investment would be 'in similar circumstances' to domestic Investors and their Investments, and the measure would be contrary to Article 10.

2.3 Justification

The final question is whether distinctive treatment of like situations may still be justified. Most authorities accept it as a relevant consideration. But there is some uncertainty as to where it fits best in the analytical framework. States appear to be more comfortable characterising it as relevant for either 'likeness' or 'distinction', perhaps because the language of 'justification' does not usually appear in the national treatment obligations in an explicit manner. Footnote 14 to the CPTPP, excerpted at Section 1, is similar in substance to the documents that follow.

Final Act of the European Energy Charter Conference, Declaration 4

... In determining whether a differential treatment of Investors and Investments is consistent with Article 10,[29] two basic factors must be taken into account. The first factor is the policy objectives of Contracting Parties in various fields insofar as they are consistent with the principles of non-discrimination set out in Article 10. Legitimate policy objectives may justify differential treatment of foreign Investors or their Investments in order to reflect a dissimilarity of relevant circumstances between those Investors and Investments and their domestic counterparts. For example, the objective of ensuring the integrity of a country's financial system would justify reasonable prudential measures with respect to foreign Investors or Investments, where such measures would be unnecessary to ensure the attainment of the same objectives insofar as domestic Investors or Investments are concerned. Those foreign Investors or their Investments would thus not be 'in similar circumstances' to domestic Investors or their Investments. Thus, even if such a measure accorded differential treatment, it would not be contrary to Article 10.

---

[28] [Eds: The first factor is the policy objectives, excerpted in the next subsection.]

[29] [Eds: The relevant part of Art. 10 of the Energy Charter Treaty provides: 'Such Investments shall also enjoy the most constant protection and security and no Contracting Party shall in any way impair by unreasonable or discriminatory measures their management, maintenance, use, enjoyment or disposal.']

CPTPP Drafters' Note on Interpretation of 'In Like Circumstances' under Article 9.4 (National Treatment) and Article 9.5 (Most-Favoured-Nation Treatment)

5. NAFTA tribunals have also accepted distinctions in treatment between investors or investments that are plausibly connected to legitimate public welfare objectives, and have given important weight to whether investors or investments are subject to like legal requirements. See, e.g., *Grand River Enterprises Six Nations Ltd., et al. v. United States of America*, UNCITRAL, Award (12 January 2011), at paras. 166–167 ('NAFTA tribunals have given significant weight to the legal regimes applicable to particular entities in assessing whether they are in "like circumstances" under Articles 1102 [National Treatment] or 1103 [Most-Favoured-Nation Treatment] ... The reasoning of these cases shows the identity of the legal regime(s) applicable to a claimant and its purported comparators to be a compelling factor in assessing whether like is indeed being compared to like for purposes of Articles 1102 and 1103'); *GAMI Investments Inc. v. United Mexican States*, UNCITRAL, Award (15 November 2004), at paras. 111–115 (holding that foreign investor [*sic*] was not 'in like circumstances' with domestic investors because the difference in treatment was 'plausibly connected with a legitimate goal of policy ... and was applied neither in a discriminatory manner nor as a disguised barrier to equal opportunity'); *Pope & Talbot Inc. v. Canada*, UNCITRAL, Award on the Merits of Phase 2 (10 April 2001), at paras. 78–79 (the tribunal's assessment included whether the difference in treatment had a 'reasonable nexus to rational government policies' and was not based on nationality).

Arbitral decisions, summarised by the *Quiborax* v. *Bolivia* tribunal,[30] tend to separate justification out as the third question. The *Bilcon* v. *Canada* tribunal explained its approach in the following manner.

William Ralph Clayton and Others v. Canada, PCA Case No. 2009–04, Award on Jurisdiction and Liability, 17 March 2015 (Simma, McRae, Schwartz), paras 720–723 (footnotes omitted)

720. If a *prima facie* case is made under the three-part *UPS* [v. *Canada*] test,[31] can a host state still show that there is no breach because the discriminatory treatment identified is somehow justified, or that the discriminatory treatment is not sufficiently linked to nationality, but merely an incidental effect of the reasonable pursuit of domestic policy objectives?

---

[30] *Quiborax* v. *Bolivia*, para. 247.

[31] [Eds: The tribunal earlier described Canada's argument as to what the investor would have to provide, by reference to the *United Parcel Service* v. *Canada* case, in the following terms: 'a government accorded Bilcon or its investment "treatment" during the environmental assessment' and 'that the same government accorded treatment to other domestic or foreign investors or investments'; that the treatment was 'less favorable' than that accorded other domestic or foreign proponents; and 'the government accorded the allegedly discriminatory treatment in question "in like circumstances"' (para. 717). Note that this three-part test is different from the three-part test that structures this section, and would cover only the first two questions.]

721. Article 1102 is not attached to any 'justification' clause, such as Article XX of GATT, 1947, which permits an exception to its norms in cases where a state has adopted reasonable measures to pursuing certain domestic policy objectives. Article XX reads in part:

Subject to the requirement that such measures are not applied in a manner which would constitute a means of arbitrary or unjustifiable discrimination between countries where the same conditions prevail, or a disguised restriction on international trade, nothing in this Agreement shall be construed to prevent the adoption or enforcement by any contracting party of measures ...

(b) necessary to protect human, animal or plant life or health.

722. The Tribunal in *Pope & Talbot* [v. *Canada*], however, held that:

Differences in treatment will presumptively violate Article 1102(2), unless they have a reasonable nexus to rational government policies that (1) do not distinguish, on their face or *de facto*, between foreign-owned and domestic companies, and (2) do not otherwise unduly undermine the investment liberalizing objectives of NAFTA.

723. The approach taken in *Pope & Talbot*, would seem to provide legally appropriate latitude for host states, even in the absence of an equivalent of Article XX of the GATT, to pursue reasonable and non-discriminatory domestic policy objectives through appropriate measures even when there is an incidental and reasonably unavoidable burden on foreign enterprises. Consistently with the approach taken in the *Feldman* [v. *Mexico*] case, however, the present Tribunal is also of the view that once a *prima facie* case is made out under the three-part *UPS* test, the onus is on the host state to show that a measure is still sustainable within the terms of Article 1102. It is the host state that is in a position to identify and substantiate the case, in terms of its own laws, policies and circumstances, that an apparently discriminatory measure is in fact compliant with the 'national treatment' norm set out in Article 1102.

In some cases, cited in paragraph 5 of the CPTPP drafters' note excerpted above, tribunals have accepted reasonable justifications for apparent distinctiveness in treatment. For example, *Pope & Talbot Inc.* v. *Canada*[32] was an investment claim brought against the broader backdrop of US–Canada lumber disputes. The tribunal concluded that Canada's conduct was reasonably related to various rational policies, including removing the threat of countervailing duty actions,[33] providing for new entrants[34] and rational choice of remedies in the inter-State dispute,[35] and therefore no breach had occurred. In other cases, tribunals have rejected the argument, including in *Bilcon* v. *Canada*.[36] In *Mercer* v. *Canada*,

---

[32] *Pope & Talbot Inc.* v. *Canada*, UNCITRAL, Award on the Merits of Phase 2, 10 April 2001.
[33] *Ibid.*, para. 87.
[34] *Ibid.*, para. 93.
[35] *Ibid.*, para. 102.
[36] *Bilcon* v. *Canada*, para. 724 ('In the present case the Tribunal is unable to discern any justification for the differential and adverse treatment accorded to Bilcon that would satisfy the *Pope & Talbot* test with respect to the standard of evaluation under the laws of federal Canada. The "community core values" approach

the tribunal was 'generally influenced' by Canada's submissions, which it considered under the rubric of 'policy defence'.[37]

3. MOST-FAVOURED-NATION TREATMENT AND PRIMARY OBLIGATIONS

National treatment, discussed so far, aims to discipline the inappropriately distinctive treatment between foreign investments and investors, on the one hand, and domestic investments and investors, on the other. MFN treatment obligation has a similar structure, but is directed at inappropriate distinctiveness between foreign investors or investment of different nationalities. One might have expected, perhaps, that claims regarding discrimination between various foreigners would be rather rare, thus making the MFN treatment obligation one of limited practical importance. The premise may be largely true,[38] but the clause has played a surprisingly significant role in investment arbitration as a gateway to more favourable rules in third-party treaties.

The example of an MFN treatment clause is taken from the BIT applicable in the *EDF International SA and Others* v. *Argentina* case, which is discussed further below.

Argentina–France BIT, Art. 4

Within its territory and in its maritime zone, each Contracting Party shall provide to the investors of the other Party, with respect to their investments and activities associated with such investments, a treatment no less favourable than that accorded to its own investors or the treatment accorded to investors of the most favoured Nation if the latter is more advantageous.

In 2015 the ILC adopted Summary Conclusions on the Most-Favoured-Nation Clause,[39] on the basis of the ILC Study Group Final Report on the Most-Favoured-Nation Clause.[40] Excerpts below from both documents summarise the key interpretative issues.

ILC Study Group on the Most-Favoured-Nation Clause, Final Report (2015), paras 79–80 (footnotes omitted)

79. The final interpretative issue is the scope of the right being accorded under an MFN clause. In other words, what does 'treatment' encompass? This question was identified by the Commission in 1978 in article 9 of the draft articles when it provided that an MFN

---

adopted by the JRP was not a "rational government policy"; it was at odds with the law and policy of the CEAA. The approach of the JRP was not consistent with the investment liberalizing objectives of NAFTA; indeed the Tribunal has found it to be incompatible with Article 1105').

[37] *Mercer* v. *Canada*, paras 7.41–7.44.

[38] But note claims made by Crystallex (although rejected by the tribunal) regarding discrimination in favour of a Chinese investor (para. 616).

[39] https://legal.un.org/ilc/texts/instruments/english/draft_articles/1_3_2015.pdf (accessed 26 September 2020).

[40] https://legal.un.org/ilc/reports/2015/english/annex.pdf (accessed 26 September 2020).

clause applies to 'only those rights that fall within the subject matter of the clause'. This, as the Commission pointed out in its commentary, is known as the *ejusdem generis* rule.

80. The question of the scope of the treatment to be provided under an MFN provision has become one of the most vexed interpretative issues under international investment agreements. The problem concerns the applicability of an MFN clause to procedural provisions, as distinct from the substantive provisions of a treaty. It also involves the larger question of whether any rights contained in a treaty with a third State, which are more beneficial to an investor, could be relied upon by such an investor by virtue of the MFN clause.

ILC, Summary Conclusions on the Most-Favoured-Nation Clause (2015), (b)–(c)

(b) The Commission underlines the importance and relevance of the Vienna Convention of the Law of Treaties (VCLT), as a point of departure, in the interpretation of investment treaties. The interpretation of MFN clauses is to be undertaken on the basis of the rules for the interpretation of treaties as set out in the VCLT;

(c) The central interpretative issue in respect of the MFN clauses relates to the scope of the clause and the application of the *ejusdem generis* principle. That is, the scope and nature of the benefit that can be obtained under an MFN provision depends on the interpretation of the MFN provision itself.

It is a trite point that, while there are boilerplate investment protection obligations, significant differences exist between various treaties both at the level of the small print of drafting of particular obligations and in their presence or omission in particular treaties. The mainstream view of the function of MFN treatment clauses is, to put it in the technically accurate parlance, that the scope and content of this obligation is articulated in terms of a parameter that varies, depending on which third-party treaty provided the most favourable treatment. The annulment committee in the *MTD* v. *Chile* case put the point briskly, in relation to a somewhat oddly drafted MFN treatment clause that appeared to connect MFN treatment with fair and equitable treatment.

MTD Equity Sdn Bhd and MTD Chile SA v. Chile, ICSID Case No. ARB/01/07, Decision on Annulment, 21 March 2007 (Guillaume, Crawford, Ordóñez Noriega), para. 64

... The most-favoured-nation clause in Article 3(1) is not limited to attracting more favourable levels of treatment accorded to investments from third States only where they can be considered to fall within the scope of the fair and equitable treatment standard. Article 3(1) attracts any more favourable treatment extended to third State investments and does so unconditionally.

The mainstream view (that an MFN treatment clause, whatever controversies might relate to its applicability to international dispute settlement, is applicable to more favourable primary obligations in third-party treaties) was recently confirmed by another annulment committee.

EDF International SA and Others **v.** *Argentina*, **ICSID Case No. ARB/03/23, Decision on Annulment, 5 February 2016 (Greenwood, Cheng, Taniguchi), paras 237–238 (footnotes omitted)**

237. The Committee considers that the Tribunal's employment of the MFN clause involved no annullable error. The language of the MFN clause, which is quoted in paragraph 228, above, is quite broad enough to embrace the use of an umbrella clause in another BIT. The clause refers to 'treatment' accorded to investors of the most favoured nation. If German investors in Argentina have the benefit of a treaty provision requiring the Host State to honour commitments undertaken (or entered into) in relation to their investment, then they are being accorded a form of treatment which is not expressly granted to French investors by the Argentina–France BIT. That situation falls squarely within the terms of the MFN clause. Even if Argentina is right in arguing that MFN clauses should be subjected to an *ejusdem generis* limitation – as to which, it is unnecessary for the Committee to comment – the umbrella clause is part of the same *genus* of provisions on substantive protection of investments as the fair and equitable treatment clause and other similar provisions which feature in the Argentina–France BIT.

238. The Committee considers that *Hochtief* [v. *Argentina*] dealt with an entirely different issue, namely whether an MFN clause can be employed so as to give the investor claiming under one BIT the benefit of a more generous arbitration provision in another BIT. That issue has divided tribunals with roughly equal numbers of decisions upholding and rejecting the application of the MFN clause to an arbitration provision. The present case, however, concerns the use of an MFN clause to take advantage of a provision on substantive treatment. On that question, there has been a far greater degree of unanimity. It is true that the comment in *Hochtief* quoted above (see paragraph 234, above) is cast in broader terms but it has to be seen in the context of the issue actually confronting the tribunal in that case. Moreover, as the Committee has already stated, the obligation to honour commitments undertaken with regard to investments is part of the same *genus* of treatment of investments protected by provisions in the Argentina–France BIT. The Committee thus rejects the argument that there was a manifest excess of powers when the Tribunal applied the MFN provision to allow the Claimants to rely upon the umbrella clauses in other Argentine BITs.

The mainstream view has been challenged by two developments in recent years. First (and more broadly) is the mere presence of a more favourable international obligation in a third party 'treatment' for the purposes of an MFN treatment clause?

EU–Canada Comprehensive Economic and Trade Agreement, Art. 8.7(4)

For greater certainty, the 'treatment' referred to in paragraphs 1 and 2 does not include procedures for the resolution of investment disputes between investors and states provided for in other international investment treaties and other trade agreements. Substantive obligations in other international investment treaties and other trade agreements do not in themselves constitute 'treatment', and thus cannot give rise to a breach of this Article, absent measures adopted or maintained by a Party pursuant to those obligations.

Second, if the language of the clause calls for 'a similar situation', does the mere presence of a more favourable international obligation in a third party satisfy the requirement?

İçkale İnşaat Ltd Şirketi v. Turkmenistan, ICSID Case No. ARB/10/24, Award, 8 March 2016 (Heiskanen, Lamm, Sands), paras 328–329, 332 (footnotes omitted)

328. The Tribunal has carefully considered the meaning and effect of the MFN clause in Article II(2) of the BIT, in light of the general rule of treaty interpretation in Article 31 of the Vienna Convention. The ordinary meaning of the terms of the MFN clause, when read in their context and in light of the object and purpose of the Treaty, suggests that each State party to the Treaty agreed to treat investments made in its territory by investors of the other State party in a manner that is no less favorable than the treatment they accord in similar situations to investments by investors of any third State. Thus the legal effect of the MFN clause, properly interpreted, is to prohibit discriminatory treatment of investments of investors of a State party (the home State) in the territory of the other State (the host State) when compared with the treatment accorded by the host State to investments of investors of any third State. However, this obligation exists only insofar as the investments of the investors of the home State and those of the investors of the third State can be said to be in 'a similar situation'. Conversely, the MFN treatment obligation does not exist if and when an investment of an investor of the home State is not in a 'similar situation' to that of the investments of investors of third States; in such a situation, there is *de facto* no discrimination.

329. The terms 'treatment accorded in similar situations' therefore suggest that the MFN treatment obligation requires a comparison of the factual situation of the investments of the investors of the home State and that of the investments of the investors of third States, for the purpose of determining whether the treatment accorded to investors of the home State can be said to be less favorable than that accorded to investments of the investors of any third State. It follows that, given the limitation of the scope of application of the MFN clause to 'similar situations', it cannot be read, in good faith, to refer to standards of investment protection included in other investment treaties between a State party and a third State. The standards of protection included in other investment treaties create legal rights for the investors concerned, which may be more favorable in the sense of being additional to the standards included in the basic treaty, but such differences between applicable legal standards cannot be said to amount to 'treatment accorded in similar situations', without

effectively denying any meaning to the terms 'similar situations'. Investors cannot be said to be in a 'similar situation' merely because they have invested in a particular State; indeed, if the terms 'in similar situations were to be read to coincide with the territorial scope of application of the treaty, they would not be given any meaning and would effectively become redundant as there would be no difference between the clause 'treatment no less favorable than that accorded in similar situations ... to investments of investors of any third country' and 'treatment no less favorable than that accorded ... to investments of investors of any third country'. Such a reading would not be consistent with the generally accepted rules of treaty interpretation, including the principle of effectiveness, or *effet utile*, which requires that each term of a treaty provision should be given a meaning and effect.

...

332. The Tribunal concludes that the Claimant's argument that it is entitled to import substantive standards of protection not included in the Treaty from other investment treaties concluded by Turkmenistan, and to rely on such standards of protection in the present arbitration, must be rejected. When including the terms 'similar situations' in Article II(2) of the BIT, the State parties must be considered to have agreed to restrict the scope of the MFN clause so as to cover discriminatory treatment between investments of investors of one of the State parties and those of investors of third States, insofar as such investments may be said to be in a factually similar situation. Nor do Article II(4) or Article VI of the BIT create any such entitlement. The Claimant is therefore only entitled to invoke those investment protection standards specifically included in the BIT. These standards include the entitlement to MFN treatment 'in similar situations'.

It remains to be seen whether these challenges will affect the apparent consensus view expressed by the *MTD* v. *Chile* and *EDF* v. *Argentina* annulment committees, either in general terms or in relation to particularly worded MFN treatment clauses.[41]

4. MOST-FAVOURED-NATION TREATMENT AND INTERNATIONAL DISPUTE SETTLEMENT

Different investment protection treaties provide different rules on international dispute settlement. Reasonable people have disagreed on whether MFN treatment can apply to rules more favourable to the particular investor.[42] This section will first introduce the

---

[41] See S. Batifort and J. Benton Heath, 'The New Debate on the Interpretation of MFN Clauses in Investment Treaties: Putting the Brakes on Multilateralization' (2017) 111 *AJIL* 873; M. Paparinskis, 'MFN Clauses and Substantive Treatment: A Law of Treaties Perspective of the "Conventional Wisdom"' (2018) 112 *AJIL* Unbound 49.

[42] See, among many others, Z. Douglas, 'The MFN Clause in Investment Arbitration: Treaty Interpretation off the Rails' (2011) 2(1) *JIDS* 97; F. Orrego-Vicuña, 'Reports of [Maffezini's] Demise Have Been Greatly Exaggerated' (2012) 3(2) *JIDS* 299; C. Greenwood, 'Reflections on "Most Favoured Nation" Clauses in Bilateral Investment Treaties' in D. Caron, S. W. Schill, A. Cohen Smutny and E. E. Triantafilou (eds), *Practising Virtue: Inside International Arbitration* (Oxford: Oxford University Press, 2015), 556; S. Schill,

issue and then set out various approaches adopted in practice, drawing largely upon the 2015 ILC Study Group's Final Report.

Impregilo SpA v. *Argentina*, ICSID Case No. ARB/07/17, Decision of the Ad Hoc Committee on the Application for Annulment, 24 January 2014 (Oreamuno, Zuleta, Cheng), paras 135–137 (footnotes omitted)

135. The Tribunals in cases that have ruled on the most favored nation clause in relation to jurisdictional issues have expressed divergent positions. In *Mafezzini* (Argentine investor) v. *Spain*, the Arbitration Tribunal applied this clause contained in the Argentina–Spain BIT and, based on it, referred to the provisions of the Treaty between the Kingdom of Spain and the Republic of Chile and assumed jurisdiction. In *Siemens* (German investor) v. *Argentina*, the Tribunal, based on the most favored nation clause of the Argentina–Germany BIT had recourse to the current treaty between the Republics of Argentina and Chile and declared that it had jurisdiction to hear the case. In *Gas Natural* (Spanish company) v. *Argentina* the Tribunal, based on the MFN clause of the Argentina–Spain BIT referred to the Treaty between the United States and Argentina and also decided that it had jurisdiction. In the opposite direction, Argentina cited the case of *ICS* (UK investor) against that nation, in which the Tribunal applied the provisions of the Argentina–United Kingdom BIT, denied that the MFN clause was applicable to jurisdictional issues and stated that it had no jurisdiction. In *Salini* (Italian investor) v. *Jordan* the Tribunal analyzed the MFN clause in the Italy–Jordan BIT and considered the treaties signed between Jordan and the United States and Great Britain. It held that it could not extend the procedural rights of the dispute resolution clause under those treaties to circumvent the requirement to have recourse to the mechanisms established under the investment contract. In the *Plama* case (Cypriot company) v. *Bulgaria*, the Tribunal analyzed the most favored nation clause and the treaty between Bulgaria and Finland and concluded that the claimant could not rely on other treaties signed by Bulgaria to access ICSID.

136. The above cited decisions suggest that there are two extreme positions on this issue: one supports the application of the MFN clause to dispute resolution mechanisms as a means of access to ICSID jurisdiction, the other considers that the MFN clause cannot be given effect for jurisdictional purposes. In each particular case the wording of the Treaty, the circumstances of the dispute and the evidence and arguments submitted have had a substantial role in the decision of Tribunals as to whether or not to apply the MFN clause to jurisdictional issues. Thus, this matter should be analyzed on a case-by-case basis and it is not possible to establish, for the purposes of the annulment of an award, a general rule that an MFN clause applies or does not apply to jurisdictional

---

'*Maffezini v. Plama*: Reflections on the Jurisprudential Schism in the Application of Most-Favored-Nation Clauses to Matters of Dispute Settlement' in M. Kinnear G. Fischer, J. Minguez Almeida, *et al.* (eds), *Building International Investment Law: The First 50 Years of ICSID* (Alphen aan den Rijn: Kluwer Law International, 2015).

issues. If the Treaty – as some do – expressly prohibits the application of the MFN clause to jurisdictional issues and the tribunal disregards such prohibition and applies the MFN clause to assume competence; or if the Treaty expressly extends the MFN clause to jurisdictional issues and the Tribunal does not assume jurisdiction, regardless of the clear wording of the clause, one could say that there is a manifest excess of powers. In such events, the mere comparison between the text of the Treaty and the decision of the tribunal could lead to the conclusion that there is an excess of powers, and that such excess would be evident.

137. The issue is different, however, when there is no express prohibition or authorization and the applicability or non-applicability of the MFN clause to jurisdictional matters requires, inter alia, an interpretation of the provisions of the given Treaty, a review of the intent of the parties and the evidence and arguments submitted in the case at hand. Such are the cases that give rise to controversy and to a division in the reasoning of the tribunals.

ILC, Summary Conclusions on Most-Favoured-Nation Clause (2015), (d)–(e)

(d) The application of MFN clauses to dispute settlement provisions in investment treaty arbitration, rather than limiting them to substantive obligations, brought a new dimension to thinking about MFN provisions and perhaps consequences that had not been foreseen by parties when they negotiated their investment agreements. Nonetheless, the matter remains one of treaty interpretation;

(e) Whether MFN clauses are to encompass dispute settlement provisions is ultimately up to the States that negotiate such clauses. Explicit language can ensure that an MFN provision does or does not apply to dispute settlement provisions. Otherwise the matter will be left to dispute settlement tribunals to interpret MFN clauses on a case-by-case basis.

4.1 Applicable, with Public Policy Exceptions

The first approach was adopted in *Maffezini* v. *Spain*.[43] The tribunal took the view that the broadly worded MFN treatment clause could apply to rules of international dispute settlement in third-party treaties, unless certain public policy considerations excluded it. In the particular case, the MFN clause was applied to displace the requirement to litigate for a certain period in domestic courts before bringing the investment claim.

---

[43] ICSID Case No. ARB/97/7, Decision of the Tribunal on Objections to Jurisdiction, 25 January 2000 (Orrego Vicuña, Buergenthal, Wolf).

ILC Study Group on the Most-Favoured-Nation Clause, Final Report (2015), paras 86–90 (footnotes omitted)

86. In respect of the *ejusdem generis* principle, the *Maffezini* tribunal took the view that dispute settlement arrangements, in the current economic context, are inextricably related to the protection of foreign investors, and that dispute settlement is an extremely important device which protects investors. Therefore, such arrangements were not to be considered as mere procedural devices but arrangements designed to better protect the rights of investors by recourse to international arbitration.

87. From this, the tribunal concluded that,

'... if a third party treaty contains provisions for the settlement of disputes that are more favourable to the protection of the investor's rights and interests than those in the basic treaty, such provisions may be extended to the beneficiary of the most favoured nation clause as they are fully compatible with the *ejusdem generis* principle'.

88. This application of the MFN clause to dispute settlement arrangements would, in the view of the tribunal, result in the 'harmonization and enlargement of the scope of such arrangements'. However, the tribunal was conscious of the fact that its interpretation of the MFN clause was a broad one, and could give rise, *inter alia*, to 'disruptive treaty shopping'. It noted that,

'As a matter of principle, the beneficiary of the clause should not be able to override public policy considerations that the contracting parties might have envisaged as fundamental conditions for their acceptance of the agreement in question, particularly if the beneficiary is a private investor, as will often be the case. The scope of the clause might thus be narrower than it appears at first sight.'

89. Thereafter, the tribunal went on to set out four situations in which, in its view, an MFN provision could not be invoked:

- where one Contracting Party had conditioned its consent to arbitration on the exhaustion of local remedies, because such a condition reflects a 'fundamental rule of international law';
- where the parties had agreed to a dispute settlement arrangement which includes a so-called 'fork in the road' provision, because to replace such a provision would upset the 'finality of arrangements' that countries consider important as matters of public policy;
- where the agreement provides for a particular arbitration forum, such as the International Centre for Settlement of Investment Disputes (ICSID), and a party wishes to change to a different arbitration forum; and
- where the parties have agreed to a highly institutionalized system of arbitration that incorporates precise rules of procedure (e.g. NAFTA), because these very specific provisions reflect the precise will of the contracting parties.

90. The tribunal also left open the possibility that 'other elements of public policy limiting the operation of the clause will no doubt be identified by the parties or tribunals'.

The *Maffezini* v. *Spain* decision left itself open to criticism from two distinct perspectives: on the one hand, the very idea of applying MFN clauses to dispute settlement was challenged; on the other, the fit of 'public policy' within the framework of sources and interpretation of international law was questioned.

4.2 Inapplicable, Unless Explicitly Provided For

The first challenge to *Maffezini* v. *Spain* was taken up by a number of sceptical tribunals, of which *Plama Consortium Ltd* v. *Bulgaria*[44] was the most elaborate. In that dispute, the investor invoked the MFN clause to rely on consent on jurisdiction in a third-party treaty.

ILC Study Group on the Most-Favoured-Nation Clause, Final Report (2015), paras 101–103 (footnotes omitted)

101. In *Plama*, the tribunal treated the question of the scope of an MFN clause as one of agreement to arbitrate, stating that '[i]t is a well established principle, both in domestic and international law, that such an agreement should be clear and unambiguous'. As a result, 'the intention to incorporate dispute settlement provisions must be clearly and unambiguously expressed'. Therefore, the party seeking to apply an MFN clause to a question of jurisdiction bears the burden of proving such application was clearly intended – a high threshold to meet. This view was endorsed fully by the tribunal in *Telenor* [v. *Hungary*] and is echoed in *Wintershall* [v. *Argentina*].

102. However, this approach has been met with considerable opposition. It was rejected in *Austrian Airlines* [v. *Slovakia*], and in *Suez* [v. *Argentina*], where the tribunal said 'dispute resolution provisions are subject to interpretation like any other provisions of a treaty, neither more restrictive nor more liberal'. Jurisdictional clauses, the tribunal said, must be interpreted as any other provision of a treaty, on the basis of the rules of interpretation set out in articles 31 and 32 of the VCLT.

103. The view that because the application of MFN to dispute settlement matters is a question of jurisdiction there is a higher burden on a party seeking to invoke an MFN provision has found little support in the decisions of more recent investment tribunals, although it has been endorsed by at least some commentators. Those opposing the approach have also claimed that it is inconsistent with general international law on the interpretation of jurisdictional provisions. However, the *ICS* [v. *Argentina*] tribunal has suggested that the *Plama* tribunal was not establishing a jurisdictional rule; it was simply pointing out that consent to jurisdiction could not be assumed.

---

[44] ICSID Case No. ARB/03/24, Decision on Jurisdiction, 8 February 2005 (Salans, van den Berg, Veeder).

4.3 Applicable to Admissibility, but Not to Jurisdiction

A way of reconciling the results – if not the explicit rationale – of *Maffezini* v. *Spain* and *Plama* v. *Bulgaria* would be to draw the distinction between (applicability of MFN clauses to) admissibility matters in the former case and (inapplicability of MFN clauses to) jurisdictional matters in the latter case. The principled concern about this position is that the distinction does not easily flow from the application of principles of interpretation of treaties. The pragmatic concern is that the line between jurisdiction and admissibility is itself rather controversial (as discussed in Chapter 5); therefore, one should hesitate to explain one contested concept by means of introducing another and possibly even more contested one.

ILC Study Group on the Most-Favoured-Nation Clause, Final Report (2015), paras 111–112 (footnotes omitted)

111. The approach taken in *ICS* [v. *Argentina*] was reiterated in *Daimler Financial Services AG v. Argentine Republic* where the tribunal concluded that the 18-month delay requirement was a condition precedent to the exercise of jurisdiction. Accordingly, it could not be modified by the application of MFN. A similar result was reached in *Kılıç İnşaat İthalat İhracat Sanayi ve Ticaret Anonim Şirketi* v. *Turkmenistan*, where the tribunal took the view that the respondent State's consent to arbitration was conditioned on the fulfilment of the conditions stated in the BIT, including an 18-month delay requirement. Since failure to comply with such a provision had the effect of denying jurisdiction, the matter could not be cured by the application of an MFN provision. Similarly, in *ST-AB GmbH (Germany) v. Republic of Bulgaria*, non-compliance with the 18-month delay requirement was also found to deprive the tribunal of jurisdiction.

112. However, the tribunal in *Hochtief* [v. *Argentina*] took the view that an 18-month domestic litigation requirement is not a matter of jurisdiction. Rather, it is a matter of admissibility – something that could be raised as an objection by a party to the dispute, but need not be. The tribunal distinguished between a provision affecting a right to bring a claim (jurisdiction) and a provision affecting the way in which a claim has to be brought (admissibility). Thus, the fact that the claimant had ignored the 18-month litigation requirement under the Germany–Argentina BIT and relied instead on the dispute settlement provisions of the Argentina–Chile BIT did not affect its jurisdiction.

4.4 Applicable to Objectively Unfavourable Treatment

Arbitral decisions and legal writers usually discuss the possible applicability of MFN clauses through a variety of dyads: substance/procedure, jurisdiction/admissibility and presence/absence of consent. But one may also pick on the textual expression of the clause – 'most *favoured* nation' – and ask a different question: are various regimes of dispute settlement sufficiently similar to be commensurable in terms of greater or lesser favourability in the first place?[45]

ILC Study Group on the Most-Favoured-Nation Clause, Final Report (2015), paras 137–139 (footnotes omitted)

137. The difficulty of determining which treatment is less favourable is illustrated where MFN is used to replace one form of dispute settlement with another. Some tribunals have questioned whether the correct comparison is being made when third party treaty provisions are being compared with basic treaty provisions. If the basic treaty contains an 18-month litigation requirement, while the third party treaty has no 18-month litigation requirement but includes a fork in the road provision, is it correct that the third party treaty provides more favourable treatment? On the one hand, there is an 18-month delay before invoking the dispute settlement provisions of the BIT under the basic treaty, but the investor gets access to both domestic and international processes. On the other hand, the investor under the third party treaty gets access to international dispute settlement earlier but loses having both international and domestic dispute settlement available. Which treatment is the more favourable?

138. The *ICS* [v. *Argentina*] tribunal took the view that an investor relying on an MFN provision to avoid the 18-month litigation requirement would be subject to the fork in the road provision of the third party treaty. The *Garanti Kos* [v. *Turkmenistan*] tribunal took the view that it was difficult to say that ICSID arbitration was objectively more favourable than UNCITRAL arbitration, but that they were 'indisputably different'. In the end the tribunal concluded that choice was better than no choice and allowed the claimant to import ICSID arbitration on the basis of the MFN provision in the basic treaty.

139. The question of whether the provision in the third party treaty sought to be relied on is in fact more favourable than the provision in the basic treaty that is sought to be avoided was not considered in any detail in the earlier decisions of investment tribunals. Generally it has been assumed that not having to litigate in domestic courts for 18 months is more favourable than having to wait and litigate. However, this might be questioned unless negative assumptions are made about the domestic courts in question.

4.5 Recent Developments

Three somewhat disjointed points may be noted in relation to recent developments. First, States increasingly include clauses in the new treaties that explicitly exclude the application of MFN treatment clauses to dispute settlement. Article 8.7(4) of the CETA is a fairly representative example: 'For greater certainty, the "treatment" referred to in paragraphs 1 and 2 does not include procedures for the resolution of investment disputes between

---

[45] M. Paparinskis, 'Moving beyond Maffezini and Plama?' (2011) 26(2) *ICSID Review – FILJ* 14, 34–56.

investors and states provided for in other international investment treaties and other trade agreements.' Plainly, such clauses have dispositive effect for the treaties in which they are included. Creative lawyers will probably argue that the 'for greater certainty' proviso also signifies the position of parties to treaties, in general terms, that certain legal consequence would follow from the ordinary wording itself, and therefore could have an impact on interpretation of their other treaty obligations even without an explicit proviso. In a pragmatic sense, even though contemporaneity as a principle of treaty interpretation will demand otherwise, some tribunals may hesitate to follow the assumptions of *Maffezini* v. *Spain* and similar cases about the breadth of States' intentions, when many States in their more recent treaties have explicitly indicated a different preference.

Second, the result, if not the rationale, of *Maffezini* v. *Spain* was followed in a number of cases throughout the 2000s and 2010s, disposing of domestic litigation-related conditions.[46] The tea leaves of the more recent decisions appear to suggest that tribunals are increasingly hesitant to follow this approach. Determination of application of MFN clauses by distinguishing between jurisdiction and admissibility led many tribunals, as discussed in Chapter 5, to characterise these conditions as jurisdictional. There are also doubts about whether domestic litigation or particular conditions attached to international arbitration are less favourable in an objective sense, which would (for some) be required for triggering the MFN clause. It remains to be seen whether practice in favour of *Maffezini* will crystallise in a coherent rationale that would persuade future tribunals. In that sense, recent practice may suggest a reversal of the common wisdom of the 2000s that MFN clauses are applicable to domestic litigation-related conditions. The recent award in *Itisaluna Iraq* v. *Iraq* is a good example of that uncertainty, with three arbitrators essentially adopting three positions: applicability in principle but not in the particular instance, applicability only when so indicated and applicability in principle and in the particular instance.

Itisaluna Iraq LLC and Others v. *Iraq*, ICSID Case No. ARB/17/10, Award, 3 April 2020 (Bethlehem, Peter, Stern) para. 195, Dissenting Opinion of Arbitrator Peter, paras 195, 235 (footnotes omitted)

195. ... notwithstanding the debate about the scope of application of MFN clauses, there is a sufficiently settled body of consistent investment treaty law in favour of the proposition that MFN clauses are capable of applying, as a matter of principle, to dispute settlement provisions. Arbitrator Stern wants to be more precise on this point, considering indeed that

---

[46] As a recent annulment committee put it, 'the Tribunal's jurisdictional decision was at the very least reasonable and, in fact, consistent with all prior and subsequent decisions on the scope of the MFN clause in the Spanish treaty. Yet, even if a full merits review were available, Argentina has failed to show any jurisdictional error at all. Extensive case law supports the use of MFN clauses in the present circumstances': *Suez, Sociedad General de Aguas de Barcelona S.A., and Interagua Servicios Integrales del Agua S.A. v. Argentina*, ICSID Case No. ARB/03/17, Decision on Argentina's Application for Annulment, 14 December 2018 (McRae, Jones, Abraham), para. 102.

it is not entirely excluded that an MFN clause could apply to dispute settlement provisions, but only when so indicated in the treaty containing the MFN clause. As mentioned in her Dissenting and Concurring Opinion in *Impregilo*, she considers that there is a 'presumption that dispute-resolution provisions do never fall within the scope of an MFN provision in a BIT, unless the contrary is plainly demonstrated'.

...

235. ... Arbitrator Peter considers and agrees with the majority that 'the right to resort to arbitration is a right or privilege accorded to investors' and 'MFN clauses are capable of applying, as a matter of principle, to dispute settlement provisions'. However, he disagrees with the application of these principles in connection with Article 8(1) of the OIC Agreement.

Third, a number of recent cases have also challenged the other plank of common wisdom – that MFN clauses cannot create jurisdiction. In the *Garanti Koza* v. *Turkmenistan* case, a tribunal took the view that an MFN clause in a treaty that provided for only UNCITRAL arbitration could be relied upon to constitute consent to ICSID arbitration in a third-party treaty.[47] In *Venezuela US* v. *Venezuela*, a tribunal took the view that an MFN clause in a treaty that, due to denunciation of the ICSID Convention by Venezuela, did not provide for any effective consent, could be relied upon to constitute consent to UNCITRAL arbitration in a third-party treaty.[48] In both of these cases, the MFN clauses explicitly referred to the provisions on international dispute settlement, which disposed of some of the objections to *Maffezini* v. *Spain* posed by *Plama* v. *Bulgaria* (but not all, as the dissenting arbitrators in both cases pointed out, since applicability to a *genus* of rules in principle, and greater favourability of a particular rule, may be different matters).

CONCLUSION

Non-discrimination in investment protection law is not what it once used to be, and its role in the practice of investment dispute settlement is much less important than that of fair and equitable treatment or expropriation. But it is not entirely irrelevant.

National treatment obligations are commonly included in investment protection treaties. Prohibition of inappropriately distinctive treatment of similar circumstances often appears as a stand-alone provision, but it is also a standard condition of lawfulness for expropriation, and may even be implicit in fair and equitable treatment. Tribunals tend to approach claims of national treatment by asking three questions: (1) are circumstances like, (2) is treatment different and (3) is there a reasonable justification for that? Tribunals

---

[47] *Garanti Koza* v. *Turkmenistan*, ICSID Case No. ARB/11/20, Decision on Objection to Jurisdiction for Lack of Consent, 3 July 2013 (Townsend, Lambrou, Boisson de Chazournes). But see Dissenting Opinion by Arbitrator Boisson de Chazournes, 3 July 2013.

[48] *Venezuela US, SRL* v. *Venezuela*, PCA Case 2013-34, Interim Award on Jurisdiction (on the Respondent's Objection to Jurisdiction *Ratione Voluntatis*), 26 July 2016 (Tomka, Fortier, Kohen). But see Dissenting Opinion by Arbitrator Kohen, 26 July 2016.

have not been entirely consistent on whether competitive relationships are relevant for determination of likeness. It may be that the preference of a majority of recent cases, in line with State practice, is to treat competitive relationships as one of the relevant factors, particularly if identical comparators do not exist. Determination of differences in treatment has been an easier endeavour. Tribunals have concluded that it applies to de jure as well as de facto distinctions, probably requires treatment accorded to the best treated domestic investor, and that discriminatory intent is neither sufficient nor necessary for a finding of discrimination. Finally, while there is some uncertainty on where justification fits within the analytical framework – States view it as an aspect of inquiry into likeness, tribunals tend to apply it as a separate step of analysis – it is accepted as a relevant, and at times decisive, consideration.

The MFN treatment has been important less at the level of disciplining inappropriate distinctions drawn between various foreigners than at the systemic level of acting as conduit for more favourable substantive rules and rules of international dispute settlement from third-party treaties. For both points, recent practice has raised questions about the received wisdom. The traditional position, confirmed in a number of leading arbitral decisions, is that MFN clauses can act as a conduit to more favourable substantive rules. Conversely, some elements in recent State practice and arbitral decisions have queried the proposition that mere divergence at the level of international obligations, without any conduct by the State, is 'treatment' that applies to investors 'in similar circumstances'. For rules of international dispute settlement, the dichotomy between the broader principle of *Maffezini* v. *Spain* and the narrower reading of *Plama* v. *Bulgaria* had already been articulated in the early 2000s. The common wisdom in the 2000s was that, whatever the best rationale, it was permissible in practice to dispose of insignificant procedural conditions, but not to establish jurisdiction via MFN clauses. Recent practice has cast doubts on both parts of this certainty: there is increasing scepticism about MFN clauses and dispute settlement in general terms, but two cases, based on somewhat atypically worded clauses, have found jurisdiction on its basis. It remains to be seen whether old certainties will be confirmed or challenged by future practice.

QUESTIONS

1. Why has national treatment been less important in the practice of investment arbitration than other investment obligations?
2. Explain the legal principle and considerations relevant for the application of 'likeness of circumstances' and 'distinctiveness of treatment'.
3. What is the role played by 'reasonable justification' in reasoning about national treatment?
4. On MFN clauses, the award in *İçkale İnşaat Ltd Şirketi* v. *Turkmenistan* is incompatible with the annulment decisions in *MTD* v. *Chile* and *EDF* v. *Argentina*. Discuss.
5. Can MFN clauses be applied to rules of international dispute settlement in investment protection matters?

SUGGESTIONS FOR FURTHER READING

1. UNCTAD, 'Most-Favoured-Nation Treatment' in *UNCTAD Series on Issues in International Investment Agreements II* (UNCTAD, 2010), http://unctad.org/en/Docs/diaeia20101_en.pdf (accessed 26 September 2017).
2. C. Greenwood, 'Reflections on "Most Favoured Nation" Clauses in Bilateral Investment Treaties' in D. Caron, S. W. Schill, A. Cohen Smutny and E. E. Triantafilou (eds), *Practising Virtue: Inside International Arbitration* (Oxford University Press, 2015).
3. A. Reinisch, 'National Treatment' in M. Bungenberg, J. Griebel, S. Hobe and A. Reinisch (eds), *International Investment Law*: A Handbook (Baden-Baden: C. H. Beck/Hart/Nomos, 2015)
4. J. Kurtz, *The WTO and International Investment Law: Converging Systems* (Cambridge University Press, 2016), chapter 3.
5. S. Batifort and J. Benton Heath, 'The New Debate on the Interpretation of MFN Clauses in Investment Treaties: Putting the Brakes on Multilateralization' (2017) 111 *AJIL* 873.

14

Expropriation

CHAPTER OUTLINE

This chapter examines one of the most common claims brought by foreign investors against host States – an expropriation claim. It is a general rule of international law, around which very few exceptions are hedged, that the taking of foreign-owned property by a State should serve a public purpose, be met by the payment of prompt, adequate and effective compensation, and be carried out in accordance with due process. This rule finds expression in investment treaties which expressly guard against the arbitrary and uncompensated taking of property rights, as well as other rights that fall within the treaty definition of a protected investment. Whether an expropriation claim is well founded depends on three things: first, whether the investor holds rights that are capable of being expropriated; second, whether there is an actual taking or substantial deprivation of those rights by the State; and third, whether the expropriation meets the conditions for a lawful expropriation. To this end, Section 1 analyses the object, Section 2 the existence and Section 3 the legality of an expropriation. To illustrate the importance of distinguishing the object, existence and legality of an expropriation, Section 4 addresses an intriguing category of expropriation claims – judicial expropriation.

INTRODUCTION

The right to expropriate inheres in every State. This right is recognised under national law, as well as under international law. An act of expropriation, in and of itself, is prohibited by neither national law nor by international law. An expropriation is not objectionable so long as it satisfies prescribed cumulative conditions for lawfulness. These typically include the pursuit of public purpose, the payment of prompt, adequate and effective compensation, and the observance of due process, which may include non-discrimination. The crux of the challenge to host State activity in an expropriation claim brought by a foreign investor is the legality of the expropriation. The strength of the challenge is assessed in three stages.

The first stage verifies that the rights which the investor seeks to protect can form the object of expropriation. The object of expropriation is not limited to property or property rights. Certain contractual rights, for instance, may be expropriated. Moreover, when an expropriation claim is brought pursuant to an investment treaty, any right that falls within the treaty definition of a protected investment ought to reap the protection of the expropriation clause. In some cases, there are doubts over whether the investor is the proper party to defend the affected right through an expropriation claim. In this event, the tribunal needs to ensure that the investor is the holder of the rights that it seeks to defend, before proceeding to the next stage of the assessment.

The second stage verifies the existence of expropriation. Stock examples of expropriation include the repossession or confiscation of land and buildings by the State, while other examples include State activity that interferes with the exercise (but not termination) of contractual rights or which precipitates the devaluation (but not destruction) of shareholdings. It is generally accepted that only State activity which completely or substantially deprives the investor of the enjoyment or benefit of the rights in question amounts to an expropriation. And only if the State activity complained of amounts to an expropriation does the assessment proceed to the third and final stage.

The third stage verifies if the expropriation satisfies the cumulative conditions for lawfulness. This means that the investor need only establish that *one* condition is unmet to prevail on a claim of unlawful expropriation, while the State needs to establish that *all* the conditions have been met to defeat it. Of the various conditions for legality, the condition over which investors and States typically clash is compensation.[1] Certain expropriations, like those carried out in the exercise of a State's police powers to secure the betterment of public welfare, which are also known as regulatory takings, are non-compensable. The respondent State that raises the defence of a regulatory taking to justify the absence of compensation bears the burden of proving the validity of this defence.[2]

1. THE OBJECT OF EXPROPRIATION

Customary international law recognises property rights as objects of expropriation. In contrast, investment treaties recognise protected investments, which include property and non-property rights, as objects of expropriation. There is a greater variety of rights that can form the basis of an expropriation claim brought under an investment treaty than one brought under customary international law.

The fidelity to property deprivation as the basis for an expropriation claim under customary international law reflects the perception among States that a key role of international law is the protection of aliens and alien property. The international law on expropriation developed from that perception. For some time, the proliferation of investment treaties which simply recorded the desire of States to protect foreign *investment* rather than foreign *property* meant that property was no longer the only genre of assets belonging to foreigners that international law was being enlisted to safeguard. However, newer generation investment treaties qualify objects of expropriation as property, as

---

[1] B. A. Wortley, *Expropriation in Public International Law* (Cambridge University Press, 1959), 40–57.
[2] See Chapter 8, Section 1.1.

rights arising from property, or as rights bearing proprietary characteristics.[3] Therefore, whether an investment qualifies as a protected investment, which in turn qualifies as an object of expropriation, depends on the wording of the applicable treaty.

As the majority of expropriation claims are brought under investment treaties, this section relies on treaty language and select pertinent arbitral jurisprudence to flesh out three broad categories of rights that can found expropriation claims in investment arbitration. They are: property rights (Section 1.1), contractual rights (Section 1.2) and shareholder rights (Section 1.3).

1.1 Property Rights

The taking of property with a corporeal form, such as a hotel, by the State is the classic example of an expropriation.[4] This is illustrated in *Wena Hotels Ltd* v. *Egypt*,[5] where the expropriation claim was governed by Articles 1 and 5 of the Agreement between the Government of the United Kingdom of Great Britain and Northern Ireland and the Government of the Arab Republic of Egypt for the Promotion and Protection of Investments (UK–Egypt BIT).[6]

UK–Egypt BIT, Arts 1(a)(i) and 5(1)

1(a)(i) For the purposes of this Agreement, 'investment' means every kind of asset and in particular, though not exclusively, includes: movable and immovable property and any other property rights such as mortgages, liens or pledges.

...

5(1) Investments of nationals or companies of either Contracting Party shall not be nationalized, expropriated or subjected to measures having effect equivalent to nationalization or expropriation (hereinafter referred to as 'expropriation') in the territory of the other Contracting Party except for a public purpose related to the internal needs of that Party and against prompt, adequate and effective compensation. Such compensation shall amount to the market value of the investment expropriated immediately before the expropriation itself or before there was an official Government announcement that expropriation would be effected in the future, whichever is the earlier, shall be made without delay, be effectively realizable and be freely transferable. The national or company affected shall have a right, under the law of the Contracting Party making the expropriation to prompt review, by a judicial or other independent authority of that Party, of whether the expropriation is in conformity with domestic law and of the valuation of his or its investment in accordance with the principles set out in this paragraph.

[3] See for instance the Association of South East Asian Nations Comprehensive Investment Agreement (ACIA) (signed 26 February 2009, entered into force 24 February 2012), Annex 2(1) which provides: 'An action or a series of related actions by a Member State cannot constitute an expropriation unless it interferes with a tangible or intangible property right to property interest in a covered investment.'

[4] The taking is usually manifested by the dispossession of the investor of the property in question, which can involve formal eviction of the investor and/or its personnel from the premises: see, e.g., *Mr. Franck Charles Arif* v. *Moldova*, ICSID Case No. ARB/11/23, Award, 8 April 2013 (Cremades, Hanotiau, Knieper).

[5] ICSID Case No. ARB/98/4, Award, 8 December 2000 (Leigh, Fadlallah, Wallace).

[6] Signed 11 June 1975, entered into force 24 February 1976.

Wena Hotels v. Egypt, ICSID Case No. ARB/98/4, Award, 8 December 2000 (Leigh, Fadlallah, Wallace), paras 17–18, 75, 96, 99 (footnotes omitted)

17. On August 8, 1989, Wena and the Egyptian Hotels Company ('EHC'), 'a company of the Egyptian Public Sector affiliated to the General Public Sector Authority for Tourism' entered into a 21 year, 6 month 'Lease and Development Agreement' for the Luxor Hotel in Luxor, Egypt. Pursuant to the agreement, Wena was to 'operate and manage the "Hotel" exclusively for [its] account through the original or extended period of the "Lease", to develop and raise the operating efficiency and standard of the "Hotel" to an upgraded four star hotel according to the specification of the Egyptian Ministry of Tourism or upgratly [sic] it to a five star hotel if [Wena] so elects ...' The agreement provided that EHC would not interfere 'in the management and/or operation of the "Hotel" or interfere with the enjoyment of the lease' by Wena and that disputes between the parties would be resolved through arbitration. The lease was awarded to Wena in a competitive bid, after Wena agreed to pay a higher rent than another potential investor.

18. On January 28, 1990, Wena and EHC entered into an almost identical, 25-year agreement for the El Nile Hotel in Cairo, Egypt. Wena also entered into an October 1, 1989 Training Agreement with EHC and Egyptian Ministry of Tourism 'to train in the United Kingdom ... Egyptian nationals in the skills of hotel management ...'

...

75. In its Memorial on the Merits, Wena claims that 'Egypt violated the IPPA, Egyptian law and international law by expropriating Wena's investments without compensation'. ...

...

96. The Tribunal also agrees with Wena that Egypt's actions constitute an expropriation and one without 'prompt, adequate and effective compensation', in violation of Article 5 of the [UK–Egypt BIT] ...

...

99. Here, the Tribunal has no difficulty finding that the actions previously described constitute such an expropriation. Whether or not it authorized or participated in the actual seizures of the hotels, Egypt deprived Wena of its 'fundamental rights of ownership' by allowing EHC forcibly to seize the hotels, to possess them illegally for nearly a year, and to return the hotels stripped of much of their furniture and fixtures. Egypt has suggested that this deprivation was merely 'ephemeral' and therefore did not constitute an expropriation. The Tribunal disagrees. Putting aside various other improper actions, allowing an entity (over which Egypt could exert effective control) to seize and illegally possess the hotels for nearly a year is more than an ephemeral interference 'in the use of that property or with the enjoyment of its benefits'.

1.2 Contractual Rights

Rights conferred by a contract are recognised as protected investments in many investment treaties. Therefore, contractual rights per se can, to the extent allowed by the applicable treaty, be the object of expropriation. And investors often argue that the non-performance of a contractual obligation, or the termination of a contract by the host State, amounts to an expropriation. However, some arbitral tribunals exhibit reluctance to treat every contractual interference as an expropriation, even in the absence of treaty language qualifying contractual rights as objects of expropriation. Arbitral jurisprudence proffers two ways of distinguishing contractual interference by a host State that can found an expropriation claim, and contractual interference that cannot.

The first, which was articulated by the tribunal in *Emmis International Holding BV and Others* v. *Hungary*,[7] regards an affected contractual right as expropriable only if it has proprietary features (Section 1.2.1).[8] The second, which was endorsed by the tribunal in *Vigotop Ltd* v. *Hungary*,[9] ascertains if the interference was carried out in a contractual or sovereign capacity, with only the latter capable of amounting to an expropriation (Section 1.2.2).[10]

1.2.1 Contract as Property

In *Emmis International Holding BV and Others* v. *Hungary*, the Dutch and Swiss claimants contended that they held a contractual right to have their broadcasting licence renewed. They construed the eventual non-renewal, following a competitive tender where the claimants, through their affiliates, entered losing bids, as an expropriation by Hungary. One expropriation claim was brought under Article 4 of the Agreement between the Kingdom of the Netherlands and the Hungarian People's Republic for the Encouragement and Reciprocal Protection of Investments (Netherlands–Hungary BIT),[11] and another under Article 6 of the Agreement between the Swiss Confederation and the Hungarian People's Republic on the Reciprocal Promotion and Protection of Investments (Switzerland–Hungary BIT).[12] The Switzerland–Hungary BIT expressly recognises 'rights given ... by contract' as a protected investment,[13] but the Netherlands–Hungary BIT does not. Rather, Article 1(a)(iii) of the Netherlands–Hungary BIT lists 'title to money, goodwill and other assets and to any performance having an economic value' as a protected investment.[14] The tribunal found on the facts that the claimants had no contractual right to have their licence renewed,[15] but even if they did, such a right had to display proprietary features to qualify as an object of expropriation.

---

[7] ICSID Case No. ARB/12/2, Award, 16 April 2014 (McLachlan, Lalonde, Thomas).
[8] See also *Accession Mezzanine Capital LP and Another* v. *Hungary*, ICSID Case No. ARB/12/3, Award, 17 April 2015 (Rovine, Lalonde, Douglas), paras 153–154; and *Oxus Gold* v. *Uzbekistan*, UNCITRAL, Final Award, 17 December 2015 (Tercier, Stern, Lalonde (partially dissenting)), para. 301, where the tribunal held that the right to formal negotiations was not proprietary in nature and could not be the object of an expropriation.
[9] ICSID Case No. ARB/11/22, Award, 1 October 2014 (Sachs, Bishop, Heiskanen).
[10] Earlier support for the same proposition can be found in *Consortium RFCC* v. *Morocco*, ICSID Case No. ARB/00/6, Sentence Arbitrale, 22 December 2003 (Briner, Cremades, Fadlallah), paras 61, 69, 87; *Parkerings-Compagniet AS* v. *Lithuania*, ICSID Case No. ARB/05/8, Award, 11 September 2007 (Lévy, Lew, Lalonde), paras 442–456; and *Biwater Gauff (Tanzania) Ltd* v. *Tanzania*, ICSID Case No. ARB/05/22, Award, 24 July 2008 (Hanotiau, Born, Landau), paras 458–460.
[11] Signed 2 September 1987, entered into force 1 June 1988.
[12] Signed 5 October 1988, entered into force 16 May 1989.
[13] Art. 1(2)(e).
[14] The parallel provision in the Switzerland–Hungary BIT is Art. 1(2)(c).
[15] Award, paras 178–255.

Netherlands–Hungary BIT, Art. 4(1)

Neither Contracting Party shall take any measures depriving, directly or indirectly, investors of the other Contracting Party of their investments unless the following conditions are complied with:

(a) the measures are taken in the public interest and under due process of law;

(b) the measures are not discriminatory or contrary to any undertaking which the former Contracting Party may have given;

(c) the measures are accompanied by provision for the payment of just compensation. Such compensation shall represent the genuine value of the investments affected and shall, in order to be effective for the claimants, be paid and made transferable, without undue delay, to the country designated by the claimants concerned and in the currency of the country of which the claimants are nationals or in any freely convertible currency accepted by the claimants.

Switzerland–Hungary BIT, Art. 6(1)

Neither of the Contracting Parties shall take, either directly or indirectly measures of expropriation, nationalization or any other measure having the same nature or the same effect against investments belonging to investors of the other Contracting Party, unless the measures are taken in the public interest, on a non-discriminatory basis, and under due process of law, and provided that provisions be made for effective and adequate compensation. The amount of compensation, interest included, shall be settled in the currency of the country of origin of the investment and paid without delay to the person entitled thereto, without regard to its residence or domicile.

Emmis and Others v. *Hungary*, ICSID Case No. ARB/12/2, Award, 16 April 2014 (McLachlan, Lalonde, Thomas), paras 158–159, 163–164, 169 (excerpted, footnotes omitted)

158. Claimants assert claims of expropriation derived from three legal sources:

(a) Article 4 of the Netherlands BIT, which provides that '[n]either Contracting Party shall take any measures depriving, directly or indirectly, investors of the other Contracting Party of their investments ...';

(b) Article 6 of the Switzerland BIT (headed 'Expropriation and compensation'), which provides that '[n]either of the Contracting Parties shall take, either directly or indirectly measures of expropriation, nationalization or any other measure having the same nature or the same effect against investments belonging to investors of the other Contracting Party ...'; and,

(c) The customary international law protection against 'expropriation without compensation of Claimants' investments'.

159. In view of the fact that the only cause of action within the Tribunal's jurisdiction is that of expropriation, Claimants must have held a property right of which they have been

deprived. This follows from the ordinary meaning of the term. The Oxford English Dictionary defines 'expropriate' as '(of the state or an authority) take (property) from its owner for public use or benefit'/'dispossess (someone) of property'. Its origin is from the medieval Latin *expropriate* – 'taken from the owner', from the verb *expropriare*, from *ex* – 'out, from' + *proprium* 'property', neuter singular of *proprius* 'own'.

...

163. There is no doubt, as the Treaty definitions emphasise, that the notion of property or assets is not to be narrowly circumscribed. For this reason, tribunals have rejected a restriction to tangible property, emphasising that expropriation may equally protect intangible property. So, too, tribunals have held that the rights protected from expropriation as not limited to rights *in rem*. This is confirmed by the Treaties which include within their definition of assets qualifying as investments numerous other rights in addition to 'movable and immovable property as well as any other rights in rem'. This is unsurprising, since the definition of investment must apply compendiously to assets created under the law of the different municipal legal systems of the Contracting States. It is not to be circumscribed by technical distinctions that may have a different import under different municipal legal systems. The test is substantive, not technical.

164. A right conferred by contract may therefore constitute an asset for this purpose. Article 1(2)(e) of the Swiss[–Hungary] BIT expressly so states. The position is in any event well established in customary international law, and has been followed by investment arbitral tribunals.

...

169. Pausing at this point in the analysis, the Tribunal summarises the legal position under international law in the following way: the loss of a right conferred by contract may be capable of giving rise to a claim of expropriation but only if it gives rise to an asset owned by the claimant to which a monetary value may be ascribed. The claimant must own the asset at the date of the alleged breach. It is the asset itself – the property interest or chose in action – and not its contractual source that is the subject of the expropriation claim. Contractual or other rights accorded to the investor under host state law that do not meet this test will not give rise to a claim of expropriation.

1.2.2 Sovereign Contractual Interference

In *Vigotop* v. *Hungary*, the tribunal had to determine if the cancellation of a concession for the development of touristic sites in Hungary amounted to an expropriation regulated by Article 4 of the Agreement between the Government of the Republic of Cyprus and the Government of the Hungarian People's Republic on Mutual Promotion and Protection of Investments (Cyprus–Hungary BIT).[16] Like the Netherlands–Hungary BIT excerpted above, the Cyprus–Hungary BIT does not expressly recognise rights arising from contracts as

---

[16] Signed 24 May 1989, entered into force 25 May 1990.

protected investment. Nonetheless, the tribunal readily accepted that contractual rights are expropriable,[17] and focused instead on the manner in which Hungary interfered with Vigotop's contractual rights. To this end, it devised a three-pronged test to ascertain when contractual interference by a host State amounts to an expropriation.

The first prong examines if Hungary had public policy reasons for terminating the concession. An affirmative answer to the first query indicates that the cancellation is potentially expropriatory, and leads to the application of the second prong, which examines if Hungary was exercising a contractual right to terminate. A negative answer to the second query confirms that the cancellation is expropriatory, while an affirmative answer leads to the application of the third prong, which examines if Hungary abused its contractual right to terminate in order to avoid compensating the investor for expropriating its investment. A negative answer to the third query directs the tribunal to find that contractual interference was not expropriatory, while an affirmative answer places the cancellation squarely within the province of an expropriation. The tribunal found on the facts that there was no expropriation because Hungary had contractual grounds for termination and was neither acting in a sovereign capacity, nor abusing its contractual powers.

Cyprus–Hungary BIT, Art. 4(1)

Neither Contracting Party shall take any measures depriving, directly or indirectly, investors of the other Contracting Party of their investments unless the following conditions are complied with:

(a) the measures are taken in the public interest and under due process or law;
(b) the measures are not discriminatory;
(c) the measures are accompanied by provision for the payment of just compensation.

Vigotop Ltd v. *Hungary*, ICSID Case No. ARB/11/22, Award, 1 October 2014 (Sachs, Bishop, Heiskanen), paras 328–331 (excerpted, footnotes omitted)

328. The Tribunal will therefore begin its analysis by focusing on the key question: whether ... Respondent 'stepped out of the contractual shoes' and, in fact, acted in its sovereign capacity when it terminated the Concession Contract. Accordingly, the Tribunal will first examine whether, as alleged by Claimant, Respondent had 'a hidden political agenda', which was the true reason for its termination of the Concession Contract, meaning that Respondent in fact took this decision in order to give effect to a change in government policy, and thus in its sovereign capacity. If this were not the case, this would exclude the

---

[17] See also *Crystallex International Corp.* v. *Venezuela*, ICSID Case No. ARB(AF)/11/2, Award, 4 April 2016 (Lévy, Gotanda, Boisson de Chazournes), para. 663; cf. *Accession Mezzanine* v. *Hungary*, paras 153–154.

finding of an expropriation regardless of whether Respondent acted in accordance with the terms of the Concession Contract and Hungarian law. However, even if the Tribunal were to conclude that Respondent indeed had public policy reasons to terminate the Concession Contract, this would not necessarily in itself lead to a finding that the termination amounted to an expropriation because Respondent could at the same time have had contractual grounds for terminating the Concession Contract.

329. In the latter case, the Tribunal would therefore have to continue its analysis by examining, as a second step, whether contractual grounds for terminating the Concession Contract in fact existed. In the Tribunal's view, a finding that none of the contractual grounds invoked by Respondent were sufficiently well-founded, while not being dispositive of the expropriation question in itself, could indicate that they were merely a pretext designed to conceal a purely expropriatory measure. If, on the other hand, the Tribunal were to reach the contrary conclusion, *i.e.*, that Respondent had contractual termination grounds in addition to its public policy reasons, this would require a further analysis.

330. In the event of such a parallel cause (public policy reasons and contractual grounds), the Tribunal would thus have to examine, as a third and final step, whether the contractual termination was legitimate, *i.e.*, consistent with the good faith principle. To be specific, the Tribunal would have to determine whether the termination constituted an abuse of the contractual right in order to avoid liability to compensate, that is, whether it involved a 'fictitious' or 'malicious' exercise of the right to terminate.

331. If the Tribunal were ultimately to conclude that it was indeed legitimate for Respondent to invoke its contractual grounds for terminating the Concession Contract, this would exclude a finding of an expropriation, despite the parallel existence of public policy reasons. The issues for determining an expropriation in the context of a contract termination are (i) whether the contract is terminated by the contractual procedure rather than a legislative act or executive decree, and (ii) whether there exists a legitimate contractual basis for termination, *i.e.*, (a) the contract or the governing law provides the ground for termination, (b) the evidence substantiates a factual basis for invoking the contractual ground, and (c) the State acts in good faith, not abusing its right by a fictitious or malicious exercise.

The *Emmis* test recalls the fidelity to property protection under customary international law, and disqualifies contractual rights that do not possess proprietary features from becoming objects of expropriation. The *Vigotop* test is different. By pivoting a finding of expropriation on the manner of contractual interference, and not on the traits of the affected rights, the *Vigotop* test accepts, as its starting point, that all contractual rights are capable of being expropriated. Whether an expropriation claim is properly founded on rights which are objects of expropriation is likely to differ depending on which test is applied. The right to contract renewal, which may not qualify as an object of expropriation under the *Emmis* test and therefore cannot give rise to an expropriation claim, may be expropriated under the *Vigotop* test. Strictly speaking, the *Vigotop* test addresses the existence of an expropriation, the subject of Section 2. However, the far more liberal reading of the expropriability of contractual rights by the *Vigotop* v. *Hungary* tribunal than the *Emmis* v. *Hungary* tribunal reveals sharp differences in opinion among arbitral tribunals over the status of contracts as objects of expropriation.

1.3 Shareholder Rights

The relative infrequency of expropriation claims founded on interference with share-holder rights may be due to the fact that the challenged measures often leave the ownership and exercise of shareholder rights intact, even if they undermine the value of the shareholding. Expropriation claims arising from property confiscation as in *Wena Hotels* v. *Egypt*, or from contractual termination as in *Vigotop* v. *Hungary*, depict an investor who is effectively precluded from drawing further benefit from its investment. The grounds for complaint are less clear-cut for devalued shareholdings because the investor may still receive dividends, albeit reduced. However, rights conferred by shares are usually recognised as protected investments in investment treaties, so shareholder rights per se can, to the extent allowed by the applicable treaty, be objects of expropriation. The analysis of the tribunal in *Enkev Beheer BV* v. *Poland*,[18] interpreting Articles 1 and 5 of the Agreement between the Kingdom of the Netherlands and the Republic of Poland on Encouragement and Reciprocal Protection of Investments (Netherlands–Poland BIT),[19] offers guidance for when engineered depreciation in share value amounts to an expropriation by the State of shareholder rights.

Netherlands–Poland BIT, Arts 1(a)(ii) and 5

1(a)(ii). For the purposes of this Agreement: the term 'investments' shall comprise every kind of asset and more particularly, though not exclusively: ... rights derived from shares ...

...

5. Neither Contracting Party shall take any measures depriving, directly or indirectly, investors of the other Contracting Party of their investments unless the following conditions are complied with:
   (a) the measures are taken in the public interest and under due process of law;
   (b) the measures are not discriminatory or contrary to any undertaking which the former Contracting Party may have given;
   (c) the measures are accompanied by provision for the payment of just compensation. Such compensation shall represent the real value of the investments affected and shall, in order to be effective for the claimants, be paid and made transferable, without undue delay, to the country designated by the claimants concerned in any freely convertible currency accepted by the claimants.

---

[18] UNCITRAL-PCA Case No. 2013–01, First Partial Award, 29 April 2014 (Veeder, van den Berg, Sachs).
[19] Signed 7 September 1992, entered into force 1 February 1994.

Enkev Beheer v. Poland, UNCITRAL-PCA Case No. 2013–01, First Partial Award, 29 April 2014 (Veeder, van den Berg, Sachs), paras 332, 336, 339–341 (footnotes omitted)

332. *Indirect Deprivation*: Accordingly, the relevant question here is whether the Claimant has been 'indirectly' deprived of its rights in Enkev Polska's shares. As regards Article 5, the Claimant submits that the relevant test is whether there exists such unreasonable interference with the use, enjoyment or disposal of property as to justify an inference that the property owner will not be able to use, enjoy or dispose of its property within a reasonable period of time after the inception of such interference. The Claimant submits that, whatever the position might have been before the 'new developments', the position with such developments is now clear with the formal notification of 7 January 2014 of the 'Decision' of 30 December 2013 to commence decision-making on a motion for an immediately enforceable expropriation decision by the City of Lódź, namely Exhibit C-150 (the 'Notification').

...

336. The current predicament facing Enkev Polska is well described in the Claimant's Submission of 17 February 2014 to the Tribunal, in regard to the Notification's immediate legal effect under Polish law, namely Article 11d, section 9 and 10 of the Road Legislation [Exhibit C-19]. According to the Claimant, as a matter of Polish law, Enkev Polska can no longer transfer any of its rights pertaining to its real property to any third person, including its use, as security in order to obtain funding to find alternative business premises. Again, according to the Claimant, the legal effect of the Notification encompasses the entirety of Enkev Polska's real property and not only that part which is likely to be the subject of expropriation by the City of Lódź; i.e., only 6,760 m^2 of a total area of 22,306 m^2 (30 percent).

...

339. Despite these legal effects since 7 January 2014, it remains a fact that no actual decision has yet been taken by the Respondent to expropriate any part of Enkev Polska's premises under the Road Legislation, still less any actual expropriation of any part of Enkev Polska's premises. Moreover, as decided above, the Claimant's investment is limited to its shares in Enkev Polska (with associated rights) and does not extend to Enkev Polska's own property. The Claimant's shares in Enkev Polska have not been expropriated and, on the evidence available to the Tribunal, these shares will not be expropriated under the Road Legislation.

340. In the Tribunal's view, however, there can be little doubt that, as of now, the commercial value of the Claimant's rights in its shareholding in Enkev Polska has been adversely affected, albeit not destroyed, by the predicament facing Enkev Polska. The question therefore arises whether such diminution in value amounts in this case to an indirect deprivation of the Claimant's investment within the meaning of Article 5 of the Treaty.

341. As regards such indirect deprivation, the Tribunal considers that Article 5 of the Treaty requires the Claimant to establish that the practical effect upon its investment of Enkev Polska's predicament, as regards severity and duration, is materially the same as if its investment in Enkev Polska had been directly deprived by the Respondent. In other words, the Claimant must prove, on the facts of this case, that its investment in the form of shares in Enkev Polska and rights deriving from such shares has lost all or almost all significant commercial value.

To date, tribunals in investment treaty arbitration do not appear troubled by the expropriability of property or shareholder rights. However, the reservation towards contractual rights as objects of expropriation injects some uncertainty into the prospect of expropriation claims that are founded on a breach or termination of contract.

2. THE EXISTENCE OF EXPROPRIATION

The international law threshold for the existence of an expropriation by a State, or an entity whose conduct can be attributed to the State,[20] is the substantial deprivation of an asset or a right that is recognised by the law pursuant to which the right was conferred.[21] What the State intended when enacting or failing to enact measures that precipitated the deprivation is irrelevant at this stage of the inquiry. Investment arbitration tribunals accept and apply this threshold to the facts to determine the existence of expropriation. A measure or measures that substantially deprive(s) a protected investor of its investment can be direct (Section 2.1) or indirect (Section 2.2). Direct expropriation is usually illustrated by the straightforward physical dispossession of property, as in the case of *Wena Hotels* v. *Egypt*, and is generally easier to identify. However, many expropriation claims involve State measures that, whether alone or combined, indirectly deprive an investor of the benefits or enjoyment that its investment promised. The imminent devaluation of shares in a company brought on by a governmental decree that anticipates reclaiming the premises on which the company conducts its business, as in the case of *Enkev Beheer* v. *Poland*, is an example of indirect expropriation. Whether the challenged State measures evince direct or indirect interference with the protected investment, the result must be substantial deprivation of the protected investment in order for there to be an expropriation on the facts.

---

[20] See Articles 4–8 of the International Law Commission's (ILC) Articles on State Responsibility (ASR) 2001: Articles on Responsibility of States for Internationally Wrongful Acts, UN Doc. A/56/83 (2001). It is necessary to show that the challenged act was either taken by or attributable to the State because expropriation is an inherently sovereign act: see *Waste Management, Inc.* v. *United Mexican States ('No. 2')*, ICSID Case No. ARB(AF)/00/3, Award, 30 April 2004 (Crawford, Civiletti, Magallón Gómez), para. 174.

[21] M. Sornarajah, *The International Law on Foreign Investment*, 4th edn (Cambridge University Press, 2017), 435–437.

2.1 Direct Expropriation

A direct expropriation is discernible through several distinctive, uncontroversial features. If there is an outright seizure of a protected investment by the State, a formal transfer of legal title in a protected investment to the State, or if the State becomes the beneficiary of an essential component of a right arising from a protected investment, then the challenged measure is an act of direct expropriation. The following excerpts demonstrate how findings of direct expropriation are usually underpinned by a single act, whose impact on the protected investment is so apparent and significant that no elaboration is required.

> ### *El Paso Energy International Co.* v. Argentina, ICSID Case No. ARB/03/15, Award, 31 October 2011 (Caflisch, Bernadini, Stern), para. 265
>
> Although the Claimant has complained about direct expropriation, it can be declared by the Tribunal from the outset, without extensive reasoning, that no such expropriation occurred. It is enough here to recall the definition given to direct expropriation by Professor Sacerdoti: 'the coercive appropriation by the State of private property, usually by means of individual administrative measures'.[207] In direct expropriation, there is a formal transfer of the title of ownership from the foreign investor to the State engaged in the expropriation or to a national company of that State.
>
> [Fn 207: Giorgio Sacerdoti, 'Bilateral Treaties and Multilateral Instruments on Investment Protection' 269 *Collected Courses, Hague Academy of International Law* (1997) at p. 379.]

> ### *Enron Corp. and Another* v. Argentina, ICSID Case No. ARB/01/3, Award, 22 May 2007 (Orrego Vicuña, van den Berg, Tschanz), para. 243
>
> In fact, the Tribunal does not believe there can be a direct form of expropriation if at least some essential component of property rights has not been transferred to a different beneficiary, in particular the State.[22]

> ### *Crystallex International Corp.* v. Venezuela, ICSID Case No. ARB(AF)/11/2, Award, 4 April 2016 (Lévy, Gotanda, Boisson de Chazournes), para. 667
>
> ... It is generally understood that a 'direct' expropriation occurs where the investor's investment is taken through formal transfer of title or outright seizure.[23]

---

[22] An identically worded understanding of direct expropriation can be found in *Sempra Energy International v. Argentina*, ICSID Case No. ARB/02/16, Award, 28 September 2007 (Orrego Vicuña, Lalonde, Morelli Rico), para. 280.

[23] See also *Spyridon Roussalis v. Romania*, ICSID Case No. ARB/06/1, Award, 7 December 2011 (Hanotiau, Giardina, Reisman), para. 327.

2.2 Indirect Expropriation

More often, though, an expropriation claim is founded on indirect expropriation, which can refer to a single act whose effect is to substantially undermine the economic value of a protected investment, or a series of acts and/or omissions that beget the same result. When the effect of a measure or series of measures is central to the determination of the existence of an indirect expropriation, this is known as the 'sole effects doctrine'.[24] The latter type of indirect expropriation is also known as 'creeping' or 'constructive' expropriation.[25] The tribunal in *Spyridon Roussalis* v. *Romania* provided an outline of the different types of indirect expropriation.

Spyridon Roussalis v. *Romania*, ICSID Case No. ARB/06/1, Award, 7 December 2011 (Hanotiau, Giardina, Reisman), paras 327–329 (excerpted)

327. ... Indirect expropriation may occur when measures 'result in the effective loss of management, use or control, or a significant depreciation of the value, of the assets of a foreign investor' (UNCTAD Series on issues in international investment agreements, *Taking of Property*, 2000, p. 2).

328. On the other hand, in order to determine whether an indirect expropriation has taken place, the determination of the effect of the measure is the key question. Acts that create impediments to business do not by themselves constitute expropriation. In order to qualify as indirect expropriation, the measure must constitute a deprivation of the economic use and enjoyment, as if the rights related thereto, such as the income or benefits, had ceased to exist (*Tecmed v. Mexico*, Award, May 29, 2003, 43 ILM (2004) 133, para. 115). In *Telenor*, the Tribunal decided that: '[t]he conduct complained of must be such as to have a major adverse impact on the economic value of the investment', as 'substantially to deprive the investor of the economic value, use or enjoyment of its investment' (*Telenor Mobile Communications A.S. v. Republic of Hungary*, ICSID Case No. ARB/04/15, Award, September 13, 2006, 64–65).

329. Expropriation may occur in the absence of a single decisive act that implies a taking of property. It could result from a series of acts and/or omissions that, in sum, result in a deprivation of property rights. This is frequently characterized as a 'creeping' or 'constructive' expropriation. In the *Biloune* case the arbitration panel found that a series of governmental acts and omissions which 'effectively prevented' an investor from pursuing his investment project constituted a 'constructive expropriation'. Each of these actions, viewed in isolation, may not have constituted expropriation. But the sum of them caused an 'irreparable cessation of work on the project' (*Biloune and Marine Drive Complex Ltd. v. Ghana Investments Centre and the Government of Ghana*, UNCITRAL ad hoc Tribunal, Award on Jurisdiction and Liability of October 27, 1989, 95 ILR 183, 209).

---

[24] R. Dolzer, 'Indirect Expropriations: New Developments?' (2003) 11 *NYU Env'l LJ* 64, 79 et seq.

[25] See generally B. Weston, '"Constructive Takings" under International Law: A Modest Foray into the Problem of "Creeping Expropriation"' (1975–1976) 16 *Vanderbilt J Int'l L* 103.

In addition to comparisons with fact patterns in other investment disputes to determine the existence of an indirect expropriation, tribunals interpreting newer generation investment protection agreements, such as the investment chapter in the European Union–Canada Comprehensive Economic Trade Agreement (CETA),[26] are likely to find assistance in illustrative criteria. These criteria are usually subject to an important caveat – that takings in pursuit of public welfare objectives, such as health or environmental protection, do not, in most circumstances, constitute indirect expropriations.

CETA, Annex 8–A

The Parties confirm their shared understanding that:
1. Expropriation may be direct or indirect:
   (a) direct expropriation occurs when an investment is nationalised or otherwise directly expropriated through formal transfer of title or outright seizure; and
   (b) indirect expropriation occurs if a measure or series of measures of a Party has an effect equivalent to direct expropriation, in that it substantially deprives the investor of the fundamental attributes of property in its investment, including the right to use, enjoy and dispose of its investment, without formal transfer of title or outright seizure.
2. The determination of whether a measure or series of measures of a Party, in a specific fact situation, constitutes an indirect expropriation requires a case-by-case, fact-based inquiry that takes into consideration, among other factors:
   (a) the economic impact of the measure or series of measures, although the sole fact that a measure or series of measures of a Party has an adverse effect on the economic value of an investment does not establish that an indirect expropriation has occurred;
   (b) the duration of the measure or series of measures of a Party;
   (c) the extent to which the measure or series of measures interferes with distinct, reasonable investment – backed expectations; and
   (d) the character of the measure or series of measures, notably their object, context and intent.
3. For greater certainty, except in the rare circumstance when the impact of a measure or series of measures is so severe in light of its purpose that it appears manifestly excessive, non-discriminatory measures of a Party that are designed and applied to protect legitimate public welfare objectives, such as health, safety and the environment, do not constitute indirect expropriations.

Assessing the existence of an expropriation is an objective exercise. While the existence or non-existence of direct expropriation is unlikely to lend itself to disagreement, the threshold of substantial deprivation of economic value, benefits and rights arising from protected investments for indirect expropriation may be debatable. However, findings of indirect expropriation tend to be made only when the value of a protected investment

---

[26] Signed 30 October 2016, not yet in force.

is entirely or almost entirely wiped out. Some depreciation in value will not satisfy the threshold of substantial deprivation, no matter how aggrieved the investor is.[27] It is therefore extremely unlikely that a claimant whose investment has not been rendered worthless by State measures or omissions will succeed in showing that an indirect expropriation has taken place. The presence of public welfare objectives can, according to Annex 8-A of the CETA, for instance, have a direct bearing on the existence of an indirect expropriation. It also has a direct bearing on the legality of an expropriation, since one feature of a lawful expropriation is the presence of a public purpose. Legality is the third and final stage of the assessment of an expropriation claim, to which the discussion now turns.

3. THE LEGALITY OF EXPROPRIATION

An expropriation is not, in and of itself, unlawful. The cumulative customary international law conditions for a lawful expropriation, which are mirrored in investment treaties, are the presence of a public purpose (Section 3.1), the payment of compensation (Section 3.2) and compliance with due process (Section 3.3). Some investment treaties list non-discrimination as a fourth, discrete condition for a lawful expropriation. However, non-discrimination may be regarded as one manifestation of due process. Therefore, this section will address three instead of four cumulative conditions of lawfulness. States contesting expropriation claims also have the option of pleading that the circumstances justify the taking of the challenged measure(s), thereby precluding wrongfulness (Section 3.4). Even if the expropriation does not satisfy all the conditions for lawfulness, the State bears no responsibility under international law for its occurrence. When an expropriation claim is brought under customary international law, the different circumstances precluding wrongfulness are set out in Articles 20 to 26 of the ILC Articles on Responsibility of States for Intentionally Wrongful Acts 2001. In contrast, when an expropriation claim is brought under an investment treaty, the expropriatory act will not be subject to the treaty conditions for lawfulness if it can be successfully characterised as a non-precluded measure.

3.1 Public Purpose

Public purpose is an expansive category that encompasses urban planning,[28] national security[29] and economic development,[30] among others. As an investor need only establish that *one* of the cumulative conditions for lawfulness has not been met to prevail

---

[27] See, for instance, *Telenor Mobile Communications AS* v. *Hungary*, ICSID Case No. ARB/04/15, Award, 13 September 2006 (Goode, Allard, Marriot), paras 79–80; *National Grid Plc* v. *Argentina*, UNCITRAL, Award, 3 November 2008 (Rigo Sureda, Garro, Kessler), para. 154; and *Walter Bau AG (In Liquidation)* v. *Thailand*, UNCITRAL, Award, 1 July 2009 (Barker, Lalonde, Bunnag), para. 10.18.

[28] See, e.g., *Mamidoil Jetoil Greek Petroleum Products Société SA* v. *Albania*, ICSID Case No. ARB/11/24, Award, 30 March 2015 (Knieper, Banifatemi, Hammond).

[29] See, e.g., *Gemplus SA and Others* v. *Mexico* and *Talsud SA* v. *Mexico*, ICSID Case Nos. ARB(AF)/04/3 and ARB(AF)/04/4, Award, 16 June 2010 (Veeder, Fortier, Magallón Gómez).

[30] See, e.g., *Ioannis Kardassopoulos and Ron Fuchs* v. *Georgia*, ICSID Case Nos ARB/05/18 and ARB/07/15, Award, 3 March 2010 (Fortier, Orrego Vicuña).

on its expropriation claim, there is a tendency to eschew challenging the purpose of an expropriation, in favour of showing that it was not complemented by any or adequate compensation. This is because questioning the motive underlying the State's decision to expropriate requires the tribunal to investigate and critique the official stance, like a shadow policymaker, a task which few tribunals appear enthusiastic or equipped to undertake.[31]

3.2 Compensation

Expropriation is normally accompanied by compensation (Section 3.2.1). The 'prompt, adequate, and effective' standard of compensation, also known as the Hull formula,[32] is commonly found in investment treaties and is regarded as the de rigueur standard of compensation for expropriation. Most treaties peg the amount of compensation payable to the fair market value of the investment immediately prior to the moment of expropriation. There are several ways of ascertaining the fair market value of an investment. The World Bank Report to the Development Committee and Guidelines on the Treatment of Foreign Direct Investment (World Bank Guidelines),[33] suggests discounted cash flow (DCF) value,[34] liquidation value[35] and replacement,[36] or book value[37] as possible valuation methods, which some tribunals have applied.[38] Another valuation method which is popular

---

[31] Restraint may matter even more should investors bring expropriation claims under investment treaties challenging drastic measures, such as nationwide lockdowns, taken by States to contain the COVID-19 pandemic. It is difficult to imagine an arbitral tribunal impugning, with the benefit of hindsight but without the benefit of experience in governance, emergency measures taken to minimize the extremely serious threat that COVID-19 poses to public health. Cf. *ADC Affiliate Ltd and Another* v. *Hungary*, ICSID Case No. ARB/03/16, Award of the Tribunal, 2 October 2006 (Kaplan, Brower, van den Berg), para. 430.

[32] The formula is named after a former US Secretary of State Cordell Hull, who proposed it in his diplomatic correspondence with Mexico as the standard of compensation that Mexico should meet for the 1917 nationalisation of US investments: see 'Statement for the Press by the Secretary of State, 30 March 1938', *Foreign Relations of the United States – Diplomatic Papers 1938* (Washington, DC: US Government Printing Office, 1956), vol. V, p. 662.

[33] Created 1 January 1992, disclosed 7 January 2010, vol. 2, https://documents.worldbank.org/en/publication/documents-reports/documentdetail/955221468766167766/guidelines (accessed 31 July 2020), Art. IV(6).

[34] This is defined in the World Bank Guidelines as: 'the cash receipts realistically expected from the enterprise in each future year of its economic life as reasonably projected minus that year's expected cash expenditure, after discounting this net cash flow for each year by a factor which reflects the time value of Money, expected inflation, and the risk associated with such cash flow under realistic circumstances. Such discount rate may be measured by examining the rate of return available in the same market on alternative investments of comparable risk on the basis of their present value'.

[35] This is defined in the World Bank Guidelines as: 'the amounts at which individual assets comprising the enterprise or the entire assets of the enterprise could be sold under conditions of liquidation to a willing buyer less any liabilities which the enterprise has to meet'.

[36] This is defined in the World Bank Guidelines as: 'the cash amount required to replace the individual assets of the enterprise in their actual state as of the date of the taking'.

[37] This is defined in the World Bank Guidelines as: 'the difference between the enterprise's assets and liabilities as recorded on its financial statements or the amount at which the taken tangible assets appear on the balance sheet of the enterprise, representing their cost after deducting accumulated depreciation in accordance with generally accepted accounting principle'.

[38] Valuation is discussed in greater detail in Chapter 17.

among investment arbitration tribunals where the object of expropriation is a contract is *damnum emergens* (sunk costs) plus *lucrum cessans* (lost profits).[39]

3.2.1 The Rule of Compensation for Expropriation

An expropriation claim seeking compensation in accordance with the treaty standard for an expropriation is a claim for compensation for *lawful* expropriation. In contrast, a claim challenging the *total absence* of compensation, due to the lack of domestic recourse to compensation or the persistent lack of State response to requests for compensation, is a claim for damages for *unlawful* expropriation. For the latter, the standard of reparation is not normally articulated in the relevant treaty. As the following excerpt illustrates, the tribunal in *Kardassopoulos and Fuchs* v. *Georgia* distinguished the standards of compensation/reparation for lawful and unlawful expropriations, locating the standard of reparation for an unlawful expropriation claim in customary international law.

Ioannis Kardassopoulos and Ron Fuchs v. *Georgia*, ICSID Case Nos ARB/05/18 and ARB/07/15, Award, 3 March 2010 (Fortier, Orrego Vicuña, Lowe), paras 501–605, 517 (footnotes omitted)

501. Article 13(1) of the ECT provides that any expropriation shall be 'accompanied by the payment of prompt, adequate and effective compensation', which compensation shall further consist of the following:

'Article 13 Expropriation ... Such compensation shall amount to the fair market value of the Investment expropriated at the time immediately before the Expropriation or impending Expropriation became known in such a way as to affect the value of the Investment (hereinafter referred to as the "Valuation Date"). Such fair market value shall at the request of the Investor be expressed in a Freely Convertible Currency on the basis of the market rate of exchange existing for that currency on the Valuation Date. Compensation shall also include interest at a commercial rate established on a market basis from the date of Expropriation until the date of payment.'

502. The Parties appear to agree that in the event of a lawful expropriation, the applicable standard of compensation is 'prompt, adequate and effective compensation', which shall amount to the FMV [fair market value] of the investment as of the date immediately before the expropriation became known so as to affect the value of the investment. However, consistent with the Tribunal's findings in respect of liability, we are no longer in the realm of a lawful expropriation.

---

[39] This method of valuation is discussed in greater detail in Chapter 17, Section 3.2; see, e.g., *SARL Benvenuti and Bonfant* v. *Congo*, ICSID Case No. ARB/77/2, Award, 8 August 1980 (Trolle, Bystricky, Razafindralambo); *Société Ouest Africaine des Bétons Industriels* v. *Senegal*, ICSID Case No. ARB/82/1, Award, 25 February 1988 (Broches, Mbaye, Schultsz); and *Autopista Concesionada de Venezuela CA (Aucoven)* v. *Venezuela*, ICSID Case No. ARB/00/5, Award, 23 September 2003 (Kaufmann-Kohler, Böckstiegel, Cremades).

503. The Parties differ in their appreciation of the appropriate standard of compensation for an unlawful expropriation, although they begin their analysis in the same place. In particular, both Parties rely on the statement of the PCIJ [Permanent Court of International Justice] in *Chorzów Factory* to the effect that 'reparation must, as far as possible, wipe out all the consequences of the illegal act and re-establish the situation which would, in all probability, have existed if that act had not been committed'.[40]

504. The *Chorzów Factory* standard is reflected today in the ILC's Articles on State Responsibility, and in particular in their compensation provision, which provides as follows:

'Article 36. Compensation

1. The State responsible for an internationally wrongful act is under an obligation to compensate for the damage caused thereby, insofar as such damage is not made good by restitution.

2. The compensation shall cover any financially assessable damage including loss of profits insofar as it is established.'

505. The Commentary to Article 36 confirms that this compensation is generally assessed on the basis of the FMV of the property rights lost:

'(21) The reference point for valuation purposes is the loss suffered by the claimant whose property rights have been infringed. This loss is usually assessed by reference to specific heads of damage relating to (i) compensation for capital value; (ii) compensation for loss of profits; and (iii) incidental expenses.

(22) Compensation reflecting the capital value of property taken or destroyed as the result of an internationally wrongful act is generally assessed on the basis of the "fair market value" of the property lost. The method used to assess "fair market value", however, depends on the nature of the asset concerned. Where the property in question or comparable property is freely traded on an open market, value is more readily determined. In such cases, the choice and application of asset-based valuation methods based on market data and the physical properties of the assets is relatively unproblematic, apart from evidentiary difficulties associated with long outstanding claims. Where the property interests in question are unique or unusual, for example, art works or other cultural property, or are not the subject of frequent or recent market transactions, the determination of value is more difficult. This may be true, for example, in respect of certain business entities in the nature of a going concern, especially if shares are not regularly traded.'

...

517. The Tribunal therefore finds that the appropriate standard of compensation from which to approach the calculation of the damage sustained by Mr. Kardassopoulos is the FMV of the early oil rights (including export rights) as of 10 November 1995. Whilst this pre-dates the expropriation effected by Decree No. 178, the Tribunal considers that the

---

[40] [Eds: *Case Concerning the Factory at Chorzów* (*Germany* v. *Poland*) (Merits) (1928) PCIJ Rep. Series A No. 17.]

> circumstances of this case require it to value Mr. Kardassopoulos' investment as of the day before passage of Decree No. 477 precisely to ensure full reparation and to avoid any diminution of value attributable to the State's conduct leading up to the expropriation. This compensation is, in effect, the amount that Mr. Kardassopoulos should have been paid as a result of the compensation process which the Respondent was obliged to put in place promptly after the taking of the Claimants' investment.

There are two exceptions to the general rule of compensation for expropriation. The first is when the expropriated investment is valued at nil (Section 3.2.2), and the second is when the expropriation qualifies as a regulatory taking (Section 3.2.3).

3.2.2 The First Exception to the Rule of Compensation for Expropriation: Investment Valued at Nil

The absence of hard and fast rules on the valuation methods to adopt when assessing the fair market value of an expropriated investment often turns the valuation exercise into a battle between the disputing parties' valuation experts.[41] No compensation is due if the tribunal is persuaded that the fair market value of the expropriated investment is zero. This unusual finding was made in the wake of the nationalisation of Northern Rock by the United Kingdom. In litigations brought by Northern Rock shareholders before the European Court of Human Rights and the English courts, the judges agreed with the independent valuer that the value of Northern Rock shares just prior to the expropriation was nil.[42] To date, there is no known investment arbitration award where the tribunal accepted that the fair market value of the expropriated investment was zero. In *Guaracachi America, Inc. and Another* v. *Bolivia*, the tribunal agreed with the claimants' valuation expert that the expropriated company had a 'positive value', thereby putting Bolivia in breach of its treaty obligation to compensate upon expropriation by refusing to pay any compensation.[43]

3.2.3 The Second Exception to the Rule of Compensation for Expropriation: Regulatory Taking

An expropriation that qualifies as a regulatory taking is not compensable. This is particularised as 'the right to protect, through non-discriminatory actions, inter alia, the environment, human health and safety, market integrity and social policies'.[44] This right to protect may also be framed as the State's exercise of its police powers. Newer generation investment protection agreements, like Annex 8-A of the CETA reproduced in

---

[41] B. Sabahi, *Compensation and Restitution in Investor-State Arbitration: Principles and Practice* (Oxford University Press, 2011), 183–185.

[42] *Case of Grainger and Others* v. *UK* (Application No. 34940/10) (2012) 55 EHRR SE13, paras 20–22, 35–43.

[43] PCA Case No. 2011–17, Award, 31 January 2014 (Júdice, Conthe, Vineusa), para. 438.

[44] C. Yannaca-Small, '"Indirect Expropriation" and the "Right to Regulate" in International Investment Law' (2004), p. 22, https://www.oecd.org/daf/inv/investment-policy/WP-2004_4.pdf (accessed 31 July 2020).

Section 2.2, also specify that regulatory takings cannot be construed as indirect expropriations by the State which attract the obligation to compensate. There is a dearth of general guidelines on how a State can prove that the expropriation was regulatory in nature, thereby confining findings on regulatory takings to the facts of a specific case.[45] However, bare assertions by a respondent State, unsupported by evidence, that an uncompensated expropriation was in fact a regulatory taking are unlikely to satisfy an arbitral tribunal.[46]

3.3 Due Process

Due process refers to the procedures for redress that a host State makes available to foreign investors. These procedures may be judicial or extra-judicial. An example of a judicial procedure is the option for investors to challenge or seek judicial review of an expropriation order before host State courts. Examples of extra-judicial procedures include: the opportunity for an investor to be heard by the relevant State department carrying out the expropriation, with the possibility of forestalling an expropriation order, and the opportunity to apply for and be awarded compensation pursuant to an expropriation.

Compliance with due process also means that States must ensure there is no discrimination among investors trying to access the available redress mechanisms. An illustration of discrimination leading to the absence of due process is the exclusion of investors from accessing redress solely on the basis of their nationality. Discrimination can also appear at the stage of expropriation. An illustration of a discriminatory expropriation is the nationalisation of one investor's investment, while leaving untouched similar investments belonging to other investors, or the blanket taking of investments belonging to investors of a certain nationality. A finding of discrimination requires a showing that the differentiated treatment of investments or investors was unreasonable.[47] Therefore, if investments belonging to investors of a certain nationality are expropriated because they represent exceptionally inequitable bargains struck with the host State, the expropriation will not be regarded as discriminatory.[48]

Although discrimination and the absence of due process may surface while expropriation is underway, this marker of legality is rarely invoked or discussed in detail in

---

[45] In particular, there are very few records of States prevailing on the argument that no compensation was due because the expropriation was carried out pursuant to the exercise of its police powers. One rare example is the United States before the Iran–US Claims Tribunal in *Emanuel Too* v. *Greater Modesto Insurance Associates*, Award, 29 December 1989 (Briner, Khalilian, Aldrich), 23 Iran–United States Cl. Trib. Rep. 378, paras 24–27.

[46] *ADC* v. *Hungary*, Award of the Tribunal, paras 403, 423–424.

[47] M. N. Shaw, *International Law*, 6th edn (Cambridge University Press, 2008), 842; and *Antoine Goetz et Consorts* v. *Burundi*, Affaire CIRDI ARB/95/3, Sentence, 10 February 1999 (Weil, Bedjaoui, Bredin), para. 121.

[48] This is especially so in the case of long-term petroleum concessions concluded between Anglo-American investors and Gulf States in the 1950s, and whose profit-sharing arrangement promised a windfall for the investors at the expense of the developing host State. There is great reluctance to view the systematic termination or renegotiation of these types of concessions as discriminatory: see Z. A. Al-Qurashi, 'Renegotiation of International Petroleum Agreements' (2005) 22(4) *J Int'l Arb* 261, 262–268.

expropriation claims. The tribunal in *Burlington Resources Inc.* v. *Ecuador* observed that a discriminatory tax measure could amount to an expropriation if it results in a substantial deprivation of the value of the investment.[49] However, as the challenged tax measure did not meet the threshold of substantial deprivation,[50] the tribunal did not proceed to consider whether the tax was discriminatory. To date, the most lucid description of due process in the context of expropriation comes from the tribunal in *ADC* v. *Hungary*. As Hungary failed to prove the existence of any redress to foreign investors with expropriated investments, the tribunal found that Hungary breached its obligation under the Cyprus–Hungary BIT to guarantee due process when expropriating protected investments.[51]

ADC v. Hungary, ICSID Case No. ARB/03/16, Award of the Tribunal, 2 October 2006 (Kaplan, Brower, van den Berg), para. 435

The Tribunal agrees with the Claimants that 'due process of law', in the expropriation context, demands an actual and substantive legal procedure for a foreign investor to raise its claims against the depriving actions already taken or about to be taken against it. Some basic legal mechanisms, such as reasonable advance notice, a fair hearing and an unbiased and impartial adjudicator to assess the actions in dispute, are expected to be readily available and accessible to the investor to make such legal procedure meaningful. In general, the legal procedure must be of a nature to grant an affected investor a reasonable chance within a reasonable time to claim its legitimate rights and have its claims heard. If no legal procedure of such nature exists at all, the argument that 'the actions are taken under due process of law' rings hollow. And that is exactly what the Tribunal finds in the present case.

3.4 Circumstances Precluding Wrongfulness and Non-Precluded Measures

Under customary international law, a State is not responsible for breaching an international obligation by which it is bound, if the breach occurred under one or more circumstance(s) precluding the wrongfulness of that breach.[52] When a State invokes a customary circumstance precluding wrongfulness as a defence to liability, the State accepts that a violation of international law has occurred, but denies that liability for the violation attaches. The six circumstances precluding wrongfulness, namely consent, self-defence, countermeasures, force majeure, distress and necessity, are set out in Chapter V of the ASR.

---

[49] ICSID Case No. ARB/08/5, Decision on Liability, 14 December 2012 (Kaufmann-Kohler, Stern, Orrego Vicuña), para. 393.

[50] Decision on Liability, para. 456.

[51] Art. 4(1)(a).

[52] For a more detailed discussion of the topic covered in this section, see Chapter 16.

ASR, Arts 20–25

Article 20
Consent
Valid consent by a State to the commission of a given act by another State precludes the wrongfulness of that act in relation to the former State to the extent that the act remains within the limits of that consent.

Article 21
Self-defence
The wrongfulness of an act of a State is precluded if the act constitutes a lawful measure of self-defence taken in conformity with the Charter of the United Nations.

Article 22
Countermeasures in respect of an internationally wrongful act
The wrongfulness of an act of a State not in conformity with an international obligation towards another State is precluded if and to the extent that the act constitutes a countermeasure taken against the latter State in accordance with chapter II of part three.

Article 23
Force majeure
1. The wrongfulness of an act of a State not in conformity with an international obligation of that State is precluded if the act is due to force majeure, that is the occurrence of an irresistible force or of an unforeseen event, beyond the control of the State, making it materially impossible in the circumstances to perform the obligation.
2. Paragraph 1 does not apply if:
    (a) the situation of force majeure is due, either alone or in combination with other factors, to the conduct of the State invoking it; or
    (b) the State has assumed the risk of that situation occurring.

Article 24
Distress
1. The wrongfulness of an act of a State not in conformity with an international obligation of that State is precluded if the author of the act in question has no other reasonable way, in a situation of distress, of saving the author's life or the lives of other persons entrusted to the author's care.
2. Paragraph 1 does not apply if:
    (a) the situation of distress is due, either alone or in combination with other factors, to the conduct of the State invoking it; or
    (b) the act in question is likely to create a comparable or greater peril.

Article 25
Necessity
1. Necessity may not be invoked by a State as a ground for precluding the wrongfulness of an act not in conformity with an international obligation of that State unless the act:

(a) is the only way for the State to safeguard an essential interest against a grave and imminent peril; and

(b) does not seriously impair an essential interest of the State or States towards which the obligation exists, or of the international community as a whole.

2. In any case, necessity may not be invoked by a State as a ground for precluding wrongfulness if:

(a) the international obligation in question excludes the possibility of invoking necessity; or

(b) the State has contributed to the situation of necessity.

Under investment treaties, a State is not internationally responsible for a measure which otherwise violates its treaty obligation(s) if the measure qualifies as a non-precluded measure as defined by the relevant treaty. When relying on a non-precluded measure as a defence to liability, the State asserts that the treaty does not apply to the challenged measure, thereby denying the very existence of a violation of the treaty. An example of a treaty clause setting out non-precluded measures is Article XI of the Treaty between the United States of America and the Argentine Republic Concerning the Reciprocal Encouragement and Protection of Investment (US–Argentina BIT).[53]

US–Argentina BIT, Art. XI

This Treaty shall not preclude the application by either Party of measures necessary for the maintenance of public order, the fulfillment of its obligations with respect to the maintenance or restoration of international peace or security, or the Protection of its own essential security interests.

There is an important difference between a State invoking a customary circumstance precluding wrongfulness and a State invoking a treaty-approved, non-precluded measure as a defence to a claim that it has violated an international obligation owed towards protected investments or investors. In the former scenario, the State accepts that it has taken a measure contrary to its international obligation, and international responsibility attaches but for the circumstance precluding wrongfulness. In the latter scenario, the State is asserting that the measure it has taken is outside the purview of the treaty and therefore cannot be construed as a violation of the treaty. In other words, the State in one case is justifying an internationally wrongful measure and in the other is arguing that there is no internationally wrongful measure. Given the distinction in the operative effect of circumstances precluding wrongfulness and of non-precluded measures, these are discrete defences to liability.[54] For example, in expropriation claims submitted to investment treaty arbitration and where the applicable treaty provides for non-precluded measures,

---

[53] Signed 14 November 1991, entered into force 20 October 1994.

[54] *CMS Gas Transmission Co.* v. *Argentina*, ICSID Case No. ARB/01/8, Decision on Annulment, 25 September 2007 (Guillaume, Elaraby, Crawford), para. 129; *Sempra Energy International* v. *Argentina*, ICSID Case No. ARB/02/16, Decision on Annulment, 29 June 2010 (Söderlund, Edward, Jacovides), para. 200; see also *Continental Casualty Co.* v. *Argentina*, ICSID Case No. ARB/03/9, Award, 5 September 2008 (Sacerdoti,

the State can characterise a taking whose legality is impugned as a non-precluded measure. The consequence of a successful characterisation is a finding that the legality of the taking is not governed by the expropriation clause in the treaty, and therefore cannot, in any event, amount to a breach of treaty. The State can also invoke the customary defence of necessity set out in Article 25 of the ASR. The consequence of a successful invocation of this defence is a finding that, although a taking is unlawful under the terms of the treaty, the State is exonerated from international responsibility because the taking was necessary.

The bone of contention between investors and States over the lawfulness of an expropriation is often the absence or inadequacy of compensation, and less frequently the absence of public purpose or non-compliance with due process. If the respondent State raises a defence to liability for expropriation that is external to the customary and treaty conditions for lawfulness, evaluating this defence is the final phase of the inquiry into legality. A defence successfully invoking customary circumstances precluding wrongfulness excuses the State from having carried out an unlawful expropriation, while a defence successfully characterising the expropriation as a non-precluded measure deems the expropriation unfettered by treaty constraints.

4. JUDICIAL EXPROPRIATION

Investment arbitration tribunals do not appear to adhere to the object-existence-legality analytical framework set out in Sections 1, 2 and 3 when the allegedly expropriatory act is attributed to the host State's judiciary. Instead, existing arbitral jurisprudence appears to treat judicial expropriation as a special type of expropriation, distinct from legislative or executive expropriation, which warrants its own assessment criteria.

The singling out of judicial expropriation from other types of expropriatory conduct attributable to the host State by investment arbitration tribunals is a fairly recent phenomenon. It began in 2009 when the tribunal in *Saipem S.p.A.* v. *The People's Republic of Bangladesh* (*Saipem* v. *Bangladesh*) held that in order for a ruling of a Bangladeshi court to be construed as an expropriation, any substantial deprivation of a right or asset also had to be 'illegal'.[55] Absent 'illegal' conduct, such as the violation of an international obligation or capricious behaviour, there can be no expropriation. The facts of *Saipem* v. *Bangladesh* were unusual. The claimant Saipem invoked an International Chamber of Commerce (ICC) arbitration clause over a contractual dispute with State-owned entity Petrobangla. After the ICC tribunal dismissed Petrobangla's objections to jurisdiction and denied several of its procedural requests, Petrobangla successfully sought an order from the courts in Dhaka, the seat of the arbitration, revoking the authority of the ICC tribunal. However, the arbitration continued and the ICC tribunal eventually rendered an award in favour of Saipem.

Veeder, Nader), paras 167–168; but cf. *LG&E Energy Corp. and Others* v. *Argentina*, ICSID Case No. ARB/02/1, Decision on Liability, 3 October 2006 (Markelt, Rezek, van den Berg), para. 245; *El Paso Energy International Co.* v. *Argentina*, ICSID Case No. ARB/03/15, Award, 31 October 2011 (Caflisch, Bernadini, Stern), para. 613.

[55] ICSID Case No. ARB/05/07, Award, 30 June 2009 (Kaufmann-Kholer, Schreuer, Otton), para. 134.

Petrobangla then moved to have the ICC award set aside before the Supreme Court of Bangladesh. The Supreme Court held that since the ICC award was rendered by a tribunal whose authority had previously been revoked, it was a 'nullity in the eye of the law' and such a 'non-existent award can neither be set aside nor can it be enforced'.[56] Saipem sued Bangladesh under the Agreement Between the Government of the Republic of Italy and the Government of the People's Republic of Bangladesh on the Promotion and Protection of Investments,[57] claiming that the sum effect of the court orders amounted to an unlawful expropriation of its 'rights to arbitration and under the Award'.[58]

The tribunal in *Saipem* v. *Bangladesh* justified its departure from the 'sole effects doctrine' with the additional criterion of illegality on the fear that future decisions of national courts setting aside arbitral awards may be construed as expropriations. And although it cautioned that its twist on the 'sole effects doctrine' was necessitated by the unusual factual circumstances, later tribunals, as the following extracts show, seemed to elevate the *Saipem* v. *Bangladesh* tribunal's one-off requirement of illegality to a standard requirement for determining the existence of judicial expropriation.

Saipem v. Bangladesh, ICSID Case No. ARB/05/07, Award, 30 June 2009 (Kaufmann-Kohler, Schreuer, Otton), paras 133–134, 159, 166–167, 170 (emphasis added, footnotes omitted)

133. As a preliminary matter, the Tribunal wishes to emphasize that according to the so-called 'sole effects doctrine', the most significant criterion to determine whether the disputed actions amount to indirect expropriation or are tantamount to expropriation is the impact of the measure. As a matter of principle, case law considers that there is expropriation if the deprivation is substantial, as it is in the present case ... That said, given the very peculiar circumstances of the present interference, the Tribunal agrees with the parties that the substantial deprivation of Saipem's ability to enjoy the benefits of the ICC Award is not sufficient to conclude that the Bangladeshi courts' intervention is tantamount to an expropriation. *If this were true, any setting aside of an award could then found a claim for expropriation, even if the setting aside was ordered by the competent state court upon legitimate grounds.*

134. In effect, both parties consider that the actions of (or the actions attributable to) Bangladesh must be 'illegal' in order to give rise to a claim of expropriation. They have

---

[56] Award, para. 50.
[57] Signed 20 March 1990, entered into force 20 September 1994. The relevant provision is Article 5(1)(2), which reads: 'Investments of investors of one of the Contracting Parties shall not be directly or indirectly nationalized, expropriated, requisitioned or subjected to any measures having similar effects in the territory of the other Contracting Party, except for public purposes, or national interest, against immediate full and effective compensation, and on condition that these measures are taken on a non-discriminatory basis and in conformity with all legal provisions and procedures.'
[58] *Saipem* v. *Bangladesh*, Award, para. 84(vi).

devoted a major part of their submissions to the issue of illegality. For the sake of clarity, the Tribunal emphasizes that the following analysis should not be understood as a departure from the 'sole effects doctrine'. It is due to the particular circumstances of this dispute and to the manner in which the parties have pleaded their case, both being in agreement that the unlawful character of the actions was a necessary condition.

...

b) Abuse of right

...

159. ... the Tribunal considers that the Bangladeshi courts abused their supervisory jurisdiction over the arbitration process. It is true that the revocation of an arbitrator's authority can legitimately be ordered in case of misconduct. It is further true that in making such order national courts do have substantial discretion. However, they cannot use their jurisdiction to revoke arbitrators for reasons wholly unrelated with such misconduct and the risks it carries for the fair resolution of the dispute. Taken together, the standard for revocation used by the Bangladesh courts and the manner in which the judge applied that standard to the facts indeed constituted an abuse of right.

...

d) Violation of the New York Convention?

...

166. Bangladesh is right that Article II(3) of the New York Convention requires courts of member states to refer the parties to arbitration 'when seized of an action in a matter in respect of which the parties have made an [arbitration] agreement'. However, Article II(1) of the New York Convention imposes on Bangladesh a wider obligation to 'recognize' arbitration agreements.

167. Based on that obligation, it is for instance generally acknowledged that the issuance of an anti-arbitration injunction can amount to a violation of the principle embedded in Article II of the New York Convention. One could think that the present case is different, however, from an anti-arbitration injunction. Technically, the courts of Bangladesh did not target the arbitration or the arbitration agreement in itself, but revoked the authority of the arbitrators. However, it is the Tribunal's opinion that a decision to revoke the arbitrators' authority can amount to a violation of Article II of the New York Convention whenever it de facto 'prevents or immobilizes the arbitration that seeks to implement that [arbitration] agreement' thus completely frustrating if not the wording at least the spirit of the Convention.

...

170. In the light of these developments, the Tribunal concludes that the revocation of the arbitrators' authority was contrary to international law, in particular to the principle of abuse of rights and the New York Convention.

> *Swisslion DOO Skopje* v. *The Former Yugoslav Republic of Macedonia*, ICSID Case No. ARB/09/16, Award, 6 July 2012 (Guillaume, Price, Thomas), paras 313–314 (footnotes omitted)
>
> 313. One of the cases on which the Claimant placed reliance, *Saipem* v. *Bangladesh*, noted that the claimant itself in that case recognized that a predicate for alleging a judicial expropriation is unlawful activity by the court itself. The award recounts the claimant's acknowledgement that it is '*an illegal action of the judiciary* which has the effect of depriving the investor of its contractual or vested rights constitutes an expropriation which engages the State's responsibility'. This point, with which the respondent in that case agreed, was accepted by the tribunal, which noted that it concurred 'with the parties that expropriation by the courts *presupposes that the courts' intervention was illegal* ... ' [Emphasis added.]
>
>   314. In the Tribunal's view, the courts' determination of breach of the Share Sale Agreement and its consequential termination did not breach the Treaty and therefore was not unlawful. The internationally lawful termination of a contract between a State entity and an investor cannot be equated to an expropriation of contractual rights simply because the investor's rights have been terminated; otherwise, a State could not exercise the ordinary right of a contractual party to allege that its counterparty breached the contract without the State's being found to be in breach of its international obligations. Since there was no illegality on the part of the courts, the first element of the Claimant's expropriation claim is not established.

> *Garanti Koza LLP* v. *Turkmenistan*, ICSID Case No. ARB/11/20, Award, 19 December 2016 (Townsend, Lambrou, Boisson de Charzournes), para. 365
>
> A seizure of property by a court as the result of normal domestic legal process does not amount to an expropriation under international law unless there was an element of serious and fundamental impropriety about the legal process. Actions by state courts to enforce contract rights, including rights to terminate a contract, have generally not been held by investment arbitration tribunals to amount to expropriation, regardless of whether the state or an instrument of the state is the contract party enforcing its rights.

Unless the national court offered no or dubious reasons for its order which substantially deprives the investor of the benefit of his investment, property, or asset, such being the exceptional case in *Saipem* v. *Bangladesh*, the requirement of illegality is a powerful obstacle to a finding of judicial expropriation. It has been suggested that this line of arbitral awards may encourage States to channel all expropriatory decisions through their courts.[59] In the absence of illegality on the part of the judiciary, there is no expropriation,

---

[59] M. Jarrett, 'The Only Thing We Have to Fear about Judicial Expropriation is the Fear of It', 20 May 2020, https://opiniojuris.org/2020/05/20/the-only-thing-we-have-to-fear-about-judicial-expropriation-is-the-fear-of-it/ (accessed 31 July 2020).

and therefore no corresponding obligation on the State to compensate the affected party or parties. The tribunal in *Krederi Ltd.* v. *Ukraine*, while applying the requirement of illegality to rule out judicial expropriation on the facts, nonetheless expressed discomfort at the differentiated treatment of judicial expropriation.

Krederi Ltd. v. Ukraine, ICSID Case No. ARB/14/17, Award, 3 July 2018 (Reinisch, Wirth, Griffith), paras 709–710, 713, 718 (footnotes omitted)

709. While it is possible that judicial action amounts to expropriation, it is the exception rather than the norm. In any kind of private law dispute over ownership of movable or immovable property, courts will make a decision which of the disputing parties claiming ownership rights prevails. This will result in a finding that one party will be entitled to ownership whereas the other (or others) will not. Such judicial determinations do not constitute expropriation. Similarly, where property transfers are held to be invalid, the resulting transfers of ownership do not amount to expropriation.

710. In this regard the Tribunal concurs with the view expressed by the *Saipem* v. *Bangladesh* tribunal which found that, in the specific circumstances, the host State's judicial actions annulling an ICC award amounted to indirect expropriation, but held that in the peculiar case of a judicial expropriation the 'substantial deprivation' of ownership rights in itself was not sufficient for a finding of expropriation because otherwise 'any setting aside of an award could then found a claim for expropriation, even if the setting aside was ordered by the competent state court upon legitimate grounds'. Rather, an additional element of illegality was required in order to turn a judicial decision into an indirect expropriation of the intangible rights under an arbitral award. In this case, the tribunal found that the 'Bangladeshi courts abused their supervisory jurisdiction over the arbitration process' and interfered with the arbitral process contrary to the New York Convention.

...

713. The Tribunal recognizes that Claimant also understands that for judicial action to amount to expropriation a due process violation is required. In order to avoid a situation whereby any title annulment would constitute indirect expropriation or a measure tantamount to expropriation it is therefore necessary to ascertain whether an additional element of procedural illegality or denial of justice was present. Only then may a judicial decision be qualified as a measure constituting or amounting to expropriation.

...

718. For the reasons stated above, the Tribunal dismisses all claims. The Tribunal nonetheless notes what it considers an unsatisfactory outcome of this case: In the result the investor has lost the properties it purchased without being recouped the original sale price paid to, and retained by, the City of Kiev. Although the legal process leading to that result has been held not to violate applicable standards, and the Respondent has flagged that local remedies may be available to deal with that situation, the Tribunal remains uncomfortable with the result.

In addition to the potentially unjust outcome of depriving deserving investors of compensation, reading an illegality requirement into judicial expropriation is also conceptually problematic because it conflates the inquiry into the *existence* of an expropriation with the inquiry into the *legality* of an expropriation. The excerpted awards in *Saipem* v. *Bangladesh* and *Krederi Ltd* v. *Ukraine* proffer two possible motivations for this conflation, neither of which necessitate a conflation of otherwise separate inquiries. The first possible motivation is the concern that the exercise of common court functions, like the setting aside of arbitral awards (*Saipem* v. *Bangladesh*) and the determination of ownership rights over property (*Krederi Ltd* v. *Ukraine*), will be susceptible to challenge as expropriatory acts. This concern may be overstated. A party to an arbitration clause has a contractual right to arbitrate covered disputes, but no right to a favourable award or to the enforcement of a favourable award. Domestic arbitration legislation as well as international instruments, such as the Convention on the Recognition and Enforcement of Foreign Arbitral Awards ('New York Convention'),[60] do not guarantee the enforcement of every arbitral award. Similarly, a losing party in an ownership dispute does not, without more, possess a right to property that can be enforced in a different forum. In these cases, the more pertinent question to ask is whether the claimant had any rights that could be expropriated? If not, there is no *object* of expropriation and the claim is a non-starter.

The second possible motivation builds on the first by flagging the possibility of misconduct in a judiciary's discharge of its adjudicatory functions and holding such misconduct to the sanctionable standard of denial of justice (*Krederi Ltd* v. *Ukraine*). Leaving aside the fact that denial of justice is a distinct cause of action in international law and should not be passed off as expropriation,[61] there is no compelling reason why an examination of 'procedural illegality', whether symptomatic of denial of justice or not, cannot be undertaken during the inquiry into the legality of an expropriation. Addressing any judicial 'procedural illegality' during the inquiry into the legality rather than the existence of a judicial expropriation would have resulted in a less uncomfortable holding for the tribunal in *Krederi Ltd* v. *Ukraine*. Since the claimant had rights to properties (object) which were later subject to total deprivation by court order (existence) without an offer of compensation or an explanation by the authorities on why no compensation was due (legality), the claimant remains entitled to compensation by the City of Kiev.[62] Making an

---

[60] Signed 10 June 1958, entered into force 7 June 1959, 330 UNTS 3 ('New York Convention'), Art. VII. Cf. Convention on the Settlement of Investment Disputes between States and Nationals of Other States (signed 18 March 1965, entered into force 14 October 1966) 575 UNTS 159 (ICSID Convention), Art. 54(1): 'Each Contracting State shall recognize an award rendered pursuant to this Convention as binding and enforce the pecuniary obligations imposed by that award within its territories as if it were a final judgment of a court in that State. A Contracting State with a federal constitution may enforce such an award in or through its federal courts and may provide that such courts shall treat the award as if it were a final judgment of the courts of a constituent state.' Unlike a party seeking enforcement of an arbitral award under the New York Convention, a party seeking enforcement of an ICSID award has the right to enforcement of a favourable award by virtue of Article 54(1) of the ICSID Convention.

[61] M. Sattorova, 'Denial of Justice Disguised? Investment Arbitration and the Protection of Foreign Investors from Judicial Misconduct' (2012) 61(1) *ICLQ* 223, 234–235.

[62] As the parties' claims and prayers for relief have been redacted in the Award, it might be unwise to speculate on whether Krederi brought a claim for unlawful expropriation or for lawful expropriation against

arbitral order to this effect, which the claimant can then enforce through judicial avenues in the absence of voluntary satisfaction by Ukraine, may be preferable to dismissing the claim in its entirety and regretting having to leave the claimant to fend for itself. And since Ukraine has invited the claimant to pursue local remedies, it should have no reservations complying with an arbitral award that expresses those remedies in monetary terms.

The arbitral jurisprudence on judicial expropriation is arguably settled but unsatisfactory. Requiring proof of illegality before an expropriation by the courts can be found to exist unnecessarily muddles the discrete assessments on the existence and legality of an expropriation. Fears of unmeritorious claims against national courts can be dispelled simply by asking if the claimant is in possession of rights that can be expropriated, in other words, whether there is an object of expropriation. And in cases that reveal judicial misconduct, such as *Saipem* v. *Bangladesh*, that misconduct is likely to be captured by the due process limb in the inquiry into the legality of judicial expropriation. Future investment arbitration tribunals hearing judicial expropriation claims may wish to consider paying equal attention to the object, the existence and the legality of the challenged measures.

CONCLUSION

Expropriation claims are among the most common claims submitted to investment arbitration. Under some investment treaties, only expropriation claims can be submitted to investment arbitration.[63] The success or failure of an expropriation claim, which involves a complaint that an expropriation carried out by the host State falls short of cumulative customary or treaty conditions for a lawful expropriation, rests on three factors.

The first factor is the existence of an object of expropriation. Customary international law requires claimants to be in possession of property or rights akin to property rights, while investment treaties require claimants to be in possession of protected investments, such as tangible and intangible property rights, contractual rights and shareholder rights, as potential objects of expropriation. As expropriation clauses in many older generation

---

Ukraine. That said, as Ukraine does not appear to have intimated a refusal to compensate, the substance of Krederi's claim is more likely to be one for lawful expropriation. Had the tribunal established the existence of expropriation, Krederi would have been entitled to compensation in accordance with the treaty standard of 'prompt, adequate and effective compensation'. For a more detailed discussion of the standards and valuation of compensation for expropriation, see Chapter 17, Sections 2.1, 3 and 4.

[63] See, e.g., Cyprus–Hungary BIT, Art. 7:

'1. Any dispute between either Contracting Party and the investor of the other Contracting Party concerning expropriation of an investment shall, as far as possible, be settled by the disputing parties in an amicable way. If such disputes cannot be settled within six months from the date either party requested amicable settlement, it shall, upon request of the investor, be submitted to one of the following:

(a) The Arbitration Institute of the Arbitral Tribunal of the Chamber of Commerce in Stockholm;

(b) The Arbitral Tribunal of the International Chamber of Commerce in Paris;

(c) The International Centre for the Settlement of Investment Disputes in case both Contracting Parties have become members of the Convention of 18 March 1965 on the Settlement of Investment Disputes between States and Nationals of Other States.'

investment treaties refer and apply to all protected investments, any investment that satisfies the treaty definition of a protected investment can be the object of expropriation. However, the insistence of some investment treaty tribunals, as well as the wording in newer generation investment treaties, that objects of expropriation must bear proprietary features heralds a revival of the customary position to separate protected investments into those with proprietary features and those without, with only the former susceptible to expropriation.

The second factor is the existence of an expropriation. An expropriation can be direct, where there is a transfer of title or outright seizure of assets. An expropriation can also be indirect, where a single measure or a series of measures result in the destruction or diminishment of the enjoyment or benefits that were previously derived from the protected investment. The litmus test for when a measure(s) that interfere(s) with a protected investment cross(es) the line and become(s) expropriatory is the attributability of the measure to the State and the 'sole effects doctrine' of substantial deprivation. Deprivation is not limited to physical takings. Measures that precipitate the severe drop in the economic value of a protected investment can also satisfy the threshold of substantial deprivation.

The third factor is the legality of the expropriation. Expropriation by a host State of foreign investment is not in and of itself unlawful. An expropriation that is undertaken in pursuit of a public purpose, accompanied by compensation and in compliance with due process, is lawful because it respects the cumulative customary and treaty conditions for a lawful expropriation. In contrast, an expropriation that is missing a public purpose, or (barring the exceptions of investments valued at zero and regulatory takings, which are non-compensable) is undertaken without compensation, or is undertaken in disregard of due process, is unlawful. However, the analysis on legality does not end here if the State invokes customary defences to liability or argues that the expropriation is a non-precluded measure to which substantive provisions of the treaty do not apply. A successful showing of the existence of a circumstance precluding wrongfulness, such as necessity, means that the expropriation may be unlawful, but the State bears no international responsibility for it. A successful characterisation of an expropriation as a non-precluded measure means that the legality of the expropriation is above treaty regulation and cannot ever amount to a treaty violation for which the State bears international responsibility.

Although the object-existence-legality analytical framework is applicable to all expropriation claims, arbitral tribunals hearing disputes over judicial expropriation to date appear to eschew this framework to focus on ascertaining the second of the three factors – the existence of an expropriation. To this end, tribunals have converged on the requirement of illegality, in addition to attribution and substantial deprivation, to substantiate a finding of judicial expropriation. Absent illegality, there is no expropriation by the courts of the host State and no obligation on the State to compensate the affected investor. The prevailing arbitral approach to judicial expropriation merits reconsideration because there are neither theoretical nor sufficient practical justifications for the conflation of distinct inquiries into the existence and legality of an expropriation. While arbitral tribunals may be informed by the findings of earlier tribunals, they are not bound by these findings.

QUESTIONS

1. Do or can objects of expropriation share common or core features? If so, what are these features, and how are they deduced? If not, why not?

2. Some claimants (see, for example *Anglia Auto Accessories Ltd* v. *Czech Republic*, SCC Arbitration Case V 2014/181, Final Award, 10 March 2017 (Banifatemi, Reinisch, Sands)) liken the non-satisfaction of an arbitral award, be it through design or delay, to an expropriation. Are there rights to payment arising from arbitral awards and if so, can such rights be objects of expropriation? If so, why, and if not, why not?

3. Must compensation for expropriation always reflect the fair market value of the property or protected investment? And must reparation for an unlawful expropriation always fully restore the claimant to the position it was in before the expropriation occurred? Are there circumstances, such as the conduct of the claimant or the impecuniosity of the host State or other considerations, that might warrant a reduction in the amount of compensation or reparation ordered?

4. To date, there is no consensus, or even a general guideline for debate and refinement, on the scope and indicia of a State's police powers. An expropriation carried out in the exercise of a State's police powers is a regulatory taking that does not amount to an indirect expropriation and is therefore non-compensable. What are some possible indicia of takings made in pursuit of police powers? How do these indicia distinguish non-compensable takings from compensable expropriations?

5. Are there characteristics of judicial expropriation that set it apart from expropriations carried out by other branches of government? What do you think these characteristics might be and do they help to explain why the criterion of illegality should be maintained when assessing the existence of an expropriation by the courts?

SUGGESTIONS FOR FURTHER READING

1. A. Mouri, *The International Law of Expropriation as Reflected in the Work of the Iran–US Claims Tribunal* (The Hague: Martinus Nijhoff, 1994).

2. B. Weston, '"Constructive Takings" under International Law: A Modest Foray into the Problem of "Creeping Expropriation"' (1975–1976) 16 *Vanderbilt J Int'l L* 103.

3. V. Lowe, 'Regulation or Expropriation?' (2002) 55 *Curr Leg Probl* 447.

4. T. Wälde and A. Kolo, 'Environmental Regulation, Investment Protection and "Regulatory Taking" in International Law' (2001) 50 *ICLQ* 811.

5. Z. Douglas, 'Property, Investment and the Scope of Investment Protection Obligations' in Z. Douglas, J. Pauwelyn and J. E. Viñuales (eds), *The Foundations of International Investment Law: Bringing Theory into Practice* (Oxford University Press, 2014), 363.

15

Umbrella Clauses

CHAPTER OUTLINE

This chapter deals with treaty clauses which stipulate that the host State shall observe the undertakings which it has assumed towards a protected investor, including but not limited to any obligations which the host State has assumed under an investor–State contract. We will explore the different interpretations given to various umbrella clauses by investment tribunals. These interpretations are varied and inconsistent. There is as yet no real consensus on the precise scope and even the nature or character of the protection conferred by umbrella treaty clauses. Section 1 explains what umbrella clauses are and the lurking presence of the theory of internationalised contracts explained earlier in Chapter 2 of this book. Section 2 contains excerpts of some of the main arbitral awards. They show at least four different views adopted by tribunals regarding umbrella clauses. Section 3 contains illustrations of contemporary treaty umbrella clauses. Some ways in which tribunals have sought to limit the potentially very wide scope and effect of umbrella clauses are discussed in the Conclusion.

INTRODUCTION

An umbrella clause or 'observance of undertakings' clause may be defined as a treaty clause which extends the independent protection of the treaty to breaches of contractual or other commitments made by the host State in relation to the foreign investor's investment.[1] We have seen how investment disputes are, today, often treaty-based. Prior to the

---

[1] For the literature, see, e.g., T. Wälde, 'The "Umbrella" (or Sanctity of Contract/Pacta Sunt Servanda) Clause in Investment Arbitration' (2004) 4 *TDM* 1; T. Wälde, 'The "Umbrella" Clause in Investment Arbitration – A Comment on Original Intentions and Recent Cases' (2005) 6(2) *JWIT* 183; E. Gaillard, 'Treaty-Based Jurisdiction: Broad Dispute Resolution Clauses' (2005) 234(68) *New York LJ* 1; E. Gaillard, 'Investment Treaty Arbitration and Jurisdiction over Contracts Claims – the SGS Cases Considered' in T. Weiler (ed.), *International Investment Law and Arbitration: Leading Cases from the ICSID, NAFTA, Bilateral Treaties and Customary International Law* (London: Cameron May, 2005), 326; J. Wong, 'Umbrella Clauses in Bilateral Investment Treaties: Of Breaches of Contract, Treaty Violations, and the Divide between Developing and Developed Countries in Foreign Investment Disputes' (2006) 14 *George Mason LR* 135; A. C. Sinclair, 'The Umbrella Clause Debate' in A. K. Bjorklund, I. A. Laird and S. Ripinsky (eds), *Investment Treaty Law – Current Issues III* (London: BIICL, 2009), 275; J. O. Voss, *The Impact of Investment Treaties on Contracts between Host States and Foreign Investors* (The Hague: Martinus Nijhoff, 2010), 238.

growth of investment treaty arbitration since the 1990s, the field had been dominated by investment contract arbitrations. That process of evolution from investment contract to investment treaty protection, and from contractual to treaty-based arbitrations, has led to complex questions surrounding those situations in which a treaty requires the host State to fulfil its contractual undertakings: in other words, situations in which contractual and treaty obligations exist together.

1. THE UMBRELLA CLAUSE

The umbrella clause is sometimes attributed to Prosper Weil's Hague Lectures.[2] According to Weil, there can be an 'umbrella treaty' between the host and home State 'which turns the obligation to perform the contract into an international obligation of the contracting State'. It 'transforms contractual obligations into international obligations'. We have already seen the notion that contractual obligations may be transformed into international obligations in the discussion on the theory of the internationalised contract.[3] In the special context of umbrella treaty clauses, it is not the contract itself which is the source of its 'internationalisation', but a treaty clause which, according to Emmanuel Gaillard, creates a 'mirror effect' in the treaty law realm of the obligations contained in a contract.[4] In *SGS* v. *Pakistan*, in which Gaillard served as counsel, the point was put by counsel in the following way.

> *SGS Société Générale de Surveillance* v. *Pakistan*, ICSID Case No. ARB/01/13, Decision on Objections to Jurisdiction, 6 August 2003 (Judge Florentino P. Feliciano, President; Mr André Faurès; Mr J. Christopher Thomas), para. 99
>
> ... I myself prefer to call it a mirror effect clause, because in fact it is a mirror effect which it creates.
>
> You have a violation of the contract, and the Treaty says, as if you had a mirror, that this violation will also be susceptible to being characterised as a violation of the Treaty. So the same facts, the same breach will be a violation of the contract in itself, and a violation of the Treaty.

---

[2] P. Weil, 'Problèmes relatifs aux contrats passés entre un Etat et un particulier' (1969) 128 *RCADI* 95, 130; see Wälde, 'The "Umbrella" (or Sanctity of Contract/Pacta Sunt Servanda) Clause', 30; Wälde, 'The "Umbrella" Clause in Investment Arbitration', 202 n. 68. It has also been credited to F. A. Mann, 'British Treaties for the Promotion and Protection of Investments' (1981) 52 *BYbIL* 241, 246; and to I. Seidl-Hohenveldern – see T. W. Wälde and K. Hobér, 'The First Energy Charter Treaty Arbitral Award' in C. Leben (ed.), *Le contentieux arbitral transnational relatif à l'investissement* (Paris: LGDJ, 2006), 307, 318 n. 13. Others credit Sir Elihu Lauterpacht's recommendation given in respect of the Anglo-Iranian Oil Company's claim against Iran in 1954, which was subsequently adopted in Art. II of the Abs-Shawcross Draft Convention, discussed further in Section 3; see, e.g., J. W. Salacuse, *The Law of Investment Treaties* (Oxford University Press, 2010), 276.
[3] See Chapter 2 of this book.
[4] Gaillard, 'Investment Treaty Arbitration and Jurisdiction over Contracts Claims', 344–345. See also E. Gaillard, 'L'arbitrage sur le fondement des traités de protection des investissements – Les Etats dans le contentieux économique international, I. Le contentieux arbitral' (2003) *Rev de l'Arb* 853, 868; cited and translated in Voss, *The Impact of Investment Treaties on Contracts*, 240.

> And,
>
> If I am the government and if I breach a contract, by the same token I will breach a treaty, so the useful effect of this is to create this mirror effect, to say that I will elevate in essence, and that's what it does, it may be far-reaching but that's what it does, to elevate breaches of contract as breaches of a treaty.

Such metaphors of transformation, 'mirror effect' or the 'elevation' of the contractual obligation onto the international plane have left a lasting impression. In *SGS* v. *Pakistan*, the tribunal itself adopted the metaphor of the elevation of the contractual obligation.

The controversy which today surrounds this type of clause may be explained by asking three distinct questions:

(1) Whether a treaty can require a State to behave in a way which is also required by a contract to which that State is a party. The answer to this question must be 'yes', since no one sees an objection to any overlap between a treaty and a contract in terms of what each prescribes.
(2) Whether a treaty can do so by having a rule which simply requires a State to do, or abstain from, whatever it is that a contract to which that State has or may become party requires or proscribes. The difference between this and the first question is that the treaty rule may not spell out in express terms what the contractual terms are beforehand. As such, the host State may not know the scope and content of its treaty obligation at the time the host State commits itself to that obligation. The treaty clause can refer to any future contract, and this has become the basis of an objection to umbrella clauses for being overly broad.
(3) Whether the underlying contractual obligation must necessarily be 'transformed', as Weil says, into an international obligation by the treaty clause into an 'international contractual obligation'.

The potentially broad effect of umbrella clauses; their ability to transform garden-variety contractual obligations into international legal obligations which trigger the application of the international law rules of State responsibility, in other words, their ability to 'elevate' domestic private law obligations onto the international plane; and the seeming ability of an umbrella clause to 'mirror' all the contents of a private law contract in the realm of international law – these are all a part of the explanation for the current controversy over umbrella clauses.

Others have also been credited with the invention of the umbrella clause, among them Elihu Lauterpacht, whose recommendation that the consortium agreement which had been proposed to settle the Anglo-Iranian Oil Company's dispute with Iran in the 1950s should be protected by a further treaty undertaking was, however, directed to a specifically identifiable agreement and set of obligations. That treaty never materialised, but the idea made its way in its broader form into the Abs–Shawcross Draft, discussed in Section 3.[5]

---

[5] See Salacuse, *The Law of Investment Treaties*, 276.

Thus, it could be said that the original idea was always more limited than the current potential scope and effect of umbrella clauses.

2. THE AWARDS

The excerpts below are intended to illustrate resistance to umbrella clauses in *SGS* v. *Pakistan* (Section 2.1), endorsement of such clauses in *SGS* v. *Philippines* (Section 2.2), an attempt to reconcile the conflicting cases by noting carefully the drafting differences in the various forms of treaty language in *Noble Ventures* v. *Romania* (Section 2.3), the continued salience of the two *SGS* cases as shown in *El Paso* v. *Argentina* (Section 2.4), separate but potentially interdependent analyses of treaty law and contract law in *Compañia de Aguas del Aconquija SA and Vivendi Universal* v. *Argentina* and also in *CMS* v. *Argentina* (Section 2.5), and the special problem of contractual forum selection clauses which conflict with the investment treaty's provision for investment arbitration (Section 2.6).

2.1 *SGS* v. *Pakistan*

The controversy surrounding umbrella clauses is usually illustrated by pointing to the manner in which the *SGS* v. *Pakistan* tribunal had rejected the clause in the Switzerland–Pakistan BIT, while the *SGS* v. *Philippines* tribunal went on to uphold what, at least at first glance, appeared to be a similar clause in the Philippines–Switzerland BIT. Both cases concerned contracts for pre-shipment inspection services.

It would be misleading, however, to accord undue attention merely to the differences in outcome in the two cases. Article 11 of the Switzerland–Pakistan BIT considered in *SGS* v. *Pakistan* had been drafted in the following way: 'Either Contracting Party shall constantly guarantee the observance of the commitments it has entered into.' The tribunal in *SGS* v. *Pakistan* concluded that the underlying contractual claims were not to be taken to have been 'elevated' to the level of a treaty claim.[6] Counsel's – Mr Gaillard's – metaphor that the contractual commitment had become 'elevated' to the international plane appears to have backfired by purporting to confer an extremely wide legal effect and heightened significance to the clause, at least in the view of the tribunal. Mr Gaillard, having advanced the argument at its highest level, had put the cat among the pigeons.

> *SGS Société Générale de Surveillance* v. *Pakistan*, ICSID Case No. ARB/01/13, Decision on Objections to Jurisdiction, 6 August 2003 (Judge Florentino P. Feliciano, Mr André Faurès, Mr J. Christopher Thomas), paras 166–173 (original emphasis)
>
> 166. Firstly, textually, Article 11 falls considerably short of saying what the Claimant asserts it means. The 'commitments' the observance of which a Contracting Party is to 'constantly guarantee' are not limited to contractual commitments.[175] The commitments referred to

---

[6] *SGS* v. *Pakistan*, paras 166–173; also discussed by the tribunal in *Noble Ventures*, para. 47.

may be embedded in, e.g., the municipal legislative or administrative or other unilateral measures of a Contracting Party. The phrase 'constantly [to] guarantee the observance' of some statutory, administrative or contractual commitment simply does not to our mind, necessarily signal the creation and acceptance of a new international law obligation on the part of the Contracting Party, where clearly there was none before. Further, the 'commitments' subject matter of Article 11 may, without imposing excessive violence on the text itself, be commitments of the State itself as a legal person, or of any office, entity or subdivision (local government units) or legal representative thereof whose acts are, under the law on state responsibility, attributable to the State itself. As a matter of textuality therefore, the scope of Article 11 of the BIT, while consisting in its entirety of only one sentence, appears susceptible of almost indefinite expansion. The text itself of Article 11 does not purport to state that breaches of contract alleged by an investor in relation to a contract it has concluded with a State (widely considered to be a matter of municipal rather than international law) are automatically 'elevated' to the level of breaches of international treaty law. Thus, it appears to us that while the Claimant has sought to spell out the consequences or inferences it would draw from Article 11, the Article itself does not set forth those consequences.

> [Footnote 175 is informative, and it reads: 'The Claimant has, for instance, not tried to distinguish between (a) a contract between a Contracting Party and an investor of the other Contracting Party, the applicable law of which is the national law of the Contracting Party and (b) a State contract with a private investor the applicable law of which is specified as "international law" or "general principles of law." The seminal lectures of Prosper Weil, *Problèmes Relatifs aux Contrats Passés Entre un État et un Particulier,* Hague Recueil des Cours (Vol. III, 1969), Tome 128, pp. 157-188, explored the theoretical consequences of "internationalization" of contracts the lex contractus of which is determined to be international law or general principles of law, such as the natural resources concessions granted, in an earlier day, by, e.g., Iran, Abu Dhabi and Qatar. The Claimant's reading of Article 11 of the BIT apparently extends to every contract, or other commitment, that a Contracting Party has entered into or assumed, or may in the future enter into or undertake with respect to an investor of the other Contracting Party.']

167. Considering the widely accepted principle with which we started, namely, that under general international law, a violation of a contract entered into by a State with an investor of another State, is not, by itself, a violation of international law, and considering further that the legal consequences that the Claimant would have us attribute to Article 11 of the BIT are so far-reaching in scope, and so automatic and unqualified and sweeping in their operation, so burdensome in their potential impact upon a Contracting Party, we believe that clear and convincing evidence must be adduced by the Claimant. Clear and convincing evidence of what? Clear and convincing evidence that such was indeed the shared intent of the Contracting Parties to the Swiss-Pakistan Investment Protection Treaty in incorporating Article 11 in the BIT. We do not find such evidence in the text itself of Article 11. We have

not been pointed to any other evidence of the putative common intent of the Contracting Parties by the Claimant.

168. The consequences of accepting the Claimant's reading of Article 11 of the BIT should be spelled out in some detail. Firstly, Article 11 would amount to incorporating by reference an unlimited number of State contracts, as well as other municipal law instruments setting out State commitments including unilateral commitments to an investor of the other Contracting Party. Any alleged violation of those contracts and other instruments would be treated as a breach of the BIT. Secondly, the Claimant's view of Article 11 tends to make Articles 3 to 7 of the BIT substantially superfluous. There would be no real need to demonstrate a violation of those substantive treaty standards if a simple breach of contract, or of municipal statute or regulation, by itself, would suffice to constitute a treaty violation on the part of a Contracting Party and engage the international responsibility of the Party. A third consequence would be that an investor may, at will, nullify any freely negotiated dispute settlement clause in a State contract. On the reading of Article 11 urged by the Claimant, the benefits of the dispute settlement provisions of a contract with a State also a party to a BIT, would flow only to the investor. For that investor could always defeat the State's invocation of the contractually specified forum, and render any mutually agreed procedure of dispute settlement, other than BIT-specified ICSID arbitration, a dead-letter, at the investor's choice. The investor would remain free to go to arbitration either under the contract or under the BIT. But the State party to the contract would be effectively precluded from proceeding to the arbitral forum specified in the contract unless the investor was minded to agree. The Tribunal considers that Article 11 of the BIT should be read in such a way as to enhance mutuality and balance of benefits in the inter-relation of different agreements located in differing legal orders.

169. Another consideration that appears to us to support our reading of Article 11 of the BIT, is the location of Article 11 in the BIT. The context of Article 11 includes the structure and content of the rest of the Treaty. We note that Article 11 is not placed together with the substantive obligations undertaken by the Contracting Parties in Articles 3 to 7: promotion and admission of investments in accordance with the laws and regulations of the Contracting Party (Article 3); prohibition of impairment, by 'unreasonable or discriminating measures,' of the management, use, enjoyment, *etc.* of such investments and according 'fair and equitable treatment' to investors of the other Contracting Party (Article 4); free cross-border transfer of payments relating to the protected investments (Article 5); prohibition of expropriation or other measures having the same nature or effect, unless taken in the public interest, on a non-discriminatory basis, under due process of law and with provision for effective and adequate and prompt compensation (Article 6); and the most-favored–investor provision (Article 7). These substantive standards are marked off by Article 8 ('Principle of Subrogation') from the two dispute settlement procedures recognized in the BIT: investor v. Contracting Party (Article 9); and Contracting Parties *inter se* (Article 10). Then follows Article 11 ('Observance of Commitments') which in turn is followed by the 'Final Provisions' (Article 12) and the signature clause.

170. Given the above structure and sequence of the rest of the Treaty, we consider that, had Switzerland and Pakistan intended Article 11 to embody a substantive 'first order' standard obligation, they would logically have placed Article 11 among the substantive 'first order' obligations set out in Articles 3 to 7. The separation of Article 11 from those obligations by the subrogation article and the two dispute settlement provisions (Articles 9 and 10), indicates to our mind that Article 11 was *not* meant to project a substantive obligation like those set out in Articles 3 to 7, let alone one that could, when read as SGS asks us to read it, supersede and render largely redundant the substantive obligations provided for in Articles 3 to 7.

171. We believe, for the foregoing considerations, that Article 11 of the BIT would have to be considerably more specifically worded before it can reasonably be read in the extraordinarily expansive manner submitted by the Claimant. The appropriate interpretive approach is the prudential one summed up in the literature as *in dubio pars mitior est sequenda*, or more tersely, *in dubio mitius*.

172. The Claimant vigorously submits that any view of Article 11 of the BIT other than the one urged by it, would render Article 11 inutile, a result abhorrent to the principle of effectiveness in treaty interpretation. We are not persuaded that rejecting SGS's reading of Article 11 would necessarily reduce that Article to 'pure exhortation', that is, to a non-normative statement. At least two points may be usefully made in this connection. Firstly, we do not consider that confirmation in a treaty that a Contracting Party is bound under and pursuant to a contract, or a statute or other municipal law issuance is devoid of appreciable normative value, either in the municipal or in the international legal sphere. That confirmation could, for instance, signal an implied affirmative commitment to enact implementing rules and regulations necessary or appropriate to give effect to a contractual or statutory undertaking in favor of investors of another Contracting Party that would otherwise be a dead letter. Secondly, we do not preclude the possibility that under exceptional circumstances, a violation of certain provisions of a State contract with an investor of another State might constitute violation of a treaty provision (like Article 11 of the BIT) enjoining a Contracting Party constantly to guarantee the observance of contracts with investors of another Contracting Party. For instance, if a Contracting Party were to take action that materially impedes the ability of an investor to prosecute its claims before an international arbitration tribunal (having previously agreed to such arbitration in a contract with the investor), or were to refuse to go to such arbitration at all and leave the investor only the option of going before the ordinary courts of the Contracting Party (which actions need not amount to 'denial of justice'), that Contracting Party may arguably be regarded as having failed 'constantly [to] guarantee the observance of [its] commitments' within the meaning of Article 11 of the Swiss–Pakistan BIT. The modes by which a Contracting Party may 'constantly guarantee the observance of' its contractual or statutory or administrative municipal law commitments with respect to investments are not necessarily exhausted by the instant transubstantiation of contract claims into BIT claims posited by the Claimant.

173. The Tribunal is not saying that States may not agree with each other in a BIT that henceforth, all breaches of each State's contracts with investors of the other State are forthwith converted into and to be treated as breaches of the BIT. What the Tribunal is stressing is that in this case, there is no clear and persuasive evidence that such was in fact the intention of both Switzerland and Pakistan in adopting Article 11 of the BIT. Pakistan for its part in effect denies that, in concluding the BIT, it had any such intention. SGS, of course, does not speak for Switzerland. But it has not submitted evidence of the necessary level of specificity and explicitness of text. We believe and so hold that, in the circumstances of this case, SGS's claim about Article 11 of the BIT must be rejected.

2.2 SGS v. Philippines

The tribunal was to adopt a markedly different approach in *SGS* v. *Philippines*. The umbrella clause in the Philippines–Switzerland BIT was worded quite differently from the Switzerland–Pakistan BIT clause. It had stated – with added emphasis – that 'Each Contracting Party *shall observe any obligation it has assumed* with regard to *specific investments* in its territory by investors of the other Contracting Party'.[7] The tribunal in *SGS* v. *Philippines* duly observed that the word 'shall' suggested the existence of a legal obligation, and that the phrase 'any obligation' included future obligations which the host State would assume. It considered that the principle of effectiveness in treaty interpretation surely requires effect to be given to the clause contained in a treaty whose object and purpose was, after all, the 'the promotion and reciprocal protection of investments'. The tribunal reasoned that it was therefore perfectly consistent with the BIT that contractual commitments which were intended to be binding under their own applicable law should also have been brought within the scope of the BIT umbrella clause's protection, and also that disputes concerning the scope and application of that protective umbrella would be subsumed within the investor–State arbitration clause in the BIT.[8]

SGS Société Générale de Surveillance SA v. *Philippines*, ICSID Case No. ARB/02/6, Decision on Jurisdiction, 29 January 2004 (Dr Ahmed S. El-Kosheri, President; Professor James Crawford; Professor Antonio Crivellaro), paras 115–116, 127

115. Article X(2) is different. It reads:
'Each Contracting Party shall observe any obligation it has assumed with regard to specific investments in its territory by investors of the other Contracting Party.'

---

[7] Art. X(2) Philippines–Switzerland BIT.
[8] The reasoning of the tribunal in *SGS* v. *Philippines* was endorsed by the tribunal in *Eureko BV* v. *Poland*, UNCITRAL, Partial Award, Ad Hoc Arbitration, 19 August 2005, paras 255–258.

This is not expressed as a without prejudice clause, unlike Article X(1). It uses the mandatory term 'shall', in the same way as substantive Articles III–VI. The term 'any obligation' is capable of applying to obligations arising under national law, e.g. those arising from a contract; indeed, it would normally be under its own law that a host State would assume obligations 'with regard to specific investments in its territory by investors of the other Contracting Party'. Interpreting the actual text of Article X(2), it would appear to say, and to say clearly, that each Contracting Party shall observe any legal obligation it has assumed, or will in the future assume, with regard to specific investments covered by the BIT. Article X(2) was adopted within the framework of the BIT, and has to be construed as intended to be effective within that framework.

116. The object and purpose of the BIT supports an effective interpretation of Article X(2). The BIT is a treaty for the promotion and reciprocal protection of investments. According to the preamble it is intended 'to create and maintain favourable conditions for investments by investors of one Contracting Party in the territory of the other'. It is legitimate to resolve uncertainties in its interpretation so as to favour the protection of covered investments.

...

127. To summarize, for present purposes Article X(2) includes commitments or obligations arising under contracts entered into by the host State. The basic obligation on the State in this case is the obligation to pay what is due under the contract, which is an obligation assumed with regard to the specific investment (the performance of services under the CISS Agreement). But this obligation does not mean that the determination of how much money the Philippines is obliged to pay becomes a treaty matter. The extent of the obligation is still governed by the contract, and it can only be determined by reference to the terms of the contract.

2.3 A Matter of Treaty Construction?

Then came *Noble Ventures v. Romania.* Article II(2)(c) of the US–Romania BIT of 1992 stated, again with added emphasis, that 'Each Party *shall observe any obligation it may have entered into* with regard to investments.' The tribunal looked to the ordinary meaning of the treaty language, and considered supplementary materials to be a useful means of confirming that meaning. Like the *SGS* v. *Philippines* tribunal, it too applied the principle of effectiveness, and just as with the *SGS* v. *Philippines* tribunal, the *Noble Ventures* tribunal observed the word 'shall' and considered that the phrase 'any obligations it may have entered into' could not be a reference to anything other than to such obligations which were contained in investment contracts with private parties. This was since States do not usually enter into inter-State investment agreements. The treaty reference to such contracts was specific because investment contracts are specific as to legal rights. The words 'entered into' also suggest an intention to include particular commitments, in comparison with the general commitments found in legislative acts. Put another way, the US–Romania umbrella clause resembled Lauterpacht's notion of an umbrella treaty commitment limited only to specific and identifiable undertakings, and while that clause broadened the scope of the original idea to include a variety of different agreements, at least it plainly intended to do so.

Noble Ventures v. *Romania*, ICSID Case No. ARB/01/11, Award, 12 October 2005 (Professor Karl–Heinz Böckstiegel, President; Sir Jeremy Lever QC; Professor Pierre-Marie Dupuy), paras 46–55 (original emphasis)

46. Considering that the Claimant's case comprises some claims which concern alleged breaches of contractual relationships purportedly concluded with the Respondent, the question for the Tribunal is whether Art. II(2)(c) BIT is an 'umbrella clause' that transforms contractual undertakings into international law obligations and accordingly makes it a breach of the BIT by the Respondent if it breaches a contractual obligation that it has entered into with the Claimant. Art. II(2)(c) reads as follows: '*Each Party shall observe any obligation it may have entered into with regard to investments.*'

47. As indicated by the parties, a similar question arose in other recent ICSID cases. Thus an important case to address the problem was *SGS Société Générale de Surveillance S.A. v. Islamic Republic of Pakistan* (ICSID Case No. ARB/01/13; *SGS v. Pakistan*), which was heavily relied on by the Respondent in the present case. The Tribunal was there concerned with Article 11 of an Agreement between the Swiss Confederation and the Islamic Republic of Pakistan on the Promotion and Reciprocal Protection of Investments (*Swiss–Pakistan BIT*) which reads as follows: '*Either Contracting Party shall constantly guarantee the observance of the commitments it has entered into with respect to the investments of the investors of the other Contracting Party.*' The Tribunal found that '*(T)he text itself of Art. 11 does not purport to state that breaches of contract alleged by an investor in relation to a contract it has concluded with a State (widely considered to be a matter of municipal rather than international law) are automatically "elevated" to the level of breaches of international treaty law. Considering the widely accepted principle with which we started, namely, that under general international law, a violation of a contract entered into by a State with an investor of another State, is not, by itself, a violation of international law, and considering further that the legal consequences that the Claimant would have us attribute to Art. 11 of the BIT are so far-reaching in scope, and so automatic and unqualified and sweeping in their operation, so burdensome in their potential impact upon a Contracting Party, we believe that clear and convincing evidence must be adduced by the Claimant that such was indeed the shared intent of the Contracting Parties to the Swiss–Pakistan Investment Protection Treaty in incorporating Article 11 in the BIT. We do not find such evidence in the text itself of Article 11. We have not been pointed to any other evidence of the putative common intent of the Contracting Parties by the Claimant*' (see paras. 166 and 167 of the Decision). Consequently, the Tribunal declined to regard Art. 11 as an umbrella clause.

48. Another important case to address the 'umbrella clause' problem was *SGS Société Générale de Surveillance S.A. v. Republic of the Philippines* (ICSID Case No. ARB/02/6; *SGS v. Philippines*). That case was referred to by the Claimant in the present case in support of its position. The relevant clause in that case (Art. X(2) of the Agreement between the Swiss Confederation and the Republic of the Philippines on the Promotion and Reciprocal Protection of Investments) reads as follows: '*Each Contracting Party shall observe any obligation it has assumed with regard to specific investments in its territory by investors of the other Contracting Party.*' The Tribunal interpreted the clause by reference to its wording and the object and purpose of the bilateral investment treaty so as to apply it to *inter alia* contractual obligations (paras. 115 and 116) and accordingly found that the contractual commitment was incorporated and brought within the framework of the bilateral investment treaty by Article X(2): '*To summarize, for present purposes Article X(2) includes commitments or obligations arising under contracts entered into by the host State*' (para. 127).

49. A third case concerned with a clause regarded by one of the parties to the dispute as an umbrella clause is *Salini Costruttori S.p.A. v. The Hashemite Kingdom of Jordan* (No. ARB/02/13; *Salini v. Jordan*). The case was decided only shortly before the end of the written proceedings in this case. In *Salini v. Jordan* the Tribunal was concerned with a clause in the bilateral investment treaty between Italy and Jordan which read as follows (Art. 2(4)): '*Each Contracting Party shall create and maintain in its territory a legal framework apt to guarantee the investors the continuity of legal treatment, including compliance, in good faith, of all undertakings assumed with regard to each specific investor.*' Regarding the terms of Art. 2(4) to be appreciably different from the provisions in *SGS v. Pakistan* and *SGS v. Philippines* the Tribunal found that '*(U)nder Art. 2(4), each contracting Party committed itself to create and maintain in its territory a "legal framework" favorable to investments. This legal framework must be apt to guarantee to investors the continuity of legal treatment. It must in particular be such as to ensure compliance of all undertakings assumed under relevant contracts with respect to each specific investor. But under Article 2(4), each contracting Party did not commit itself to "observe" any "obligation" it had previously assumed with regard to specific investments of the investor of the other party as did the Philippines. It did not even guarantee the observance of commitments it had entered into with respect to investments of the investors of the other Contracting Party as did Pakistan. It only committed itself to create and maintain a legal framework apt to guarantee the compliance of all undertakings assumed with regard to each specific investor.*'

50. With regard to Art. II(2)(c) of the bilateral investment treaty which is of relevance in the present case, it has to be observed that there are differences between the wording of the clause and the clauses in the other cases. Therefore, it is necessary, first, to interpret Art. II(2)(c) regardless of the other cases. In doing so, reference has to be made to Arts. 31 *et seq.* of the Vienna Convention on the Law of Treaties which reflect the customary international law concerning treaty interpretation. Accordingly, treaties have to be interpreted in good faith in accordance with the ordinary meaning to be given to the terms of the treaty in

their context and in the light of the object and purpose of the Treaty, while recourse may be had to supplementary means of interpretation, including the preparatory work and the circumstances of its conclusion, only in order to confirm the meaning resulting from the application of the aforementioned methods of interpretation. Reference should also be made to the principle of effectiveness (*effet utile*), which, too plays an important role in interpreting treaties.

51. Considering that Art. II(2)(c) BIT uses the term 'shall' and that it forms part of the Article which provides for the major substantial obligations undertaken by the parties, there can be no doubt that the Article was intended to create obligations, and obviously obligations beyond those specified in other provisions of the BIT itself. Since States usually do not conclude, with reference to specific investments, special international agreements in addition to existing bilateral investment treaties, it is difficult to understand the notion 'obligation' as referring to obligations undertaken under other 'international' agreements. And given that such agreements, if concluded, would also be subject to the general principle of *pacta sunt servanda*, there would certainly be no need for a clause of that kind. By contrast, in addition to the BIT, what are often concluded concerning investments are so-called investment contracts between investors and the host State. Such agreements describe specific rights and duties of the parties concerning a specific investment. Against this background, and considering the wording of Art. II(2)(c) which speaks of 'any obligation [a party] may have *entered into* with regard to *investments*', it is difficult not to regard this as a clear reference to investment contracts. In fact, one may ask what other obligations can the parties have had in mind as having been 'entered into' by a host State with regard to an investment. The employment of the notion 'entered into' indicates that specific commitments are referred to and not general commitments, for example by way of legislative acts. This is also the reason why Art. II(2)(c) would be very much an empty base unless understood as referring to contracts. Accordingly, the wording of Article II(2)(c) provides substantial support for an interpretation of Art. II(2)(c) as a real umbrella clause.

52. The object and purpose rule also supports such an interpretation. While it is not permissible, as is too often done regarding BITs, to interpret clauses exclusively in favour of investors, here such an interpretation is justified. Considering, as pointed out above, that any other interpretation would deprive Art. II(2)(c) of practical content, reference has necessarily to be made to the principle of effectiveness, also applied by other Tribunals in interpreting BIT provisions (see *SGS v. Philippines*, para. 116 and *Salini v. Jordan*, para. 95). An interpretation to the contrary would deprive the investor of any internationally secured legal remedy in respect of investment contracts that it has entered into with the host State. While it is not the purpose of investment treaties *per se* to remedy such problems, a clause that is readily capable of being interpreted in this way and which would otherwise be deprived of practical applicability is naturally to be understood as protecting investors also with regard to contracts with the host State generally in so far as the contract was entered into with regard to an investment.

53. An umbrella clause is usually seen as transforming municipal law obligations into obligations directly cognizable in international law. The Tribunal recalls the well established rule of general international law that in normal circumstances *per se* a breach of a contract by the State does not give rise to direct international responsibility on the part of the State. This derives from the clear distinction between municipal law on the one hand and international law on the other, two separate legal systems (or orders) the second of which treats the rules contained in the first as facts, as is reflected in *inter alia* Article Three of the International Law Commission's Articles on State Responsibility adopted in 2001. As stated by Judge Schwebel, former President of the International Court of Justice, 'it is generally accepted that, so long as it affords remedies in its Courts, a State is only directly responsible, on the international plane, for acts involving breaches of contract, where the breach is not a simple breach … but involves an obviously arbitrary or tortious element … ' (in *International Arbitration: Three Salient Problems* (1987), at 111). It may be further added that, inasmuch as a breach of contract at the municipal level creates at the same time the violation of one of the principles existing either in customary international law or in treaty law applicable between the host State and the State of the nationality of the investor, it will give rise to the international responsibility of the host State. But that responsibility will co-exist with the responsibility created in municipal law and each of them will remain valid independently of the other, a situation that further reflects the respective autonomy of the two legal systems (municipal and international) each one with regard to the other.

54. That being said, none of the above mentioned general rules is peremptory in nature. This means that, when negotiating a bilateral investment treaty, two States may create within the scope of their mutual agreement an exception to the rules deriving from the autonomy of municipal law, on the one hand and public international law, on the other hand. In other words, two States may include in a bilateral investment treaty a provision to the effect that, in the interest of achieving the objects and goals of the treaty, the host State may incur international responsibility by reason of a breach of its contractual obligations towards the private investor of the other Party, the breach of contract being thus 'internationalized', i.e. assimilated to a breach of the treaty. In such a case, an international tribunal will be bound to seek to give useful effect to the provision that the parties have adopted.

55. Thus, an umbrella clause, when included in a bilateral investment treaty, introduces an exception to the general separation of States obligations under municipal and under international law. In consequence, as with any other exception to established general rules of law, the identification of a provision as an 'umbrella clause' can as a consequence proceed only from a strict, if not indeed restrictive, interpretation of its terms and, more generally, in accordance with the well known customary rules codified under Article 31 of the Vienna Convention of the Law of Treaties (1969). As was stated by the International Court of Justice in the *ELSI* Case:

> 'an important principle of international law should not be held to have been tacitly dispensed with by international agreement, in the absence of words making clear an intention to do so': *Elettronica Sicula Spa – ELSI – United States* v. *Italy*, 1989, ICJ 15 at 42.

The *Noble Ventures* tribunal then went on to analyse the precise wording of treaty umbrella clauses in past disputes. In addition to the clauses in the Switzerland–Pakistan and Philippines–Switzerland BITs, the tribunal referred to the wording of the Italy–Jordan BIT, which was considered in *Salini* v. *Jordan*.[9]

Noble Ventures v. Romania, ICSID Case No. ARB/01/11, Award, 12 October 2005 (Professor Karl-Heinz Böckstiegel, President; Sir Jeremy Lever QC; Professor Pierre-Marie Dupuy), paras 56–62 (original emphasis)

56. In the present case, in order to identify the intention of the United States and Romania when they negotiated Art. II(2)(c) of the BIT, a key element is provided by the exact formulation of that provision. Indeed, it is the differences in the wording of Art. II(2)(c) of the BIT and of provisions in other bilateral investment treaties that have been relied on as umbrella clauses in other ICSID cases that go far to explain the different positions taken by different ICSID tribunals that have in recent times had to consider such clauses.

57. In *Salini v. Jordan, supra*, it is evident that the obligation laid down at Art. 2(4) of the bilateral investment treaty between Italy and Jordan plainly justifies the conclusion reached by the Tribunal. A provision creating and maintaining a 'legal framework' favourable to investment deals only with the setting of norms and establishment of institutions aimed at facilitating investment by investors of the other Party; it does not entail that each Party becomes responsible under international law for the breach of any of its contractual obligations *vis-à-vis* the private investors of the other Party.

58. In *SGS v. Pakistan, supra*, the relevant provision of the bilateral investment treaty (Art. 11) does not simply speak of a 'legal framework'; and the provision could be interpreted as laying down a kind of general obligation for the host State as a public authority to facilitate foreign investment, namely an obligation to 'guarantee' the observance of the commitments that the host State has entered into towards investors of the other Party, being an obligation to be implemented by, in particular, the adoption of steps and measures under its own municipal law to safeguard the guarantee. In other words, the formulation of Art. 11 of the bilateral investment treaty in *SGS v. Pakistan, supra*, may be interpreted as implicitly setting an international obligation of result for each Party to be fulfilled through appropriate means at the municipal level but without necessarily elevating municipal law obligations to international ones.

59. By contrast, in *SGS v. Philippines, supra*, the treaty clause was formulated so as to assimilate the host State's contractual obligations to its treaty obligations under the bilateral investment treaty by saying that each Party 'shall observe any obligation it has assumed' with regard to investments made by the investors of the other Party. It is then understandable that, without necessarily having recourse to completely different reasoning, the Tribunal in that case reached a position different from that adopted in *SGS v. Pakistan, supra*.

---

[9] *Salini v. Jordan*, ICSID Case No. ARB/02/13, Decision on Jurisdiction, 9 November 2004.

60. In the present case, the formulation adopted at Art. II(2)(c), which is even more general and straightforward than that in the bilateral investment treaty that fell to be considered in *SGS v. Philippines*, clearly falls into the category of the most general and direct formulations tending to an assimilation of contractual obligations to treaty ones; not only does it use the term 'shall observe' but it refers in the most general terms to 'any' obligations that either Party may have entered into 'with regard to investments'.

61. However, it is unnecessary for the Tribunal to express any definitive conclusion as to whether therefore, despite the consequences of the exceptional nature of umbrella clauses, referred to at paragraph 55 above, Art. II(2)(c) of the BIT perfectly assimilates to breach of the BIT *any* breach by the host State of *any* contractual obligation as determined by its municipal law *or* whether the expression 'any obligation', despite its apparent breadth, must be understood to be subject to some limitation in the light of the nature and objects of the BIT. Since, on the facts of the present case, as will appear from what follows, the Tribunal's ultimate conclusions would not be affected one way or the other by the resolution of that question, the Tribunal proceeds on the basis that, in including Art. II(2)(c) in the BIT, the Parties had as their aim to equate contractual obligations governed by municipal law to international treaty obligations as established in the BIT.

62. By reason therefore of the inclusion of Art. II(2)(c) in the BIT, the Tribunal therefore considers the Claimant's claims of breach of contract on the basis that any such breach constitutes a breach of the BIT.

2.4 The Spectre of 'the Two SGS Arbitrations' Lurks

Nonetheless, the tension between the two approaches taken in *SGS* v. *Pakistan* and *SGS* v. *Philippines* continues to exert an important influence. The tribunal in the subsequent dispute in *El Paso* v. *Argentina* demonstrates the continued presence of the more restrictive view taken in *SGS* v. *Pakistan*, and so the controversy remains very much alive.

El Paso Energy International Co. v. Argentina, ICSID Case No. ARB/03/15, Decision on Objections to Jurisdiction, 27 April 2006 (Professor Lucius Caflisch, President; Professor Brigitte Stern; Professor Piero Bernadini), paras 76–77 (original emphasis)

76. This Tribunal should like to stress, on the contrary, that the interpretation given in *SGS v. Philippines* does not only deprive one single provision of far-reaching consequences but renders the whole Treaty completely useless: indeed, if this interpretation were to be followed – the violation of *any legal obligation* of a State, and not only of any contractual obligation with respect to investment, is a violation of the BIT, whatever the source of the obligation and whatever the seriousness of the breach – it would be sufficient to include a so-called 'umbrella clause' and a dispute settlement mechanism, and no other articles

setting standards for the protection of foreign investments in any BIT. If any violation of any legal obligation of a State is *ipso facto* a violation of the treaty, then that violation needs not amount to a violation of the high standards of the treaty of 'fair and equitable treatment' or 'full protection and security'. Apart from this general and very important remark, the Tribunal also wishes to point to the fact that quite contradictory conclusions have been drawn by the Tribunal in *SGS v. Philippines*: among other things, the Tribunal stated that, although the umbrella clause transforms the contract claims into treaty claims, first 'it does not convert the issue of the *extent* or *content* of such obligations into an issue of international law' (Decision, § 128, original emphasis), which means that the 'contract claims/treaty claims' should be assessed according to the national law of the contract and not the treaty standards, and, second, that the umbrella clause does not 'override specific and exclusive dispute settlement arrangements made in the investment contract itself' (Decision, § 134), which explains that the Tribunal has suspended its proceedings until the 'contract claims/treaty claims would be decided by the national courts in accordance with the dispute settlement provisions of the contract', stating that 'the Tribunal should not exercise its jurisdiction over a contractual claim when the parties have already agreed on how such a claim is to be resolved, and have done so exclusively' (Decision, § 155). In other words, the Tribunal asserts that a treaty claim should not be analysed according to treaty standards, which seems quite strange, and that it has jurisdiction over the contract claims/treaty claims, but at the same time that it does not really have such jurisdiction – until the contract claims are decided. This controversy has been going on ever since these two contradictory decisions.

The *El Paso* tribunal was therefore critical of the tribunal in *SGS* v. *Philippines* for giving so wide a scope and effect to the treaty clause as would coincide with the scope of the contractual breach itself while, at the same time refusing to analyse the contractual breach simply as a treaty breach. It was also troubled by the question of the forum selected under the contract.

One thing is clear. Investment tribunals are not prevented from analysing contractual claims as such. An investment tribunal can undertake contractual analysis if the parties have given the tribunal the mandate to do so. In the absence of such party agreement, various institutional rules (e.g. ICSID, UNCITRAL) accord the tribunal the discretion to apply domestic contract law either directly, or subsequent to the tribunal's application of the choice-of-law rules of the appropriate domestic legal system.[10] Thus, the real difficulty is not to do with the scope of the investment tribunal's jurisdiction, but rather the need to resolve the conflict of jurisdiction between the contractually selected forum and the investment tribunal.

---

[10] A. K. Bjorklund, 'Applicable Law in International Investment Disputes' in C. Giorgetti (ed.), *Litigating International Investment Disputes: A Practitioner's Guide* (Leiden: Martinus Nijhoff, 2014), 261, 271–272. Consent to these rules therefore amounts to consent to the tribunal's application of domestic laws.

El Paso Energy International Co. v. Argentina, ICSID Case No. ARB/03/15, Decision on Objections to Jurisdiction, 27 April 2006 (Professor Lucius Caflisch, President; Professor Brigitte Stern; Professor Piero Bernadini), para. 77 (original emphasis)

Some have adopted the *SGS v. Philippines* position but not drawn the same consequences from it. Thus, in *Eureko B. V. v. Poland* (Partial Award of 19 August, 2005), the Tribunal, presided by Mr. Yves Fortier, accepted the idea that, as a result of the umbrella clause in the BIT – Article 3(5) of the BIT provided that '[e]ach Contracting Party shall observe any obligation it may have entered into with regard to investors of the other Contracting Party' –, the smallest obligation of a State with regard to investments was protected by the BIT and could give rise to an ICSID obligation. This decision was, however, accompanied by a strong dissent of the arbitrator Rajski, who emphasised the systemic consequences a broad interpretation of so-called 'umbrella clauses' could entail:

> 'It is worth to note that by opening a wide door to foreign parties to commercial contracts concluded with a State owned company to switch their contractual disputes from normal jurisdiction of international commercial arbitration tribunals or state courts to BIT Tribunals, the majority of this Tribunal has created a potentially dangerous precedent capable of producing negative effects on the further development of foreign capital participation in privatizations of State owned companies' (Dissenting Opinion, § 11).

In *Noble Ventures Inc. v. Romania* (above, § 69), the Tribunal, presided by Professor Bockstiegel, followed the same line of reasoning, stating quite generally that '[a]n umbrella clause is usually seen as transforming municipal law obligations into obligations directly cognizable in international law' (Award, § 53). The Tribunal, while it considered the umbrella clause as an exception to the 'well established rule of general international law that in normal circumstances *per se* a breach of a contract by the State does not give rise to direct international responsibility on the part of the State', certainly did not interpret that exception restrictively, as exceptions should be interpreted, although it mentioned the necessity theoretically to adopt such an interpretation when it stated: 'as with any other exception to established general rules of law, the identification of a provision as an umbrella clause can as a consequence proceed only from a strict, if not indeed restrictive, interpretation of its terms' (Decision, § 55). In the words used by the Tribunal in *Noble Ventures Inc. v. Romania*, the breach of a contract being assimilated by the umbrella clause to a breach of the BIT, is thus 'internationalized' (Decision, § 54). Again, the problem faced by such reasoning, according to this Tribunal, is that, by necessary implication, *all municipal law commitments* must necessarily be as well '*internationalised*', as the so-called umbrella clause does not differentiate among obligations; it refers to *any* obligation and not specifically to *contractual* obligations, the consequence being that the division between the national legal order and the international legal order is completely blurred. One of the arguments presented by the ICSID Tribunal in *Noble Ventures* was that the 'elevation' theory was prompted by the object and purpose of the BIT, and that '[a]n interpretation to the contrary would deprive the investor of any internationally secured legal remedy in respect of investment contracts that it has entered into with the host State' (Decision, § 52). In this Tribunal's opinion, this is not a good reason, and it can explain why. Either the foreign investor has a commercial contract with an autonomous State entity or it has an investment agreement with the State, in which some 'clauses exorbitantes du droit commun' are inserted. In both cases, it is more than likely that the foreign investor will have managed to insert a dispute settlement mechanism into the contract; usually, in a purely commercial contract, that mechanism will be commercial arbitration or the national courts, while in an investment agreement it will generally be an international arbitration mechanism such as that of ICSID. In other words, in the so-called State contracts, there is usually an 'internationally secured legal remedy', while in the mere commercial contracts governed by national law, there is no reason why such a mechanism should be available, as stated by Judge Schwebel, when he said that 'it is generally accepted that, so long as it affords remedies in its Courts, a State is only directly responsible, on the international plane, for acts involving breaches of contract, where the breach is not a simple breach ... but involves an obviously arbitrary or tortious element ... ' (*International Arbitration: Three Salient Problems*, Cambridge, Cambridge University Press, 1987, p. 111).

2.5 Distinguishing Treaty Law from Contract Law

It need hardly be added that, in particular cases, the contract may not fall within the scope of the umbrella clause at all.[11] Where the contract does do this, however, tribunals continue to be haunted by the spectre of the internationalisation of contractual commitments wholesale by treaty. Arguably, the unfortunate metaphors of transformation, 'mirror effect' and elevation have done a disservice to clarity of thought. Whether any breach of the underlying contract will automatically amount to a treaty breach, or whether a treaty breach occurs only where there has also been a non-simple breach of the contract involving an 'obviously arbitrary or tortious element',[12] what role if any remains for contractual analysis? Once it is accepted that the investment tribunal may have the jurisdiction to address contractual claims, nothing prevents either (1) the idea that treaty clauses could make contractual disputes breaches of treaty violation, or (2) that in determining whether there has been a treaty breach or following such a finding the investment tribunal could – indeed, should in particular cases – perform a contractual analysis. In *SGS* v. *Philippines*,[13] the tribunal stated that the treaty breach 'does not mean that the

---

[11] In *WNC Factoring Ltd* v. *The Czech Republic*, PCA Case No. 2014–34, Award, 22 February 2017 (Dr Gavan Griffith QC, President; Professor Robert Volterra; Judge James Crawford), the tribunal considered that there was a requirement of privity under the proper law of the contract. Since the share purchase agreement was not concluded between the claimant and the Czech Republic but rather through a subsidiary, the tribunal had no jurisdiction under the umbrella clause. That clause required the existence of a specific, clear and direct commitment by the Czech Republic to the benefit of the claimant.

[12] S. Schwebel, *International Arbitration: Three Salient Problems* (Cambridge University Press, 1987), 111, cited by the tribunal in *El Paso Energy International Co.* v. *Argentina*, Decision on Objections to Jurisdiction, para. 77.

[13] *SGS* v. *Philippines*, para. 127.

determination of how much money the Philippines is obliged to pay [also] becomes a treaty matter' since '[t]he extent of the obligation is still governed by the contract, and it can only be determined by reference to the terms of the contract'.

The following extracts also illustrate the need in other kinds of cases to bear in mind the distinction between treaty and contract. It is in this regard that the idea of a complete assimilation of the two, the ideas of a 'transformation' of the contractual obligations or a 'mirror effect' may fail to capture situations such as in *Compañia de Aguas del Aconquija SA and Vivendi Universal* v. *Argentina*, excerpted below, where the contract says one thing but the treaty says another. The short extract from *CMS Gas Transmission Co.* v. *Argentina* which follows is a further reminder that tribunals have treated the obligations under contract as well as the governing or proper law of the contract as being unchanged.[14]

Compañia de Aguas del Aconquija SA and Vivendi Universal v. Argentina, ICSID Case No. ARB/97/3, Decision on Annulment, 3 July 2002 (Mr L. Yves Fortier, CC, QC, President; Professor James R. Crawford, SC, FBA; Professor José Carlos Fernández Rozas), paras 95–97 (footnote omitted)

95. As to the relation between breach of contract and breach of treaty in the present case, it must be stressed that Articles 3 and 5 of the BIT do not relate directly to breach of a municipal contract. Rather they set an independent standard. A state may breach a treaty without breaching a contract, and vice versa, and this is certainly true of these provisions of the BIT. The point is made clear in Article 3 of the ILC Articles, which is entitled 'Characterization of an act of a State as internationally wrongful':

> The characterization of an act of a State as internationally wrongful is governed by international law. Such characterization is not affected by the characterization of the same act as lawful by internal law.

96. In accordance with this general principle (which is undoubtedly declaratory of general international law), whether there has been a breach of the BIT and whether there has been a breach of contract are different questions. Each of these claims will be determined by reference to its own proper or applicable law – in the case of the BIT, by international law; in the case of the Concession Contract, by the proper law of the contract, in other words, the law of Tucumán. For example, in the case of a claim based on a treaty, international law rules of attribution apply, with the result that the state of Argentina is internationally responsible for the acts of its provincial authorities. By contrast, the state of Argentina is not liable for the performance of contracts entered into by Tucumán, which possesses separate legal personality under its own law and is responsible for the performance of its own contracts.

---

[14] See again *El Paso Energy International Co.* v. *Argentina*, para. 76, discussing *SGS* v. *Philippines*.

97. The distinction between the role of international and municipal law in matters of international responsibility is stressed in the commentary to Article 3 of the ILC Articles, which reads in relevant part as follows:

(4) The International Court has often referred to and applied the principle. For example in the Reparation for Injuries case, it noted that '[a]s the claim is based on the breach of an international obligation on the part of the Member held responsible ... the Member cannot contend that this obligation is governed by municipal law'. In the *ELSI* case, a Chamber of the Court emphasized this rule, stating that:

'Compliance with municipal law and compliance with the provisions of a treaty are different questions. What is a breach of treaty may be lawful in the municipal law and what is unlawful in the municipal law may be wholly innocent of violation of a treaty provision. Even had the Prefect held the requisition to be entirely justified in Italian law, this would not exclude the possibility that it was a violation of the FCN Treaty.'

Conversely, as the Chamber explained:

'... the fact that an act of a public authority may have been unlawful in municipal law does not necessarily mean that that act was unlawful in international law, as a breach of treaty or otherwise. A finding of the local courts that an act was unlawful may well be relevant to an argument that it was also arbitrary; but by itself, and without more, unlawfulness cannot be said to amount to arbitrariness ... Nor does it follow from a finding by a municipal court that an act was unjustified, or unreasonable, or arbitrary, that that act is necessarily to be classed as arbitrary in international law, though the qualification given to the impugned act by a municipal authority may be a valuable indication.'

...

(7) The rule that the characterization of conduct as unlawful in international law cannot be affected by the characterization of the same act as lawful in internal law makes no exception for cases where rules of international law require a State to conform to the provisions of its internal law, for instance by applying to aliens the same legal treatment as to nationals. It is true that in such a case, compliance with internal law is relevant to the question of international responsibility. But this is because the rule of international law makes it relevant, e.g. by incorporating the standard of compliance with internal law as the applicable international standard or as an aspect of it. Especially in the fields of injury to aliens and their property and of human rights, the content and application of internal law will often be relevant to the question of international responsibility. In every case it will be seen on analysis that either the provisions of internal law are relevant as facts in applying the applicable international standard, or else that they are actually incorporated in some form, conditionally or unconditionally, into that standard.

> **CMS Gas Transmission Co. v. Argentina, ICSID Case No. ARB/01/8, Decision on Annulment, 25 September 2007 (Judge Gilbert Guillaume, President; Judge Nabil Elaraby; Professor James R. Crawford), para. 95(c)**
>
> The effect of the umbrella clause is not to transform the obligation which is relied upon into something else; the content of the obligation is unaffected, as is its proper law.

2.6 Forum Selection Clauses

What then of the contractual forum selection clause? Were it not given effect where effect is given to the investor–State arbitration provision in the treaty, the host State would lose its ability to choose between commercial and investment arbitration, whereas the investor would still be granted that choice. Here lies a troublesome asymmetry of rights and obligations.

In *SGS* v. *Philippines*, the tribunal had upheld the umbrella clause, while also upholding the contract's forum selection clause. The *SGS* v. *Philippines* tribunal explained that the BIT arbitration clause did not refer to any specific investment or contract. However, the contractual forum selection clause did and was therefore to be treated as *lex specialis*.[15] This was criticised in *El Paso*, in which the tribunal assumed the answer to its own question by asking how the contractual forum selection clause could operate where the umbrella clause had already 'overridden' the contract.[16] The dissenting arbitrator in *SGS* v. *Philippines*, Professor Crivellaro, had his own answer to this – the BIT had been concluded after the contract, and therefore it had expanded the rights of the investor by giving the investor the right to elect a choice of forum in addition to the options stipulated in the contractual forum selection clause.[17] Yet, if we might so suggest, the umbrella clause could also have created a *renvoi* by directing the tribunal to the contractual forum selection clause.[18] Both the Crivellaro and *renvoi* solutions can be applied together where the contract is concluded before the BIT.

***

Umbrella clauses lend themselves, it appears, to at least four different approaches. First, umbrella clauses do not elevate contractual obligations to the international plane regardless of the wording of an applicable umbrella clause. They have, if at all, a negligible effect on investment protection. Second, umbrella clauses do confer concrete protection

---

[15] *SGS* v. *Philippines*, para. 141.
[16] *El Paso* v. *Argentina*, para. 76. See also Wong, 'Umbrella Clauses in BITS', 137, 156 et seq.
[17] Declaration by Arbitrator Crivellaro, 29 January 2004, paras 2–4, 10.
[18] In other words, if the treaty clause, properly interpreted, points to the application of the forum selection clause by way of *renvoi*, or if on its plain meaning the umbrella clause is taken not to have been intended to interfere with the contractual balance between the investor and the host State, thus presenting both the option of forum selection. The fear of an expansion of the scope of treaty commitments remains and this view could be treated as just another species of internationalisation. Conceptually, it is different from the elevation or internationalisation theory because it would still require the tribunal to engage in a contractual analysis.

without any element of 'internationalisation'. Their effect is subtle, but not negligible, entailing the adjudication of a dispute by an investment treaty tribunal in accordance with the applicable law, which can also be domestic law. Third, umbrella clauses have whatever effect the ordinary meaning of an applicable umbrella clause conveys. If this ordinary meaning, ascertained in accordance with the usual canons of treaty interpretation, points to the internationalisation of contractual obligations, then this is the effect that umbrella clauses should have. Fourth, the practical effect of an umbrella clause could depend upon the existence of a forum selection clause in the underlying contract. When a claimant bound by a contractual forum selection clause elects to bring a claim for the breach of an umbrella clause, the umbrella clause could point to the application of the forum selection clause as the *lex specialis*. The criticism would be that this robs the umbrella clause of its effect, but there is no reason to think this an objectionable outcome at least where the forum selection clause is contained in a contract which is concluded after the treaty.

3. EXAMPLES OF UMBRELLA CLAUSES

In the Abs–Shawcross Draft Convention on Investments Abroad, named after Hermann Abs and Lord Shawcross, the formulation read as follows:

Draft Convention on Investments Abroad, 1959, Article II

Each Contracting party shall at all times ensure the observance of any undertakings which it may have given in relation to investment made by nationals of any other party.

The Abs–Shawcross formulation has been repeated in various guises. Here are but a few examples.

United Kingdom–Argentina BIT, 11 December 1990, Art. 2(2)

Each Contracting Party shall observe any obligation it may have entered into with regard to the investments of investors of the other Contracting Party.

United States–Argentina BIT, 14 November 1991, Art. II(2)(c)

Each Party shall observe any obligation it may have entered into with regard to investments.

However, there are umbrella clauses that clearly do not follow the Abs–Shawcross formulation. Therefore, one is at least reminded that it pays to take note of the language of the specific treaty clause. The following examples suffice.

Italy–Jordan BIT, 21 July 1996, Art. 2(4)

Each Contracting party shall create and maintain in its territory a legal framework apt to guarantee to investors the continuity of treatment, including the compliance, in good faith, of all obligations assumed with regard to each specific investor.

Doubt has correctly been expressed as to whether the example of the Italy–Jordan BIT has the same legal effect as the Abs–Shawcross formulation and UK–Argentina BIT examples above.[19] A more complex example is the 'umbrella clause' used currently by the United States.

2012 US Model BIT, Arts 1, 24, 26, 30

Article 1: Definitions

...

'investment agreement' means a written agreement between a national authority of a Party and a covered investment or an investor of the other Party, on which the covered investment or the investor relies in establishing or acquiring a covered investment other than the written agreement itself, that grants rights to the covered investment or investor:
  (a) with respect to natural resources that a national authority controls, such as for their exploration, extraction, refining, transportation, distribution, or sale;
  (b) to supply services to the public on behalf of the Party, such as power generation or distribution, water treatment or distribution, or telecommunications; or
  (c) to undertake infrastructure projects, such as the construction of roads, bridges, canals, dams, or pipelines, that are not for the exclusive or predominant use and benefit of the government.

...

Article 24: Submission of a Claim to Arbitration
1. In the event that a disputing party considers that an investment dispute cannot be settled by consultation and negotiation:
  (a) The claimant, on its own behalf, may submit to arbitration under this Section a claim
      (i) That the respondent has breached

          ...

          (C) an investment agreement;

      ...

Provided that a claimant may submit pursuant to subparagraph (a)(i)(C) ... a claim for breach of an investment agreement only if the subject matter of the claim and the claimed damages directly relate to the covered investment that was established or acquired, or sought to be established or acquired, in reliance on the relevant investment agreement.[20]
...

Article 26: Conditions and Limitations on Consent of Each Party

...

2. No claim may be submitted to arbitration under this Section unless:
  (a) The notice of arbitration is accompanied,
      (i) For claims submitted to arbitration under Article 24(1)(a), by the claimant's written waiver

---

[19] See the *Noble Ventures* Award.
[20] [Eds: There are equivalent provisions in Art. 24(1)(b) for claims by a claimant 'on behalf of an enterprise of the respondent that is a juridical person that the claimant owns or controls directly or indirectly'.]

...

of any right to initiate or continue before any administrative tribunal or court under the law of either Party, or other dispute settlement procedures, any proceeding with respect to any measure alleged to constitute a breach referred to in Article 24.

...

Article 30: Governing Law

...

2. Subject to paragraph 3 and the other terms of this Section, when a claim is submitted under Article 24(1)(a)(i)(B) or (C), or Article 24(1)(b)(i)(B) or (C), the tribunal shall apply:
   (a) the rules of law specified in the pertinent investment authorization or investment agreement, or as the disputing parties may otherwise agree; or
   (b) if the rules of law have not been specified or otherwise agreed:
      (i) the law of the respondent, including its rules on the conflict of laws; and
      (ii) such rules of international law as may be applicable.

Finally, there are examples of clauses which have attempted to narrow down the seemingly wide effect of umbrella clauses. The example of the Greece–Mexico BIT excerpted below narrows the clause down to commitments in writing, and also pre-empts uncertainty over the application of a contractual forum selection clause. The examples that follow demonstrate an attempt to achieve the latter objective.

Greece–Mexico BIT, 30 November 2000, Art. 19(2)

Each Contracting party shall observe any other obligation it may have entered into in writing, with regard to the specific investment of an investor of the other Contracting Party. The disputes arising from such obligations shall be settled only under the terms and conditions of the respective contract.

Germany–Pakistan BIT, 1 December 2009, Art. 7(2)

Each Contracting Party shall observe any obligation it has assumed with regard to investments in its territory by investors of the other Contracting State, with disputes arising from such obligations being redressed under the terms of the contracts underlying the obligations.

Trans-Pacific Partnership Agreement 2016, Annex 9-L(A), Agreements with selected international arbitration clauses[21]

1. An investor of a Party may not submit to arbitration a claim for breach of an investment agreement under Article 9.19.1(a)(i)(C) (Submission of a Claim to Arbitration) or Article 9.19.1(b)(i)(C) if the investment agreement provides the respondent's consent for the investor to arbitrate the alleged breach of the investment agreement and further provides that:

---

[21] Not in force, and the Trump Administration has since withdrawn the United States' signature. Except for Annex 9-L(A), the TPP's umbrella clause provisions resemble Arts 1, 24.1(a)(i)(C) and 30.2 of the 2012 US Model BIT. See TPP Arts 9.1, 9.19.1(a)(i)(C) and 9.25.2 but compare Annex 9-L(A) with Art. 26 of the Model BIT.

(a) a claim may be submitted for breach of the investment agreement under at least one of the following alternatives:

   (i) the ICSID Convention and the ICSID Rules of Procedure for Arbitration Proceedings, provided that both the respondent and the Party of the investor are parties to the ICSID Convention;

   (ii) the ICSID Additional Facility Rules, provided that either the respondent or the Party of the investor is a party to the ICSID Convention;

   (iii) the UNCITRAL Arbitration Rules;

   (iv) the ICC Arbitration Rules; or

   (v) the LCIA Arbitration Rules; and

(b) in the case of arbitration not under the ICSID Convention, the legal place of the arbitration shall be:

   (i) in the territory of a State that is party to the New York Convention; and

   (ii) outside the territory of the respondent.

CONCLUSION

Given the potentially sweeping nature of umbrella clauses, there have been various attempts to limit their potential scope and effect. There have been attempts to:

(1) distinguish between commercial and investment commitments, such that only investment commitments, strictly construed, are said to attract the protection of an umbrella clause;[22]

(2) distinguish between the acts of the host State in its sovereign as opposed to its commercial capacity, the argument being that a commercial act does not involve the host State–investor relationship and cannot therefore breach an umbrella clause;[23]

(3) require breach of another, substantive treaty obligation (for example, the fair and equitable treatment standard) as opposed to treatment of a mere breach of the underlying private law obligation as being in any way sufficient;[24]

(4) invoke the doctrine of privity of contract so that host States can be held to account only for breaches of contractual obligations to which they are party.[25]

---

[22] *Joy Mining* v. *Egypt*, ICSID Case No. ARB/03/11, Award on Jurisdiction, 6 August 2004, paras 78–82.

[23] *Impregilo* v. *Pakistan*, ICSID Case No. ARB/03/3, Decision on Jurisdiction, 22 April 2005, para. 260; see also *CMS Gas Transmission Co.* v. *Argentina*, ICSID Case No. ARB/01/8, Award, 12 May 2005, paras 299–303. The Award was subsequently annulled. The view that a distinction between sovereign and merchant acts can be drawn in this way has not been universally accepted by any means, and was rejected in *SGS Société Générale de Surveillance* v. *Paraguay*, ICSID Case No. ARB/07/29, Decision on Jurisdiction, 12 February 2010, paras 164, 167–168.

[24] The suggestion that fair and equitable treatment clauses may operate as de facto umbrella clauses is related: see I. A. Laird, B. Sahabi, F. G. Sourgens, *et al.*, 'International Investment Law and Arbitration: 2012 in Review' in A. K. Bjorklund (ed.), *Yearbook of International Investment Law and Policy 2012–2013* (Oxford University Press, 2014), 109, 150; see also *El Paso Energy International Co.* v. *Argentina*, ICSID Case No. ARB/03/15, Decision on Jurisdiction, 27 April 2006, paras 82, 84.

[25] N. Gallus, 'An Umbrella Just for Two? BIT Obligations Observance Clauses and the Parties to a Contract' (2008) 24 *Arb Int'l* 157, 159–161.

A more direct way of limiting any tendency of tribunals to treat umbrella clauses as tools of internationalisation is for States to be explicit about what the intended effect of the clause is when concluding investment treaties. Notice, however, that while the original concerns expressed by the *SGS* v. *Pakistan* tribunal had less to do with any deficiency in the treaty clause and more to do with the tribunal's fears about the potentially wide scope and effect of the clause, the tribunal had also stated that had there been clear and convincing evidence that an umbrella clause was what the treaty parties truly intended, the outcome might have been different. More drastically, States can leave out umbrella clauses altogether. It was observed in the 2015 World Investment Report that many recent investment treaties do not contain umbrella clauses.[26]

QUESTIONS

1. Do umbrella clauses elevate every contractual obligation onto the international plane? Do such clauses create Gaillard's 'mirror effect' on the international treaty plane in respect of every contractual obligation?
2. If so, would that entail a breach of treaty for any breach of the underlying contract?
3. If not, what kinds of contractual breach in light of the existence of an umbrella clause would occasion a treaty violation?
4. To what extent can the conflicting jurisprudence be explained by differences in the language of specific umbrella clauses?
5. Does a forum selection clause in the underlying contract fall away if the claimant, inconsistently with that clause, wishes to bring an investment treaty claim instead?

SUGGESTIONS FOR FURTHER READING

1. E. Gaillard, 'Treaty-Based Jurisdiction: Broad Dispute Resolution Clauses' (2005) 234(68) *New York LJ* 1.
2. A. C. Sinclair, 'The Umbrella Clause Debate' in A. K. Bjorklund, I. A. Laird and S. Ripinsky (eds), *Investment Treaty Law – Current Issues III* (London: BIICL, 2009), 275.
3. C. L. Lim, 'Is the Umbrella Clause Not Just Another Treaty Clause?' in C. L. Lim (ed.), *Alternative Visions of the International Law on Foreign Investment: Essays in Honour of Muthucumaraswamy Sornarajah* (Cambridge University Press, 2016), 349.

---

[26] UN Conference on Trade and Development (UNCTAD), 'World Investment Report 2015 – Reforming International Investment Governance', 25 June 2015, 113.

16

Defences

CHAPTER OUTLINE

This chapter addresses defences in investment protection law. Section 1 introduces the concept and delineates its boundaries. Section 2 discusses defences that are expressed or necessarily implicit in investment protection obligations, illustrated by the case study of indirect expropriation. Section 3 addresses defences that are drafted as exceptions. It discusses both the much-litigated non-precluded-measures clause in the US–Argentina Bilateral Investment Treaty (BIT) and general exceptions included in the newest generation of investment treaties. Section 4 considers circumstances precluding wrongfulness in law of State responsibility. It addresses in greater detail three circumstances that have played a role in the practice of investment arbitration: consent (Section 4.1), countermeasures (Section 4.2) and necessity (Section 4.3).

INTRODUCTION

The first investment treaty arbitrations in the 1990s drew attention to a previously perhaps unappreciated puzzle: how is the balance struck between competing interests in international investment law? Vaughan Lowe posed the question in the following terms in an important early article: how should we draw the line between legitimate regulatory measures and illegitimate interference with the rights and interests of investors?

V. Lowe, 'Regulation or Expropriation?' (2002) 55 *Current Legal Problems* 447, 450

BITs, like most treaties, represent a balance between competing interests. The balance here, however, is not between the interests of the signatories, the two States Parties. Rather, it is between the host State and the investors, individual and corporate, who are nationals of the other State.

...

States are simply required to treat investments fairly; and that requirement by no means deprives the host State of the right to exercise its regulatory powers.

One of the elements of the puzzle is that investment protection obligations, at least of the type usually concluded in the 1990s, were quite explicit in articulating obligations that, reflecting interests of investors, bound host States. It was less obvious where rules reflecting interests of host States were expressed. Rules on fair and equitable treatment, full protection and security, expropriation and national treatment (discussed in Chapters 12 to 14) were usually articulated without rule-specific exceptions, and treaties rarely provided for general exceptions either.

If investment law is put in the comparative perspective with other regimes of international law that discipline the behaviour of States regarding individuals, the contrast is clear. The European Convention on Human Rights, Article 6, and Article 1 of Protocol 1, which are sometimes described as functionally analogous to investment obligations on denial of justice,[1] expropriation, and fair and equitable treatment, are drafted in a very different manner. The European Court of Human Rights has identified implied limitations within particular rights, and rights overall may be subject to derogations in accordance with Article 15 of the European Convention on Human Rights. The General Agreement on Tariffs and Trade (GATT), which is again sometimes described as a comparable regime of international economic law, provides for general exceptions in Article XX and security exceptions in Article XXI.[2] Why is investment protection law different?

The first and the broadest response is, that to focus on the treaty instrument is to not see the wood for the trees, without appreciating issues properly governed by municipal law and (as shown in the excerpt below) the broader legal order(s) within which investment treaties fit.

V. Lowe, 'Book Review of *Commentaries on Selected Model Investment Treaties/* edited by Chester Brown. ISBN 978–0–19–964519–0, £180.00' (2015) 30(1) *ICSID Review – FILJ* 275, 276

... the current debate over the acceptability of BITs and the question of their denunciation might generate a little less heat and a little more light if the treaties were considered not as self-sufficient monads but as components in a legal process that moves through overlapping legal orders, national, regional and international.

For example, it makes no sense to criticize a BIT for being an unbalanced instrument favouring investors at the expense of host States, if one looks only at the provisions of the BIT. One of the main functions of a BIT is to operate as a counterweight to the plenary sovereign powers of the host State. BITs may be criticized on the ground that they provide too little or too much of a counterweight, or on the ground that their procedures are ineffective or deficient: but to criticize a BIT on the ground that it only gives rights to investors is like criticizing a screwdriver for only being useful for attaching screws.

---

[1] J. Paulsson, *Denial of Justice* (Cambridge University Press, 2005), chapters 4, 6 and 7.
[2] J. Kürtz, *The WTO and International Investment Law: Converging Systems* (Cambridge University Press, 2016), chapter 5.

These are general systemic questions and are addressed elsewhere in this book (see Chapters 1 and 20). This chapter will instead consider four possible answers of a more technical character.

The second response is that interests of States that might have been articulated as defences have rather been drafted in different technical terms, for example by excluding particular matters of public importance from the tribunals' jurisdictions or by providing objections to admissibility. These issues will be briefly noted in Section 1. The third response is that interests of States may be articulated through a proper interpretation and application of obligations (Section 2). The fourth response is that investment protection law, just like international trade law, needs explicit across-the-board exceptions, and their absence in some of the earlier treaties is not a reflection of systemic peculiarity, but an omission which recent treaties mostly address (Section 3). The fifth response is that exceptions will be provided by the broader system of the international legal order, in particular circumstances precluding wrongfulness in the law of State responsibility (Section 4).

1. CONCEPTS OF DEFENCES

There are many arguments that a respondent State could raise in an investment dispute to avoid its responsibility. The International Law Commission (ILC) made the point in the following terms when introducing the concept of circumstances precluding wrongfulness (on which, see more at Section 4) into the 2001 ILC Articles on Responsibility of States for Internationally Wrongful Acts (2001 ILC Articles).

2001 ILC Articles on Responsibility of States for Internationally Wrongful Acts, Part One, Chapter V, Commentary 7

Circumstances precluding wrongfulness are to be distinguished from other arguments which may have the effect of allowing a State to avoid responsibility. They have nothing to do with questions of the jurisdiction of a court or tribunal over a dispute or the admissibility of a claim. They are to be distinguished from the constituent requirements of the obligation, i.e. those elements which have to exist for the issue of wrongfulness to arise in the first place and which are in principle specified by the obligation itself. In this sense the circumstances precluding wrongfulness operate like defences or excuses in internal legal systems, and the circumstances identified in chapter V are recognized by many legal systems, often under the same designation.

This chapter takes a broad view of what may be considered to fall under the rubric of 'defences', including both what the ILC described as 'the constituent requirements of the obligation' (which will be addressed in Sections 2 and 3) and circumstances precluding wrongfulness in the technical sense (Section 4). But a treaty-maker that wants to draft a rule that would permit the State to avoid responsibility has considerable flexibility in choosing whether to articulate it as a matter of jurisdiction or admissibility, as a condition in the obligation as a rule or as a condition in the obligation as an exception, or to leave it to customary law of State responsibility.

> **M. Paparinskis, 'International Investment Law and European Union Law: A Response to Catharine Titi' (2015) 26(3) *EJIL* 663, 665**
>
> ... any interpreter, whether operating in an arbitral or a less formalized setting, will have to examine a variety of different rules – on jurisdiction, admissibility, the scope and content of obligations, exceptions in primary rules and applicable secondary rules – to determine the existence of responsibility or the success of a particular claim. A rule-by-rule comparison may miss the overall systemic effect of individual changes – for example, the knock-on effect that changes to rules on jurisdiction, admissibility or exceptions will have on the manner of issues that substantive obligations address.

Earlier treaties of the more sophisticated pedigree as well as more recent treaties tend to, as it were, front-load avoidance of responsibility to matters of jurisdiction and admissibility. For example, in order to avoid responsibility in relation to sovereign debt restructuring, the EU–Canada Comprehensive Economic and Trade Agreement (CETA)[3] excludes it from investment arbitration. In the absence of such a rule, if claims about sovereign debt passed the requisite jurisdictional musters,[4] they could be considered on the merits and might raise questions about availability of defences.

EU–Canada Comprehensive Economic and Trade Agreement, Annex 8–B(2) (Public Debt)

No claim that a restructuring of debt of a Party breaches an obligation under Sections C and D may be submitted, or if already submitted continue, under Section F if the restructuring is a negotiated restructuring at the time of submission, or becomes a negotiated restructuring after such submission, except for a claim that the restructuring violates Article 8.6 or 8.7.

States may also avoid responsibility by listing in reservations domestic rules that cannot be challenged,[5] by drafting carve-outs for particular types of measures (for example, tax and financial), or – in a somewhat dated fashion – by limiting the scope of the tribunal's jurisdiction to particular substantive obligations (on jurisdiction and admissibility, see Chapter 5). Of course, these rules do not relate to defence in the technical sense, but they have the effect of avoiding determination of responsibility by an arbitral tribunal just as if they had been presented as a defence. To repeat the earlier point, if such rules exist, a State need not resort to defence to avoid its responsibility in the particular arbitral

---

[3] 30 October 2016.
[4] Which they did not in *Poštová banka a.s. and ISTROKAPITAL SE* v. *Greece*, ICSID Case No. ARB/13/8, Award, 9 April 2015 (Zuleta, Stern, Townsend), upheld on annulment, ICSID Case No. ARB/13/8, Decision on Poštová banka's Application for Partial Annulment of the Award, 29 September 2016 (Kettani, Edward, Shin).
[5] *Mobil Investments Canada & Murphy Oil Corp.* v. *Canada*, ICSID Case No. ARB(AF)/07/4, Decision on Liability and Principles of Quantum, 22 May 2012 (van Houtte, Janow, Sands); Partially Dissenting Opinion of Professor Philippe Sands, 17 May 2012.

proceedings. One preliminary objection that operates in a manner similar to defence, in the sense of avoiding responsibility even if the State has acted in breach of its investment protection obligations, is denial of benefits (indeed, the denial of benefits clause of CETA is located in a section on 'Reservations and Exceptions').

EU–Canada Comprehensive Economic and Trade Agreement, Art. 8.16 (Denial of benefits)

A Party may deny the benefits of this Chapter to an investor of the other Party that is an enterprise of that Party and to investments of that investor if:
- (a) an investor of a third country owns or controls the enterprise; and
- (b) the denying Party adopts or maintains a measure with respect to the third country that:
  - (i) relates to the maintenance of international peace and security; and
  - (ii) prohibits transactions with the enterprise or would be violated or circumvented if the benefits of this Chapter were accorded to the enterprise or to its investments.

Reasonable tribunals have disagreed about the temporal effect of invocation of denial of benefits clauses. In the Energy Charter Treaty (ECT) cases, tribunals have taken the view that the effect is only prospective.[6]

Liman Caspian Oil BV and NCL Dutch Investment BV v. Kazakhstan, ICSID Case No. ARB/07/14, Award, 22 June 2010 (Böckstiegel, Hobér, Crawford), paras 224–225

224. ... the Tribunal notes that there is no disagreement between the Parties on the point that Article 17 contains a notification requirement to the effect that a state must expressly invoke Article 17(1) of the ECT to rely on the rights under that provision. The Tribunal agrees that this is the only interpretation that can be drawn from the wording that the host state 'reserves the right to deny the advantages of this Part'. To reserve a right, it has to be exercised in an explicit way.

225. With regard to the question of whether the right under Article 17(1) of the ECT can only be exercised prospectively, the Tribunal considers that the above mentioned notification requirement – on which the Parties agree – can only lead to the conclusion that the notification has prospective but no retroactive effect. Accepting the option of a

---

[6] Art. 17 of the Energy Charter Treaty provides that: 'Each Contracting Party reserves the right to deny the advantages of this Part to: (1) a legal entity if citizens or nationals of a third state own or control such entity and if that entity has no substantial business activities in the Area of the Contracting Party in which it is organized; or (2) an Investment, if the denying Contracting Party establishes that such Investment is an Investment of an Investor of a third state with or as to which the denying Contracting Party: (a) does not maintain a diplomatic relationship; or (b) adopts or maintains measures that: (i) prohibit transactions with Investors of that state; or (ii) would be violated or circumvented if the benefits of this Part were accorded to Investors of that state or to their Investments.'

retroactive notification would not be compatible with the object and purpose of the ECT, which the Tribunal has to take into account according to Article 31(1) of the VCLT, and which the ECT, in its Article 2, expressly identifies as 'to promote long-term co-operation in the energy field'. Such long-term co-operation requires, and it also follows from the principle of legal certainty, that an investor must be able to rely on the advantages under the ECT, as long as the host state has not explicitly invoked the right to deny such advantages. Therefore, the Tribunal finds that Article 17(1) of the ECT does not have retroactive effect.

In a case decided on the basis of the Dominican Republic–Central America Free Trade Agreement (DR–CAFTA),[7] a tribunal took the view that a properly invoked denial of benefits clause could dispose of an already commenced case.

Pac Rim Cayman LLC v. *El Salvador*, ICSID Case No. ARB/09/12, Decision on the Respondent's Jurisdictional Objections, 1 June 2012 (Veeder, Tawil, Stern), paras 4.83–4.85, 4.90

4.83 There is no express time-limit in CAFTA for the election by a CAFTA Party to deny benefits under CAFTA Article 10.12.2. In a different case under different arbitration rules, this third question might have caused this Tribunal certain difficulties given the importance of investor-state arbitration generally and, in particular, the potential unfairness of a State deciding, as a judge in its own interest, to thwart such an arbitration after its commencement. In this case, however, no such difficulties arise for three reasons.

4.84. First, the Tribunal accepts that, given that this was the first denial of benefits by any CAFTA Party under CAFTA Article 10.12.2, denying benefits to the Claimant under CAFTA was a decision requiring particular attention by the Respondent, to be exercised upon sufficient and ascertainable grounds. Inevitably, such a decision requires careful consideration and, inevitably, also time. It is not apparent to the Tribunal that the Respondent thereby deliberately sought or indeed gained any advantage over the Claimant, by waiting until

---

[7] Art. 10.12 of DR–CAFTA provides that:
1. A Party may deny the benefits of this Chapter to an investor of another Party that is an enterprise of such other Party and to investments of that investor if persons of a non-Party own or control the enterprise and the denying Party: (a) does not maintain diplomatic relations with the non-Party; or (b) adopts or maintains measures with respect to the non-Party or a person of the non-Party that prohibit transactions with the enterprise or that would be violated or circumvented if the benefits of this Chapter were accorded to the enterprise or to its investments.
2. Subject to Articles 18.3 (Notification and Provision of Information) and 20.4 (Consultations), a Party may deny the benefits of this Chapter to an investor of another Party that is an enterprise of such other Party and to investments of that investor if the enterprise has no substantial business activities in the territory of any Party, other than the denying Party, and persons of a non-Party, or of the denying Party, own or control the enterprise.

1 March 2010 (as regards notification to the USA) or 3 August 2010 (for its invocation of denial of benefits to the Claimant).

4.85. Second, this is an arbitration subject to the ICSID Convention and the ICSID Arbitration Rules, as chosen by the Claimant under CAFTA Article 10.16(3)(a). Under ICSID Arbitration Rule 41, any objection by a respondent that the dispute is not within the jurisdiction of the Centre, or, for other reasons, is not within the competence of the tribunal 'shall be made as early as possible' and 'no later than the expiration of the time limit fixed for the filing of the counter-memorial'. In the Tribunal's view, that is the time-limit in this case here incorporated by reference into CAFTA Article 10.12.2. Any earlier time-limit could not be justified on the wording of CAFTA Article 10.12.2; and further, it would create considerable practical difficulties for CAFTA Parties inconsistent with this provision's object and purpose, as observed by Costa Rica and the USA from their different perspectives as host and home States (as also by the Amicus Curiae more generally). In the Tribunal's view, the Respondent has respected the time-limit imposed by ICSID Arbitration Rule 4.

...

4.90. As regards ICSID Article 25(1), the Tribunal accepts the Respondent's submission to the effect that the Respondent's consent to ICSID Arbitration in CAFTA Article 10.16.3(a) is necessarily qualified from the outset by CAFTA Article 10.12.2. It is not possible for the Tribunal to arrive at any different interpretation without distorting the meaning of Article 10.12.2, contrary to the applicable rules for treaty interpretation under international law. Accordingly, a CAFTA Party's denial of benefits invoked after the commencement of an ICSID arbitration cannot be treated as the unilateral withdrawal of that Party's consent to ICSID arbitration under ICSID Article 25(1).

While not being defences in the technical sense, the successful invocation of these rules would have the similar effect, to borrow the phrase from the ILC, 'of allowing a State to avoid responsibility'.

2. DEFENCES IN OBLIGATIONS

Interests of States could also be given effect through appropriate drafting and application of investment obligations as such. A good example for this proposition is the concept of indirect expropriation (discussed in greater detail in Chapter 14). Some of the earlier decisions focused on the effect of the State's measures to determine whether (compensable) expropriation had taken place, which was perceived by some as providing an insufficient role to the public interest of States to regulate in the public interest. In response, tribunals and treaty drafters identified an exception that would preclude a finding of expropriation, (by implication) whatever the effect of the State's measures might be.

Chemtura Corp. v. Canada, UNCITRAL Case, Award, 2 August 2010 (Kaufmann-Kohler, Brower, Crawford), para. 266 (footnote omitted)

Irrespective of the existence of a contractual deprivation, the Tribunal considers in any event that the measures challenged by the Claimant constituted a valid exercise of the Respondent's police powers. As discussed in detail in connection with Article 1105 of NAFTA, the PMRA took measures within its mandate, in a non-discriminatory manner, motivated by the increasing awareness of the dangers presented by lindane for human health and the environment. A measure adopted under such circumstances is a valid exercise of the State's police powers and, as a result, does not constitute an expropriation.

EU–Canada Comprehensive Economic and Trade Agreement, Annex 8-A(3) (Expropriation)

For greater certainty, except in the rare circumstance when the impact of a measure or series of measures is so severe in light of its purpose that it appears manifestly excessive, non-discriminatory measures of a Party that are designed and applied to protect legitimate public welfare objectives, such as health, safety and the environment, do not constitute indirect expropriations.

In an influential case, the investor argued that there was no defence of this kind against expropriation. The tribunal disagreed.

Philip Morris Brands Sàrl and Others v. Uruguay, ICSID Case No. ARB/10/7, Award, 8 July 2016 (Bernandini, Born, Crawford), paras 289–291 (footnotes omitted)

289. .... In the Claimants' view, the State's exercise of police powers does not constitute a defense against expropriation, or exclude the requirement of compensation. The Claimants add that there is no room under Article 5(1) or otherwise in the BIT for carving out an exemption based on the police powers of the State.

290. The Tribunal disagrees. As pointed out by the Respondent, Article 5(1) of the BIT must be interpreted in accordance with Article 31(3)(c) of the VCLT requiring that treaty provisions be interpreted in the light of '[a]ny relevant rules of international law applicable to the relations between the parties', a reference 'which includes ... customary international law'. This directs the Tribunal to refer to the rules of customary international law as they have evolved.

291. Protecting public health has since long been recognized as an essential manifestation of the State's police power, as indicated also by Article 2(1) of the BIT which permits contracting States to refuse to admit investments 'for reasons of public security and order, public health and morality'.

If the *Chemtura* v. *Canada* and *Philip Morris* v. *Uruguay* decisions and the CETA definition are right, it seems appropriate to characterise the 'State's police power' as a defence against expropriation.

The argument may be particularly prominent in the law of expropriation, but is not limited to it. A good example of similarity of considerations involved in the application of fair and equitable treatment and necessity (on which, see more at Section 4.3) is provided by the following excerpt, where the tribunal explicitly engages with the comparison in (excerpted) footnote 200.

Hochtief AG v. *Argentina*, ICSID Case No. ARB/07/31, Decision on Liability, 29 December 2014 (Lowe, Brower, Thomas), paras 243–244 (some footnotes omitted, original emphasis)

243. The majority has thus concluded that pesification of debts alone did not breach the treaty, and that if appropriate and timely steps had been taken by Respondent to restore Claimant to the position (in terms of the commercial balance of the Contract) that had been secured in the Contract, there would have been no breach of the duty to treat Claimant fairly and equitably.

244. The position might have been different if Respondent had made a deliberate choice to abandon peso-dollar parity in circumstances in which parity could have been maintained and Respondent had freedom of choice in determining its exchange-rate policy. But in the view of the Tribunal, that was not the case in Argentina during the period in question. The majority of the Tribunal accepts that although the abandonment of parity was obviously effected by a deliberate act of the Respondent – the enactment of the pesification law – and was in that narrow sense Respondent's 'choice', that act was an acceptance of what foreign exchange markets had already shown to be an economic fact: the unsustainability of parity. The IMF had endorsed the economic policies pursued by Argentina prior to the crisis; and the Emergency Law adopted in January 2002 by the Respondent was regarded by a range of expert commentators as a sound and coherent approach to the unavoidable facts of the extraordinary financial crisis then confronting Argentina.[220]

> [Fn 220: To avoid any possible doubt, it should be emphasized that although these factors are similar to those that would be taken into account in the context of a consideration of the defence of necessity, they are here wholly independent of the necessity defence. The factors do not bear upon the issue raised in the context of necessity: namely, whether in the circumstances the Respondent should be excused for what is on the face of it a breach of its international obligations. Here they bear on the question whether, in order to treat the Claimant with fairness and equity, it was absolutely essential that Respondent maintain parity at all costs. That is a question as to the precise scope of the obligation that was owed by Respondent to Claimant. Was it unfair or inequitable to Claimant for Argentina to depart from parity? In particular, was it unfair to do so in circumstances where Respondent undertook to rebalance the commercial contract in order to address the losses sustained by Claimant as a consequence of pesification?]

3. DEFENCES IN EXCEPTIONS

Most investment protection treaties concluded in the 1990s and arbitrated in the 2000s did not include explicit exceptions. However, the US–Argentina BIT did contain a so-called non-precluded-measures clause, which was extensively – if somewhat inconclusively – arbitrated in the aftermath of the Argentinian crisis of the early 2000s (Section 3.1). Recent treaties are much more likely to provide exceptions, indeed often of an extensive and multi-layered character (Section 3.2).

3.1 Non-Precluded-Measures Clause

Article XI of the US–Argentina BIT may be one of the most contested rules of international investment law.

US–Argentina BIT, Art. XI

This Treaty shall not preclude the application by either Party of measures necessary for the maintenance of public order, the fulfilment of its obligations with respect to the maintenance or restoration of international peace or security, or the Protection of its own essential security interests.

The application of this rule has raised a number of important questions. First, is the judgment on necessity entirely self-judging, subject to a good-faith review or objectively reviewable? Second, what is the legal standard for evaluating whether measures are 'necessary'? Third, what is the legal effect of successful reliance on the clause?

Argentina argued in a number of cases that Article XI was self-judging. All tribunals rejected this argument.

El Paso Energy International Co. v. *Argentina*, ICSID Case No. ARB/03/15, Decision on the Application for Annulment of Argentina, 22 September 2014 (Oreamuno, Cheng, Knieper), paras 195–196 (footnotes omitted)

195. The Tribunal analyzed the position of Argentina in connection with the self-judging nature of Article XI of the BIT ... it referred to the evidence that Argentina filed, including documents to show that one year after the signing of the BIT the State Department of the United States of America introduced similar treaties and a model treaty to the Senate and in the latter the self-judging nature of a provision similar to Article XI of the BIT was established; it also cited a statement by the U.S. Senate in favor of the self-judging nature of Article XI of the BIT. The Tribunal held that such evidence was irrelevant. The Committee notes that the Tribunal assessed the evidence provided by Argentina to interpret the BIT in light of the Vienna Convention; later on the Tribunal considered other evidence. The Tribunal conducted an analysis of the wording of Article XI of the BIT; then went on to analyze the context of that Article; it also considered subsequent practices (Article 31(3) of the Vienna

Convention) and the object and purpose of the treaty. The Tribunal concluded that Article XI is not self-judging and that said body had the power to interpret it.

196. From the above summary, the Committee concludes that the Tribunal analyzed, from different points of view and with diverse methods of interpretation, the alleged self-judging nature of Article XI of the BIT. The analysis is *lege artis* and thorough.

Even if international lawyers tend to be sceptical about arguments of self-judgment unless treaty drafters have been fairly explicit in that regard, how should the tribunal approach the argument by a State that it has adopted 'measures necessary'? Should the tribunal evaluate whether the State itself thought measures necessary, whether the State acted within its margin of appreciation, whether the State acted reasonably or whether the measures were the only way to address an overwhelming crisis?

The first possible response is to adopt the latter approach outlined above, relying for interpretative support on necessity as a circumstance precluding wrongfulness from Article 25 of the 2001 ILC Articles (on which, see more at Section 4.3, including its excerpted text), which would result in a restrictive reading of the provision. This approach was adopted in the first ICSID cases that addressed the Argentinian crisis, starting from *CMS Gas Transmission Co.* v. *Argentina*.[8]

Annulment committee decisions were, however, critical of this approach, explaining in some detail why Article XI should *not* be read by reference to the customary law of necessity (if, understandably in light of the limited functions of annulment committees, saying less on how it should be read). The *CMS* v. *Argentina* annulment committee criticised the tribunal for conflating the exception provided in the primary treaty obligation with a circumstance precluding wrongfulness in customary law, and therefore failing to properly interpret the treaty obligation.

CMS Gas Transmission Co. v. Argentina, ICSID Case No. ARB/01/8, Decision of the Ad Hoc Committee on the Application for Annulment of Argentina, 25 September 2007 (Guillaume, Elaraby, Crawford), paras 122–123, 129–130, 135 (footnotes omitted)

122. With respect to the defense based on Article XI of the BIT, the Tribunal examined the Parties' arguments and concluded first that 'there is nothing in the context of customary international law or the object and purpose of the Treaty that could on its own exclude major economic crises from the scope of Article XI'. Then it addressed the debate which the parties had chosen to engage in as to whether Article XI is self-judging. The Tribunal concluded that under Article XI it had the authority to proceed to a substantive review and

[8] ICSID Case No. ARB/01/8, Award, 12 May 2005 (Orrego Vicuña, Lalonde, Rezek).

that 'it must examine whether the state of necessity or emergency meet the conditions laid down by customary international law and the treaty provisions and whether it thus is or is not able to preclude wrongfulness'.

123. The problem is, however, that the Tribunal stopped there and did not provide any further reasoning at all in respect of its decision under Article XI.

...

129. The Committee observes first that there is some analogy in the language used in Article XI of the BIT and in Article 25 of the ILC's Articles on State Responsibility. The first text mentions 'necessary' measures and the second relates to the 'state of necessity'. However Article XI specifies the conditions under which the Treaty may be applied, whereas Article 25 is drafted in a negative way: it excludes the application of the state of necessity on the merits, unless certain stringent conditions are met. Moreover, Article XI is a threshold requirement: if it applies, the substantive obligations under the Treaty do not apply. By contrast, Article 25 is an excuse which is only relevant once it has been decided that there has otherwise been a breach of those substantive obligations.

130. Furthermore Article XI and Article 25 are substantively different. The first covers measures necessary for the maintenance of public order or the protection of each Party's own essential security interests, without qualifying such measures.

...

135. ... As admitted by CMS, the Tribunal gave an erroneous interpretation to Article XI. In fact, it did not examine whether the conditions laid down by Article XI were fulfilled and whether, as a consequence, the measures taken by Argentina were capable of constituting, even *prima facie*, a breach of the BIT.

If customary law of necessity becomes suspect as authority, another possible source of guidance could be the World Trade Organization's (WTO) law, which would call for weighing and balancing of values furthered by the challenged measures, contribution of the measure to the end pursued, and availability of alternative and less restrictive measures.

Continental Casualty Co. v. Argentina, ICSID Case No. ARB/03/9, Award, 5 September 2008 (Sacerdoti, Veeder, Nader), paras 192, 196 (footnotes omitted)

192. The Tribunal is thus faced with the task of determining the content of the concept of necessity in Art. XI, in order to decide whether the various Measures challenged by the Claimant were indeed necessary, as a matter of causation. With regard to the necessity test required for the application of the BIT, for the reasons stated above relating to the different role of Art. XI and of the defense of necessity in customary international law, the Tribunal does not share the opinion that 'the treaty thus becomes inseparable from the customary law standard insofar as to the conditions for the operation of the state of necessity are

concerned', ... Since the text of Art. XI derives from the parallel model clause of the U.S. FCN treaties and these treaties in turn reflect the formulation of Art. XX of GATT 1947, the Tribunal finds it more appropriate to refer to the GATT and WTO case law which has extensively dealt with the concept and requirements of necessity in the context of economic measures derogating to the obligations contained in GATT, rather than to refer to the requirement of necessity under customary international law.

...

196. According to these principles, the next step for us is to assess whether the Measures contributed materially to the realization of their legitimate aims under Art. XI of the BIT, namely the protection of the essential security interests of Argentina in the economic and social crisis it was facing. More specifically, whether the Measures were apt to and did make such a material or a decisive contribution to this end.

A tribunal that approaches Article XI from such a perspective is more likely to find its requirements to be satisfied, as the summary of the *Continental Casualty* v. *Argentina* tribunal's findings by the annulment committee suggests.

Continental Casualty Co. v. Argentina, ICSID Case No. ARB/03/9, Decision on the Applications for Partial Annulment, 16 September 2011 (Griffith, Söderlund, Ajibola), para. 125 (footnotes omitted)

The Tribunal found that Article XI applied to relevant measures taken by Argentina in this case because they were taken 'in the face of the social and economic crisis', and found that they 'were sufficient in their design to address the crisis and were applied in a reasonable and proportionate way at the end of 2001–2002'. However, while the Tribunal reached this conclusion in respect of the measures taken by Argentina in 2001–2002, it reached a contrary conclusion in relation to the restructuring of the LETEs[9] through Decree 1735/04, a measure that was adopted in December 2004. One of the reasons for finding that Article XI did not apply to Decree 1735/04 was that by that time 'Argentina's financial conditions were evolving towards normality'.

A third approach, perhaps less appreciated by commentators who focus on the decisions of the 2000s, was adopted by the tribunal in the *El Paso Energy International Co.* v. *Argentina* case.[10] Not entirely dissimilarly from the first approach criticised by the *CMS* v. *Argentina* annulment committee, it identified a general principle of international law precluding invocation of Article XI where the State itself had contributed to the crisis (cf. Article 25(2)(b) of the 2001 ILC Articles), and therefore dismissed Argentina's

[9] [Eds: Argentine Government Treasury Bills.]
[10] ICSID Case No. ARB/03/15, Award, 31 October 2011 (Caflisch, Bernandini, Stern).

arguments.[11] The tribunal in *Mobil Exploration and Development Argentina Inc. Suc. Argentina and Mobil Argentina Sociedad Anónima* v. *Argentina*[12] adopted a similar position. Consequently, the third approach, just as the first approach, found Article XI to be inapplicable; the *Continental Casualties* v. *Canada* tribunal, on the contrary, found it to be partially applicable.

Finally, what effect would successful reliance on Article XI have on compensation? The *CMS* v. *Argentina* annulment committee provided a concise response to this question.

CMS Gas Transmission Co. v. Argentina, ICSID Case No. ARB/01/8, Decision of the Ad Hoc Committee on the Application for Annulment of Argentina, 25 September 2007 (Guillaume, Elaraby, Crawford), para. 146

... the Tribunal should have considered what would have been the possibility of compensation under the BIT if the measures taken by Argentina had been covered by Article XI. The answer to that question is clear enough: Article XI, if and for so long as it applied, excluded the operation of the substantive provisions of the BIT. That being so, there could be no possibility of compensation being payable during that period.

The uncertainties regarding interpretation and application of non-precluded measures clauses are illustrated by two more recent cases against India on the basis of the same facts and similar treaty clauses regarding taking back of the S-band spectrum from foreign investors. One tribunal concluded that 60 per cent of allocation of the spectrum was directed to the national security interests and to that extent benefited from the non-precluded measures clause; the second tribunal, echoing a dissenter to the first award, found that the clause was fully inapplicable.

CC/Devas (Mauritius) Ltd., Devas Employees Mauritius Private Limited and Telcom Devas Mauritius Limited v. India, PCA Case No. 2013–09, Award on Jurisdiction and Merits, 25 July 2016 (Lalonde, Haigh, Singh), paras 211, 353–355, 371, 373 (footnotes omitted)

211. Article 11(3) of the Treaty provides:

The provisions of this Agreement shall not in any way limit the right of either Contracting Party to apply prohibitions or restrictions of any kind or take any other action which is directed to the protection of its essential security interests, or to the protection of public health or the prevention of diseases in pests or animals or plants.

...

---

[11] Paras 613–626, 649–665. But see paras 666–670, where Arbitrator Stern agrees with the theoretical point about contribution, but finds that it was not satisfied in the circumstances.

[12] ICSID Case No. ARB/04/16, Decision on Jurisdiction and Liability, 10 April 2013 (Möller, Bernandini, Remiro Brotóns).

353. Article 11(3) constitutes an important exception to the provisions of the Treaty and, while proper deference must be given to State authority in defining what its essential security interests are, it must be interpreted in accordance with the provisions of the VCLT.

354. The problem in the present case is that the decision of the CCS [Indian Cabinet Committee on Security] itself contains a mix of objectives. Even though there is nowhere in the CCS decision any specific reference to the Respondent's 'essential security interests', the Tribunal, by majority, has no difficulty concluding that the reservation of spectrum for the needs of defence and para-military forces can be classified as 'directed to the protection of its essential security interests', coming under the exclusion covered in Article 11(3) of the Treaty; however, the same cannot be said when it comes to taking over the spectrum allocated to the Claimants for 'railways and other public utility services as well as for societal needs, and having regard to the needs of the country's strategic requirements', as stated in the CCS decision.

355. While it could quite properly expropriate the Claimants' rights under Article 6 of the Treaty for 'public utility services as well as for societal needs', it could not have recourse to Article 11(3) for such purposes and confiscate their rights.

...

371. The Tribunal, by majority, therefore concludes that, although the CCS decision of 2011 appears to have been in part 'directed to the protection of its essential security interests', that part remained undefined and several other objectives were included in that decision, which had nothing to do with national security. In the circumstances, the Tribunal rules that, although the Respondent was fully entitled to reassign the S-spectrum to non-commercial use, the part which was not reserved for military or paramilitary purposes would be subject to the provisions of Article 6 of the Treaty concerning expropriation.

...

373. On the basis of the evidence submitted to it as described above and bearing in mind that the Respondent had already reserved to itself 10% of the spectrum in question, the Tribunal, by majority, is of the view that a reasonable allocation of spectrum directed to the protection of the Respondent's essential security interests would not exceed 60% of the S-band spectrum allocated to the Claimants, the remaining 40% being allocated for other public interest purposes and being subject to the expropriation conditions under Article 6 of the Treaty. It will be up to the Tribunal, in the next phase of this arbitral process (damages), to establish the compensation due to the Claimants in that respect.

Deutsche Telekom AG v. India, PCA Case No. 2014–10, Interim Award, 13 December 2017 (Kaufmann-Kohler, Price, Stern), paras 287–288 (footnotes omitted)

287. ... Had there been any essential security interests necessary to protect, there would have been no protracted debate lasting almost four years among organs of the Government about the use of this spectrum for strategic and societal purposes, on the one hand, or commercial

auctioning purposes, on the other hand. The Tribunal thus agrees with the Dissenting Opinion [of Arbitrator Haig] in the Mauritius BIT Arbitration [*CC/Devas* v. *India*], whereby:

> 'In these circumstances, it is impossible to say that the decision of the CCS was directed towards the "essential security interests" of India. The question of S-band spectrum allocation remained open in February 2011 and the debate as to where that S-band spectrum could have gone could just as readily have favoured DOT's preference for public auction by terrestrial users as it could have gone to DOS and or MOD to be used for military purposes or disaster management or railway tracking. As long as these various potential uses remained under consideration and subject to debate, there was no identified purpose for the CCS decision. There were only possible uses and until it was determined, there was no action directed at the protection of essential security interests or the military interests no matter what the MOD or its several different arms may have requested or wished for.'

288. Thus, in light of the evidence presented before it, including certain unredacted portions of documents which may not have been available to the Mauritius BIT tribunal, this Tribunal cannot reach the same conclusion as the one reached by that tribunal on the fulfilment of the essential security interest clause, including as to a 60/40 apportionment of spectrum between essential security interests and other concerns. The Tribunal also wishes to underscore that the non-precluded measures clause in the BIT applicable in this case requires it to find that a measure was 'necessary' to protect essential security interest, and not merely 'directed at the protection' of such interests as was required under the treaty at issue in the Mauritius BIT Arbitration. In the Tribunal's view, the phrase 'to the extent necessary' implies a more stringent nexus between the measure at issue and the interests pursued. Given the lack of determinacy of the CCS decision and the protracted debate between branches of the Government which ensued, the Tribunal finds that India has not established the presence of such nexus in the circumstances of this case.

3.2 Modern Exceptions

Perhaps the simple point of the decade of convoluted litigation about Article XI of the US–Argentina BIT is that it is not a well – or at least sufficiently clearly – drafted exception. That seems to be the lesson taken by the drafters of recent treaties.

The general exceptions clause of the CETA (excerpted below) is notable for a number of reasons. First, it explicitly borrows from the law and practice of the WTO. Second, rather than tailoring an exception to investment protection matters,[13] across-the-board exceptions are applied. Third, general exceptions do not apply to Section D (Investment protection) of Chapter Eight (Investment), which among other things provides rules for fair and equitable treatment and expropriation. One possible implication is that the treaty drafters thought that properly drafted and applied obligations (of the kind discussed in Section 2 in relation to expropriation) already reflect the public interests expressed through general exceptions.

[13] Although see Art. 8.15 (Reservations and exceptions).

EU–Canada Comprehensive Economic and Trade Agreement, Art. 28.3 (General exceptions)

1. For the purposes of ... Sections B (Establishment of investment) and C (Non-discriminatory treatment) of Chapter Eight (Investment), Article XX of the GATT 1994 is incorporated into and made part of this Agreement. The Parties understand that the measures referred to in Article XX(b) of the GATT 1994 include environmental measures necessary to protect human, animal or plant life or health. The Parties understand that Article XX(g) of the GATT 1994 applies to measures for the conservation of living and non-living exhaustible natural resources.

2. For the purposes of ... Sections B (Establishment of investments) and C (Non-discriminatory treatment) of Chapter Eight (Investment), subject to the requirement that such measures are not applied in a manner which would constitute a means of arbitrary or unjustifiable discrimination between the Parties where like conditions prevail, or a disguised restriction on trade in services, nothing in this Agreement shall be construed to prevent the adoption or enforcement by a Party of measures necessary:

   (a) to protect public security or public morals or to maintain public order;
   [Fn 33: The public security and public order exceptions may be invoked only where a genuine and sufficiently serious threat is posed to one of the fundamental interests of society].

   (b) to protect human, animal or plant life or health; or
   [Fn 34: The Parties understand that the measures referred to in subparagraph (b) include environmental measures necessary to protect human, animal or plant life or health.]

   (c) to secure compliance with laws or regulations which are not inconsistent with the provisions of this Agreement including those relating to:
   (i) the prevention of deceptive and fraudulent practices or to deal with the effects of a default on contracts;
   (ii) the protection of the privacy of individuals in relation to the processing and dissemination of personal data and the protection of confidentiality of individual records and accounts; or
   (iii) safety.

The national security clause is notable for its subtle but important differences from Article XI of the US–Argentina BIT.

EU–Canada Comprehensive Economic and Trade Agreement, Art. 28.6 (National security) (footnote omitted)

Nothing in this Agreement shall be construed:

   (a) to require a Party to furnish or allow access to information if that Party determines that the disclosure of this information would be contrary to its essential security interests; or

(b) to prevent a Party from taking an action that it considers necessary to protect its essential security interests:

(i) connected to the production of or traffic in arms, ammunition and implements of war and to such traffic and transactions in other goods and materials, services and technology undertaken, and to economic activities, carried out directly or indirectly for the purpose of supplying a military or other security establishment;

(ii) taken in time of war or other emergency in international relations; or

(iii) relating to fissionable and fusionable materials or the materials from which they are derived; or

(c) prevent a Party from taking any action in order to carry out its international obligations for the purpose of maintaining international peace and security.

Recall the language of 'measures necessary for ... the Protection of its own essential security interests', which, in Argentina's view – not shared by any of the tribunals – signified its self-judging character. The analogous clause in CETA speaks about 'an action that *it [Party] considers* necessary to protect its essential security interests' (emphasis added), which is much more suggestive of a self-judging character. It does not mean that, as a matter of legal principle, all the tribunals interpreting Article XI got it wrong. But it may suggest, as a matter of policy, that when States reflected upon how Argentina's arguments had been handled, they felt that it would be sensible to provide an additional safety valve for matters of such importance.

This is not to suggest that modern exceptions clauses raise no interpretative controversies; they are simply different. Interpretation and application of the general exceptions in Canadian treaties has raised a question about their relationship with justifications within particular primary obligations. The tribunal in *Bear Creek* v. *Peru* took a view that a general exceptions clause ruled out implicit qualifications within primary obligations such as police powers regarding expropriation; a Canadian submission in a later case regarding a similarly drafted exceptions clause suggested, to the contrary, that exceptions do not affect the scope of primary obligations. (Also note the partial dissent in *Bear Creek* on the third layer of defences, to be considered in Section 4, articulated as circumstances precluding wrongfulness.)

Bear Creek Mining Corporation v. Peru, ICSID Case No. ARB/14/21, Award, 30 November 2017 (Böckstiegel, Pryles, Sands), paras 472–474

472. Article 2201.1 of the FTA [Canada–Peru Free Trade Agreement] provides for the following 'Exceptions':

3. For the purposes of Chapter Eight (Investment), subject to the requirement that such measures are not applied in a manner that constitute arbitrary or unjustifiable discrimination between investments or between investors, or a disguised restriction on international trade or investment, nothing in this Agreement shall be construed to prevent a Party from adopting or enforcing measures necessary:

(a) to protect human, animal or plant life or health, which the Parties understand to include environmental measures necessary to protect human, animal or plant life or health;

(b) to ensure compliance with laws and regulations that are not inconsistent with this Agreement; or

(c) the conservation of living or non-living exhaustible natural resources.

473. The Tribunal considers that already the title of Article 2201 'General Exceptions' shows that otherwise Chapter Eight (investment) remains applicable including its Articles 812 and, by the express footnote to the title of Article 812, as well as Article 812.1. Further, the list is not introduced by any wording (e.g. 'such as') which could be understood that it is only exemplary. It must therefore be understood to be an exclusive list. Also in substance, in view of the very detailed provisions of the FTA regarding expropriation (Article 812 and Annex 812.1) and regarding exceptions in Article 2201 expressly designated to 'Chapter Eight (Investment)', the interpretation of the FTA must lead to the conclusion that no other exceptions from general international law or otherwise can be considered applicable in this case.

474. There is, thus, no need to enter into the discussion between the Parties regarding the jurisprudence concerning any police power exception for measures addressed to investments.

Bear Creek Mining Corporation v. *Peru*, ICSID Case No. ARB/14/21, Partial Dissenting Opinion of Professor Philippe Sands QC, 12 September 2017, para. 41 (footnotes omitted)

The only other point I wish to make concerns the legitimate right of a Party to the Canada-Peru FTA 'to regulate and to exercise its police power in the interests of public welfare', a point made by Canada in its submission. The Majority has ruled at paragraph 473 that Article 2201.1 of the FTA, which provides for a list of exceptions that fall within a State's legitimate exercise of police powers, is exhaustive. I do not disagree with this analysis, but wish to make clear that my support for this conclusion is without prejudice to the application of Article 25 of the ILC Articles on State Responsibility, which deals with acts of Necessity. As the Annulment Committees in *CMS* and *Sempra* made clear, the operation of a *lex specialis* in a BIT does not have the effect (unless the BIT explicitly provides otherwise) of precluding the operation of Article 25, which continues to function as a 'secondary rule of international law' operating even when an exception under the *lex specialis* is not available ... whatever the requirements of the FTA, the possibility of having resource to Article 25, as a rule precluding wrongfulness, is not excluded by the FTA.

Eco Oro Minerals Corp. v. *Colombia*, ICSID Case No. ARB/16/41, Non-Disputing Party Submission of Canada, 27 February 2020, paras 19–23 (footnotes, omitted, original emphasis)

Relation Between the General Exceptions in Article 2201(3) and the Investment Obligations

19. Many of the investment provisions contain their own internal flexibilities that determine whether regulatory action is legitimate or if it amounts to a breach of an obligation. For example, States can differentiate between investments on the basis of a broad range of policy objectives without breaching the national treatment obligation because the treatment was not accorded in like circumstances in light of the policy objectives pursued.

20. As a result, legitimate regulatory actions will rarely need to be justified on the basis of the general exception in Article 2201(3) [Canada–Colombia Free Trade Agreement] because they will not constitute breaches of the investment obligations in the first place. In this sense, the general exceptions are an additional tool or a final 'safety net' to protect the State's exercise of regulatory powers in pursuit of the specific legitimate objectives identified in the exceptions.

21. While some of the considerations that relate to a finding of breach of one of the investment obligations may be similar to those that would form part of the general exceptions analysis, whether a measure is justified under Article 2201(3) is a distinct enquiry that must be viewed through a different lens.

22. Only if a tribunal concludes that the measure breaches a Chapter Eight (Investment) obligation can there be consideration of the application of the general exception in Article 2201(3) to justify the breach. Because the exception in Article 2201(3) applies generally to all obligations in Chapter Eight (Investment), its relevance to a specific measure or to an alleged breach may vary.

23. The exceptions in Article 2201 cannot be used to broaden the scope of the primary obligations. Such a reading would have unintended consequences. Thus, for example, environmental measures that have the effect of depriving investors of the use and enjoyment of their property or vested rights must therefore first and foremost be considered in light of Annex 811.2 to determine whether there is a compensable expropriation. The Parties' intention was never to limit the scope of legitimate policy objectives that States can pursue and that would not breach the investment obligations in the first place.

4. DEFENCES IN CIRCUMSTANCES PRECLUDING WRONGFULNESS

This chapter has so far discussed various ways in which a respondent State could avoid responsibility through arguments related to interpretation and application of the investment protection obligation itself. But some defences are also provided by the broader international legal order within which investment protection law is situated, even if they are not explicitly referred to – in the technical parlance of the law of State responsibility, these are circumstances precluding wrongfulness. One of them has already been encountered in the discussion of interpretation of non-precluded measures in Section 3.1, and the rest of this section will discuss three circumstances that have been of importance in the practice of investment arbitration: consent (Section 4.1), countermeasures (Section 4.2) and necessity (Section 4.3), and will conclude by briefly considering the effect of their successful invocation (Section 4.4). Before discussing these matters, it bears noting that there is some disagreement on whether (some of) the circumstances precluding wrongfulness are best viewed as justifications or excuses, a question that may have a bearing on compensation.

> **V. Lowe, 'Precluding Wrongfulness or Responsibility: A Plea for Excuses' (1999) 10 EJIL 405, 406**
>
> My concern is with the small but important question of the nature of the 'defences'. There is behaviour that is right; and there is behaviour that, though wrong, is understandable and excusable. The distinction between the two is the very stuff of classical tragedy. No dramatist, no novelist would confuse them. No philosopher or theologian would conflate them. Yet the distinction practically disappears in the Draft Articles.

4.1 Consent

2001 ILC Articles on Responsibility of States for Internationally Wrongful Acts, Art. 20 (Consent)

Valid consent by a State to the commission of a given act by another State precludes the wrongfulness of that act in relation to the former State to the extent that the act remains within the limits of that consent.

2001 ILC Articles on Responsibility of States for Internationally Wrongful Acts, Art. 20, Commentary 10 (footnotes omitted)

Article 20 envisages only the consent of States to conduct otherwise in breach of an international obligation. International law may also take into account the consent of non-State entities such as corporations or private persons. The extent to which investors can waive the rules of diplomatic protection by agreement in advance has long been controversial, but under the Convention on the Settlement of Investment Disputes between States and Nationals of other States (art. 27, para. 1), consent by an investor to arbitration under the Convention has the effect of suspending the right of diplomatic protection by the investor's national State. The rights conferred by international human rights treaties cannot be waived by their beneficiaries, but the individual's free consent may be relevant to their application. In these cases the particular rule of international law itself allows for the consent in question and deals with its effect.

Can investors consent to what otherwise would be a breach of an investment protection obligation, or consent not to bring an arbitral claim? One of the first tribunals to discuss umbrella clauses noted, in passing, its doubts regarding this proposition.

SGS Société Générale de Surveillance SA v. *Philippines*, ICSID Case No. ARB/02/6, Decision on Objections to Jurisdiction, 29 January 2004 (El-Kosheri, Crawford, Crivellaro), para. 154 (footnote omitted)

The jurisdiction of the Tribunal is determined by the combination of the BIT and the ICSID Convention. It is, to say the least, doubtful that a private party can by contract waive rights or dispense with the performance of obligations imposed on the States parties to those treaties under international law. Although under modern international law, treaties may confer rights, substantive and procedural, on individuals, they will normally do so in order to achieve some public interest. Thus the question is not whether the Tribunal has jurisdiction: unless otherwise expressly provided, treaty jurisdiction is not abrogated by contract.

Later decisions have been more open to the idea that consent or waiver of treaty rights may be given effect, and have rather focused on whether that effect is achieved by particular drafting (the case in the first excerpt), and whether giving effect to a waiver could have possible detriment to the public interest (the second excerpt).

Hochtief AG v. *Argentina*, ICSID Case No. ARB/07/31, Decision on Liability, 29 December 2014 (Lowe, Brower, Thomas), paras 191–192 (footnotes omitted, original emphasis)

191. The Tribunal considers that there is no legal reason why effect should not be given to an agreement between an investor and a host State either to limit the rights of the investor or to oblige the investor not to pursue any remedies, including its BIT remedies, in certain circumstances. Such an agreement does not purport to alter the terms of the Treaty. Nor does it necessarily purport to bar action in respect of extant responsibilities of the Grantor: it may constitute an agreement by a particular investor to limit the range of matters for which the Grantor carries the risk and responsibility. It may also be regarded as an agreement by the investor not to rely upon certain treaty provisions and extant rights in the specified circumstances.

192. The majority of the Tribunal considers that Article 22.2 is such a provision, and that it operates so as to bar 'any claim', including claims under the Treaty, by a signatory to the Concession Contract, such as Claimant, against the Respondent *in so far as the claim is made by the signatory in its capacity as a lender*. Neither the Concession Contract nor the BIT contains any provision that expressly nullifies Article 22.2 or subordinates it to the protections afforded by the Treaty. The Concession Contract is governed by Argentine law, and there is no suggestion that Argentine law imposes any such nullification or subordination upon Article 22.2.

MNSS BV and Recupero Credito Acciaio N.V. v. Montenegro, ICSID Case No.
ARB(AF)/12/8, Award, 4 May 2016 (Rigo Sureda, Gaillard, Stern), paras 163–165
(footnotes omitted)

163. ... in the view of the Tribunal, the public interest may not be ignored. The Tribunal
agrees with Professor Scheuer that 'Investor-State arbitration serves not only the investor's
interests but has an important function in the public interest for the relations between the
States concerned'. Thus the question is not whether the rights may or may not be waived,
but to what extent, if they have been waived, the waiver is in detriment of the public
purpose pursued by the State parties to the BIT.

164. In the case before the Tribunal, it is undisputed that the waiver in question was
freely negotiated and agreed to by MNSS by way of the Assignment Agreement. It is
significant that, as interpreted by the Tribunal, the waiver is limited to contractual disputes
and that MNSS may resolve contractual disputes arising from the Privatization and
Assignment Agreements by 'ad hoc arbitration in accordance with UNCITRAL Arbitration
Rules without recourse to the ordinary courts of law'. The ability of the investor and the
State to settle their contractual disputes by arbitration is evidently congruent with the
public purpose pursued by the State parties to the BIT.

165. Based on these considerations the Tribunal concludes that MNSS validly waived its
right under the BIT to pursue contractual claims based on Article 3(4).

4.2 Countermeasures

**2001 ILC Articles on Responsibility of States for Internationally Wrongful Acts,
Arts 22, 49**

Article 22 (Countermeasures in respect of an internationally wrongful act)
The wrongfulness of an act of a State not in conformity with an international obligation
towards another State is precluded if and to the extent that the act constitutes a
countermeasure taken against the latter State in accordance with chapter II of
Part Three.
...

Article 49 (Object and limits of countermeasures)
1. An injured State may only take countermeasures against a State which is responsible
   for an internationally wrongful act in order to induce that State to comply with its
   obligations under Part Two.
2. Countermeasures are limited to the non-performance for the time being of international
   obligations of the State taking the measures towards the responsible State.
3. Countermeasures shall, as far as possible, be taken in such a way as to permit the
   resumption of performance of the obligations in question.

Countermeasures constitute an integral element of the classic international legal order: implementation of international responsibility through the self-help of breach of international obligations. On the face of it, countermeasures inhabit an entirely different universe from investment treaty arbitrations. Their interplay might have remained merely a fascinating academic query, if not for reliance by Mexico on countermeasures against the United States as an excuse for its breach of obligations under the North American Free Trade Agreement (NAFTA) in three investor–State arbitrations relating to discriminatory taxation of soft drinks. The excerpt below discusses the role of countermeasures in investment law, with a particular focus on the soft drinks arbitrations.[14]

> ### M. Paparinskis, 'Circumstances Precluding Wrongfulness in International Investment Law' (2016) 31(2) *ICSID Review – FILJ* 484, 493–496 (footnotes omitted)
>
> Can a State preclude wrongfulness for the breach of primary obligations of investment protection by invoking countermeasures in response to an anterior breach of international law? [...] Under contemporary international law, countermeasures are plainly accepted as a circumstance precluding wrongfulness. But an international investment lawyer could find it slightly odd if a respondent State, in response to an investment claim, were to say: 'Awfully sorry for mistreating your investment in breach of my investment obligations but you must appreciate that it is not personal; just a gentle nudge to your home State to resume compliance with its own obligations, precisely what international law on implementation of responsibility is about.' It may be convenient to address in turn two ways in which the normative intuition of oddness may be articulated in legal terms: first, can countermeasures be invoked in principle to preclude wrongfulness for the breach of investment obligations and, second, can countermeasures be realistically invoked in relation to investment obligations, as they are drafted?
>
> The starting point for thinking about the first question is that the right to take countermeasures is a dispositive rule and may be superseded by *lex specialis*. Has this taken place in international investment law? The argument in favour of an affirmative answer could be presented in several ways. The first would rely on subject matter. International investment law addresses important and sensitive issues, which would be greatly harmed by arbitrary interferences of States, by reference to inter-State disputes. On its own, such a reliance on the content of primary obligations would be insufficient. Second, if States owe obligations directly to investors, could they really be permitted to breach them in response to the conduct of other States? This is a valid point, but it conflates exclusion of secondary rules in principle and the practical limitations of their application to primary rules drafted in a particular manner. Another argument would be to look more broadly

---

[14] Mexico's argument was rejected in all three cases, but with important differences in rationale between, on the one hand, *Archer Daniels Midland Co. and Tate & Lyle Ingredients Americas, Inc. v. Mexico*, ICSID Case No. ARB(AF)/04/05, Award, 21 November 2007 (Cremades, Rovine, Siqueiros), and on the other, *Corn Products International, Inc. v. Mexico*, ICSID Case No. ARB(AF)/04/01, Decision on Responsibility, 15 January 2008 (Greenwood, Lowenfeld, Serrano de la Vega) and *Cargill, Inc. v. Mexico*, ICSID Case No. ARB(AF)/05/2, Award, 18 September 2009 (Pryles, Caron, McRae).

at the system of international investment law and rely on its efficiency and coherence, particularly as reflected in the recent mega-regional treaties and proposals, to suggest that the backdrop of general rules on implementation of responsibility must fade in comparison to this special structure. A yet different, or at least differently focused, argument would rely upon the framing of modern investment dispute settlement law around the investor–State axis as excluding the application of remedies and procedures from traditional inter-State law. The *lex specialis* argument was considered in three NAFTA claims against Mexico regarding soft drinks. One Tribunal rejected it explicitly,[15] one by necessary implication,[16] one did not address it at all[17] and one arbitrator wrote a short separate opinion, finding countermeasures inapplicable due to a mixture of purposive and procedural arguments.[18] There is something to be said for a generalist preference regarding the question of principle, at least partly because the practicalities for successful invocation may often be insurmountable.

One starting point for thinking about the practicalities is the position regarding countermeasures and international human rights law – which, for the purposes of State responsibility, is a regime similar to investment law in that it also permits invocation of responsibility by non-State actors on their own account and without the intermediation of any State. The 2001 ILC Articles address the issue in Article 50(1)(a), which provides that '[c]ountermeasures shall not affect ... obligations for the protection of fundamental human rights'. The rationale of this proposition is unclear [...] Various readings of the rationale of these general rules on countermeasures could have a different impact for investment law [...]

The three NAFTA Tribunals dealing with soft drink claims read the law of responsibility, at least by implication, along the lines suggested by the Fifth Special Rapporteur [James Crawford] in his third report:

> The position with respect to human rights is at one level the same as the position with respect to the rights of third States. Evidently, human rights obligations are not owed to States as the primary beneficiaries, even though States are entitled to invoke those obligations and to ensure respect for them. Thus it is obvious that human rights obligations (whether or not qualified as 'basic' or 'fundamental') may not themselves be subject to countermeasures ... and that conduct inconsistent with human rights obligations may not be justified or excused except to the extent provided for by the applicable regime of human rights itself.

To determine whether '[t]he position with respect to [investor] rights is at one level the same as the position with respect to the rights of third States', the right question to ask is

---

[15] [Eds: *Archer Daniels Midland Company and Tate & Lyle Ingredients Americas, Inc* v. *Mexico*, ICSID Case No. ARB(AF)/04/05, Award, 21 November 2007 (Cremades, Rovine, Siqueiros) (*ADM* v. *Mexico*), paras 120–123.]

[16] [Eds: *Corn Products International, Inc* v. *Mexico*, ICSID Case No. ARB(AF)/04/01, Decision on Responsibility, 15 January 2008 (Greenwood, Lowenfeld, Serrano de la Vega), para. 165.]

[17] [Eds: *Cargill, Inc* v. *Mexico*, ICSID Case No. ARB(AF)/05/2, Award, 18 September 2009 (Pryles, Caron, McRae), para. 429.]

[18] [Eds: *Corn Products* v. *Mexico*, Separate Opinion by Arbitrator Lowenfeld, 15 January 2008.]

whether primary obligations under investment law are owed to investors. Reasonable people may disagree about the general issue. However, the answer to this particular question will be provided by the interpretation of the particular obligation in the particular treaty, to which the discussion [by the International Court of Justice] regarding 'individual rights' in the *LaGrand* case could provide some methodological guidance. Tribunals have answered the interpretative question differently. For (the majority of) one Tribunal[19], Chapter 11 of NAFTA expresses primary obligations only at the inter-State level; therefore, countermeasures can preclude wrongfulness for their breach, provided that other criteria of countermeasures – particularly adoption in response to an alleged breach and proportionality of the measures – have been met (they were not). For two Tribunals,[20] as well as one arbitrator of the first Tribunal writing separately,[21] investors did have rights under NAFTA, and countermeasures regarding their home State could not be opposed to these rights. Consequently, while Mexico's argument was rejected in all cases, the first, but not the second, position leaves open the possibility of successful invocation of countermeasures, provided that structural and procedural conditions are complied with. (The usual caveat is that these decisions turned on the interpretation of NAFTA, and, therefore, one should carefully consider the extent to which their reasoning is transposable to other rules regarding investment protection.)

No publicly available arbitral decisions appear to have engaged with countermeasures since the soft drinks awards of the late 2000s. A critical reflection on the current majority position – that countermeasures cannot be opposed to investors – is most likely to occur at the intersection of investment law with the two areas where countermeasures regarding economic interests are taken in a systematic manner in contemporary practice: the WTO[22] and third-party countermeasures (colloquially referred to as 'sanctions').

4.3 Necessity

2001 ILC Articles on Responsibility of States for Internationally Wrongful Acts, Art. 25

1. Necessity may not be invoked by a State as a ground for precluding the wrongfulness of an act not in conformity with an international obligation of that State unless the act:
   (a) is the only way for the State to safeguard an essential interest against a grave and imminent peril; and

---

[19] [Eds: *ADM* v. *Mexico*.]

[20] [Eds: *Corn Products* v. *Mexico*; *Cargill* v. *Mexico*.]

[21] [Eds: *ADM* v. *Mexico*, Concurring Opinion of Arbitrator Rovine.]

[22] Some investment treaties synchronise investment protection obligations with institutionalised trade countermeasures via the exceptions provisions – e.g. Trans-Pacific Partnership, Art. 29.1(4): 'Nothing in this Agreement shall be construed to prevent a Party from taking action, including maintaining or increasing a customs duty, that is authorised by the Dispute Settlement Body of the WTO or is taken as a result of a decision by a dispute settlement panel under a free trade agreement to which the Party taking action and the Party against which the action is taken are party.'

(b) does not seriously impair an essential interest of the State or States towards which the obligation exists, or of the international community as a whole.

2. In any case, necessity may not be invoked by a State as a ground for precluding wrongfulness if:

(a) the international obligation in question excludes the possibility of invoking necessity; or

(b) the State has contributed to the situation of necessity.

Argentina invoked necessity as a defence in investment arbitrations relating to the Argentinian financial crisis. Some of the early arbitral tribunals constituted on the basis of the US–Argentina BIT discussed necessity in quite some detail, as part of interpretation of the non-precluded measures clause in Article XI. However, as discussed in greater detail at Section 3.1, the persuasiveness of that interpretative approach is subject to some doubt.

M. Paparinskis, 'Circumstances Precluding Wrongfulness in International Investment Law' (2016) 31(2) *ICSID Review – FILJ* 484, 493–496 (footnotes omitted)

The story of interaction between modern investment law and necessity can be told, almost exclusively, through the rich and diverse decisions in the International Centre for Settlement of Investment Disputes (ICSID) cases on claims regarding the Argentinean crisis of the early 2000s, mostly those brought by US investors.

...

What is it that Argentinean cases tell us about necessity? Taking stock of the whole body of decisions rendered, one possible response is 'not much'. The first ICSID awards in the mid-2000s did revolve around the substance of necessity, due to the (somewhat peculiar) manner in which Argentina presented its argument on the crisis. However, gradually the focus shifted elsewhere, as international lawyers preferred to talk about any topic – be it primary and secondary rules, law and economics, primary rules expressed as obligations or primary rules expressed as exceptions – provided that they could evade addressing necessity as a secondary rule head on. The combined effect of these methodological and normative qualifications, if accepted, is to cast significant doubts on key assumptions underpinning everything said about necessity in the early decisions. If read with the most critical eye, Argentinean decisions confirm that necessity can be invoked regarding economic and financial crises – a proposition that would not have surprised international lawyers a century ago. Even more charitable commentators might take the view that these decisions do little to contribute to consensus. The muddying of waters by arbitral or doctrinal authority for nearly every imaginable construction of necessity makes discussion of the application of necessity to investment obligations challenging.

It may be convenient to consider in turn a number of questions. First, is the definition of necessity provided in Article 25 of the 2001 ILC Articles accurate and applicable in investment arbitration?

EDF International SA and Others v. Argentina, ICSID Case No. ARB/03/23, Decision on Annulment, 5 February 2016 (Greenwood, Cheng, Taniguchi), para. 319 (footnotes omitted)

... It is true that Argentina questioned whether all of the detail of Article 25 reflected customary international law and disputed what it described as the Claimants' propensity to 'refer to each of the paragraphs of Article 25 as though it were the final text of a treaty in full force and effect'. At no point, however, did Argentina indicate what aspects of Article 25 it considered did not reflect customary international law. Nor, more importantly, did it at any stage advance a positive case in favour of a standard of necessity materially different from that set out in Article 25. On the contrary, Argentina joined issue with the Claimants on each of the principal requirements of Article 25.

Most tribunals have taken a similar view.[23]

Second – since space precludes detailed consideration of application of separate elements – is it likely that a State could satisfy the cumulative and prima facie rather stringent criteria, particularly the 'only way' and non-contribution elements? Not entirely surprisingly, investment arbitration decisions regarding Argentina and more recently regarding Zimbabwe cast some doubt on that proposition. *Total SA* v. *Argentina*[24] dismissed Argentina's defence of various measures because they were either not the only way to safeguard an interest or were not adopted to protect an essential interest. *EDF International and Others* v. *Argentina*[25] concluded that Argentina's defence failed on both the 'only way' and non-contribution planks. *Hochtief AG* v. *Argentina*[26] also rejected the argument of necessity, albeit for the narrow reason that '[t]he economic crisis had ended by the time that the losses for which reparation is due were sustained'. *Bernhard Friedrich Arnd Rüdiger von Pezold and Others* v. *Zimbabwe*,[27] which addressed occupation of land, carefully examined invocation of necessity and rejected it on all grounds. *Union Fenósa Gas* v. *Egypt*,[28] which addressed interference with the supply of gas within the broader context of revolution and social revolution, again carefully examined invocation

---

[23] *Bernhard Friedrich Arnd Rüdiger von Pezold and Others* v. *Zimbabwe*, ICSID Case No. ARB/10/15, Award, 28 July 2015 (Fortier, Williams, Hwang), para. 624. But see *Urbaser SA and Other* v. *Argentina*, ICSID Case No. ARB/07/26, Award, 8 December 2016 (Bucher, Martinez-Fraga, McLachlan), at n. 245: 'While there are good reasons to accept the application of rules of international law to investment disputes, some reservation is to be observed in respect of the ILC Articles that address the responsibility of States and do so together with the self-containment rule of Article 33, para. 2, stating that these rights arising from the States' responsibility are "without prejudice to any right ... which may accrue directly to any person or entity other than a State".' Note, though, that reliance on Art. 33(2) of the 2001 ILC Articles may be not entirely accurate, since that provision refers to Part Two of the 2001 ILC Articles, and Art. 25 is in Part One.

[24] ICSID Case No. ARB/04/1, Decision on Liability, 27 December 2010 (Sacerdoti, Alvarez, Herrera Marcano), paras 223, 483–484.

[25] ICSID Case No. ARB/03/23, Award, 11 June 2012 (Park, Kaufmann-Kohler, Remón), para. 1171.

[26] ICSID Case No. ARB/07/31, Decision on Liability, 29 December 2014 (Lowe, Brower, Thomas), para. 301.

[27] ICSID Case No. ARB/10/15, Award, 28 July 2015 (Fortier, Williams, Hwang), paras 626 et seq.

[28] ICSID Case No. ARB/14/4, Award, 31 August 2018 (Veeder, Rowley, Clodfelter) para. 8.59.

of necessity and rejected it on all grounds except contribution, which 'does not fit easily with long term macro-economics' (a perspective significantly different from the early Argentinian cases). Indeed, the only explicit recent example to accept necessity, *Urbaser SA and Other* v. *Argentina*,[29] took a markedly more flexible approach to evaluation of alternative measures (perhaps somewhat similarly to interpretation of Article XI in *Continental Casualty* v. *Argentina*, discussed at Section 3.1).

4.4 Consequences

What is the effect of a successful invocation of a circumstance precluding wrongfulness?

2001 ILC Articles on Responsibility of States for Internationally Wrongful Acts, Art. 27 (Consequences of invoking a circumstance precluding wrongfulness)

The invocation of a circumstance precluding wrongfulness in accordance with this chapter is without prejudice to:

    (a) compliance with the obligation in question, if and to the extent that the circumstance precluding wrongfulness no longer exists;

    (b) the question of compensation for any material loss caused by the act in question.

2001 ILC Articles on Responsibility of States for Internationally Wrongful Acts, Art. 27, Commentaries 5–6 (footnotes omitted)

(1) Subparagraph (b) is a proper condition, in certain cases, for allowing a State to rely on a circumstance precluding wrongfulness. Without the possibility of such recourse, the State whose conduct would otherwise be unlawful might seek to shift the burden of the defence of its own interests or concerns onto an innocent third State. This principle was accepted by Hungary in invoking the plea of necessity in the *Gabčíkovo-Nagymaros Project* case. As ICJ noted, 'Hungary expressly acknowledged that, in any event, such a state of necessity would not exempt it from its duty to compensate its partner'.

(2) Subparagraph (b) does not attempt to specify in what circumstances compensation should be payable. Generally, the range of possible situations covered by chapter V is such that to lay down a detailed regime for compensation is not appropriate. It will be for the State invoking a circumstance precluding wrongfulness to agree with any affected States on the possibility and extent of compensation payable in a given case.

The 2001 ILC Articles and the Commentary say little about compensation. This is deliberate: as the *CMS* v. *Argentina* annulment decision put it, 'Article 27 itself is a "without prejudice" clause, not a stipulation. It refers to "the question of compensation" and does not attempt to specify in which circumstances compensation could be due, not withstanding the state of necessity'.[30]

---

[29] ICSID Case No. ARB/07/26, Award, 8 December 2016 (Bucher, Martínez-Fraga, McLachlan), paras 710–732.

[30] *CMS* v. *Argentina,* Decision of the Ad Hoc Committee on the Application for Annulment of the Argentine Republic, 25 September 2007, para. 147.

EDF International SA and Others v. *Argentina*, ICSID Case No. ARB/03/23, Decision on Annulment, 5 February 2016 (Greenwood, Cheng, Taniguchi), para. 330 (footnotes omitted)

The third requirement, namely to restore the *status quo* or compensate the Claimants, requires more discussion. That requirement, which the Committee derived from Article 27 of the ILC Articles, had not been the subject of such detailed argument by Argentina (although it had been raised by the Claimants). Nevertheless, the Committee cannot accept that it was 'invented' by the Tribunal. The Tribunal's analysis on this point seems to the Committee to reflect what is inherent in the very concept of necessity. If a departure from a legal obligation can be justified by a state of necessity, it can be justified for only so long as that state of necessity exists. That limitation is clearly stated in the correspondence between the British and United States Governments in the *Caroline* case, which is generally regarded as a critical instance of State practice leading to the development of the modern law of necessity.

It would be plausible to expect that some circumstances precluding wrongfulness, like consent and countermeasures, preclude compensation as well. The position may be different regarding necessity, although this is an issue where the finer legal points remain to be developed.

CONCLUSION

How is the balance struck between competing interests in international investment law? Investment protection obligations, at least of the type usually created in the 1990s, were quite explicit in articulating obligations that, in reflecting interests of investors, bound host States. It was less obvious where rules reflecting interests of host States were expressed. Where, then, are the defences in investment protection law?

First, there are many arguments that a respondent State could raise in an investment dispute to avoid its responsibility, not all of them drafted as defences. Earlier treaties of the more sophisticated pedigree as well as more recent treaties tend to, as it were, front-load avoidance of responsibility to matters of jurisdiction and admissibility – for example, reservations, carve-outs and narrow jurisdictional clauses. One preliminary objection that operates in a manner similar to defence (in the sense of avoiding responsibility even if the State has acted in breach of its investment protection obligations) is denial of benefits. This rule has been interpreted by some tribunals as operating in a retrospective manner.

Second, defences could also be given effect through appropriate drafting and application of investment obligations as such. A good example for this proposition is the concept of indirect expropriation, where both arbitral decisions and treaty-makers have recognised (what very much looks like) a defence of police powers of States. In some cases, considerations involved in the application of fair and equitable treatment and necessity may be quite similar.

Third, defences may be articulated through exceptions that are drafted as being applicable across the board. Most investment protection treaties concluded in the 1990s and arbitrated in the 2000s did not include explicit exceptions. However, the US–Argentina BIT did contain a so-called non-precluded-measures clause. This rule was extensively arbitrated in the aftermath of the Argentinian financial crisis of the early 2000s, with tribunals variously searching for interpretative inspiration in general principles, customary law and international trade law. Recent treaties often provide more elaborate exceptions, at least to some extent, with language suggestive of self-judging character. Disputes about the relationship between exceptions clauses in Canadian treaties and primary obligations, as well as secondary circumstances precluding wrongfulness, suggest that the search for certainty and clarity may be elusive, with different questions arising regarding the differently drafted clauses.

Finally, some defences are also provided by the broader international legal order within which investment protection law is situated, even if they are not explicitly referred to – in the technical parlance of the law of State responsibility, circumstances precluding wrongfulness. Consent, countermeasures and necessity have played some role in the practice of investment arbitration (the latter two in an explicit manner). One imagines that the most interesting developments will occur at the intersections between investment law and these general defences, and between the application of these defences within investment law and the operation of other regimes of international law.

QUESTIONS

1. Why did investment protection law of the 1990s and 2000s, unlike human rights and trade law, lack explicit defences?
2. The approach of *CC/Devas* v. *India* and *Deutsche Telekom* v. *India* tribunals to interpretation and application of non-precluded measures clauses is incompatible. Discuss.
3. What, if any, is the role of general exceptions in interpreting and applying primary obligations? Discuss by reference to *Bear Creek* v. *Peru* and Canada's submission in *Eco Oro* v. *Colombia*.
4. Can a State rely on countermeasures against the home State of the investor to defend its breach of investment protection obligations?
5. Arbitral decisions regarding Argentinian, Zimbabwean and Egyptian invocations of necessity show that necessity does not fit within investment law. Discuss.

SUGGESTIONS FOR FURTHER READING

1. UNCTAD, 'The Protection of National Security in IIAs' in *UNCTAD Series on Issues in International Investment Agreements* (UNCTAD, 2009), http://unctad.org/en/Docs/diaeia20085_en.pdf (accessed 7 September 2020).
2. C. Binder, 'Circumstances Precluding Wrongfulness' in M. Bungenberg, J. Griebel, S. Hobe and A. Reinisch (eds), *International Investment Law: A Handbook* (Baden-Baden: C. H. Beck/Hart/Nomos, 2015).

3. P. Tomka, 'Defenses Based on Necessity under Customary International Law and on Emergency Clauses in Bilateral Investment Treaties' in M. Kinnear, G. Fischer, J. Minguez Almeida *et al.* (eds), *Building International Investment Law: The First 50 Years of ICSID* (Alphen aan den Rijn: Kluwer Law International, 2015).

4. F. Paddeu, *Justification and Excuse in International Law* (Cambridge University Press, 2018).

5. UNCTAD, *UNCTAD's Reform Package for the International Investment Regime* (UNCTAD, 2018), https://investmentpolicy.unctad.org/uploaded-files/document/UNCTAD_Reform_Package_2018.pdf (accessed 7 September 2020), 33–47.

17

Remedies

CHAPTER OUTLINE

This chapter discusses the remedies awarded by investment arbitration tribunals upon a finding that the host State is liable for the breach of an international obligation. Section 1 establishes the principle of reparation for internationally wrongful acts by which investment arbitration tribunals are guided, while Section 2 examines how this principle is borne out in the award of compensation and restitution. Section 3 sets out the principal methods for quantifying pecuniary remedies, and Section 4 considers the award of interest on pecuniary remedies.

INTRODUCTION

The award, categorisation and quantification of remedies make up what is possibly the most critical and complex topic in international investment law and arbitration. This is because aggrieved investors lodge claims against host States for violating international obligations, with the overriding objective of obtaining concrete relief for the wrongs they have suffered. A finding by the arbitral tribunal that the host State has violated international law, whether by breaching a customary or treaty obligation, is a necessary precondition to the award of remedies. That said, whether it was ultimately worth an investor's while to bring a claim boils down to the nature and amount of relief awarded. Foreign investment often involves substantial capital outlay. The inability to recoup this outlay because of host State interference with the investment compels the affected investor to seek recompense for its losses elsewhere. Obtaining declaratory relief that the host State has violated its investment protection obligations is important for showing there is a strong legal basis for a claim, but it is the order for defaulting host States to pay that provides the most tangible form of satisfaction of a successful claim.

Although remedies in investment arbitration are not limited to monetary relief, this is the most commonly sought and awarded type of remedy. The discussion in this chapter reflects this emphasis. There are four considerations in the award of remedies in investment arbitration. The first is the principle of full reparation, a remedial rule of customary status, that is applied when a State is found liable for the commission of an internationally wrongful act. The second is the character of the loss suffered and the type of remedy that is best suited for restoring the claimant to a pre-loss position. The third, and arguably most significant, consideration is the quantification of the remedy awarded on the basis of the first two considerations, which affixes a monetary value to unlawful host State interference. The fourth is the calculation of interest on the awarded payout, which can be substantial if the payout is large. This chapter surveys how investment arbitration tribunals have addressed each of these considerations.

1. THE PRINCIPLE OF FULL REPARATION FOR INTERNATIONALLY WRONGFUL ACTS

The principle that the commission of an internationally wrongful act calls for the default-ing State to return the victim to a position where the act had not been committed is a principle of international law. The *locus classicus* is the 1928 decision of the Permanent Court of International Justice (PCIJ) in the *Case Concerning the Factory at Chorzów.*[1] The PCIJ found that Poland had unlawfully expropriated the contractual rights of the German owner of a nitrite factory located at Chorzów. As a result, Germany, on behalf of its national, was entitled to full reparation.

Case Concerning the Factory at Chorzów (Claim for Indemnity – Merits) (1928) PCIJ Rep. Series A No. 17, p. 47

The essential principle contained in the actual notion of an illegal act – a principle which seems to be established by international practice and in particular by the decisions of arbitral tribunals – is that reparation must, as far as possible, wipe out all the consequences of the illegal act and re-establish the situation which would, in all probability, have existed if that act had not been committed. Restitution in kind, or, if this is not possible, payment of a sum corresponding to the value which a restitution in kind would bear; the award, if need be, of damages for loss sustained which would not be covered by restitution in kind or payment in place of it – such are the principles which should serve to determine the amount of compensation due for an act contrary to international law.

Investment arbitration tribunals endorse the principle of full reparation for internation-ally wrongful acts, with frequent pronouncements that host States are obliged to make full reparation within the framework laid down by the PCIJ. The following excerpt is illustrative of how tribunals regard the principle as a common starting point for deter-mining how investor's losses should be remedied.[2]

---

[1] Claim for Indemnity – Merits, (1928) PCIJ Rep. Series A No. 17.
[2] See also *El Paso Energy International Co.* v. *Argentina*, ICSID Case No. ARB/03/15, Award, 31 October 2011 (Caflisch, Bernadini, Stern), paras 700–701.

> *Biwater Gauff (Tanzania) Ltd* v. *Tanzania*, ICSID Case No. ARB/05/22, Award, 24 July 2008 (Hanotiau, Born, Landau), paras 776–777 (footnote omitted)
>
> 776. For claims other than expropriation (breach of fair and equitable treatment, unreasonable and discriminatory measures, violation of full protection and security, and of the principle of unrestricted transfer of funds), the BIT [bilateral investment treaty] does not offer any guidance for evaluating the damages arising from such breaches. On the basis that this does not mean that compensation is excluded, the common starting point is the broad principle articulated in the well-known *Factory at Chorzow* case, according to which any award should:
>
> > 'as far as possible wipe out all the consequences of the illegal act and re-establish the situation which would, in all probability, have existed if that act had not been committed'.
>
> 777. The application of this broad principle has been the subject of detailed analysis in many commentaries and decisions, albeit that in many BIT cases, arbitral tribunals appear to have simply deployed the fair market value of the investment in question as the measure of damages both for claims of expropriation and breaches of other treaty standards.

The principle of full reparation applies upon a finding of unlawfulness. Reparation that wipes out the consequences of the unlawful act can take the form of monetary compensation, material restitution or a combination of the two. Tribunals thus have the flexibility to determine how best to remedy the losses suffered by an investor due to the unlawful acts of the host State.

2. COMPENSATION AND RESTITUTION

The form of compensation and restitution in investment arbitration is predominantly pecuniary. This is because compensation or restitution in kind, such as *restitution in integrum*, which may require a State to invalidate acts or enacted legislation that interferes with a protected investment, or to return confiscated assets, is essentially an order for specific performance that international courts and tribunals hesitate to impose on States. In addition to being extremely difficult to supervise and enforce, compelling a State to perform a specified act is a possible affront to the dignity of that State.[3] While a few investment arbitration tribunals consider that specific performance can, in principle, be ordered should the circumstances call for and permit this,[4] only two tribunals have, to

---

[3] S. M. Schwebel, 'Speculations on Specific Performance of a Contract between a State and a Foreign National' in Southwestern Legal Foundation International and Comparative Law Center, *Rights and Duties of Private Investors Abroad* (New York: M. Bender, 1965), 210.

[4] *Burlington Resources Inc. and Others* v. *Ecuador and Another*, ICSID Case No. ARB/08/5, Procedural Order No. 1, 29 June 2009 (Kaufmann-Kohler, Stern, Orrego Vicuña), para. 70; *Mohammad Ammar Al-Bahloul* v. *Tajikistan*, SCC Arbitration No. V (064/2008), Final Award, 8 June 2010 (Hertzfeld, Happ, Zykin), paras 47–51; cf. *CMS Gas Transmission Co.* v. *Argentina*, ICSID Case No. ARB/01/8, Award, 12 May 2005 (Orrego Vicuña, Lalonde, Rezek), para. 406; and *LG&E Energy Corp. and Others* v. *Argentina*, ICSID Case No. ARB/02/1, Decision on Liability, 3 October 2006 (de Maekelt, Rezek, van den Berg), para. 87.

date, ordered a host State to take positive steps to restore the right that a protected investor was seeking to exercise.[5] Moreover, it is exceptional that the damage sustained by the investor cannot be adequately remedied with monetary relief, but only with, or coupled with, an order for specific performance.

Oft-requested pecuniary remedies include compensation for expropriation (Section 2.1), compensation for violation of treaty obligations other than compensable expropriation (Section 2.2) and moral and punitive damages (Section 2.3).

2.1 Compensation for Expropriation

The standard of compensation for lawful expropriation is 'prompt, adequate and effective' compensation, while the amount of compensation due is the fair market value of the investment immediately prior to the moment of expropriation.[6] In contrast, it is generally agreed that the standard of compensation for unlawful expropriation is full reparation, as set out in the *Case Concerning the Factory at Chorzów*. Although the standard of compensation for unlawful expropriation may differ from that for lawful expropriation, both standards oblige the host State to indemnify the investor for the fair market value of the expropriated investment. However, the fair market value will differ depending on whether the date of valuation is set as the date of expropriation, or as a later date. Valuation as of the later date is likely to obtain a higher market value because it accounts for variables such as inflation, and is only warranted when full reparation is sought and ordered. When the date of valuation is fixed at the date of expropriation, the legality of the expropriation has no bearing on the calculation of the fair market value. Therefore, investors bringing claims for unlawful expropriation will receive more compensation than investors seeking compensation for lawful expropriations *only if* the date of valuation comes after the date of expropriation. The subtle distinction between compensation due for an unlawful expropriation and that due for a lawful expropriation was carefully explained by the tribunal in *Crystallex International Corp.* v. *Venezuela*.[7]

Crystallex International Corp. v. *Venezuela*, ICSID Case No. ARB(AF)/11/2, Award, 4 April 2016 (Lévy, Gotanda, Boisson de Chazournes), paras 841–846 (footnotes omitted)

841. The Treaty vests the Tribunal with the power to award 'monetary damages and any applicable interest' in case of breach of an obligation contained in the Treaty (Article XII(9) of the BIT). It does not, however, as is generally the case with BITs, detail any standard of compensation which the Tribunal must apply when awarding such monetary damages. The

---

[5] *Texaco Overseas Petroleum Co./California Asiatic Oil Co.* v. *Libya*, 53 ILR 389, Award on the Merits, 19 January 1977 (Dupuy), pp. 507–509; *ATA Construction, Industrial and Trading Co.* v. *Jordan*, ICSID Case No. ARB/08/2, Award, 18 May 2010 (Fortier, El-Kosheri, Reisman), paras 129–132.

[6] See discussion at Chapter 14, Section 3.2.1.

[7] ICSID Case No. ARB(AF)/11/2, Award, 4 April 2016 (Lévy, Gotanda, Boisson de Chazournes).

only reference to a standard of compensation is the one contained in Article VII(1) of the Treaty. Article VII(1) of the BIT provides that:

> 'Investments or returns of investors of either Contracting Party shall not be nationalized, expropriated or subjected to measures having an effect equivalent to nationalization or expropriation (hereinafter referred to as "expropriation") in the territory of the other Contracting Party, except for a public purpose, under due process of law, in a non-discriminatory manner and against prompt, adequate and effective compensation. Such compensation shall be based on the genuine value of the investment or returns expropriated immediately before the expropriation or at the time the proposed expropriation became public knowledge, whichever is the earlier, shall be payable from the date of expropriation with interest at a normal commercial rate, shall be paid without delay and shall be effectively realizable and freely transferable.'

842. It is undisputed that such reference concerns the compensation requirement for an expropriation to be considered compliant with Article VII(1) of the Treaty. The Parties are, however, in dispute as to whether such standard also applies to expropriations not meeting one or more of the Treaty requirements and to violations of other Treaty standards (such as FET [fair and equitable treatment] or FPS [full protection and security]), or whether in such cases the 'full reparation' standard set out in *Chorzów* should apply.

843. While in other cases this question may have important consequences, the Tribunal considers that in this particular case this discussion is rather theoretical and devoid of significant practical effects. In the Tribunal's view, to follow the BIT expropriation standard as opposed to 'full reparation' under *Chorzów* may in particular produce different outcomes where the BIT standard would lead to a valuation date as of the date of the expropriation, whereas full reparation may require, under certain circumstances, the valuation date to be fixed at the date of the award.

844. In this case, however, neither Party has argued in favor of the application of a valuation date as of the date of the award. Rather, as the Tribunal will explain *infra* when dealing with the valuation date, both Parties agree that the valuation date in this case should be the date of expropriation (they disagree on whether such date should be fixed in April 2008 or February 2011, which, however, is a different question).

845. Furthermore, the Parties agree that monetary damages must be assessed by reference to the fair market value (which is both the standard required under customary international law, and the one applicable under the BIT which speaks of 'genuine value' or 'valeur réelle' or 'valor genuino'). As rightly noted by the Respondent, the Parties' disagreement over the applicable standard of reparation is thus 'ultimately largely irrelevant'.

846. With these considerations in mind, the Tribunal wishes to make the following remarks in relation to the standard of compensation applicable in this case. First, as a general matter, the Tribunal considers that the standard of compensation contained in Article VII(1) of the Treaty is not the appropriate standard of compensation in cases of

breaches of that provision, i.e., when the requirements set out in Article VII(1) are not met. One particular question is whether the BIT standard is, however, applicable in cases of expropriations merely lacking compensation. This point may be left open here, as in any event the Tribunal is of the view that the Article VII(1) 'standard' is only concerned with expropriation, and not breaches of other BIT standards. Because the Tribunal has found breaches of FET (in addition to an expropriation), the Tribunal considers that the 'full reparation' principle under customary international law must be applied as a consequence of its decision on liability. In other words, given the cumulative nature of the breaches that the Tribunal must compensate, and especially in view of its findings on FET that the Respondent's conduct caused all the investments made by Crystallex to become worthless, the Tribunal will apply the full reparation standard according to customary international law.

2.2 Compensation for Violations of Other Treaty Standards

In order to maximise their chances of being indemnified for their losses, investors invoking investment treaty protection seldom bring claims against host States alleging the violation of a single treaty obligation. State conduct that interferes with a protected investment is usually construed as giving rise to several treaty violations, the more commonly pleaded being denial of fair and equitable treatment (FET),[8] denial of full protection and security (FPS)[9] and uncompensated expropriation.[10] Other treaty violations include the breach of a most-favoured-nation (MFN) treatment clause[11] and the breach of an umbrella clause.[12] However, when an investor alleges that State conduct simultaneously violates several treaty obligations, located in a single or several investment treaties, this raises the issue of whether the investor is entitled to remedy for every treaty obligation that is violated.

The rule of thumb is that no investor is entitled to double recovery. When the loss inflicted on a protected investment can be attributed to several, discrete treaty violations, the investor can only be indemnified for one treaty violation. No distinction is drawn between compensation for denial of FET, FPS, MFN, unlawful expropriation and the breach of an umbrella clause. This implies that the loss flowing from the breach of one treaty obligation is deemed identical to the loss flowing from the breach of a different treaty obligation. Tribunals avoid double recovery in one of two ways, both of which adhere to the principle of full reparation. The first and more popular approach simply selects one violated treaty obligation to indemnify. This is also why some tribunals do not proceed to consider the rest of the investor's claims once a treaty violation is established. If the violation of one treaty obligation already entitles the investor to recovery, whether additional treaty obligations were breached is irrelevant. The second approach directs the tribunal to spread the losses across all the treaty violations established, so that the final

---

[8] See discussion at Chapter 12.
[9] *Ibid.*
[10] See discussion at Chapter 14.
[11] See discussion at Chapter 13.
[12] See discussion at Chapter 15.

sum awarded will place the investor in a position where none of the violations occurred. The following excerpts from *Gemplus SA and Others* v. *Mexico* and *Talsud SA* v. *Mexico*,[13] and *SAUR International SA* v. *Argentina*,[14] illustrate the first and second approaches to compensation whenever loss is occasioned by two or more treaty breaches.

Approach 1: *Gemplus SA and Talsud SA* v. *Mexico*, ICSID Case Nos ARB(AF)/04/3 and ARB(AF)/04/4, Award, 16 June 2010 (Veeder, Fortier, Magallón Gomez), paras 12-51–12-52 (footnote omitted)

12-51 *Chorzów Factory*: As to the general approach to the assessment of compensation, the Tribunal accepts the general guidance provided by the well-known passage in the PCIJ's decision in *Chorzów Factory* 1928 PCIJ, Series A, No 17 (Merits), 47, as invoked by both the Claimants and the Respondent in these arbitration proceedings (summarised above):

'The essential principle contained in the actual notion of an illegal act – a principle which seems to be established by international practice and in particular by the decisions of arbitral tribunals – is that reparation must, as far as possible, wipe out all the consequences of the illegal act and reestablish the situation which would, in all probability, have existed if that act had not been committed. Restitution in kind, or, if this is not possible, payment of a sum corresponding to the value which a restitution in kind would bear; the award, if need be, of damages for loss sustained which would not be covered by restitution in kind or payment in place of it – such are the principles which should serve to determine the amount of compensation due for an act contrary to international law.'

The Tribunal is likewise guided by Article 31 of the ILC's draft Articles of State Responsibility, being declaratory of international law.

12-52 *FET & Expropriation*: The Tribunal accepts the Claimants' submissions, as summarised above, that this is an appropriate case in which the Tribunal should be guided by the same measure for breach of the FET standards in the two BITs, as for unlawful expropriation under the BITs: see the *Enron* award and *Chorzów Factory*. Accordingly, the Tribunal does not hereafter distinguish between compensation for unlawful expropriation and compensation for breach of the FET standards.

Approach 2: *SAUR International SA* v. *Argentina*, ICSID Case No. ARB/04/4, Award, 22 May 2014 (Fernández-Armesto, Hanotiau, Tomuschat), para. 165 (authors' translation from original French)

The principle of full reparation requires the Tribunal to incorporate the two violations [unlawful expropriation and denial of FET] into one damages model and calculate the value of the investment at the moment of the first violation, in order to return the investment to a position where neither violation was committed.

---

[13] ICSID Case Nos ARB(AF)/04/3 and ARB(AF)/04/4, Award, 16 June 2010 (Veeder, Fortier, Magallón Gomez).
[14] Affaire CIRDI No. ARB/04/4, Sentence, 22 May 2014 (Fernández-Armesto, Hanotiau, Tomuschat).

2.3 Moral and Punitive Damages

Moral and punitive damages refer to compensation that goes beyond indemnifying tangible loss occasioned by the breach of a treaty obligation. Moral damages may be claimed for reputational or emotional injury suffered by the investor as a result of the host State's acts of interference with its investment, while punitive damages may be claimed on the basis that a breach of treaty was particularly egregious. Investment arbitration tribunals broadly agree that it is within their powers to award moral damages,[15] although few tribunals have exercised this power. In stark contrast, the handful of tribunals that have considered the role of punitive damages in investor–State disputes are generally unwilling to introduce a punitive dimension to compensation.[16] For tribunals hearing disputes submitted under the North American Free Trade Agreement (NAFTA), there was no room for discretion, as the treaty expressly forbade tribunals from awarding punitive damages.[17] To date, no tribunal has ordered a State to pay punitive damages for investment treaty infractions.

On the rare occasion when moral damages have been awarded, this was a result of the investors and/or their personnel having been threatened with physical violence or subject to harassment. The first investment treaty tribunal to award moral damages in this context was the tribunal in *Desert Line Projects LLC* v. *Yemen*.[18] The facts of this case are memorable. The Omani claimant signed a total of eight road construction contracts with Yemen. Yemen defaulted on various progress payments and the matter was referred to arbitration in Yemen. The arbitrators held that the Yemeni government owed a substantial debt to the claimant, but despite the binding validity of this arbitral award on Yemen, no payment was forthcoming. Yemen subsequently concluded a settlement agreement with the reluctant claimant, where the amount judged owing in the earlier arbitral award was reduced by half. More importantly, the tribunal noted that Yemen relied on a potent mix of financial duress – refusal to pay which brought the claimant to the brink of bankruptcy just prior to the signing of the settlement – and physical duress – harassment of the claimant's work sites by armed men, arrests and threats to the personal safety of the

---

[15] See, for instance, *Oxus Gold Plc* v. *Uzbekistan*, UNCITRAL, Final Award, 17 December 2015 (Tercier, Stern, Lalonde (dissenting)), paras 895–900.

[16] This tendency mirrors the position in general international law where there is little authority to support claims for aggravated damages that comport a punitive and deterrent function. As a result, such claims are generally rejected.

[17] Signed 17 December 1992, entered into force 1 January 1994, 32 ILM 289, Art. 1135(3): 'A Tribunal may not order a Party to pay punitive damages.' Since the publication of the first edition of this book, the NAFTA has been updated and renamed the Agreement Between the United States of America, the United Mexican States, and Canada (signed 30 November 2018, entered into force 1 July 2020) (USMCA). The prohibition against punitive damages remains as Art. 14.D.13(6) of the USMCA, which provides: 'A tribunal shall not award punitive damages.' This prohibition may gain traction in other multilateral agreements. As the second edition of this book goes to press, the European Union proposed that the Energy Charter Treaty (signed 17 December 1994, entered into force 16 April 1998) 2080 UNTS 100 should be revised to, amongst other things, preclude tribunals from awarding punitive damages to investors: 'EU text proposal for the modernization of the Energy Charter Treaty (ECT)', 29 May 2020, https://trade.ec.europa.eu/doclib/docs/2020/may/tradoc_158754.pdf (accessed 31 July 2020).

[18] ICSID Case No. ARB/05/17, Award, 6 February 2008 (Tercier, Paulsson, El-Kosheri). A more recent example is *Bernhard Friedrich Arnd Rüdiger von Pezold and Others* v. *Zimbabwe*, ICSID Case No. ARB/10/15, Award, 28 July 2015 (Fortier, Williams, Hwang), paras 921–923.

claimant's employees – to coerce the claimant into signing the settlement agreement. These acts of coercion persuaded the tribunal that not only had Yemen violated the FET standard in the Oman–Yemen BIT,[19] but it had done so maliciously, thereby entitling the investor to moral damages.

The only known instance where substantial moral damages in the ballpark of USD 30 million were awarded for injury to an investor's business reputation is *Mohamed Abdulmohsen Al-Kharafi & Sons Co. v. Government of Libya and Others* (*Al-Kharafi v. Libya*).[20] The dispute arose from various stop-work orders issued by Libya on the performance of a touristic development concession, which led to its eventual termination. There was no applicable investment treaty. Despite the large payout, the tribunal's cursory discussion on moral damages renders uncertain the extent of reputational loss required to satisfy a request for moral damages,[21] diminishing the instructive value of this award.

***

The principle of full reparation guides tribunals in the award of compensation and restitution for violations of investment treaty obligations. To restore the investor to a position where the violations never happened, it suffices to indemnify the investor for violation of a single treaty obligation, even if several treaty violations can be established on the facts. Allowing the investor to claim separate indemnities from violations that cause damage to the same investment will result in double recovery. Regardless of whether a violation pertains to the expropriation, FET, FPS, MFN or umbrella clause, the amount of compensation is identical. Therefore, prevailing on one ground of a treaty claim, even if several grounds are pleaded, is all it takes for the loss suffered to be remedied. Exceptionally, investors may be awarded moral damages if State interference with a protected investment encompasses threats to physical well-being or reputational standing. However, the very low incidence of successful requests for moral damages suggests that real or projected physical and reputational harm must be severe.

3. METHODS OF VALUATION

When the compensation due for the breach of one treaty obligation is equivalent to the compensation due for the breach of another, the same valuation method can be employed across the spectrum of treaty obligations. Once a tribunal finds that there is a treaty violation by the State, it will proceed to determine the valuation method for calculating the exact amount of compensation due to the investor.

The World Bank Report to the Development Committee and Guidelines on the Treatment of Foreign Direct Investment (World Bank Guidelines) suggests discounted cash flow (DCF) value, liquidation value and replacement, or book, value as possible valuation methods.[22]

---

[19] Signed 20 September 1998, entered into force 1 April 2000. English translation from the original Arabic of relevant provisions found in *Desert Line* v. *Yemen*, Award.

[20] Unified Agreement for the Investment of Arab Capital in the Arab States, Final Arbitral Award, 22 March 2013 (El-Ahdab, Fawzi, El-Kamoudi El-Hafi).

[21] *Ibid.*, paras 368–369.

[22] Created 1 January 1992, disclosed 7 January 2010, vol. 2, http://documents.worldbank.org/curated/en/955221468766167766/Guidelines (accessed 31 July 2020), Art. IV(6).

Additionally, many tribunals arrive at a compensatory sum by adding an investor's sunk costs to its projected profits, or *damnum emergens* plus *lucrum cessans* (DELC). To date, the most frequently employed valuation methods, which will be discussed in this section, are the DCF method (Section 3.1) and the DELC method (Section 3.2).

Valuation in investor–State disputes is a complex exercise that is rarely undertaken without the benefit of expert valuation reports prepared by certified accountants. And in any dispute, parties are likely to submit valuation reports that propose different valuation methods and/or attach different amounts to the various categories of loss. Tribunals will review these reports in order to determine the appropriate valuation method as well as the accuracy of the submitted figures. Although some tribunals in the past offered limited insight into how they arrived at a figure of compensation,[23] the tendency towards brevity is losing purchase among modern-day tribunals. The section on payable compensation in an arbitral award is open to scrutiny and challenge just like any other section in the award. The tribunal in *Venezuela Holdings, BV and Others* v. *Venezuela*[24] was admonished by the Ad Hoc Committee in Venezuela's application for annulment for miscalculating the amount of compensation due to the claimant investors.[25] By omitting to apply the upper limit to compensation amounts fixed by the underlying contract between the disputing parties and by Venezuelan law, thereby overcompensating the investors, the tribunal had failed to state the reasons on which its award on compensation was based.[26] This led to the Ad Hoc Committee annulling the portions of the award that dealt with compensation. Tribunals therefore take pains to ensure that their valuation analysis is sufficiently detailed, cogent and accurate to bear up to scrutiny and challenge.

3.1 Discounted Cash Flow (DCF)

Article IV(6) of the World Bank Guidelines defines DCF as:

> [T]he cash receipts realistically expected from the enterprise in each future year of its economic life as reasonably projected minus that year's expected cash expenditure, after discounting this net cash flow for each year by a factor which reflects the time value of Money, expected inflation, and the risk associated with such cash flow under realistic circumstances. Such discount rate may be measured by examining the rate of return available in the same market on alternative investments of comparable risk on the basis of their present value.

---

[23] *Compañia del Desarrollo de Santa Elena SA* v. *Costa Rica*, ICSID Case No. ARB/96/1, Final Award, 17 February 2000 (Fortier, Lauterpacht, Weil), paras 93–95.

[24] ICSID Case No. ARB/07/27, Award, 9 October 2014 (Guillaume, Kaufmann-Kohler, El-Kosheri), paras 307–389.

[25] Decision on Annulment, 9 March 2017 (Berman, Abraham, Knieper), paras 137–187.

[26] Convention on the Settlement of Investment Disputes between States and Nationals of Other States (signed 18 March 1965, entered into force 14 October 1966) 575 UNTS 159 (ICSID Convention), Art. 52(1)(e): 'Either party may request annulment of the award by an application in writing addressed to the Secretary General on one or more of the following grounds ... that the award has failed to state the reasons on which it is based.' See further discussion on the ICSID annulment process at Chapter 19.

The DCF method is usually applied when the investment is a going concern, such as a factory that is already operating and earning revenue.[27] Lieblich explains how the DCF method works and why it is particularly well suited to the calculation of compensation for expropriated assets.[28]

W. C. Lieblich, 'Determining the Economic Value of Expropriated Income-Producing Property in International Arbitrations' (1991) 8 *J Int'l Arb* 59, 72–75 (footnotes omitted)

A. An Overview of the Discounted Cash Flow Method

...

The DCF method can be used to value cash flows received either before or after the valuation date, and the valuation date can be any date one chooses, whether past, present or future. In normal practice involving the valuation of businesses, the valuation date is generally the time at which the valuation is carried out, and the cash flows valued are usually those that the business is expected to generate in the future. In valuing an expropriated business, however, the valuation date should be the date on which the expropriation took place, which conforms to the customary international law rule that, at least in cases of lawful takings, the value of the expropriated property should be measured in light of the facts and circumstances known to exist as of the date of the taking.

To apply the DCF method in valuing an enterprise, one calculates the cash receipts the enterprise is expected to generate in each year subsequent to the valuation date, and then subtracts that year's expected cash expenditures in order to obtain the net cash flow for the year. The net cash flow for each future year must then be discounted (i.e. reduced) to determine its value on the valuation date (usually referred to as its 'present value'), to reflect the fact that cash to be received in the future is worth less than the same amount of cash received today. This discounting involves the application of a discount factor that is derived from a discount rate. The sum of the present values of the net cash flows for all future years is the value of the enterprise as determined by the DCF method.

...

The discount rate that is used to determine the present value of each year's net cash flows is the result of three considerations: (a) when the receipt of cash is delayed, the intended recipient loses the opportunity to use that cash to earn more cash (e.g. by investing it) during the period of delay; (b) any inflation expected between today and the expected date of receipt will reduce the purchasing power of the cash received; and (c) the person who expects to receive cash in the future bears the risk that the amount of

---

[27] World Bank Guidelines, Art. VI(i).
[28] Also, see generally S. K. Khalilian, 'The Place of Discounted Cash Flow in International Commercial Arbitrations: Awards by Iran–United States Claims Tribunal' (1991) 8 *J Int'l Arb* 31, 31–50.

cash actually received will be different from the amount expected. The first two of these considerations (i.e. the time value of money and inflation) affect all investments equally, while the extent of the third (i.e. risk) is specific to the investment being valued.

B. The Advantages of the Discounted Cash Flow Method in an Arbitral Context

...

[B]ecause of the nature of an adversarial proceeding, the DCF method is well-suited to provide the tribunal with the necessary information to carry out its responsibilities. The tribunal is greatly assisted by the process of open discussion and challenging of assumptions and data. It can then decide for itself which party has presented the more convincing arguments and evidence – for example, which expert witnesses appeared to be more highly qualified and presented more reasonable opinions, which party used the best evidence available as of the valuation date, which party's projections appeared to be more likely in the circumstances? These may be difficult judgments in specific cases, but tribunals are frequently called upon to determine difficult and controversial issues and to decide between opposing points of view of expert witnesses on matters for which they may lack expertise themselves. Once a tribunal has made these judgments, it can then translate them into a conclusion with respect to value by incorporating them in its own DCF calculation. In an age when powerful personal computers are in widespread use, such a calculation is a relatively simple matter.

The DCF method's great flexibility is a crucial aspect of its usefulness to tribunals in deciding expropriation valuation disputes. Basically, the DCF method breaks the question of value down into its constituent parts and enables the parties and the tribunal to focus on each of them. This means that the tribunal is not forced to choose between the values advocated by the parties, but can instead reach its own conclusions regarding each element of the valuation analysis and combine them into a single conclusion concerning value. For example, if the tribunal concludes that both parties' projections concerning future prices are off the mark, it can make its own projections based on the evidence before it. It can do the same with each element of the analysis, taking care to be consistent in its assumptions. When it performs its DCF calculation, its conclusion will almost certainly differ from those of both parties.

The tribunal in *Tidewater Inc. and Others* v. *Venezuela* applied the DCF method to establish the amount of compensation due to the investor for the unlawful expropriation of its marine transportation business.[29] DCF analyses in arbitral awards are invariably lengthy. However, the analysis in *Tidewater Inc.* v. *Venezuela* was selected from the large pool of awards where the tribunal adopted the DCF method as an illustration, because it provides a clear road map for the application of the DCF method to concrete facts, identifying the different factors relevant to a DCF calculation.

---

[29] ICSID Case No. ARB/10/5, Award, 13 March 2015 (Mclachlan, Rigo Sureda, Stern).

Tidewater Inc and Others v. *Venezuela*, ICSID Case No. ARB/10/5, Award, 13 March 2015 (McLachlan, Rigo Sureda, Stern), paras 165, 169, 182–190, 197–202 (footnotes omitted)

165. The Tribunal considers that in the present case, it is appropriate to determine the fair market value of Claimants' investment in SEMARCA [Tidewater Marine Service CA] by reference to a discounted cash flow analysis for the following reasons: (a) SEMARCA was, immediately prior to the date of the taking, a going concern with a proven track record of profitability; (b) it had been operating successfully in Venezuela for some fifty years, and (c) in the five years prior to the taking, it had recorded substantial operating income as recorded in its income statements. Thus, in the Tribunal's view, it is not appropriate to determine the fair market value by reference to either the liquidation value of the assets of the SEMARCA Enterprise, or the book value of those assets, as Respondent contends. Such methods would likely only be appropriate, as the World Bank Guidelines point out, where the enterprise was not a proven going concern.

...

169. There are six variables adopted in the experts' reports that have a material effect on the valuation of Claimants' investment in SEMARCA:
  (a) Scope of business: Whether SEMARCA's business is assumed to be limited to its operations on Lake Maracaibo, or whether one adds operations existing in 2009 outside Lake Maracaibo (and, if so, whether one includes services provided to international oil companies or only to PDVSA [Petróleos de Venezuela, S.A] and its subsidiaries);
  (b) Accounts receivable: Whether the outstanding accounts receivable from PDVSA are to be included in the value of the company at the valuation date or excluded from it;
  (c) Historical cash-flow: Whether to include the whole period from 2006 to March 2009 or to exclude 2009 (on the basis that the cash flow is disproportionately high in comparison to earlier years);
  (d) Equity risk: Whether to apply an equity risk premium at 5% or 6.5%;
  (e) Country risk: Whether to apply a country risk of 1.5% (Claimants' expert) or 14.75% (Respondent's experts);
  (f) Business risk: Whether to make an adjustment for single customer concentration at an assumed rate of 25% per annum or no such adjustment.
[The tribunal then proceeds to analyse each of the six variables in detail. The discussion on variable (e), country risk premium, is reproduced in full to illustrate.]

(e) Country risk premium

182. An element of greatest difference between the approaches of the experts is the premium to be applied to the risk of investing in a particular country, here Venezuela. Claimants' expert adopted a country risk premium of 1.5%, while Respondent's experts adopted 14.75%.

183. Claimants' expert, Mr. Kaczmarek, accepted in answer to a question from a member of the Tribunal that Venezuela 'quite possibly is one of the highest risk countries' in the world in which to invest. The reason why his country risk premium is so low is that he considers that political risk ought to be excluded from the country risk premium. This opinion is in turn based upon a view about the legal implications of the existence of the investment protections contained in the Venezuela-Barbados BIT. This, he considers, entitled him to exclude the 'real risks of the Government acting in a very negative way towards any private investment'. He considers that, in the light of such protections, to include such risks would confer an illegitimate benefit on the State:

> If the State can create these risks that it controls, threaten businesses, ... lower the value of the business, and then they expropriate, if we're going to take all that risk into account, then they get to purchase the company at a very steep discount because of their own risks that they have created hostile towards those companies.

184. In the Tribunal's view, Claimants' expert conflates two separate elements in a legal claim of this kind. The first element is a question of liability: are the protections of Article 5 of the BIT engaged by the specific actions of the host State, such that the investor is entitled to be awarded compensation for the loss of his property? As the Tribunal has already observed, the BIT does not prohibit all State taking of private property. Rather it requires a taking for a public interest to be compensated and provides a mechanism by which the appropriate level of compensation can be awarded by an international tribunal. Doubtless, the Treaty seeks to encourage investment between the Contracting States. But it is not an insurance policy or guarantee against all political or other risks associated with such investment.

185. If the Tribunal finds liability, then, at the second quantum stage, the Tribunal must determine the 'market value' of the investment. This second element in the claim is in essence an economic question. It depends upon the value that the market would attribute to the investment in question. Returning to the World Bank Guidelines, this is an amount that a willing buyer would pay to a willing seller of the investment immediately prior to the taking in question. Where this is determined by use of a discounted cash flow analysis, the Guidelines specifically invite a consideration of 'the risk associated with such cash flow under realistic circumstances'.

186. This is not a matter of permitting a respondent State to profit from its own wrong. On the contrary, the damages that the Tribunal is empowered by virtue of the Treaty to award are designed to ensure that the private investor is compensated for the loss of its investment. But, in determining the amount of that compensation by reference to a discounted cash flow analysis, the Tribunal should consider the value that a willing buyer would have placed on the investment. In determining this value, one element that a buyer would consider is the risk associated with investing in a particular country. Such a factor is not specific to the particular State measure that gives rise to the claim. That measure must be left out of account in arriving at a valuation, since, according to Article 5, the market valuation must be arrived at 'immediately before the expropriation or before the impending expropriation became public knowledge, whichever is the earlier'. Rather the country risk

premium quantifies the general risks, including political risks, of doing business in the particular country, as they applied on that date and as they might then reasonably have been expected to affect the prospects, and thus the value to be ascribed to the likely cash flow of the business going forward.

187. The inclusion of a country risk premium is a very common feature of tribunals' calculations of compensation, since, as one tribunal observed 'the fundamental issue of country risk [is] obvious to the least sophisticated businessman'. For example, in one recent decision concerning Venezuela, the tribunal adopted a country risk rate of 18%.

188. For these reasons, the Tribunal rejects Mr. Kaczmarek's view as to the appropriate basis on which to approach country risk.

189. Respondent's experts for their part advanced a country risk premium of 14.75%. This was derived from the Ibbotson-Morningstar International Cost of Capital Report for 2009 and validated by comparison with the method adopted by Professor Damodaran.

190. In the Tribunal's view, a country risk premium for Venezuela in 2009 of 14.75% represents a reasonable, indeed conservative, premium. In the light of its rejection of Claimants experts' reasoning, it adopts this premium for the purpose of its valuation of the investment.

...

(g) Conclusion on DCF calculation

197. The Tribunal therefore applies the elements that it has found to be appropriate, using the DCF analysis:

    (a) A business consisting of the services performed by the 15 vessels that SEMARCA operated in or from Lake Maracaibo;

    (b) Including the outstanding accounts receivable, both as an element supporting the working capital of the ongoing business and as being recoverable in itself;

    (c) Taking the average of the historic cash flows of the business for the four years 2006 – 2009;

    (d) Applying an equity risk of 6.5%;

    (e) Applying a country risk of 14.75%;

    (f) But with no additional discount for single customer concentration.

198. As mentioned above, during the hearing the Tribunal requested the experts to prepare additional calculations using their existing models including, inter alia, these variables. The experts prepared additional tables of calculations that they presented to the Tribunal in the course of the Parties' closing submissions. These tables have proved of very considerable assistance to the Tribunal in its deliberations. They produced a significantly greater convergence in figures than had been the case in the experts' reports that were filed in the written phase. Nevertheless, there continue to be material differences in the approach adopted by the experts, which in turn affect the figures presented.

199. <u>Accounts receivable</u>: Claimants' expert extracts the outstanding large amount of accounts receivable from his calculations. He presents this as an additional sum that would

have to be valued and included as a separate line item. After adjustments, he calculates the total non-recurring working capital to be added in this way to be US$16,484,677 (from the total due from PDVSA and PetroSucre as at 8 May 2009 of US$44,888,040). Respondent's experts present only the effect of including the accounts receivable as working capital within their calculations.

200. Scope of business: Claimants' expert assumes that the total size of SEMARCA's business in May 2009 includes the two vessels chartered to Chevron, thus presenting figures for either 11 vessels only (those actually operating on Lake Maracaibo) or 17 vessels. Respondent's experts limit their calculations of additional business to 15 vessels. As the Tribunal has already found that it should exclude the two vessels chartered to Chevron from its analysis, this has the consequence that the two sets of figures cannot be directly compared.

201. With these qualifications, the spread of figures presented by the two experts are as follows:

  (a) Claimants: US$31.959 million (11 vessels only) (an earnings multiple of 3.79) + US$16.484 million non-recurring accounts receivable = US$48.443 million;

  (b) Respondent: US$27.407 million (15 vessels with 100% recoverability of accounts receivable).

202. The Tribunal has already observed that the determination of an appropriate level of compensation based upon a discounted cash flow analysis of this kind is not and cannot be an exact science, but is rather a matter of informed estimation. The Tribunal considers that a willing buyer would have valued the business at approximately US$30 million, but that it would also have been prepared to pay an additional amount of US$16.4 million for the non-recurring accounts receivable, which it would have been entitled to recover in full from PDVSA upon acquisition of the business. The Tribunal therefore arrives at a valuation (excluding pre-award interest) for the purposes of compensation of US$46.4 million.

There is an important postscript to *Tidewater Inc.* v. *Venezuela*. One of the grounds for Venezuela's application for annulment of the award was the tribunal failing to state the reasons for fixing the value of SEMARCA at USD 30 million,[30] which is slightly rounded down from the value of USD 31.959 million proposed by the claimants. The Ad Hoc Committee was alerted by Venezuela to the fact that the tribunal arrived at the approximate value of USD 30 million by applying a country risk premium of 1.5 per cent, instead of 14.75 per cent, the latter being the figure proposed by Venezuela's expert, and the figure that the tribunal professed to adopt.[31] Had the tribunal applied a risk premium of 14.75 per cent, it would have arrived at a value of USD 19.997 million.[32] In light of the miscalculation, the Ad Hoc Committee annulled the portion of the Award dealing with the amount of compensation for SEMARCA's business value.[33]

[30] *Tidewater Inc. and Others* v. *Venezuela*, ICSID Case No. ARB/10/5, Decision on Annulment, 27 December 2016 (Ahmed Yusuf, Abraham, Knieper), para. 66; see also ICSID Convention, Art. 52(1)(e).
[31] *Ibid.*, Award, paras 189–190.
[32] Decision on Annulment, para. 191.
[33] Decision on Annulment, para. 212.

3.2 *Damnum Emergens* Plus *Lucrum Cessans* (DELC)

The DELC method of valuation permits the recovery of necessary expenditures made in reliance of the opposing party performing its end of the bargain (*damnum emergens*), as well as expected profits flowing from the mutual performance of the bargain (*lucrum cessans*). It is the principal valuation method employed by courts for contractual breaches under some national laws,[34] and is also popular among investment arbitration tribunals for quantifying expropriation claims that are contractual in origin.[35] According to the tribunal in *Siemens AG* v. *Argentina*, the DELC method is an optimal valuation method because '[u]nder customary international law, Siemens is entitled not just to the value of its enterprise as of May 18, 2001, the date of expropriation, but also to any greater value that enterprise has gained up to the date of this Award, plus any consequential damages'.[36]

The DELC method was employed in *Karaha Bodas Co. LLC* v. *Pertamina and PT (Persoro) PLN*.[37] In the early 1990s, Indonesia courted private foreign investment to develop its vast geothermal energy reserves. Through a State entity, Pertamina, it concluded a series of build-operate-and-transfer energy sales contracts with foreign investors.[38] In the wake of the 1997 Asian financial crisis, Indonesia was unable to continue making payments under the various energy sales contracts. Several contracts, including two concluded with Karaha Bodas, were suspended indefinitely. Karaha Bodas brought a claim in arbitration seeking damages for a breach of contract, and was awarded more than USD 260 million for incurred expenses and lost profits.

Karaha Bodas v. *Pertamina and Another*, 16 Mealey's International Arbitration Reports C1, Final Award, 18 December 2000 (Derains, Bernadini, El-Kosheri), paras 92, 98, 108, 121–122, 136

92. The necessary correlation between the rights and obligations of the Parties inherent to such contractual structure leads to the logical and inevitable conclusion that whenever the foreign investor is prevented from pursuing the performance of the binding

---

[34] For the position in the United Kingdom, see *C & P Haulage* v. *Middleton* [1983] 1 WLR 1461 (English Court of Appeal), p. 1467 (per Lord Ackner); for the position in the United States, see *L Albert & Son* v. *Armstrong Rubber Co.* (1949) 178 F2d 182 (US Court of Appeals of the Second Circuit), p. 189 (per Learned Hand CJ); for the position in Canada, see *Bowlay Logging Ltd* v. *Domtar Ltd* [1978] 4 WWR 105 (British Columbia Supreme Court), p. 117 (per Lord Berger). See also the position under French administrative law, synopsised in P. Frier and J. Petit, *Droit Administratif*, 8th edn (Paris: Librairie LGDJ, 2013), 596–600.

[35] See, for instance, *Sapphire International Petroleums Ltd* v. *National Iranian Oil Co.*, 35 ILR 136, Award, 15 March 1963 (Cavin); *Starrett Housing Corp. and Another* v. *Iran and Others*, 16 Iran–USCTR 112, Final Award, 14 August 1987; *Patua Power Ltd (Bermuda)* v. *PT (Persoro) PLN (Indonesia)*, 14 Mealey's International Arbitration Reports B1, Award, 4 May 1999 (Paulsson, de Fina, Setiawan); *Autopista Concesionada de Venezuela CA (Aucoven)* v. *Venezuela*, ICSID Case No. ARB/00/5, Award, 23 September 2003 (Kaufmann Kohler, Böckstiegel, Cremades).

[36] ICSID Case No. ARB/02/8, Award, 6 February 2007 (Rigo Sureda, Brower, Bello Janeiro), para. 352.

[37] 16 Mealey's International Arbitration Reports C1, Final Award, 18 December 2000 (Derains, Bernadini, El Kosheri).

[38] See also Chapter 2, Section 3.3 for varieties of BOT contracts.

contracts it relies upon for reasons beyond its control which were imposed upon it by the public authorities of the host country, the foreign investor should not bear the consequences thereof. In other words, in this case the foreign investor is entitled to seek recoupment of its entire investment as an essential element of compensation, in the sense that due to the frustration of its legitimate expectations in reliance on the contracts previously concluded it has to be reimbursed for what he incurred as proven expenditure.

...

98. Taking into account all the above-stated considerations, the Arbitral Tribunal is of the opinion that the Claimant has to be awarded as *damnum emergens* the aggregate of the expenditures incurred in reliance on the two Contracts concluded with the Respondents ...

...

108. ... The Arbitral Tribunal condemns jointly and severally the Respondents to pay to the Claimant an amount of US$ 111.1 million as damage for lost expenditures.

...

121. Indonesian law, like numerous other legal systems, provides for the recovery of lost profit ('*lucrum cessans*') as a component of the damages to which the innocent party is entitled in case of inexcusable breach of contract, in addition to the other damages component, the '*damnum emergens*'. As in other legal systems, recovery is limited to damages that were foreseeable when the contract was made and that are the immediate and direct result of the breach.

122. There is no doubt in the Arbitral Tribunal's opinion that the Claimant is entitled to obtain the benefit of its bargain in addition to recovering the expenditures it has incurred ...

...

136. ... The Arbitral Tribunal, after careful consideration of all elements involved in this analysis as enumerated above, and in the exercise of its inherent power to assess the quantum of damages on the basis of the evidence submitted by both parties, fixes at US$ 150 million (one hundred and fifty million US dollars), the amount of lost profits to which the Claimant is entitled ...

The tribunal in *Karaha Bodas* v. *Pertamina and Another* was criticised by Harvard economist Louis Wells for engaging in 'double counting'.[39] Wells argued that the DELC valuation method allowed 'double counting' because lost future profits (*lucrum cessans*) would have already been factored into the current value of the investment (*damnum emergens*). Allowing recovery of *lucrum cessans* in addition to *damnum emergens* will therefore lead to excessive awards on compensation.

[39] L. T. Wells, 'Double Dipping in Arbitration Awards? An Economist Questions Damages Awarded to Karaha Bodas Company in Indonesia' (2003) 19(4) *Arb. Int'l* 471.

L. T. Wells, 'Double Dipping in Arbitration Awards? An Economist Questions Damages Awarded to Karaha Bodas Company in Indonesia' (2003) 19(4) *Arb. Int'l* 471, 474–477 (footnotes omitted)

Although the award document makes it frustratingly difficult to determine exactly how the arbitrators calculated the profits part of the award, from an economist's point of view, the total amount awarded was likely excessive.

In most involuntary or efficient takings of investments, the goal of compensation ought to be to leave the investor in the same position it would have been in had the property not been taken. The principal guideline for calculating compensation is fair market value (FMV) of the property. Such a standard will usually lead to Pareto optimal results: the party initiating the breach will be better off (the Indonesians will not have to pay for unneeded electricity) and the other party (KBC) will not be worse off than if the event had not occurred.

In calculating the FMV of commercial property, or an ongoing business, analysts are likely to begin with the net present value (NPV) of the expected future stream of cash flow from the project as a measure. They would not add to the resulting figure the amount of investment. Rather, if the investment had a residual value to the investor at the end of the calculation period, that residual would be discounted and included in the NPV. In the case of KBC, there was no residual value; the project, including all assets and improvements, reverted free of cost to Pertamina at the end of 30 years. Projecting the stream of earnings for 30 years requires some heroic assumptions, especially for a project that has not yet been completed and thus has no track record; in some cases, such projections are essential, as uncertain as they might be; but there are advantages in seeking another approach when another is feasible.

When the investment is very recent, or still in the process of being made, there is an obvious and often easier alternative to using NPV of future cash flow to determine FMV. If the project was expected to generate 'normal' rates of return for the business, then the amount of investment itself provides a reasonable starting point for determining FMV. In most cases, the FMV of recently acquired assets is unlikely to be substantially different from the cost of those assets. Cost of investment will approximate what a buyer might pay; moreover, the investor who receives his investment back can invest the sum in another project, earn normal returns, and be equally well off. For most unfinished projects, this should end the calculations.

If one starts with investment as a measure of FMV, however, one must be willing to ask whether there are reasons why the market value might differ substantially from the amount spent, and make appropriate adjustments. There are indeed reasons that might justify modifications. First, if some of the investment was wasteful, or represented over-invoiced transactions with affiliates, the market value would be less than the amount invested. Indonesians [*sic*] claimed that this was the case in KBC without deciding whether any portion of the investment was wasteful or over invoiced, the arbitrators determined that even wasteful investment should be reimbursed in full, a position sharply at odds with FMV as the standard. Second, if the investor brought some kind of technology or other intangible asset to the project that added to its future cash flow but was not reflected in the investment figures, the project might have an FMV greater than the reported investment. That does not seem to support a case for greatly increasing the valuation of the KBC project over the amount invested; the geothermal projects are not at the forefront of technology, or at least no argument was reported in the arbitral decision that investors brought important proprietary technology or other intangible assets to the project. Third, adjustments might be required for an investment that was in 'exploratory' or 'research'-type activities; that is, if the investor undertook a significant gamble. If the exploration yielded negative results by the time of the taking, the project would have an FMV less than the investment, perhaps even zero, and the award should be reduced accordingly. If the gamble turned out positive, the FMV would be higher than the investment. KBC does seem to have faced some risk in terms of the geothermal resources; it is not clear, however, whether KBC had resolved questions about the amount of steam available by the time of the postponement of the project. Although the NPV approach might be an easier measure of FMV in a 'gambling' project, the arbitrators did not use that argument to explain the award to KBC. Fourthly, the FMV might be different from the amount of investment if the deal reflected corruption, lack of competitive 'bidding', or ignorance on the part of the other party. Under this argument, the tribunal would have to assess the ability of an investor to continue to collect the resulting abnormally high return; the FMV might be more, or possibly even less, than the investment. In fact, the defendant alleged that at least one of the latter conditions was present in the KBC project, an allegation that KBC denied. However, even if a party in KBC's position advanced such an argument (and KBC did not), it is not clear that the tribunal ought to make an award based on adjustments to reflect extra value accruing from these factors. Finally, a tribunal might subtract the value of those future earnings that result from an inappropriate monopoly position.

In sum, one could estimate FMV by starting with either the investment or the NPV of expected cash flows, but they should not be added together. It appears from the award document that the arbitrators in the case double counted in determining the amounts owed by Pertamina and PLN by awarding the amount of the investment (with no adjustment of the kinds indicated above) plus the NPV of expected cash flows.

Notably, Wells' argument has not won over any tribunals in the years since it was made. There are two possible reasons for this.

First, Wells assumes that *lucrum cessans* is NPV, or, based on the way he defines NPV, the economic value of a commercial entity calculated using the DCF method. This is not a uniformly held assumption because the DCF method is normally recommended as an accounting tool for 'a going concern with a proven record of profitability'.[40] It may

---

[40] World Bank Guidelines, Art. VI(i).

therefore be less apposite to situations where an investment contract is expropriated shortly after the commencement of works and where there is no 'going concern' to speak of. Moreover, nowhere was it indicated in *Karaha Bodas* v. *Pertamina and Another* that *lucrum cessans* was being calculated using the DCF method. As the tribunal reduced the claim for lost profits from USD 512 million to USD 150 million with no explanation, Wells correctly observes that it was 'frustratingly difficult to determine exactly how the arbitrators calculated the profits part of the award'. However, this observation casts doubt on the correctness of his formulation of how the Karaha Bodas tribunal allowed double recovery through DELC, namely, 'amount of the investment [DE] ... plus the NPV of expected cash flows [LC]'.

Second, even if tribunals rely on the DCF method to calculate lost profits, this does not have to result in 'double counting' when *lucrum cessans* are awarded in conjunction with *damnum emergens*. As explained by two other tribunals hearing claims arising from the same factual context as *Karaha Bodas* v. *Pertamina and Another*, 'when the victim of a breach of contract seeks recovery of sunken costs, confident that it is entitled to its damnum, it may go on to seek lost profits only with the proviso that its computations reduce future net cash flows by allowing a proper measure of amortisation'.[41]

***

There are no hard and fast rules governing the choice of valuation method by investment arbitration tribunals. That said, of the various valuation methods recommended in the World Bank Guidelines, tribunals tend to favour the DCF method, which projects the rate of return of an investment that is a going concern, and the DELC method, which adds lost profits to incurred costs when the investment is pre-operational or contract-based. Whichever valuation method the tribunal employs, the objective of valuation is to arrive at a fair market value of the investment. Therefore, tribunals have to remain vigilant to the risk of inflated claims, speculative claims and 'double counting'.

4. INTEREST

An award of compensation will normally be accompanied by an award of interest. This can be simple interest or compound interest. Simple interest is calculated on the principal amount of compensation per annum, while compound interest is calculated on the principal amount of compensation plus accumulated interest per annum.

For example, an order for compensation of USD X payable for a lawful expropriation that took place three years ago at a simple interest rate of 4.5 per cent will mean a final payment of USD [X + (0.045(X) multiplied by three years)]. And an order for compensation of USD X payable for an unlawful expropriation that took place three years ago at a compound interest rate of 4.5 per cent will mean a final payment of USD [X + 0.045(X)

---

[41] *Patua Power* v. *PT (Persoro) PLN*, Award, para. 359–60; *Himpurna California Energy Ltd (Bermuda)* v. *PT (Persero) PLN (Indonesia)*, Award, 4 May 1999 (Paulsson, de Fina, Setiawan), in A. J. van den Berg (ed.), *Yearbook of Commercial Arbitration* (The Hague: Kluwer Law International, 2000), vol. XXV, paras 241–242.

[Year 1] + (0.045(X + 0.045(X))[Year 2] + (0.045(X + 0.045(X) + 0.045(X + 0.045(X)))
[Year 3]]. When compound interest is awarded, the final figure of compensation payable
is necessarily higher than if simple interest had been awarded.

The award of compound rather than simple interest for unlawful State activities has
been justified on the basis that compound interest reflects the principle of full reparation.[42] Investment arbitration tribunals appear to share this view and exhibit a strong
tendency to award compound interest for unlawful expropriations.[43] Compensation provisions in investment treaties often provide for the payment of interest at a 'commercial
rate'. As banks typically 'compound interest due and unpaid on a quarterly basis', 'commercial rate' connotes treaty authorisation for the award of compound interest.[44]

CONCLUSION

The guiding principle in the award of remedies in investment arbitration is full reparation
for the internationally wrongful act committed by the State. This entails restoring the
claimant, whether through pecuniary compensation or compensation in kind, to a position where the internationally wrongful act had not occurred. To this end, tribunals must
determine the form and quantum of compensation.

Form: Although full reparation can take different forms, tribunals tend to award monetary compensation. This is due to the difficulty of supervising a State to ensure compliance with an order to do or undo a specific act. On the rare occasion where *restitution in
integrum* or specific performance is ordered, this may be because the State has previously
indicated its willingness to comply with such an order. Investors who prevail on their
claims will be awarded compensation that repairs the damage caused by the breach of an
international obligation. They may also seek and be awarded moral damages, over and
above compensation for the breach, if the State engages in conduct that threatens the
physical well-being or health of the investors or their personnel.

Quantum: In determining the amount of compensation due, tribunals are guided by
any applicable standard of compensation, such as the ubiquitous 'prompt, adequate, and
effective' standard for expropriations and the rule against double recovery. Therefore,
even if an investor shows that the loss suffered by a protected investment was the result
of the violation of several international obligations by the State, only one violated obligation will be considered for valuation purposes. The valuation methods adopted, with
the DCF and DELC methods being the most popular, must also be carefully applied to
avoid overcompensating the investor. Tribunals have been called out, and the relevant
portions of their awards annulled, for miscalculating the amount of compensation due.

---

[42] F. A. Mann, 'Compound Interest as an Item of Damage in International Law' (1987-1988) 21 *UC Davis
L Rev* 577; S. M. Schwebel, 'Compound Interest in International Law' in S. M. Schwebel (ed.), *Justice in
International Law: Further Selected Writings* (Cambridge University Press, 2011), 302.

[43] See, for instance, *OI European Group BV* v. *Venezuela*, ICSID Case No. ARB/11/25, Award, 10 March 2015
(Fernández-Armesto, Orrego Vicuña, Moure), paras 948-949; *Quiborax SA and Another* v. *Bolivia*, ICSID
Case No. ARB/06/2, Award, 16 September 2015 (Kaufmann-Kohler, Lalonde, Stern), paras 523-524.

[44] *Tidewater Inc. and Others* v. *Venezuela*, Award, paras 207-209.

Finally, investors who prevail are also entitled to compound interest on the amount of compensation awarded.

QUESTIONS

1. Is the principle of full reparation for internationally wrongful acts laid down in the *Case Concerning the Factory at Chorzów* the proper juridical basis for the award of remedies in all investor–State disputes? If so, why, and if not, why not?
2. Is the standard of compensation for lawful expropriation different from the standard of compensation for unlawful expropriation? If so, what is the difference? If not, should there be different standards and why?
3. Awarding moral damages is a slippery slope to arbitrariness. Often, requesting parties and tribunals offer little explanation for how they arrived at an amount that will repair moral damage. Discuss.
4. As disputing parties normally submit conflicting expert valuation reports, tribunals normally elect to follow one report or incorporate elements from both in its valuation analysis. Given the highly technical nature of accounting practices, is there a case for tribunals appointing independent valuation experts to serve as tie-breakers? What are some possible impediments to the execution of this proposal?
5. In the interest of the finality of arbitral awards, the grounds for annulment in Article 52(1) of the ICSID Convention have to be interpreted narrowly. The recent trend of Ad Hoc Committees partially annulling remedial portions of awards for miscalculation of compensation due should be discouraged. Miscalculation is an error of fact, and not, as the respondent States argue and the Ad Hoc Committees agree, a failure to state reasons. Discuss.

SUGGESTIONS FOR FURTHER READING

1. S. Ripinsky and K. Williams, *Damages in International Investment Law* (London: British Institute of International and Comparative Law, 2008).
2. B. Sabahi, *Compensation and Restitution in Investor-State Arbitration* (Oxford University Press, 2011).
3. M. Kantor, *Valuation for Arbitration* (Alphen aan den Rijn: Kluwer Law International, 2008).
4. S. M. Schwebel, 'Speculations on Specific Performance of a Contract between a State and a Foreign National' in Southwestern Legal Foundation International and Comparative Law Center, *Rights and Duties of Private Investors Abroad* (New York: M. Bender, 1965), 201.
5. P. Nevill, 'Awards of Interest by International Courts and Tribunals' (2007) 78 *BYbIL* 255.

18

Costs and Legal Fees

CHAPTER OUTLINE

This chapter deals with how costs and fees are viewed and how they are awarded by arbitral tribunals in international investment arbitration. Costs comprise both arbitration costs, meaning the cost of the tribunal including any institutional fees, and also legal costs. The latter can be substantial and may form a critical part of the relief sought by claimants. Such costs are not sought only by winning claimants – they may also be sought from losing claimants by winning respondent host States. Section 1 introduces counsel's concerns, while Section 2 describes the two main types of costs in international investment arbitration. Section 3 discusses the main considerations that guide tribunals in awarding costs. Sections 4 and 5 address related concerns of contemporary interest in this rapidly evolving area – the ever-growing prominence and importance of the 'loser-pays' principle, and the availability of security for costs as a preliminary measure. The discussion on security for costs overlaps with the discussion in Chapter 9 on provisional measures, but is considered in greater detail in the present chapter. Although third-party funding is mentioned in passing for its relevance to tribunal cost allocation, a more general discussion of alternative fee arrangements and legal expenses insurance, such as after-the-event insurance, which seeks to protect against adverse costs orders, fall outside our present focus. For readers interested in the broader debate on alternative fee arrangements in international investment arbitration, such as contingent fees and third-party funding, an item is included in the suggestions for further reading.

INTRODUCTION

The issue of costs is the first obstacle that a claimant faces in practice. It forms a critical aspect of the choice made by the claimant to initiate a claim. Costs comprise arbitration costs (how much it costs to run the proceedings) and legal costs (how much it costs to engage counsel, experts and witnesses). The issue is equally important for the respondent State. Counsel will be required to advise on the issue in circumstances less certain than he, she or the client would prefer. This is separate from but related to the usual concerns about financing the legal case, but just as with concerns about financing, the issue of costs may be critical to a decision about whether the claim should be initiated.

1. THE QUESTION OF COSTS IN THE CONTEXT OF INVESTMENT ARBITRATION

To the question 'How much?', the answer is: 'It depends'.

M. Bradfield and G. Verdirame, 'Costs in Investment Treaty Arbitration' in C. Giorgetti (ed.), *Litigating International Investment Disputes: A Practitioner's Guide* (Leiden/Boston, MA: Brill, 2014), 411

Investment arbitration can be complex and lengthy, with costs often reaching millions of dollars and sometimes tens of millions. Lawyers experienced in this field will form a view as to a plausible range of costs and share that with their clients. Any such view will be provided subject to the caveat that unforeseen events can derail early assessments. In addition to these 'unknown unknowns' there will also be 'known unknowns' – for example on the type and extent of evidence that is required, the length of the hearings, the possibility of bifurcation of proceedings – which are difficult to quantify.

Another difficulty concerns the assessment of risk in connection to the liability for the other side's costs. The current state of the law does not allow the lawyer to offer straightforward advice such as: 'if we win, they pay us; if we lose, we pay them'; or 'whatever happens, each side will pay its own costs and half the costs of the Tribunal'. Much as it frustrates clients, the answer should be: 'It depends'. The variables include the degree of success; the conduct of the parties; the complexity of the case; and considerations of equity and fairness.

Understandably, there is currently much debate and there are reforms underway in particular jurisdictions on alternative fee arrangements, particularly in respect of resort to third-party funding, which we will come to later. Such funding involves financial enterprises which have no legal interest in the dispute paying a portion or the whole of the costs in return for a share of the winnings on a 'non-recourse' basis – i.e. where the funder looks not to the legal party for repayment, but to that party's winnings. At common law, contingent fee arrangements (i.e. 'no win no pay') had for long offended against the rule prohibiting maintenance (i.e. meddling without justification in another's legal claim) on account of the funder having no legitimate legal interest in the claim itself, and the rule against champerty, which is defined as maintenance given in return for a share of the spoils gained in the event of the claim's success. In England, Lord Justice Steyn (as he then was) quoted Bentham thus:

> A mischief, in those times it seems but too common, though a mischief not to be cured by such laws, was, that a man would buy a weak claim, in hopes that power might convert it into a strong one, and that the sword of a baron, stalking into court with a rabble of retainers at his heels, might strike terror into the eyes of a judge upon the bench. At present, what cares an English judge for the swords of a hundred barons? Neither fearing nor hoping, hating nor loving, the judge of our days is ready

with equal phlegm to administer, on all occasions, that system, whatever it be, of justice or injustice, which the law has put into his hands.[1]

That describes the original justification against third-party funding of disputes before the courts. Its relevance, or at least its attractiveness, in the sphere of the private dispensation of justice, of which investment arbitration is sometimes declared to be a subset, is now questioned.[2] It may require no great stretch of the imagination to suppose that one might someday encounter an investment claim brought by a disappointed third-party funder who claims to have 'invested' in the investment claim. The investment arbitration system would then have become the snake which devours its own tail.

2. TYPES OF COSTS

There are in essence two types of costs: namely, the costs of the arbitration (Section 2.1), and legal costs (Section 2.2). The following excerpts deal with them in turn. A finding by Mathew Hodgson suggests that mean arbitration or tribunal costs – consisting of the arbitrators' fees and expenses as well as any institutional charges – were USD 746,000 at the end of 2012. Mean costs for an UNCITRAL arbitration were found to be USD 853,000, according to this finding, compared to a figure of USD 769,000 for ICSID proceedings and USD 480,000 for an SCC arbitration. Evidently, ICSID's cap on arbitrators' fees (currently fixed at USD 3,000 per day) may have had a role to play.[3] Some of those figures have since been updated. The mean arbitration costs, taking into account only the data since 2013, have risen to USD 1,118,000 from the previous figure of USD 746,000. The mean figure for UNCITRAL arbitrations is now USD 1,384,000, whereas for ICSID arbitrations that figure is USD 1,042,000.[4] Taking the pre-2013 and post-2013 figures together, the mean figure for the former category is USD 1,089.000 and USD 920,000 for the latter.

2.1 'Arbitration Costs' or 'Costs of the Proceedings'

What do arbitration costs comprise?

---

[1] *Giles* v. *Thompson* [1993] 3 All ER 321, 329a; quoted in Jeremy Morgan QC, 'Third Party Funding – Legal Aspects', paper presented to the London Common Law and Commercial Bar Association on Wednesday 12 March 2008, available at www.39essex.com/docs/articles/JMO_Third_Party_Funding_March2008.pdf (accessed 7 September 2020).

[2] There has been recent reform of arbitration legislation in various places, for example in Singapore and Hong Kong, which aims to accommodate third-party-funding in arbitration. The considerations which apply to commercial arbitration, which is what such reforms may have primarily in mind, may not, however, apply as well to investment arbitration between claimants and host States. This is due to the public regulatory aspects which typically are involved in investment arbitration. Should a sovereign State subordinate itself in any way to a third-party funder in the management of the claim, especially where the dispute concerns that State's sovereign regulatory powers?

[3] Allen & Overy, 'Investment Treaty Arbitration: How Much Does It Cost? How Long Does It Take?', 18 February 2014; M. Hodgson, 'Counting the Costs of Investor Treaty Arbitration', GAR Online News, 24 March 2014, 3 ('Original 2014 Hodgson/Allen & Overy Study').

[4] Matthew Hodgson and Alistair Campbell, 'Damages and Costs in Investment Treaty Arbitration Revisited', *GAR*, 14 December 2017 (hereafter, Hodgson and Campbell, 'Revisited')

M. Bradfield and G. Verdirame, 'Costs in Investment Treaty Arbitration' in C. Giorgetti (ed.), *Litigating International Investment Disputes: A Practitioner's Guide* (Leiden/Boston, MA: Brill, 2014), 412–414

Arbitration costs normally include the costs of the tribunal, the arbitral institution, and the hearing venue. These costs are met through the payment of fees, and advances on costs during the proceedings.

Tribunal fees and expenses are the main arbitration costs. They include each arbitrator's fees for work undertaken in connection with the proceedings, travel costs, and other direct expenses reasonably incurred (for example, the costs of communications, photocopying and typing). Accordingly, they will depend on such factors as the length and complexity of the proceedings, the location of the hearings, and the need for the tribunal to appoint any experts and/or clerical staff.

In ICSID arbitrations, the arbitrators' fees are determined by the Secretary-General with the approval of the Chairman of the Administrative Council. These fees are currently set at US$3,000 per day. ICSID tribunals are also entitled to receive a *per diem* allowance (when away from their normal place of residence) and travel expenses, both of which are set by reference to the 'norms established from time to time for the Executive Directors of the [World] Bank'. It is possible (albeit highly unusual) for the tribunal to request, or the parties to agree to, higher rates of remuneration.

In UNCITRAL proceedings, the tribunal *prima facie* has greater flexibility in determining the fees and expenses it may recover from the parties. However, the UNCITRAL Rules provide the following safeguards: first, the tribunal is obliged to take into account the method for determining fees set by any applicable appointing authority; and, second, after being constituted the tribunal has to inform the parties promptly how it proposes to determine its fees and expenses, following which the parties may refer the proposal to the relevant appointing authority for review and, if necessary, adjustment.

Parties will also bear the costs of the arbitral institution. A party wishing to commence an ICSID arbitration is required, upon submitting the request for arbitration, to pay to the ICSID Centre a non-refundable fee, currently set at US$25,000. Until this payment is received, the Secretary-General of the ICSID Centre is not obliged to take any step, other than acknowledging receipt of the request.

No such payment is normally required when commencing an UNCITRAL arbitration, as (unless the parties have agreed to the contrary) no institution will provide an equivalent administrative function to that of the Centre. An exception is where an appointing authority is required to appoint an arbitrator, in which case the default position is that the Secretary-General of the Permanent Court of Arbitration ('PCA') will designate an appointing authority upon payment of a fee.

In ICSID arbitrations, the Centre administers the arbitral process in return for which it requires payment of: (a) an administrative fee following the constitution of the tribunal, currently set at US$32,000; and (b) further administrative fees on an annual basis thereafter. As stated above, in UNCITRAL arbitrations there is normally no arbitral institution. However, the parties may agree, or the tribunal may request, that a body such as the PCA be appointed to act as registrar or administrative secretary. This can help to make the arbitral process more efficient and, despite the associated costs involved, may save the parties costs that they would otherwise incur in payments to the tribunal or in legal fees concerning minor administrative issues.

The final arbitration cost is the hire of the hearing venue. The default position under the ICSID Convention is that hearings take place at the seat of the Centre, namely the principal office of the World Bank in Washington, D.C. If the parties rely on this default position, the associated expense will be requested from the parties in an advance on costs. Under the UNCITRAL Rules, the parties and the tribunal agree on the venue for any hearing. The parties will pay for costs of the venue directly or request that the tribunal does so, in which case they will be required first to put the tribunal in funds by way of a deposit.

2.2 'Legal' or 'Party' Costs

Legal costs comprise lawyers' fees and disbursements (travel, communications, translation), and the costs of witnesses and experts, including experts' fees. The 2014 Hodgson/ Allen & Overy study found that average claimants' costs stood at USD 4,437,000, while average respondents' costs stood at USD 4,559,000.[5] However, this figure is distorted by certain very high value claims. An average mid-value claim would be closer to USD 3,145,000 for claimants and USD 2,286,000 for respondents. Claimants' costs are presumed to be higher because they bear the burden of proof, possess a less acute costs sensitivity compared to respondents, and also because of the availability of in-house respondent legal teams.[6] As to the last, it is well known that Argentina soon developed a capable in-house legal team. The updated figures based upon information after 2013 are USD 7,414,000 for claimants' costs and USD 5,188,000 for respondents' costs. Taking the pre-2013 and post-2013 figures together, average claimants' costs were found by the Hodgson/Allen & Overy study to be USD 6,019,000, and average respondents' costs to be USD 4,855,000.[7]

---

[5] The 2014 Hodgson/Allen & Overy study had been based on 176 awards. Other estimates include the OECD's estimate of combined arbitration and legal costs exceeding USD 8 million on average, based on a study of 143 awards from August 2011, and it is this more dramatic figure which UNCTAD also cites. See Jeffery P. Commission, 'How Much Does an ICSID Arbitration Cost? A Snapshot of the Last Five Years', *Kluwer Arbitration Blog*, 29 February 2016. Commission's study of ICSID arbitrations between 2011 and 2015 reveals figures closer to the Hodgson/Allen & Overy study's figures. Commission found legal costs to have been around USD 5.6 million on average for claimants, and slightly less than USD 5 million on average for respondents. Tribunal costs during this period were on average around USD 880,000.
[6] M. Hodgson, 'Counting the Costs of Investment Treaty Arbitration', GAR Online News, 24 March 2014, 2.
[7] Hodgson and Campbell, 'Revisited'.

It is also important to bear in mind the distinction between arbitration and legal costs. To illustrate, assume a simple contingency fee arrangement (e.g. 'no win no pay'). Lawyers may be able to enter into such an arrangement where permissible under legal professional rules. However, even where permissible, such arrangements are likely to cover only the cost of the lawyers' fees, but not necessarily the arbitration costs and other party costs.

Traditionally, the rule has been to have the parties pay their own costs and to divide the costs of the tribunal between them, sometimes known as the 'American Approach'. But as we have seen from Bradfield and Verdirame, there is increasingly less certainty and much attention has been drawn in recent years to a possible trend towards the loser-pays principle, or the principle that 'costs follow the event' (CFtE), otherwise known as the 'English Approach'.[8] The issue has to do with how a tribunal would, and should, allocate costs between the parties. More will be said in Section 3 on costs allocation.

***

To summarise the discussion so far, arbitration costs include the tribunal's fees and expenses, the costs charged by the arbitral institution administering the arbitration and the cost of hiring the arbitration venue. According to the Hodgson/Allen & Overy study, arbitration costs can range from around USD 500,000 to more than USD 800,000, depending on the arbitral institution selected. Legal costs refer to the charges and expenses of counsel, experts and witnesses. According to the same study, legal costs range from around USD 2 million to more than USD 4 million.

3. COST ALLOCATION BY THE TRIBUNAL

How does a tribunal approach the matter?

3.1 UNCITRAL and ICSID Rules

Subject to a party agreement, there is at present a wide divergence in tribunal cost allocation practices. There are several possibilities. A tribunal could split the costs of the arbitration and make each party bear both its own legal and other costs, under what is euphemistically referred to as 'pay your own way'. It could instead apportion both legal costs and the cost of the arbitration on the basis that costs follow the event (i.e. 'loser pays'), or it could confine the application of the loser-pays rule to party costs but not to arbitration costs, thereby making the respondent pay for the claimant's party costs only

---

[8] See, Hodgson, 'Counting the Costs', 8, where the study shows that cost adjustment of some manner occurred in 35 per cent of cases prior to 2006, while the figures after that date show a rise to 49 per cent. One caveat is that cost-adjusted outcomes do not always reflect the application of a costs-follow-the-event approach even when that is used as a starting point. For example, this approach may not show in the outcome because of some element of 'misconduct' by the successful party. See *Eastern Sugar* v. *Czech Republic*, where the tribunal ordered the successful party to pay a part of the losing party's tribunal costs. This was due to the winning party having claimed an overlarge amount where it managed only to secure approximately 25 per cent of the sum claimed: Hodgson, 'Counting the Costs', 6; *Eastern Sugar* v. *Czech Republic*, UNCITRAL, SCC 088/2004, Final Award on Tribunal Costs, 12 April 2007, para. 6 (Dr Pierre A. Karrer, Chairman; Mr Robert A. Volterra; Professor Emmanuel Gaillard).

if the respondent loses, and vice versa. Furthermore, in applying the costs-follow-the-event rule at the outset, the tribunal need not end up allocating to the loser all the costs of the winner, but may grant only a portion of such costs, as the tribunal in *International Thunderbird Gaming* v. *Mexico* did (excerpted below).[9]

The first thing to notice is that the ICSID and UNCITRAL rules on cost allocation are worded differently, the principal difference being that the rule that costs should follow the event is expressly stated in what had been Article 40(1) of the 1976 UNCITRAL Arbitration Rules. The rule is now stated in Article 42(1) of the 2010 UNCITRAL Arbitration Rules.

UNCITRAL Arbitration Rules 2010, Art. 42

1. The costs of the arbitration shall in principle be borne by the unsuccessful party or parties. However, the arbitral tribunal may apportion each of such costs between the parties if it determines that apportionment is reasonable, taking into account the circumstances of the case.
2. The arbitral tribunal shall in the final award or, if it deems appropriate, in any other award, determine any amount that a party may have to pay to another party as a result of the decision on allocation of costs.

Compare the UNCITRAL Arbitration Rules to Article 61(2) of the ICSID Convention. Article 61(2) states the ICSID rule on cost allocation as follows:

Convention on the Settlement of Investment Disputes between States and Nationals of Other States

Article 61

...

(2) In the case of arbitration proceedings the Tribunal shall, except as the parties otherwise agree, assess the expenses incurred by the parties in connection with the proceedings, and shall decide how and by whom those expenses, the fees and expenses of the members of the Tribunal and the charges for the use of the facilities of the Centre shall be paid. Such decision shall form part of the award.

This difference between the two rule formulations is said to have had a visible effect on the recovery of costs before tribunals.[10]

3.2 Tribunal Considerations

Gotanda has made the following suggestions for improving the costs regime in investment arbitration.

---

[9] See also *Eastern Sugar* v. *Czech Republic.*

[10] According to Hodgson, 'Counting the Costs', 9, successful parties recover costs in 69 per cent of UNCITRAL cases compared to a figure of 36 per cent for ICSID claims.

J. Y. Gotanda, 'Consistently Inconsistent: The Need for Predictability in Awarding Costs and Fees in Investment Treaty Arbitration' (2013) 28 *ICSID Review – FILJ* 420, 434–435 (footnote omitted)

First, tribunals should regularly request the parties to separately brief issues relating to the award of costs and fees after the tribunal has held a hearing on the other claims. This procedure is contemplated, but not mandated, by ICSID Rule 28(2). Tribunals could also consider holding a separate hearing on the issue of costs and fees if such argument would assist the tribunal in more fully understanding the issues related to costs and fees, particularly where costs and fees are substantial. In certain cases, it may be advantageous for parties to address issues relating to costs and fees after a decision on the merits, which would allow them to draw upon aspects of the decision on the merits in arguing for a particular outcome with respect to awards of costs and attorneys' fees. This would also give tribunals an opportunity to address special factors, such as 'when a party has engaged in bad faith or misconduct during the proceedings or when an award of costs and fees may cause undue hardship'. In short, this procedure would allow the parties more appropriately to tailor their arguments, and enable tribunals to examine more closely how costs should be allocated under the circumstances and whether the amounts claimed are reasonable.

Second, tribunals should consider the success of the parties as the major factor in allocating costs and fees. Emphasizing this factor would give effect to the main justification for the costs-follow-the-event approach – to make successful parties whole. In this regard, factors such as the complexity of the case and the quality of the arguments should not be considered in allocating costs and fees. These factors are irrelevant to the primary purpose of the costs-follow-the-event rule. However, they may affect whether the amounts claimed are reasonable.

Third, because the costs-follow-the-event method is not as objective as when mandating parties bear their own expenses, the goals of transparency and legitimacy would be better served by tribunals adopting a general practice of providing detailed explanations for their awards of costs and fees. Currently, many tribunals award costs and fees without discussion.

Two points which therefore deserve consideration have to do with the desirability of tribunals adopting a broad-brush approach towards costs, and the factors which should be considered relevant. The following study, capturing the early trend towards the adoption of a loser-pays approach, contains a useful summary of the principal factors which may matter to a tribunal. As we have seen, Gotanda would reject factors such as the complexity of the case and the quality of the legal arguments.

N. Rubins, 'The Allocation of Costs and Attorney's Fees in Investor-State Arbitration' (2003) 18 *ICSID Review – FILJ* 109, 126–129 (footnotes omitted)

Primary Factors

The relative success of the parties, the conduct of each side and its counsel, and the novelty of legal issues involved in the dispute at hand recur in almost every investment arbitration costs award where some kind of reasoning is presented.

(1) Proportion of success. The most common factor in arbitrators' cost allocation consideration appears to be the element of victory. But simply 'prevailing' as a formal matter appears to be insufficient for most tribunals to justify full cost shifting. Instead, arbitrators frequently review the extent to which each party can be considered 'successful', including the percentage of damages requested that were actually awarded, as well as recognition of the validity of particular defenses or objections.

(2) Conduct during the proceedings. Considering that dilatory or otherwise uncooperative behavior frequently increases legal fees and the costs of arbitration for both parties, arbitrators have often considered each party's conduct in setting the allocation of costs. In particular, obstruction of discovery, delay of proceedings, raising frivolous claims and defenses, and other apparent bad-faith behavior have increased the final costs burden on the offending party. Where a respondent State refuses to participate (a circumstance that appears more common in investment arbitration than the private, commercial variety), tribunals have often awarded some measure of costs or fees to the claimant in recognition of the delay and expense that such unresponsiveness creates.

(3) Novelty of legal issues. When issuing costs awards, tribunals regularly take into account the lack of legal clarity in the relatively novel field of investment arbitration. In this regard, arbitrators may consider that a party's submission of a groundless claim or defense was nevertheless reasonable and understandable, given that little or no legal guidance as to the interpretation of treaties and customary international law was available. It remains to be seen whether the continuing development of international investment jurisprudence will reduce the importance of this factor over time.

Secondary Factors

There is far more disagreement concerning the utility of factors such as the gravity of the respondent's international law breach, the position of the host state's national law, and concerns of equity and public policy in properly allocating the costs and expenses of arbitrating investment disputes. For now, none of these elements appears with any great frequency in the costs allocation section of arbitration awards, but because some influential tribunals have from time to time relied upon them, these three factors could increase in importance in future cases.

(1) Gravity of breach. While the seriousness of the respondent's illegal conduct towards the successful claimant is not always a factor in the cost allocation analysis, and in *S.D. Myers* the tribunal opined that it should never be, there is some indication that where a

host state has behaved with particular malice towards the claimant, the arbitrators may be more likely to order the respondent to cover a larger proportion of costs and legal fees.

(2) Local law of Respondent State. To date, *Himpurna* and *CME* are among only a handful of decisions on costs to take account of the position of the local law of the respondent state on the issue. This is in a sense surprising, since most bilateral investment treaties and many concession contracts that provide jurisdiction for investment arbitration tribunals contain a choice-of-law provision designating the local law as at least one of the applicable sources of law. While it could be argued that cost allocation is a purely procedural matter, and therefore outside the ambit of the choice-of-law clause, some jurisdictions categorize cost-shifting as substantive. In future, tribunals convened under investment treaties may begin to consider more seriously the host state's law in determining who should bear the costs of arbitration.

(3) Equitable concerns. Considerations of justice and equity may play some role in the cost allocation process, particularly when the losing party is not ordered to pay the winner's expenses. Where the claimant has failed to establish either jurisdiction or liability for 'technical' reasons, a tribunal that is nevertheless sympathetic to its predicament or the way it was treated by the state respondent may express this through an equal division of costs and expenses. Similarly, where a respondent state has lost its case and is condemned to pay damages, arbitrators appear occasionally to take account of the economic situation in the country and the potential impact on the population of a further award of costs, exercising discretion to refrain from imposing the 'loser pays' rule.

***

In sum, neither the UNICTRAL Arbitration Rules nor the ICSID regime oblige tribunals to allocate costs in a particular manner, although the UNCITRAL Rules provide that arbitration costs should, generally, be borne by the losing party. Tribunals therefore have considerable leeway to determine how costs should be allocated in international investment arbitrations. Factors that tribunals may take into account in their awards on costs include the proportion of success of each party, the conduct of the parties during the proceedings, the novelty or even complexity[11] of the issues raised, the gravity of the breach by the respondent State and the local law of the respondent State, as well as equitable concerns.

4. THE 'LOSER-PAYS' PRINCIPLE, OR 'COSTS AFTER THE EVENT'

Until fairly recently, the view was that unless parties had agreed otherwise, a tribunal would – following the practice in public international law – usually split the costs of the arbitration and make each party bear their own costs. In this regard, the NAFTA Chapter 11 Awards in *Methanex Corp.* v. *US* and *International Thunderbird Gaming* v. *Mexico*

---

[11] *EuroGas Inc. and Belmont Resources Inc.* v. *Slovak Republic*, ICSID Case No. ARB/14/14, Award, 18 August 2017 (Mayer, President; Gaillard; Stern), para. 473.

represent a notable development which suggests a trend towards adopting a loser-pays approach since the beginning of the twenty-first century.

Methanex Corp. v. United States, UNCITRAL (NAFTA) Arbitration, Final Award, 3 August 2005, Part V, paras 3, 4–5, 9–12 (footnote omitted)

3. Article 40 of the UNCITRAL Rules provides, in material part, as follows:

1. Except as provided in paragraph 2, the costs of arbitration shall in principle be borne by the unsuccessful party. However, the arbitral tribunal may apportion each of such costs between the parties if it determines that apportionment is reasonable, taking into account the circumstances of the case.

2. With respect to the costs of legal representation and assistance referred to in article 38, paragraph (e), the arbitral tribunal, taking into account the circumstances of the case, shall be free to determine which party shall bear such costs or may apportion such costs between the parties if it determines that apportionment is reasonable ...

4. The Tribunal addresses separately below: (i) the Costs of the Arbitration under Articles 38(a), (b), (c) and (f) and 39(1)1 of the UNCITRAL Rules; and (ii) the Disputing Parties' Legal Costs under Article 38(e) of the UNCITRAL Rules.

5. The Tribunal determines that there is no compelling reason not to apply the general approach required by the first sentence of article 40(1) of the UNCITRAL Rules. Although over the last five years, Methanex has prevailed on certain arguments and other issues against the USA, Methanex is the unsuccessful party both as to jurisdiction and the merits of its Claim. There is no case here for any apportionment under Article 40(1) of the Rules or other departure from this general principle. Accordingly, the Tribunal decides that Methanex as the unsuccessful party shall bear the costs of the arbitration.

...

9. Both Disputing Parties have claimed an award in respect of their respective legal costs. The Tribunal has taken into account the practices of certain arbitration tribunals where no order is made in respect of legal costs. The practices of international tribunals vary widely. Certain tribunals are reluctant to order the unsuccessful party to pay the costs of the successful party's legal representation unless the successful party has prevailed over a manifestly spurious position taken by the unsuccessful party. Other arbitral tribunals consider that the successful party should not normally be left out of pocket in respect of the legal costs reasonably incurred in enforcing or defending its legal rights.

10. In the present case, the Tribunal favours the approach taken by the Disputing Parties themselves, namely that as a general principle the successful party should be paid its reasonable legal costs by the unsuccessful party.

11. In this case, the USA has emerged as the successful party, as regards both jurisdiction and the merits. The Tribunal has borne in mind that, at the time of the Partial Award, it could have been argued that the USA had lost several important arguments on the admissibility issues; but over time the Partial Award does not affect the end-result of the dispute overall, as decided by this Final Award. Likewise, the issues on which the USA did

not prevail in this Award were of minor significance. The Tribunal does not consider any apportionment appropriate under Article 40(2) of the UNCITRAL Rules.

12. Accordingly, the Tribunal decides that Methanex shall pay to the USA the amount of its legal costs reasonably incurred in these arbitration proceedings. The Tribunal assesses that amount in the sum claimed by the USA, namely US $2,989,423.76, which the Tribunal deems to be reasonable in the circumstances within the meaning of Article 38(e) of the UNCITRAL Rules. It is also far inferior to the sum claimed by Methanex in respect of its own legal costs, namely US $11–12 million.

International Thunderbird Gaming Corp. v. *Mexico*, UNCITRAL (NAFTA) Arbitration, Award, 26 January 2006, paras 212–221 (Professor Dr Albert Jan van den Berg, President; Professor Thomas Wälde; Lic. Augustín Portal Ariosa)

212. ... Articles 40 (1) and (2) of the UNCITRAL Rules provide as follows:

1. Except as provided in paragraph 2, the costs of arbitration shall in principle be borne by the unsuccessful party. However, the arbitral tribunal may apportion each of such costs between the parties if it determines that apportionment is reasonable, taking into account the circumstances of the case.

2. With respect to the costs of legal representation and assistance referred to in article 38, paragraph (e), the arbitral tribunal, taking into account the circumstances of the case, shall be free to determine which party shall bear such costs or may apportion such costs between the parties if it determines that apportionment is reasonable.

213. The majority view in *S.D. Myers v. Canada* believed that there is a 'subtle distinction' between these two paragraphs, the first emphasizing 'success', and the second 'the circumstances of the case'. The present Arbitral Tribunal does not see the distinction between the two paragraphs in that way. The first paragraph too refers to 'the circumstances of the case' whilst the second, as conceded by the majority view in *S.D. Myers*, also implies success. Rather, the difference between the two paragraphs is that the first paragraph sets forth a rule with an exception to that rule, whereas the second paragraph gives an arbitral tribunal unfettered discretion. According to the first paragraph, the costs of the arbitration 'shall in principle be borne by the unsuccessful party', whilst according to the second paragraph, an arbitral tribunal 'shall be free' to determine which party bears the costs of legal representation (or may apportion such costs). In the present case, the Arbitral Tribunal does not see a reason to rely on that distinction, as the more objective benchmark for both types of costs is the rate of success of a party.

214. It is also debated whether 'the loser pays' (or 'costs follow the event') rule should be applied in international investment arbitration. It is indeed true that in many cases, notwithstanding the fact that the investor is not the prevailing party, the investor is not condemned to pay the costs of the government. The Tribunal fails to grasp the rationale of this view, except in the case of an investor with limited financial resources where

considerations of access to justice may play a role. Barring that, it appears to the Tribunal that the same rules should apply to international investment arbitration as apply in other international arbitration proceedings.

215. It may be added that Article 1135 of the NAFTA explicitly contemplates the possibility for a tribunal to award costs: '[a] tribunal may also award costs in accordance with the applicable arbitration rules'. The treaty does not contain any limitation in regard of the award of costs.

216. The parties to the present case have themselves each claimed an award of costs (see Notice of Arbitration at ¶34 and SoD at ¶372). Although Thunderbird has contended that it is rarely appropriate for costs to be awarded to an unsuccessful NAFTA claimant, it has at the same time recognized: '[n]o NAFTA provisions exist which would modify the application of [Articles 38 and 40 of the UNCITRAL] arbitration rules. Accordingly, it lies within the discretion of this Tribunal to award costs in the manner it determines to be the most appropriate and reasonable in the circumstances' (see PSoC at p.121).

217. The Tribunal is mindful of other NAFTA awards such as the decision in *Azinian v. Mexico*, in which the tribunal considered four factors for deciding that the losing investor need not pay the costs of the respondent (state party):

> The claim has failed in its entirety. The Respondent has been put to considerable inconvenience. In ordinary circumstances it is common in international arbitral proceedings that a losing claimant is ordered to bear the costs of the arbitration, as well as to contribute to the prevailing respondent's reasonable costs of representation. This practice serves the dual function of reparation and dissuasion.
>
> In this case, however, four factors militate against an award of costs. First, this is a new and novel mechanism for the resolution of international investment disputes. Although the Claimants have failed to make their case under the NAFTA, the Arbitral Tribunal accepts, by way of limitation, that the legal constraints on such causes of action were unfamiliar. Secondly, the Claimants presented their case in an efficient and professional manner. Thirdly, the Arbitral Tribunal considers that by raising issues of defective performance (as opposed to voidness *ab initio*) without regard to the notice provisions of the Concession Contract, the Naucalpan Ayuntamiento may be said to some extent to have invited litigation. Fourthly, it appears that the persons most accountable for the Claimants' wrongful behaviour would be the least likely to be affected by an award of costs; Mr. Goldenstein is beyond this Arbitral Tribunal's jurisdiction, while Ms. Baca – who might as a practical matter be the most solvent of the Claimants – had no active role at any stage.

218. With respect to the first factor, investment arbitration in general and NAFTA arbitration in particular have become so well known and established as to diminish their novelty as dispute resolution mechanisms. Thus, this factor is no longer applicable when considering apportionment of costs in international investment disputes. As for the second factor, although it may be said that the Parties here presented their case in an efficient and professional manner, the Tribunal does not find it a decisive factor for awarding costs

in deviation of the general principle. Finally, the third and fourth *Azinian* factors are not applicable in the present case.

219. In the present case, the Tribunal has found that Mexico is the successful party, except on issues of jurisdiction and/or admissibility.

220. Accordingly, the Tribunal finds that Mexico may in principle recover an appropriate portion of the costs of its legal representation and assistance. In this regard, the amount of US$ 1,502,065.84 claimed by Mexico appears to be reasonable in light of the scope and length of the present arbitral proceedings. Mexico did not however prevail on all issues. In consideration of this fact, the Tribunal shall exercise its discretion and allocate the costs on a ¾–¼ basis. Accordingly, the Tribunal hereby determines that Thunderbird shall reimburse Mexico in the amount of US$ 1,126,549.38 in respect of the costs of legal representation for this arbitration.

221. As regards the fees of the arbitrators, the Arbitral Tribunal has determined the fees of the Arbitrators to be US$405,620. The disbursements of the arbitration, including rent of hearing rooms, travel, hotel accommodation and court reporters amount to US$99,632.08. Consequently, the costs of the arbitration amount to US$505,252.08 and will be paid out of the deposits made by the Parties. For the same reasons as expressed in the preceding paragraph, the costs referred to in this paragraph shall be allocated between Thunderbird and Mexico on a ¾–¼ basis. Accordingly, the Arbitral Tribunal hereby determines that Thunderbird shall reimburse Mexico in the amount of US$126,313.02 in respect of the aforementioned deposits made by Mexico.

International Thunderbird Gaming was something of a watershed.[12] Recall that the rules on cost allocation are worded differently under the ICSID Convention and the UNCITRAL Rules, and that neither *Methanex* nor *International Thunderbird Gaming* were themselves ICSID disputes. This is not to say that there have not been an increasing number of ICSID cases in which a costs-follow-the-event approach was taken.[13] *Libananco* v. *Turkey* illustrates this.

Libananco Holdings v. *Turkey*, ICSID Case No. ARB/06/8, Award, 2 September 2011 (Mr Michael Hwang SC, President; Mr Henri C. Alvarez QC; Sir Franklin Berman QC), paras 562–568

562. An explanation of why each Party has incurred its costs and expenses is not the same thing as a justification of their necessity. Many national jurisdictions that follow a practice of awarding costs to the successful party also make a distinction between the costs actually incurred by a litigating party and those which are assessed by the court as

---

[12] Bradfield and Verdirame, 'Costs in Investment Treaty Arbitration', 417.

[13] See the table in T. H. Webster, 'Efficiency in Investment Arbitration: Recent Decisions on Preliminary and Costs Issues' (2009) 25 *Arb. Int'l* 469, 507–514.

having been reasonably and necessarily incurred for the purposes of the litigation, and base their award of costs on the latter not the former. Without being in any way bound by national practice of this kind, the Tribunal regards the underlying approach as suitable for international arbitration, and intends to follow it in the present case. In this regard, the Tribunal has considered, among other things, the following factors (in no particular order of importance):

    (a) the importance of the matter to the Parties and the value of money or property involved, namely the sum of some US$ 10.1 billion claimed by the Claimant (which the Tribunal understands to be the largest claim in ICSID arbitration at the time the Request for Arbitration was filed);

    (b) the amount and extent of factual and expert evidence adduced in these proceedings in relation to the issue of whether Libananco acquired ownership of the share certificates in question by 12 June 2003;

    (c) the conduct of the Parties during the proceedings; and

    (d) the circumstances in which the work or parts of it were done (which the Tribunal understands to have taken place across multiple jurisdictions and involving extensive arrangements for travel, translation and investigation made by both Parties).

563. Although many ICSID tribunals have ruled that each party should bear its own costs, others have applied the principle that 'costs follow the event', or else have proceeded to an allocation *pro rata*, i.e. an allocation proportionate to the tribunal's assessment of the relative merits of all claims made by the parties. The present Tribunal is of the view that a rule under which costs follow the event serves the purposes of compensating the successful party for its necessary legal fees and expenses, of discouraging unmeritorious actions and also of providing a disincentive to over-litigation. It also allows a tribunal sufficient leeway to take due account of specific issues on which the overall losing party has nevertheless succeeded, and to take account as well of the costs implications of procedural motions raised by one or another party. The Tribunal accordingly considers that it is appropriate to apply here the principle that 'costs follow the event' and that a costs order should be made in favour of the Respondent, on the basis that the Claimant has not been able to prove its ownership of the investment that forms the essential foundation for these lengthy and hard fought proceedings.

564. However, the Tribunal has also to take into account those issues where it is not appropriate for costs to be awarded in favour of the ultimate prevailing Party, because it was not the winner on that particular issue or 'event' or indeed because there was no decision as to who won or lost ...

565. Further, the Tribunal is inclined to exercise some restraint in assessing the reasonable amount of costs and expenses that should be awarded to the Respondent pursuant to paragraph 563 above. While the Respondent's wish to assemble a powerful battery of legal and other resources is well understood, given the magnitude of the claim against it, other underlying aspects of the tensions between the Parties (reflected in the way the case was argued on both sides), lend themselves less well to being reflected in a costs order by an

ICSID tribunal. Specifically, although the Tribunal is conscious that the claim was for a sum in excess of US$ 10 billion, the Tribunal is mindful that:

    (a) the claim for costs and expenses is significantly larger than any claim for costs previously made in an ICSID arbitration, as well as significantly larger than any previous award for costs and expenses made by any previous ICSID tribunal;

    (b) the Award in this case is on a jurisdictional issue (albeit hotly contested as to facts and law) and a selection of other preliminary issues; and

    (c) there needs to be some proportionality in the award (as opposed to the expenditure) of legal costs and expenses. A party with a deep pocket may have its own justification for heavy spending, but it cannot expect to be reimbursed for all its expenditure as a matter of course simply because it is ultimately the prevailing party.

566. The Tribunal is also not in the position of a national court which can undertake a detailed assessment on an item by item basis of a party's claim for legal costs and expenses. Following contemporary international arbitration practice, the Tribunal takes a 'broad-brush' approach to the task of determining a reasonable figure to award for such legal costs and expenses.

567. For these reasons, the Tribunal considers that it is appropriate to order the Claimant to pay the Respondent the sum of US$ 15,000,000 in respect of legal fees and out of pocket expenses, representing what in the Tribunal's view amounts to an appropriate figure to award, having regard to the principles and reasons set out above, and to all the circumstances of this case.

568. The above excludes the question of the costs of the arbitration (i.e. the fees and expenses of the Members of the Tribunal and of the ICSID Secretariat), which amount to approximately US$ 1,205,000. As a result, each Party's share of the costs of arbitration amounts to approximately US$ 602,500. The decision of the Tribunal is that such costs should follow the ultimate event, and must be paid in full by the Claimant.

One should therefore be wary of exaggerating the differences in wording between the ICSID and UNCITRAL regimes, while still being mindful of the statistical suggestion in the Hodgson study. The true comparison is with international commercial arbitration in which costs follow the event is the usual method. On this, Webster states that the loser-pays principle is now to be considered the dominant approach in investment arbitration of all kinds.[14] This view is supported by a number of studies, the latest showing that costs follow the event, at least in its pro rata variant, has been applied in the majority of Awards surveyed between 2000 and 2014.[15] It must be remembered, however, that the

---

[14] T. H. Webster, *Handbook of Investment Arbitration* (London: Sweet & Maxwell, 2012), 291; Bradfield and Verdirame, 'Costs in Investment Treaty Arbitration', 407.

[15] I. Uchkunova and O. Temnikov, 'Allocation of Costs in ICSID Arbitration', *Kluwer Arbitration Blog*, 3 December 2014, http://arbitrationblog.kluwerarbitration.com/2014/12/03/allocation-of-costs-in-icsid-arbitration/ (accessed 7 September 2020); Hodgson, 'Counting the Costs'.

point is not purely statistical. Other commentators have emphasised the lack of predictability in light of awards in recent years.[16]

5. SECURITY FOR COSTS

Once it is admitted that the respondent may recover its costs on a 'loser-pays' basis, the question of security for the respondent's costs also arises. This is a cost allocation issue, but it is also more than that. It also presents a method for handling unmeritorious or 'frivoulous' claims, which is a matter of genuine concern to host States.

T. H. Webster, *Handbook of Investment Arbitration* (London: Sweet & Maxwell, 2012), 291

[T]he prevailing tendency is to award costs based at least substantially on the principle that costs follow the event. For Respondents there can be a serious issue of whether the Claimant will be able to pay any cost order. Although substantial cost orders have been issued against Claimants it is not clear the extent to which they have been recovered. Nevertheless Claimants are generally not required to provide for security for costs of the Respondent in ICSID arbitration. One of the concerns in this respect is that granting an order for security could effectively bar Claimants with legitimate claims from bringing proceedings. A Claimant must already finance its share of the ICSID costs (including the deposit of the fees for the arbitrators) and pay or make arrangements to pay its legal costs. The burden of having to provide security in addition may create a bar to bringing proceedings on which the Claimant could have been successful.

T. H. Webster, 'Efficiency in Investment Arbitration: Recent Decisions on Preliminary and Costs Issues' (2009) 25 *Arb. Int'l* 469, 472–474

Ultimately, the sanction for unmeritorious claims should be costs that are awarded and paid. In international commercial arbitration, it is submitted that the basic starting point for allocation of costs is that 'costs follow the event' ... and that this has been the case for some time. There are notable distinctions in practice and it should be emphasised that the 'costs follow the event' principle is simply the starting point for allocating costs in international commercial arbitration. Nevertheless, it is a starting point, and in the 100 ICC cases we have not located a single instance where a tribunal expressly challenged the applicability of this principle. However, in investment arbitration, arbitral tribunals

---

[16] Bradfield and Verdirame, 'Costs in Investment Treaty Arbitration', 417; D. Smith, 'Shifting Sands: Cost-and-Fee Allocation in International Investment Arbitration' (2011) 51 *Virginia J Int'l L* 749, 776; J. Y. Gotanda, 'Consistently Inconsistent: The Need for Predictability in Awarding Costs and Fees in Investment Treaty Arbitration' (2013) 28 *ICSID Review – FILJ* 420, 422; J. Power, 'Investment Arbitration – Determination of Costs in ICSID Arbitration' in C. Klausegger, P. Klein, F. Kremslehner *et al.* (eds), *Austrian Yearbook of International Arbitration* (Munich: C. H. Beck, 2010), 351.

have been reluctant to link costs to the results of the case. In investment arbitration cases up to 2005, generally unsuccessful claimants do not appear to have been required to pay successful respondent's costs, as is illustrated in the summary appended to the dissent in the *International Thunderbird* case, and there is widespread uncertainty of the cost allocation principles in investment arbitration. The practice in investment arbitration appears to be changing. In the cases from 2005 to 2009 ... tribunals are divided. However, in more than half of the cases, tribunals have adopted the 'costs follow the event' principle. Therefore, not only is there a trend to apply the principle, but that trend appears to be becoming dominant. One suspects that, once tribunals are conscious of this trend, there will be an even greater tendency for tribunals to apply the principle in investment arbitration and in effect conform the practice in investment arbitration to international commercial arbitration in general. As regards unmeritorious claims (as opposed to unsuccessful claims in general), it is submitted that there is no justification for not applying the principle that 'costs follow the event' and that the effect of application of that principle should be to discourage those claims. If the principle that 'costs follow the event' is accepted as a starting point for allocating costs, then an even thornier issue of security for costs arises. Awarding costs against an unsuccessful claimant is of little effect if the claimant cannot be forced to pay the costs. In international commercial arbitration, where the same concern exists, security for costs is rarely ordered. Security for costs may be ordered in international commercial arbitration where special circumstances present themselves, such as a significant change in the financial condition of a claimant. One very legitimate justification for the reluctance to order security for costs is the concern that such an order may deprive legitimate claimants of the opportunity of presenting their cases. It is submitted that this concern should be balanced against the concern that awards on costs, in order to be effective, must have some consequences or the principle that costs that are awarded should be paid will be undermined. A discussion of this issue in investment arbitration may be viewed as premature. Nevertheless, it is submitted that there is a difference between full security for costs and building in a disincentive for unmeritorious claims. For example, arguably it is qualitatively different for a tribunal to order security in the amount of US$5 million for all legal costs than for a tribunal to order security for the arbitration costs of the respondent itself (which may amount to US$500,000) or for a portion of legal fees. Ordering a claimant to provide security of US$5 million may well act to chill the arbitration (and be designed to have exactly that effect) even where a claim has merit. Ordering security for the costs of arbitration arguably would not deter a claimant with a reasonable claim, as the claimant usually must budget a reasonable amount for its share of the arbitration costs and its legal fees in any event. In a sense, ordering security for costs, be it only partial, is one way that a tribunal can seek to deal with the situation where a claim appears to be unmeritorious.

What the author proposes, therefore, is a limited scope for tribunals to order the claimant to provide security for the respondent State's costs, precisely so as to deter unmeritorious claims. This, however, assumes that smaller claimants would not be placed at a disadvantage. One tribunal has, it appears, responded to this concern by linking the issue of security to the availability of third-party funding.

RSM Production Corp. v. *St Lucia*, ICSID Case No. ARB/12/10, Decision on St Lucia's Request for Security for Costs, 13 August 2014 (Professor Siegfried H. Elsing, President; Dr Gavan Griffith QC; Judge Edward W. Nottingham (dissenting)), paras 54–56, 83–84

54. The Tribunal, by majority, agrees with the general proposition that security for costs can be ordered based on Article 47 ICSID Convention and ICSID Arbitration Rule 39. The fact that ordering security for costs is not expressly provided for in those provisions does not exclude the Tribunal's jurisdiction to issue such measure. Rather, such provisions are phrased broadly and encompass 'any provisional measures' the Tribunal, after carefully balancing the Parties' interests deems appropriate 'to preserve the respective right of either party' under the given circumstances. The fact that other sets of arbitration rules (such as Art. 25.2 of the London Court of International Arbitration Rules) expressly provide for the possibility to order security for costs does not lead to a different conclusion: The broad wording does not address any particular measure but rather leaves it entirely to the Tribunal's discretion which measure it finds necessary and appropriate under the circumstances of the individual case.

55. The fact that Article 47 ICSID Convention and ICSID Arbitration Rule 39 do not expressly make reference to security for costs in particular – nor to any other particular measure – can easily be explained by the time at which the ICSID Convention was drafted. In 1965, issues such as third party funding and thus the shifting of the financial risk away from the claiming party were not as frequent, if at all, as they are today. Hence, the omission does not allow any negative inference.

56. Moreover, the reference to other arbitration rules such as Art. 25.2 of the LCIA Rules and the explicit mention of security for costs as a provisional measure does not provide a valid argument against ordering such measure under the ICSID regime. Institutional arbitration rules are constantly subject to review and modernization as deemed necessary by the drafters. By contrast, there is no comparable mechanism with regard to the ICSID Convention. Amending the ICSID Convention in general and in particular to the effect that security for costs as a provisional measure is expressly dealt with would require considerably more effort. Hence, stating that such amendment has not been made cannot serve as a ground for assuming that the drafters of the ICSID Convention intended to exclude security for costs.

...

83. Moreover, the admitted third party funding further supports the Tribunal's concern that Claimant will not comply with a costs award rendered against it, since, in the absence

of security or guarantees being offered, it is doubtful whether the third party will assume responsibility for honoring such an award. Against this background, the Tribunal regards it as unjustified to burden Respondent with the risk emanating from the uncertainty as to whether or not the unknown third party will be willing to comply with a potential costs award in Respondent's favor.

84. Claimant's argument that also Respondent used third party funding, is merely based on suspicion and not substantiated.

Ultimately, the power of an ICSID tribunal to order security for costs remains controversial.[17] Notably, Judge Nottingham dissented on the following grounds in *RSM* v. *St Lucia*.

RSM v. *St Lucia*, ICSID Case No. ARB/12/10, Dissenting Opinion of Edward Nottingham, paras 1, 17–18

1. Relying on Article 47 of the ICSID Convention and Rule 39 of the ICSID Arbitration Rules, the Majority orders Claimant to post a $750,000 bank guarantee to secure payment of any monies that the Tribunal may award Respondent as costs and attorney fees in this proceeding. In my view, the language of Article 47 and Rule 39, properly interpreted, does not support this unprecedented result. I must therefore respectfully dissent, for two reasons. First, I do not think that an order requiring Claimant to secure costs which may be awarded to Respondent is encompassed within the class of 'provisional measures' which may 'be taken to preserve the rights' of Respondent. Second, entry of an 'order' simply flies in the face of the explicit direction in both Article 47 and Rule 39 that a tribunal may 'recommend' provisional measures.

...

17. In reaching its decision concerning security for costs, the Majority relies in part on its conclusion, based on the sketchiest of records, that Claimant has third party funding to finance its case. (Maj. Op. ¶ 82.) It also justifies its broad interpretation of tribunals' powers under Article 47 and Rule 39 by observing that, in 1965, when the ICSID Convention was drafted, 'issues such as third party funding and thus the shifting of the financial risk away from the claiming party were not as frequent, if at all, as they are today' (Maj. Op. ¶ 57). In my view, this rationale illustrates the wisdom of tribunals' hewing closely to the words of the governing documents (the Convention and Arbitration Rules) and the mischief which can follow if individual tribunals adjudicating particular cases latch on to broad language in the governing documents as a warrant to address matters which, if they were matters of general concern, could and should be addressed by the ICSID Administrative Council after input and consultation with all interested parties.

---

[17] The power of an ICSID tribunal to 'recommend' provisional measures was discussed in Chapter 9.

18. The Majority's conclusion that there is third-party funding here and that the existence of such funding supports its decision is based on a one-sentence admission elicited from Claimant's counsel during the Tribunal's First Session. (Maj. Op. ¶ 75, citing Transcript of First Session of October 4, 2013 at 116 ll. 10–11.) There is no evidence concerning the identity of the funder or any other information about the funder. There is no evidence of the funder's financial means. There is nothing in the record about the arrangement between Claimant and the funder.

In a subsequent dispute, the tribunal in *Dirk Herzig* v. *Turkmenistan* rescinded its own previous order[18] for security for costs. The majority of the tribunal considered that, notwithstanding the existence of third-party funding, the claimant would have been prevented from bringing his claim as he had been unable to obtain security on reasonable terms. Thus requiring security would have led instead to a denial of justice.[19]

CONCLUSION

One could begin by saying that the claimant has a right to bring a claim, and that being so, the claimant therefore should not be punished for having brought it, even when the claimant loses. The counter-argument is that the respondent State has a right to defend itself and ought not to be punished for having simply done so.[20] There lies a basic philosophical difference in debates about moving to a general loser-pays approach. In response to the counter-argument, it might be said that the respondent State has no right, however, to violate the claimant's treaty rights. Thus, at least where the claimant succeeds, the respondent State should be made to pay the claimant's costs, for otherwise can it truly be said that the respondent, having breached an international legal obligation owed to the claimant, has made reparation? In the well-known words of the Permanent Court of International Justice in the *Chorzów Factory* case:

> The essential principle contained in the actual notion of an illegal act – a principle which seems to be established by international practice and in particular by the decisions of arbitral tribunals – is that reparation must, as far as possible, wipe out all the consequences of the illegal act and re-establish the situation which would, in all probability, have existed if that act had not been committed. Restitution in kind, or, if this is not possible, payment of a sum corresponding to the value which a restitution in kind would bear; the award, if need be, of damages for loss sustained which would not be covered by restitution in kind or payment in place of it – such are the principles

---

[18] *Dirk Herzig as Insolvency Administrator over the Assets of Unionmatex Industrieanlagen GmbH* v. *Turkmenistan*, ICSID Case No. ARB/18/35, Decision on the Respondent's Request for Security for Costs and the Claimant's Request for Security for Claim, 27 January 2020 (Reed, President; Sands; Prof. Voser).
[19] Cosmo Sanderson, 'ICSID Panel Rescinds Security for Costs Order', *GAR*, 12 June 2020.
[20] Uchkunova and Temnikov, 'Allocation of Costs'.

which should serve to determine the amount of compensation due for an act contrary to international law.[21]

Applying the costs-follow-the-event, or loser-pays, rule against the respondent does seem fair in such a case. Having said that, the pro-claimant argument has sometimes gone as far as to suggest that only the respondent State should pay if the claimant wins, but that the claimant should never be made to pay unless its claim was spurious to begin with. This is, however, a variant of the view that the claimant has a *right* to bring a claim. Against this should be held in mind the reality of inflated legal claims and costs, and a key psychological effect which costs after the event can also have on claimants. The claimant will be incentivised to inflate costs by adopting an 'all-or-nothing' approach. In England, Lord Woolf had this to say:

> [T]oo robust an application of the 'follow the event principle' encourages litigants to increase the cost of litigation, since it discourages litigants from being selective as to the points they take. If you recover all your costs as long as you win, you are encouraged to leave no stone unturned in your effort to do so.[22]

In comparison, the pay-your-own-way approach, in which each party bears its own party or legal costs and half the costs of the arbitration or proceedings, contributes at least to certainty.[23] Yet it is not difficult to appreciate that such certainty will benefit the claimant who is contemplating whether or not to bring a claim. The question of costs is, after all, typically one of the first strategic questions the claimant and the claimant's legal advisers are confronted with.

Finally, the question of costs goes to the heart of contemporary debate about the reform of investor–State arbitration. The question of security for costs could also become increasingly important as a possible way of screening out spurious claims. The interests of smaller claimants will, however, have to be taken into account. Host States should also beware of drawing the conclusion that the seemingly straightforward notion that a costs-follow-the-event approach will deter frivolous claims is always advantageous to the host State. As Nicholson and Gaffney have argued, such an approach could also encourage strong claims:

> Under CFtE, confident claimants with strong claims are more likely to come forward than they would under the more traditional approach, especially if they have a smaller claim, because CFtE increases their payoff if they prevail; claimants with strong claims will necessarily accord less weight to the cost implications of losing. CFtE therefore increases the incentive for confident claimants to come forward with their cases.[24]

---

[21] *Case Concerning the Factory at Chorzów (Indemnity) (Germany v. Poland)* (Merits) (1928) PCIJ Rep. Series A No. 17, pp. 4, 47.

[22] *AEI Rediffusion Music v. Phonographic Performance* [1999] 1 WLR 1507.

[23] Gotanda, 'Consistently Inconsistent', 434.

[24] J. Nicholson and J. Gaffney, 'Cost Allocation in Investment Arbitration: Forward toward Incentivisation', *Columbia FDI Perspectives*, No. 123, 9 June 2014, 2.

The subject of costs is not only one of practicality; it also raises important questions of principle which may guide the 'rebalancing' of investment treaties, where BITs are beginning to provide expressly for cost allocation, and the reform of investment arbitration more broadly.

QUESTIONS

1. Should a large multinational enterprise expect its legal costs to be paid by a small, developing nation?

2. Should a small company have to bear its own costs even if it prevails against a large, wealthy nation which has promised investors a right to bring an investment arbitration claim? Should that nation be permitted to extract its legal costs from the small investor?

3. Would it surprise you that, in one sample study, successful claimants tended not to recover much of their costs, while respondents recovered their costs in full a third of the time?

4. Cost-adjusted outcomes do not always reflect the mere application of the loser-pays approach even when that approach is used as a starting point. Should they? If not, what factors should the tribunal take into account? How should those factors be weighed?

5. To what extent can an appropriate costs regime address cotemporary allegations that investment arbitration is unfair to host countries?

SUGGESTIONS FOR FURTHER READING

1. M. Hodgson, 'Counting the Costs of Investment Treaty Arbitration', GAR Online News, 24 March 2014.
2. D. Smith, 'Shifting Sands: Cost-and-Fee Allocation in International Investment Arbitration' (2011) 51 *Virginia J Int'l L* 749.
3. S. D. Franck, 'Rationalising Costs in Investment Treaty Arbitration' (2011) 88 *Wash Univ L Rev* 769.
4. 'TDM Special Issue: Contingent Fees and Third-Party Funding in Investment Arbitration Disputes', *TDM* 4 (2011).

19

Challenging and Enforcing Awards, and the Question of Foreign State Immunities

CHAPTER OUTLINE

This chapter discusses the enforcement of awards and challenges to enforcement. It distinguishes between ICSID and other kinds of arbitral awards. Section 1 deals with the basic regime for set aside, enforcement and challenges to the enforcement of an international arbitral award, before introducing the ICSID regime, which applies specifically to ICSID awards. Section 2 discusses the case of non-ICSID arbitration in greater detail, while Section 3 discusses in greater depth the special case of ICSID arbitration, where enforcement and annulment of the award are matters governed solely under the ICSID Convention. Section 4 then deals with foreign state immunity. Notwithstanding the exceptions to foreign State immunity which allow the enforcement of investment arbitration awards, foreign sovereign assets continue to enjoy a broad immunity from execution and attachment. It might matter not at all that the immunity of the Respondent host State has already been lifted from suit and even enforcement, either in the non-ICSID situation by way of a 'commercial exception' typically found under various national rules, or in the case of an ICSID arbitration under the terms of the ICSID Convention. Immunity from execution and attachment is therefore the 'last refuge' of the host State. In practical terms, attachment of foreign sovereign assets will depend upon how favourable the rules are in the particular domestic jurisdiction, and this is discussed in Section 5.

INTRODUCTION

Options for challenge and enforcement differ between ICSID and 'non-ICSID' arbitral awards. An ICSID award is enforceable under the terms of the 1965 Convention on the Settlement of Investment Disputes between States and the Nationals of Other States (ICSID Convention),[1] whereas a non-ICSID Convention award will have to rely upon the 1958 Convention on the Recognition and Enforcement of Arbitral Awards ('New York

---

[1] 18 March 1965, 575 UNTS 159.

Convention').[2] Examples of non-ICSID awards include the award of an ad hoc tribunal, perhaps administered by the Permanent Court of Arbitration under the UNCITRAL Arbitration Rules, as well as those of other arbitral institutions such as the Stockholm Chamber of Commerce (SCC), London Court of International Arbitration (LCIA), Hong Kong International Arbitration Centre (HKIAC) or Singapore International Arbitration Centre (SIAC). Many arbitral bodies which have had distinguished histories in commercial arbitration, and even newer bodies, have begun to develop rules tailored to investment arbitration. This does not preclude investment arbitration tribunals from applying arbitration rules that were originally designed for commercial arbitration, the UNCITRAL Rules being a prime example.

1. ICSID AND 'NON–ICSID' AWARDS

Commonly, a 'non-ICSID' award would be enforceable under the 1958 New York Convention. Article III of the New York Convention states that: 'Each Contracting State shall recognize arbitral awards as binding and enforce them.' The Convention provides in Article V for certain limited ways in which enforcement of an award may be challenged. This is distinct from an award being set aside by the courts of the place of the seat of the tribunal under its national arbitration law.[3] It may help the reader to consider the matter in the following way. An award may be resisted in two places – in the place of the seat of the tribunal or where the award of the tribunal is intended to take practical effect – in other words, its place of enforcement. Treating set aside separately from challenges to the enforcement of an award may be seen to have resulted from the way in which international commercial arbitration has developed from what originally were domestic arbitrations in an earlier era. In the purely domestic situation, the award is handed down in the same place as its place of enforcement. One can imagine that before the advent of international commercial arbitration, when commercial arbitration was merely a domestic or national matter, the rules on set aside and challenges to enforcement would have tended to be the same. With the growth of international commercial arbitration, disputing parties came from different countries while the arbitration would be seated in a third, neutral country. With this, there emerged the phenomenon of an award being obtained in a place different from its place of enforcement, or put more bluntly, different from the location of the losing party's assets. Typically, the award would be given in a neutral country, while the losing party's assets would be in that party's home state or elsewhere in the world.[4] This applies equally where the losing party is a sovereign government. Thus, the first thing to observe is the need to distinguish the rules on set aside and challenges to enforcement. However, the history

---

[2] 10 June 1958, 330 UNTS 3.

[3] Which in those national legal orders which are 'Model Law jurisdictions' would typically, although not always, apply Art. 34 of the UNCITRAL Model Law with or without modification.

[4] See A. J. van den Berg, 'Should the Setting Aside of the Arbitral Award Be Abolished?' (2014) 29 *ICSID Review – FILJ* 263, 265–266.

of set asides and challenges to enforcement will already suggest to the reader that the respective rules are at least similar.

As with Article III of the New York Convention, the ICSID Convention also requires the enforcement of ICSID Awards. In other words, the obligation to enforce the award is a treaty obligation. Article 54(1) of the ICSID Convention states that: 'Each Contracting State shall recognize an award rendered pursuant to this Convention as binding and enforce the pecuniary obligations imposed by that award within its territories as if it were a final judgment of a court in that State.' Under the ICSID Convention, there is, however, no distinction between set asides and challenges to enforcement. Rather, there is a unitary procedure for seeking the annulment of an ICSID tribunal's award by an ICSID annulment committee.

In Section 2 we will look at set aside, enforcement and challenges to enforcement in the case of a non-ICSID award. We will then turn (in Section 3) to the equivalent regime under the ICSID Convention.

2. 'NON-ICSID' ARBITRATION

Simply put, the rules which are relevant to international commercial arbitration apply to non-ICSID arbitration. Thus, an award, be it a commercial arbitration award or a non-ICSID investment arbitration award, may be sought to be set aside or its enforcement may be challenged, or indeed it *generally* may be successfully enforced, in the usual manner befitting an international commercial arbitration award.

One says 'generally' for there is sometimes doubt and difficulty which arises due to the fact that the usual rules which apply to commercial arbitration awards could still be treated by certain national courts as inappropriate for the enforcement of an investment arbitration award. The argument may be raised that an investment arbitration award cannot be enforced under the New York Convention.[5] Putting such wrinkles aside, the New York Convention remains in practical terms a crucially important treaty for the enforcement of investment arbitration awards outside the ICSID regime.

UN Convention on the Recognition and Enforcement of Foreign Arbitral Awards (New York, 10 June 1958), Arts III, IV, V

Article III
Each Contracting State shall recognize arbitral awards as binding and enforce them in accordance with the rules of procedure of the territory where the award is relied upon, under the conditions laid down in the following articles. There shall not be imposed substantially more onerous conditions or higher fees or charges on the recognition or enforcement of arbitral awards to which this Convention applies than are imposed on the recognition or enforcement of domestic arbitral awards.

---

[5] Similarly, the (bilateral investment) treaty basis of an investment arbitration claim has been said to be non-justiciable before a domestic court, and this is discussed later in Section 5.

Article IV

1. To obtain the recognition and enforcement mentioned in the preceding article, the party applying for recognition and enforcement shall, at the time of the application, supply:

   (a) The duly authenticated original award or a duly certified copy thereof;

   (b) The original agreement referred to in article II or a duly certified copy thereof.

2. If the said award or agreement is not made in an official language of the country in which the award is relied upon, the party applying for recognition and enforcement of the award shall produce a translation of these documents into such language. The translation shall be certified by an official or sworn translator or by a diplomatic or consular agent.

Article V

1. Recognition and enforcement of the award may be refused, at the request of the party against whom it is invoked, only if that party furnishes to the competent authority where the recognition and enforcement is sought, proof that:

   (a) The parties to the agreement referred to in article II were, under the law applicable to them, under some incapacity, or the said agreement is not valid under the law to which the parties have subjected it or, failing any indication thereon, under the law of the country where the award was made; or

   (b) The party against whom the award is invoked was not given proper notice of the appointment of the arbitrator or of the arbitration proceedings or was otherwise unable to present his case; or

   (c) The award deals with a difference not contemplated by or not falling within the terms of the submission to arbitration, or it contains decisions on matters beyond the scope of the submission to arbitration, provided that, if the decisions on matters submitted to arbitration can be separated from those not so submitted, that part of the award which contains decisions on matters submitted to arbitration may be recognized and enforced; or

   (d) The composition of the arbitral authority or the arbitral procedure was not in accordance with the agreement of the parties, or, failing such agreement, was not in accordance with the law of the country where the arbitration took place; or

   (e) The award has not yet become binding on the parties, or has been set aside or suspended by a competent authority of the country in which, or under the law of which, that award was made.

2. Recognition and enforcement of an arbitral award may also be refused if the competent authority in the country where recognition and enforcement is sought finds that:

   (a) The subject matter of the difference is not capable of settlement by arbitration under the law of that country; or

   (b) The recognition or enforcement of the award would be contrary to the public policy of that country.

The scheme, under the New York Convention, was to have a treaty which, under Article III, compels the recognition and enforcement of foreign arbitral awards, with limited exceptions provided in Article V for challenges to enforcement. But what about awards which have been set aside? The extract below reproduces the rules of the 1985 UNCITRAL Model Law for setting an award aside. The Model Law is precisely what it says it is – a model for national legislatures to adopt in their national arbitration laws. Thus, the Model Law reflects, at least in the numerous countries which adopt it, common rules on setting aside an award.

> ## UNCITRAL Model Law on International Commercial Arbitration (United Nations document Al40117, annex I) (as adopted by the United Nations Commission on International Trade Law on 21 June 1985), Chapter VII, Art. 34

Chapter VII Recourse Against Award

Article 34. Application for setting aside as exclusive recourse against arbitral award

(1) Recourse to a court against an arbitral award may be made only by an application for setting aside in accordance with paragraphs (2) and (3) of this article.

(2) An arbitral award may be set aside by the court specified in article 6 only if:

    (a) the party making the application furnishes proof that:

        (i) a party to the arbitration agreement referred to in article 7 was under some incapacity; or the said agreement is not valid under the law to which the parties have subjected it or, failing any indication thereon, under the law of this State; or

        (ii) the party making the application was not given proper notice of the appointment of an arbitrator or of the arbitral proceedings or was otherwise unable to present his case; or

        (iii) the award deals with a dispute not contemplated by or not falling within the terms of the submission to arbitration, or contains decisions on matters beyond the scope of the submission to arbitration, provided that, if the decisions on matters submitted to arbitration can be separated from those not so submitted, only that part of the award which contains decisions on matters not submitted to arbitration may be set aside; or

        (iv) the composition of the arbitral tribunal or the arbitral procedure was not in accordance with the agreement of the parties, unless such agreement was in conflict with a provision of this Law from which the parties cannot derogate, or, failing such agreement, was not in accordance with this Law; or

    (b) the court finds that:

        (i) the subject-matter of the dispute is not capable of settlement by arbitration under the law of this State; or

        (ii) the award is in conflict with the public policy of this State.

(3) An application for setting aside may not be made after three months have elapsed from the date on which the party making that application had received the award or, if a

request had been made under article 33, from the date on which that request had been disposed of by the arbitral tribunal.

(4) The court, when asked to set aside an award, may, where appropriate and so requested by a party, suspend the setting aside proceedings for a period of time determined by it in order to give the arbitral tribunal an opportunity to resume the arbitral proceedings or to take such other action as in the arbitral tribunal's opinion will eliminate the grounds for setting aside.

The United Kingdom did not adopt the UNCITRAL Model Law, and for the law in England and Wales the reader may wish to refer to sections 67 and 68 of the English Arbitration Act of 1996 for the detailed provisions there on challenging an award on the grounds of substantive jurisdiction (s. 67) or serious irregularity (s. 68).[6] In *Ecuador* v. *Occidental Production and Development Co.*,[7] Ecuador had initiated proceedings to set aside an award against it under the 1996 Act, specifically, on the basis that the arbitrators had exceeded their authority since the dispute had involved matters of taxation which fell outside the scope of the US–Ecuador BIT. Under section 67 of the UK Act, the question is whether the arbitrators were correct in deciding upon their jurisdiction. Occidental, which had won before the tribunal, argued that questions concerning the scope of the arbitrators' jurisdiction were 'non-justiciable' before the courts of England and Wales since the dispute had involved a treaty between Ecuador and the United States. The non-justiciability point was heard on appeal from an order of Aiken J by the Court of Appeal, which held the dispute to be justiciable.[8] Aiken J went on to refuse to set aside the award of the arbitrators. The non-justiciability point is discussed in Section 4.

In *The Republic of Korea* v. *Mohammad Reza Dayyani and Others*,[9] Korea had similarly sought unsuccessfully to set aside an investment arbitration award in England under section 67 of the 1996 Act, i.e. on the ground that the tribunal lacked substantive jurisdiction. Korea had argued that this was because rights under a share purchase agreement, contract deposits and such did not constitute 'property or assets' and therefore did not constitute an 'investment', lacked the characteristics of an investment, and were not made in Korea; that the Dayyani brothers, the Respondents, were not investors within the meaning of the Korea–Iran bilateral investment treaty, also because they were merely shareholders; and that there was no dispute arising out of an investment between an investor and a Contracting Party.

What if the challenge had succeeded? What becomes of an award that has been set aside? Logically, it should no longer exist. It is important to notice, here, that the New York

---

[6] For an example of an application under s. 67, challenging on jurisdictional grounds an investment tribunal's award on jurisdiction, see *GPF GP S.à.r.l.* v. *The Republic of Poland* [2018] EWHC 409, most notably that under s. 67 there is a re-hearing of the jurisdictional question (*per* Bryan J): see paras 64–71 which contain a useful summary of the English authorities including *Dallah Real Estate* v. *Pakistan* [2010] UKSC 46; [2011] 1 AC 763. Also, unlike the Model Law, the Arbitration Act preserves appeals on a point of law, in other words on the basis that the tribunal applied the law wrongly, in s. 69.

[7] [2006] EWHC 345 (Comm).

[8] *Occidental Exploration and Production Co.* v. *Ecuador* [2005] EWCA Civ. 1116; see Section 4 of this chapter.

[9] [2019] EWHC 3580.

Convention does not say that. Rather, it states in Article V(1) that recognition and enforcement of an award which has been set aside *may* be refused. With those remarks, we can now turn to the regime under the ICSID Convention for ICSID arbitrations.

3. ICSID ARBITRATION

The position is more straightforward in the case of an ICSID award. ICSID Convention Member States are obligated to recognise and enforce ICSID tribunal awards. Rather than being subjected to the complexity of set aside and enforcement challenges and, as we have seen, suffer questions about the complex interaction of a set aside and an enforcement challenge, the losing party may seek annulment of an ICSID Award by an Ad Hoc Annulment Committee constituted under the ICSID Convention.[10] ICSID arbitration therefore has a unitary procedure for annulment and enforcement. The grounds for annulment are, however, similar in many respects to the grounds for challenging the enforcement of a non-ICSID award before a national court.

Convention on the Settlement of Investment Disputes between States and Nationals of other States, 18 March 1965, 575 UNTS 159, Section 5 Interpretation, Revision and Annulment of the Award, Art. 52

(1) Either party may request annulment of the award by an application in writing addressed to the Secretary-General on one or more of the following grounds:
   (a) that the Tribunal was not properly constituted;
   (b) that the Tribunal has manifestly exceeded its powers;
   (c) that there was corruption on the part of a member of the Tribunal;
   (d) that there has been a serious departure from a fundamental rule of procedure; or
   (e) that the award has failed to state the reasons on which it is based.
(2) The application shall be made within 120 days after the date on which the award was rendered except that when annulment is requested on the ground of corruption such application shall be made within 120 days after discovery of the corruption and in any event within three years after the date on which the award was rendered.
(3) On receipt of the request the Chairman shall forthwith appoint from the Panel of Arbitrators an ad hoc Committee of three persons. None of the members of the Committee shall have been a member of the Tribunal which rendered the award, shall be of the same nationality as any such member, shall be a national of the State party to the dispute or of the State whose national is a party to the dispute, shall have been designated to the Panel of Arbitrators by either of those States, or shall have acted as a conciliator in the same dispute. The Committee shall have the authority to annul the award or any part thereof on any of the grounds set forth in paragraph (1).
(4) The provisions of Articles 41–45, 48, 49, 53 and 54, and of Chapters VI and VII shall apply *mutatis mutandis* to proceedings before the Committee.

[10] See further R. Doak Bishop and S. M. Marchili, *Annulment Under the ICSID Convention* (Oxford University Press, 2012).

(5) The Committee may, if it considers that the circumstances so require, stay enforcement of the award pending its decision. If the applicant requests a stay of enforcement of the award in his application, enforcement shall be stayed provisionally until the Committee rules on such request.

(6) If the award is annulled the dispute shall, at the request of either party, be submitted to a new Tribunal constituted in accordance with Section 2 of this Chapter.

Thus, ICSID Awards may only be annulled in limited situations: where a tribunal is improperly constituted, in other words in the context of challenges to the appointment of an arbitrator; or where the tribunal has acted in 'manifest excess' of its 'powers' such as where it exceeds its jurisdiction, fails to apply the applicable law or had decided *ex aequo et bono*; on grounds of corruption, or because of a serious procedural irregularity, for example in failing to hear both sides; or finally, for issuing an unreasoned award.[11]

Perhaps the most well-known annulments thus far have concerned the Argentinian Gas Cases, in respect of four comparable awards. The four tribunals ruled on issues arising from practically identical facts, involving investments in the Argentinian gas industry by CMS, Enron, Sempra and LG&E. Following the Argentinian financial crisis, the Argentinian Central Bank had suffered a liquidity crisis, causing Argentina to remove its dollar peg, revise gas concession regulations and gas tariffs, and replace dollar-denominated tariff payments with gas payments denominated in the Argentinian peso (dubbed 'pesoisation' or 'pesification'). The issue in all four cases concerned whether a treaty clause allowing emergency action by Argentina should be read against the high threshold for invoking a defence of necessity under customary international law. Three awards – involving CMS's, Enron's and Sempra's claims – went one way, with the tribunals there saying 'yes', while a final award involving LG&E's claim said 'no' and took a more deferential approach towards Argentinian emergency action.[12] Of the former category, two of those awards were subsequently annulled. In the *CMS* case, the Annulment Committee considered that the award had contained a 'manifest error of law', but that this nonetheless did not amount to a 'manifest excess' in the exercise of the tribunal's powers.

> **CMS Gas Transmission v. Argentina, ICSID Case No. ARB/01/8, Decision of the Ad Hoc Committee on the Application for the Annulment of the Argentine Republic, 25 September 2007 (Judge Gilbert Guillaume, President; Judge Nabil Elaraby, Professor James R. Crawford), paras 128, 130–132, 135–136**
>
> *Manifest excess of powers*
> 128. As indicated above the Tribunal, as likewise the parties, assimilated the conditions necessary for the implementation of Article XI of the BIT to those concerning the existence of the state of necessity under customary international law. Moreover, following Argentina's presentation, the Tribunal dealt with the defense based on customary law before dealing

---

[11] See further, for example, Katia Yannaca-Small (ed.), *Arbitration under International Investment Agreements*, 2nd edn (Oxford University Press, 2018), chapter 27.

[12] See E. Martinez, 'Understanding the Debate over Necessity: Unanswered Questions and Future Implications of Annulments in the Argentine Gas Cases' (2012) 23 *Duke J Int'l Comp L* 149, 153–155.

with the defense drawn from Article XI. Argentina submits before the Committee that in doing so, the Tribunal on both points manifestly exceeded its powers.

...

130. ... Article XI and Article 25 are substantively different. The first covers measures necessary for the maintenance of public order or the protection of each Party's own essential security interests, without qualifying such measures. The second subordinates the state of necessity to four conditions. It requires for instance that the action taken 'does not seriously impair an essential interest of the State or States towards which the obligation exists, or of the international community as a whole', a condition which is foreign to Article XI. In other terms the requirements under Article XI are not the same as those under customary international law as codified by Article 25, as the Parties in fact recognized during the hearing before the Committee. On that point, the Tribunal made a manifest error of law.

131. Those two texts having a different operation and content, it was necessary for the Tribunal to take a position on their relationship and to decide whether they were both applicable in the present case. The Tribunal did not enter into such an analysis, simply assuming that Article XI and Article 25 are on the same footing.

132. In doing so the Tribunal made another error of law

...

135. These two errors made by the Tribunal could have had a decisive impact on the operative part of the Award. As admitted by CMS, the Tribunal gave an erroneous interpretation to Article XI. In fact, it did not examine whether the conditions laid down by Article XI were fulfilled and whether, as a consequence, the measures taken by Argentina were capable of constituting, even *prima facie*, a breach of the BIT. If the Committee was acting as a court of appeal, it would have to reconsider the Award on this ground.

136. The Committee recalls, once more, that it has only a limited jurisdiction under Article 52 of the ICSID Convention. In the circumstances, the Committee cannot simply substitute its own view of the law and its own appreciation of the facts for those of the Tribunal. Notwithstanding the identified errors and lacunas in the Award, it is the case in the end that the Tribunal applied Article XI of the Treaty. Although applying it cryptically and defectively, it applied it. There is accordingly no manifest excess of powers.

Compare, however, *Malaysian Historical Salvors Sdn. Bhd.* v. *Government of Malaysia.* This case concerned a salvage contract between the claimant, a marine salvage company, and the government of Malaysia. A dispute arose over payment and the claimant claimed that its performance had also constituted an 'investment' under the UK–Malaysia BIT. The Respondent, the government of Malaysia, argued that the claimant's performance did not qualify as an investment within the terms of Article 25 of the ICSID Convention. The arbitrator, Mr Michael Hwang,[13] had ruled that the salvage contract did not entail a significant contribution to Malaysia's economic development, and therefore was not a qualifying investment under the 'Salini' criteria.[14] Mr Hwang had considered the various Salini criteria to be indecisive, or only partially decisive, but ultimately found no

---

[13] ICSID Case No. ARB/05/10, Award on Jurisdiction, 17 May 2007.

[14] *Salini* v. *Morocco*, ICSID Case No. ARB/00/4, Decision on Jurisdiction, 23 July 2001. Discussed in Chapter 10 of this book.

contribution which the salvors had made to the economic development of Malaysia. The following extract is from the decision which annulled Hwang's award in *Malaysian Historical Salvors*.[15]

Malaysian Historical Salvors Sdn Bhd v. *Government of Malaysia*, ICSID No. ARB/05/10, Decision on the Application for Annulment, 16 April 200974 (Judge Stephen M. Schwebel, President; Judge Mohamed Shahabuddeen dissenting, Judge Peter Tomka), paras 61–63, 66–70 (footnotes omitted)

61. It follows that, by the terms of the Agreement, and for its purposes, the Contract is an investment. There is no room for another conclusion. The Sole Arbitrator did not reach another considered conclusion in respect of the Agreement. He rather chose to examine, virtually exclusively, the question of whether there was an investment within the meaning of Article 25(1) of the ICSID Convention. Finding that there was not, he found that 'it is unnecessary to discuss whether the Contract is an 'investment' under the BIT'. Nevertheless the Sole Arbitrator observed that, 'while the Contract did provide some benefit to Malaysia', there was not 'a sufficient contribution to Malaysia's economic development to qualify as an "investment" for the purposes of Article 25(1) or Article 1(a) of the BIT'. He provided an extensive analysis in support of his conclusion in respect of the ICSID Convention, but none in respect of his conclusion in respect of the BIT. The Committee is unable to see what support the Sole Arbitrator could have mustered to sustain the conclusion that the Contract and its implementation did not constitute an investment within the meaning of that Agreement ...

62. ... Unlike some other BITs, no third party dispute settlement options are provided in the alternative to ICSID. It follows that, if jurisdiction is found to be absent under the ICSID Convention, the investor is left without international recourse altogether. That result is difficult to reconcile with the intentions of the Governments of Malaysia and the United Kingdom ...

63. What of the intentions of the Parties in concluding the Washington Convention? The term 'investment' was deliberately left undefined. But light is shed on the intentions of the Parties in respect of that term by the Convention's *travaux préparatoires* as well as the Convention's interpretation by the Executive Directors of the International Bank for Reconstruction and Development in adopting and opening it for signature.

...

66. ... the prevailing view was that there should be no monetary limit on claims submitted and that the contribution of money or other asset of economic value need not be for an indefinite period or for not less than five years. More than this, a British proposal that omitted any definition of the term 'investment', on the ground that a definition would only create jurisdictional difficulties, 'was adopted by a large majority in the Legal Committee'.

67. That result was consistent with the position of the General Counsel of the Bank, Mr. Broches, who served as chairman of the regional meetings of legal experts of governments and of the Legal Committee. Thus, Mr. Broches called attention to the fact that the document did not limit or define the types of disputes which might be submitted

---

[15] References to the views of Aaron Broches cite *History of the ICSID Convention* (Washington, DC: World Bank, 1968), vol. II-1, 54, 566.

to conciliation or arbitration under the auspices of the Center. It was difficult to find a satisfactory definition. There was the danger that recourse to the services of the Center might in a given situation be precluded because the dispute in question did not precisely qualify under the definition of the convention. There was the further danger that a definition might provide a reluctant party with an opportunity to frustrate or delay the proceedings by questioning whether the dispute was encompassed by the definition. These possibilities suggested that it was inadvisable to define narrowly the kinds of disputes that could be submitted. Moreover, Mr. Broches added, a contracting state would be free to announce that it did not intend to use the facilities of the Center for particular kinds of disputes.

68. Mr. Broches elsewhere explained that:

since the jurisdiction of the Center is limited by the overriding condition of consent, the exclusions desired by the one or the other delegation could be achieved by a refusal of consent in those cases in which in their view there was no proper case for use of the facilities of the Center. Refusal of consent would be an adequate safeguard for host States.

The purpose of Section 1 is not to define the circumstances in which recourse to the facilities of the Center would in fact occur, but rather to indicate the outer limits within which the Center would have jurisdiction provided the parties' consent had been attained. Beyond these outer limits no use could be made of the facilities of the Center even with such consent.

69. However it is important to note that the *travaux préparatoires* do not support the imposition of 'outer limits' such as those imposed by the Sole Arbitrator in this case. Little more about the nature of outer limits is indicated in the *travaux* than is contained in Article 25(1), namely that, '[t]he jurisdiction of the Centre shall extend to any legal dispute arising directly out of an investment ... ' It appears to have been assumed by the Convention's drafters that use of the term 'investment' excluded a simple sale and like transient commercial transactions from the jurisdiction of the Centre. Judicial or arbitral construction going further in interpretation of the meaning of 'investment' by the establishment of criteria or hallmarks may or may not be regarded as plausible, but the intentions of the draftsmen of the ICSID Convention, as the *travaux* show them to have been, lend those criteria (and still less, conditions) scant support.

70. The Report of the Bank's Executive Directors is similarly illuminating. In the debate over the draft of that Report, Mr. Broches recalled that none of the suggested definitions for the word 'investment' had proved acceptable. He suggested that while it might be difficult to define the term, an investment in fact was readily recognizable. He proposed that the Report should say that the Executive Directors did not think it necessary or desirable to attempt a definition. After some further debate, the Report was adopted ...

...

74. In the light of this history of the preparation of the ICSID Convention and of the foregoing analysis of the Report of the Executive Directors in adopting it, the Committee finds that the failure of the Sole Arbitrator even to consider, let alone apply, the definition of investment as it is contained in the Agreement to be a gross error that gave rise to a manifest failure to exercise jurisdiction.

One genuine concern, illustrated by *Malaysian Historical Salvors* above, has had to do with whether ICSID Awards are too easily annulled, in which case – or so the argument goes – the annulment mechanism becomes, in effect, an appeals mechanism.

M. Burgstaller and C. B. Rosenberg, 'Challenging International Arbitral Awards: To ICSID or Not to ICSID?' (2011) 27 *Arb. Int'l* 91, 96–97

Commentators ... have voiced concerns that ICSID annulment committees have improperly re-examined the merits of a case, thereby effectively transforming an annulment proceeding into an appeal. Annulment statistics may support these views. In ICSID's history, there have been a total of 41 annulment proceedings. Eleven of these proceedings were pending at the time of this writing, while six had been settled or discontinued prior to an annulment decision. In the remaining 24 proceedings, ad hoc committees annulled 11 awards in full or in part: an astounding 46 per cent. Moreover, there has been a growing trend for the losing party to submit an adverse ICSID award for annulment. ICSID registered its first annulment application in 1985. Between 1986 and 2000, another four applications were registered. Twelve applications were registered between 2000 and 2006, and in the last five years, 22 annulment applications (more than half of all annulment applications) were registered.

The annulment in *Eiser* v. *Spain*, discussed earlier in Chapter 7 of this book in the context of challenges brought against arbitrators, is likely to be viewed in certain quarters in a similar light. Should what originally was an unsuccessful challenge brought against an arbitrator lead to the annulment of an eventual award on the ground that the tribunal was, instead, improperly constituted? Would this increase, rather than reduce, confidence in ICSID arbitration? If so, whose confidence – that of members of the public or users of ICSID arbitration?

Eiser Infrastructure Limited and Energía Solar Luxembourg S.à r.l. v. *Spain*, ICSID Case No. ARB/13/36, Decision on Annulment, 11 June 2020 (Prof. Ricardo Ramírez Hernández, President; Mr. Makhdoom Ali Khan, Judge Dominique Hascher), paras 217–219 (excerpted, footnotes omitted)

219. Arbitrators should either not sit in cases or be prepared to be challenged and/or disqualified where, on an objective assessment of things, assessed by a fair minded and informed third party observer, they may not be perceived as independent and impartial. The role of a third party observer, when these matters are challenged, in annulment proceedings, is performed by annulment committees. It matters not that Dr. Alexandrov may not even have been conscious of the insidious effects of this association. What matters is that an independent observer, on an objective assessment of all the facts, would conclude that there was a manifest appearance of bias on the part of Dr. Alexandrov.

An ICSID award may also be revised, in which case in the meantime it is stayed provisionally.[16] But unlike an annulled award, the award is otherwise binding. Each Contracting State is obligated to recognise and enforce an ICSID award in its territory as if it were the final judgment of a court in that Contracting State. As we shall see in Section 4, matters could become more complicated when it comes to attaching the 'losing' foreign State's assets, due to the ICSID Convention's preservation of the immunity of foreign state assets from attachment (where this is provided under the law of the place in which attachment is sought).

ICSID Convention, Section 6 Recognition and Enforcement of the Award, Arts 53–55

Article 53

(1) The award shall be binding on the parties and shall not be subject to any appeal or to any other remedy except those provided for in this Convention. Each party shall abide by and comply with the terms of the award except to the extent that enforcement shall have been stayed pursuant to the relevant provisions of this Convention.

(2) For the purposes of this Section, 'award' shall include any decision interpreting, revising or annulling such award pursuant to Articles 50, 51 or 52.

Article 54

(1) Each Contracting State shall recognize an award rendered pursuant to this Convention as binding and enforce the pecuniary obligations imposed by that award within its territories as if it were a final judgment of a court in that State. A Contracting State with a federal constitution may enforce such an award in or through its federal courts and may provide that such courts shall treat the award as if it were a final judgment of the courts of a constituent state.

(2) A party seeking recognition or enforcement in the territories of a Contracting State shall furnish to a competent court or other authority which such State shall have designated for this purpose a copy of the award certified by the Secretary-General. Each Contracting State shall notify the Secretary-General of the designation of the competent court or other authority for this purpose and of any subsequent change in such designation.

(3) Execution of the award shall be governed by the laws concerning the execution of judgments in force in the State in whose territories such execution is sought.

Article 55

Nothing in Article 54 shall be construed as derogating from the law in force in any Contracting State relating to immunity of that State or of any foreign State from execution.

Before turning to the question of immunity, a recent judgment of the English High Court, for the first time, stayed enforcement of an ICSID Award on the ground that there had been a European Commission decision that payment under the award would constitute unlawful State aid under EU law while an appeal was pending against the Commission's

---

[16] See *Victor Pey Casado and President Allende Foundation* v. *Chile*, ICSID Case No. ARB/98/2, Revision Decision, 18 November 2009.

decision. However, Mr Justice Blair declined to set aside registration of the award.[17] The dispute had concerned Romania's withdrawal of investment incentives because of the application of EU State aid rules following its entry into the European Union. The claimant had won before an investment arbitration tribunal but the Commission decided that enforcement and execution of the tribunal's award would itself comprise unlawful State aid. There was an appeal against Mr Justice Blair's decision to the Court of Appeal, which upheld the stay,[18] and subsequently to the UK Supreme Court, which decided that the stay was unwarranted because the English courts are obligated under the ICSID Convention, or more precisely under the Arbitration (International Investment Disputes) Act 1966, to give effect to the ICSID award.

Micula and others v. *Romania* [2020] UKSC 5 (Lord Lloyd-Jones and Lord Sales (Lady Hale, Lord Reed and Lord Hodge agreeing)), paras 65–86

65. At first instance, Blair J dismissed the application by Romania to set aside the order of Burton J registering the award. In Blair J's view, registration of the award would not place Romania in breach of the Commission Decision. However, he stayed enforcement of the award pending the resolution of the annulment proceedings in the GCEU [General Court of the European Union] on the basis that under the ICSID Convention and under section 2 of the 1966 Act an arbitral award was to be equated for the purposes of enforcement with a judgment of the High Court. As the High Court would not enforce a domestic judgment which conflicted with a decision of the Commission, it could not enforce the Award pending the outcome of the annulment proceedings. Accordingly, article 351 TFEU [Treaty on the Functioning of the European Union] (set out at para 90, below) did not apply because there was no conflict between the obligations of the United Kingdom under the ICSID Convention and the EU Treaties.

66. The Court of Appeal unanimously dismissed the appeal against the order for a stay. The majority (Arden and Leggatt LJJ) held that while section 2 (1) of the 1966 Act did not have the effect of making an ICSID award registered under section 1 equivalent for all purposes to an ordinary domestic judgment, the domestic court could grant a stay of execution if in the circumstances of the case it was just to do so, provided the stay was temporary and consistent with the purposes of the ICSID Convention. Hamblen LJ (dissenting on this point) held that the ICSID Convention and the 1966 Act conferred on a registered award the same status as a final domestic judgment. Since such a judgment would not be enforced where inconsistent with EU law, there was no inconsistency with the ICSID Convention or the 1966 Act in not enforcing an award where inconsistent with EU law.

67. On behalf of the Claimants it is submitted that Blair J and the Court of Appeal were in error in granting a stay because the ICSID Convention and the 1966 Act do not permit a

---

[17] *Viorel Micula, Ioan Micula, SC European Food SA, SC Starmill SRI, SC Multipack SRI* v. *Romania* [2017] EWHC 31 (Comm).

[18] *Viorel Micula and Others* v. *European Commission* [2018] EWCA Civ. 1801.

stay in such circumstances. Distinguishing between enforcement and execution, they submit that a stay of enforcement may only be granted pursuant to articles 50–52 of the ICSID Convention. Article 54 imposes a duty on national courts to enforce awards and does not permit a national court to refuse enforcement where it would refuse to enforce a domestic judgment. They accept that the national court has control over the execution of an award, including power to grant a temporary stay; however, this is strictly for procedural (not substantive) reasons and only where no inconsistency arises with the duties to recognise and enforce the award. They submit that the stay granted in these proceedings was not a stay of execution but a stay of enforcement pending the determination of the GCEU proceedings, which the Court had no power to order.

68. The provisions of the 1966 Act must be interpreted in the context of the ICSID Convention and it should be presumed that Parliament, in enacting that legislation, intended that it should conform with the United Kingdom's treaty obligations. It is a notable feature of the scheme of the ICSID Convention that once the authenticity of an award is established, a domestic court before which recognition is sought may not re-examine the award on its merits. Similarly, a domestic court may not refuse to enforce an authenticated ICSID award on grounds of national or international public policy. In this respect, the ICSID Convention differs significantly from the New York Convention on the Recognition and Enforcement of Foreign Arbitral Awards 1958. The position is stated in this way by Professor Schreuer in his commentary on article 54(1) …

…

69. Contracting States may not refuse recognition or enforcement of an award on grounds covered by the challenge provisions in the Convention itself (articles 50–52). Nor may they do so on grounds based on any general doctrine of *ordre public*, since in the drafting process the decision was taken not to follow the model of the New York Convention. However, although it is recognised that this is the general position under the Convention, it is arguable that article 54(1), by framing the relevant obligation as to enforcement as an obligation to treat an award under the Convention as if it were a final judgment of a local court, allows certain other defences to enforcement which are available in local law in relation to such a final judgment to be raised.

70. The principle that arbitration awards under the ICSID Convention should be enforceable in the courts of all Contracting States and with the same status as a final judgment of the local courts in those States, as eventually set out in article 54(1), was a feature from an early stage in the drafting of the Convention. Mr Aron Broches, General Counsel of the World Bank at the time who chaired the regional consultative meetings ('the Regional Consultative Meetings') that occurred as part of the Convention's drafting, explained to delegates that by virtue of this formula Contracting States would be entitled to apply their local law of sovereign or state immunity with regard to the enforcement of awards, and thereby avoid or minimise possible embarrassment at having to enforce awards against other friendly Contracting States. Accordingly, it was made clear that article 54(1) had the substantive effect of introducing to some degree a principle of equivalence between

a Convention award and a local final judgment as regards the possibility of applying defences in respect of enforcement. See ICSID, *History of the ICSID Convention* (Washington DC, 1968) vol II-1: Doc 22 (20 September 1963) 'Memorandum of the discussion by the Executive Directors, September 10, 1963, Discussion of the First Preliminary Draft Convention', p 177); Doc 25, (30 April 1964) 'Summary Record of Proceedings, Addis Ababa Consultative Meetings of Legal Experts, December 16–20, 1963', p 242; Doc 31 (20 July 1964) 'Summary Record of Proceedings, Bangkok Consultative Meetings of Legal Experts, April 27-May 1, 1964', p 520.

71. In his report on the Regional Consultative Meetings, Mr Broches referred to certain comments that had dealt with the effect of what was then draft section 15 (which became article 54(1)) on existing law with respect to sovereign immunity. Mr Broches 'explained that the drafters had no intention to change that law. By providing that the award could be enforced as if it were a final judgment of a local court, section 15 implicitly imported the limitation on enforcement which in most countries existed with respect to enforcement of court decisions against Sovereigns. However, this point might be made explicit in order to allay the fears expressed by several delegations' (*History*, vol II-1: Doc 33 (9 July 1964) 'Chairman's Report on the Regional Consultative Meetings of Legal Experts', p 575; and see Doc 27 (12 June 1964) 'Summary Record of Proceedings, Santiago Consultative Meetings of Legal Experts, February 3–7, 1964', pp 342 et seq, where Mr Broches again indicated that this was the intended effect of what became article 54(1), but that it could be made completely clear to allay concerns).

72. Accordingly, the provision which eventually became article 55 was included in what was designated as the First Draft of the Convention and was retained in the final version of the Convention (*History*, vol I, 254; vol II-1, Doc 43 (11 September 1964) 'Draft Convention: Working Paper for the Legal Committee', p 636). The official Report of the Executive Directors on the Convention confirmed that this provision was introduced for the avoidance of doubt (as its text indicates): see ICSID, *Report of the Executive Directors of the International Bank for Reconstruction and Development on the Convention on the Settlement of Investment Disputes between States and Nationals of Other States* (Washington DC, 1965), para 43; Mr Broches made the same point in his Memorandum to the Executive Directors (*History*, vol II-2, Doc 128 (19 January 1965) 'Memorandum from the General Counsel and Draft Report of the Executive Directors to accompany the Convention', paras 43–44). The law of State immunity varies from State to State, and the Convention made no attempt to harmonise it. As Professor Schreuer points out in his commentary on article 54, persons seeking to enforce arbitration awards made pursuant to the Convention will tend to choose to do so in those jurisdictions which have the least generous rules of State immunity for the protection of the assets of other Contracting States (Schreuer, p 1124, para 27).

73. The fact that the specific qualification of the obligation to enforce an award like a final court judgment relating to state immunity was expressly dealt with in article 55 for the avoidance of doubt indicates that article 54(1) was itself understood to have the

effect of allowing the possibility of certain other defences to enforcement if national law recognised them in respect of final judgments of local courts.

74. The travaux préparatoires also indicate that it was accepted that further defences available in national law in relation to enforcement of court judgments could be available in exceptional circumstances by virtue of the formulation of the obligation in article 54(1). Mr Broches pointed out 'that the First Draft went further than the Secretariat draft since treating awards in the same way as court judgments implied that exceptional grounds only could be invoked to prevent recognition and enforcement' (Aron Broches, 'Awards Rendered Pursuant to the ICSID Convention: Binding Force, Finality, Recognition, Enforcement, Execution', (1987) ICSID Rev 287, 312). But he also resisted a proposal by the Austrian representative to delete the words (in what became article 54(1)) requiring an award to be enforced 'as if it were a final judgment [of a local court]', so as to make the obligation in that provision an unqualified one, since the Austrian representative noted that 'there were several possibilities for annuling [sic] judgments even after they had been declared final' (*History*, vol II-2, Doc 120 (11 January 1965) 'Summary Proceedings of the Legal Committee meeting, December 11, morning', p 901). Mr Broches stated that in his opinion 'by making an award the equivalent of a final judgment one had reached the maximum obtainable' (that is to say, in practical terms, given the issues raised in the drafting meetings) (Broches, p 314). So, for example, there was discussion of the possibility in English law of applying to have a final judgment of a national court set aside on the grounds that it was obtained by fraud, and Mr Broches confirmed that this would also be applicable in relation to a Convention award: see *History*, vol II-2, Doc 113 (11 January 1965) 'Summary Proceedings of the Legal Committee meeting, December 10, afternoon', p 889 ('If a final judgment against a sovereign State could not be executed, then an award could not be executed either; and in the same way, if a final judgment was open to some extraordinary remedy in the case of fraud or similar occurrence, that would be true for the award as well.'). Later, Mr Broches resisted a suggestion that what is now article 55 should be expanded so as also to 'cover the cases where there were laws which, although not related to immunities, might limit the execution of the award against the State', on the grounds that he 'thought this was unnecessary because full recognition had been given to the laws of the State in article [54]' and '[article 55] dealt with one specific problem on which certain delegations had expressed concern' (*History*, vol II-2, Doc 120, p 905).

75. In his commentary on article 54, Professor Schreuer observes that at the stage of recognition and enforcement of awards '[t]he otherwise self-contained nature of the Convention does not apply' (p 1120, para 10). At, pp 1142–1143, para 91 he says (omitting references):

'The fact that article 54(1) assimilates ICSID awards to final judgments of domestic courts implies that enforcement may be resisted in countries where national rules provide for an exceptional refusal to enforce a final judgment. Though this possibility was already acknowledged during the drafting of the Convention, it has not yet been relied upon in practice in order to defy recognition and enforcement of ICSID awards. Instead, past attempts to resist enforcement of awards have relied upon immunity from execution.'

76. Article 54(3) of the Convention is concerned with execution of awards. Its effect is that the available processes of execution will be those in the law of the State where enforcement is sought. It does not require that State to make available any other processes of execution. This provision does not limit the obligation on Contracting States to enforce awards. Once again, the matter is explained by Professor Schreuer in his commentary: having regard to all the authentic language versions of the Convention, no distinction is to be drawn between enforcement and execution (p 1134, para 64). He observes in his commentary on article 54(3):

'The drafting history and the context of article 54(3) make it clear that the laws of the enforcing State that govern execution of an ICSID award are of a procedural nature only. Article 54(3) does not detract from the obligation of every State party to the Convention to enforce awards. In particular, the laws of the enforcing State may not serve as a standard for the review of awards. Article 54(3) does not affect the finality and non-reviewability of awards ... ' (p 1149, para 112)

77. Articles 50(2), 51(4) and 52(5) make specific provision for staying enforcement of an award in certain specific situations, none of which applies here. Section 2(2) of the 1966 Act and CPR [Civil Procedure Rules] 62.21(5) make corresponding provision in domestic law for the grant of a stay in such situations. These stays pursuant to the Convention are available only in the context of interpretation, revision and annulment of awards addressed by those articles. In the present case, Romania has already exercised and exhausted its right under article 52 of ICSID to seek annulment of the Award. The ICSID *ad hoc* Committee upheld the Award on 26 February 2016.

78. However, in light of the wording of articles 54(1) and 55 and the travaux préparatoires reviewed above, it is arguable that there is scope for some additional defences against enforcement, in certain exceptional or extraordinary circumstances which are not defined, if national law recognises them in respect of final judgments of national courts and they do not directly overlap with those grounds of challenge to an award which are specifically allocated to Convention organs under articles 50 to 52 of the Convention. Mr Broches proposed at the drafting meeting on 11 December 1964 referred to above that representatives 'should consciously accept something that was of necessity not precise, which each country in good faith would seek to translate into appropriate local law. He thought that it was necessary to leave some freedom to the Contracting States to interpret in good faith the principal concept laid down in the Convention' (ie the obligation in article 54(1)) (*History*, vol II-2, Doc 120, 903).

79. In the Court of Appeal Hamblen LJ accepted Romania's submission that the relevant obligation of the United Kingdom under article 54(1) was one of 'equivalence'. He considered that, while there will be different national rules and procedures relating to enforcement, provided the same rules and procedures are applied to registered awards as to final court judgments in the State concerned article 54 will be complied with. In his view, the effect of

section 2(1) of the 1966 Act was to make an ICSID award registered under section 1 of the Act equivalent for all purposes to a judgment of the High Court given in ordinary domestic proceedings. As a result, in his view, if the present award had been a final decision of the English court there could be little doubt that the English court would stay enforcement because payment was prohibited by a subsequent Commission decision. On that basis, he considered that enforcement of the Award had to be stayed. The courts have general powers under the CPR to order a stay where that would be appropriate outside the specific situations dealt with in CPR 62.21: see in particular CPR 3.1(2)(f), CPR 40.8A and CPR 83.7(4).

80. Hamblen LJ's view on the general question whether article 54(1) operates on the basis of a principle of 'equivalence' gains some support from the points set out above and the travaux préparatoires referred to. But as appears below, even if he is right on that point, consideration of the effect of article 351 TFEU means that it does not follow that Romania succeeds in showing that the enforcement of the Commission Award should be refused under the ICSID Convention and the 1966 Act.

81. On the other hand, it might be said that this reading of the obligation of each Contracting State under article 54(1) to enforce the pecuniary obligations imposed by an ICSID award 'as if it were a final judgment of a court in that State' fails to take proper account of the scheme of the ICSID Convention as described above. It is arguable that there is countervailing force in the view of Arden and Leggatt LJJ in the Court of Appeal that it would be inconsistent with that scheme for a national court to refuse to enforce an award on the ground that, if it had been an ordinary domestic judgment, giving effect to it would be contrary to a provision of national law and that the only circumstances in which the validity or enforceability of an ICSID award can be challenged are those set out in the ICSID Convention itself. It is arguable that the words 'as if it were a final judgment of a court in that State' in article 54(1) should not be read as referring to the circumstances in which an award is enforceable in the State concerned or as importing national standards as a requirement of enforceability. Rather it is arguable that, as Leggatt LJ put it (at para 258), albeit without consideration of the travaux préparatoires, 'the purpose of equating an award with a final judgment of a court in the state where enforcement is sought is to give legal force to an award for the purpose of executing it and to provide machinery for that purpose'. If that is right, then section 2(1) of the 1966 Act, which implements article 54(1), would not entitle courts in this jurisdiction to refuse to enforce an award on grounds that would justify staying enforcement of a domestic judgment. On this view, article 54(1) simply provides a legal basis for execution. If anything, this might be said to emerge even more clearly from section 2(1) which provides that an award shall 'be of the same force and effect *for the purposes of execution* ... ' (emphasis added) as a domestic judgment (although clearly that provision should be read so as to conform with article 54(1), to which it is intended to give effect).

82. Nevertheless, despite the view they took about the effect of article 54(1), Arden and Leggatt LJJ came to the conclusion that it was open to the court to grant a stay. In their view

article 54(3) gave the national court control over the process of execution which includes its manner and timing and that was reflected in section 2(1)(c) of the 1966 Act. Rules of court, CPR 40.8A and CPR 83.7(4), confer wide discretionary powers to stay the execution of a final judgment. Accordingly, it was open to courts in this jurisdiction to grant a stay of execution if in the particular circumstances of the case it was just to do so, provided that the stay was temporary and consistent with the purposes of the ICSID Convention (Arden LJ at paras 122–126; Leggatt LJ at paras 260–262). Both emphasised, however, that this power could not extend to declining to enforce an award because of a substantive objection to it or staying enforcement of an award permanently or indefinitely (at paras 125, 262).

83. The difference between Hamblen LJ on the one hand and Arden and Leggatt LJJ on the other regarding the proper interpretation of article 54(1) of the ICSID Convention is something which ultimately could only be authoritatively resolved by the International Court of Justice. There are valid arguments on both sides. It is perhaps not altogether surprising that there is some doubt about the true meaning and effect of article 54, given that the work on drafting that provision was carried out 'under great time pressure and is described by Broches as being characterized by great fluidity, sometimes bordering on confusion' (Schreuer, p 1135, para 66). However, the important point for present purposes is that whichever view is correct, it does not assist Romania in this case.

84. We first address the position which arises on the interpretation of article 54(1) preferred by Arden and Leggatt LJJ. We agree with them that courts in this jurisdiction have the power to stay execution of an ICSID award in the limited circumstances which they describe. However, we consider that in granting a stay of execution of the Award in the present case pending the determination of the annulment proceedings in the GCEU (or further order in the meantime) they exceeded the proper limits of that power. The grant of a stay in these circumstances was not consistent with the ICSID Convention, on their interpretation of it, under which the United Kingdom and its courts had a duty to recognise and enforce the Award. This was not a limited stay of execution on procedural grounds, but a prohibition on enforcement of the Award on substantive grounds until the GCEU had ruled on the apparent conflict between the ICSID Convention and the EU Treaties. Effect was given to the Commission Decision until such time as the GCEU might pronounce upon it. The logic of the position adopted by Arden and Leggatt LJJ was that if the GCEU upheld the Commission Decision, the stay would continue indefinitely (and the same would be true if the CJEU allows the Commission's appeal against the decision of the GCEU). But the grounds of objection raised by the Commission, even if upheld before the EU courts, were not valid grounds of objection to the Award or its enforcement under the ICSID Convention, as interpreted by Arden and Leggatt LJJ. The principle laid down in article 53(1) that awards are binding on the parties and are not subject to any appeal or other remedy except those provided under the Convention and reflected in article 54 (on their interpretation of it) was disregarded. In substance, the Court of Appeal made use of powers to stay execution granted by domestic law in order to thwart enforcement of an award which had become enforceable under the ICSID Convention.

85. On the other hand, if article 54(1) incorporates the principle of equivalence, in line with Hamblen LJ's interpretation, it remains the case that Romania's submission in answer to the Claimants' cross-appeal cannot succeed. This is because article 351 TFEU has the effect that any obligation on the UK courts to give effect to a decision such as the Commission Decision pursuant to the duty of sincere co-operation which might arise under the Treaties in other circumstances does not arise in this case. The discussion below of Original Ground 4 of the cross-appeal, explains that the United Kingdom owes relevant obligations to non-EU member states under the ICSID Convention, a treaty to which the United Kingdom was party before it became a member state. By virtue of article 351 TFEU this means that the obligations on the United Kingdom arising from the ICSID Convention are 'not ... affected by the provisions of the Treaties'.

86. Leaving aside the Treaties, in the circumstances of the present case the English courts are obliged under article 54(1) of the ICSID Convention to give effect to the Award in favour of the Claimants and this is not a case in which any of the exceptional possible types of defence to enforcement contemplated by Mr Broches and Professor Schreuer arise. Leaving the Treaties out of the analysis, if the Award were a final judgment of an English court it would be enforced without question. Similarly, on Hamblen LJ's interpretation of article 54(1) involving the principle of equivalence, it must follow that the Award would be enforced in the same way. Article 351 TFEU means that this obligation cannot be affected by anything in the Treaties, which are the foundation for the legal effect of Commission rulings and for the obligation of sincere co-operation on which Romania seeks to rely. Romania's attempt to pray in aid the obligation of sincere co-operation is an attempt to pull itself up by its own bootstraps. It cannot make out the necessary foundation for its argument, since it cannot show that the obligation of sincere co-operation has any application at all.

4. FOREIGN STATE IMMUNITY, ACT OF STATE AND NON-JUSTICIABILITY

4.1 Foreign State Immunity

Even if an award is recognised and enforced, the difficulties do not end there. A distinction should be drawn between recognition and enforcement on the one hand, which are likely to be less of a problem, and the execution of the award, say by way of the attachment of foreign State assets, on the other. Execution and attachment are likely to encounter genuine difficulties arising from the immunities of the foreign State. We will deal with recognition and enforcement of awards in this section, as well as the related issues of Act of State and non-justiciability, before turning to the problem of execution and attachment in Section 5.

First, regarding recognition and enforcement, the ICSID Convention lifts immunity from proceedings brought in national courts to have ICSID awards recognised and enforced. Typically, national legislation such as the UK Arbitration Act, seen above in *Micula* v.

Romania, is used to implement this Convention obligation.[19] In the case of non-ICSID tribunal awards, things are more convoluted. Reliance may be placed on the 'restrictive theory' of foreign State immunity (sometimes termed 'foreign sovereign immunity', particularly in the United States) by which a foreign State which acts like a merchant is treated as one, rather than as a sovereign.[20] That is the theory, at least, and as with any theory it has its adherents and detractors. Still, industrialised Western nations are broadly speaking adherents, indeed proponents, of the restrictive immunity theory – i.e. they have adopted a restrictive view of immunity. The restrictive immunity theory is now also contained in the UN Convention on the Jurisdictional Immunities of States and Their Property. That UN Convention aims to provide a uniform global code on foreign state immunity. Currently, it has twenty-eight signatories, but only twenty-one parties. It will only enter into force 30 days after the deposit of the thirtieth instrument of ratification, acceptance, approval or accession. The point is that there is a trend towards increasing the scope of application of the restrictive theory, and that at least is a promising development from the viewpoint of the recognition and enforcement of non-ICSID investment arbitration awards.

The following extracts include a recent, somewhat surprising case from Hong Kong which had applied the opposite view to the restrictive theory – termed the 'absolute' theory of immunity. There follow some relevant provisions of the UN Convention which, if and when ratified by China, will change even the Chinese position, and thus the current Hong Kong position. The brief commentary on the provisions of the Convention contained in this chapter compares the Convention to the modern practice of national legal systems.

Let us begin with the unusual, contemporary example of the actual operation of the absolute theory of immunity. Precedents today are few and far between except, perhaps, for this case from Hong Kong, and it is for this reason that the case is noteworthy. The case, dubbed the *Congo* case, involved an unsuccessful attempt to enforce two ICC arbitration awards in Hong Kong. Although the awards were commercial arbitration awards, as opposed to investment arbitration awards, the principles are the same as those which would apply to the enforcement of a non-ICSID Award under the New York Convention.[21] The case was noteworthy as Hong Kong had itself, prior to its 1997 handover to China, once practised the restrictive theory of sovereign immunity. The *Congo* case is today perhaps the only example of a jurisdiction, indeed of a key global financial centre, which has since reversed its position away from a prior acceptance of the restrictive immunity theory. The decision, obtained by a majority of 3:2, was widely criticised in light of modern-day commercial expectations, as it should be, for it is an anachronism and did little to further Hong Kong's reputation as a global centre for international arbitration.

---

[19] For Singapore, see for example the Arbitration (International Investment Disputes Act) (Cap. 11).

[20] For the modern subject of State immunity, see H. Fox and P. Webb, *The Law of State Immunity*, 3rd edn (Oxford University Press, 2013); R. O'Keefe and C. J. Tams (eds), *The United Nations Convention on Jurisdictional Immunities of States and Their Property* (Oxford University Press, 2013).

[21] In this case, the New York Convention was seen to be inapplicable by virtue of the Democratic Republic of Congo being a non-signatory thereto.

Democratic Republic of the Congo v. FG Hemisphere Associates LLC (No. 1) (2011) 14 HKCFAR 95 (Court of Final Appeal, Hong Kong) (Mr Justice Chan PJ, Mr Justice Ribeiro PJ and Sir Anthony Mason NPJ), paras 201–203, 211, 224–226

201. ... Reyes J [the lower court judge] noted the contents of the 1st OCMFA [Office of the Commissioner of the Ministry of Foreign Affairs in Hong Kong's – i.e. the Chinese Foreign Ministry's] Letter and recognized that there was no doubt 'that until recently the Mainland took the absolute immunity position'. However, he was troubled that the Letter did not discuss the signing by the PRC [People's Republic of China] in September 2005 of the United Nations Convention on Jurisdictional Immunities of States and Their Property 2004 ('the UN Convention') which adopts a restrictive approach to state immunity. Even though he noted that the UN Convention had not secured sufficient signatories to enter into force, Reyes J thought that 'having signed the Convention, the PRC Government must be taken to have at least indicated its acceptance of the wisdom of the provisions therein'. He therefore did not think the CPG's [Central People's Government of the People's Republic of China's] position was 'as clear-cut as the Letter states' and that it was therefore not an obstacle to his reaching the provisional view expressed.

B.4 The 2nd OCMFA Letter

202. FGH [FG Hemisphere] filed its Notice of Appeal against Reyes J's decision on 18 December 2008. Before the appeal came on for hearing, the Secretary for Justice placed before the Court a further letter from the OCMFA dated 21 May 2009 ('the 2nd OCMFA Letter'), designed to explain the CPG's position regarding the UN Convention. After referring to the 1st OCMFA Letter, it states (in translation) as follows:

> 'Having been duly authorized, the (OCMFA) in the (HKSAR [Hong Kong Special Administrative Region]) makes the following statement as regards the signature of China of the UN Convention on Jurisdictional Immunities of States and Their Property (hereinafter referred to as the "Convention"):
>
> 1. China considers that the issue of state immunity is an important issue which affects relations between states. The long-term divergence of the international community on the issue of state immunity and the conflicting practices of states have had adverse impacts on international intercourse. The adoption of an international convention on this issue would assist in balancing and regulating the practices of states, and will have positive impacts on protecting the harmony and stability of international relations.
>
> 2. In the spirit of consultation, compromise and cooperation, China has participated in the negotiations on the adoption of the Convention. Although the final text of the Convention was not as satisfactory as China expected, but as a product of compromise by all sides, it is the result of the coordination efforts made by all sides. Therefore, China supported the adoption of the Convention by the United Nations General Assembly.
>
> 3. China signed the Convention on 14 September 2005, to express China's support of the above coordination efforts made by the international community. However,

until now China has not yet ratified the Convention, and the Convention itself has not yet entered into force. Therefore, the Convention has no binding force on China, and moreover it cannot be the basis of assessing China's principled position on relevant issues.

4. After signature of the Convention, the position of China in maintaining absolute immunity has not been changed, and has never applied or recognized the so-called principle or theory of "restrictive immunity" (annexed are materials on China's handling of the Morris case).'

203. Annexed were copies of a letter dated 25 January 2006 and a legal memorandum from the Chinese Embassy in Washington DC to the United States Department of State setting out China's position on state immunity and asserting absolute immunity in respect of a claim sought to be made by one Marvin L Morris Jr against the PRC on the basis of certain bonds issued by the then Chinese government in 1913.

...

211. The Secretary for Justice placed before the Court a further letter from the OCMFA dated 25th August 2010 which, after referring to the first two OCMFA Letters and the decision of the Court of Appeal, stated (in translation) as follows:

'The judgment held that there was no evidence suggesting that the sovereignty of China would be prejudiced if the common law as applied in the Hong Kong Special Administrative Region incorporated the principle of "restrictive immunity"; in practice, the application of the principle of "restrictive immunity" by the courts of the SAR would neither prejudice the sovereignty of China nor place China in a position of being in breach of international obligations under the Convention; there was also no mention in the above-mentioned two letters of the Office of the Commissioner of the Ministry of Foreign Affairs in the Hong Kong Special Administrative Region that the application of the principle of "restrictive immunity" in the Hong Kong Special Administrative Region would prejudice the sovereignty of China.

Given the inconsistencies between the above understanding as stated in the judgment of the Court of Appeal of the High Court of the Hong Kong Special Administrative Region and the actual situation, the Office of the Commissioner of the Ministry of Foreign Affairs in the Hong Kong Special Administrative Region, having been duly authorized, further makes the following statement as regards the issue of state immunity:

...

4. Before 30 June 1997, the United Kingdom extended the State Immunity Act 1978 to Hong Kong. That Act involved matters of foreign affairs and the so-called principle or theory of "restrictive immunity" reflected therein was inconsistent with the consistent position of China in maintaining absolute immunity. Furthermore, from 1 July 1997, the Central People's Government would be responsible for the foreign affairs relating to the Hong Kong Special Administrative Region. Therefore, the above-mentioned State Immunity Act

of the United Kingdom was not localized as were most other British laws that previously applied in Hong Kong when the issue of localization of Hong Kong laws was being dealt with during the transitional period. The principle of "restrictive immunity" which was reflected in the Act no longer applied in the Hong Kong Special Administrative Region upon the resumption of the exercise of sovereignty by China over Hong Kong. At that time, the representatives of the Central People's Government also made it clear in the Sino-British Joint Liaison Group that the uniform regime of state immunity of China would be applicable in the Hong Kong Special Administrative Region from 1 July 1997.

5. If the Hong Kong Special Administrative Region were to adopt a regime of state immunity which is inconsistent with the position of the state, it will undoubtedly prejudice the sovereignty of China and have a long-term impact and serious prejudice to the overall interests of China:

   (1) The issue of state immunity obviously involves the understanding and application of the principle of state sovereignty by China, and concerns relations between states. If the position of the Hong Kong Special Administrative Region on this issue were not consistent with that of the state, the overall power and capacity of the Central People's Government in uniformly conducting foreign affairs would be subjected to substantial interference, which would not be consistent with the status of the Hong Kong Special Administrative Region as a local administrative region.

   (2) The consistent position of China in maintaining absolute immunity on the issue of state immunity has already been widely acknowledged by the international community. Being an inalienable part of China, if the Hong Kong Special Administrative Region were to adopt the principle of "restrictive immunity", the consistent position of China in maintaining absolute immunity would be open to question.

   (3) The Central People's Government is responsible for the foreign affairs relating to the Hong Kong Special Administrative Region, which entails that in the area of foreign affairs, the international rights and obligations concerned would be assumed by the Central People's Government. If the courts of the Hong Kong Special Administrative Region were to apply its jurisdiction over foreign states and their property by adopting the principle of "restrictive immunity", it would be possible for the state concerned to make representations to the Central People's Government, and accordingly the Central People's Government may have to assume state responsibility, thus prejudicing the friendly relations between China and the state concerned. As a matter of fact, since the inception of the case *FG Hemisphere Associates LLC v Democratic Republic of the Congo and Others*, the Government of the Democratic Republic of the Congo has repeatedly made representations to the Central People's Government through the diplomatic channel.

(4) The consistent principled position of China to maintain absolute immunity on the issue of state immunity is not only based on the fundamental international law principle of "sovereign equality among nations", but also for the sake of protecting the security and interests of China and its property abroad. If the principle of "restrictive immunity", which is not consistent with the principled position of the state on absolute immunity, were to be adopted in the Hong Kong Special Administrative Region, the states concerned may possibly adopt reciprocal measures to China and its property (which are not limited to the Hong Kong Special Administrative Region and its property), thus threatening the interests and security of the property of China abroad, as well as hampering the normal intercourse and co-operation in such areas as economy and trade between China and the states concerned.

(5) The international community has been supporting the economic development of impoverished states and the improvement of the livelihood in these states through debt relief initiatives and assistance schemes. Supporting the economic development of developing states has also been one of the foreign policies of China. In recent years, certain foreign companies have acquired the debts of impoverished African states and profited from claiming those debts through judicial proceedings, thus adding to the financial burden of these impoverished states and hampering the efforts of the international community in assisting these states. Such practice is inequitable and some states have even enacted legislation to impose restrictions on the same. If the Hong Kong Special Administrative Region were to adopt a regime of state immunity that is not consistent with that of the state and thereby facilitate the pursuance of the above-mentioned practice, it would be contradictory to the above-mentioned foreign policy of China and tarnish the international image of China.'

...

224. The 'consistent and principled position of China' in relation to state immunity is unequivocally stated in the OCMFA Letters referred to above. It is 'that a state and its property shall, in foreign courts, enjoy absolute immunity, including absolute immunity from jurisdiction and from execution'. There is no room for doubting that such is and has consistently been the policy of the State of the PRC. None of the parties have sought to suggest otherwise, although they differ as to the effect and weight to be attributed to those letters.

225. The fundamental question which falls to be determined in the present appeal is whether, after China's resumption of the exercise of sovereignty on 1st July 1997, it is open to the courts of the HKSAR to adopt a legal doctrine of state immunity which recognizes a commercial exception to absolute immunity and therefore a doctrine on state immunity which is different from the principled policy practised by the PRC.

226. In our view, for the reasons developed below, the answer is clearly 'No'. As a matter of legal and constitutional principle, it is not open to the HKSAR courts to take such a course.

Against this, the specific application of the restrictive theory in the arbitration context has also yielded a specialised 'arbitration exception'. A foreign state's very submission to arbitration, it is said, suffices to lift foreign state immunity. The question will be whether the forum state adopts this specialised exception. In this regard, it is to be noticed that the UN Convention[22] does.

UN Convention on the Jurisdictional Immunities of States and their Property, 2004, Arts 17–19

Article 17 Effect of an arbitration agreement
If a State enters into an agreement in writing with a foreign natural or juridical person to submit to arbitration differences relating to a commercial transaction, that State cannot invoke immunity from jurisdiction before a court of another State which is otherwise competent in a proceeding which relates to:
  (a) the validity, interpretation or application of the arbitration agreement;
  (b) the arbitration procedure; or
  (c) the confirmation or the setting aside of the award, unless the arbitration agreement otherwise provides.

Article 18 State immunity from pre-judgment measures of constraint
No pre-judgment measures of constraint, such as attachment or arrest, against property of a State may be taken in connection with a proceeding before a court of another State unless and except to the extent that:
  (a) the State has expressly consented to the taking of such measures as indicated:
      (i)   by international agreement;
      (ii) by an arbitration agreement or in a written contract; or
      (iii) by a declaration before the court or by a written communication after a dispute between the parties has arisen; or
  (b) the State has allocated or earmarked property for the satisfaction of the claim which is the object of that proceeding.

Article 19 State immunity from post-judgment measures of constraint
No post-judgment measures of constraint, such as attachment, arrest or execution, against property of a State may be taken in connection with a proceeding before a court of another State unless and except to the extent that:
  (a) the State has expressly consented to the taking of such measures as indicated:
      (i)   by international agreement;
      (ii) by an arbitration agreement or in a written contract; or
      (iii) by a declaration before the court or by a written communication after a dispute between the parties has arisen; or
  (b) the State has allocated or earmarked property for the satisfaction of the claim which is the object of that proceeding; or

---

[22] Not, as yet, in force.

(c) it has been established that the property is specifically in use or intended for use by the State for other than government non-commercial purposes and is in the territory of the State of the forum, provided that post-judgment measures of constraint may only be taken against property that has a connection with the entity against which the proceeding was directed.

Several, notable, jurisdictions worldwide also independently treat an arbitration agreement as being sufficient in and of itself to waive immunity from the jurisdiction of domestic courts.[23] The problem, however, is that even where the recognition and enforcement of an award may be relatively unproblematic, the actual attachment of State assets is not. Some jurisdictions have, at various times, extended the 'arbitration exception' to the attachment of assets, thereby lifting immunity automatically. When such is the case, it will be welcome news for the winning claimant in an investment arbitration. Such jurisdictions would treat submission to arbitration by the foreign state as amounting to a waiver of immunity from the attachment of that foreign state's assets.[24] There is one final, minor point to add for the sake of comprehensiveness. Notice that Articles 18(a)(ii) and 19(a)(ii) of the UN Convention require an 'express' waiver of immunity from the pre- and post-judgment attachment of foreign state assets in the arbitration agreement. Much will depend upon how this provision is interpreted when the UN Convention enters into force.

4.2 Pleas of Act of State and Non-Justiciability

We will go on to discuss the issue of award execution and asset attachment, but before we do so, there is a doctrine – mentioned earlier – which is often viewed in association with, but which is conceptually distinct from, foreign State immunity. It is the idea that some matters ought not to be treated as being 'justiciable' before the courts of another State. That is the broad principle referred to as the doctrine of 'non-justiciability'. Where this broad principle involves the need to adjudicate upon the action of a foreign State in its own territory, it is known more specifically as the 'Act of State' doctrine.[25]

---

[23] See, e.g., the United Kingdom's State Immunity Act 1978, s. 9; the US Foreign Sovereign Immunities Act 1976, s. 1605(a)(6); Singapore's State Immunity Act 1979, s. 11; Australia's Foreign States Immunities Act 1985, s. 17; South Africa's Foreign States Immunities Act 1981, s. 10; Pakistan's State Immunity Ordinance 1981, s. 10.

[24] See the decision of the French Court of Cassation, First Civil Chamber, *Creighton v. Qatar*; Cass. Civ. 1, 28 September 2011, the decision of the US Court of Appeals, Fifth Circuit, in *Walker International Holdings Ltd v. Congo*, 395 F3d 229, 234 (2004) and the Canadian decision in *Collavino Inc. v. Tihama Development Authority* [2007] 9 WWR 290 (Alta QB) (construing s. 12(1)(a) of the 1980 Canadian State Immunity Act).

[25] For the Anglo-American and Anglo-Commonwealth doctrines, see, e.g., J. Crawford, *Brownlie's Principles of Public International Law*, 8th edn (Oxford University Press, 2012), 72–87; C. McLachlan, *Foreign Relations Law* (Cambridge University Press, 2016), 523–545. For non-justiciability from a comparative perspective, see Crawford, *Brownlie's Principles*, 103–110. The reader will find the judgment of Lord Justice Rix in *Yukos Capital SARL v. OJSC Rosneft Oil Co.* [2012] EWCA Civ. 855 particularly useful. The *locus classicus* is Lord Wilberforce's judgment in *Buttes Gas and Oil Co. v. Hammer (No. 3)* [1982] AC 888.

Occidental Exploration and Production Co. v. Ecuador [2005] EWCA Civ. 1116 (Lord Justice Mance), paras 1–3, 11–13, 16–19, 23–26, 29–30, 32–33, 38, 41

1. This is the judgment of the Court. The appeal, from a judgment and order of Aikens J dated 29th April 2005, concerns the extent to which the English Courts may under s.67 of the Arbitration Act 1996 consider a challenge to the jurisdiction of an award made by arbitrators appointed under provisions to be found in a Bilateral Investment Treaty. The Treaty was signed on 27th August 1993 between the United States of America ('USA') and the Republic of Ecuador ('Ecuador') ... One of the options provided was arbitration subject to the Arbitration Rules of the United Nations Commission on International Trade Law ('UNCITRAL'), as here occurred. The arbitration was between Occidental Exploration and Production Company ('Occidental'), a Californian corporation, and Ecuador. There was a distinguished panel of arbitrators consisting of the Honourable Charles N. Brower, Dr Patrick Barrera Sweeney and, as chairman, Professor Francisco Orrego Vicuña. Their final award was dated 1st July 2004.

2. ... Occidental and Ecuador were unable to agree upon a place, and the arbitrators by decision dated 1 August 2003 determined that it should be London ...

3. By their award the arbitrators determined the dispute in favour of Occidental, save on one point relating to whether there had been expropriation, which was not in the event relevant to the result. Ecuador by claim form dated 11 August 2004 seeks to have the award set aside under both ss.67 and 68 of the 1996 Act. Also on 11 August 2004, Occidental issued a claim form seeking, in the event of a challenge to the award by Ecuador and if necessary, to re-visit the point on expropriation. But by application notice dated 24 November 2004 Occidental raised a prior objection, that Ecuador's challenge requires the English court to interpret provisions of the Bilateral Investment Treaty between the USA and Ecuador, in contravention of a rule of English law making such an issue 'non-justiciable' ...

   ...

11. Before us, the issues have mirrored those argued extensively before Aikens J. In bare outline, Mr Greenwood QC for Occidental submits that Ecuador's challenge to the tribunal's jurisdiction under s.67 raises issues upon which English Courts cannot or should not adjudicate. First, it would require the Court to enforce or interpret the terms of the Treaty, contrary to a principle stated in *J H Rayner (Mincing Lane) Ltd. v. DTI* ('the *Tin Council* case') [1990] 2 AC 418. Secondly and in any event, it would require the Court to 'adjudicate upon the transactions of foreign sovereign states' contrary to a wider principle of 'judicial restraint or abstention' stated by Lord Wilberforce in *Buttes Gas and Oil Co. v. Hammer* [1982] AC 888, 931 G. The first principle may be viewed as a particular concretisation of the second wider principle. In support of these submissions, Mr Greenwood suggests (though less emphatically than before the judge) that the rights and duties in issue in the arbitration should be seen as state rights – Occidental was in other words claiming no more than to enforce the rights which the United States of America would have in international law against Ecuador in respect of any

breach of the Treaty towards a United States national or company. But, assuming that Occidental was in the arbitration claiming in its own right, Mr Greenwood submits that any adjudication by an English Court upon the question whether the arbitrators acted within their jurisdiction would still depend upon the application or interpretation of an international treaty and be impermissible. The underlying rationale of the House of Lords authorities which, on his case, lead to this conclusion is, he submits, judicial restraint in the national and international interests, reinforced in the specific area of unincorporated treaties by the constitutional consideration that it is for Parliament, and not the United Kingdom Government or the Courts, to introduce new law at a domestic level. As to the need for the judicial restraint, he submits that a decision on the scope of the matters submitted to arbitration could involve a decision upon the scope of the rights enforceable not just by Occidental but necessarily also by the USA, and could have international implications.

12. Mr Lloyd Jones QC for Ecuador submits in response that the Court is concerned with an agreement to arbitrate, arising in a manner contemplated by the Treaty but nonetheless separate from the Treaty and made between different parties, only one of them party to the Treaty. English law having become the curial law of the arbitration (albeit only as a result of a decision of the arbitrators pursuant to the terms of the agreement to arbitrate), he submits that neither of the principles which Mr Greenwood invokes should be understood as precluding the English Court from considering and determining an objection to the arbitrators' jurisdiction under s.67 of the Arbitration Act 1996, even if this would involve construing those parts of the Treaty (particularly Articles VI and X, and possibly also Article III) at which it is necessary to look in order to determine the scope of the matters falling within the scope of Ecuador's offer to arbitrate which Occidental accepted.

13. With regard to the nature of the rights pursued in the arbitration, the judge concluded that investors like Occidental were not enforcing rights of the USA, but were given 'the right to pursue, in their name and for themselves, claims against the other State party' (paragraph 61). He then held, and this was not in issue before us, that Occidental's substantive claims were governed by principles of international law (in the same way that any claims arising between the USA and Ecuador would be). He held that the arbitration agreement coming into existence between Occidental and Ecuador was likewise subject to international law. This is in issue before us, although neither side suggests that the answer is crucial to its own case. Finally, the judge held, and it is common ground before us, that the arbitral procedure was governed by the law of England as the law of the place of arbitration. Hence, the possibility of applications under the Arbitration Act 1996. Turning to the issues of justiciability, the judge did not consider that examination by the Court of Ecuador's challenge under s.67 to the arbitrators' jurisdiction would 'infringe any of the "rules" of non-justiciability ... set out by Lord Oliver' in the Tin Council case (paragraphs 72 to 81). He accepted the distinction advanced by Mr Lloyd Jones between adjudication upon rights operating purely at the

international level and adjudication upon international rights intended to be exercised in a tribunal subject to control under municipal laws; and he considered that s.67 gave a 'foothold' in domestic law to challenge the jurisdictional ruling of the tribunal.

...

16. Bilateral investment treaties such as the present introduce a new element, and create a 'very different' situation (cf *Zachary Douglas* in *The Hybrid Foundations of Investment Treaty Arbitrations* (2003) BYIL 151, 169). The protection of nationals is crystallised and in the present Treaty expanded to cover every kind of investment 'owned or controlled directly or indirectly by nationals or companies of the other Party' (Article 1), but the investor is given direct standing to pursue the State of the investment in respect of any 'investment dispute'. An investment dispute is defined as 'a dispute ... arising out of or relating to (a) an investment agreement between that Party and such national or company; (b) an investment authorisation granted by that Party's foreign investment authority to such national or company; or (c) an alleged breach of any right conferred or created by this Treaty with respect to an investment'.

...

17. Where a dispute arises out of or relates to a commercial agreement made with the investor, it would seem to us both artificial and wrong in principle to suggest that the investor is in reality pursuing a claim vested in his or its home State, and that the only improvement by comparison with the traditional State protection for investors is procedural. It would potentially undermine the efficacy of the protection held out to individual investors, if such protection was subject to the continuing benevolence and support of their national State. *Douglas*, at p.170 in the article already cited, draws attention to arbitrations where the national State by intervention or in submissions opposed its investor's claims or the tribunal's jurisdiction to hear them; but, if the claims were the State's, such opposition should have been of itself fatal.

18. In the case of a claim of type (c) – and probably also (b) – any substantive right would have to be found in the Treaty. The Treaty would have to be regarded as conferring or creating direct rights in international law in favour of investors either from the outset, or at least (and in this event retrospectively) as and when they pursue claims in one of the ways provided. These alternative analyses are advanced by *Douglas* at pp.182–4. The former analysis is in our view natural and preferable, but it does not matter which applies.

19. That treaties may in modern international law give rise to direct rights in favour of individuals is well established, particularly where the treaty provides a dispute resolution mechanism capable of being operated by such individuals acting on their own behalf and without their national state's involvement or even consent. *Oppenheim's International Law* (9th Ed.), para. 375 put the matter in this way in 1992:

'States can, ... and occasionally do, confer upon individuals, whether their own subjects or aliens, international rights *strictu sensu*, ie rights which they can acquire without the intervention of municipal legislation and which they can enforce in their own name before international tribunals'.

...

23. We turn to the core aspect of Mr Greenwood's case, non-justiciability. The wider basis on which this is asserted was identified by Lord Wilberforce in *Buttes Gas*. The civil claims pursued between private individuals or concerns in that case were not founded on any investment treaty, or even on any private law contract referring to the provisions of any treaty. But the defence of justification raised by Mr Hammer and Occidental as defendants (in response to Buttes Gas's libel claim) and Occidental's counterclaim for conspiracy to defraud could, on the unusual facts of that case, only have been decided by considering a range of extremely contentious international matters: an allegation that the Ruler of Sharjah had back-dated a decree extending his territorial waters; a claim to sovereignty by the Government of Iran made subsequent to such decree; instructions to the ruler of Umm al Qaiwain by the United Kingdom political agent; intervention by Her Majesty's naval, air and military forces then operating in the relevant area under treaty arrangements; and further intervention by the Iranian Government. In the single full speech given by Lord Wilberforce, these issues were held to be non-justiciable, on the basis of a general principle of English law that 'the courts will not adjudicate upon the transactions of foreign sovereign states' (p.931 G and 932A). This was explained as a matter of 'judicial restraint or abstention' and to be 'inherent in the very nature of the judicial process' (p.931 G and 932A). In applying this principle to the facts of the case, Lord Wilberforce said 'the important inter-state issues and/or issues of international law which would face the court': '... have only to be stated to compel the conclusion that these are not issues upon which a municipal court can pass ... [T]here are ... no judicial or manageable standards by which to judge these issues, or to adopt another phrase ... the court would be in a judicial no-man's land: the court would be asked to review transactions in which four sovereign states were involved, which they had brought to a precarious settlement, after diplomacy and the use of force, and to say that at least part of these were 'unlawful' under international law. I would just add ... that it is not to be assumed that these matters have now passed into history, so that they now can be examined with safe detachment.'

...

24. In *British Airways Board v. Laker Airways Ltd.* [1985] AC 58, Lord Diplock, with whose speech all other members of the House agreed, said that:

'The interpretation of treaties to which the United Kingdom is a party but the terms of which have not either expressly or by reference been incorporated in English domestic law by legislation is not a matter that falls within the interpretative jurisdiction of an English court of law.'

This was however in the context of a claim that the US Government had been in breach of treaty obligations (so that the considerations later identified in *Buttes Gas* were potentially in play). The case was not concerned with a situation where the interpretation of treaty wording may be relevant to the construction of an agreement with a private party, or with any investment treaty ...

25. On the other hand, in *Kuwait Airways Corporation v. Iraqi Airways Company (Nos. 4 and 5)* [2002] 2 AC 883, the House of Lords held that the principle in *Buttes Gas* did not prevent the English courts from identifying the plain breach of the United Nations Charter involved in Iraq's invasion of Kuwait and subsequent expropriation of the Kuwait civil aviation fleet. The problems of adjudication confronting the court in *Buttes Gas* were absent, the standard to be applied was clear and manageable and the outcome not in doubt: see at paras 25, 113, 125 and 146 per Lords Nicholls, Steyn, Hoffmann and Hope. Lord Steyn regarded the proposition that *Buttes Gas* established 'an absolute rule ... that courts in England will not adjudicate upon acts done abroad by virtue of sovereign authority' as 'too austere and unworkable an interpretation of the *Buttes* case' (p.1101E).

26. The narrower and more clear-cut basis on which Mr Greenwood advances his case was stated in the *Tin Council* case ...

    ...

29. The unenforceability in the United Kingdom of unincorporated treaties under the reasoning in the *Tin Council* case was at the heart of the further decisions of the House of Lords in *R. v. Home Secretary, ex p. Brind* [1991] 1 AC 696 ...

30. In *ex p. Brind*, the House again acknowledged that reference might be made to an unincorporated treaty (in that case the European Convention on Human Rights) to resolve an ambiguity in English primary or secondary legislation ...

    ...

32. The answer to this question can in our view only be found by taking into account, first, the special character of a bilateral investment treaty such as the present and, second, the agreement to arbitrate which it is intended to facilitate and which is both recognized under English private international law rules and (since England is the place of arbitration) subject to the Arbitration Act 1996. The Treaty involves, on any view, a deliberate attempt to ensure for private investors the benefits and protection of consensual arbitration; and this is an aim to which national courts should, in an internationalist spirit and because it has been agreed between States at an international level, aspire to give effect ...

33. Further, as Mr Greenwood accepts, the agreement to arbitrate which results by following the Treaty route is not itself a treaty. It is an agreement between a private investor on the one side and the relevant State on the other ...

    ...

38. In the case of an ICSID arbitration, no recourse to the English court is currently possible under the Arbitration Act 1996: see the Arbitration (International Investment Disputes) Act 1966 s.3(2). The ICSID scheme also differs in having its own enforcement mechanism, so that the New York Convention is inapplicable. Neither of these factors suggests to us that the English Court should refrain from exercising jurisdiction under s.67 in respect of an arbitration conducted under Article VI.3(a)(iii) and UNICITRAL rules.

    ...

41. We see no good reason why any arbitration held pursuant to such an agreement, or any supervisory role which the court of the place of arbitration may have in relation to any such arbitration, should be categorised as being concerned with 'transactions between States' so as to invoke the principle of non-justiciability in *Buttes Gas*.[26]

Banco Nacional de Cuba v. *Sabbatino*, 376 US 398 (1964), at 398, 401, 416, 421, 423, 427–428, 439–440 (US Supreme Court)

Respondent American commodity broker contracted with a Cuban corporation largely owned by United States residents to buy Cuban sugar. Thereafter, subsequent to the United States Government's reduction of the Cuban sugar quota, the Cuban Government expropriated the corporation's property and rights. To secure consent for shipment of the sugar, the broker, by a new contract, agreed to make payment for the sugar to a Cuban instrumentality which thereafter assigned the bills of lading to petitioner, another Cuban instrumentality, and petitioner instructed its agent in New York to deliver to the broker the bills of lading and sight draft in return for payment. The broker accepted the documents, received payment for the sugar from its customer, but refused to deliver the proceeds to petitioner's agent. Petitioner brought this action ... The District Court concluded that the corporation's property interest in the sugar was subject to Cuba's territorial jurisdiction, and acknowledged the 'act of state' doctrine, which precludes judicial inquiry in this country respecting the public acts of a recognized foreign sovereign power committed within its own territory. The court nevertheless rendered summary judgment against the petitioner, ruling that the act of state doctrine was inapplicable when the questioned act violated international law, which the District Court found had been the case here. The Court of Appeals affirmed, additionally relying upon two State Department letters which it took as evidencing willingness by the Executive Branch to a judicial testing of the validity of the expropriation.

MR. JUSTICE HARLAN delivered the opinion of the Court.

The question which brought this case here, and is now found to be the dispositive issue, is whether the so-called act of state doctrine serves to sustain petitioner's claims in this litigation. Such claims are ultimately founded on a decree of the Government of Cuba expropriating certain property, the right to the proceeds of which is here in controversy. The act of state doctrine in its traditional formulation precludes the courts of this country from inquiring into the validity of the public acts a recognized foreign sovereign power committed within its own territory.

...

The classic American statement of the act of state doctrine, which appears to have taken root in England as early as 1674, *Blad v. Bamfield*, 3 Swans. 604, 36 Eng. Rep. 992,

---

[26] [Eds: Cited with approval, for example, by the Singapore High Court in *Government of Laos* v. *Sanum Investments Ltd* [2015] SGHC 15 (reversed on appeal, but not on this point).]

and began to emerge in the jurisprudence of this country in the late eighteenth and early nineteenth centuries ... is found in *Underhill v. Hernandez*, 168 U. S. 250, where Chief Justice Fuller said for a unanimous Court (p. 168 U. S. 252):

> 'Every sovereign state is bound to respect the independence of every other sovereign state, and the courts of one country will not sit in judgment on the acts of the government of another, done within its own territory. Redress of grievances by reason of such acts must be obtained through the means open to be availed of by sovereign powers as between themselves.'

...

We do not believe that this doctrine is compelled either by the inherent nature of sovereign authority, as some of the earlier decisions seem to imply ... or by some principle of international law. If a transaction takes place in one jurisdiction and the forum is in another, the forum does not, by dismissing an action or by applying its own law, purport to divest the first jurisdiction of its territorial sovereignty; it merely declines to adjudicate, or makes applicable its own law to parties or property before it.

...

The act of state doctrine does, however, have 'constitutional' underpinnings. It arises out of the basic relationships between branches of government in a system of separation of powers. It concerns the competency of dissimilar institutions to make and implement particular kinds of decisions in the area of international relations. The doctrine, as formulated in past decisions, expresses the strong sense of the Judicial Branch that its engagement in the task of passing on the validity of foreign acts of state may hinder, rather than further, this country's pursuit of goals both for itself and for the community of nations as a whole in the international sphere.

...

If the act of state doctrine is a principle of decision binding on federal and state courts alike, but compelled by neither international law nor the Constitution, its continuing vitality depends on its capacity to reflect the proper distribution of functions between the judicial and political branches of the Government on matters bearing upon foreign affairs. It should be apparent that the greater the degree of codification or consensus concerning a particular area of international law, the more appropriate it is for the judiciary to render decisions regarding it, since the courts can then focus on the application of an agreed principle to circumstances of fact, rather than on the sensitive task of establishing a principle not inconsistent with the national interest or with international justice. It is also evident that some aspects of international law touch much more sharply on national nerves than do others; the less important the implications of an issue are for our foreign relations, the weaker the justification for exclusivity in the political branches. The balance of relevant considerations may also be shifted if the government which perpetrated the challenged act of state is no longer in existence, as in the *Bernstein* case, for the political interest of this country may, as a result, be measurably altered. Therefore, rather than laying down or reaffirming an inflexible and all-encompassing rule in this case, we decide only that the

Judicial Branch will not examine the validity of a taking of property within its own territory by a foreign sovereign government, extant and recognized by this country at the time of suit, in the absence of a treaty or other unambiguous agreement regarding controlling legal principles, even if the complaint alleges that the taking violates customary international law.

There are few if any issues in international law today on which opinion seems to be so divided as the limitations on a state's power to expropriate the property of aliens.

...

Against the force of such considerations, we find respondents' countervailing arguments quite unpersuasive. Their basic contention is that United States courts could make a significant contribution to the growth of international law, a contribution whose importance, it is said, would be magnified by the relative paucity of decisional law by international bodies. But, given the fluidity of present world conditions, the effectiveness of such a patchwork approach toward the formulation of an acceptable body of law concerning state responsibility for expropriations is, to say the least, highly conjectural. Moreover, it rests upon the sanguine presupposition that the decisions of the courts of the world's major capital exporting country and principal exponent of the free enterprise system would be accepted as disinterested expressions of sound legal principle by those adhering to widely different ideologies.

...

MR. JUSTICE WHITE, dissenting

I am dismayed that the Court has, with one broad stroke, declared the ascertainment and application of international law beyond the competence of the courts of the United States in a large and important category of cases. I am also disappointed in the Court's declaration that the acts of a sovereign state with regard to the property of aliens within its borders are beyond the reach of international law in the courts of this country. However clearly established that law may be, a sovereign may violate it with impunity, except insofar as the political branches of the government may provide a remedy. This backward-looking doctrine, never before declared in this Court, is carried a disconcerting step further: not only are the courts powerless to question acts of state proscribed by international law, but they are likewise powerless to refuse to adjudicate the claim founded upon a foreign law; they must render judgment, and thereby validate the lawless act. Since the Court expressly extends its ruling to all acts of state expropriating property, however clearly inconsistent with the international community, all discriminatory expropriations of the property of aliens, as for example the taking of properties of persons belonging to certain races, religions or nationalities, are entitled to automatic validation in the courts of the United States. No other civilized country has found such a rigid rule necessary for the survival of the Executive Branch of its government; the Executive of no other government seems to require such insulation from international law adjudications in its courts; and no other judiciary is apparently so incompetent to ascertain and apply international law.

5. ATTACHMENT OF ASSETS: THE 'FINAL REFUGE'

Returning to the subject of asset attachment, the first thing to observe is that, even in the case of an ICSID arbitration, the ICSID Convention (Articles 54(3) and 55, reproduced in Section 3 above) defers to national rules on what is termed the 'execution' of the award and the attachment of foreign State assets. Saunders and Salomon explain this aspect of the matter.[27]

M. Saunders and C. Salomon, 'Enforcement of Arbitral Awards against States and State Entities' (2007) 23 *Arb. Int'l* 467, 468–469

The ICSID Convention provides a comprehensive procedure for investment arbitrations, and excludes the application of national arbitration law. There is no seat or place of arbitration in an ICSID arbitration which would operate to trigger the application of a national law on arbitration. Accordingly, enforcement of an ICSID award is governed by the ICSID Convention and not the New York Convention (which applies to arbitrations rendered in a seat that is a New York Convention contracting state).

Article 54 of the ICSID Convention requires contracting states to enforce an ICSID award 'as if it were a final judgment of a court in that state'. There are no grounds for refusal of enforcement, although Article 55 makes clear that the Convention does not derogate from the law in force in any ICSID Convention contracting state relating to immunity of the state from execution; thus, the minefield that is domestic law on the issue of sovereign immunity remains to be negotiated.

...

Immunity from execution arises when execution measures (following the court's recognition and enforcement of an arbitral award) are to be taken against a state's assets. States continue to apply such immunity, with the consequence that a successful ICSID claimant may suffer a Pyrrhic victory unless assets owned by the state but not immune from enforcement/execution (commonly those in use for commercial purposes) can be identified.

Having gone to the significant costs of obtaining an ICSID award, and leave to enforce the award (pursuant to Article 54(2) of the ICSID Convention), the claimant may find itself unable to obtain satisfaction thereunder.

There is an apparent contradiction in a state's waiver of immunity from jurisdiction under Article 54 of the ICSID Convention (thereby enabling the successful party to obtain leave to enforce the award) but not from execution (pursuant to Article 55 of the ICSID Convention). This incongruity may be resolved by considering that the failure to waive immunity from execution does not imply that the successful party cannot execute against any of the state's assets. It is simply that such execution is subject to laws on immunity which restrict the categories of state assets which may be executed against. Of course, the practical reality is that there are very few state assets which will not fall under the protective cloak of immunity.

---

[27] For a concise – albeit somewhat practical – introduction to the attachment of foreign sovereign assets, see also C. L. Lim, 'Worldwide Litigation over Foreign Sovereign Assets' (2016) 10 *Dispute Resolution Int'l* 145.

The reader might ask what the difference is between 'enforcement' of an award domestically and the 'execution' of the award by way of asset attachment. The simple answer is that, depending on the specific national procedure involved, enforcement may indeed be indissociable from execution and attachment, and that is perhaps the more logical view. However, it is not a universal view and it is not the view at common law. That explains why the framers of the UN Convention declined even to lift immunity under the restrictive theory in respect of an action to 'enforce' an arbitral award (i.e. to prevent immunity from being automatically lifted for cases where enforcement means, or is simply a procedural prelude to, the execution and attachment of foreign State assets).[28]

'Enforcement', at least under English law by way of example, refers merely to the jurisdiction of the English courts to adjudicate upon enforcement (i.e. to the English court's 'adjudicative jurisdiction'). The position may be the same in places like Germany.[29] Because of procedural differences elsewhere, however, where enforcement may be taken to be tantamount to execution, the UN Convention therefore refuses to treat submission to arbitration as an implied waiver of immunity even from enforcement, for fear that it may amount to a waiver of immunity from the attachment of the foreign State's assets.[30] A separate express waiver of the foreign State will be required.

In contrast, under Anglo-American law, submission to arbitration would already (i.e. automatically) lift immunity from attachment as a waiver of immunity is implied under the restrictive theory of immunity.[31] Thus, all is not lost where the foreign State's assets may be pursued for the purpose of attachment in such jurisdictions which do extend the 'commercial exception' under the restrictive theory to the attachment of foreign State assets.

CONCLUSION

Enforcement is typically governed by treaty, be it under the ICSID Convention or in the case of non-ICSID (such as ad hoc) arbitration *if* the arbitration is seated in a New York Convention country. The bilateral investment treaty may itself require the arbitration to be seated thus, and NAFTA is but one example of an investment treaty which imposes such a requirement. Thus, treaty rules, be they rules under the ICSID Convention or the New York Convention, restrict the grounds of challenge. The grounds themselves are broadly similar under the two treaty regimes, and they are similar to the grounds for setting aside an award in the place of the seat of an arbitration under the UNCITRAL Model Law.

There is, in effect then, a high degree of harmonisation of the rules at play, more so than might first appear to the naked eye. The basic idea remains that an international

---

[28] C. Annecker and R. T. Greig, 'State Immunity and Arbitration' (2004) 15 *ICC Bulletin* 70, 71–72.
[29] See the *Walter Bau Case*, Case No. III ZB 40/12.
[30] Art. 17 of the UN Convention on the Jurisdictional Immunities of States and Their Property.
[31] UK State Immunity Act 1978, s. 9; *Svenska* v. *Lithuania* [2007] 2 WLR 876, CA, [117]–[122], per Moore-Bick LJ; US Foreign Sovereign Immunities Act 1976, s. 1605(a)(1), (6); *Ipitrade International SA* v. *Nigeria*, 465 F. Supp. 824 (DDC 1978) (applying only to awards to which the New York Convention applies). The position in France may be more complex.

investment arbitration award should be as easily enforceable as an international commercial award. However, a characteristic which is indissociable from investment arbitration is that the respondent is a sovereign, and thus questions of foreign sovereign or foreign state immunity, and the related doctrines of Act of State and non-justiciability, loom large, even if they are not unique to investment arbitration.

QUESTIONS

1. How is an ICSID award enforced in comparison with a non-ICSID award?
2. How does the annulment of an ICSID award differ from the set aside and challenges to the enforcement of a non-ICSID award?
3. What is the distinction between the enforcement of an award on the one hand, and execution and attachment on the other?
4. Why is immunity from attachment still an issue, notwithstanding the requirement in Article 54(1) of the ICSID Convention that awards shall be 'recognised' and 'enforced'?

SUGGESTIONS FOR FURTHER READING

1. M. Burgstaller and C. B. Rosenberg, 'Challenging International Arbitral Awards: To ICSID or Not to ICSID' (2011) 27 *Arb Int'l* 91.
2. E. Martinez, 'Understanding the Debate over Necessity: Unanswered Questions and Future Implications of Annulments in the Argentine Gas Cases' (2012) 23 *Duke J Int'l Comp L* 149.
3. M. L. Seelig and A. G. Tevini, 'Revision Proceedings under the ICSID Convention' (2010) 26 *Arb Int'l* 467.
4. M. Saunders and C. Salomon, 'Enforcement of Arbitral Awards against States and State Entities' (2007) 23 *Arb Int'l* 467.
5. C. L. Lim, 'Worldwide Litigation over Foreign Sovereign Assets' (2016) 10 *Dispute Resolution Int'l* 145.

20

New Directions in International Investment Law and Arbitration

CHAPTER OUTLINE

This concluding chapter discusses the current backlash against investment arbitration and investment treaties. Section 1 discusses the backlash to investment arbitration under Chapter 11 of the NAFTA in the early 2000s, and the consequent 'rebalancing' of the US Prototype BIT of 1994 in 2004. The chapter goes on to discuss how the backlash grew, beginning in 2007, from Bolivia's, Ecuador's and Venezuela's terminations of their participation in the ICSID Convention and other similar terminations worldwide, to various countries' efforts to 'rebalance' (i.e. rewrite) their own BITs and other investment agreements. Section 2 highlights some of the latest treaty clauses which have emerged from this worldwide rebalancing effort, focusing on some of the most important substantive clauses, namely FET and expropriation clauses, particularly in connection with the controversy over the continued ability of host States to enact environmental, health and other public welfare measures. The chapter then turns to current procedural innovations and proposals for reform, such as the proposal for an appellate mechanism. Section 3 concludes this chapter with the European Union's current proposal to replace investment arbitration altogether with a 'Multilateral Investment Court'. Today, the system for settling investment disputes through investment arbitration faces proposals for its improvement, as well as for its demise, or at least its diminution as the principal mode of investment dispute settlement. Yet here is a field which has always seen such shifts in sentiment, and little of what has been said in this book will likely be irrelevant in understanding what the future brings.

INTRODUCTION

For more than a decade there has been a global backlash against investment treaties and investment treaty arbitration. The early signs had showed in attempts to achieve more 'balanced' BITs in the 2004 US and Canadian Model BITs. The year 2004 also saw the *Methanex* arbitration.[1] Following *Methanex*, 'expropriation safeguards' – meaning new

---

[1] *Methanex* v. *USA*, UNCITRAL (NAFTA), Ad Hoc Arbitration, Final Award, 3 August 2005. See M. Sornarajah, *Resistance and Change in the International Law on Foreign Investment* (Cambridge University Press, 2015),

forms of treaty language which guard against potentially overbroad findings of expropriation, particularly of indirect or regulatory expropriation – have come into focus. The
Methanex Award has since been cited by, among others, the tribunal in *Saluka* for the
general proposition that general, non-discriminatory regulation commonly accepted to
be within the scope of a State's police powers will not be taken to amount to indirect
expropriation.[2] The rewriting of treaty expropriation clauses is but a part of what, presently, is referred to as the global 'rebalancing' of contemporary BITs and other investment
agreements by treaty draftsmen.

The signs of a full-blown backlash did not, however, emerge until around 2007,[3] beginning with the discontent with investment arbitration in Latin America. Discontent with
the way in which BITs had been drafted then spread to South Africa, and then other
places like India, Indonesia and Europe, in the course of which these events soon dis-
credited the view, perhaps all-too-hastily expressed, that the Latin American events were
merely an isolated phenomenon,[4] or that 'it was only the Latin American economies'.

This began in 2007 when Bolivia denounced the ICSID Convention with effect
from November 2007. That denunciation was effected under Article 71 of the ICSID
Convention.[5] Then followed Ecuador's and Venezuela's own denunciations, which took
effect, respectively, from January 2010 and July 2012.[6] Notice that unlike the broader
non-governmental backlash against economic globalisation which had begun earlier
in the late 1990s, the backlash against investment treaties had become an official or
governmental backlash. Capitols were in revolt.

Initially, as we have seen, these were limited to events in Latin America. However,
a new phase began when dissatisfaction with BITs spread to South Africa, which in
November 2012 began to terminate its European BITs. Then, in early 2014, Indonesia
declared an intention to terminate the Netherlands–Indonesia BIT. In 2015, India released
a new Draft Model BIT for consultation in March before its finalisation later that year.
It has been the expectation since 2017 that Indonesia will eventually announce a new

399–400, also reproduced in Section 1.2. Fear of overreach by tribunals had already prompted the NAFTA parties to issue a 'binding interpretation', which the parties are entitled to do under NAFTA, in 2001; see NAFTA Free Trade Commission, *Notes of Interpretation of Certain Chapter 11 Provisions* (Washington, DC, 31 July 2001). For trenchant criticism of that interpretation, see, e.g., C. N. Brower, 'Why the FTC Notes of Interpretation Constitute a Partial Amendment of NAFTA Article 1105' (2006) 46 *Virginia J Int'l L* 347; both the binding interpretation and its criticism are discussed further below.
[2] See further *Methanex* v. *USA*, para. IV.D.7; *Saluka Investments BV* v. *Czech Republic*, Partial Award (ad hoc arbitration under the 1976 UNCITRAL Rules), PCA, Decision of 17 March 2006, paras 262–263; discussed in K. Tienhaara and T. Tucker, 'Regulating Foreign Investment: Methanex Revisited' in C. L. Lim (ed.), *Alternative Visions of the International Law on Foreign Investment* (Cambridge University Press, 2016), 255, esp. 262–264, 273 et seq.
[3] See, further, M. Waibel, C. Balchin, L. Kyo-Hwa Chung and A. Kaushal (eds), *The Backlash against Investment Arbitration* (The Hague: Kluwer Law International, 2010).
[4] See T. G. Nelson, '"History Ain't Changed": Why Investor-State Arbitration Will Survive the "New Revolution"' in Waibel *et al.*, *The Backlash against Investment Arbitration*, 555.
[5] For the law on withdrawals, see, further, C. Schreuer, 'Denunciation of the ICSID Convention and Consent to Arbitration' in Waibel *et al.*, *The Backlash against Investment Arbitration*, 353.
[6] B. Bland and S. Donnan, 'Indonesia to Terminate More than 60 Bilateral Investment Treaties', *Financial Times*, London, 26 March 2014; S. Ripinsky, 'Venezuela's Withdrawal from ICSID: What It Does and Does Not Achieve', *Investment Treaty News*, 13 April 2012, available at https://cf.iisd.net/itn/2012/04/13/vene-zuelas-withdrawal-from-icsid-what-it-does-and-does-not-achieve/ (accessed 7 September 2020).

model BIT following its earlier announcement that it would 'terminate its BITs or at least allow its existing BITs to lapse'. In Europe, in the context of the US–European Union Trans-Atlantic Trade and Investment Partnership (TTIP), the European Union first proposed an investment court regime to replace investment arbitration, an initiative which is already found in the recent (and recently concluded) EU treaties with Canada, Vietnam and Singapore.

For the present, investment arbitrations go on unabated, but the entire subject is facing a tectonic shift in the refinement of both procedural rules and in attempts to address more substantive concerns.

1. THE BACKLASH

1.1 The Backlash to NAFTA and in the United States, 2001–2004

As with subsequent events in Latin America, the initial attempt by the United States to rebalance its Model BIT in 2004 was met with denial and disbelief in some quarters. This had followed events in 2001 when the United States and the other parties to the North American Free Trade Agreement (NAFTA), namely Canada and Mexico, had issued a binding 'interpretation' of NAFTA Chapter 11 following NAFTA parties' experience of some early cases which were part of the beginning of the explosion of modern investment arbitrations in the 1990s. The scope and application of investment treaties were being rethought, incredibly at the time in the United States – a harbinger of a pattern of behaviour to be repeated not only in North America, but elsewhere in the ensuing two decades.

Judge S. M. Schwebel, 'A Critical Assessment of the U.S. Model BIT', Keynote Address, Twelfth ITF Public Conference, London, British Institute of International and Comparative Law, 15 May 2009

For more than 150 years, the policy of the United States in respect of foreign investment was positive. Initially as a developing country, from the time of the Revolutionary War to the early decades of the Nineteenth Century, the United States needed and welcomed foreign investment from the traditional source of that investment, Europe, Great Britain in particular. In the post-Civil War years, the industrialization of the United States, and the inventiveness of its citizenry, accelerated; capital as well as immigrants from Europe poured in. At the same time, investment by citizens and companies of the United States abroad grew and, by and during the Twentieth Century, it became the world's main engine of overseas investment. The attachment of the United States to capital creation and investment, and to legal principles and institutions, conduced to its support for the promotion and protection of foreign investment, through treaty-making as well as other means.

That virtually unbroken pattern changed with the publication in 2004 of a new model bilateral investment treaty. The United States did not abandon its policy on foreign investment but it significantly modified its policy.

...

Why? Essentially because it dawned on the bureaucracy – and the Congress – that bilateral investment treaties are bilateral, that they actually operate in more than one direction, that not only do BITs enable American companies to initiate arbitral proceedings against foreign governments but they enable foreign companies to bring arbitrations against the Government of the United States. This elemental perception was forced upon the bureaucracy, and commanded the attention of labor, environmental and other lobbies of non-governmental organizations, and eventually of members of Congress, not in a bilateral but trilateral context. Six NAFTA cases were filed by Canadian companies against the U.S. Government. The reaction was: What? They are suing us? And through arbitration? Don't they know that the United States protects foreign investment better than anyone and that our Constitution and courts provide all the recourse that could be desired?

One might have expected that a mature capitalist society, protective of foreign investment whatever the direction of its flow, would have taken six cases in its stride.

...

The U.S. 1994 Model BIT provided, as BITs generally do, that, 'Each Party shall at all times accord to covered investments fair and equitable treatment and full protection and security, and shall in no case accord treatment less favorable than that required by international law.'

In contrast, the 2004 Model BIT provides, in an article denominated 'Minimum Standard of Treatment':

'1. Each Party shall accord to covered investments treatment in accordance with customary international law, including fair and equitable treatment and full protection and security.

2. For greater certainty, paragraph 1 prescribes the customary international law minimum standard of treatment of aliens as the minimum to be accorded to covered investments. The concepts of "fair and equitable treatment" and "full protection and security" do not require treatment in addition to or beyond that which is required by that standard, and do not create additional substantive rights ... '

The differences between the 1994 Prototype and the 2004 Model BIT are striking. 1994 provided, directly, comprehensively, and flatly, as BITs the world over typically do, that the Parties shall at all times accord investments of nationals of the other Party 'fair and equitable treatment' etc., and in no case treatment less favorable than that required by international law.

The 2004 BIT retreats from these categoric and far reaching prescriptions. Each Party shall accord to foreign investments no more than 'treatment in accordance with customary international law, including fair and equitable treatment and full protection and security.' What was the floor has become the ceiling. What is more, 'The concepts' – not the prescriptions but the concepts – 'of fair and equitable treatment and full protection and security do not require treatment in addition to or beyond that required by that standard and do not create additional rights.'

> The profound, and startling, deficiency of the 2004 provision is that there is no agreement within the international community on the content of the minimum standard of customary international law on which the 2004 BIT so centrally relies. There is not even agreement on whether the minimum standard exists.
>
> ...
>
> Rather than concluding treaties that invite controversy, why does not the United States adhere to provisions accepted more than two thousand times by the vast majority of States, including the United States before 2004? How can it make sense for the United States to jettison the characteristic protections of BITs against unfair and inequitable treatment in favor of invocation of a minimum standard that is hardly accepted as such?
>
> Article 6 of the 2004 BIT is a normal provision on expropriation, except insofar as it imports a reference to the 'Minimum Standard of Treatment'. But an Annex elaborates that Article 6 is intended to 'reflect customary international law concerning the obligation of States with regard to expropriation'. That is a remarkable proviso, since it is incontestable that the content of customary international law on expropriation is contentious.

A number of further observations can be made. First, the 2004 US Model BIT contains a 'qualified' clause in its provision on the Minimum Standard of Treatment (MST), which – as Judge Schwebel explains – serves to link MST, including the standards of fair and equitable treatment (FET) and full protection and security (FPS), to whatever the prevailing customary law standard is.[7] Second, because the customary standard is itself contentious, Schwebel argues that the new clause will result in a more textured – or, put unkindly, conflicting – arbitral jurisprudence, and this will only fuel further criticism of inconsistencies of approach in investment arbitration. Third, more recent attempts at treaty rebalancing have seen attempts to define, in the BIT itself, what 'customary international law' means. We see this in the 2012 Model BIT which originated from former US President Barack Obama's campaign pledge to further revisit US BITs, and in this aspect the 2012 Model BIT preserves the changes first seen in the 2004 US Model BIT.[8] Fourth, this rebalancing is now a worldwide phenomenon as emulators of US rebalancing proliferate, even in Beijing's evolving treaty policy.[9]

It should not be thought, however, that originally there were not also substantive reasons for reforming the United States' MST clause. In other words, the reasons for doing so

---

[7] See Chapter 12, Section 4 of this book.

[8] See 2004 US Model BIT, Annex A; 2012 US Model BIT, Annex A.

[9] Examples are pre-establishment national treatment, which China agreed with the United States as a precondition to the US–China BIT negotiations; using the test of 'like circumstances' in MFN and NT clauses – for example, in Arts 3 and 4 of the China–Uzbekistan BIT, 19 April 2011 and Arts 3 and 4 of the China–Japan–Korea Trilateral Investment Treaty (C–J–K TIT), 13 May 2012; employing an express clause for indirect expropriation; applying the US 'three-part test' for indirect expropriation under para. 2 of Annex B.10 of the China–Canada BIT, 9 September 2012 and para. 2(b) of the Protocol to the C–J–K TIT; and finally using a 'rare' or 'exceptional circumstances' clause to contain claims for regulatory expropriation, such as in Annex B.10, para. 3 of the China–Canada BIT, 9 September 2012, Art. 6(3) of the China–Uzbekistan BIT, 13 March 1992 and para. 2(c) of the Protocol to the C–J–K TIT.

were not simply political, driven by dissatisfaction over the outcome of particular awards. There was also dissatisfaction with tribunal reasoning which led to those outcomes. Put simply, the clause was vague from the beginning. At the same time, the 2004 revision of the US Model BIT merely sought to codify a refinement which had already been introduced as an afterthought in the NAFTA context in 2001. The reasons in 2001 had to do with perceived ambiguities surrounding the MST clause in the NAFTA and its corollary – the 1994 Prototype BIT. All this is discussed in the following extract by Professor Charles N. Brower II.

Charles N. Brower II, 'Why the FTC Notes of Interpretation Constitute a Partial Amendment of NAFTA Article 1105' (2006) 46 *Virginia J Int'l L* 347, 351–352, 353

Nearly five years ago, the Free Trade Commission (FTC) created by the North American Free Trade Agreement (NAFTA) issued 'Notes of Interpretation' (Notes) purporting to restrict the minimum standard of treatment under the NAFTA's investment chapter (Chapter 11) to the requirements of customary international law.

...

During the first wave of Chapter 11 claims, Article 1105(1)'s vague text quickly raised interpretive questions, which the investor-driven, uncoordinated dispute settlement process could not resolve to the NAFTA Parties' satisfaction. For disputes arising under Article 1105(1), interpretive debate focused on two phrases: 'international law' and 'fair and equitable treatment'. With regard to 'international law', disputes called on tribunals to decide whether the term referred to all sources of international law or whether it contained an unstated restriction to customary international law. With regard to 'fair and equitable treatment', disputes required tribunals to identify the proper reference points for assessing the fairness and equity of measures adopted or maintained by host states. Given the dearth of precedent and the substantial dollar amounts in controversy, tribunals undertook a difficult task in the face of intense scrutiny.

After Mexico successfully defended an arbitration in which Article 1105(1) played a peripheral role, tribunals articulated broad interpretations of the same provision and imposed liability on the respondent states in a series of three cases decided under Chapter 11. In *Metalclad Corp. v. United Mexican States*, the tribunal construed 'fair and equitable treatment' to encompass obligations of transparency similar to those articulated in other chapters of NAFTA. Later, in *S.D. Myers, Inc. v. Canada*, the tribunal held that the infringement of any 'rule of international law ... specifically designed to protect investors will tend to weigh heavily in favour of finding a breach of Article 1105'. Applying this logic, a majority of the tribunal held that Canada's 'breach of Article 1102 [relating to national treatment] essentially establishe[d] a breach of Article 1105 as well'. Finally, in *Pope & Talbot, Inc. v. Canada*, the tribunal held that, despite textual indications to the contrary, fair and equitable treatment requires not only compliance with international law, but also with the 'ordinary standards' of fairness 'applied in the [domestic legal systems of the] NAFTA countries'.

Taken as a whole, the *Metalclad*, *S.D. Myers*, and *Pope & Talbot* awards created both the opportunity and the motive for the FTC to issue an 'interpretation' of Article 1105(1).

...

Surrendering to opportunity and motive, the FTC adopted its first (and, to date, only) Notes of Interpretation on July 31, 2001. The Notes provide, in relevant part, that:

> Article 1105(1) prescribes the customary international law minimum standard of treatment of aliens as the minimum standard of treatment ... The concept of 'fair and equitable treatment' ... do[es] not require treatment in addition to or beyond that which is required by the customary international law minimum standard of treatment ... A determination that there has been a breach of another provision of the NAFTA, or of a separate international agreement, does not establish that there has been a breach of Article 1105(1).

Evidently, the Notes represented an effort to 'overrule' the *Metalclad*, *S.D. Myers*, and *Pope & Talbot* awards by limiting NAFTA Article 1105(1) to the obligations established by customary international law. Thus, the first sentence in the Notes connects the minimum standard of treatment to customary international law. The second sentence excludes from the minimum standard all legal obligations that exceed the scope of customary international law. For good measure, the third sentence provides that the minimum standard does not require compliance with free-standing treaty obligations.

1.2 The Global Backlash Begins in Earnest, 2007 to Date

Still, the domestic rewriting of the US Model BIT, and a similar Canadian effort, were only early examples of a 'backlash', demonstrating a change of heart which is not attributable simply to non-governmental, activist and popular public concerns. The backlash had become official, and was no longer the monopoly of civil society activists and anti-globalisation protests. The spread of the backlash to official circles also began to extend worldwide, which perhaps is what Judge Schwebel had anticipated would happen. There were, of course, other factors. One of them, especially hotly contested, is whether the arbitration industry, specifically the behaviour of tribunals and tribunal awards, helped to contribute to the spread of a global backlash.

M. Waibel, A. Kaushal, L. Kyo-Hwa Chung and C. Balchin, 'The Backlash against Investment Arbitration: Perceptions and Reality' in M. Waibel, A. Kaushal, L. Kyo- Hwa Chung and C. Balchin (eds), *The Backlash against Investment Arbitration* (The Hague: Kluwer Law International, 2010), xxxvii–xxxviii, xl–xli, xlix

Even before the current boom of investment arbitration, Jan Paulsson presciently highlighted its fragile foundations: 'Future prospects for this development in international arbitration may depend on whether national governments – many of whom may not have appreciated the full implications ... take fright and reverse tracks. That may in turn depend on the degree of sophistication shown by arbitrators when called upon to pass judgment on governmental actions. Arbitration without privity is a delicate mechanism. A single incident of an adventurist arbitrator going beyond the proper scope of his jurisdiction in a sensitive case may be sufficient to generate a backlash.'

...

Contentions that the international investment regime lacks legitimacy come from many directions. Some suggest that ad hoc tribunals produce inconsistent law, which undermines the ultimate goals of stability and predictability. Others point to the reduced scope for state regulation. Still others claim that the regime is systematically biased in favor of business interests and capital exporting states. Another concern is that the regime leads to the reverse discrimination of domestic investors. Finally, some contend that the regime imprudently uses private commercial dispute resolution tools to resolve public disputes. These are telling signs of the turbulent climate for investment arbitration.

...

The critiques aimed at the investment regime tend to divide into two categories: procedural and substantive. For several years now, particularly following the entry into force of the North American Free Trade Agreement (NAFTA), academics and civil society groups have called for additional procedural safeguards. These demands fall under the broad banner of transparency, comprising, among other aspects, publicity and administrative fairness.

In 2001, the following powerful indictment of NAFTA Chapter 11 proceedings in the *New York Times* gained notoriety:

> Their meetings are secret. Their members are generally unknown. The decisions they reach need not be fully disclosed. Yet the way a small number of international tribunals handles disputes between investors and foreign governments has led to national laws being revoked, justice systems questioned and environmental regulations challenged.

This quote encapsulates serious qualms about the operation and effects of investment arbitration, especially from those who have not been directly involved in arbitrations: an alleged lack of democratic accountability, a shrinking of domestic policy space, pervasive confidentiality, and a lack of transparency. Moreover, some arbitration practitioners are increasingly questioning the traditional advantages of this tailor-made method of crossborder dispute resolution – such as speed, low cost, and neutral forum. There are growing concerns that international arbitration may be losing its long-standing edge over litigation in domestic courts.

Other reasons for the looming backlash include doubts about whether BITs increase foreign investment and thus live up to their promise; inadequate representation of developing countries among the panels of arbitrators; alleged institutional bias or unfairness by major arbitral institutions; the tension, and at times subordination, of the public interest to commercial interests; conflicts of interest and a vested interest in the future growth of investment arbitration. These alleged conflicts are another procedural criticism leveled at the investment regime.

...

Despite these growing concerns, some progress toward procedural transparency has been achieved since that article appeared in the *New York Times*. International arbitral tribunals have permitted third party participation through the submission of *amicus curiae* briefs, and NAFTA tribunals have opened up their hearings to the public. Developed country investors and host states alike seem to understand the importance of securing democratic legitimacy. Nonetheless, pleadings and even decisions often remain confidential, making meaningful *amicus curiae* participation difficult and leaving the public to speculate about the allegations and reasoning behind the result.

...

Agreement on the substantive problems of investment arbitration and desirable modifications is more elusive. Progress is hard to assess by any standard.

...

States – the most important stakeholders – have also started to assume a critical position. Bolivia denounced the ICSID Convention in 2007 and attempted to renegotiate all of its BITs. One aim was to steer dispute resolution to domestic fora rather than international arbitration. Bolivia alleged bias and expressed concern about the lack of appeals mechanism and the confidentiality of ICSID proceedings. This rupture with ICSID generated alarm among international investment lawyers. Yet most took comfort in the fact that Bolivia's economy was too small to really matter; that the move did not trigger a domino effect, as some had feared in Argentina, in particular; that the effects of denunciation remain unclear and contested; and that many of Bolivia's BITs provide for non-ICISD arbitration, such as under UNCITRAL rules.

Ecuador recently joined Bolivia in turning its back on ICSID. Other states, in particular in Latin America, have mooted similar moves, including Nicaragua and Venezuela.

Ecuador notified ICSID in December 2007 that it was withdrawing its consent for investment arbitrations in the mining and energy sectors. Argentina, the state that appears most often as a respondent, thus far remains committed to ICSID. However, the country has assumed a combative stance, for instance, by seeking the annulment of every single award. Other countries plan to renegotiate or else terminate their BITs.

In addition, several developed countries, which given their history of capital exports should presumptively favor the free flow of foreign investment, have adopted legislation to screen foreign investments for national security, a substantial barrier to admission of new investments.

The following extracts by Sornarajah and Johnson place the contemporary backlash not only against the recent history of disputes and tribunal awards, but also larger events. They discuss the most recent attempt by the United States, between 2009 and 2012, to further 'rebalance' the already reformed 2004 US Model BIT.

M. Sornarajah, *Resistance and Change in the International Law on Foreign Investment* (Cambridge University Press, 2015), 399–400

The year 2004 is taken as the beginning of the period of conflict. As indicated, the US and Canada model treaties of 2004 presaged change. Yet just a few years before, the awards in the first few Argentine cases had signalled the opportunity for establishing an expansionist framework. The Argentinian cases are important as the early cases show the expansionist scope of the newly discovered fair and equitable standard, but, as the cases progressed, the exploration of the defences of national security and necessity began to succeed, undermining the inflexibility of investment protection. There were arbitrators who resisted the enhancement of investment protection through the creative interpretation of treaty provisions. The extensions were not supportable in terms of the strict application of the law. Some arbitrators doubted the legitimacy of an investment tribunal taking a role in actively expanding the law and going beyond the consent disclosed in the investment treaty, A classic instance is the dissent of the distinguished French international lawyer, Prosper Weil, who was the president of the tribunal in *Tokios Tokeles v. Ukraine* (2004), who expressed the fear that the expansionist trends may come to undermine investment treaty arbitration.

The scope and extent of the fair and equitable clause came to be limited in cases like *Saluka*. The use of the MFN clause to enhance jurisdiction initiated in *Maffezini v. Spain* was challenged in a series of awards.[10]

The year 2004 may be taken as crucial in this period. It is the year of the US Model Treaty (as well as the Canadian Model Treaty), It was also the year of *Methanex*, where the United States was making the argument that regulations prohibiting a carcinogenic substance used as an additive in petroleum were regulatory measures and therefore could not amount to a compensable expropriation. The argument proved successful. That year, when negotiating the US–Singapore FTA, the principal negotiators, in an exchange of letters, signalled that indirect regulatory takings were not to be considered compensable except in exceptional circumstances. The exception contained in the letters passed into a firm statement in the US Model Treaty of 2004. It was actually a rediscovery of a rule that had always existed, but it took the United States to articulate it and to have measures that it had taken vindicated on the basis of the rule on regulatory expropriation.

A new type of balanced treaty took the place of treaties geared solely to investment protection. The period may be taken as lasting until around 2008, the year of the global economic crisis. States were beginning, rather belatedly, to recognize that the policy of minimal market regulation did not provide for market failures. They realized that more assertive action would become necessary in the event of imperfections developing within the market. Such assertive action could be violations of investment treaties, as they would amount to legal changes that depreciate the value of foreign investment. Investment treaties stood in the way of necessary changes. The developed states began to see the need for the creation of regulatory space. They also became conscious of the fact that they

---

[10] [Eds: see Chapter 4, Section 2 and Chapter 13 of this book.]

were becoming massive recipients of direct investment from industrializing states such as China, India and Brazil. On the political level, the unipolar order under the hegemony of the United States was declining and a multipolar order was coming to replace it. Greater concern with human rights and the environment had to be accommodated. The effect of the growth of NGOs on international politics had to recognized. The moorings of investment treaties, which lay in the North–South divide, was shifting with these developments. New models had to be thought up. New approaches had to be taken to meet new situations.

The result was the spate of balanced treaties recognizing areas in which regulatory measures had to be taken. Defences were provided for measures taken in the public interest.

The balanced treaties were favourable towards the recognition of measures taken to protect the environment and labour standards as requiring separate treatment. Taxation and prudential measures in the financial sector were provided for separately. The balanced treaties made by developing country regional associations have been different. They leave no room for any view other than that there is an unreviewable regulatory right in the state to take measures in definite areas of public interest. These treaties move away significantly from the aim of investment protection. They clearly no longer buy into the idea that investment protection given by the treaties is necessary for investment flows that are so beneficial to the host state that it should overlook other considerations.

During this period, the Argentine cases, which arose out of the economic crisis, also began to take a different turn. The early cases showed that the promises that Argentina had made to court foreign investment, such as the tying of gas prices to the American price indices and the parity between the dollar and the peso, had given rise to legitimate expectations that were violated. Compensation became due for the violation of the fair and equitable treatment provision. The plea of necessity that was taken up both under the treaty and as a defence available under public international law was rejected. The outcome in the cases changed. The annulment tribunal in *CMS* was trenchant in its criticism of the award's treatment of the necessity plea. It thought that the plea under the treaty provision should have been considered separately from the customary international law plea of necessity as they function differently. The Annulment Committee ruled that there was an error of law, though it had no power to annul the award on that ground.[11]

The doubt on the scope of the necessity was enhanced when three awards allowed necessity for the period of the economic crisis. The Argentine cases have introduced new uncertainties into the law. The issue of whether arbitral tribunals had assumed jurisdiction without waiting for the exhaustion of the period of eighteen months during which local remedies had to be tried out will also cause problems for existing awards. This is despite a ruling by the US Supreme Court that it will not review such awards. The decision will leave a bitter taste in that there is little means of challenging what was objectively a wrong

---

[11] [Eds: see Chapter 19, Section 3 of this book.]

decision, particularly in view of the fact that a later Argentine case has refused jurisdiction precisely on the point that the waiting period had not been satisfied. As time passes, the appropriateness of the views that a state takes when confronted with economic crises will undergo change. The United States and Europe have undergone similar economic crises, and have taken similar measures, including nationalisations, following the global economic crisis. There are cases arising from the measures that Greece and Belgium took during the crisis. There could be more. One will have to await the awards in these cases to see whether views different from those in the Argentinian cases emerge. As the treaties come to be drafted differently to provide for secure defences such as those taken by Argentina during its economic crisis, it is highly unlikely that disputes like the fifty-two cases against Argentina will be brought to arbitration again.

There were also high-profile disputes that involved Latin American states. None received greater attention than the *Cochahamba* water dispute. It was the result of the privatization of the water supply in the Bolivian city of *Cochahamba*. Bechtel an American company had obtained the concession to supply water previously supplied by a public corporation. Its subsidiary raised the price of water by over 50 per cent, leading to riots in the city. Bechtel had to leave but brought an arbitration under the Bolivia–Netherlands treaty after 'migrating' to the Netherlands. Worldwide protests continued during the arbitration, which lasted for more than four years. The notion of migration and the denial of efforts at *amicus curiae* briefs gave publicity to the case. Bechtel eventually settled the case, but the controversy highlighted the commodification of water by a global company and the denial of the human right to water to the poor of the city. It brought investment arbitration to global attention.

Bolivia, obviously, was keen to withdraw from arbitrations after the episode and did so.

Both the Argentine cases as well as the many arbitrations brought against other Latin American states resulted in widespread concern over investor-state arbitration in Latin America. In April 2007, at the meeting of the Bolivarian Alliance for the Americas (ALBA), Nicaragua, Bolivia and Ecuador announced that they would withdraw from the ICSID 'in order to guarantee the sovereign right of states to regulate foreign investment on their territories'. In May 2007, Bolivia denounced the ICSID, Ecuador joined ALBA in May 2007 and also denounced the ICSID. Venezuela followed in January 2012. Withdrawals from the ICSID do not matter unless existing investment treaties are terminated in accordance with their termination provisions. These provisions often permit protection to existing investments for periods of up to ten years. Venezuela now has twenty arbitrations pending at ICSID.

It is certain to default on all unfavourable awards, having moved its assets back into its own jurisdiction or into states like China or Russia which still retain absolute immunity for state assets. Brazil did not sign investment treaties. After its experience with investment arbitration, the only reason why Argentina may want to stay on the bandwagon is the experience it has obtained in defending arbitrations brought by investors. It appears that the interlude of Latin American states with liberalization and privatization is over. Latin

America is back to the Calvo Doctrine.[12] At least one part of the world, where the story of [the] international law of foreign investment began has come a full circle. Having gone from the Calvo Doctrine to liberalization and privatization, Latin America has now come back to the Calvo Doctrine. This analysis will of course depend on the political situation remaining the same at least in the near future ... There may be displeasure beginning in other countries as well. In India, the *White Industries* Award, which held that an arbitral award was an asset under the Australia–India BIT and that delay by the local courts in its enforcement would amount to a breach of the fair and equitable standard, has caused consternation. It comes at a time when there are other threats of arbitration against India in several sectors. The bribery scandal involving the allocation of spectrums involve several companies affected by the order of the Indian Supreme Court that the allocations should be cancelled and fresh tenders called. Some foreign companies have threatened to bring arbitrations under BITs.

Similarly, in the *Novartis* litigation, the Indian courts have held that the local manufacturing of generic drugs was permissible, resulting again in the threat of arbitration. In the light of these developments, India has shelved future BITs. South Africa has similar reservations after its black empowerment programme was challenged. Indonesia has announced that it will not conclude investment treaties in the future. Another area in which a storm is gathering is an unrelated area kept away from discussion of the law on investment arbitration involving the increasing concern over the violation of human rights and the environment by global business. Despite Bhopal and similar disasters, the misconduct of global business did not affect the rationale that investment is good for economic development that underpinned investment protection under the treaties and the law made through investment arbitration. With reports by the UN Special Representative on Business and Human Rights that situation was ending. His studies showed the need for concern in the area. It was no longer possible to hold onto the myth that investment flows were always to the benefit of developing host states. There are a growing number of studies on corporate responsibility of multinational corporations. The law that emerges in this field must have an impact on the issue of investment protection. Two separate laws will merge at some future point.

An increasing number of economic studies also began to question the assumption that investment protection through treaties is necessary to promote flows of investment to developing countries. The correlation between the treaties could not be established in clear terms. This resulted in the querying of the making of the treaties, which appeared to involve the surrender of sovereignty for virtually no benefit, the assumption that investment flows take place being unfounded. The period ended with considerable scepticism with the existing network of investment treaties and the system of investment arbitration on which it is based.

---

[12] [Eds: see Chapter 1, Section 2 of this book.]

L. Johnson, 'The 2012 US Model BIT and What the Changes (or Lack Thereof) Suggest about Future Investment Treaties', *Political Risk Insurance Newsletter*, vol. VIII, Issue 2, November 2012

The Obama Administration launched its formal review of the 2004 Model BIT in early 2009.

...

[C]ontinued endorsement of the 2004 Model is notable because when that version was adopted, it departed in significant respects from the previous versions. Changes that were made in the 2004 version primarily (though not exclusively) included those that were made to be more, rather than less, protective of governments' regulatory authority and discretion. The modifications included those that: clarified and narrowed the definition of covered investments; changed and added language to explain and constrain the meaning of the 'minimum standard of treatment' and expropriation obligations and closely guide arbitral tribunals' interpretations of those provisions; provided for exceptions to the agreements' prohibitions on performance requirements; codified the stance adopted by the US government in other areas of international law and some earlier investment treaties by expressly declaring that the essential security exception is self-judging; added language to protect host-state authority to take measures relating to financial services; and modified some aspects of investor-state dispute settlement, such as adding a statute of limitations, and giving state parties to the treaty additional or clearer authority to determine issues of treaty interpretation and application that would be binding on investor-state tribunals.

Some aspects of the 2004 Model also aimed to address issues of broader public concern. These included, for example, language expressly giving investor-state tribunals authority to accept submissions from amicus curiae and providing for public disclosure of information regarding the disputes; articles on labor rights and environmental protection; and text in the preamble clarifying that investment protection aims to improve living standards and should be pursued consistent with the protection of health, safety, and the environment, and the promotion of internationally recognized labor rights.

Together, the amendments, additions, and clarifying provisions in the 2004 Model BIT differentiated and continue to differentiate it from the more skeletal models and treaties of many other states, particularly European countries.

...

Nevertheless, the 2012 US Model BIT does contain some new features falling into three broad categories: modifications that impose additional burdens and restrictions on host states in order to facilitate and protect foreign investment; provisions that add slight protections for government authority in the area of financial services regulation; and new language on environmental and labor issues that may better address and help avoid some of the possible negative effects that can be associated with foreign investment.

...

One aspect of the 2012 Model that negotiating partners may particularly push back against or seek modifications in is Section B on investor-state dispute settlement.

Dissatisfaction with all or part of the current system of investor-state arbitration is mounting among a number of states including Australia and India, countries with which the US is or may soon be negotiating bilateral or multilateral agreements, raising questions of whether the US will be able to successfully incorporate that dispute settlement mechanism in all of its future investment treaties. Even among states that have not formally renounced investor-state arbitration, there appear to be increasing concerns regarding state signatories' ability (or inability) to ensure that tribunals adjudicating investor-state disputes give the treaties the meaning intended by the state parties. These concerns, in turn, may be prompting states to consider expressly reserving more power for themselves in terms of interpreting and/or applying all or part of the treaties.

Adding to those pressures from states, discontent with the current practice of investor-state dispute settlement also appears to be rising from the main beneficiaries of that mechanism, the investors, who have complained about the length and costs of proceedings, and difficulties in enforcing awards. Whether and how these issues manifest themselves and are resolved in future treaties are open questions and developments to be watched.

1.3 The Treaty Terminations Begin

The following extracts discuss the termination of BITs. After the Latin American withdrawals from the ICSID, there followed the phenomenon of declarations by States of their intent to terminate their BITs, from Venezuela to South Africa, the Czech Republic (albeit for reasons connected with internal EU arrangements), then India and Indonesia. No longer could it be said that the backlash was a Latin American phenomenon, or that large economies were not involved. At the same time, what the threat of BIT terminations showed was that withdrawing from the ICSID, as Bolivia, Ecuador and Venezuela had done, would be insufficient. Another point to observe is the uncertain line between a declaration of an avowed intention to terminate a State's BITs and the underlying intention merely to renegotiate these treaties.

A. Carska-Sheppard, 'Issues Relevant to the Termination of Bilateral Investment Treaties' (2009), 26 J Int'l Arb 755, 755–756, 758–759, 761–763

It appears that when it comes to the termination of a BIT, there is very little experience compared with the wealth of knowledge associated with the cancellation of investment contracts. Nevertheless, the issue of termination of BITs is not uncommon. For instance, Venezuela has surprised the Dutch government by sending 'a formal communication in which it signaled its intention to terminate the treaty as of November 1, 2008, on the fifteen year anniversary'. The Dutch government responded by expressing their interest to renegotiate the BIT when the communication of unilateral termination had already been sent. As another example, reports circulated in the autumn of 2008 that the Czech government would be talking to its partners regarding the termination of BITs.

...

The Vienna Convention on the Law of Treaties ('Vienna Convention') codifies the customary international law on termination of treaties. Article 56 of the Vienna Convention addresses situations of denunciation of, or withdrawal from, a treaty which has no specific provision regarding termination, denunciation, or withdrawal. In such a case, a treaty is not subject to denunciation or withdrawal unless 'it is established that the parties intended to admit the possibility of denunciation or withdrawal or a right of denunciation or withdrawal may be implied by the nature of the treaty.' Where a treaty falls under Article 56, the notice of intention to denounce or withdraw from a treaty must be no less than twelve months.

The Vienna Convention identifies such circumstances as supervening impossibility of performance (Article 61) and fundamental change of circumstances (Article 62) which can be invoked by a party terminating or withdrawing from the treaty. Over the years, the jurisprudence of the International Court of Justice (I.C.J.) has developed very high thresholds for their application. It is clear that a breach by one party (including unlawful denunciation) does not automatically terminate the treaty, and even material breach can be invoked as a ground for terminating or suspending a treaty and does not effectuate termination of the treaty itself.

...

In *Germany v. Iceland*, the I.C.J. has set a high threshold for treaty termination on the ground of fundamental change of circumstances. The I.C.J. has ruled, inter alia, that Iceland was not entitled unilaterally to exclude their fishing vessels from the disputed area. The I.C.J. responded to Iceland's argument of fundamental change of circumstances referring to Article 62 of the Vienna Convention on the Law of Treaties. The I.C.J. stated that:

> International law admits that a fundamental change in the circumstances which determined the parties to accept a treaty, if it has resulted in a radical transformation of the extent of the obligations imposed by it, may, under certain conditions, afford the party affected a ground for invoking the termination or suspension of the treaty. Moreover, in order that a change of circumstances may give rise to a ground for invoking the termination of a treaty it is also necessary that it should have resulted in a radical transformation of the extent of the obligations still to be performed.

The I.C.J. described the changes as 'rendering the performance something essentially different from that originally undertaken'.

Iran–United States Claims Tribunal Case No. 56 confirmed that a change of circumstances never automatically terminates a treaty. The Tribunal analyzed the procedure for termination of a treaty and it noted that the:

> formal notification of treaty termination is not necessary in every case. The intent of a party to terminate a treaty can be implied from its conduct. Yet such conduct may be construed as an implicit denunciation only if it clearly demonstrates the intent of the party concerned to terminate the treaty.

...

The least intrusive solution to termination of a BIT which will not erode the perception of a sufficient degree of legal stability is termination in accordance with the terms of a BIT. A sample survey of BITs ... shows that they tend to be for terms of an initial period of ten years, and after expiry of this stated period, may be denounced by either party subject to the proper notice of termination, which is generally one year. The BITs take into account long-term objectives of investors in the host state by providing extended protection for investments prior to the date of termination.

As this brief survey shows, the language of the extended protection found in different BITs is not uniform. Article 13(3) of the Chinese Model BIT (2003) provides the following protection: '[w]ith respect to investments made prior to the date of termination of this Agreement, the provisions of Articles 1 to 12 shall continue to be effective for a further period of ten years from such a date of termination'; Article 12 of the French Model BIT provides that 'les investissements effectués pendant qu'il était en vigueur continueront de bénéficier de la protection de ses dispositions pendant une période supplémentaire de vingt ans'; Article 14(3) of the German Model BIT (2005) states that '[i]n respect of investments made prior to the date of termination of this Treaty, the provisions of the proceeding Articles shall continue to be effective for a further period of twenty years from the date of termination of this Treaty'. Article 14 of the UK Model BIT (2005) is more specific and makes reference to rules of general international law: '[p]rovided that in respect to investments made whilst the Agreement is in force, its provisions shall continue in effect with respect to such investments for a period of twenty years after the date of termination and without prejudice to the application thereafter of the rules of general international law.' The drafters of the US Model BIT (2004) also use more specific termination language, providing that '[f]or ten years from the date of termination, all other Articles shall continue to apply to covered investments established or acquired prior to the date of termination, except insofar as those Articles extend to the establishment or acquisition of covered instruments'. 'Covered investment' is defined with respect to a party as 'an investment in its territory of an investor of the other party in existence as of the date of entry into force of this Treaty or established, acquired, or expanded thereafter'. Article 14(3) of the Agreement Between Australia and the Czech Republic on the Reciprocal Promotion and Protection of Investment refers not only to extended protection for the 'investments made' but adds the alternative term 'investments acquired'.

These provisions indicate that BITs typically provide extended protection in the range of ten years to twenty years. Depending on the type of investment, this period may not be long enough to adequately restructure the investments and to prepare for the loss of the BIT protection. In the case of natural expiration of the BIT, the terms of the BIT need to be honored and the investors have no recourse. However, they will face a different situation if a state renounces the BIT before its natural expiration.

...

> Suppose, where a state makes a decision to renounce a BIT prior to its natural expiry, and as such alters the term of the agreement, the nonbreaching party which is willing but unable to perform can sue for breach of the BIT. The premature termination of the BIT may trigger two kinds of disputes, one between contracting states, the other investor-state cases.
>
> ...
>
> The mere fact that the state has initiated its own proceedings will not preclude the investor-state proceedings.
>
> ...
>
> From the state's perspective, it may be better to wait a decade and let the BIT expire rather than expose the state to the risk of claims by aggrieved investors asserting their rights under the BIT.

As the author goes on to point out, the consequences of a breach of a treaty is governed by Article 60 of the Vienna Convention on the Law of Treaties of 1969, and also by customary international law. Two issues might be added before concluding on this point. First, a treaty may not have a clause specifying that it is for a definite duration, and/or the issue could be governed purely by the termination clause. In other words, a treaty may be designed to be terminated at will, provided sufficient notice is given. Second, as the authors show in the extract below, nothing prevents a State from seeking to renegotiate the termination and survival clauses in the treaty, or for that matter any clause governing the duration of the treaty. There are many variations upon the theme, in which not only could the line between termination and renegotiation come into play, but the line between renegotiation and reinterpretation could also enter the mix. India, at the time of writing, had earlier proposed an interesting approach to renegotiation, which is to renegotiate a class of older treaties but to issue joint interpretations in respect of a class of newer treaties.

> **T. Voon and A. D. Mitchell, 'Denunciation, Termination and Survival: The Interplay of Treaty Law and International Investment Law' (2016) 31 *ICSID Review – FILJ* 413, 430–431 (footnote omitted)**
>
> This article previously explained the view that the parties to an IIA [international investment agreement] may override a survival clause as a general matter, so that it has no effect, by agreeing to extinguish it at the same time as they agree to terminate the treaty. The underlying justification for this view is that an IIA is a treaty entered into between States parties, and it depends on their continuing consent for its operation, notwithstanding the benefits that investors may obtain under the treaty. For similar reasons, we consider that the States parties to an IIA could terminate the IIA by mutual consent even within the initial period of entry into force, agreeing to abrogate any provision in the treaty requiring such a period before allowing notice of unilateral termination. Furthermore, Catharine Titi suggests, giving even more weight to the current intentions of the negotiating States parties, that if the

parties terminate a treaty by consent and replace it with a new treaty, the survival clause in the original treaty is automatically extinguished without the need for an express agreement to that effect. Two relatively recent examples of State practice – coupled with other examples that are detailed elsewhere – show that at least some States ascribe to this view.

First, the Czech Republic has arranged for mutual termination of seven BITs with other EU Member States on the basis that such BITs are no longer necessary, as discussed above. In four or five of these instances (with Slovenia, Denmark, Malta, Estonia and possibly Italy), the agreement to terminate the treaty is reported to have been accompanied by a simultaneous agreement to modify the survival clause to preclude its further application. In addition, in some instances of mutual termination, the parties appear to have agreed to terminate the treaty before the expiry of the initial period of entry into force. For example, Article 16 of the Czech Republic–Denmark BIT provides:

> (1) This Agreement shall remain in force for a period of ten years and shall continue in force thereafter unless, after the expiry of the initial period of ten years, either Contracting Party notifies in writing the other Contracting Party of its intention to terminate this Agreement. The notice of termination shall become effective one year after it has been received by the other Contracting Party.

> (2) In respect of investments made prior to the date when the notice of termination of this Agreement becomes effective, the provisions of Articles 1 to 10 shall remain in forc[e] for a further period of ten years from that date.

Articles 1–10 of this Treaty cover matters such as definitions; substantive protections such as fair and equitable treatment, expropriation and non-discrimination and both State–State and investor–State dispute settlement (in the latter case, pursuant to the ICSID Convention or the UNCITRAL Arbitration Rules). In one view, the survival clause in Article 16(2) should be interpreted in the context of its position next to Article 16(1), such that the 'notice of termination' referred to in Article 16(2) is properly understood as signifying the unilateral notice of termination permitted under Article 16(1). In thiscase, no amendment of Article 16(2) is necessary to prevent the survival of any provisions following mutual termination. However, to remove uncertainty and debate, States may prefer to indicate expressly their agreement to reduce or eliminate any survival period, as they are entitled to do pursuant to the law of treaties and as the Czech Republic and Denmark apparently did.

As foreshadowed earlier, the Argentina–Indonesia BIT provides a second, more recent, instance in which the parties are reported to have agreed to terminate the treaty while, at the same time, extinguishing the survival clause. Article 13 follows the same format as the Czech Republic–Denmark BIT, providing for an initial period of entry into force of 10 years, after which either party may unilaterally terminate the agreement by giving 12 months' notice to the other party (Article 13(1)). For investments made before the termination takes effect, Articles 1–12 remain in force for an additional 10 years (Article 13(2)). Articles 1–12 of the Argentina-Indonesia BIT cover matters including substantive investment protection (for example, fair and equitable treatment, expropriation and non-discrimination) and dispute settlement (both State–State and investor–State under either the ICSID Convention or the UNCITRAL Arbitration Rules).

2. THE NEW TREATY CLAUSES

In everyday, practical terms, the current backlash has been wrapped up in the rewriting of substantive rules, as well as the reform of the investment arbitration procedure. Revolution cannot always be distinguished from reform of a more prosaic nature. It is not simply a political phenomenon, but goes to the heart of the emergence of new forms of treaty rule design which will affect the practice of investment treaty arbitration and dispute settlement for years to come.

2.1 Reform of Treaty Substantive Rules in Recent Treaties

2.1.1 Reform of the FET Rule

In Section 1, we saw how the MST rule has been reformed in the United States, which led to the benchmarking of the FET and FPS standards to a customary international law standard which serves as a ceiling. This began in 2001 with the NAFTA and continued through the incorporation of that new rule in the 2004 US Model BIT. In turn, that reform was reflected in the 2012 US Model BIT.

More recently, further refinements have been added to the MST rule in the 2012 US Model BIT and in more contemporary US treaties such as the beleaguered and now moribund Trans-Pacific Partnership Agreement (TPP),[13] itself very much a victim of the current backlash. These refinements include stating the content of the concept of 'fair and equitable treatment' more precisely. Thus, the TPP, in keeping with the 2012 US Model BIT, states that FET includes denials of justice and violations of due process rights in an attempt to articulate, albeit in an open-ended way, some of the FET concept's core features. The TPP also addresses more recent developments discussed earlier in this book,[14] such as the emergence of a legitimate expectations doctrine. The TPP, going beyond the 2012 US Model BIT, states additionally that:[15]

> For greater certainty, the mere fact that a Party takes or fails to take an action that may be inconsistent with an investor's expectations does not constitute a breach of this Article, even if there is loss or damage to the covered investment as a result.

That is not the only approach taken today to rebalance treaty FET clauses. The TPP's approach may be compared, for example, with the approach taken in the 2016 Canada–EU Comprehensive Economic and Trade Agreement (CETA). CETA lists the characteristics of FET more comprehensively than the US approach in the TPP and the 2012 US Model BIT. CETA, Article 8.10, stipulates that:[16]

---

[13] This was an agreement signed between the United States, Canada, Mexico, Chile, Peru, Japan, Vietnam, Brunei, Singapore, Malaysia, Australia and New Zealand. In January 2017, US President Donald Trump signed an executive order withdrawing the United States from the TPP, thus throwing any such future treaty into doubt. On the TPP more generally, albeit written in more hopeful times, see C. L. Lim, D. K. Elms and P. Low (eds), *The Trans-Pacific Partnership: A Quest for a Twenty-First Century Trade Agreement* (Cambridge University Press, 2012).

[14] See Chapter 12, Section 2.

[15] Art. 9.6(4) TPP.

[16] Art. 8.10(2)(a)–(f) CETA.

2. A Party breaches the obligation of fair and equitable treatment referenced in paragraph 1 if a measure or series of measures constitutes:

   (a) denial of justice in criminal, civil or administrative proceedings;

   (b) fundamental breach of due process, including a fundamental breach of transparency, in judicial and administrative proceedings;

   (c) manifest arbitrariness;

   (d) targeted discrimination on manifestly wrongful grounds, such as gender, race or religious belief;

   (e) abusive treatment of investors, such as coercion, duress and harassment; or

   (f) a breach of any further elements of the fair and equitable treatment obligation adopted by the Parties in accordance with paragraph 3 of this Article.

3. The Parties shall regularly, or upon request of a Party, review the content of the obligation to provide fair and equitable treatment. The Committee on Services and Investment, established under Article 26.2.1(b) (Specialised committees), may develop recommendations in this regard and submit them to the CETA Joint Committee for decision.

It reflects many of the 'heads' of FET claim discussed earlier in this book.[17] CETA then goes on to spell out precisely what would constitute a breach of an investor's legitimate expectation: namely, that a tribunal 'may' take into account 'a specific representation' which 'created a legitimate expectation, and upon which the investor relied in deciding to make or maintain the covered investment, but that the Party subsequently frustrated'.[18]

There are now signs of similar reform in East Asia.

W. Shan and H. Chen, 'China–US BIT Negotiation and the Emerging Chinese BIT 4.0' in C. L. Lim (ed.), *Alternative Visions of the International Law on Foreign Investment* (Cambridge University Press, 2016), 223, 238

The difference appears to be that the approach taken by the US is open ended, whilst the EU's approach is a closed list. In other words, The US' approach offers more flexibility whilst the EU's approach guarantees more certainty. However, a closer look reveals that the difference is not as significant as it appears. The US model attempted to achieve certainty by not only referring to the international minimum standard to define FET, but also by explicitly referring to denial of justice as a demonstration of a breach of the standard. On the other hand, the EU approach also leaves significant room for flexibility, as terms such as 'fundamental', 'manifest' and 'abusive' are not defined and are therefore subject to discretionary interpretation.

It is unclear which approach China will take for the new generation BIT. The China–Canada BIT generally follows the US approach by referring to the minimum standard of treatment under international law, which effectively means customary international law as

---

[17] See Chapter 12, Section 2.
[18] Art. 8.10(4) CETA.

defined under Article 38 of the ICJ Statute. The trilateral investment treaty (TIT) between China, Japan and Korea also refers to international law but uses the term 'generally accepted rule of international law'. Such practice suggests that China is also qualifying the standard to make sure that it is not misused. It remains to be seen whether China adopts the EU approach in further defining the standard of treatment. The China–EU BIT presents the perfect opportunity to observe developments in this regard.

Note that the China–EU BIT is, however, still under negotiation at the time of writing, as with the China–US BIT, although the latter may be closer to fruition. However, the 2012 China–Japan–Korea Trilateral Investment Treaty (the C-J-K TIT) adopts the NAFTA approach of linking the FET standard to the customary international law standard as a ceiling, and as Brower had described in relation to the NAFTA clause, states 'for good measure' also that 'the minimum standard does not require compliance with free-standing treaty obligations'.[19] The C-J-K TIT states, in Article 5, that:

> 1. Each Contracting Party shall accord to investments of investors of another Contracting Party fair and equitable treatment and full protection and security. The concepts of 'fair and equitable treatment' and 'full protection and security' do not require treatment in addition to or beyond any reasonable and appropriate standard of treatment accorded in accordance with generally accepted rules of international law. A determination that there has been a breach of another provision of this Agreement, or of a separate international agreement, does not ipso facto establish that there has been a breach of this paragraph.

As Professor Shan and Dr Chen have tried to suggest, we will have to watch closely to see how far the draftsmen of Beijing, and indeed we might add the other emulators of Washington in Seoul and Tokyo, will continue to track the evolution of US FET clauses. However, as the following discussion of expropriation clauses shows, these draftsmen of Beijing have already shown a disposition towards emulating the draftsmen of Washington, DC.[20] Contextual factors will matter. China now exports more capital than it imports. It is the third largest exporter of capital in the world after the United States and Japan. The shoe is now on the other foot in Beijing. Unlike in the past, it will have to balance the need to preserve its regulatory space against the need to protect Chinese investments abroad.

2.1.2 Reform of the Expropriation Rule

As for reform of the expropriation rule in today's BITs, Judge Schwebel has observed of the 2004 US Model BIT that there was an Annex which 'elaborates that Article 6 is intended to "reflect customary international law concerning the obligation of States with

---

[19] Brower, 'Why the FTC Notes of Interpretation Constitute a Partial Amendment'.
[20] See, further, C. L. Lim, 'Finding a Workable Balance between Investor Protection and the Public Interest in the Trans-Pacific Partnership' in B. Kingsbury, D. Malone, R. B. Stewart and A. Sunami (eds), *Megaregulation Contested: Global Economic Ordering After TPP* (Oxford University Press, 2019), 551.

regard to expropriation"', saying: 'That is a remarkable proviso, since it is incontestable that the content of customary international law on expropriation is contentious.'[21]

The current US rule for expropriation is reflected in the 2012 US Model BIT, and also in contemporary, heavily US-influenced treaties such as the TPP and, following the Trump Administration's withdrawal from the TPP, the Comprehensive and Progressive Agreement for Trans-Pacific Partnership (CPTPP).[22] The 2012 US Model BIT formulation is that expropriation would be unlawful except where taken for a public purpose, without discrimination, on payment of compensation, and in accordance with due process as well as the minimum standard of treatment.[23] In an Annex,[24] the 2012 Model BIT contains the old 'NAFTA footnote' linking the expropriation standard to the customary international law standard:

> The Parties confirm their shared understanding that:
> 1. Article 6 [Expropriation and Compensation] is intended to reflect customary international law concerning the obligation of States with respect to expropriation.

As for indirect expropriation, the 2012 Model BIT employs a 'three-part' test derived from American constitutional jurisprudence:[25]

(a) The determination of whether an action or series of actions by a Party, in a specific fact situation, constitutes an indirect expropriation, requires a case-by-case, fact-based inquiry that considers, among other factors:

    (i) the economic impact of the government action, although the fact that an action or series of actions by a Party has an adverse effect on the economic value of an investment, standing alone, does not establish that an indirect expropriation has occurred;

    (ii) the extent to which the government action interferes with distinct, reasonable investment-backed expectations; and

    (iii) the character of the government action.

The 2012 Model BIT goes on to state that 'except in rare circumstances, non-discriminatory regulatory actions by a Party that are designed and applied to protect legitimate public welfare objectives, such as public health, safety, and the environment, do not constitute indirect expropriations'.[26] This 'rare circumstances' clause is significant, for it has been

---

[21] Schwebel, Keynote Address.

[22] As discussed in Chapter 4 of this book, the TPP did not enter into force and, prior to the Trump Administration's withdrawal, had included twelve nations as signatories. It was until then hailed as a model for an Asia–Pacific-wide investment treaty. CPTPP is intended to consist of the remaining eleven members, and though it is now in force following six ratifications, that aim, in terms of membership, has not been accomplished. At the same time, CPTPP is open to new entrants.

[23] See, e.g., 2012 US Model BIT, Art. 6(1); TPP, Art. 9.8(1). Note, however, that the TPP clause does not link the expropriation rule to compliance with the MST clause, unlike the 2012 US Model BIT.

[24] 2012 US Model BIT, Annex B, para. 1. This footnote does not, however, appear in the TPP, although a footnote in the TPP clarifies that the concept of 'public purpose' is customary; fn. 17, TPP.

[25] 2012 US Model BIT, Annex B, para. 4(a). See, further, Lim, 'Finding a Workable Balance'.

[26] 2012 US Model BIT, Annex B, para. 4(b).

used not just in the recent ill-fated TPP;[27] that type of clause is also reflected, with some variation in the form of greater detail and specificity, in China's, Japan's and South Korea's treaty practice.[28] Accompanying the official backlash is a global comparative exercise in treaty drafting which ought to be of great interest to those who practise in the investment treaty arbitration field.

2.1.3 Other Innovations in Substantive Standards of Treaty Protection

Other more radical changes which are to be found today include the deletion of most-favoured-nation (MFN) clauses altogether, the removal of tax measures from the scope of investment treaty commitments and provision for host State counterclaims against the investor. Such has been the case, for example, with India in the latest Indian Model BIT.[29]

2.1.4 Enter the United States–Mexico–Canada Agreement

By the time this edition is published, the United States–Mexico–Canada Agreement (USMCA) will have entered into force on 1 July 2020.[30] It will have replaced the NAFTA. As a result, and because the USMCA does not offer investment arbitration between the US and Canada, investment treaty arbitration is abolished between them,[31] allowing only a three-year grace period for claims in respect of existing investments to continue to be brought under the NAFTA, i.e. in respect of investments made prior to 1 July 2020.[32] As for Canada and Mexico, investment arbitration will be preserved outside the USMCA by other treaties such as the CPTPP, of which mention has already been made.

Turning to the US and Mexico, the same three-year grace period applies,[33] and following that period investment treaty arbitration will continue to exist under the USMCA but with severe restrictions. Foremost of these restrictions is that, barring – in the absence of – the existence of a 'covered government contract' in a 'covered sector',[34] protection under the FET standard and against indirect expropriation would be excluded,[35] as would treaty protection during the pre-establishment phase of the investment.[36] In other words,

---

[27] Which includes Japan, Vietnam, Brunei, Singapore, Malaysia, Australia and New Zealand, in addition to Canada, Mexico, Chile and Peru.

[28] See the 2012 China–Canada BIT, Annex B.10, para. 3; 1992 China–Uzbekistan BIT, Art. 6(3); 2012 C–J–K TIT, Protocol, para. 2(c).

[29] M. Mohan, 'Asian Perspectives on Investment Agreements and Arbitration: An Evolving Marcottage' in A. K. Bjorklund (ed.), *Yearbook on International Investment Law and Policy (2014–2015)* (Oxford University Press, 2016), 317; A. Rajput, 'India and Investment Protection' in C. L. Lim (ed.), *Alternative Visions of the International Law on Foreign Investment* (Cambridge University Press, 2016); K. Singh, 'An Analysis of India's New Model Bilateral Investment Treaty' in K. Singh and B. Ilge (eds), *Rethinking Bilateral Investment Treaties: Critical Issues and Policy Choices* (Delhi: Madhyam, 2016), 69. On the new Indian Model BIT generally, see also G. Hanessian and K. Duggal, 'The Final India Model BIT: Is This the Change the World Wishes to See?' (2017) 32 *ICSID Review – FILJ* 216.

[30] Agreement between the United States of America, the United Mexican States, and Canada, 30 November 2018, revised 10 December 2019.

[31] Art. 14.2.4.

[32] Annex 14-C.

[33] Annex 14-D.

[34] Annex 14-E.

[35] Annex 14-D, para. 3.

[36] *Ibid.*

such 'non-covered sector' investments would be limited to national treatment and MFN treatment protection only post-establishment, with pre-establishment/market access protection excluded, and claims for only direct expropriation.[37]

For the purpose of the current discussion, an important question is whether this signals a lasting change in the US approach to investment treaty protection. A tentative view may be that, as between the US and Mexico, the USMCA is less about rebalancing investment treaty arbitration – as a new generation US Model BIT – and still less about the abolition of investment treaty protection. Rather, investment treaty arbitration is abolished at Canada's insistence and preserved in a drastically reduced manner between the US and Mexico.[38] For the US and Mexico, the USMCA preserves investment treaty protection (including FET protection) where there is a specifically and closely defined contractual relationship while, at the same time, such protection is not limited simply to umbrella clause-type protection or a treaty 'internationalisation' as such of the underlying contract. Instead, the existence of a defined contractual relationship triggers a wide range of the usual forms of investment treaty protection, but only if such a relationship exists. It fits with, although only very, very imperfectly, the long-held criticism in the context of the global backlash that investment treaty arbitration, as distinguished from investment contract arbitration, should be abolished altogether.

The USMCA's other large innovation is procedural, imposing what may be characterised as, in effect, a treaty-grounded exhaustion of local remedies rule. This will require a claimant to pursue a claim in domestic courts for a period of at least 30 months.[39]

G. Sacerdoti, 'Is USMCA Really "The New Gold Standard" of Investment Protection?', *Columbia FDI Perspectives,* **No. 281, 29 June 2020**

Direct arbitration is restricted to US-Mexico relations, in practice in favor of US nationals investing in Mexico. Moreover, it is fully available for breaches of all of the substantive standards provided in the treaty only to investors having entered 'covered governmental contracts' with either host country. Canada opted out from this mechanism altogether, as advocated by its civil society in light of the many cases in which US investors had successfully challenged Canadian restrictive measures under NAFTA, mainly enacted by provinces.

Chapter 14 is the result of a novel development. The more limited protection compared to NAFTA does not reflect acceptance of the persistent criticism of the investment regime, specifically investor-state dispute settlement (ISDS), expressed by certain developing

---

[37] O. F. Cabrera C, 'The US-Mexico-Canada Agreement: the New Gold Standard to Enforce Investment Treaty Protection?', *Columbia FDI Perspectives*, No. 269, 13 January 2020.

[38] G. Sacerdoti, 'Is USMCA Really "The New Gold Standard" of Investment Protection?', *Columbia FDI Perspectives*, No. 281, 29 June 2020.

[39] Annex 14-D, para. 5(1)(b).

countries circles (and UNCTAD), civil society (the 'no-globals') and some think-tanks in the north. The origin is the Trump administration's novel theory that international treaty protection granted to US investors abroad encourages the delocalization of US companies to the detriment of US workers, and hence is incompatible with its 'America First' policy.

In this political context, Canada found no resistance from the US in removing ISDS. As to Mexico, the NAFTA-level procedural protections for US investors (i.e., full ISDS) have been maintained only for the big business sectors that advocated it most energetically, had the best political connections and are least affected by the 'American-jobs-first' policy because of their capital-intensive character.

...

[T]he most protected investments appear to be the most capital-intensive and environment-unfriendly sectors (oil and gas). The least protected is manufacturing, which is the most labor-intensive and hence the most important to fight poverty, unemployment and workers' exploitation in a developing country such as Mexico.

2.2 Procedural Innovations

There is a similar ongoing process of purely procedural innovations. These include current efforts to make investment arbitration more transparent. The Mauritius Convention on Transparency is merely a vehicle by which parties consent to apply the 2014 UNCITRAL Rules on Transparency.[40] The Mauritius Convention operates by making the UNCITRAL Rules on Transparency apply to investment treaty arbitrations which are brought pursuant to treaties concluded before 1 April 2014, irrespective of their applicable arbitration rules.[41] These transparency reforms are linked to the admission of *amicus curiae* briefs. There are now treaty clauses permitting such submissions in explicit terms, and which also state the applicable procedures to be followed. Other innovations include treaty clauses which provide expressly for summary proceedings in order to address the risk of unmeritorious claims, clauses which penalise frivolous claims with cost orders, and also the bespoke arbitrator codes of conduct in the newer BITs. Regarding the latter, the backlash is in part a result of perceptions of unacceptable arbitrator conflicts of interest having been tolerated too easily in the past. All of the issues listed above are also reflected in the 2016 TPP treaty text, and now in the CPTPP,[42] including a clause which reflects the UNCITRAL Transparency Rules.[43]

---

[40] See, further, UN Convention on Transparency in Treaty-based Investor-State Arbitration, New York, 2014 ('Mauritius Convention on Transparency'), and the 2014 UNCITRAL Rules in Treaty-based Investment Arbitration.

[41] See, e.g., 'Mauritius Convention and UNCITRAL Rules on Transparency in SCC cases', SCC, 15 February 2016.

[42] See, e.g., TPP/CPTPP, Art. 9.23.3; US Model BIT, Art. 28.3 (*amicus* briefs); TPP/CPTPP, Arts 9.23.4–9.23.6, 2012 US Model BIT, Arts 28.4–28.6 (applying the 'loser-pays' principle to costs, following summary dismissal of a claim).

[43] TPP/CPTPP, Art. 9.24.

L. Johnson and N. Bernasconi-Osterwalder, 'New UNCITRAL Arbitration Rules on Transparency: Application, Content and Next Steps' (CIEL, IISD, CCSI, August 2013)

ICSID's administrative and financial regulations ... require the Secretary-General to publish awards if both disputing parties consent to publication. In cases when both parties do not consent to publication of the award, the ICSID Arbitration Rules require ICSID to 'promptly include in its publications excerpts of the legal reasoning of the Tribunal'.

Apart from the ICSID Arbitration Rules, the rules used in investor-State arbitrations, including the UNCITRAL Arbitration Rules, have largely been crafted to apply to commercial disputes between private parties. It is therefore not surprising that the drafters of these arbitration rules did not incorporate provisions that require transparency, facilitate the development of international law or that otherwise attempt to take into account public rights and interests raised or touched on by the disputes.

Indeed, most arbitration rules referred to in investment treaties are essentially silent on the matter of transparency, neither mandating confidentiality nor requiring disclosure. The rules allow the disputing parties significant latitude to determine – individually or through agreement – the degree of openness of the proceedings. Restrictions on disclosure, where they are present, are primarily directed at the arbitrators and arbitral institutions, not the parties themselves. As a consequence, arbitrations conducted under these rules can, to a large extent, be transparent if at least one party so desires, and the tribunal does not explicitly require confidentiality.

Nothing in the SCC, ICC, ICSID or UNCITRAL (1976 or 2010) arbitration rules, for example, prevents either party to the dispute from unilaterally disclosing information regarding the initiation and core of the case. Those rules do not preclude either disputing party from releasing the notice of arbitration, pleadings, or briefs. Thus, there are a number of these documents generated at the commencement and during the course of the proceedings that are available in the public domain.

The rules of the SCC, ICC and ICSID do not expressly prevent either disputing party unilaterally disclosing orders, decisions and final awards issued by the tribunal. On this issue, the UNCITRAL Arbitration Rules have long stood out as being more restrictive than the others. Article 32(5) of the 1976 UNCITRAL Arbitration Rules provides that '[t]he award may be made public only with the consent of both parties'. Pursuant to this provision, a State must seek and obtain approval from the investor to publish an award, and vice versa. The 2010 UNCITRAL Arbitration Rules are slightly more open. They state in Article 34(5) that '[a]n award may be made public with the consent of all parties or where and to the extent disclosure is required of a party by legal duty, to protect or pursue a legal right or in relation to legal proceedings before a court or other competent authority'. Yet, like the 1976 UNCITRAL Arbitration Rules, the 2010 rules generally require both disputing parties to consent to disclosure of awards.

Treatment of hearings is the one aspect of investor-State arbitrations where the various sets of arbitral rules can all generally be said to have actively restricted public access. The rules of ICSID, UNCITRAL (1976 & 2010), the ICC and the SCC all require the consent of both disputing parties for hearings to be open to those not involved in the proceedings. Other than by mutual consent, hearings in treaty-based investor-State disputes will only be open when required by the underlying treaty.

Therefore, with the exception of the rather frequently used restrictions on access to hearings, and the UNCITRAL Arbitration Rules' restrictions on disclosure of awards, rules used in investor-State arbitrations have not excluded the possibility of public access to information and, at least in the case of the ICSID Arbitration Rules, have required a certain amount of disclosure. The new Rules on Transparency thus represent not a complete upending of the approach to transparency in arbitration, but, instead, a shift in the underlying presumption toward openness, rather than privacy, in treaty-based investor-State arbitrations.

...

The new Rules on Transparency ensure transparency in treaty-based investor-State arbitration from the beginning to the end of a dispute. Article 1 of the Rules on Transparency governs the scope and manner of application of those provisions. Article 1 of the general UNCITRAL Arbitration Rules have [sic] also been amended to expressly indicate that they incorporate the Rules on Transparency. Then, in terms of content, the Rules on Transparency contain three articles mandating disclosure and openness (Articles 2, 3, and 6); two governing participation by non-disputing parties (Articles 4 and 5); one setting forth exceptions from the disclosure requirements (Article 7); and one regarding management of disclosure through a specific repository (Article 8).

Another idea which is being actively discussed, and which treaty texts already acknowledge as a future possibility, is that of having an investment disputes appellate mechanism.[44]

A Joubin-Bret, 'Why We Need a Global Appellate Mechanism for International Investment Law', *Columbia FDI Perspectives*, No. 146, 27 April 2015

The European Union's (EU) proposal to include an appellate mechanism in its international investment agreements (IIAs) is a response to concerns about the inconsistency of awards rendered by investment-treaty arbitration tribunals and to criticism about the legitimacy of investor-state arbitration.

The proposal is not new. It had already been included in the IIAs concluded by the United States (US) since 2004, to respond to similar concerns, and had been discussed in 2006 as part of the revision process of the rules of the International Centre for Settlement of Investment Disputes (ICSID). While it can be argued that provisions regarding the

---

[44] See, further, I. M. Ten, 'International Arbitration and the Ends of Appellate Review' (2012) 44 *NYU JILP* 1109.

establishment of an appellate mechanism have remained open-ended, and that contracting parties have not shown a strong appetite for their implementation, there was always the excuse that a future multilateral regime, to which the contracting parties to any IIA could adhere, was preferable to an appellate mechanism set up treaty-by-treaty.

As an appellate mechanism for investment treaty arbitration gains renewed momentum, its discussion should not be carried out solely by the EU and Canada in the context of their Comprehensive Economic and Trade Agreement (CETA), or with the US in the context of the Transatlantic Trade and Investment Partnership (TTIP) negotiations with the EU, or with a focus on each individual treaty.

...

This could be achieved by an initiative along the lines of the ICSID Additional Facility Rules, or by a specific convention such as the one adopted in July 2014 by UNCITRAL on transparency, to which treaty parties can then decide to opt in or out. This was suggested by ICSID in a 2004 paper that proposed an Appeals Facility for cases under ICSID, UNCITRAL and other rules. Such an approach offers the best hope for enhancing consistency and coherence.

J. Karl, 'An Appellate Body for International Investment Disputes: How Appealing Is It?', *Columbia FDI Perspectives,* **No. 147, 11 May 2015**

The debate about a reform of the international investment agreement (IIA) regime is gaining momentum. One suggestion currently being discussed is the establishment of an appellate body for investor-state dispute settlement (ISDS) cases, as a means to review first instance awards, thereby enhancing the coherence and predictability of jurisprudence and contributing to legal security. However, more discussion is needed on how such a body could be set up, and to what extent it could achieve its purpose.

One option is to establish a standing appellate body as exists for trade disputes under World Trade Organization (WTO) rules. The second is an ad hoc appellate body, following the example of the International Centre for Settlement of Investment Dispute (ICSID) regarding the annulment of arbitral awards. Either type of appellate body would not only have the right to annul awards, but also to amend them.

...

Certainly, a serious shortcoming of an ad hoc appellate body – independent of whether it is based on a bilateral, regional or multilateral treaty – is its limited ability to promote coherence in treaty interpretation. Since none of these tribunals would have supremacy over the others, there would be a considerable risk that different ad hoc appellate bodies would decide the same legal issue differently, thus perpetuating a common drawback in current arbitration practice. This risk would exist both with regard to a consistent interpretation of one and the same IIA, and in respect of similar IIA provisions deriving from different treaties.

... it appears that inclusion into future IIAs would be the fastest way toward an appellate body in ISDS. An ad hoc tribunal could review decisions of the first instance and thereby address a major concern of critics of the existing arbitration system. However, for promoting the equally important objective of coherence and predictability in international arbitration practice, it would need a permanent appellate body with broad jurisdiction over the existing IIA regime.

In addition, the ICSID secretariat initiated consultations in 2016 in its now ongoing fourth rule amendment process. The aims are similar: to address inconsistency in awards and questions about arbitrator impartiality, independence, transparency, time and costs.[45]

3. THE EUROPEAN PROPOSAL FOR A MULTILATERAL INVESTMENT COURT

More far-reaching than all of this, and which indeed is in a way akin to earlier Latin American withdrawals from the ICSID Convention, is the European Union's proposal for the complete replacement of international investment arbitration with international investment adjudication. The proposal is for the establishment of a Multilateral Investment Court (MIC). Three treaties which the European Union now has with Canada, Singapore and Vietnam already include a bilateralised version of this proposed system, a model which reportedly is also intended to be adopted by the European Union in its future negotiations with 'Australia, Chile, China, Indonesia, Myanmar, New Zealand, the Philippines and Tunisia'.[46]

European Commission, Inception Impact Assessment: 'Establishment of a Multilateral Investment Court for Investment Dispute Resolution', DG Trade – F2, 1 August 2016

[Investor-to-State Dispute Settlement (ISDS)] has grown up as an effective means to ensure that international law can be enforced without requiring an investor to pass by its government, which may or may not be willing to bring its case. It has developed since the 1960s, and is now contained in virtually all of the more than 3000 such agreements in place. It is often the case that international law is not enforceable in the domestic legal system and that therefore an international investor cannot always be sure that the treatment which the country has accepted that it will provide in the international investment treaty will in fact be provided. ISDS only provides for the possibility of compensation, not for the reversal of laws or decisions, and the substantive rules are

---

[45] See R. Codeço and H. Martins Sachetim, 'ICSID Rule Amendment: An Attempt to Remedy Some of the Concerns Regarding ISDS Identified by UNCITRAL WG III', *Investment Treaty News*, 2 October 2019. The Secretariat published Working Paper #4 on 28 February 2020.

[46] 'EU's Malmström Makes Global Investment Court Pitch to Stakeholders', *Bridges*, vol. 21(7), 2 March 2017.

designed in such a way so as to ensure that the right to regulate of countries is not undermined.

There are a limited set of rules in the field of investment dispute resolution, such as the 1965 Washington Convention, which established the International Centre for Settlement of Investment Disputes (ICSID). The arbitration rules of the United Nations Commission for International Trade Law (UNCITRAL) or of other international arbitral institutions (such as the Permanent Court of Arbitration or the International Arbitration Court of the International Chamber of Commerce) are also used to adjudicate international investment disputes.

With the entry into force of the Lisbon Treaty in 2009, investment became part of the common commercial policy, which is an exclusive competence of the EU. The Commission's Communication COM(2010)343 *'Towards a comprehensive European international investment policy'* had already outlined the Commission's vision on how to develop a European investment policy, by incorporating investment protection disciplines – building on those that have been earlier negotiated by EU Member States – in its free trade agreement (FTA) negotiations or in stand-alone investment agreements.

The 2010 Communication had identified certain characteristics of the ISDS system, which presented challenges that should be addressed in the EU's international investment policy: transparency, consistency, predictability and the possibility to appeal featured explicitly amongst those challenges.

In the years that followed, EU level negotiations of investment protection rules, notably in the context of the Transatlantic Trade and Investment Partnership (TTIP) agreement, raised public awareness of ISDS. There was growing controversy and concern about the perceived insufficient legitimacy, neutrality and transparency of the ISDS system. That concern has been raised in the last couple of years both within the EU but also internationally due to prominent ISDS cases such as *Philip Morris vs Australia, Vattenfall vs Germany* etc.

After an extensive reflection process, which also included a public consultation in 2014 on the EU's approach to investment protection and investment dispute resolution in TTIP, the Commission published on 5 May 2015 a Concept Paper *'Investment in TTIP and beyond – the path for reform'*, which set out the EU's future path with regard to its policy on investment protection and investment dispute resolution, including in particular the establishment of the investment court system in bilateral agreements.

On that basis, the EU agreed in November 2015 on a new EU level policy on investment protection and investment dispute settlement to be proposed for TTIP and other EU negotiations for FTA or stand-alone investment agreements. The policy consists of two distinct but inter-related elements: (1) the replacement of ISDS by an institutionalised investment dispute resolution system (the Investment Court System (ICS) with both a Tribunal of First Instance and an Appeal Tribunal) with permanent judges appointed by the EU and its trade and/or investment agreement partners, with the objective of increasing the legitimacy, effectiveness and independence of the dispute settlement system in EU agreements; and (2) the inclusion of clearer and more precise provisions on investment protection, including on the right to regulate in order to strike the right balance between ensuring a high level of protection for investments and safeguarding the right of states to regulate in the public interest.

The EU has made significant progress in implementing this new policy, now included in two concluded FTA negotiations (the Comprehensive Economic and Trade Agreement with Canada (CETA) and the EU–Vietnam FTA, both concluded in the beginning of 2016).

The Concept Paper of 5 May 2015 also foresaw the establishment of a multilateral system for the resolution of investment disputes. This idea was put forward by a number of stakeholders in the public consultation conducted in 2014.

Building on this, the '*Trade for all*' Communication from October 2015 sets out that the Commission will – in parallel with its bilateral efforts – 'engage with partners to build consensus for a fully-fledged, permanent International Investment Court'.

At the public release on 12 November 2015 of the EU's proposed text for TTIP on investment protection and investment dispute settlement, the Commission stated that the 'Commission will start work, together with other countries, on setting up a permanent International Investment Court ... The objective is to, over time, replace all investment dispute resolution mechanisms in EU agreements, in EU Member States' agreements with third countries, and trade and investment treaties concluded between non-EU countries, with the International Investment Court. This would lead to the full replacement of the "old ISDS" mechanism with a modern, efficient, transparent and impartial system for international investment dispute resolution.'

European Commission, 'European Commission Launches Public Consultation on a Multilateral Reform of Investment Dispute Resolution', Brussels, 21 December 2016

The European Commission today launched a public consultation to gather stakeholders' views on possible options for multilateral reform of the way investment disputes are resolved, including the possible establishment of a permanent Multilateral Investment Court.

The idea of multilaterally reforming investment dispute settlement first emerged in the context of the 2014 public consultation on investment protection, where a number of stakeholders pointed to the idea that the reform of investment dispute resolution would be best undertaken multilaterally rather than through bilateral reforms. The Commission also put forward the idea in its 2015 Concept Paper on '*Investment in TTIP – the path beyond*' and it has been largely supported by the European Parliament and Member States.

For the EU, the permanent Multilateral Investment Court would replace the bilateral Investment Court Systems (ICS) that have been thus far included in the EU trade agreements with Canada and Viet Nam and that is being proposed in all ongoing EU negotiations. The Multilateral Investment Court would apply to all international investment agreements if the Parties to those agreements agreed to resort to it.

2. Members shall not, directly or indirectly, incur any obligation or accept any benefit that would in any way interfere or appear to interfere, with the proper performance of their duties.

3. Members may not use their position to advance any personal or private interests and shall avoid actions that may create the impression that they are in a position to be influenced by others.

4. Members may not allow financial, business, professional, family or social relationships or responsibilities to influence their conduct or judgment.

5. Members must avoid entering into any relationship or acquiring any financial interest that is likely to affect their impartiality or that might reasonably create an appearance of impropriety or bias.

Article 6
Obligations of Former Members
All former members must avoid actions that may create the appearance that they were biased in carrying out their duties or derived advantage from the decisions or awards of the Tribunal or Appeal Tribunal.

As we can see from this text, a fifteen-member Tribunal of First Instance and six-member Appellate Tribunal were proposed.[50] This model was then adopted in the EU–Canada CETA's investor–State dispute provisions, which constitute a bilateralised version of the MIC proposal. The EU–Canada CETA has in turn become the basis for similar provisions in other treaties. Where CETA provides for fifteen members of a first instance 'Tribunal'[51] and an 'Appellate Tribunal',[52] the EU–Vietnam Investment Protection Agreement envisages that there shall be nine first instance tribunal members[53] and six appellate tribunal members.[54] The EU–Singapore Investment Protection Agreement states that there shall be six members of a 'Tribunal of First Instance'[55] and three Appellate Body Members.[56]

The latest iteration of the European Union's proposal lies in its submission – Working Paper 159 (WP 159) – to the United Nations Commission on International Trade Law's Third Working Group (UNCITRAL WG III).[57] WP 159 offers three possibilities – (1) having the originally proposed two-tier MIC, comprising a first instance court to replace investor–State arbitration and an appeals court rather than the ICSID mechanism for the annulment of tribunal awards, (2) having only a free-standing appeals mechanism, thus

---

[50] TTIP negotiating text tabled in 2015, Chapter 3, Section 3, Arts 9 and 10.

[51] The lower Tribunal consists of five Canadians, five European Union nationals and five third country nationals, sitting in divisions of three. This is the same number as for an ICSID Annulment Committee and for WTO Appellate Body Divisions. However, parties may choose to have only one member: EU–Canada CETA, Art. 8.27.

[52] Leaving the precise number of Appellate Tribunal members to be decided later: see EU–Canada CETA, Art. 8.28.

[53] EU–Vietnam IPA, 30 June 2019, Art. 3.38.

[54] *Ibid.*, Art. 3.39.

[55] EU–Singapore IPA, 15 October 2018, Art. 3.09.

[56] *Ibid.*, Art. 3.10.

[57] UN Doc. A/CN.9/WG.III/WP.159, Add. 1.

preserving investor–State arbitration, or (3) making the appellate function of an eventual MIC available in any event to those who choose nonetheless to preserve investor–State arbitration (i.e. such States can 'opt in' to the use of the 'upper tier' of the MIC).[58]

Much of the impetus for the idea of replacing investment arbitration stems from many of the issues discussed in Chapter 7 of this book. Some spectacular challenges have fueled public dissatisfaction, not all of which have been discussed in this book. The problem, to risk simplification, is three-fold. First, there is already only a small club of arbitrators – but will not a fixed number of adjudicators be smaller still?

A second reason lies in so-called 'double-hatting'.[59] Although few probably would argue that having worked as counsel before assuming a decision-making role results in a mind so inevitably prejudiced and corrupt that it can no longer remain open, one argument is that an award delivered today is done so with an eye toward emerging as counsel tomorrow armed with that same award. Still, which tribunal would be so gullible or easily swayed? Putting this narrow situation aside, need an 'open' mind be a vacant or 'empty' one?[60] Thus, counsel pursues a point which subsequently is somehow reflected while serving, separately, as arbitrator. Can it be said, always, that this proves a mind which has closed? We come back to the improbable picture of a mind corrupted by a professional lifetime's lawyering. The problem so carefully outlined by Philippe Sands in a seminal paper is a truism – that our experiences inform us; but Sands did add, by way of a caveat, the words: 'speaking for myself'.[61] Others may feel that what countless formal decision-makers do daily is to put their personal views and prejudices aside in a conscious manner. Sands is, however, correct: 'The issue is not whether she thinks it can be done, but whether a reasonable observer would so conclude.'[62] And therein lies the rub: justice must be seen to be done while remaining more than a mere public relations exercise.

A final reason has to do with multiple appointments as arbitrator; but there is also party autonomy to be considered, and the fact that a State facing a sudden multitude of claims will, if the criticism is taken only on its face, have to obtain a fresh arbitrator for each separate arbitration.[63]

Finally, re-politicisation lurks in the shadow of reform. Brigitte Stern sounds a note of warning: 'This [the proposal for an MIC] is not at all a step forward and certainly introduces again politics ... who will be the nominees of the States? Probably retired diplomats,

---

[58] *Ibid.*, para. 3.16. For how the present reform proposal was inspired by the WTO in Geneva's trade dispute settlement system, see, for example, C. L. Lim, 'Reaching for Utopia: Geneva as Inspiration for Investment Disputes' in M. K. Lewis, J. Nakagawa, R. J. Neuwirth, C. B. Picker and P. T. Stoll (eds), *A Post-WTO International Legal Order: Utopian, Dystopian and Other Scenarios* (Berlin: Springer, 2020), 167. An interest in representing an observer entity only in WGIII discussions is hereby declared.

[59] P. Sands, 'Conflict and Conflicts in Investment Treaty Arbitration: Ethical Standards for Counsel' in C. Brown and K. Miles (eds), *Evolution in Investment Treaty Law and Arbitration* (Cambridge University Press, 2011), 19, 23–24.

[60] Remark by Stanimir A. Alexandrov, *Proceedings of the ISDS Reform Conference 2019* (Hong Kong: AAIL/ HKSAR DOJ, 2019), 208.

[61] Sands, 'Conflict and Conflicts', 23–24.

[62] *Ibid.*

[63] Brigitte Stern, *Proceedings of the ISDS Reform Conference 2019*, 258.

retired judges, civil servants that have the State and have always been on good terms with the State. I think it might be re-politicised.'[64]

CONCLUSION

The backlash against investment treaties and arbitration has had an impact on the latest treaty clauses on both substantive protection and procedure. Reform of treaty clauses is not the only result of this, even if it may yet prove to be the backlash's most lasting legacy. The impetus for reform is now official and it comes from the various State capitals. Some capitals have, in a sense, resumed where they had left off in the final days of the twentieth-century movement for a New International Economic Order.[65] The pendulum swings anew.[66] The forces driving change in the European Union threaten to alter the very landscape of investment arbitration. The disapplication in the USMCA of investment treaty arbitration between Canada and the US may be viewed in the same light, especially following Canada's conclusion of the EU–Canada CETA. However, one thing should not be overlooked. This is a discipline which has witnessed such shifts before. Although given due emphasis in this book as its principal subject, the law and practice surrounding investment arbitration is only a part of a longer tradition of foreign investment dispute settlement. As in the past, through the rise and fall of various modalities and mechanisms for the settlement of international investment disputes, little of our present learning and experience is likely to be irrelevant in the future.

QUESTIONS

1. What differences, if any, exist between the context surrounding the NAFTA parties' original reaction to over-broad tribunal interpretations in the early 2000s and events today?
2. Are the newly 'rebalanced' treaty clauses significantly different or do they only reflect slight tinkering around the edges? Will the results satisfy critics of the current system of investment arbitration?
3. How does an 'appellate mechanism' for investment arbitration differ from the proposal for a Multilateral Investment Court?
4. What constraints should be imposed upon the members of a Multilateral Investment Court? Should its judges be allowed to continue to act as counsel in arbitrations and/or arbitrators? If not, how long should they be expected to avoid entering into private practice as counsel and/or arbitrators after stepping down from the bench? Who will be attracted to an appointment to the court?
5. How will the decisions of the Multilateral Investment Court be enforced worldwide?

---

[64] *Ibid.*, 193–194 and more generally 190–201.
[65] Discussed in Chapter 1, Section 2 of this book.
[66] The image of a pendulum which swings occasionally in favour of the investor, but at other times in favour of the host State, back and forth over the decades, was conceived by Professor Muthucumaraswamy Sornarajah: see Lim, *Alternative Visions*, 34, 449, 452.

SUGGESTIONS FOR FURTHER READING

1. M. Kantor, 'Little Has Changed in the New US Model Bilateral Investment Treaty' (2012) 27 *ICSID Review – FILJ* 335.
2. C. L. Lim, 'The Many-Headed Hydra and Laws that Rage of Gain, a Chapter in Conclusion' in C. L. Lim (ed.), *Alternative Visions of the International Law on Foreign Investment: Essays in Honour of Muthucumaraswamy Sornarajah* (Cambridge University Press, 2016), 431.
3. G. Hanessian and K. Duggal, 'The Final India Model BIT: Is This the Change the World Wishes to See?' (2017) 32 *ICSID Review – FILJ* 216.
4. A. Reinisch, 'Will the EU's Proposal Concerning an Investment Court System for CETA and TTIP Lead to Enforceable Awards? – The Limits of Modifying the ICSID Convention and the Nature of Investment Arbitration' (2016) 19 *JIEL* 761.
5. M. Wood, 'Choosing between Arbitration and a Permanent Court: Lessons from Inter-State Cases' (2017) 32 *ICSID Review – FILJ* 1.

Index

absolute sanctity of contract, 39, 50, 55
absolute theory of immunity, 557
Abs–Shawcross Draft Convention on Investments
    Abroad (1959), 64, 453
ACIA. *See* Association of South East Asian Nations
    (ASEAN) Comprehensive Investment
    Agreement (ACIA)
Act of State doctrine, 14, 563–571
  benchmark American ruling, 569
ad hoc appellate bodies, 603
ad hoc ICSID annulment committees, 103, 547
ad hoc investment arbitration
  ICSID, comparison with, 109–113
ad hoc investment tribunal system, 82
admissibility. *See* jurisdiction and admissibility
adverse inferences, 246
  low incidence, 247
adverse third party
  arbitrators, 211
Agreement between Australia and Japan for an
    Economic Partnership (Australia–Japan EPA)
  linking FET standard to customary international law,
    82
agreements must be kept. *See pacta sunt servanda*
appellate tribunals, 82
arbitral awards. *See also* New York Convention
  challenging, 109
  protected investments, 290–296
arbitral clause, 23, 43, 48
arbitration clauses, 51, 127, 175, 455
  right to arbitrate covered disputes, 428
arbitration costs, 513, 515–517
Arbitration Rules of the Centre, 29
arbitration without privity, 88, 89–94
arbitrators
  appointment, 179
    ICSID, 180–184
    UNCITRAL, 185
    UNCITRAL/Permanent Court of Arbitration, 185–188
  background of, 174–179
  challenges against, issues
    double-hatting, 224–225

    parties influence, 208–217
    previous opinions, 217–223
  challenges against, procedure
    ICSID, 196–197
    Stockholm Chamber of Commerce (SCC), 197
    UNCITRAL, 198
  challenges against, substance
    IBA, 205, 207
    ICSID, 199–204
    Stockholm Chamber of Commerce (SCC), 205
    UNCITRAL, 205
  challenges, procedure, 189
  double-hatting, 228
  justifiable doubts standard, 203
  key figures, 173
  multiple appointments
    relationship of adversity, 215
    same counsel, 214–215
    same party, 213–214
Argentina–Chile BIT, 393
Argentina–France BIT, 384
Argentina–Germany BIT, 389
Argentina–Indonesia BIT, 593
Argentina–Spain BIT, 389
Argentinian gas cases, 543
ASEAN Treaty for the Promotion and Protection of
    Investments
  Article IV, 68
Asian–African Legal Consultative Organisation, 109
ASR
  Articles 20–25, 421
asset attachment, 572–573
Association of South East Asian Nations (ASEAN)
    Comprehensive Investment Agreement (ACIA)
  Article 28, 322
  Article 4, 283, 300
  Article 8.10, 79
Australia–India BIT, 587
Australia–Japan EPA
  Article 14.6, 82
award enforcement
  arbitration

Manufactured by Amazon.ca
Acheson, AB

11173682R00376